Maryland Monster Movie Memories

Baltimore-Washington Area Horror Hosts and More! (1957-1987)

Maryland Monster Movie Memories

Baltimore-Washington Area Horror Hosts and More! (1957-1987)

by John Carter Stell

Midnight Marquee Press, Inc.

Baltimore, Maryland, USA

Copyright © 2022 John Carter Stell
Layout and Cover Design: A. Susan Svehla
Copy Editor: Janet Atkinson

Without limiting the rights under copyright reserved above, no part of this publication may be reproduced, stored in or introduced into a retrieval system, or transmitted, in any form, or by any means (electronic, mechanical, photocopying, recording or otherwise), without the prior written permission of the copyright owner or the publishers of the book.

ISBN 978-1-64 430-127-2
Library of Congress Catalog Card Number 20229380 80
Manufactured in the United States of America
First Printing June 2022

To George "Ghost Host" Lewis
and Dick "Count Gore" Dyszel
for all those wonderful late Saturday Nights.

FIRST TV SHOWING
FRANKENSTEIN

Starring

BORIS KARLOFF

COLIN CLIVE
MAE CLARK

TONIGHT
10 PM

THE SPINE CHILLING STORY THAT SHOCKED GENERATIONS WITH ITS RAW HORROR!!!

"SHOCK" THEATRE

Table of Contents

8	Acknowledgements
10	Introduction
16	Chapter 1: Before Shock!: TV's State of Terror Pre-1957
27	Chapter 2: Dr. Lucifer (1957-1959)
34	Chapter 3: The Great Zucchini (1967-1970)
40	Chapter 4: Sir Graves Ghastly (1970-1971)
50	Chapter 5: Ghost Host (1971-1987)
78	Chapter 6: Count Gore De Vol (1973-1987)
96	Chapter 7: Un-hosted Horror Theaters
169	Chapter 8: And the Rest: Additional Local Airings
220	Chapter 9: Life After September 5, 1987: Final Memories, Thoughts, and Reflections
223	Chapter 10: Baltimore Horror Film Fandom
246	Appendix 1: Filmography
355	Appendix 2: Network Airings
361	Bibliography

Acknowledgements

This book did not start out as a book. I just wanted a filmography of what aired on *Ghost Host Theatre*. Some quick internet searches produced no results. I knew that if I wanted such a list, I was going to have to build it myself. Therefore, I began, first taking advantage of online newspaper archive sites and then visiting Baltimore and DC libraries to fill in missing schedule holes. As I perused the weekly and sometimes daily television listings, I realized just how much genre television graced the airwaves during the 1970s and 1980s. My curiosity sent me back into the 1960s and then into the 1950s, when the Universal Monsters first appeared on the TV screen. Before I knew it, I had an obscene spreadsheet file with numerous tabs, listing films by host or theater. I next gathered all I could find on the horror hosts whose analog signals reached the Baltimore area during their respective reigns. The realization that others who grew up studying the weekly TV supplement in search of what horror flicks were airing that week might be interested in the rotten fruits of my labors resulted in what you hold in your hands.

The end result, however, was hardly a solo undertaking. There are many people to thank (or blame) for *Maryland Monster Movie Memories* as it exists now. First, I must thank my personal horror hosts: George "Ghost Host" Lewis and Dick "Count Gore" Dyszel. You both made growing up so much fun. In fact, you both have helped make adulthood enjoyable too, thanks to the memories you helped create. (The child is the father of the man after all.) I hope I have adequately expressed my appreciation for your efforts in the pages that follow.

Count Gore does a live show at FANEX 5, a local horror film convention that ran for 16 years, most which were attended by your author. Fans were able to meet most of their classic horror film idols. FANEX 5 hosted Yvette Vickers and John Agar.

My parents, John and Dorothy Stell, let me stay up Saturday night after Saturday night (and more often during the summer) watching films that many parents would have seen as unhealthy. They also bought me the occasional horror film book from the Scholastic Book Club whose catalogue surely offered worthier purchases. The trips to the library to borrow horror-related books and records (Disney's *Chilling Thrilling Sounds of the Haunted House* was a favorite) were numerous. Thanks Mom and Dad!

There is probably no bigger *Ghost Host* fan than my friend Gene Crowell. When I asked if he would help with the *Ghost Host* chapter, he went beyond the call of duty. He arranged interviews, provided stills, shared facts he had learned throughout the years, lent me a cassette tape of an interview he had conducted with George Lewis himself, and tracked down VHS tapes of the horror host pan-

el held during 1993's *Nostalgia Vision* convention. Gene's enthusiasm, support, and feedback were invaluable. I thank him for his generosity and friendship.

Gary and Susan Svehla launched Midnight Marquee Press in 1995 and I was thankfully there at the beginning. They have endlessly encouraged and supported my writing, from the early years where I focused on horror film appreciation, through the more recent years when I began writing my fictional *Tracy Brubaker Mystery* series. I could not be happier that Midnight Marquee agreed to publish *Maryland Monster Movie Memories*. The Svehlas help keep such memories alive, after all.

Many thanks to Count Gore himself, Dick Dyszel, for graciously spending an hour of his time speaking with me about his years at Channel 20 and the many things he's done since leaving the D.C. airwaves. Count Gore is a pioneering horror host legend whose upkeep with technology has made him even more popular today given his audience is now international! May all *your* blood be warm, Count!

My sincerest thanks go out to Tracy Lewis Collins (one of George Lewis' five daughters), Tammy Petrides (Captain Chesapeake Fan Club!), and James "Traffic Jam Jimmy" Uhrin (Channel 45) for a most enjoyable afternoon where they reminisced for two hours about George Lewis and the *Ghost Host* years, sharing the warmest of memories.

I am deeply grateful for Gregory William Mank taking time out of his very busy schedule to share his recollections of Dr. Lucifer, aka Richard Dix. Greg Mank is of course one of the most respected writers in the field of classic horror. His contributions to the Dr. Lucifer chapter gave it the personal touch it would have otherwise lacked. Thank you, Mr. Mank!

I'd like to thank Shawn "Vintage Horror" McCracken for making available many of the more obscure films that aired during the horror host era. Thanks to him I was able to watch nearly every "monster" movie for Appendix 1.

I also want to give a shout out to the Baltimore City Enoch Pratt Library staff members who retrieved over 30 years of *TV Guide* magazine on microfiche during my weeklong opening-to-closing-no-lunchbreak visit during May 2018. They were so helpful that they had the next day's reels ready and waiting for me. I know that it is, technically speaking, their job. Nevertheless, I thank them for doing it so well.

Of course, I want to thank my family for their continued support for this writing thing. I especially want to thank my wife Mena who, even though she does not particularly care for these kinds of films, has been my biggest cheerleader. She has also been a great marketer: sending emails and telling friends about her husband's latest effort. Thanks for your patience and tolerance, especially during this last year when I spent nearly every night watching three or so films in order to complete the review section. Thanks love!

Author John Stell as Kolchak is surrounded by vampires at a Halloween Party given by The Horror and Fantasy Film Society.

Introduction

Immortality: that seems to be a universal trait shared by many a movie monster. Vampires can live hundreds of years; high priests have repeatedly summoned mummies throughout the ages; and mad scientists have constructed seemingly indestructible monsters. During the 1930s, the decade that redefined what a horror movie was for years to come, villagers and would-be heroes, for example, burned Frankenstein's Monster in a windmill, blew him up in a laboratory, *and* sent him tumbling into a sulfur pit. However, other than some minor scarring and a need for a recharge, he was just fine and back again for several 1940s outings. So, if the audiences kept coming back for more, so too would the monsters.

This author was not, fortunately, or unfortunately, around during this classic period of imagination. It would be more than 40 years before I first set (or averted in some cases) my eyes on Universal's *Dracula*, *Frankenstein*, *The Mummy*, and *The Wolfman* movies. It *was* fortunate for those not alive during this time, however, that these monsters did in fact achieve a certain type of immortality: preserved in camera negatives, these classic monsters survived in film prints struck and circulated, allowing them to roam the silver screen for years to come. With the debut of *Shock Theatre* in 1957, they made their way to the small screen where they have remained, in some form or another, ever since.

However, there was more to it than that. To entice viewers to tune in, purchasers of the *Shock Theatre* package were encouraged to engage a guide who would promote the movies: a horror host that would introduce, interrupt, comment, or in some other way preside over the airings. They might be dressed as mad doctors, or vampires, or ghouls, or some combination thereof. They might be nothing more than a well-dressed figure in a suit or an anonymous station employee wearing a rubber mask. To the young viewers watching though, it did not really matter what the level of sophistication was. There was something special about an adult addressing *you* and inviting you to watch, if you dared, the nightly offering. For many a youthful horror fan, having your movie hosted was as important as watching the movie itself. They became a package deal.

November 9, 1957: At 11:15 p.m. this Saturday night after the local news, Dr. Lucifer introduces the first *Shock!* (the local title) presentation in Maryland, on WBAL Channel 11. It is the 1931 classic *Frankenstein*. Very few young eyes had ever seen it. Those who were able to keep those orbs opened would never forget it. *Shock!* would prove so popular that a follow up feature called *Horror!* was added a month later. *Horror!* would also air Fridays at 1:00 a.m., following *The Tonight Show*. One wonders how many people realized Richard Dix, host of *The Officer Happy Show*, played Dr. Lucifer. Before getting his own program in March 1957, Officer Happy had hosted *Little Rascals* and *Laurel and Hardy* shorts as early as 1955 on this same station.

In April 1971, Baltimore independent station WBFF 45 began broadcasting and, among its initial programming, was *Ghost Host Theatre*. *The Dungeon of Harrow* (aka *Dungeons of Horror*) aired April 17, 1971. George Lewis played the host; during the weekdays, he served as kid-friendly Captain Chesapeake on the same station, showcasing cartoons, *Three Stooges* shorts, and other programs that children just getting up or, later, home from school might enjoy. But on Saturday nights, one would find this very same man donned in moustache and beard, wearing a brown suit, and speaking in a much deeper voice wishing everyone a "Good *evening...*" He might be

roaming through a graveyard or fiddling with beakers and test tubes. He never interfered with the movie. One would see him at the beginning, the end, and perhaps during, at some point just after a commercial break, revealing what features were on the horizon. He did not have jokes to tell or details about the movies to pass on. He was essentially a mood-setter. He moved slowly and spoke ominously; the lighting was appropriately eerie. A synthesizer played creepy background music, punctuated by the occasional wolf's howl. It may have been basic

show each week, giving an—*ahem*—full-blooded performance. In fact, Count Gore is still active today, hosting a weekly internet show, *Creature Feature: The Weekly Web Program*, as well as having his own Roku channel. The addition of Count Gore to Saturday nights, however, resulted in the occasional dilemma for any horror fan: in the decade before VCRs were atop most TV sets, what would one do if he or she wanted to watch *both* offerings on a Saturday night?

I'm getting ahead of myself though. If my mother's memory is correct, my love affair with horror *didn't* begin with the classic monster movies. It most likely started October 23, 1971 at some point past 8:00 p.m. when at age four, I watched for the first time the classic *It's the Great Pumpkin, Charlie Brown*! From there, I moved on to Saturday mornings watching *Scooby-Doo, Where are You?* while eating Count Chocula, which had just hit the market the previous March.

and uncomplicated, but oh, how those of us watching loved it.

February 3, 1973: While *Ghost Host Theatre* is offering the horror "comedy" *Ghost of Dragstrip Hollow*, Washington, D.C.'s independent station Channel 20 counters with its *Creature Feature* offering *House of Frankenstein* starting at 11:00 p.m. This night, however, is the debut of vampire host Count Gore De Vol, the creation of Dick Dyszel, who had joined the station the previous year. (Guess what film was playing on the host-less *Creature Feature* the night *Ghost Host Theatre* premiered—*Ghost of Dragstrip Hollow*!) Before Count Gore, *Creature Feature* had no host. Dyszel had worked in Paducah, Kentucky at WDXR-TV, Channel 29, before relocating to Washington. While at Channel 29, he had hosted *Night of Terror* as M.T. Graves for approximately two years. Like Richard Dix and George Lewis, he had kid-friendly alter egos: Bozo the Clown and Captain 20. Unlike the Ghost Host, however, Count Gore De Vol did in fact host his

More Memories: Sunday, January 19, 1972: my parents allow me to stay up late, and I watch *Night Gallery*. (I think I was having some medical procedure the next day, so my parents *wanted* me sleepy.) The episode this night is "The Miracle at Camafeo," the story about a conman faking blindness as part of an insurance swindle. He plans to be "healed" and then to keep the insurance money. At the end, after visiting the Shrine of Miracles, he is rendered blind. The simple effect of colorless orbs representing blindness was my first live-action horror memory. It creeped me out.

Mia Farrow in *Rosemary's Baby*

Saturday, September 22, 1973: I am in bed, supposedly asleep, while my parents are watching *Rosemary's Baby*, which is airing on Channel 13 as an ABC Movie Special. The television set's volume is loud enough so I hear Roman Castevet victoriously shout, "God is dead!" I get very upset and go to my parents tearfully asking if God really is dead. They assure me He isn't and send me back to bed.

Sometime in October 1973, I experience my first horror movie in a theater. Someone (can't remember who) takes me to see *The Legend of Hillbilly John*, most likely at the Liberty I theater. (Hey, it was G-rated after all.) For years afterward, I remember two key moments from the film that at first seem like they cannot be from the same movie. One moment has a wanderer beckoned by a beautiful woman to enter her cabin in the woods. After he enters, she closes the door, turns, and faces him, now a decrepit hag. The second scene shows an attack by a stop-motion animated, prehistoric bird. I remember it melting. It would not be until the 1990s that I was able to figure out what movie I'd seen.

Friday, February 8, 1974: There is no school the next day, so I stay up and watch Jack Palance play the title role in *Dracula*, a made-for-TV premiere. At one point, Dracula returns to his lair to discover the heroes have staked his future bride. He starts tearing the place apart, upending the casket that holds his victim. I distinctly remember asking my mother what upset him so much. "They killed his Barbie doll," my mom replied. I also remember feeling sorry for Dracula when the heroes plunged that stake into his heart because it looked, to my six-and-a-half-year-old eyes, as if he were crying.

My fondest early horror memory however is watching *Kolchak: The Night Stalker* on Friday nights during the 1974/1975 television season. Debuting on Friday September 13, the show received terrible reviews and did poorly in the ratings. Thankfully, I am blissfully ignorant of all that. I just love the show because I absolutely love the character—and the monsters. I cannot recall if I had seen the earlier TV-movies, *The Night Stalker* and *The Night Strangler*, by this point. As far as I am concerned, this show is perfection. The moment that stands out is from the "Demon in Lace" episode when the succubus comes screeching through a pair of glass doors. It freaked my little self out.

Darren McGavin and Craig R. Baxley in *The Night Stalker*

Halloween 1975: it is a Friday, which means no getting up for school the next day. It is the first time I recall staying up late—and I mean *late*. Beginning at 1:30 a.m. on Channel 2, there is a double feature of *Abbott and Costello Meet Frankenstein* and *Abbott and Costello Meet Dr. Jekyll & Mr. Hyde*. I make it through them both. I cannot remember if my younger brother did or not.

> **1.30 ② Friday Fright Movies.**
>
> "Abbott and Costello Meet Frankenstein." (1948.) Dracula and Frankenstein's monster kidnap Abbott and Costello, wanting to transfer Costello's brain to the monster. Bela Lugosi, Lon Chaney. Also, " Abbott and Costello Meet Dr. Jekyll and Mr. Hyde." (1953.) Two American police officers search for a monster terrorizing London. Boris Karloff.

At some point during 1974 or 1975, I started watching *Ghost Host Theatre*. This was the era of rabbit ears and rooftop antennae, so Channel 45 was the better bet with respect to acquiring a decent UHF signal. Regardless, by the ripe old age of seven I was a horror TV and film fanatic who lived for Saturday nights and especially Halloween. Now in my 50s, I cannot say my feelings towards the genre have changed. I do not see them ever changing.

Primarily, this book is a thank you to horror hosts in general, particularly the Baltimore-area hosts, for the immeasurable pleasure they gave their young and young-at-heart viewers throughout the years they served. For many people, their first exposure to horror films was through these hosts, and this in turn began a love affair with the genre. In fact, these friendly fiends created little movie monsters with insatiable appetites, not nearly satisfied by a once-a-week-fix. Thus, this book does not just include filmographies of local hosts, but also chapters on local television airings that would have been of interest to the budding horror fan. Some stations had dedicated "Chiller Theaters" that specialized in horrific

> CHILLER—"Unknown Terror," starring John Howard, Mala Powers and May Wynn. (1957) Second Feature—"Horror Chamber of Dr. Faustus," starring Pierre Brasseur and Alida Valli. (1962) Channel 5 at 11 P.M.

programming, even if there was no host. Other horrors frequently popped up on the more inclusive "Late Late Show." This type of programming would not last much past the 1980s, when the combination of the cable television explosion and the home video revolution sent networks scrambling to reconfigure their schedules. When a fourth network—Fox—started looking for affiliates in 1986, Baltimore and Washington ultimately bid farewell to formally independent stations, including Channel 45.

In other words, the television landscape of the late '80s was nothing like it was at the beginning of the decade. One of the casualties of this change was a decrease in local programming, and that, sadly, included our horror hosts. Count Gore aired his final weekly *Creature Feature*, 1953's *Invaders from Mars*, on May 23, 1987. Ghost Host ended his reign shortly thereafter. The Baltimore-Washington airwaves have not been nearly as scary since.

It was not all bad news though. For those who were able to take advantage, cable television and the local video store offered uncut, uninterrupted versions of

Boris Karloff as the Monster throws little Maria (Marilyn Harris) into the lake in *Frankenstein*. Karloff was very unhappy about this scene according to author Greg Mank.

Dracula and *Frankenstein*. (The 1986 VHS re-release of *Frankenstein* contained footage not shown during any previous television airing, including the infamous tossing of Maria into the lake.) One could tape a broadcast to watch later or rent their fear film of choice. However, the viewing experience was not the same. Part of this was due of course to the viewer not being the innocent they used to be. Still, at least subconsciously, we realized things had changed, and not all of it was for the better. Thus, the author feels fortunate to have grown up in the 1970s, the last decade where the horror host, at least locally, was a beloved figure and fixture of Saturday nights.

> **1.45 13 The Late Late Show.**
> "Gorgo." An undersea explosion off the coast of Ireland brings to the surface an infant monster. Later, scientists learn that the mother of the monster has begun to search for her child destroying everything in her path. Bill Travers, William Sylvester, Vincent Winter. 1961.

Baltimore's Nostalgia Vision (Feb. 1993) brought together horror hosts (L to R) Dick Dyszel (Count Gore De Vol), film historian Bill LIttman, Richard Dix (Dr. Lucifer), George Lewis (Ghost Host) and Baltimore's beloved TV personality Stu Kerr—known to generations of Baltimore area TV viewers as: the Night Janitor (1950s), Mr. Fortune (1960s), Bozo the Clown (1960s), Professor Kool (1970s), and Wormy the Word Whiz (1980s) at WMAR-TV (1952-1981).

Most likely, though, *anyone* from *anywhere* who grew up with a similar Saturday night routine shares these feelings and has similar memories.

Thus, the primary focus of this book is the period November 9, 1957 through September 5, 1987: the debut of Dr. Lucifer through the (presumed) final weekly presentation by Ghost Host. While there was no lack of horror offerings during this almost 30-year period, the *hosted* films provide the warmest viewing memories. In this way, these brave hosts have achieved their own version of immortality. A love for one's local horror host is something that is positively…universal.

Author's Note: The airdates and times contained herein were culled from numerous hours searching through more than 30 years' worth of *TV Guide* magazines and Baltimore-Washington area newspapers, as well as utilizing relevant websites, books, and magazine articles. Earnest attempts were made to reconcile any discrepancies. Real life or individual station events of course may have occurred which disrupted the planned schedule. Therefore, it is more than likely some airdates and times (although hopefully very few) are incorrect. This author remembers instances of this very thing happening and

> **12:30 (45) Ghost Host Theater.**
> "Invasion of the Body Snatchers." (1956). Southern California is invaded by seeds from giant plants. Kevin McCarthy, Dana Wynter, Larry Gates.

to this day recalls the internal rage that resulted. Sincerest apologies in advance for these possible errors; I hope you will forgive me.

—John Carter Stell
June 2019

Ghost Host holds a very special place in my heart, being a continuous part of my life for the last 40 years. When I was growing up in the late 1970s and early '80s, I wasn't interested in the normal fare. What I did like were horror movies, makeup effects and monsters. I stumbled upon Ghost Host around 1979 and it quickly became a religious experience for me. I lived for Ghost Host Saturday nights. The show featured horror films, the host setting an extremely atmospheric and creepy atmosphere. During the week I would constantly daydream about visiting the house from the opening of the show, meeting the Ghost Host and living in that world I saw on my little JC Penny TV.

I collected Halloween masks and spent as much of my free time as possible staring at my collection and waiting for another installment of Ghost Host. Those Saturday nights were very comforting and gave me great joy. Certain movies stuck with me over the years from seeing them on Ghost Host. *Twisted Brain*, *Equinox*, and *The Night Walker* are just a few examples.

In 1991, I was extremely fortunate to have had the opportunity to interview the Ghost Host himself George Lewis in his home. George and his lovely wife Dorothy were two of the nicest people I had ever met. This was my very first interview for a local monster makeup fanzine titled *Amateur Monster Maker*. George was extremely gracious to me and my girlfriend (now wife) Amy, and he loved reminiscing about his days as the Ghost Host. Sitting there in his living room and gushing about how much Ghost Host meant to me over the years, I really felt it made him feel good. Aside from Ghost Host, George talked of his role as Captain Chesapeake, his early days in broadcasting, and his adventures in meeting John F. Kennedy and local Baltimore Burlesque greats like Dagmar and Blaze Starr.

One great story George shared with me during the interview has stood out for me all these years. George was doing a personal appearance as Captain Chesapeake at a children's hospital where he was sitting with and consoling a blind child. From behind him, he heard another kid say: "Aww stop feeling so sorry for yourself!" George said he was so mad that he quickly turned around to confront the rude kid and saw it was a bedridden child, missing both arms and legs. Seeing that made him cry and he held that exchange with him ever since. He told me, whenever he had something to deal with that was heavy or stressful, he would always reflect on what that kid said, "stop feeling so sorry for yourself."

In 1993 I was asked to arrange for George Lewis to attend a local film convention as a featured guest. The FANEX *Nostalgia Vision* Convention in Towson, Maryland hosted a weekend for TV lovers. George Lewis spoke at two panels and attended a celebrity dinner on the last night. During the horror host panel, the crowd went wild with applause when we showed a video clip of the Ghost Host show opening. When the lights came back up, George had the biggest smile on his face. George was modest and was really touched by all the fans who braved the snowstorm that February weekend to come out and tell him how much his work had meant to them.

In 2013 I was asked to present a tribute panel and discussion on George Lewis and his work on Ghost Host and Captain Chesapeake for The Mid-Atl;antic Nostalgia Convention in Baltimore. It was a great honor to speak about a man I only got to meet several times but had so much affection for. The room was packed and two of his family members were in the audience!

Now in 2019, I find myself assisting on the Ghost Host portion of this book. If there is one thing I have learned over the years, it's that everyone who knew George personally or just met him once all say the same thing. Not only was George Lewis extremely kind but he also made a positive impact on everyone he met. Thank you, George for everything you did for the children of Maryland. You are remembered fondly my friend.

—Gene Crowell
June 2019

Chapter 1

Before Shock!: TV's State of Terror Pre-1957

Through a fog-enshrouded and oppressive-looking hallway, a figure moves slowly towards the camera. As the black-and-white image comes into view, we see an hourglass-shaped female, donned in a tight-fitting black dress. Her dark hair rests on her shoulders. Her eyebrows are the color of deepest night. She stops and peers into the lens. Suddenly, she emits an ear-piercing cry! Then, seductively, she smiles and calmly says, "Screaming relaxes me so." Her name is Vampira, played by actress/model Maila Nurmi. She is the host of *Lady of Horrors*, a new program airing on Los Angeles, California ABC affiliate KABC-TV. She presents *White Zombie* (1932) on May 1, 1954. Even though her show is a local production, she proves popular enough that the programmers change the title to *The Vampira Show* beginning June 5, and the June 14, 1954, edition of *Life* magazine publishes an article discussing her show. Suddenly, she is no longer just a local phenomenon, and she would eventually appear as a guest on network programs such as *The*

Red Skelton Show. Yet, despite great ratings and popularity, the powers-that-be cancel the program in March 1955 because Nurmi will not let ABC purchase the rights to her character. Despite her brief tenure, however, the female bloodsucker makes her vampiric mark, and returns to television in 1956 on Los Angeles' KHJ-TV. Today history views Vampira as one of the all-time great horror hosts—and one of the first.

Unfortunately, because it was not yet common practice to record or possibly syndicate her live show, little footage remains of Vampira's horrific antics. What *does* remain is impressive, revealing a character that was sexy, alluring, deadpan, and perhaps a little scary too. One wishes we could see more. In these early days of television, not everything was filmed or kinescoped and thus retained for posterity. One's memories are sometimes the only form of preservation these times have, which is sad for those of us who were not there to witness Vampira and others like her during their hosting years. Other people's memories will just have to suffice.

Vampira, however, was not the first of her kind. That honor *probably* belongs to Chicago's Swami Drana Badour, who hosted *Murder Before Midnight* on WBKB Channel 4. The program aired every night except Sunday, debuting in January 1950, and initially presented films in segments, as opposed to complete, since the Swami was limited to a half hour each night: 11:30 p.m. to midnight. The Swami's crystal ball provided a gateway into such fare as *The Face of Marble* (1946) and the Charlie Chan mystery *Red Dragon* (1945). The Swami was played first by television announcer Allen Harvey

Vampira (Maila Nurmi) hosted *Lady of Horrors*.

Swami Drana Badour

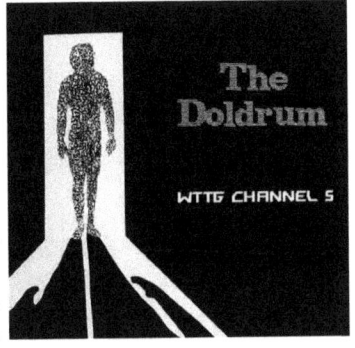

On Thursday, August 5, 1954, WTTG Channel 5 introduced a fellow named The Doldrum. Laurent described this character as, "a scar-faced Hunchback of Notre Dame." The Doldrum hosted primarily mystery films at 9:00 p.m. Although he debuted with 1948's *The Creeper*, the remainder of his output included B-thrillers such as *A Gentleman After Dark* (1942) and *13 Lead Soldiers* (1948). His last show aired September 16, 1954.

and then by radio performer Art Hern. *Murder Before Midnight* ended in September 1953 (at least according to the listings in the *Chicago Daily Tribune*). Like Vampira, only those whose TV antennas could grasp the local station's signal viewed Swami Drana Badour. No program footage appears to exist.

Closer to Maryland, beginning Tuesday, March 24, 1953, Washington, D.C. Channel 9 launched a weekly program entitled *The Black Cat*. Station employee Bob Dalton wore a black leotard and introduced Republic crime thrillers while a black cat named Thanatopsis rested, not always comfortably, on his lap. Filling the 8:00 p.m. to 9:00 p.m. slot, the show lasted only five weeks. Films shown were *Secret Service Investigator* (1948), *The Last Crooked Mile* (1946), *Crime of the Century* (1946), *Faces in the Fog* (1944), and *Double Identity* (1941).

The following year D.C.'s Channel 4 aired *Cauldron of Horrors* 11:20 p.m. Fridays, starting July 23, 1954, with *Lost Continent* (1951), and running through September 24, 1954, until the debut of *The Tonight Show*. The host was an unnamed witch, described by *Washington Post* writer Lawrence Laurent as, "a grimy old girl with straggly hair and a cracked voice." Further, she made "unkind comments about the characters." Titles aired under *Cauldron of Horrors* included *Valley of the Zombies* (1946), *Devil Bat's Daughter* (1946), *The Revenge of the Zombies* (1943), *White Pongo* (1945), *Strangler of the Swamp* (1946), *The Corpse Vanishes* (1942), and *The Lady and the Monster* (1944).

> 11:20 [4] MOVIE—Horror
> Cauldron of Horrors: Movie introduced by a "witch."

Washington Baltimore

Advance Tips on Shows: Beginning next month a top-notch group of movies will be shown on Gunther's *Premium Playhouse* (Sat., 10:30 P.M., ❷).  The pictures include "Body and Soul," with John Garfield and Lilli Palmer; "One Touch of Venus," Ava Gardner, Dick Haymes, and Eve Arden; "A Double Life," Ronald Colman, Signe Hasso, Shelly Winters; Orson Welles' "Macbeth"; and "Arch of Triumph," with Ingrid Bergman and Charles Boyer.

Miss Nancy

Channel Chatter: Still another oddity has appeared in Washington television as host to horror and mystery movies. y now you have probably seen the witch who introduces the chillers on *Cauldron of Horrors*, ([4], Fri., 11:20 P.M.). Now WTTG's new Thurs. 9:00 . . mystery series as an in e nite sort of ghoul called a Doldrum—male, chubby, and guaranteed absolutely unattractive. Apparently a Los Angeles performer named Vampira [TV GUIDE, July 17] started all this.

Mentions of both Cauldron of Horrors and The Doldrum in this Washington D.C. newspaper column.

Thus, in addition to having a local, and thus limited, audience, the hosts shared another trait: the quality of their film library. At this stage in television's development, the picture box and big screen industries were *not* friends. TV was the enemy, threatening to siphon the movie audience. Tinseltown responded with 3D and Cinemascope; there were more epics and color films produced. Drive-ins entered their heyday. It would not be until the mid-1950s that the major studios would start licensing their films to their perceived rival.

The smaller studios, however, had no such qualms; they would take anybody's money. Therefore, most of the films shown in the new medium's early years came from what have been termed Poverty Row studios: purveyors of low-budget offerings made quickly and cheaply. Monogram, Producers Releasing Corporation (PRC), and Republic were the primary studios of this type, whose horror and mystery films made up the bulk of the early television packages. As another example, here are the films, with dates, that Vampira showed during her tenure at KABC-TV.

05/01/54 *White Zombie* (1932)
05/08/54 *The Face of Marble* (1946)
05/15/54 *Revenge of the Zombies* (1943)
05/22/54 *Fog Island* (1945)
05/29/54 *Condemned to Live* (1935)
06/05/54 *Gog* (1954 [Flat black-and-white version])
06/12/54 *Devil Bat's Daughter* (1946)
06/19/54 *The Flying Serpent* (1946)
06/26/54 *The Mask of Diijon* (1946)
07/03/54 *The Strange Mr. Gregory* (1945)
07/10/54 *The Man with Two Lives* (1942)
07/17/54 *Corridor of Mirrors* (1948)
07/24/54 *Fear* (1946)
07/31/54 *Rogue's Tavern* (1936)
08/07/54 *Dangerous Intruder* (1945)
08/14/54 *Mystery of the 13th Guest* (1943)
08/21/54 *Midnight Limited* (1940)
08/28/54 *Bluebeard* (1944)
09/04/54 *The Missing Lady* (1946)
09/11/54 *Murder by Invitation* (1941)
09/18/54 *Red Dragon* (1945)
09/25/54 *The Case of the Missing Heiress* (1949)
10/02/54 *The Missing Corpse* (1945)
10/09/54 *The Fatal Hour* (1940)
10/16/54 *Phantom Killer* (1942)
10/23/54 *The Shadow Returns* (1946)
10/30/54 *King of the Zombies* (1941)
11/06/54 *Doomed to Die* (1940)
11/13/54 *House of Mystery* (1934)
11/20/54 *My Brother's Keeper* (1948)
11/27/54 *Dear Murderer* (1947)
12/04/54 *Castle of Doom* (aka *Vampyr*) (1932)
12/11/54 *The Charge is Murder* (1950)
12/18/54 *Return of the Ape Man* (1944)
12/25/54 *Man with the Grey Glove* (1948)
01/01/55 *Apology for Murder* (1945)
01/08/55 *Decoy* (1946)
01/15/55 *Murder is My Business* (1946)
01/22/55 *Phantom of 42nd Street* (1945)
01/29/55 *Case of the Guardian Angel* (1949)
02/05/55 *Lady Chaser* (1946)
02/12/55 *Killer at Large* (1947)
02/19/55 *She Shall Have Murder* (1950)
02/26/55 *The Lady Confesses* (1945)
03/05/55 *Larceny in Her Heart* (1946)

03/12/55 *Glass Alibi* (1946)
03/19/55 *Detour* (1945)
03/26/55 *Strangler of the Swamp* (1946)

As one can see from the list, after a relatively strong start, by July Vampira was showing mostly suspense and mystery pictures: lower tier Charlie Chan outings such as *Red Dragon*, or entries in Monogram's lackluster Mr. Wong series, such as *The Fatal Hour* and *Doomed to Die*. Absent are what most would consider true classics of the genre: The Universal monster films; Paramount's *Dr. Jekyll and Mr. Hyde* (1931) and *Island of Lost Souls* (1933); RKO's *King Kong* (1933) and the Val Lewton productions; or MGM's *Mad Love* (1935), as some examples. The reason for this though is understandable and forgivable: big studio pictures were expensive to license, *if* the studios would even license them at all, which at this stage they were loath to do.

Boris Karloff in the *Suspense* episode, "The Yellow Scarf," which aired June 7, 1949.

As for the networks, television was still an infant—or perhaps a toddler—in the early 1950s; its role model was radio. Thus, *Lights Out* becomes a weekly series for NBC in July 1949, ultimately settling down in a 9:00 p.m. Monday night spot until its cancellation in September 1952. *Lights Out*'s host is radio announcer Frank Gallop, who appears to be a bodiless head thanks to a black turtleneck and strategic lighting. A candle burns close by. At CBS, *Suspense* airs Tuesdays at 9:30 p.m. debuting in March 1949. It becomes a regular series for the 1949-1950 season and lasts until August 1954. *Suspense*'s host Rex Marshall, like Frank Gallop, began in radio before moving to television. Marshall was not the intimidating, spooky figure his competition was. Marshall promoted car parts and the like for the show's sponsor. In addition to their radio show origins, both series are anthologies and broadcast live, meaning many episodes are lost. Kinescopes of some surviving episodes have made it to DVD.

> 9.30—"Suspense," Boris Karloff in "The Yellow Scarf."

Lights Out and *Suspense* were each a mixture of horror, mystery, and suspense stories. In that way, they were like the offerings of the early horror hosts. Worth noting too is that past and future horror stars guested on these programs. Boris Karloff ("The Leopard Lady" for *Lights Out* and six *Suspense* episodes); Basil Rathbone ("Dead Man's Coat" for *Lights Out* and two episodes for *Suspense*); Bela Lugosi ("A Cask of Amontillado" for *Suspense*); Peter Lorre ("The Tortured Hand" for *Suspense*); and Vincent Price ("The Third Door" for *Lights Out*) are some exam-

Bela Lugosi stars in the *Suspense* episode "A Cask of Amontillado."

ples. One can easily imagine a parent and child sitting in front of the family set, viewing "The Leopard Lady" or "A Cask of Amontillado," and that parent telling their offspring, "You should have seen how scary this guy was in 1931!"

Boris Karloff also appeared in two episodes of the third network's anthology offering. In August 1951, ABC added *Tales of Tomorrow*, which aired Friday nights at 9:30 p.m., to the genre roster. (Note how these series did not compete directly against each other. That must have been great news for the budding horror or science fiction fan.) Granted, the show was more science fiction than outright horror, but it had plenty of chilling offerings: "The Children's Room," "Ice from Space," "The Fatal Flower," and "Ghost Writer" are just some of the entries that should warm a horror fan's heart.

Today, this program's most discussed episode, however, is its adaptation of *Frankenstein*, which stars Lon Chaney as the Monster. Apparently thinking it was just a rehearsal instead of the actual airing, Chaney comes to the stage moaning and groaning; picks up furniture as if he's about to destroy it; and then instead places it unharmed in its original position. John Newland plays Dr. Frankenstein. He would later create, host, and direct his own anthology series *One Step Beyond*, which debuted in January 1959. *Tales of Tomorrow* ended its run in June 1953.

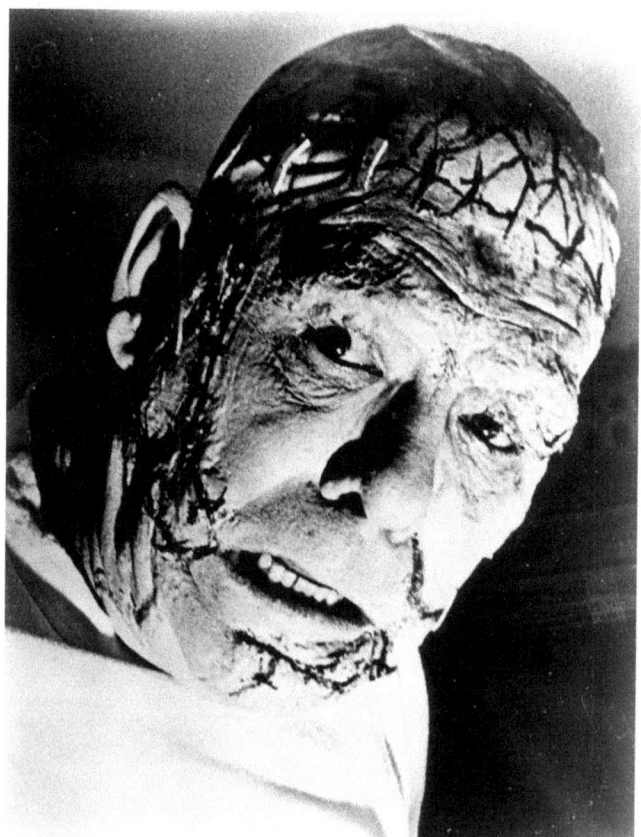

Lon Chaney, Jr. as the Frankenstein Monster in *Tales of-Tomorrow*

MATINEE — "Dracula." A revised version of Bram Stoker's scary classic, resembling neither the original novel nor the Bela Lugosi film. Count Dracula comes to England in a coffin and immediately makes a bee-line (or perhaps a bat-line) for the throats of fair young damsels. John Carradine, an old hand at this sort of thing, is properly repulsive as the royal vampire, and the climax in a creepy castle is designed for shudders. Channel 11, 3 P.M.

With *Lights Out*, *Suspense*, and *Tales of Tomorrow* all gone by the summer of 1954, the networks' horror pickings were so slim as to be nonexistent. During the 1950s the networks aired various and sundry programs that showcased live performances: NBC offered *Kraft Television Theatre*, *Matinee Theatre*, and *Hallmark Hall of Fame*; CBS produced *Studio One* and *Shower of Stars*; and ABC aired *The Elgin Hour* and *Conflict*. Each program would offer the occasional terror tale. For example, another NBC anthology, *Robert Montgomery Presents*, adapted *The Hunchback of Notre Dame* for its 1954 season and presented it in two parts, airing on November 8 and November 15, 1954. On August 6, 1956, *Matinee Theatre* aired "The Fall of the House of Usher," with Tom Tyron (*I Married a Monster from Outer Space*) as Roderick Usher. The same program offered a version of another Edgar Allan Poe story, "The Tell-Tale Heart," on November 6 of that same year. The cast included John Abbott (*The Vampire's Ghost*), John Drew Barrymore (son of John Barrymore), and John Carradine (Universal's Dracula for the two *House of...*monster rallies). Speaking of Carradine, he also played Dracula for NBC's *Matinee Theatre* adaptation that aired 3:00 p.m. on November 23, 1956. No copy of this exists. (It aired on Channel 11 according to the *Baltimore Sun*.)

The anthology series *Climax!*, which debuted in October 1954 on CBS, also provided horror stories. Small-screen versions of borderline horror films *The Thirteenth Chair* and *The Great Impersonation* aired in October 1954 and March 1955, respectively. Perhaps the most notable entry (for horror fans) in the *Climax!* catalogue is its July 28, 1955 version of "Dr. Jekyll and Mr. Hyde," which stars *The Day the Earth Stood Still*'s Michael Rennie as the title characters. Adapted by Gore Vidal, this version also stars Sir Cedric Hardwicke, whose horror résumé includes *The Ghoul* (1933), *The Hunchback of Notre Dame* (1939), *The Invisible Man Returns* (1940), *The Ghost of Frankenstein* (1942), *Invisible Agent* (1942), and *The Lodger* (1944). He also was the narrator for MGM's 1945 film version of Oscar Wilde's *The Picture of Dorian Gray*. In only a few years, young people would become very familiar with nearly all these films.

The aforementioned, as well as other, anthologies also offered thrillers, suspense pictures, science fiction stories, and fantasy outings throughout their runs. However, there were no regular trips to the crypt, so to speak, that a viewer could count on to get a weekly horror fix.

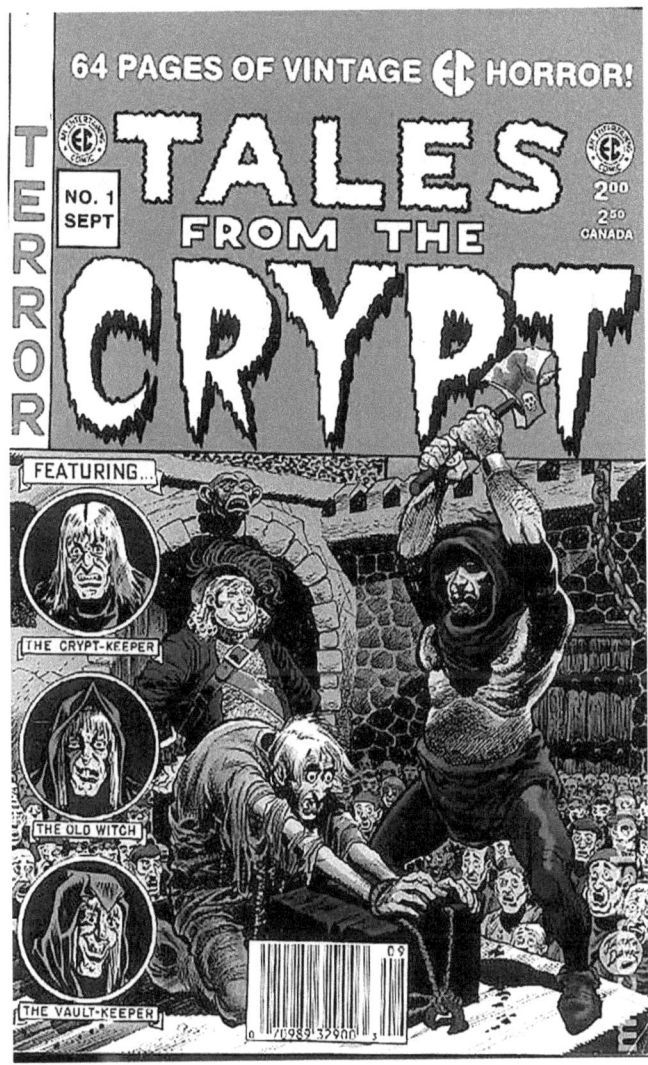

of hours to fill outside their respective network's Prime Time schedule. Network programming had started as early as 1946, with NBC and DuMont being the first to offer a mix of sports, game shows, and news programs. ABC and CBS joined in, starting in 1948. Limited programming left large gaps in the networks' schedules that paved the way for the earliest round of theatrical features coming to television. In fact, CBS and DuMont had no Saturday programming at all; ABC went local at 8:00 p.m. NBC had only 8:30 p.m. to 9:00 p.m. programmed with *Television Screen Magazine*.

Local CBS affiliate Channel 2, which went live in October 1947, thereby becoming Maryland's first station to broadcast, responded on Saturday May 8, 1948 at 8:00 p.m. with *Danger on the Air* (1938), a Universal Studios "Crime Club" mystery released to television through Astor Pictures Corporation. (The station had covered various sports events on Saturdays up until this point.) This will ultimately lead to "Film Theater of the Air" and then "Mystery Theater," when not preempted by sports coverage. Initially alternating irregularly week to week, Channel 2 will eventually air both programs back-to-back. On September 24, 1949, at 8:00 p.m. under the "Mystery Theater" title, the station airs what might be considered the first horror film shown on local television: *Tower of Terror*, a 1941 British thriller about a mad lighthouse keeper (Wilfrid Lawson) who threatens to thwart an English agent's (Michael Rennie) escape from Germany. With plot elements including a hook for

Those looking for horror stories outside of their television, however, had horror comics from which to choose. For example, EC comics offered *Tales from the Crypt*, *The Haunt of Fear*, and *The Vault of Horror* that frequented newsstands beginning in 1950 and lasting through early 1955. The comics' demise was the result of 1954 Congressional subcommittee hearings that alleged reading horror comics, and comics in general, was damaging to young minds. Bill Gaines, EC's publisher, didn't want to deal with the Comics Code Authority (CCA), a result of the hearings by which the Comics Magazine Association of America agreed to regulate itself. Publishers had to submit their Comics to the CCA for approval. While other publishers agreed to tone down or eliminate the violent imagery, the February/March 1955 issue of *Tales from the Crypt* was its final one, as well as the last of the EC horror comics overall. Gaines focused his attention instead on *Mad* magazine. Three years later, with the February 1958 publication of *Famous Monsters of Filmland-*, a fright aficionado had a new reason to make regular returns to the local newsstand.

Thus, the burden of satiating the horror fan's appetite fell on the *local* TV affiliates, and they had plenty

a hand, a possibly reincarnated wife, and a hidden body, the film fits comfortably in the psycho killer subgenre. Lawson gives an excellent performance. If one prefers more traditional horror tales, then know *The Devil Bat* (1940) aired as part of "Mystery Theater" on September 23, 1950, at 11:00 p.m. Bela Lugosi's low-budget genre fare would be seen regularly during the pre-*Shock!* years. (Boris Karloff's non-horror *Mr. Wong* films were also part of "Mystery Theater.")

Eventually, all the local affiliates added theatrical features to their programming, with the filmic floodgates opening wide in the 1950s. Baltimore's ABC affiliate Channel 13 featured "Nocturne Movies," "Night Owl Theatre," "The Early Show," and "Hollywood Film Theater." D.C.'s ABC affiliate Channel 7 gave us "Midnight Theatre," while Channel 5 (affiliate of DuMont, which ceased programming in 1956) aired their own "Night Owl Theatre." Not surprisingly, since the locals did not have big dollars to spend, nearly all the pre-*Shock!* offerings were the same programmers that Vampira and the Swami hosted during the first half of the decade.

> VILMA—Sun., Mon., Red Skelton. "Lovely to Look At." Tues., Wed., Doris Day. "The Winning Team." Thurs.-Sat., Fay Wray, "King Kong."

The good news, though, was that local movie theaters were at least screening classic horror films on occasion. Want to see the legendary 1933 *King Kong*? Take a trip to the Vilma Theatre on Belair Road in August 1952 and get your ticket. For one who prefers the Universal classics, the Horn Theatre in Baltimore City is running *Frankenstein* (1931) that same month. Do you want to catch a double feature of *Dracula's Daughter* (1936) and *Night Monster* (1942) on May 29, 1953? Better hurry: they are showing for one night only at the Hi-Rock Drive-In Theatre in Rawlings, Maryland. If you show up at the Hi-Rock Drive-In on July 4, 1952, you will be treated to fireworks at some point during the double feature presentation of *House of Frankenstein* (1944) and *House of*

Dracula (1945). In December 1954, you could catch *The Beast with Five Fingers* (1946) with Peter Lorre at the Edmondson Drive-In, located on Baltimore National Pike just outside I-695. Therefore, the most famous monsters of them all *were* available to see before finally coming to television. One just needed a ride and some coin.

> EDMONDSON DRIVE-IN—BEAST WITH FIVE FINGERS and COMBAT SQUAD.

The truth is though that the big screens were showing science fiction thrillers more than horror films for most of the '50s. The classic monsters had lost their scare power in the wake of World War II, communism paranoia, and, let's be honest, a decrease in the overall quality of the films themselves. Interest in outer space, fear of what the dropping of the atomic bomb may have wrought, and a July 8, 1947 press release discussing the recovery of a "flying disk" from a ranch near Roswell,

FLYING DISC FOUND; IN ARMY POSSESSION

New Mexico all contributed to the nation redefining its idea of what was truly scary. Thankfully, there were plenty of frightening science fiction films during the better part of the 1950s including *The Thing from Another World* (1951), *Creature from the Black Lagoon* (1954), *Them!* (1954), *Tarantula* (1955), and *Invasion of the Body Snatchers* (1956). In August 1956, an Americanized version of the 1954 Japanese film *Gojira* hits screens under the title *Godzilla*. It will become a classic, and sequels to this film continue into the 21st century. Another import—this one from Great Britain—had landed on our shores two months earlier. *The Creeping Unknown* (released in its home country the previous year as *The Quatermass Xperiment*) was made by a small studio called Hammer Film Produc-

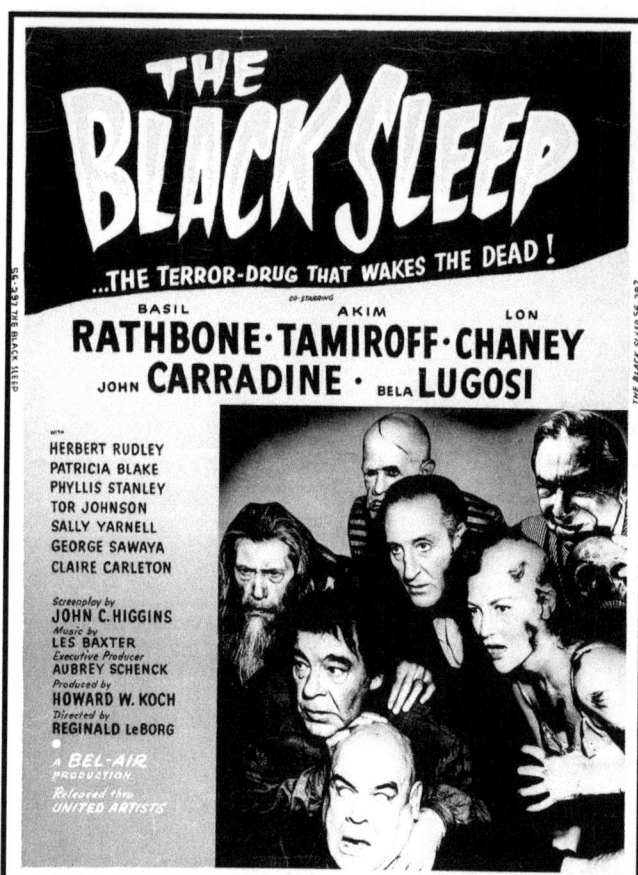

The Black Sleep—if only the movie was as great as the cast!

tions. In 1957, Hammer would be just as important to the renewed interest in Gothic style horror films as *Shock Theatre*. (In fact, *The Quatermass Xperiment*'s co-feature was *The Black Sleep*, a return to the mad scientist type of film so prevalent in the 1930s and 1940s. Among its stars are Basil Rathbone and Bela Lugosi, who co-starred in 1939's *Son of Frankenstein*, as well as Lon Chaney and John Carradine.)

However, it is not quite Fall 1957 yet. Most young people will have to settle for what their television sets offer. Listed below is a sample of the Baltimore-D.C. horror (or near-horror) offerings for the period prior to *Shock!*'s local debut in November 1957.

Alias John Preston (1956)
The Amazing Mr. X (1948)
The Ape (1940)
The Ape Man (1943)
Bedlam (1946)
The Black Doll (1938)
The Black Raven (1943)
Bluebeard (1944)
The Brute Man (1946)
Chandu On the Magic Isle (1934)
Chandu the Magician (1932)
Condemned to Live (1935)
The Corpse Vanishes (1942)
The Creeper (1948)
Dead Men Walk (1943)
Dead of Night (1945)
The Death Kiss (1932)
The Devil Bat (1941)
Devil Bat's Daughter (1946)
Devil Girl from Mars (1954)
Donovan's Brain (1953)
Dr. Jekyll and Mr. Hyde (1941)
Dr. Renault's Secret (1942)
The Face at the Window (1939)
The Face of Marble (1946)
The Flying Serpent (1946)
Fog Island (1945)
Ghost Catchers (1944)
Ghost Story (1941)
The Ghost Train (1941)
The Ghost Walks (1934)
The Girl Who Dared (1944)
Gog (1954)
Hangover Square (1945)
The Hound of the Baskervilles (1939)
House of Mystery (1934)
The Human Monster (1939)
I Walked with A Zombie (1943)
King Kong (1933)
King of the Zombies (1941)
The Lady and the Monster (1944)
The Living Ghost (1942)
The Lodger (1944)
Lost Continent (1951)
The Mad Monster (1942)
The Magnetic Monster (1953)
The Man from Planet X (1951)

> 11.15 ⑪ Million-Dollar Movie.
> "Man From Planet X."
> With Robert Clark and
> Margaret Field.

Man in Black (1949)
The Man Who Changed His Mind (1936)
The Man with Two Lives (1942)
The Mask of Diijon (1945)
Mesa of Lost Women (1953)
The Missing Corpse (1945)
The Monkey's Paw (1948)
The Monster Maker (1944)
The Monster Walks (1932)
Night Comes Too Soon (1948)
The Night Has Eyes (1942)
One Million B.C. (1940)
The Phantom Fiend (1932)

Belgium poster for *The Human Monster*

Phantom Ship (1935)
Red Planet Mars (1952)
Return of the Ape Man (1944)
Revenge of the Zombies (1943)
Revolt of the Zombies (1936)
Riders to the Stars (1954)
Rocketship X-M (1950)
Room to Let (1950)
Scared to Death (1947)
Shadow of Chinatown (1936)
Spaceways (1953)
The Spiral Staircase (1946)
The Stolen Face (1952)
The Strange Mr. Gregory (1945)
Strangler of the Swamp (1946)
Things to Come (1936)
Three Cases of Murder (1953)
Torture Ship (1939)
Tower of Terror (1941)
Valley of the Zombies (1945)
The Vampire Bat (1933)
White Zombie (1932)
Woman Who Came Back (1945)
You'll Find Out (1940)

In June 1957, Columbia Pictures' television subsidiary Screen Gems acquired the rights to syndicate over 500 Universal Studios films. Screen Gems packaged 52 of them together as *Shock!*, making them available to television markets around the country. Executives had all kinds of promotional ideas on how to get viewers to watch, including the recommendation that local talent host these shows. *Shock!* debuted in some markets as early as October the same year. In the November 3, 1957 edition of *The Sunday Sun*'s "News, Notes About Television," columnist Kathryn Geraghty writes, "Horror Appeal—With the current popularity of Boris Karloff, Bela Lugosi and similar horror films on TV, last week's *Sponsor* magazine sought to discover the reason behind the holding power of these thrillers." The conclusion reached was, "Horror pictures have a common appeal in that a central theme runs through all of them—the unmotivated lethal impulse of the monster." Unmotivated? Whatever the true reason, less than one week after the article's publication, this appeal was about to be proved. Charm City had no idea what was about to hit, bite, and/or claw them.

Chapter 2

Dr. Lucifer (1957-1959)

On page five of the November 9, 1957 edition of *The Baltimore Sun*, there is a corner ad that plainly reads, "11:15 P.M. Tonight: *Frankenstein*. Everybody's Favorite Monster. Look for him TONIGHT on Channel 11." It is the night of nights: the debut of Baltimore's *Shock!*, hosted by Dr. Lucifer, the "Grandee of the Goose Bumps," as one ad would refer to him. As winds howled and chains rattled, Dr. Lucifer rose each Saturday night from the coffin in his laboratory. Dressed in formal wear complete with top hat and cape, and donning a split moustache and goatee, the handsome, dark-haired Dr. Lucifer certainly *looked* harmless, even while ordering "shock-tales for two" in his great, booming voice.

Lucifer's (Richard Dix) real-life wife Nancy and teenage daughter Landra also appeared on the show.

The doctor was typically dabbling in experiments that thankfully never quite worked out. Antics included:

- Being caught in his own bear trap when attempting to capture Santa Claus.
- Bringing forth a weightlifter adorned in princess attire while trying to revive a 3,000-year-old-mummy.
- Dropping a marble slab on a bill collector who shows up at the laboratory.
- Firing a cannon during a live race, which inadvertently blew up nine studio lamps.
- Inserting himself in the films now and again. (Characters having a phone conversation now unknowingly have a third party.)

At times, our host was joined by his wife Grace and daughter Lucretia (Lucifer's real-life wife Nancy and teenage daughter Landra, respectively), while Baby Borgia (his son) remained off camera. On other occasions, the "Grey Ghost" would pay a visit: a dog that brought

The actor behind the slightly sinister persona was Richard Dix, a local thespian who had served in the military during World War II as a B-17 gunner and attended the American Institute of Theatre at William and Mary College in Williamsburg, Virginia before settling down to a broadcasting career. Prior to hosting *Shock!* for WBAL TV 11, he had had his own highly rated children's show for the station playing Officer Happy, hosting *Our Gang* and *The Little Rascals* shorts. During his tenure as Dr. Lucifer, he was the managing director of the Children's Theatre Association of Baltimore as well as the president of the American Federation of Television and Radio Artists local chapter. In short, Baltimore's first horror host was not an amateur suddenly thrust into some position hosting horror movies. Instead, he was a

him the severed limbs of local children. All in good fun, of course. Dr. Lucifer was popular enough that he hosted a showing of *The Fly* on August 14, 1958, at The Stanley Theatre on Howard Street. A hearse brought the Lucifers to the playhouse. "Guests of Horror" Dracula, the Frankenstein Monster, Vampirina, the Hunchback, and, of course, the Fly itself joined them onstage.

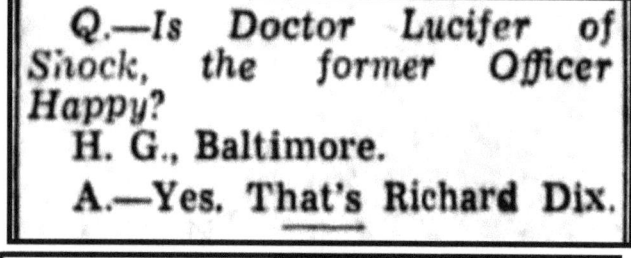

Richard Dix was a popular subject of The TV Mailbag in *The Evening Sun*.

long-standing, beloved employee with an impressive résumé when it came to the performing arts. Now in his mid-30s, he was a man who clearly enjoyed his work, as evidenced by his bringing his own family (including the family dog) onto the program. As the "Horror Appeal" article had unwittingly predicted, *Shock!* became a popular and highly successful program.

One viewer who was tuning in each week was future author/film historian/actor Gregory William Mank. Dix was a major influence on the young Mank's life, and the writer befriended the Dixes in the mid-1990s. Mank attributes his love of writing and acting to watching Officer Happy and Dr. Lucifer. "It was all because of Richard and the actual movies. I was six years old." With respect to Dix's persona, Mank recalled:

> Richard was incredible…My wife and I went to dinner with Richard and Nancy one time after they came to see a show I was in. We went to a *Bob Evans* and

Richard and Nancy Dix with Count Gore De Vol at Nostalgia Vision

he walked in and he goes up, [the hostess] asks how many and he says, "Four." And she said, "Are you an actor?" One word. She took one look at him, heard one word from him, and knew he was an actor.

Others certainly agreed Dix as Dr. Lucifer was something to behold. The show was a hit. "It was such a phenomenon at the time," Mank offered. "I think it was really kind of scandalous for Baltimore because one of the commercials they showed for *Frankenstein* that first week was the scene with him with the little girl. There was already an outcry that 'Oh my God, what are they showing on television?' The show was funny, but it wasn't silly. There were things he'd do and wouldn't do. It was a real hoot for me because I'd see him every day as Officer Happy."

In February 1993 at the Sheraton Hotel in Towson, Maryland, Richard Dix reminisced about his Dr. Lucifer days during a Horror Host panel presented as part of the *Nostalgia Vision* convention. He told the audience, "On Wednesday the films would arrive, and a fella named Lenny Levin and I, we would sit down, and we'd watch the film, and then we'd try to pick out a theme from the show." The production team would then decide where they would edit Lucifer into the program. Sometimes he would receive a kiss from the hero. Other times he might detour a car off the road.

Dr. Lucifer (portrayed by Richard Dix) is the host of "Shock," Channel 11's late Saturday night horror movie.

TV News And Notes
By WILLIAM HYDER

RICHARD DIX, formerly of WBAL-TV, has acted many roles in his time. For years he was well known to Vagabond audiences. On a Channel 11 children's show he played a Keystone Cop, Officer Happy, and as Dr. Lucifer he used to come out of a coffin to introduce the Saturday night horror movie.

Since leaving the station he has been acting in a cabaret theater in Chicago, where he was so successful in "Born Yesterday" and "Will Success Spoil Rock Hunter?" last summer that a rival club has signed him to repeat the roles this year.

But Dix's most unusual role was an impromptu impersonation of a wax dummy at the Robert E. Lee home in Arlington, Va., last month. Back in Baltimore between engagements, Dix was hired by WRC-TV, Washington, to portray Lee in a historical film. The program, "Robert E. Lee: Night of Decision," will be seen at 6 P.M. Saturday on Channel 4.

A Period Piece

Lee's home has been preserved as a historical monument, and the station got permission to shoot the film there. The rooms are barred to protect the furnishings, but one afternoon last month Dix, dressed in period costume and made up with a black mustache such as Lee wore at the beginning of the Civil War, was admitted to a sitting room.

While waiting for the camera crew he sat quietly, studying his script. The camera make-up on his face gave him an unreal look, and before long he heard a voice. "Isn't that a wonderful likeness? Look—they even put hair on the back of its hands!" Dix looked up, and the faces peering at him through the bars were startled and then embarrassed.

At this the guides taking the visitors around saw a chance to enliven their routine. As Dix studied his book, occasionally turning a page, they began to tell visitors about the wonderful new Robert E. Lee mannequin. They went on to invent a motor-driven mechanism inside it that caused the figure to turn a leaf of its book every 2½ minutes.

Gag Gets Try

Dix went along with the joke. As each group stopped at the door, the guide would point out the motorized mannequin. Any second now, they said, it would turn a page. Watch! The group would fall silent. Dix, with an actor's instinct, would let the anticipation build up. Finally, in a slow, mechanical movement, his hand would move up, turn the page and return to its place. There would be a general murmur of gratification and the group would move on to the next room.

There were those who thought the performance a sham. A group of 80 school children came through and a sharp-eyed boy remarked that the dummy seemed to be breathing. "Yes," the guide ad-libbed, "You see, in the dummy's chest there's an inflated bladder run by the same motor that drives the arm."

Soon the camera crew arrived in the room. Having been coached by the guides, they pretended to regard Dix as a waxen nonentity. The cameraman rearranged one of the arms of the motionless figure, as if to get a better composition, and a lighting man impersonally moved the feet out of the way of a power cable.

After 45 minutes of sitting still Dix tired of the joke. It was closing time, and the last visitors were straggling through. As a couple were looking through the bars debating whether the mustached figure in the chair was a man or a mannequin, Dix put down his book, stood up and settled the argument.

Highlights Of Week

TODAY
THE OPEN DOOR—Passover concert with Jan Peerce, tenor, and the CBS Symphony Orchestra. Channel 2. 10 A.M.
HALL OF FAME—"Give Us Barabbas." Drama about the criminal whose life was spared when Jesus was condemned. With James Daly. In color. Rebroadcast. Channel 11. 6 P.M.
PROJECT 20—"He Is Risen." The Crucifixion and Resurrection of Christ as shown in paintings by great masters. In color. Channel 11. 8.30 P.M.
SHOW OF THE WEEK—"The Action in New Orleans." A con man tries to bilk a widow visiting New Orleans. With Bob Cummings. In color. Channel 11. 10 P.M.

TUESDAY
RAINBOW OF STARS—Variety special combined with a tour of New York's Rockefeller Center. With Robert Goulet, Al Hirt, Nancy Walker, Dick Button, Carol Lawrence and

Edward Van Sloan and Bela Lugosi in *Dracula*, which aired on *Dr. Lucifer* December 7, 1957 at 11:15 PM.

During an airing of *Dracula's Daughter*, while an authority figure describes how the poor, deceased wretch Renfield dined on spiders, there is a cut to Dr. Lucifer enthusiastically enjoying lobster.

In an interview with Mank for *Midnight Marquee*, Dix explained the idea behind Maryland's first horror host. "My inspiration for Dr. Lucifer was Charles Addams. Both Nancy and I are fans of Addams; we had all of his cartoon books and liked his approach and sense of humor." In accordance with the macabre humor, the *Shock!* set featured actual human skulls and bones, as well as an authentic mummy, all courtesy of Johns Hopkins and similar venues. (They had trouble getting rid of these props at the end of the program because they had no death certificates!) The painted backdrop featured a ghoulish portrait "hanging" above a fireplace, with gas lamps on either side. The set would have been at home in any old dark house mystery.

> "While at WBAL, I played Dr. Lucifer, a grisly host who spoofed the late Saturday night horror movies," says Dix. "Then I was fired," he adds with a laugh. "Too long a story to go into. So I decided to try theater permanently. That was in 1959, and I have been employed in this medium ever since."

While Dr. Lucifer may have been an unsuccessful scientist, Dix continued, "He saw himself as a 'quality' scientist—he drank tea, he did all 'quality' things and he liked working on 'quality' projects. But he had no 'quality' at all—the results of his experiments were always disastrous. It was a lot of fun."

His wife Nancy agreed. She told the *Nostalgia Vision* audience, "It was fun! I always looked forward to the times when [Richard] was either sick or had another engagement, because then *I'd* take over."

Mank recalled one of the doctor's many failed experiments. "He was making a hair tonic. He had this chemical vial and pouring stuff in, and smoke was coming out. He was there talking about [the experiment] and the camera came in real close to the bottles and then stayed on his hands for a long time…and when the camera pulled back, he had a skull cap on."

There were other examples of Dr. Lucifer's playfulness. As the classic Universal globe turns and the plane circles, suddenly there's Dr. Lucifer piloting, while donned in aviator goggles and scarf. As we are looking into a microscope during *The Invisible Man Returns*, we're suddenly treated to a bikini-clad beauty as she comes into focus. And as Boris Karloff ponders his ugliness during *The Raven*, he is suddenly interrupted by an ad asking, "Do you wear dental plates?" A phony commercial offered sulfuric acid aftershave.

The show could even be risqué on occasion. As the camera pans four bottles sitting atop a laboratory shelf, we see the labels 4Q and then 4Q2. "We almost got fired at the end of *that* show," Dix told the Towson crowd. During one program, Mrs. Lucifer was supposed to boil a bunny rabbit.

And the budget to pull all this off? Dix answered, "We had no money." He added, "You took advantage of whatever you could at the moment."

One example of taking such advantage occurred when WBAL hosted a stunt whereby a man spent five days submerged in a large fish tank. Dix decided the "idiot" could serve as Lucifer's daughter's pet.

Regrettably, since the shows were performed live, there is no visual record of the fun. No kinescopes were made of the programs, and so Dr. Lucifer's antics cannot be truly appreciated by those who weren't seated in front of their sets during the bad doctor's tenure.

That tenure abruptly ended in March 1959 when new WBAL management failed to renew the *Shock!* contract. Consequently, Dr. Lucifer was suddenly off the air, and titles in the *Son of Shock* Screen Gems package were never aired as part of Baltimore's incarnation of *Shock!* When the horror titles started appearing again, they were part of Saturday's "Tonight's Best Feature" or perhaps a late-afternoon movie. There was no fanfare. There would never be another horror host on a *network* affiliate in Baltimore (D.C.'s CBS affiliate Channel 9 would be home to Sir Graves Ghastly, however), and Charm City would have to wait for over a decade before another host disgraced the airwaves.

After leaving Channel 11, Richard Dix pursued (and succeeded in) a career in the theater, where he spent the next 30 or so years. Mank relates, "I think Richard felt,

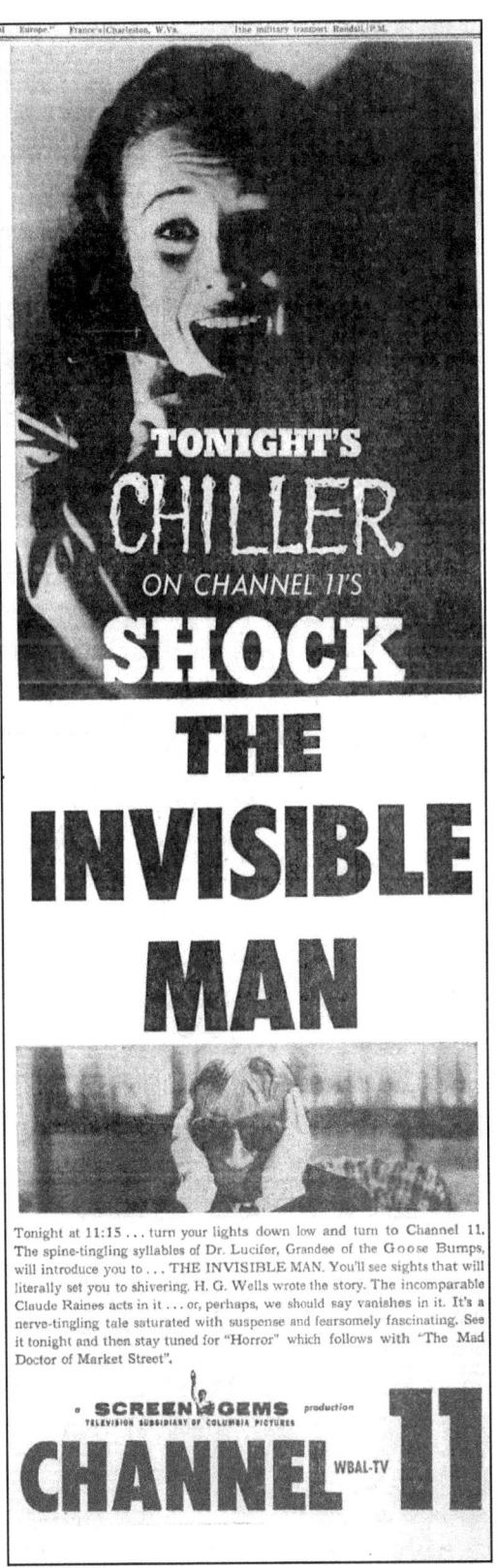

as most actors do, he could have gone a lot farther. He really was very, very talented. He hoped the big break would come. As it was, he made a living, supported himself, raised two kids…from being an actor."

Richard Dix was genuinely touched when he learned during his 1993 convention appearance that he

Dr. Lucifer... Baltimore's bumbling bogeyman haunts on WBAL-TV

A macabre figure who comes off more mocking than menacing is Dr. Lucifer, a tremendously popular fellow in Baltimore, Md. In his laboratory at WBAL-TV (1 A.M. Sat.) his fiendish brain is constantly at work experimenting and creating—but his experiments usually backfire and his creations are harmless, making him a bumbling sort of a bogeyman. As a terror he's all thumbs, and that's just the way Richard Dix, who breathes life into the luckless Lucifer, plans it. For instance, the bear trap he set to catch Santa Claus (just to prove there is a Santa Claus) caught the good doctor instead. His attempt to recreate a baby sitter from a 3,000-year-old mummy (because the label said she was young and beautiful) resulted instead in an unhappy 350-pound weight lifter in the Egyptian princess' clothing. One night Lucifer dropped a marble slab on a bill collector who was hounding him. At various times during the show he'd lift the marble and ask the man if he'd give up. Each time the answer was no, so the slab would drop again. When the collector finally gave up Lucifer let him have it again—because he hates quitters! Though Lucifer works mostly solo he is occasionally joined by the rest of his video family—his wife, Grace; a daughter, Lucretia, and Baby Borgia. The formally attired doctor is also aided—or victimized—by a Great Dane who's addicted to showing up on camera with dismembered arms and legs of neighborhood children. For this Lucifer chastises him publicly as not being neighborly. And, believe it or not, the whole thing is handled so amusingly that it comes off more "grin" than "grim." Years of acting, directing, producing and studying the dramatic arts are behind the 33-year-old Mr. Dix's week-after-week characterization. A native of Baltimore, Md., he attended City College of Baltimore and Johns Hopkins University. In addition he received a scholarship to the Institute of the Theatre in Williamsburg, Va., in 1948 and again from 1950-52. His career was interrupted by service in the U.S. Air Force from 1944-46 and 1950-51. A veteran actor, Dix has some 200 roles to his credit, including off-Broadway productions and a five-year run as lead in *The Common Glory*, a historical pageant staged annually at Williamsburg. A versatile performer, Dix has run the gamut of professional acting from such deep drama fare as *The Glass Menagerie* and *Petrified Forest* in legitimate theater, to the role of *Officer Happy* on WBAL-TV. His favorite role is that of *Scrooge* in Dickens' *Christmas Carol*, which he did on network television in 1948. At present he's a director of the Children's Theatre Association of Baltimore and president of the local AFTRA chapter. So when things go wrong on Baltimore's *Shock Theatre*, the viewers needn't get too upset, for Dr. Lucifer knows what he's doing—every stumble of the way.

40 FEBRUARY, 1959

was remembered and beloved. Baltimore's first horror host passed away September 27, 1998. Mank concluded, "He was a very versatile actor; he could do anything. He was a brilliant inspiration, personally. He was a superb actor."

By all accounts, it would certainly seem Dr. Lucifer had quality after all.

Airs at 11:15 p.m.
11/09/57 *Frankenstein* (1931)
11/16/57 *The Mummy* (1932)
11/23/57 *The Wolf Man* (1941)
11/30/57 *Frankenstein Meets the Wolf Man* (1943)
12/07/57 *Dracula* (1931)
12/14/57 Didn't air
12/21/57 *The Frozen Ghost* (1945)
12/28/57 *She-Wolf of London* (1946)
01/04/58 *The Mummy's Hand* (1940)
01/11/58 *The Invisible Man* (1933)
01/18/58 *The Black Cat* (1934)
01/25/58 *House of Horrors* (1946)
02/01/58 *Murders in the Rue Morgue* (1932)
02/08/58 *The Mad Ghoul* (1943)
02/15/58 *WereWolf of London* (1935)

02/22/58 *The Mummy's Tomb* (1942)
03/01/58 *The Raven* (1935)
03/08/58 *Night Key* (1937)
03/15/58 *The Strange Case of Dr. Rx* (1942)
03/22/58 *Nightmare* (1942)
03/29/58 *Night Monster* (1942)
04/05/58 *The Invisible Ray* (1936)
04/12/58 *Son of Frankenstein* (1939)
04/19/58 *Secret of the Blue Room* (1933)
04/26/58 *The Great Impersonation* (1935)
05/03/58 *The Wolf Man* (1941)
05/10/58 *The Third Man* (1949)
05/17/58 *The Mummy's Hand* (1940)
05/24/58 *Mystery of Edwin Drood* (1935)
05/31/58 *Dracula's Daughter* (1936)
06/07/58 *Frankenstein* (1931)
06/14/58 *She-Wolf of London* (1946)

Airs at 1:00 a.m.
06/21/58 *My Son is Guilty* (1939)
06/28/58 *Mystery of Marie Roget* (1942)
07/05/58 *Calling Dr. Death* (1943)
07/12/58 *The Invisible Man Returns* (1940)
07/19/58 *Before Midnight* (1933)
07/26/58 *Reported Missing* (1937)
08/02/58 *The Mummy's Ghost* (1944)
08/09/58 *The Undying Monster* (1942)
08/16/58 *The Cat Creeps* (1946)
08/23/58 *A Dangerous Game* (1941)
08/30/58 *The Mad Ghoul* (1943)
09/06/58 *Man Made Monster* (1941)
09/13/58 *Murders in the Rue Morgue* (1932)
09/20/58 *Pillow of Death* (1945)
09/27/58 *The Spider Woman Strikes Back* (1946)
10/04/58 *Weird Woman* (1944)
10/11/58 *Scared to Death* (1947)
10/18/58 *The Man Who Wouldn't Die* (1942)
10/25/58 *Nightmare* (1942)
11/01/58 *Calling Dr. Death* (1943)
11/08/58 *The Glass Tomb* (1955)

11/15/58 *Mystery of the White Room* (1939)
11/22/58 *The Witness Vanishes* (1939)
11/29/58 *Night Key* (1937)
12/06/58 *Dracula's Daughter* (1936)
12/13/58 *The Human Monster* (1939)
12/20/58 *The Strange Case of Dr. Rx* (1942)
12/27/58 *Mystery of Edwin Drood* (1935)
01/03/59 *The Raven* (1935)

Airs at 12:30 a.m.
01/10/59 *The Invisible Man Returns* (1940)
01/17/59 *The Mad Doctor of Market Street* (1942)
01/24/59 *Chamber of Horrors* (1940)
01/31/59 *Night Monster* (1942)
02/07/59 *Dracula* (1931)
02/14/59 *Dead Man's Eyes* (1944)
02/21/59 *Secret of the Chateau* (1934)
02/28/59 *Man Made Monster* (1941)
03/07/59 *The Mummy's Ghost* (1944)
03/14/59 *The Last Warning* (1938)
03/21/59 *The Man Who Cried Wolf* (1937)
03/28/59 *Mystery of Marie Roget* (1942)

Chapter 3

The Great Zucchini (1967-1970)

"Roll it before it rots!" The Great Zucchini hosted *Supernatural Theater* Saturday nights on WDCA Channel 20 and was, therefore, the station's first horror host and D.C.'s first host since the mid-1950s. Independent WDCA had begun broadcasting April 20, 1966, with un-hosted terror films part of the initial programming: the station presented *House of Horrors* Saturday and Sunday afternoons. The new Washington, D.C. station, however, did not yet have the *Shock!* titles as part of their programming. (Channel 9 was still running *Shock!*, albeit un-hosted, in 1967.) Instead WDCA had various film packages such as Eurpoa "33" which consisted mostly of German *krimis*, or crime films, based largely on the works of Edgar Wallace; and Screen Gems "X" package of 15 science fiction titles (e.g. *The H-Man*).

After a little over a year on the air, WDCA reshuffled its schedule to include The Great Zucchini, who resided

Bela Lugosi as Ygor in *Son of Frankenstein*

in the basement of the station, watching over the props stored therein in exchange for living quarters. The host looked like a relative of Bela Lugosi's Ygor character from *Son of Frankenstein* and *Ghost of Frankenstein*, with his shaggy hair and full beard and moustache. There were also burn marks on his face, reminders of a long-ago fire. Like Dr. Lucifer before him, the character was a hit and the fan mail started pouring in.

The man beneath the makeup was Bill Miller, a former radio announcer who had joined the station just over a month prior to assuming horror host duties. Miller was born in Spartanburg, South Carolina, and graduated from Wofford College. His first of several television gigs was with WSPA-TV Channel 7, Spartanburg's CBS affiliate. Miller had created a version of the Great Zucchini when he worked for Florence, South Carolina's WBTW, his employer just prior to joining WDCA. In fact, Miller had created multiple characters while with WBTW. Among his roles were horror hosts Gonzales the Mad Mexican and The Whistler, who presented fright fare under the banner *Creepy Inn*, which aired Friday nights after the late news. When Miller migrated to Washington's WDCA, he first served as host of the music and dance program *Wing Ding* weekdays from 4:30 p.m. to 5:30 p.m. starting April 3, 1967 (*Billboard* magazine announced his new gig!), eventually hosting the Saturday edition also. (His last *Wing Ding* show was August 26, 1967.) Less than two months later, however, he was hosting *Supernatural Theater*. In addition to his acting and vocal talents, Miller was adept at putting on his own

> **BATTLE OF BOGIES**
> For those interested in "sights" without much "sound", a curiosity has been developing during the past few months as late local televiewers tuned to Channel 13's two weekend octoplasmic extravaganzas are coming to realize.
> Spine-tinglers, Friday night's "Creepy Inn" and Sunday night's 'Directors' Choice" hosts are at it hot and heavy in what may be a television first for the area. A real knockdown, drag-out competition for "who's got the creepiest and spookiest" old movie with which to terrify the masses. The question still appears to be unresolved, but it would seem from this side of the tube that "Directors' Choice" host Stropheimer Von Nastychap is in the running slightly ahead of his dual opponents, a formidable and wicked-looking Mexican and the ghoulish Whistler (referred to by Von Nastychap as "Old Jellyface!")

YOUR HORROR MOVIE HOST

By William Hyder

MONSTERS — a regular school of them—flourished on TV seven or eight years ago as hosts of late-evening horror movies. Baltimore had its *Dr. Lucifer* (Richard Dix), a ghastly figure in a moldy dress suit who arose from a coffin every week.

It takes a lot to kill a monster—a silver bullet, or a stake driven through his heart at a crossroads, or (as in the case of the TV monsters) bad ratings. But any devotee of horror movies knows that it is a mistake to underestimate the breed's power of survival. A new generation has begun on Washington's Channel 20 (WDCA-TV) in the person of *The Great Zucchini*.

A sort of first cousin to the Phantom of the Opera, *Zucchini* was once a stage magician,, a master of legerdemain, spiritualism and illusion. A theater fire at some remote time ruined his face and with it his career. Now, a pitiful but harmless creature in a moth-eaten tuxedo, he lurks in the basement of WDCA-TV with the tacit approval of management, keeping the station's props in order in return for a place to live out his days. Once a week, at the traditional witching hour for TV horror movies, Saturdays at 11 P.M., he emerges with high-pitched laugh and off-key whistling to introduce and comment on the films.

Zucchini is the creation of Bill Miller, of the WDCA-TV announcing staff. A native of South Carolina, Miller has worked for TV stations from Miami to Washington, always combining his career in broadcasting with another in little-theater and repertory companies. He specializes in character makeup and brings the art to his TV work whenever he can.

THE Great Zucchini, for example, was born at WBTW-TV in Florence, S.C., one of several characters Miller developed for a children's show. He fit in perfectly when Miller was assigned to do the horror movie at WDCA-TV. But he requires great devotion from his creator. Miller has to do a two-hour makeup job on himself every Saturday night before *Zucchini* can limp from his lair in the station's basement.

The Great Zucchini

makeup. According to an October 22, 1967 article in *The Baltimore Sun*, it took Miller two hours to transform himself into his horror host character.

The Great Zucchini limped about WDCA's cellar during his hosting duties, laughing maniacally and carrying a cane in his gloved hands, occasionally breaking bottles while he ranted and raved, berating those around him. Miller gave his character a backstory too. Zucchini was formerly a gifted stage magician whose career was cut short due to a fire in 1935. Disfigured and bitter, he now abuses his projectionist Waldo ("You boob!") and his audience, whom he calls "boobies." Not a mad scientist like Dr. Lucifer, he nevertheless hatched horrific plans such as eliminating his competition (Channels 7 and 9) with a death ray. Always the nihilist, he created a "broken hearts club" whereby he gave awful romantic advice. In response to the popular "Up with People" tour featuring singing, upbeat high school juniors and seniors, he launched a "Down with People" campaign. However, he did at least read fan mail—whether positive or negative—on the air. He also invited viewers to send him their homemade movies. Apparently, the Great Zucchini never showed any of them.

After over three years of hosting and seeming popularity, however, the Great Zucchini's duties abruptly came to an end when Channel 20 ceased broadcasting *Supernatural Theater* in September 1970. The circumstances surrounding Bill Miller's departure from WDCA remain unclear, although one possible reason given was that he was fired when he asked for a raise. (Future Channel 20 horror host Dick "Count Gore" Dyszel told the author that *no one* ever mentioned The Great Zucchini during his 15 years at the station!) All that we know regarding the fate of Miller's host is what the sta-

tion announcer reported after the final broadcast. "The Great Zucchini and Waldo have escaped from the catacombs beneath Channel 20. They were last seen running across the studio roof." Unfortunately, like Dr. Lucifer, no footage of the Great Zucchini in action is known to exist.

After leaving WDCA, Miller eventually relocated to Atlanta, Georgia where he formed William Miller Associates, a company that produced commercials, documentaries, and political ads. During the 1990s, he returned to South Carolina where he switched careers, becoming involved in the hotel industry with great success. In 2006, he was hired by Radisson Hotel & Suites, Spartanburg as its Director of Sales and Marketing.

[Author's note: What happened to Miller after being hired by Radisson or how he felt about his stint as horror host will most likely remain a mystery, which is a true shame given his lengthy tenure. With a rather common moniker (there were both a politician and football star with the same name around the time Miller was active in D.C.) and not knowing his year of birth or any other personal information, it proved impossible to track Miller down despite various attempts.]

French poster for *Uncle was a Vampire* shown July 15, 1967

Airs at 11:00 PM
05/20/67 *The Indian Scarf* (1963)
05/27/67 *Monster from the Ocean Floor* (1954)
06/03/67 *Invaders from Mars* (1953)
06/10/67 *Sky Above Heaven* (1965)
06/17/67 *Bluebeard* (1963)
06/24/67 *No Survivors Please.* (1964)
07/01/67 *The Undying Monster* (1942)
07/08/67 *The Invisible Terror* (1963)
07/15/67 *Uncle Was a Vampire* (1959)
07/22/67 *House of Horrors* (1946)
07/29/67 *The Crawling Eye* (1958)
08/05/67 *The Ringer* (1952)
08/12/67 *The Boogie Man Will Get You* (1942)
08/19/67 *Invisible Agent* (1942)
08/26/67 *King of the Zombies* (1941)
09/02/67 *Elevator to the Gallows* (1958)
09/09/67 *Revenge of the Zombies* (1943)
09/16/67 *The Death Ray Mirror of Doctor Mabuse* (1964)
09/23/67 *The Forger of London* (1961)
09/30/67 *The Inn on the River* (1962)
10/07/67 *The Vampire Bat* (1933)
10/14/67 *Teenage Monster* (1958)
10/21/67 *The Curse of the Yellow Snake* (1963)
10/28/67 *The Invisible Dr. Mabuse* (1962)
11/04/67 *Violent Midnight* (1963)
11/11/67 *Bride of the Gorilla* (1951)
11/18/67 *Captive Wild Woman* (1943)
11/25/67 *The Testament of Dr. Mabuse* (1962)
12/02/67 *The Terrible People* (1960)
12/09/67 *The Squeaker* (1963)
12/16/67 *The Green Archer* (1961)
12/23/67 *The Ape* (1940)
12/30/67 *The Secret of the Chinese Carnation* (1964)
01/06/68 *The Face of Marble* (1946)
01/13/68 *The Creeper* (1948)
01/20/68 *The Night Has Eyes* (1942)
01/27/68 *The H-Man* (1959)
02/03/68 *The Woman Eater* (1958)
02/10/68 *Creature with the Atom Brain* (1955)
02/17/68 *The 27th Day* (1957)
02/24/68 *The Tingler* (1959)
03/02/68 *Curse of the Demon* (1957)
03/09/68 *Invaders from Mars* (1953)
03/16/68 *The Avenger* (1960)
03/23/68 *The Strangler of Blackmoor Castle* (1963)
03/30/68 *The Mad Ghoul* (1943)
04/06/68 *The Door with Seven Locks* (1962)
04/13/68 *The Undying Monster* (1942)
04/20/68 *Bela Lugosi Meets a Brooklyn Gorilla* (1952)
04/27/68 *Monster from the Ocean Floor* (1954)
05/04/68 *Invisible Agent* (1942)
05/11/68 *The Son of Dr. Jekyll* (1951)

Claudia Barrett fights off the *Robot Monster,* aired by The Great Zucchini March 15, 1969.

05/18/68 *Battle in Outer Space* (1959)
05/25/68 *The Invisible Dr. Mabuse* (1962)
06/01/68 *The Amazing Mr. X* (1948)
06/08/68 *House of Horrors* (1946)
06/15/68 *The Stranglers of Bombay* (1959)
06/22/68 *Tower of Terror* (1941)
06/29/68 *The Testament of Dr. Mabuse* (1962)
07/06/68 *The Death Ray Mirror of Doctor Mabuse* (1964)
07/13/68 *It Came from Beneath the Sea* (1955)
07/20/68 *The Electronic Monster* (1958)
07/27/68 *Sky Above Heaven* (1965)
08/03/68 *The Giant Claw* (1957)
08/10/68 *Revenge of the Zombies* (1943)
08/17/68 *The Creeper* (1948)
08/24/68 *The Living Ghost* (1942)
08/31/68 *12 to the Moon* (1960)
09/07/68 *The Woman Eater* (1958)
09/14/68 *Teenage Monster* (1958)
09/21/68 *The Black Abbot* (1963)
09/28/68 *The H-Man* (1959)
10/05/68 *Mothra* (1961)
10/12/68 *Monster from a Prehistoric Planet* (1967)
10/19/68 *Ghidorah, the Three-Headed Monster* (1964)
10/26/68 *The Mad Magician* (1954)
11/02/68 *King of the Zombies* (1941)

11/09/68 *War of the Monsters* (1966)
11/16/68 *Circus of Fear* (1966)
11/23/68 *Planet of the Vampires* (1965)
11/30/68 *Sky Above Heaven* (1965)
12/07/68 *The Undying Monster* (1942)
12/14/68 *The Death Ray Mirror of Doctor Mabuse* (1964)
12/21/68 *The Mad Ghoul* (1943)
12/28/68 *No Survivors Please.* (1964)
01/04/69 *The Red Circle* (1960)
01/11/69 *The Invisible Terror* (1963)
01/18/69 *Battle in Outer Space* (1959)
01/25/69 *Majin, Monster of Terror* (1966)
02/01/69 *The Time Travelers* (1964)
02/08/69 *The Avenger* (1960)
02/15/69 *Mars Needs Women* (1967)
02/22/69 *Violent Midnight* (1963)
03/01/69 *Attack of the Robots* (1966)
03/08/69 *The Crawling Eye* (1958)
03/15/69 *Robot Monster* (1953)
03/22/69 *Uncle Was a Vampire* (1959)
03/29/69 *Fame and the Devil* (1949)
04/05/69 *The Face at the Window* (1939)
04/12/69 *The Creeper* (1948)
04/19/69 *Revenge of the Zombies* (1943)
04/26/69 *The Face of Marble* (1946)

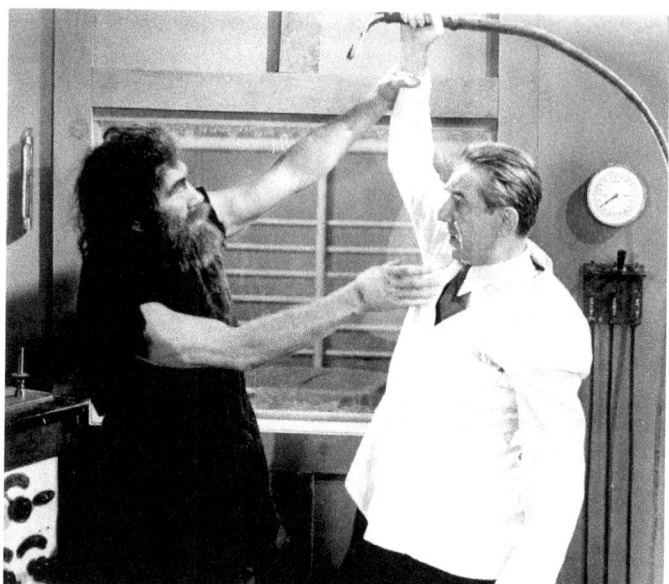

Frank Moran and Bela Lugosi in *Return of the Ape Man* which aired January 24, 1970

Oops, think we had a typo here!

05/03/69 *The Tingler* (1959)
05/10/69 *The Boogie Man Will Get You* (1942)
05/17/69 *The H-Man* (1959)
05/24/69 *The Black Abbot* (1963)
05/31/69 *The Electronic Monster* (1958)
06/07/69 *Rome Against Rome* (1964)
06/14/69 *Crimes at the Dark House* (1940)
06/21/69 *Bride of the Gorilla* (1951)
06/28/69 *Sweeney Todd: The Demon Barber of Fleet Street* (1936)
07/05/69 *What A Carve Up* (1961)
07/12/69 *The Mad Magician* (1954)
07/19/69 *The Jungle Captive* (1945)
07/26/69 *The Red Circle* (1960)
08/02/69 *Uncle Was a Vampire* (1959)
08/09/69 *The Ape* (1940)
08/16/69 *The Strange Mr. Gregory* (1945)
08/23/69 *Fog for A Killer* (1962)
08/30/69 *Horror Island* (1941)

Airs at Midnight
09/06/69 *The Living Ghost* (1942)
09/13/69 *Violent Midnight* (1963)
09/20/69 *Captive Wild Woman* (1943)
09/27/69 *The Spider Woman Strikes Back* (1946)
10/04/69 *House of Horrors* (1946)
10/11/69 *Monster from a Prehistoric Planet* (1967)
10/18/69 *Creature of Destruction* (1967)
10/25/69 *The Mad Doctor of Market Street* (1942)
11/01/69 *In the Year 2889* (1967)
11/08/69 *Bela Lugosi Meets a Brooklyn Gorilla* (1952)
11/15/69 *No Survivors Please.* (1964)
11/22/69 *The Man Who Could Work Miracles* (1936)
11/29/69 *Fog for A Killer* (1962)
12/06/69 *The Vampire Bat* (1933)

12/13/69 *The Black Abbot* (1963)
12/20/69 *Crimes at the Dark House* (1940)
12/27/69 *Fame and the Devil* (1949)
01/03/70 *The Carpet of Horror* (1962)
01/10/70 *The Spider Woman Strikes Back* (1946)
01/17/70 Didn't air

Airs at 11:00 p.m.
01/24/70 *Return of the Ape Man* (1944)
01/31/70 *The Incredibly Strange Creatures Who Stopped Living and Became Mixed-Up Zombies!!?* (1964)
02/07/70 *The Crimes of Stephen Hawke* (1936)
02/14/70 *The Unearthly* (1957)

Here is a film you don't see every day: *The Carpet of Horror*, a German film titled *Der Teppich des Grauens*. Shown by The Great Zucchini January 3, 1970. iMDB describes the plot as "An evil genius uses poison gas to avenge himself on his enemies."

02/21/70 *Mars Needs Women* (1967)
02/28/70 *Jack the Ripper* (1959)
03/07/70 *Cyclotrode "X"* (1966)
03/14/70 *Project Moonbase* (1953)
03/21/70 *Invasion of the Body Snatchers* (1956)
03/28/70 *Sweeney Todd: The Demon Barber of Fleet Street* (1936)
04/04/70 *Blood of Dracula* (1957)
04/11/70 *The Vampire Bat* (1933)
04/18/70 *Bela Lugosi Meets a Brooklyn Gorilla* (1952)
04/25/70 *Robot Monster* (1953)
05/02/70 *The Undead* (1957)
05/09/70 *Terror from the Year 5000* (1958)
05/16/70 *The Killer Shrews* (1959)
05/23/70 *A Bucket of Blood* (1959)
05/30/70 *Attack of the Giant Leeches* (1959)
06/06/70 *The Carpet of Horror* (1962)
06/13/70 *Return of the Ape Man* (1944)
06/20/70 *The Avenger* (1960)
06/27/70 *The Curse of the Hidden Vault* (1964)
07/04/70 *Revenge of the Zombies* (1943)
07/11/70 *The Living Ghost* (1942)
07/18/70 *King of the Zombies* (1941)
07/25/70 *Captive Wild Woman* (1943)
08/01/70 *Bride of the Gorilla* (1951)
08/08/70 *Crimes at the Dark House* (1940)
08/15/70 *Fame and the Devil* (1949)
08/22/70 *The Vampire Bat* (1933)
08/29/70 Didn't air
09/05/70 *The Brain Eaters* (1958)

> ⑳ **Supernatural Theater.**
> "With the Great Zucchini,"
> Bill Goodwin and Robert Lowery. 1946.

Chapter 4

Sir Graves Ghastly (1970-1971)

"Nyah-ah-ah-ah-ah! Welcome once again to that ghastly production *Sir Graves Presents*. I am your gruesome greeter-how do you like that?-Sir Graves Ghastly." This greeting (or some variation thereof) was that of D.C.'s newest horror host. WTOP Channel 9 stopped airing its un-hosted *Shock Theater* in January 1969. However, the station still had the rights to plenty of horror films. Therefore, beginning in January 1970 WTOP imported Detroit's Lawson Deming, better known to his fans as Sir Graves Ghastly, to host *Sir Graves Ghastly Presents* Friday nights and Saturday afternoons, the latter geared more to the kiddies. Deming originated his character in 1967 (the same year The Great Zucchini debuted) on Detroit, Michigan's WJBK Channel 2, where the show impressively ran until 1982, airing its last outing the day after Halloween. Ghastly's Washington career was unfortunately much, much shorter.

Actor Deming lived in Cleveland, Ohio, and would fly to D.C. and tape his host segments. Looking and dressed like a satanic vampire Ghastly would rise from his coffin and enter his graveyard each week through heavy, iron gates to sound effects borrowed from the Disney's 1964 record album *Chilling Thrilling Sounds of the Haunted House*. Ghastly himself sounded not unlike Hans Conried did when voicing Snidely Whiplash for the *Dudley Do-Right* cartoons. The last touch was a nasally cackle, inspired by the Devil character in *Damn Yankees*. "Welcome to that ghastly production *Sir Graves Ghastly Presents*," he would greet. In *Scary Monsters* Issue 21, Deming described his character as follows:

> He was sort of a half-assed vampire who had trod the boards with Will Shakespeare and got into an argument with Her Majesty the Queen and was hanged in the Tower of London. Like a bad vaccination, it didn't quite take, and so consequently, Sir Graves was able to return.

Sir Graves certainly seemed to be enjoying himself, engaging in macabre silliness when the movie wasn't playing. For example, he may be trying to call Morey Dracula's Delicatessen, a local establishment, and be connected instead with the Count Dracula residing in Transylvania.

Lawson Deming as Sir Graves Ghastly sounded like Hans Conried as Snidely Whiplash in *The Dudley Do-Right Show*

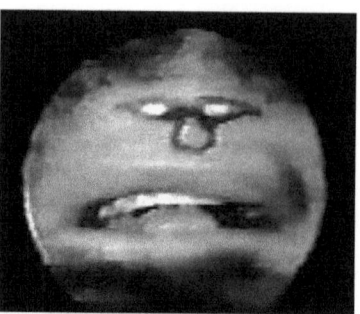

Beware of the Glob!

GHOULISH HOSTS RESURRECTED IN WASHINGTON

By William Hyder

SIR GRAVES GHASTLY is a spooky bearded man in evening clothes and a cape, who hosts horror movies on Washington's Channel 9 Fridays at 11.30 P.M. and Saturdays at 3 P.M.

A viewer who tunes in without warning might feel the way the scientists felt when a coelacanth—a fish they said had been extinct for 70 million years—turned up among an African fisherman's catch one day in 1938. At some remote period, creatures like Sir Graves Ghastly flourished briefly on TV. Baltimore had a certain Dr. Lucifer, a ghoul named Zacherle appeared on a Philadelphia station, and there were others in other cities. Then they faded away, and for 10 years it looked as if the species had disappeared from the earth like the passenger pigeon and the great auk.

But a couple of seasons ago horror thrillers and monster movies became popular again. Film packages that had been languishing in the distributors' stock rooms, marked down to bargain prices, started moving again. Rental fees suddenly went up. So it was inevitable that the creepy characters who used to host such movies would appear again.

In Detroit, at WJBK-TV, an actor named Lawson Deming worked up a new version of the familiar host and called him Sir Graves Ghastly. Sir Graves is unusually cultivated and polished, for a zombie. In life he was a Shakespearean actor. He comes out of a coffin, as Dr. Lucifer (Richard Dix) used to do, and invites viewers to pass through a pair of rusty iron gates and enter the graveyard he inhabits. There he is joined by a gallery of characters with names like Glob, Tillie Trollhaus, Walter, the Cool Ghoul, Baruba and the Voice of Doom—all played by Deming.

Deming developed his versatility during his years as a radio actor. He started in Cleveland in 1932 and played hundreds of roles requiring a variety of characterizations and dialects. He has also worked as announcer, director, producer, writer, musician and puppeteer, in TV as well as radio. Before he developed Sir Graves he did a children's show in Detroit, playing a character called Woodrow the Woodsman.

WHEN WTOP-TV bought its first package of horror films the programming department decided to import Sir Graves, who was getting good ratings in Detroit. Deming flies to Washington every other week and tapes two weeks worth of skits, weird songs, flapping bats, screams and groans.

He plays everything for laughs. This doesn't please the hard-core horror-film buffs in the audience, but it satisfies most of the viewers, who regard the show as camp. On Saturday afternoons, when the audience is made up largely of children, Deming plays even more broadly. Having raised four sons himself, he thinks he has a good idea of what makes children laugh.

Deming writes all of his own material and calls this the hardest part of the job. He likes to invent skits based on electronic effects. One of his characters, the Glob, is a close-up of Deming's mouth and chin, turned upside down by electronic means. The Glob's eyes and nose are painted on Deming's chin.

Once Deming took a full-length shot of Sir Graves with one camera and a close-up of a glass of water with another.

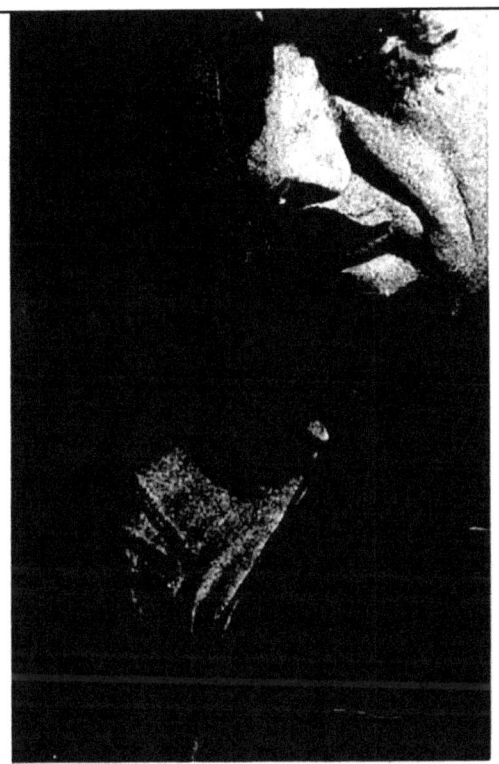

Lawson Deming

In the control room the director mixed the two images together. The result appeared to show a miniature Sir Graves submerged in the water. By fading one image out the director made Sir Graves dissolve. Then the other camera—the one aimed at the glass of water—pulled back. Sir Graves entered (now appearing full-sized), picked up the glass and drank the water.

Deming's weird carryings-on while portraying Sir Graves and his associates contrast sharply with his off-camera personality. He is a graying man of 58, compactly built and quietly dressed. The closest he comes in his private life to the horror movies he hosts is reading science fiction. "I'm a conservative actor," he says. **5**

Deming wrote all the skits for the show and created additional characters with whom Ghastly could interact through the magic of technology. Deming played all the characters. The Glob, for example, was Deming's own chin and mouth, filmed upside down, with eyes and nose painted on his chin. The Glob would be superimposed on the moon that hovered above the graveyard, and lip synch to songs such as the parody *I Wanna Bite Your Hand* (1964) by Gene Moss. Sir Graves' house cleaner Tilly Trollhouse was Leming in drag. "She" also performed songs, such as *My Funny Valentine*. Then there was Cool Ghoul, a "hep" musician mangled in a motorcycle accident. All that remained were his head and sunglasses. The Voice of Doom was a skull that told the bad jokes that viewers sent in. ("If you've got the nerve to send 'em, we've got the nerve to read 'em.") Sir Graves had an alter ego named Walter, a more genteel soul who considered Sir Graves, "sick, sick, sick," as well as a cousin called Bar-

Tilly Trollhouse

on Boogala, "who was from the Bavarian branch of the family." Sir Graves was unlike any host the area had yet

Lawson Deming

College Park Plans Silver Anniversary

College Park, (Special)—The city of College Park will celebrate its 25th anniversary as an incorporated city with a week of special events, beginning Sunday.

A parade featuring majorettes, floats and firetrucks—including a 1901 model, the oldest motor-driven fire engine in the United States—will assemble at 2 P.M. in front of Litton Industries parking lot on Calvert road.

The marchers will proceed west on Calvert to Dartmouth street, right on Dartmouth to College avenue, then left across Route 1 to the University of Maryland campus, where they will pass by the administration building and disperse at the chapel.

Old-fashioned modes of travel will highlight the procession, with horse-drawn wagons carrying the mayor and council of College Park and the Prince Georges county commissioners.

Antique Cars

Antique cars will bear the marshals. T. Raymond Burch, former Maryland legislator and one of the founding fathers of the city, will be grand marshal. Other marshals are Betty Groebli, radio and television personality, and Sir Graves Ghastly, horror show host. The university will contribute its Equestrienne Club and marching band.

Other events include a free Music Night at Ritchie Coliseum on Monday from 7 P.M. to 10 P.M., featuring singing choirs and choruses.

A Youth Council, composed of girls and boys from nearby high schools, who have been chosen by city representatives, will conduct a council meeting Tuesday.

Book Dedication

A special feature of the open meeting, to be held in the council chambers of the municipal building, will be dedication to the city's youth of a book outlining the history of the first 25 years of College Park. The author is Dr. Charles R. Davis, whose continuing service to the city incorporates 12 years as mayor and 11 years as councilman.

A full day is planned for Saturday when a Scoutarama, beginning at 9 A.M., will be held on the Rhode Island avenue recreation field and the Boys' Club will offer football games at 10 A.M. and 2 P.M. on the adjacent field.

During the day, the Branchville and College Park fire departments will both hold open house and offer fire-fighting demonstrations. Junior and senior high schoolers will be entertained at a 4 P.M. to 6 P.M. dance on the Litton lot, with music by a four-piece band.

seen. No local host ever had as many different recurring characters as *Sir Graves Ghastly Presents*.

Even though Sir Graves was hosting at a Washington D.C. station, he was popular enough to make several appearances in Maryland during his brief run. In September 1970, he was one of the antique car show marshals for College Park, Maryland's 25th Anniversary Celebration. On Saturday, January 23, 1971, he (and some of the show's other characters) hosted a kid's matinee of *Dracula* and other films at Catonsville Community College. Free soft drinks and popcorn were included. He joined the Banana Splits in hosting a children's program on March 20, 1971 at Laurel Cinema in Laurel, Maryland. (His Saturday, kid-friendly show inspired his young viewers to send in the artwork, which Sir Graves presented in his "Art Ghoulery.")

Unfortunately, despite good ratings and Sir Graves continued popularity in both D.C. and Maryland ("I got mail from people in the Pentagon, the Navy, the Army, college students."), Channel 9 effectively vaccinated *Sir*

The Lighter Side

Sir Ghastly to emcee comic chiller for tykes

By DICK WEST

WASHINGTON (UPI) — Speaking of cultural trends, a local television station, WTOP-TV, recently gave a little party in honor of its new resident ghoul, Sir Graves Ghastly, an actor who specializes in introducing horror films.

Sir Graves began plying his trade at WJBK-TV in Detroit and is now branching out to help meet the growing demand for macabre emcees.

Beginning this weekend, he will be on the air here twice a week, presiding over a midnight horror film plus hosting a Saturday afternoon comic chiller for the kiddies.

"DO YOU HAVE any feeling that this may be a case of overexposure," I asked a station executive.

"Not at all," he replied. "Television is in the midst of a horror film renaissance that has yet to reach full flower.

"Films that we wouldn't have programmed seriously five years ago now draw huge audiences and pictures that already have been shown in this area 10 times now cost more than when they had their TV premiere 10 years ago.

"IN ADDITION, there are about a half dozen books on the subject, all treating the horror film as a genuine art form. It definitely appears that we are on the threshold of the golden age of horror films."

I said, "How do you square this with the complaints about violence on television?"

"Actually, there is very little violence in the classical horror film format," he explained. "The thrill is more in the suspense than in the commission of horrifying deeds."

"Such violence as does occur usually is highly stylized so that the audience does not relate it to reality. Nobody is ever shot with a gun, for instance. Rather, the victims are run down with an eccentric millionaire's toy train, or something of the sort."

HE WENT ON to say that he regarded the horror film renaissance primarily as an offshoot of "camp," which is the humorous appreciation of things once taken seriously but now considered outlandish or banal.

Very well. As the vampires say, "I'll drink to that."

Graves Ghastly Presents when the man that hired Deming left the station. Deming told *Scary Monsters*:

> We got trapped into a funny thing in Washington. The man who hired me there was the program manager. He'd come from TV-2 in Detroit. Unfortunately, he got trapped in a political thing, so when he went, Sir Graves went—despite good ratings.

Those who were fortunate enough to be of age during its all-too-brief (local) run lovingly remember *Sir Graves Ghastly Presents*. Lawson J. Deming passed away on April 24, 2007, one day after his 94th birthday, taking all his characters with him, but leaving behind many a fine monster memory.

Airs Fridays at 11:30 p.m.
01/09/70 *The Castle of the Living Dead* (1964)
01/16/70 *Track of the Vampire* (1966)
01/23/70 *The Genie of Darkness* (1962)

"Sir Graves"—Featuring "Sir Graves," "Cool Ghoul," and others and film showings, including "Dracula ... ," (for children), Lecture Hall, Catonsville Community College, 800 South Rolling road, Catonsville, 12 noon.

Janet Leigh in the infamous shower scene in *Psycho* shown February 13, 1970, happy Valentine's Day!

Sir Graves Ghastly showed the Mexican horror film *The World of the Vampires* January 30, 1961.

01/30/70 *The World of the Vampires* (1961)
02/06/70 *WereWolf of London* (1935)
02/13/70 *Psycho* (1960)
02/20/70 *Dracula* (1931)
02/27/70 *Frankenstein* (1931)
03/06/70 *The Wolf Man* (1941)
03/13/70 *The Raven* (1935)
03/20/70 *Black Sabbath* (1963)
03/27/70 *The Eye Creatures* (1965)
04/03/70 *X* (1963)

04/10/70 *The Living Head* (1963)
04/17/70 *The Curse of the Doll People* (1961)
04/24/70 *Zontar, the Thing from Venus* (1966)
05/01/70 *Bride of Frankenstein* (1935)
05/08/70 *Son of Frankenstein* (1939)
05/15/70 *The Hunchback of Notre Dame* (1923)
05/22/70 *House of Frankenstein* (1944)
05/29/70 *Dracula's Daughter* (1936)
06/05/70 *Pyro* (1964)
06/12/70 *House of Dracula* (1945)
06/19/70 *The Mummy* (1932)
06/26/70 *The Mummy's Ghost* (1944)
07/03/70 *The Beach Girls and the Monster* (1965)
07/10/70 *Curse of the Undead* (1959)
07/17/70 *The Deadly Mantis* (1957)
07/24/70 *The Monolith Monsters* (1957)
07/31/70 *Tarantula* (1955)
08/07/70 *Hunter of the Unknown* (1966)
08/14/70 *The Terror* (1963)

(9) Sir Graves Ghastly Special:
"Dracula" Bela Lugosi and David Manners. A vampire terrorizes the countryside in its search for human blood.

08/21/70 Didn't air
08/28/70 Didn't air
09/04/70 *Queen of Blood* (1966)
09/11/70 *Dracula* (1931) *
09/11/70 *Master of the World* (1961)
09/18/70 *The Castle of the Living Dead* (1964)
09/25/70 *The Invisible Man* (1933)
10/02/70 *Black Sabbath* (1963)
10/09/70 *The Raven* (1935)
10/16/70 *Frankenstein* (1931)
10/23/70 *The Invisible Man Returns* (1940)
10/30/70 *The Black Cat* (1934)
11/06/70 *King Kong* (1933)
11/13/70 *Psycho* (1960)
11/20/70 *Son of Frankenstein* (1939)
11/27/70 *The Creature Walks Among Us* (1956)
12/04/70 *Atom Age Vampire* (1960)
12/11/70 *Bride of Frankenstein* (1935)
12/18/70 *From the Earth to the Moon* (1958)
12/25/70 Didn't air
01/01/71 *Son of Dracula* (1943)
01/08/71 *The World of the Vampires* (1961)
01/15/71 *Dracula's Daughter* (1936)
01/22/71 *Battle of the Worlds* (1961)
01/29/71 *House of Dracula* (1945)
02/05/71 *House of Frankenstein* (1944)
02/12/71 *King Kong vs. Godzilla* (1962)
02/19/71 *The Hunchback of Notre Dame* (1923)
02/26/71 *Godzilla: King of the Monsters* (1956)
03/05/71 *Curse of the Undead* (1959)
03/12/71 *The Mummy* (1932)

Michael Pate is the first Western vampire in *Curse of the Undead*, shown March 5, 1971

Eddie Parker as the Mummy is about to put a scare into Lou Costello in *Abbott and Costello Meet the Mummy*, shown by Sir Ghastly Graves January 17, 1970.

03/19/71 *Frankenstein Meets the Wolf Man* (1943)
03/26/71 *Gorgo* (1961)
04/02/71 *The Black Cat* (1934)
04/09/71 *Dracula* (1931)
04/16/71 *Frankenstein* (1931)
04/23/71 *The Invisible Man* (1933)
04/30/71 *WereWolf of London* (1935)
05/07/71 *Bride of Frankenstein* (1935)

*Special 7:30 p.m. presentation in addition to 11:30 showing.

Airs Saturday afternoons (various times)
01/10/70 *Abbott and Costello Meet Dr. Jekyll and Mr. Hyde* (1953)
01/17/70 *Abbott and Costello Meet the Mummy* (1955)
01/24/70 *Abbott and Costello Meet the Killer* (1949)
01/31/70 *Abbott and Costello Meet the Invisible Man* (1951)
02/07/70 *Black Sabbath* (1963)
02/14/70 *The Invisible Man* (1933)
02/21/70 *The Invisible Man Returns* (1940)
02/28/70 *Creature from the Black Lagoon* (1954)
03/07/70 *The Black Cat* (1934)
03/14/70 *The Ghost of Frankenstein* (1942)
03/21/70 *The Black Castle* (1952)
03/28/70 *Reptilicus* (1961)
04/04/70 *The Mole People* (1956)
04/11/70 Didn't air
04/18/70 Didn't air
04/25/70 *The Incredible Shrinking Man* (1957)
05/02/70 *Cult of the Cobra* (1955)

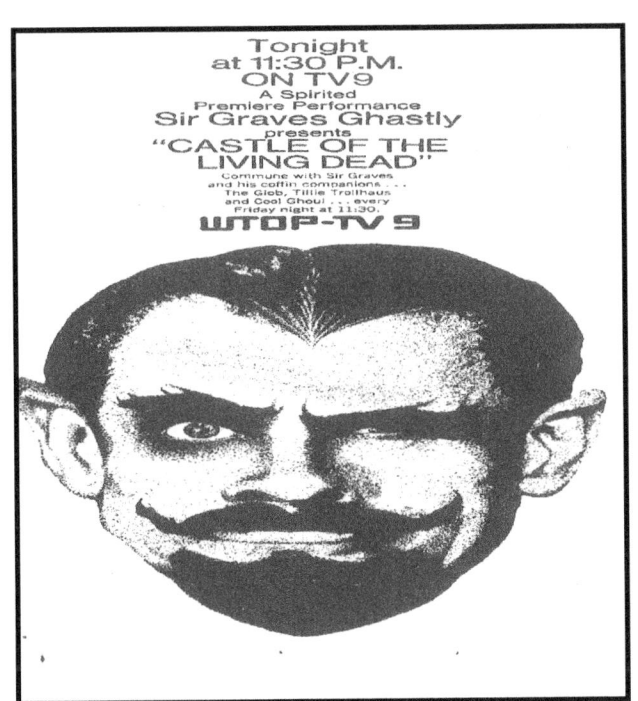

05/09/70 Didn't air
05/16/70 Didn't air
05/23/70 Didn't air
05/30/70 *Curse of the Swamp Creature* (1966)
06/06/70 *The Invisible Ray* (1936)
06/13/70 Didn't air
06/20/70 *Werewolf in a Girl's Dormitory* (1961)
06/27/70 *Frankenstein Meets the Wolf Man* (1943)
07/04/70 Didn't air
07/11/70 *The Evil Eye* (1963)
07/18/70 *The Mind Benders* (1963)
07/25/70 *Panic in Year Zero* (1962)
08/01/70 *The Blood of Nostradamus* (1962)
08/08/70 *The Curse of the Aztec Mummy* (1957)
08/15/70 *Attack of the Mushroom People* (1963)
08/22/70 Didn't air
08/29/70 *Dagora, the Space Monster* (1964)
09/05/70 *Revenge of the Creature* (1955)
09/12/70 Didn't air
09/19/70 Didn't air
09/26/70 *Creature from the Black Lagoon* (1954)
10/03/70 *WereWolf of London* (1935)
10/10/70 *Track of the Vampire* (1966)
10/17/70 *Voyage to the Planet of Prehistoric Women* (1968)
10/24/70 *The Leech Woman* (1960)
10/31/70 *The Wolf Man* (1941)
11/07/70 *Gorgo* (1961)
11/14/70 *Bride of Frankenstein* (1935)
11/21/70 *King Kong vs. Godzilla* (1962)
11/28/70 *Abbott and Costello Meet Dr. Jekyll and Mr. Hyde* (1953)

Chapter 5

Ghost Host (1971-1987)

Ghost Host Theatre began every week with the image of a (painted) creepy mansion. As rain poured, the camera moved closer towards the home as a chorus of operatic "ahs" played while trumpets blared, all part of a music score seemingly composed for some epic production. (The music was, in fact, a sampling from "Tara's Theme" from *Gone with the Wind*.) Suddenly, the words Ghost Host materialized and wiggled while the music faded, overtaken by sounds of howling wind, crashing thunder, and finally a baying wolf, before giving way to an eerie electronic score. As the camera "entered" the abode, we either followed Ghost Host down to his dungeon, found him tinkering in his laboratory, or witnessed him merely standing menacingly, just before delivering his greeting.

Except for the vocals, Ghost Host's intros didn't vary from week to week. And there is a simple explanation for that. Shortly before WBFF had even began broadcasting in 1971, George Lewis and a small crew filmed the introduction, adverts, and closing while keeping Lewis'

"Good *evening*...This *is* your Ghost Host, inviting you to watch if you dare..." With these words, Baltimore's first horror host since the 1950s welcomed viewers every Saturday night for over 16 years to *Ghost Host Theatre*. Played by George Lewis, Ghost Host was part of WBFF-TV 45's programming since it began broadcasting April 11, 1971. He is the only area horror host that can claim such a distinction. He looked not unlike Ygor from *Son of Frankenstein*, although he lacked a broken neck and had much better posture. Each week, as he tinkered with various beakers in his decidedly low-budget laboratory while creepy electronic music played, he would ominously reveal the evening's entertainment and then laugh deliberately and maniacally as the film began unspooling. Ghost Host had no shtick; he got right to the point. He would return only once or twice during the broadcast to roam a low-budget graveyard as he told viewers what to expect in the coming weeks. He would return a final time to deliver his closing line, "Here's blood in your eye."

mouth in shadow. (Lewis reported he was reciting lines from *Hamlet* Act II, Scene II during the taping.) WBFF hired Lewis in 1970 to do double duty as a production director and children's show host (to be called Captain Chesapeake). It was Lewis' idea to have a hosted show that presented the various horror films acquired as part of the various licensed film packages. His costume was a simple brown, Edwardian coat and suit, and (artificial) bushy beard. Nearly everyone (including even the station owner's son!) pitched in artistically to create the studio dungeon set. Lewis himself painted the bricks on the paper backdrop. The crew filmed the scenes of Ghost Host descending the steps at the home of Lewis' father on North Charles Street in Baltimore City. Shortly after retiring, Lewis explained to Gene Crowell in a January 13, 1991 interview conducted for *Amateur Monster Maker Magazine*,

> We didn't have any money. So, I wanted the Ghost Host—those words at the beginning—to fluctuate. So, I got a photographer's developing pan, painted it black; I painted in white letters Ghost Host, put it on the floor, filled it with water, put a camera down on it, had somebody jiggle the water. So, that refracted the light and made the Ghost Host wiggle and squirm. Eerie.

Back at Channel 45, Lewis then electronically superimposed the floating words over the painted manor. A few years after the initial filming, the production team filmed new scenes of Ghost Host wandering a graveyard (with joke tombstones). The new painted backdrop, lab, and grave markers were all created in the studio. Essentially, however, the same footage was used throughout the entire run of the program. Our beloved Ghost Host thus redefined low budget, locally speaking. Nevertheless, the minimalistic approach effectively set the mood for the evening, and there were no comedic interruptions to break the tension. As a youth, the author truly appreciated this approach.

James Uhrin was one of the people who helped bring *Ghost Host Theatre* into our living rooms every week. He joined WBFF in 1976 at the age of 18. "My first job was loading films Saturday night," Uhrin told the author. Uhrin also took over the voice of Mondy the Sea Monster, sidekick to Captain Chesapeake until Lewis' retirement in 1990. (The name Mondy is a variation on Lewis' daughter Ramonda.) Today Uhrin is still with the station, better known as Traffic Jam Jimmy, who prowls

the rush hour streets in his traffic mobile delivering live updates.

"Each Thursday [George] would record the voice track," Uhrin explained. "He'd spend between one and two hours working on it, just before doing the Captain Chesapeake show."

To create the Ghost Host's unsettling voice, Lewis got creative, utilizing an old coffee can station employees used for their cigarette butts. Lewis

George Lewis as Captain Chesapeake and Mondy the Sea Monster

explained, "I got a butt can, took out the top, and I got a microphone down in the butt can. So, that gave you the hollow, eerie thing."

Uhrin laughingly recalled, "Some of the crew would fill up that can with cigarette butts and coffee cups. [George] had to put a 'This is not a trash can' sign on it."

George Lewis was born November 24, 1926, in Atlanta, Georgia. His family moved to Baltimore the following year. He worked at various broadcast jobs before settling at WBFF-TV in 1970, including hosting a radio morning program on WCBM in Maryland and gigs in New Jersey and Kentucky. In 1957, he began working at WSAZ-TV in Huntington, West Virginia, first as a news anchor. In 1959, he produced that station's horror host program "Shockwatch" featuring Gaylord, played by Fred Briggs, who went on to become an Emmy-win-

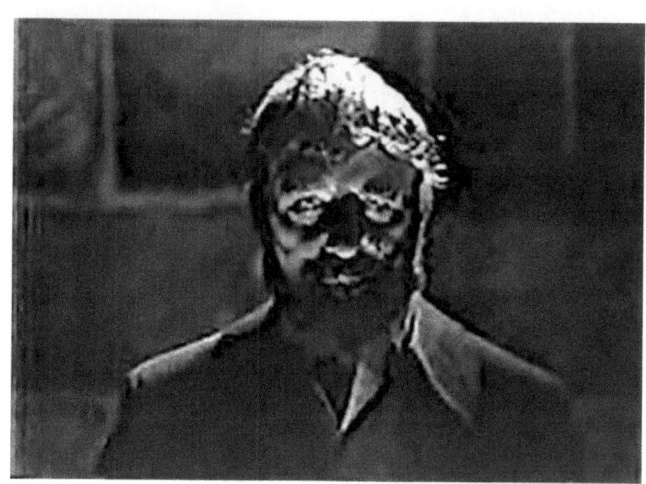

It was pouring down rain...This woman is flagging him down...So he stops...She got in the front seat and started to tell him how much he had meant to her son who had died recently. "You gave him so much joy." Daddy just hugged her and hugged her and drove her back to her car.

ning correspondent for NBC. More important for Lewis, however, was when he took over hosting the children's show and created the character Steamboat Bill, with sidekick Merlin the Sea Monster. When Lewis signed on with WBFF-TV, those characters became Captain Chesapeake and Mondy the Sea Monster, respectively. Later Lewis added Andrew Claws the Lion, and the never-seen Bruce the Bird. Thus, during the week, Lewis was the friendly captain, introducing cartoons and Three Stooges shorts.

Another character that appeared on Captain Chesapeake was Mandy the Mermaid. Tracy Lewis Collins, one of Lewis' five daughters, portrayed the character, complete with auburn wig and tale, when she was around 14. She recalled for the author the kind of impact Captain Chesapeake had on viewers by relating what happened as she and her parents were leaving a restaurant after dinner.

In his Captain Chesapeake guise, Lewis also visited hospitals to say hello to young patients. "He just loved children," his daughter related. "For birthday parties, he did magic tricks." The Captain signed off daily with the confidence building, "Be somebody important. Be yourself." However, on Saturday nights, Lewis adopted a much more sinister persona, which had quite a different effect on his youthful audience members.

Interestingly, even though Ghost Host was the de facto successor to Dr. Lucifer and *Shock!*, he didn't start showing the Universal classics until 1973, almost two years after his debut. Prior to that, the show drew from, among others, the catalogues of Columbia (Sony), Warner Bros., Allied Artists, Bel Air, Monogram, and Republic. A few weeks after Ghost Host began his long tenure, Channel 9 cancelled *Sir Graves Ghastly Presents*, making Ghost Host the only game in town for almost two years. Without any competition to speak of, the show, not surprisingly, was a hit.

In fact, *Ghost Host Theatre* proved so popular that, in December 1971, the station added a Sunday night edition, which ran until September 1972. In February 1973, a Friday late-night version joined the schedule. It lasted until April 1974. In July 1976, double features began airing Saturday nights as the start time moved from 12:30 a.m. to 11:30 p.m. Single features returned in March 1979. The double features began again in September 1985 and lasted until February 1987. The show returned to single features for the remainder of its run.

Feature.

"Horrors of the Black Museum." (1959.) A mystery writer, aided by his assistant under hypnosis, commits several gruesome crimes, baffling Scotland Yard. Michael Gough, June Cunningham, Graham Curnew. Also, "The Thing that Couldn't Die." (1958.) A girl, gifted with the power to find hidden things, discovers a chest buried for 400 years which contains a hideous head. William Reynolds, Andra Martin, Mara Corday.

On October 28, 1972, WBFF presented an all-night Halloween Special that aired five films. Author Gregory William Mank remembered watching some of it. "He did a live show one night. I started to watch it but didn't make it through. He actually talked to the camera. Some weeks later, he was on with the usual thing, and he said people had written in and asked when are you going to have another all-night show? And the answer is, 'Never!' He must have run out of steam."

Despite this popularity, however, Ghost Host did not make any public appearances until the show had been on for about six years. (Lewis made over 100 annual appearances as Captain Chesapeake.) Lewis recalled for Crowell,

> I had to be in a parade. And I thought, 'Gee, let's go with Ghost Host instead of Captain Chesapeake. It will be fun, 'cause you know Captain Chesapeake has to be smiling and happy. And the Ghost Host can be nasty.' So, I had a ball going through the crowd, and when we got to a place where they weren't applauding, I'd look at them [Lewis makes applauding motions]. It got to one point there was this pretty girl over there. She was just sitting there smiling and everyone around her was applauding. And I gave her a frown, you know? And she just smiled and laughed, and I jumped off the float and I ran over to her and grabbed her by the shoulders like I was going to bite her on the neck. And she whispers in my ear, 'You don't scare me a bit, George Lewis.'

Ghost Host bits used between commercials and the films.

BALTIMORE-WASHINGTON AREA HORROR HOSTS AND MORE! (1957-1987)

Ghost Host also attended a few theatrical horror film premiers, including the May 9, 1980 debut of *Friday the 13th* at the Patterson I on Eastern Avenue. His last public appearance was in 1987 at Baltimore City's nightclub P.T. Flaggs, near the Inner Harbor. "We broke all [attendance] records. It was the biggest night they had ever had in their history and since."

Ghost Host Theatre also ran several contests through the years, inviting viewers to write in in hopes of being selected the winner of something that would *not* be good for them. One lucky viewer received reducing pills, which shrunk her to six inches tall. Ghost Host put her in an aquarium. Ghost Host subjected another victor to brain surgery, with various pieces removed throughout the program. Red dye-dotted cauliflower served as the brain.

Ghost Host didn't haunt just the Baltimore airwaves. In 1978, former WBFF employee Ken Buschman became general manager of WPTT Channel 22, an independent station in Pennsylvania, which launched Sunday, October 1, 1978. George Lewis would travel to Pennsylvania and tape host segments for that station's kids programming as Captain Pitt. He would also dub the Ghost Host openings for those films featured on WPTT's version. WPTT, however, did not have the same film catalogue as WBFF, and it never acquired the rights to air the Universal horror films of the 1930s and 1940s. Instead, this northern variant concentrated on science fiction thrillers (e.g. *The Blob*) and 1950s shockers such as *The Four Skulls of Jonathan Drake* (1959). The Pennsylvania incarnation debuted October 7, 1978 at 11:30 p.m. with *The Beast from 20,000 Fathoms* (1953). It broadcast its final offering, *The Monster that Challenged the World* (1957), September 29, 1984. (Ghost Host's now 9:00 p.m. Saturday slot was taken over by Elvira-clone Moana, host of *Moana's Place*, starting October 6, 1984.)

It wasn't all love for the Ghost Host though. While he got lots of fan mail, he also received weekly death threats for about eight to 10 months from a "fan" in

> 12.30 ⑤ **Ghost Host.**
> "Dungeons of Horror." Two survivors of a capsized ship reach a remote island where a woman is isolated with a dread disease. Russ Harvey, Helen Hogan. 1962.

Pennsylvania. The letters included drawings of how the writer planned to kill Ghost Host. Lewis however never reported the threats to the police, and the letters eventually stopped.

For a program that ran for as long as it did and meant so much to so many, it is shocking and saddening to report how little local coverage the Ghost Host received during his incredible run. It is also unfortunate no documentation appears to exist to confirm when exactly WBFF-TV last aired the *Ghost Host Theatre* intro. In 1986, Channel 45 began its affiliation with the new Fox network. Programming was sparse during the early Fox years, and Saturday night local programming resumed at 10:00 p.m., well before Ghost Host aired. Based on the author's research, yours truly believes Ghost Host's final airing was the September 5, 1987 showing of *Revenge of the Creature*. The following week, WBFF started airing the music programs *Solid Gold* and *Hot New Tracks* from 11:00 p.m. through 1:00 a.m. prior to its genre offerings. (In fact, when Gene Crowell called the station in preparation for his interview, he was told the show ended in 1987.) While it is true that horror films did continue to run off and on late Saturday nights through 1988 and beyond, it is unlikely Lewis was being called in to loop dialogue by this point. One certainly cannot imagine Ghost Host presenting the December 12, 1987, 1:00 a.m. airing of *Return to Fantasy Island*!

George Lewis retired from WBFF-TV in 1990. The *Ghost Host Theatre* recordings, which Lewis left in his office, were apparently thrown away by station employees and not given to the Lewis family. Thus, for posterity all that exists are home recordings people may have made during the VCR era. Thankfully, some of these tapings have been posted to YouTube. So, at least anyone curious can learn exactly what viewers saw every week.

George Lewis passed in December 2000 at age 74 [his obituary did not mention his Ghost Host character],

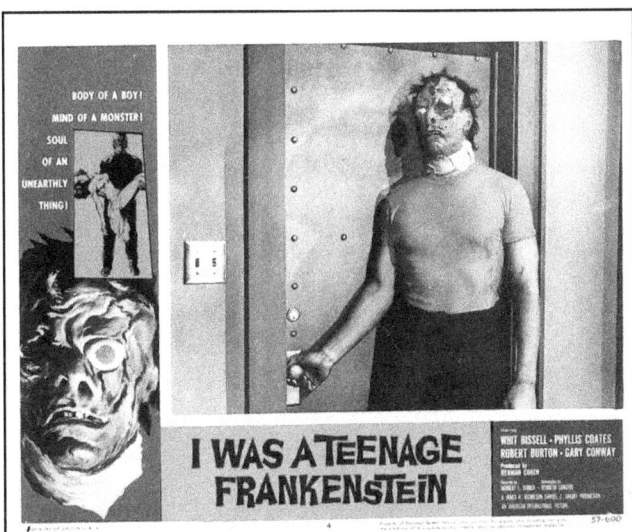

Scream, scream for your lives! It's *The Tingler* July 17, 1970

outliving the characters he created for WBFF-TV by 10-plus years. Lewis' legacy survives in the memories of those who eagerly welcomed him into their living rooms regularly, whether as the friendly Captain Chesapeake or the unnerving Ghost Host.

Saturday Night

Airs at 12:30 a.m.
04/17/71 *The Dungeon of Harrow* (1962)
04/24/71 *The Horrible Dr. Hichcock* (1962)
05/01/71 *Castle of Evil* (1966)
05/08/71 *Horror Castle* (1963)
05/15/71 *The Return of Doctor X* (1939)
05/22/71 *The Body Disappears* (1941)
05/29/71 *The Walking Dead* (1936)
06/05/71 *Donovan's Brain* (1953)
06/12/71 *The Face of Marble* (1946)
06/19/71 *King of the Zombies* (1941)
06/26/71 *The Living Ghost* (1942)
07/03/71 *The Strange Mr. Gregory* (1945)
07/10/71 *Revenge of the Zombies* (1943)
07/17/71 *The Tingler* (1959)
07/24/71 *The Son of Dr. Jekyll* (1951)
07/31/71 *Curse of the Demon* (1957)
08/07/71 *The Manster* (1959)
08/14/71 *Voodoo Island* (1957)

08/21/71 *The Undying Monster* (1942)
08/28/71 *The Return of Dracula* (1958)
09/04/71 *The Vampire* (1957)
09/11/71 *Web of Evidence* (1959)
09/18/71 *I Bury the Living* (1958)
09/25/71 *Pharaoh's Curse* (1957)
10/02/71 *The Black Sleep* (1956)
10/09/71 *The Quatermass Xperiment* (1955)
10/16/71 *Night Tide* (1961)
10/23/71 *Cry of the Bewitched* (1957)
10/30/71 *The Terror* (1963)
11/06/71 *Castle of Evil* (1966)
11/13/71 *Valley of the Zombies* (1946)
11/20/71 *The Vampire's Ghost* (1945)
11/27/71 *Devil Bat's Daughter* (1946)
12/04/71 *The Four Skulls of Jonathan Drake* (1959)
12/11/71 *Dr. Renault's Secret* (1942)
12/18/71 *Dead of Night* (1945)
12/25/71 *Chamber of Horrors* (1940)
01/01/72 *Voodoo Woman* (1957)
01/08/72 *Bride of the Monster* (1955)
01/15/72 *Black Sunday* (1960)
01/22/72 *Attack of the Mushroom People* (1963)
01/29/72 *Beast of Morocco* (1966)
02/05/72 *The Great Flamarion* (1945)

TV digest

WBFF-TV, Channel 45, will temporarily discontinue its 24-hour broadcast schedule beginning tonight to permit technical work to be done in connection with the independent station's new broadcast tower being erected on TV Hill.

The station will sign off the air nightly following the Starlite Theatre movie (which airs at midnight Monday through Thursday and 1 a.m. Fridays) and on Saturdays following the 12:30 a.m. Ghost Host Theatre.

Broadcasting via the new tower is scheduled to begin in May.

02/12/72 *Horrors of the Black Museum* (1959)
02/19/72 *I Was a Teenage Frankenstein* (1957)
02/26/72 *The Spider* (1958)
03/04/72 *The Lady and the Monster* (1944)
03/11/72 *The Cape Canaveral Monsters* (1960)
03/18/72 *King of the Zombies* (1941)

03/25/72 *The Living Ghost* (1942)
04/01/72 *The Strange Mr. Gregory* (1945)
04/08/72 *The Tingler* (1959)
04/15/72 *The Brain That Wouldn't Die* (1962)
04/22/72 *The Blancheville Monster* (1963)
04/29/72 *Night of Terror* (1933)
05/06/72 *The Devil's Messenger* (1961)
05/13/72 *The Man They Could Not Hang* (1939)
05/20/72 *The Man with Nine Lives* (1940)
05/27/72 *My Son, the Vampire* (1952)
06/03/72 *I Bury the Living* (1958)
06/10/72 *Unearthly Stranger* (1963)
06/17/72 *The Terror* (1963)
06/24/72 *The Phantom Planet* (1961)
07/01/72 *The Vampire* (1957)
07/08/72 *Dementia 13* (1963)
07/15/72 *Beginning of the End* (1957)
07/22/72 *The Unearthly* (1957)
07/29/72 *Invisible Invaders* (1959)
08/05/72 *Return of the Giant Monsters* (1967)
08/12/72 *It Came from Beneath the Sea* (1955)
08/19/72 *Valley of the Zombies* (1946)
08/26/72 *The Headless Ghost* (1959)
09/02/72 *The Magnetic Monster* (1953)
09/09/72 *Attack of the Puppet People* (1958)
09/16/72 *I Was a Teenage Frankenstein* (1957)
09/23/72 *Horrors of the Black Museum* (1959)
09/30/72 *The Vampire's Ghost* (1945)
10/07/72 *Revenge of the Zombies* (1943)
10/14/72 *King of the Zombies* (1941)
10/21/72 *Valley of the Zombies* (1946)

The Ghost Host is mixing up some terror for tots in his lab.

10/28/72 Halloween Special: *The Brute Man* (1946); *My Son, the Vampire* (1952); *Slaughter of the Vampires* (1964); *The Vampire's Ghost* (1945); *Valley of the Zombies* (1946)
11/04/72 *The Spider* (1958)
11/11/72 *The Mad Magician* (1954)
11/18/72 *The Horror of Party Beach* (1964)
11/25/72 *Dr. Renault's Secret* (1942)
12/02/72 Didn't air
12/09/72 *Devil Bat's Daughter* (1946)
12/16/72 *Zontar, the Thing from Venus* (1966)
12/23/72 *In the Year 2889* (1967)
12/30/72 *Zombies of Mora Tau* (1957)
01/06/73 *Shadow of Evil* (1964)

01/13/73 *The Curse of the Living Corpse* (1964)
01/20/73 *The Evil Eye* (1963)
01/27/73 *I Was a Teenage Werewolf* (1957)
02/03/73 *Ghost of Dragstrip Hollow* (1959)
02/10/73 *The Son of Dr. Jekyll* (1951)
02/17/73 *The Invisible Man Returns* (1940)
02/24/73 *Voodoo Woman* (1957)
03/03/73 *Invisible Ghost* (1941)
03/10/73 *The Man with Nine Lives* (1940)
03/17/73 *Night of Terror* (1933)
03/24/73 *Giant from the Unknown* (1958)
03/31/73 *She Demons* (1958)

04/07/73 *The Diabolical Dr. Z* (1966)
04/14/73 *The Incredibly Strange Creatures Who Stopped Living and Became Mixed-Up Zombies!!?* (1964)
04/21/73 *The Unearthly* (1957)
04/28/73 *The Beach Girls and the Monster* (1965)
05/05/73 *The Werewolf* (1956)
05/12/73 *The Manster* (1959)
05/19/73 *I Bury the Living* (1958)
05/26/73 *The Tingler* (1959)
06/02/73 *Terror is a Man* (1959)
06/09/73 *Chamber of Horrors* (1940)
06/16/73 *The Magnetic Monster* (1953)
06/23/73 *Konga* (1961)
06/30/73 *Goliath and the Vampires* (1961)
07/07/73 *Bride of Frankenstein* (1935)
07/14/73 *The Crime of Doctor Hallet* (1938)
07/21/73 *The Crimson Canary* (1945)
07/28/73 *Dead Man's Eyes* (1944)
08/04/73 *The Crosby Case* (1934)
08/11/73 *Dracula's Daughter* (1936)
08/18/73 *The Horror of Party Beach* (1964)
08/25/73 *Frankenstein Meets the Wolf Man* (1943)
09/01/73 *House of Frankenstein* (1944)
09/08/73 *House of Dracula* (1945)
09/15/73 *Invisible Agent* (1942)
09/22/73 *The Jungle Captive* (1945)
09/29/73 *Jungle Woman* (1944)
10/06/73 *The Mad Doctor of Market Street* (1942)
10/13/73 *The Mad Ghoul* (1943)
10/20/73 *The Invisible Man Returns* (1940)
10/27/73 *The Hatchet Man* (1932)
11/03/73 *The Man Who Cried Wolf* (1937)
11/10/73 *Secret of the Chateau* (1934)
11/17/73 *The Mummy's Curse* (1944)
11/24/73 *The Mummy's Ghost* (1944)
12/01/73 *The Mummy's Hand* (1940)
12/08/73 *The Mummy's Tomb* (1942)
12/15/73 *Mystery of Marie Roget* (1942)
12/22/73 *Mystery of the White Room* (1939)
12/29/73 *It Came from Beneath the Sea* (1955)
01/05/74 *Son of Dracula* (1943)
01/12/74 *Son of Frankenstein* (1939)
01/19/74 *WereWolf of London* (1935)
01/26/74 *The Wolf Man* (1941)
02/02/74 *Curucu, Beast of the Amazon* (1956)
02/09/74 *Curse of the Undead* (1959)
02/16/74 *The Deadly Mantis* (1957)
02/23/74 *Tarantula* (1955)
03/02/74 *The Black Castle* (1952)
03/09/74 *The Castle of the Living Dead* (1964)
03/16/74 *Track of the Vampire* (1966)
03/23/74 *Terror in the Crypt* (1964)
03/30/74 *Dr. Orloff's Monster* (1964)
04/06/74 *Creature with the Atom Brain* (1955)
04/13/74 *The Man Who Turned to Stone* (1957)
04/20/74 *The Son of Dr. Jekyll* (1951)
04/27/74 *It! The Terror from Beyond Space* (1958)
05/04/74 *Voodoo Island* (1957)
05/11/74 *The Return of Dracula* (1958)
05/18/74 *Lady of Vengeance* (1957)
05/25/74 *The Magnetic Monster* (1953)
06/01/74 *Revenge of the Creature* (1955)
06/08/74 *The Face of Marble* (1946)
06/15/74 *The Catman of Paris* (1946)
06/22/74 *Valley of the Zombies* (1946)
06/29/74 *The Vampire's Ghost* (1945)
07/06/74 *The Cobra Strikes* (1948)
07/13/74 *Devil Bat's Daughter* (1946)
07/20/74 *Bury Me Dead* (1947)
07/27/74 *The Brute Man* (1946)
08/03/74 *The Flying Serpent* (1946)
08/10/74 *King of the Zombies* (1941)
08/17/74 *The Living Ghost* (1942)

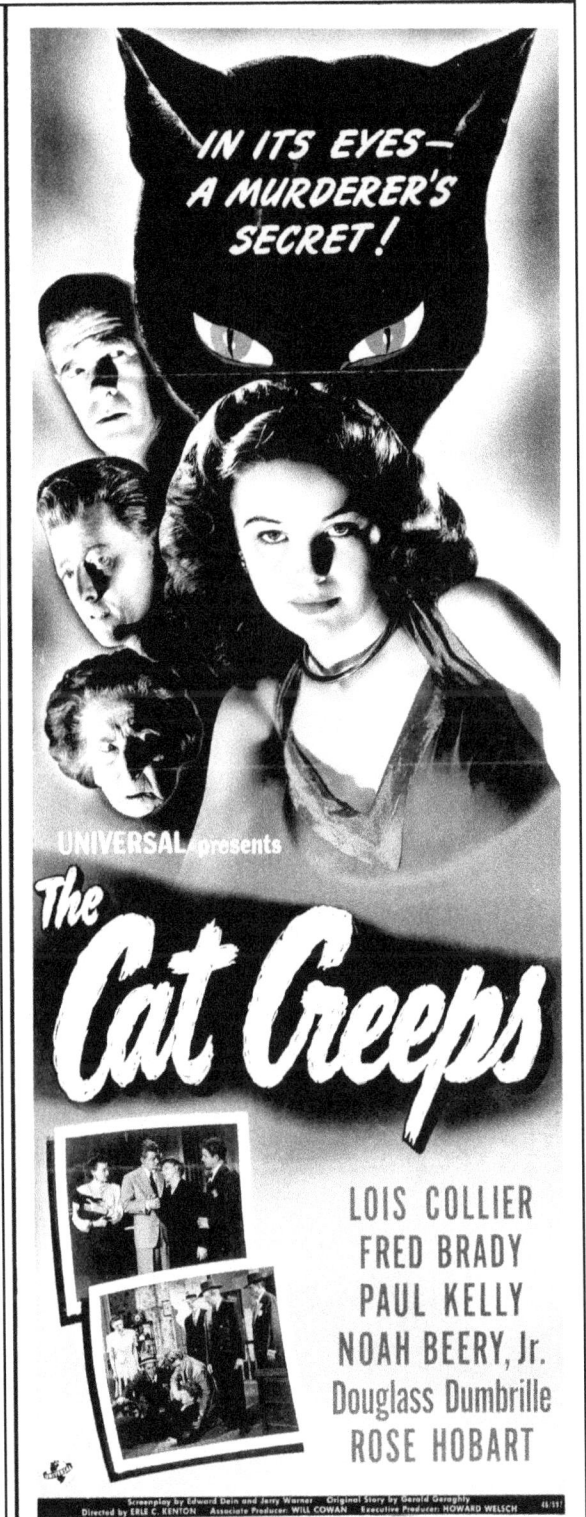

10/26/74 *Bride of Frankenstein* (1935)
11/02/74 *The Black Cat* (1941)
11/09/74 *Black Friday* (1940)
11/16/74 *Calling Dr. Death* (1943)
11/23/74 *Captive Wild Woman* (1943)
11/30/74 *The Cat Creeps* (1946)
12/07/74 *The Crime of Doctor Hallet* (1938)
12/14/74 *The Crosby Case* (1934)
12/21/74 *Dead Man's Eyes* (1944)
12/28/74 *Horror Island* (1941)
01/04/75 *The House of Fear* (1939)
01/11/75 *Frankenstein* (1931)
01/18/75 *Frankenstein Meets the Wolf Man* (1943)
01/25/75 *The Ghost of Frankenstein* (1942)
02/01/75 *House of Frankenstein* (1944)
02/08/75 *Dracula* (1931)
02/15/75 *Dracula's Daughter* (1936)
02/22/75 *House of Dracula* (1945)
03/01/75 *Son of Dracula* (1943)
03/08/75 *The Return of Doctor X* (1939)
03/15/75 *Doctor X* (1932)
03/22/75 *Terror is a Man* (1959)
03/29/75 *I Bury the Living* (1958)
04/05/75 *The Manster* (1959)
04/12/75 *The Neanderthal Man* (1953)
04/19/75 *It! The Terror from Beyond Space* (1958)
04/26/75 *Charlie Chan in the Secret Service* (1944)
05/03/75 *The Shanghai Cobra* (1945)
05/10/75 *The Chinese Cat* (1944)

08/24/74 *Revenge of the Zombies* (1943)
08/31/74 *The Strange Mr. Gregory* (1945)
09/07/74 *The Quatermass Xperiment* (1955)
09/14/74 *Pharaoh's Curse* (1957)
09/21/74 *The Black Cat* (1934)
09/28/74 *The Walking Dead* (1936)
10/05/74 *The Creature Walks Among Us* (1956)
10/12/74 *It Came from Outer Space* (1953)
10/19/74 *The Frozen Ghost* (1945)

The **GHOST HOST** presents...

"CHARLIE CHAN IN THE SHANGHAI COBRA"

There's plenty of action and suspense when Charlie plays with death to trap a killer and protect a fortune in radium.

Shortly after midnight tonight. Watch it - and then, Watch out!

TV★45

05/17/75 *The Jade Mask* (1945)
05/24/75 *The Scarlet Clue* (1946)
05/31/75 *Curse of the Faceless Man* (1958)
06/07/75 *The Man from Planet X* (1951)
06/14/75 *Coast of Skeletons* (1965)
06/21/75 *Donovan's Brain* (1953)
06/28/75 *The Face of Marble* (1946)
07/05/75 *Valley of the Zombies* (1946)
07/12/75 *Invasion of the Zombies* (1962)
07/19/75 *Giant from the Unknown* (1958)
07/26/75 *Voodoo Man* (1944)
08/02/75 *Horror Hotel* (1960)
08/09/75 *The Human Monster* (1939)
08/16/75 *Fog Island* (1945)
08/23/75 *The Vampire's Ghost* (1945)
08/30/75 *The Catman of Paris* (1946)
09/06/75 *The Ape* (1940)
09/13/75 *The Cat Creeps* (1946)
09/20/75 *Bride of the Monster* (1955)
09/27/75 *The Crosby Case* (1934)
10/04/75 *House of Horrors* (1946)
10/11/75 *The Vampire* (1957)
10/18/75 *Man Made Monster* (1941)
10/25/75 *Terror in the Crypt* (1964)
11/01/75 *The Castle of the Living Dead* (1964)
11/08/75 *Bury Me Dead* (1947)
11/15/75 *Tarantula* (1955)
11/22/75 *The Awful Dr. Orlof* (1962)
11/29/75 *Bluebeard* (1944)
12/06/75 *Revenge of the Zombies* (1943)
12/13/75 *The Living Ghost* (1942)
12/20/75 *King of the Zombies* (1941)
12/27/75 *Voodoo Island* (1957)
01/03/76 *Pharaoh's Curse* (1957)

01/10/76 *Voodoo Woman* (1957)
01/17/76 *The Headless Ghost* (1959)
01/24/76 *Cat Girl* (1957)
01/31/76 *Goliath and the Vampires* (1961)

02/07/76 *Track of the Vampire* (1966)
02/14/76 *Cry of the Bewitched* (1957)
02/21/76 *The Invisible Man* (1933)
02/28/76 *The Invisible Man Returns* (1940)
03/06/76 *The Flying Serpent* (1946)
03/13/76 *Murder in the Blue Room* (1944)
03/20/76 *It Came from Beneath the Sea* (1955)
03/27/76 *Invasion of the Body Snatchers* (1956)
04/03/76 *The Tingler* (1959)
04/10/76 *The Man They Could Not Hang* (1939)
04/17/76 *Night of Terror* (1933)
04/24/76 *Unknown World* (1951)
05/01/76 *Crucible of Terror* (1971)
05/08/76 *Horror Express* (1972)
05/15/76 *Psychomania* (1973)
05/22/76 *Zombies of Mora Tau* (1957)
05/29/76 *The Baby* (1973)
06/05/76 *Gallery of Horrors* (1967)
06/12/76 *The Return of Doctor X* (1939)

Lon Chaney, Jr. and George Irving in *Son of Dracula*, which aired on *Ghost Host* June 4, 1977

06/19/76 *Revenge of the Creature* (1955)
06/26/76 *The Strange Case of Dr. Rx* (1942)

Airs at 11:30 p.m.
07/03/76 *Horrors of the Black Museum* (1959); *The Thing That Couldn't Die* (1958)
07/10/76 *The Raven* (1935); *The Spider Woman Strikes Back* (1946)
07/17/76 *The Revenge of Frankenstein* (1958)
07/24/76 *Revenge of the Zombies* (1946); *WereWolf of London* (1935)
07/31/76 *The Strange Mr. Gregory* (1945); *Weird Woman* (1944)
08/07/76 *Terror is a Man* (1959)
08/14/76 *The Terror* (1963); *The Strange Door* (1951)
08/21/76 *The Walking Dead* (1936); *Son of Dracula* (1943)
08/28/76 *Son of Frankenstein* (1939); *The Son of Dr. Jekyll* (1951)
09/04/76 *She-Wolf of London* (1946); *Secret of the Chateau* (1934)
09/11/76 *The Shanghai Cobra* (1945)
09/18/76 *Charlie Chan in the Secret Service* (1944)
09/25/76 *The Scarlet Clue* (1945)
10/02/76 *The Jade Mask* (1945)
10/09/76 *The Chinese Cat* (1944)
10/16/76 *The Mummy's Ghost* (1944)
10/23/76 *The Missing Guest* (1938); *The Mummy's Hand* (1940)
10/30/76 *The Mummy's Tomb* (1942)
11/06/76 *The Creature Walks Among Us* (1956)
11/13/76 *Creature from the Black Lagoon* (1954); *The Black Castle* (1952)
11/20/76 *It Came from Outer Space* (1953); *Horror Island* (1941)
11/27/76 *Monster on the Campus* (1958); *The Mole People* (1956)
12/04/76 *The Leech Woman* (1960); *The Deadly Mantis* (1957)
12/11/76 *The Werewolf* (1956)
12/18/76 *Voodoo Woman* (1957); *Captive Wild Woman* (1943)
12/25/76 *The Crime of Doctor Hallet* (1938); *Dead Man's Eyes* (1944)
01/01/77 *The Frozen Ghost* (1945); *The Son of Dr. Jekyll* (1951)
01/08/77 *Pillow of Death* (1945); *Night Monster* (1942)
01/15/77 *Revenge of the Creature* (1955); *Rendezvous at Midnight* (1935)
01/22/77 *The Monolith Monsters* (1957); *Bride of Frankenstein* (1935)
01/29/77 *Curse of the Undead* (1959); *The Wolf Man* (1941)
02/05/77 *Curucu, Beast of the Amazon* (1956); *Night Key* (1937)
02/12/77 *The Black Sleep* (1956); *Murders in the Rue Morgue* (1932)
02/19/77 *The Invisible Ray* (1936); *Secret of the Blue Room* (1933)
02/26/77 *The Man Who Reclaimed His Head* (1934); *The Jungle Captive* (1945)

> **45 Ghost Host Theater.**
> "Curucu Beast of the Amazon." (1956.) The foreman of large Amazon plantations sets out with an American woman doctor to track down a legendary monster who is killing and terrorizing natives. John Bromfield, Beverly Garland, Tom Payne. (1½ hours.)

03/05/77 *Mystery of the White Room* (1939); *Mystery of Marie Roget* (1942)
03/12/77 *Dracula* (1931); *Calling Dr. Death* (1943)
03/19/77 *The Man Who Cried Wolf* (1937); *Curse of the Faceless Man* (1958)
03/26/77 *Destination Moon* (1950); *Black Friday* (1940)
04/02/77 *Murder in the Blue Room* (1944); *The Mad Ghoul* (1943)
04/09/77 *The Invisible Man's Revenge* (1944); *Invisible Invaders* (1959)
04/16/77 *The Mad Doctor of Market Street* (1942); *Jungle Woman* (1944)
04/23/77 *Castle of Evil* (1966); *The Invisible Woman* (1940)
04/30/77 *House of Dracula* (1945); *Invisible Agent* (1942)
05/07/77 *Dracula's Daughter* (1936); *The Ghost of Frankenstein* (1942)
05/14/77 *Frankenstein* (1931); *House of Horrors* (1946)
05/21/77 *Frankenstein Meets the Wolf Man* (1943); *Man Made Monster* (1941)

05/28/77 House of Frankenstein (1944); It! The Terror from Beyond Space (1958)
06/04/77 Son of Dracula (1943); I Bury the Living (1958)
06/11/77 The Four Skulls of Jonathan Drake (1959); Pharaoh's Curse (1957)
06/18/77 Gog (1954); The Manster (1959)
06/25/77 The Neanderthal Man (1953); The Return of Dracula (1958)
07/02/77 The Man with Nine Lives (1940); The Man They Could Not Hang (1939)
07/09/77 Lady of Vengeance (1957); The Ape (1940)
07/16/77 The Vampire (1957); King of the Zombies (1941)
07/23/77 The Monster that Challenged the World (1957); The Living Ghost (1942)
07/30/77 Donovan's Brain (1953); Revenge of the Zombies (1943)
08/06/77 Chamber of Horrors (1940); The Cobra Strikes (1948)
08/13/77 A Game of Death (1945); Devil Bat's Daughter (1946)
08/20/77 Horror Hotel (1960); The Catman of Paris (1946)
08/27/77 The Human Monster (1939); Invisible Ghost (1941)
09/03/77 The Cape Canaveral Monsters (1960); Voodoo Man (1944)
09/10/77 The Black Cat (1941)
09/17/77 Invasion of the Zombies (1962)
09/24/77 Frankenstein's Daughter (1958); Ghosts on the Loose (1943)

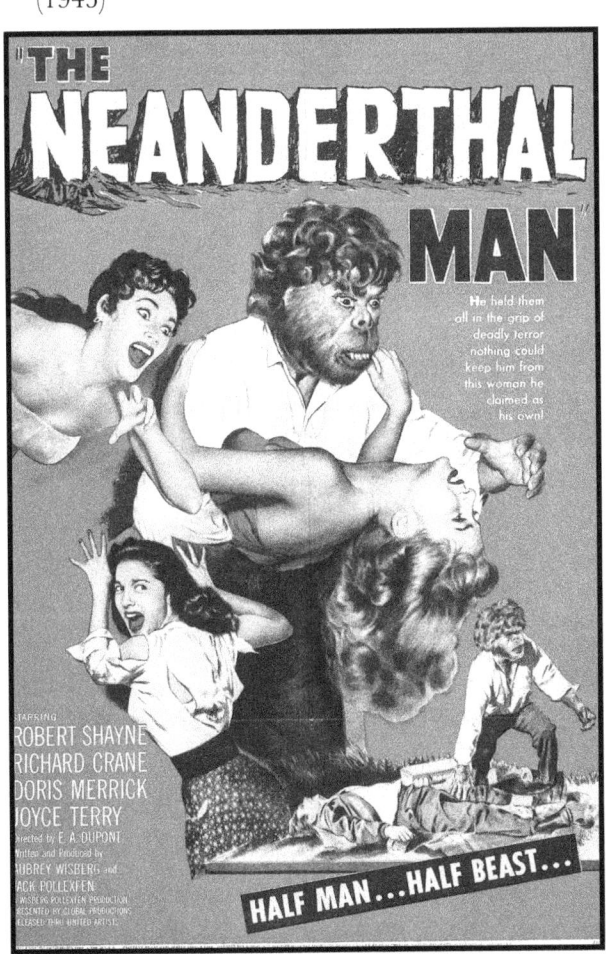

Bela Lugosi, Lucille Lund and Boris Karloff terrified the *Ghost Host* viewers in the 1934 *The Black Cat*. Lucille Lund attended FANEX 9 here in Baltimore.

10/01/77 Assignment Terror (1970); The Astro-Zombies (1968)
10/08/77 Blood and Lace (1971)
10/15/77 Creature with the Blue Hand (1967); Black Dragons (1942)
10/22/77 The Crimson Cult (1968)
10/29/77 Deathmaster (1972); Fog Island (1945)
11/05/77 Dracula vs. Frankenstein (1971); Equinox (1970)
11/12/77 Didn't air
11/19/77 Horror House (1969); The Incredible 2-Headed Transplant (1971)
11/26/77 The Bloody Judge (1970); Web of Violence (1966)
12/03/77 The Cat Creeps (1946); Tarantula (1955)
12/10/77 Horror of Dracula (1958)
12/17/77 The Undead (1957); A Bucket of Blood (1959)
12/24/77 Blood of Dracula (1957); The Screaming Skull (1958)
12/31/77 The Hound of the Baskervilles (1939); The Spider (1958)
01/07/78 Blood Mania (1970); Silent Night, Bloody Night (1972)
01/14/78 Dracula's Castle (1969); The Devil's Hand (1961)
01/21/78 Curse of Bigfoot (1975); The House of Seven Corpses (1974)

45 Ghost Host Movie

"Terror is a Man." (1960) Lone survivor of freighter drifts to desolate island where doctor conducting experiments calculated to turn panther into human being finds him. Creature gets loose causing havoc before its destruction. Francis Lederer, Greta Thussen. (1 hr. 35 min.)

01/28/78 *Footsteps on the Moon* (1969); *The Crawling Eye* (1958)
02/04/78 *The Revenge of Frankenstein* (1958); *Track of the Vampire* (1966)
02/11/78 *The Werewolf* (1956); *Curse of the Swamp Creature* (1966)
02/18/78 *The Tingler* (1959); *Black Sabbath* (1963)
02/25/78 *Curse of the Demon* (1957); *Terror in the Crypt* (1964)
03/04/78 *The Castle of the Living Dead* (1964); *The Blancheville Monster* (1963)
03/11/78 *The Invisible Man* (1933); *The Crosby Case* (1934)
03/18/78 *The Invisible Man Returns* (1940); *The Man from Planet X* (1951)
03/25/78 *Voodoo Island* (1957); *Alias John Preston* (1955)
04/01/78 *The Flame Barrier* (1958); *Terror is a Man* (1959)
04/08/78 *The Horrible Dr. Hichcock* (1962); *The Flying Serpent* (1946)
04/15/78 *The Awful Dr. Orlof* (1962); *Bury Me Dead* (1947)
04/22/78 *Bluebeard* (1944); *The Brain That Wouldn't Die* (1962)
04/29/78 *The Mask of Diijon* (1946); *The Brute Man* (1946)
05/06/78 *The Hostage* (1967); *Terrified* (1963)
05/13/78 *Nightmare in Wax* (1969); *Terror in the Jungle* (1968)
05/20/78 *Plan 9 From Outer Space* (1959); *Theatre of Death* (1967)
05/27/78 *Point of Terror* (1971); *They Saved Hitler's Brain* (1964)
06/03/78 *Stanley* (1972); *Twisted Brain* (1973)
06/10/78 *Tower of Terror* (1941); *The Spectre of Edgar Allan Poe* (1974)
06/17/78 *Death at Broadcasting House* (1934); *Demons of the Mind* (1972)
06/24/78 *Burn, Witch, Burn* (1962); *Ghost of Dragstrip Hollow* (1959)
07/01/78 *Goliath and the Vampires* (1961); *The Invisible Man's Revenge* (1944)
07/08/78 *My Son, the Vampire* (1952); *The Son of Dr. Jekyll* (1951)
07/15/78 *The Mad Magician* (1954); *The Man Who Turned to Stone* (1957)
07/22/78 *The Gamma People* (1956); *20 Million Miles to Earth* (1957)
07/29/78 *The Maze* (1953); *Earth vs. the Flying Saucers* (1956)
08/05/78 *Charlie Chan at the Circus* (1936); *The Cape Canaveral Monsters* (1960)
08/12/78 *Charlie Chan at the Race Track* (1936); *Invasion of the Body Snatchers* (1956)
08/19/78 *Charlie Chan at the Opera* (1936); *Castle of Evil* (1966)
08/26/78 *Charlie Chan at the Olympics* (1937); *Giant from the Unknown* (1958)
09/02/78 *Charlie Chan on Broadway* (1937); *The Atomic Brain* (1963)
09/09/78 *Circus of Horrors* (1960)
09/16/78 *Black Sunday* (1960)
09/23/78 *Invisible Creature* (1960)
09/30/78 *Face of Terror* (1962)
10/07/78 *The Mummy* (1932); *The Vampire's Ghost* (1945)
10/14/78 *Valley of the Zombies* (1946)
10/21/78 *The Man Who Reclaimed His Head* (1934)

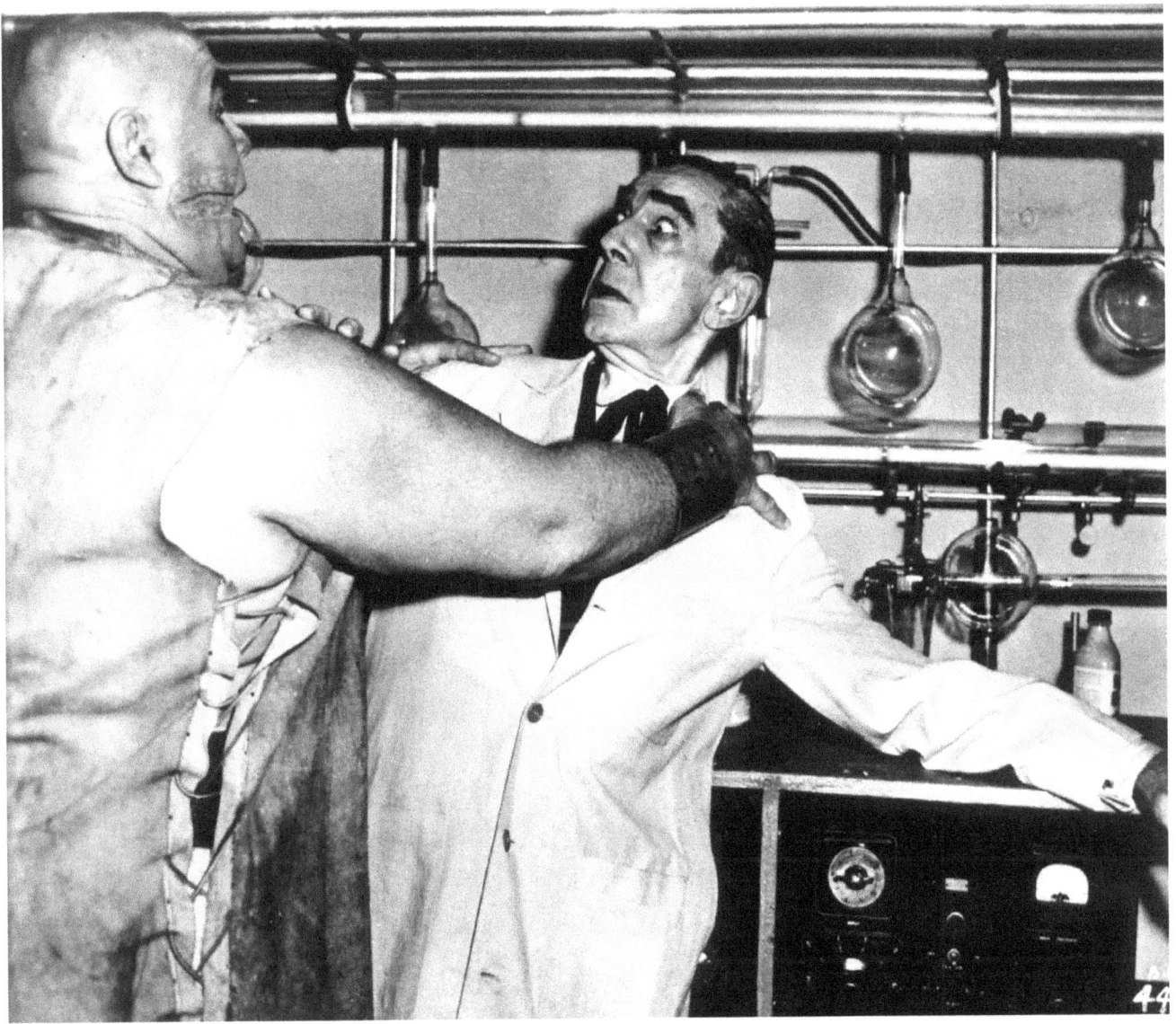
Tor Johnson and Bela Lugosi in *Bride of the Monster*

10/28/78 *Charlie Chan at the Wax Museum* (1940); *The Mummy's Ghost* (1944)
11/04/78 *Murder Over New York* (1940); *Graveyard of Horror* (1971)
11/11/78 *Black Friday* (1940); *The Missing Guest* (1938)
11/18/78 *Bride of Frankenstein* (1935); *Varan the Unbelievable* (1962)
11/25/78 *Calling Dr. Death* (1943); *Escape from Hell Island* (1963)
12/02/78 *Captive Wild Woman* (1943); *The Astro-Zombies* (1968)
12/09/78 *The Crime of Doctor Hallet* (1938); *Horror Hotel* (1960)
12/16/78 *Dracula* (1931); *The House of Seven Corpses* (1974)
12/23/78 *Dracula's Daughter* (1936); *Devil Bat's Daughter* (1946)
12/30/78 *Frankenstein* (1931); *Chamber of Horrors* (1940)
01/06/79 *The Mummy's Curse* (1944)
01/13/79 *Curucu, Beast of the Amazon* (1956)
01/20/79 *The Leech Woman* (1960); *Frankenstein's Bloody Terror* (1968)
01/27/79 *Deathmaster* (1972); *Curse of the Undead* (1959)
02/03/79 *The Giant Claw* (1957); *The Bloody Judge* (1970)
02/10/79 *Zombies of Mora Tau* (1957); *Mothra* (1961)
02/17/79 *The Stranglers of Bombay* (1959); *Die, Monster, Die!* (1965)
02/24/79 *The Thing That Couldn't Die* (1958); *The Deadly Mantis* (1957)
03/03/79 *Crucible of Terror* (1971); *Curse of the Faceless Man* (1958)
03/10/79 *The Living Ghost* (1942); *Revenge of the Zombies* (1943)
03/17/79 *The Strange Mr. Gregory* (1945)
03/24/79 *Donovan's Brain* (1953)
03/31/79 *The Four Skulls of Jonathan Drake* (1959)
04/07/79 *The Return of Dracula* (1958)
04/14/79 *Bride of the Gorilla* (1951)
04/21/79 *The Neanderthal Man* (1953)
04/28/79 *Invisible Invaders* (1959)
05/05/79 *Dracula's Castle* (1969)
05/12/79 *Curse of the Demon* (1957)

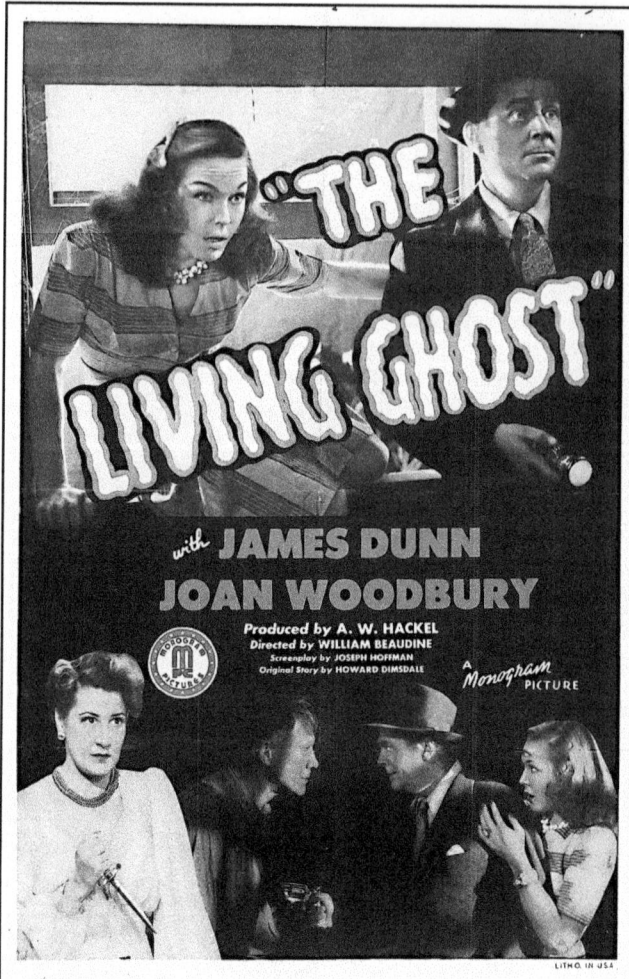

05/19/79 *The Tingler* (1959)
05/26/79 *The Beast from 20,000 Fathoms* (1953)
06/02/79 *Assignment Terror* (1970)
06/09/79 *The Awful Dr. Orlof* (1962)
06/16/79 *Bride of the Monster* (1955)
06/23/79 *Bury Me Dead* (1947)
06/30/79 *A Game of Death* (1945)
07/07/79 *Terror in the Crypt* (1964)
07/14/79 *The Brain That Wouldn't Die* (1962)
07/21/79 *The Quatermass Xperiment* (1955)
07/28/79 *Cry of the Bewitched* (1957)
08/04/79 *The Black Cat* (1934)
08/11/79 *The Black Cat* (1941)
08/18/79 *The Cat Creeps* (1946)
08/25/79 *Frankenstein* (1931)
09/01/79 *Frankenstein Meets the Wolf Man* (1943)
09/08/79 *Horror Island* (1941)
09/15/79 *House of Dracula* (1945)
09/22/79 *The House of Fear* (1939)
09/29/79 *House of Frankenstein* (1944)
10/06/79 Didn't air
10/13/79 *Man Made Monster* (1941)
10/20/79 *The Mummy's Hand* (1940)
10/27/79 *The Mummy's Tomb* (1942)
11/03/79 *Murder in the Blue Room* (1944)
11/10/79 *Murders in the Rue Morgue* (1932)
11/17/79 *Night Key* (1937)
11/24/79 *Night Monster* (1942)
12/01/79 *The Werewolf* (1956)
12/08/79 *The Man They Could Not Hang* (1939)
12/15/79 *Zombies of Mora Tau* (1957)
12/22/79 *Phantom of the Rue Morgue* (1954)
12/29/79 *The Wolf Man* (1941)
01/05/80 *Theater of Blood* (1973)
01/12/80 *Coast of Skeletons* (1965)
01/19/80 *The Black Sleep* (1956)
01/26/80 *The Brides of Dracula* (1960)
02/02/80 *The Curse of the Werewolf* (1961)
02/09/80 *The Evil of Frankenstein* (1964)
02/16/80 *Mystery of the Wax Museum* (1933)
02/23/80 *Island of Terror* (1966)
03/01/80 *Frankenstein: The True Story (Pts 1 and 2)* (1973)
03/08/80 *The Mad Doctor of Market Street* (1942)
03/15/80 *Jungle Woman* (1944)
03/22/80 *Mystery of Edwin Drood* (1935)

45 Ghost Host Movie
"Phantom of the Rue Morgue." (1954). Karl Malden, Patricia Medina. (1 hr 30 min.)

03/29/80 *The Spider Woman Strikes Back* (1946)
04/05/80 *Terror on the Beach* (1973)
04/12/80 *The Mephisto Waltz* (1971)
04/19/80 *Phantom of the Rue Morgue* (1954)
04/26/80 *Horror of Dracula* (1958)
05/03/80 *The Incredible 2-Headed Transplant* (1971)
05/10/80 *Coast of Skeletons* (1965)
05/17/80 *Horror House* (1969)
05/24/80 *Graveyard of Horror* (1971)
05/31/80 *Night Creatures* (1962)
06/07/80 *The Walking Dead* (1936)
06/14/80 *Curse of the Faceless Man* (1958)
06/21/80 *It! The Terror from Beyond Space* (1958)
06/28/80 *Gog* (1954)
07/05/80 *Mark of the Vampire* (1935)
07/12/80 *Pharaoh's Curse* (1957)
07/19/80 *Terror is a Man* (1959)
07/26/80 *The Monster that Challenged the World* (1957)
08/02/80 *Destination Moon* (1950)
08/09/80 *Twisted Brain* (1973)
08/16/80 *Women of the Prehistoric Planet* (1966)
08/23/80 *Frankenstein's Bloody Terror* (1968)
08/30/80 *Web of Violence* (1966)
09/06/80 *Blood Mania* (1970)
09/13/80 *Carnival of Crime* (1962)
09/20/80 *The Creeping Terror* (1964)

09/27/80 *The Devil's Hand* (1961) [Airs at 2:00 a.m.]
10/04/80 *Point of Terror* (1971)
10/11/80 *Dracula's Castle* (1969)
10/18/80 *Footsteps on the Moon* (1969)
10/25/80 *First Spaceship on Venus* (1960)
11/01/80 *The Hostage* (1967)
11/08/80 *The Crawling Eye* (1958)
11/15/80 *Nightmare in Wax* (1969)
11/22/80 *Terrified* (1963)
11/29/80 *Terror in the Jungle* (1968)
12/06/80 *Theatre of Death* (1967)
12/13/80 *Varan the Unbelievable* (1962)
12/20/80 *Kiss of the Vampire* (1963)
12/27/80 *Agent for H.A.R.M.* (1966)
01/03/81 *The Night Walker* (1964)
01/10/81 *The Projected Man* (1966)
01/17/81 *The Shadow of the Cat* (1961)
01/24/81 *Unknown World* (1951)
01/31/81 *Theater of Blood* (1973)
02/07/81 *Paranoiac* (1963)
02/14/81 *The House of Seven Corpses* (1974)
02/21/81 *Twisted Brain* (1973)
02/28/81 *The Day of the Triffids* (1963)
03/07/81 *The Cat Creature* (1973)
03/14/81 *The Brides of Dracula* (1960)
03/21/81 *The Brotherhood of Satan* (1971)

03/28/81 Didn't air
04/04/81 *Night Creatures* (1962)
04/11/81 *Horror of Dracula* (1958)
04/18/81 *Plan 9 From Outer Space* (1959)
04/25/81 *They Saved Hitler's Brain* (1963)
05/02/81 *Island of Terror* (1966)
05/09/81 *The Evil of Frankenstein* (1964)
05/16/81 *The Curse of the Werewolf* (1961)
05/23/81 *Frankenstein: The True Story Part 1* (1973)
05/30/81 *Frankenstein: The True Story Part 2* (1973)
06/06/81 *Assignment Terror* (1970)
06/13/81 *The Astro-Zombies* (1968)
06/20/81 *Blood and Lace* (1971)
06/27/81 *Creature with the Blue Hand* (1967)
07/04/81 *Dracula vs. Frankenstein* (1971)
07/11/81 *Deathmaster* (1972)
07/18/81 *The Crimson Cult* (1968)
07/25/81 *The Bloody Judge* (1970)
08/01/81 *The Navy vs. the Night Monsters* (1966)
08/08/81 *Tales of the Haunted: Evil Stalks this House* (1981)
08/15/81 *Equinox* (1970)
08/22/81 *Bride of the Gorilla* (1951)
08/29/81 *The Crawling Eye* (1958)
09/05/81 *Silent Night, Bloody Night* (1972)
09/12/81 *The Projected Man* (1966)
09/19/81 *The Phantom of the Opera* (1962)
09/26/81 *The Shadow of the Cat* (1961)
10/03/81 *Paranoiac* (1963)
10/10/81 *The Night Walker* (1964)
10/17/81 *The Beast from 20,000 Fathoms* (1953)
10/24/81 *Kiss of the Vampire* (1963)
10/31/81 *Phantom of the Rue Morgue* (1954)
11/07/81 *Theater of Blood* (1973)
11/14/81 *X the Unknown* (1956)
11/21/81 *The Brides of Dracula* (1960)
11/28/81 *Them!* (1954)

Baltimore-Washington Area Horror Hosts and More! (1957-1987)

Vincent Price is at his maniacal best in *Theater of Blood* with Diana Rigg, which was shown January 31, 1981

12/05/81 *The Curse of the Werewolf* (1961)
12/12/81 *Blood Mania* (1970)
12/19/81 *Carnival of Crime* (1962)
12/26/81 *The Devil's Hand* (1961)
01/02/82 *Agent for H.A.R.M.* (1966)
01/09/82 *Footsteps on the Moon* (1969)
01/16/82 *The Hostage* (1967)
01/23/82 *Nightmare in Wax* (1969)
01/30/82 *Dracula's Castle* (1969)
02/06/82 *First Spaceship on Venus* (1960)
02/13/82 *Point of Terror* (1971)
02/20/82 *Stanley* (1972)
02/27/82 *Theatre of Death* (1967)
03/06/82 *Twisted Brain* (1973)
03/13/82 *Plan 9 From Outer Space* (1956)
03/20/82 *Horror House* (1969)
03/27/82 Didn't air
04/03/82 *Graveyard of Horror* (1971)
04/10/82 *The Incredible 2-Headed Transplant* (1971)
04/17/82 *Web of Violence* (1966)
04/24/82 *Vampire Circus* (1972)
05/01/82 *Frankenstein's Bloody Terror* (1968)
05/08/82 *Countess Dracula* (1971)
05/15/82 *The House of Seven Corpses* (1974)
05/22/82 *Assignment Terror* (1970)
05/29/82 *The Mephisto Waltz* (1971)
06/05/82 *Blood and Lace* (1971)
06/12/82 *Creature with the Blue Hand* (1967)

06/19/82 *The Night Walker* (1964)
06/26/82 *Deathmaster* (1972)
07/03/82 *Equinox* (1970)
07/10/82 *Theater of Blood* (1973)
07/17/82 *The Brides of Dracula* (1960)
07/24/82 *The Crimson Cult* (1968)
07/31/82 *The Clones* (1973)
08/07/82 *The Beast from 20,000 Fathoms* (1953)
08/14/82 *The Creeping Terror* (1964)
08/21/82 *The Devil's Hand* (1961)
08/28/82 *Footsteps on the Moon* (1969)
09/04/82 *Plan 9 From Outer Space* (1959)
09/11/82 *The Castle of Fu Manchu* (1969)
09/18/82 *Fear in the Night* (1972)
09/25/82 *Phantom of the Rue Morgue* (1954)
10/02/82 *Countess Dracula* (1971)
10/09/82 *Vampire Circus* (1972)
10/16/82 *Them!* (1954)
10/23/82 *Horror of Dracula* (1958)
10/30/82 *The Legend of Hell House* (1973)
11/06/82 *Black Friday* (1940)
11/13/82 *The Brotherhood of Satan* (1971)
11/20/82 *Bride of Frankenstein* (1935)
11/27/82 *The Cat Creature* (1973)
12/04/82 *Frankenstein: The True Story Part 1* (1973)
12/11/82 *Frankenstein: The True Story Part 2* (1973)
12/18/82 *Tower of Terror* (1941)
12/25/82 *The Clones* (1973)
01/01/83 *Theater of Blood* (1973)
01/08/83 *The Cat Creeps* (1946)
01/15/83 *The Crime of Doctor Hallet* (1938)
01/22/83 *Dead Man's Eyes* (1944)
01/29/83 *Dracula* (1931)
02/05/83 *The Crimson Canary* (1945)
02/12/83 *Dracula's Daughter* (1936)
02/19/83 *Frankenstein Meets the Wolf Man* (1943)
02/26/83 *The Ghost of Frankenstein* (1942)
03/05/83 *The Frozen Ghost* (1945)
03/12/83 *The Navy vs. the Night Monsters* (1966)
03/19/83 *Bride of the Gorilla* (1951)
03/26/83 Didn't air
04/02/83 *Bela Lugosi Meets a Brooklyn Gorilla* (1952)

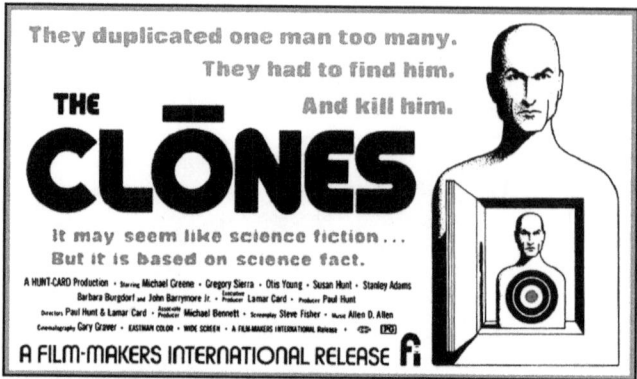

04/09/83 *Women of the Prehistoric Planet* (1966)
04/16/83 *The Clones* (1973)
04/23/83 *Fear in the Night* (1972)
04/30/83 *The Castle of Fu Manchu* (1969)
05/07/83 *Demons of the Mind* (1972)
05/14/83 *Island of Terror* (1966)
05/21/83 *Paranoiac* (1963)
05/28/83 *The Shadow of the Cat* (1961)
06/04/83 *Kiss of the Vampire* (1963)
06/11/83 *Vampire Circus* (1972)
06/18/83 *Countess Dracula* (1971)
06/25/83 *The Black Cat* (1934)
07/02/83 *Calling Dr. Death* (1943)
07/09/83 *The Brides of Dracula* (1960)
07/16/83 *The Curse of the Werewolf* (1961)
07/23/83 *The Evil of Frankenstein* (1964)
07/30/83 *Night Creatures* (1962)
08/06/83 *House of Dracula* (1945)
08/13/83 *Captive Wild Woman* (1943)
08/20/83 *The Black Cat* (1941)

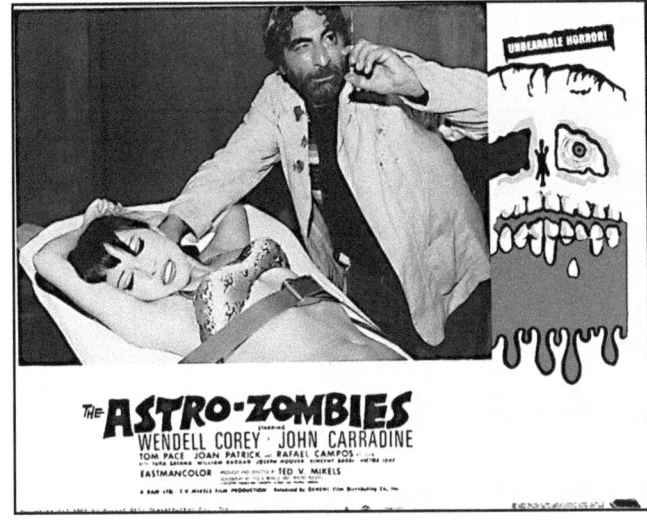

```
㊺ Movie.
"Calling Dr. Death" (1943)
Lon Chaney Jr., J. Carrol
Naish.
```

The local TV listings were not even calling it *Ghost Host* anymore.

08/27/83 *The Crosby Case* (1934)
09/03/83 *Horror Island* (1941)
09/10/83 *House of Dracula* (1945)
09/17/83 *The House of Fear* (1939)

Airs at 12:30 a.m.
09/24/83 *House of Frankenstein* (1944)
10/01/83 *House of Horrors* (1946)
10/08/83 *Invisible Agent* (1942)
10/15/83 *The Cat Creature* (1973)
10/22/83 *The Invisible Man* (1933)
10/29/83 *Friday the 13th Part 2* (1981)
11/05/83 *Assignment Terror* (1970)
11/12/83 *The Astro-Zombies* (1968)
11/19/83 *The Crimson Cult* (1968)
11/26/83 *Dracula vs. Frankenstein* (1971)
12/03/83 *The Invisible Ray* (1936)
12/10/83 *The Invisible Man Returns* (1940)
12/17/83 Didn't air
12/24/83 Didn't air
12/31/83 *The Invisible Woman* (1940)
01/07/84 *The Skull* (1965)
01/14/84 *The Man Who Could Cheat Death* (1959)
01/21/84 *When Worlds Collide* (1951)
01/28/84 *Countess Dracula* (1971)
02/04/84 *Let's Scare Jessica to Death* (1971)
02/11/84 *The Mummy* (1932)
02/18/84 *The Mummy's Curse* (1944)
02/25/84 *Graveyard of Horror* (1971)
03/03/84 *The Colossus of New York* (1958)
03/10/84 *Conquest of Space* (1955)
03/17/84 *The Mad Ghoul* (1943)
03/24/84 *Man Made Monster* (1941)
03/31/84 Didn't air
04/07/84 *The Missing Guest* (1938)
04/14/84 *The Man Who Reclaimed His Head* (1934)
04/21/84 *The Man Who Cried Wolf* (1937)
04/28/84 *The Mummy's Ghost* (1944)
05/05/84 *Blood and Lace* (1971)
05/12/84 *Creature with the Blue Hand* (1967)

Monsters and sexy girls, a horror kid's dream! Ben Chapman and Julie Adams in *Creature from the Black Lagoon*

05/19/84 *Deathmaster* (1972)
05/26/84 *Frankenstein* (1931)
06/02/84 *The Mummy's Hand* (1940)
06/09/84 *The Mummy's Tomb* (1942)
06/16/84 *Murder in the Blue Room* (1944)
06/23/84 *Mystery of Edwin Drood* (1935)
06/30/84 Didn't air
07/07/84 *The Incredible 2-Headed Transplant* (1971)
07/14/84 *Night Key* (1937)
07/21/84 *Night Monster* (1942)
07/28/84 *Pillow of Death* (1945)
08/04/84 *Mystery of Marie Roget* (1942)
08/11/84 *The Raven* (1935)

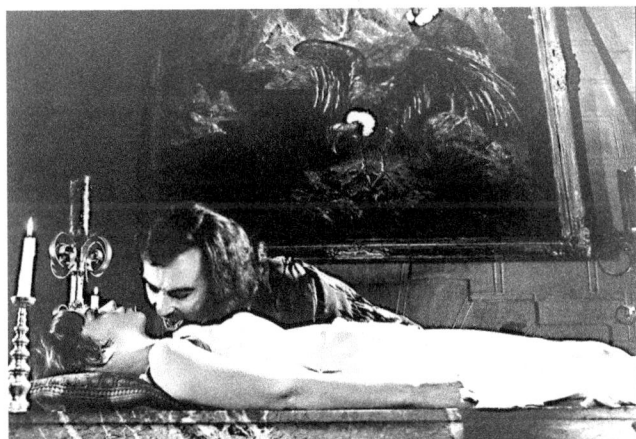

Robert Quarry and Brenda Dickson in *Deathmaster*, shown May 19, 1984. Robert was guest at the FANEX 9, The Horror and Fantasy Film Festival, held in Baltimore July 1995.

08/18/84 *Rendezvous at Midnight* (1935)
08/25/84 *Secret of the Blue Room* (1933)
09/01/84 *She-Wolf of London* (1946)
09/08/84 *They Saved Hitler's Brain* (1963)
09/15/84 *Twisted Brain* (1973)
09/22/84 *Varan the Unbelievable* (1962)

Airs at Midnight
09/29/84 *The Bribe* (1949)
10/06/84 *Murders in the Rue Morgue* (1971)
10/13/84 *Son of Dracula* (1943)
10/20/84 *Son of Frankenstein* (1939)
10/27/84 *The Brides of Dracula* (1960)
11/03/84 *The Curse of the Werewolf* (1961)
11/10/84 *The Evil of Frankenstein* (1964)
11/17/84 *Island of Terror* (1966)
11/24/84 *Night Creatures* (1962)
12/01/84 *The Night Walker* (1964)
12/08/84 *Kiss of the Vampire* (1963)
12/15/84 *Paranoiac* (1963)
12/22/84 *The Phantom of the Opera* (1962)
12/29/84 *The Shadow of the Cat* (1961)
01/05/85 *The Henderson Monster* (1980)

01/12/85 *WereWolf of London* (1935)
01/19/85 *Weird Woman* (1944)
01/26/85 *The Wolf Man* (1941)
02/02/85 *The Spider Woman Strikes Back* (1946)
02/09/85 *Secret of the Chateau* (1934)
02/16/85 *Mystery of the White Room* (1939)
02/23/85 *The Strange Case of Dr. Rx* (1942)
03/02/85 *Curucu, Beast of the Amazon* (1956)
03/09/85 *Agent for H.A.R.M.* (1966)
03/16/85 *Curse of the Undead* (1959)
03/23/85 *The Deadly Mantis* (1957)
03/30/85 Didn't air
04/06/85 *The Legend of Hell House* (1973)

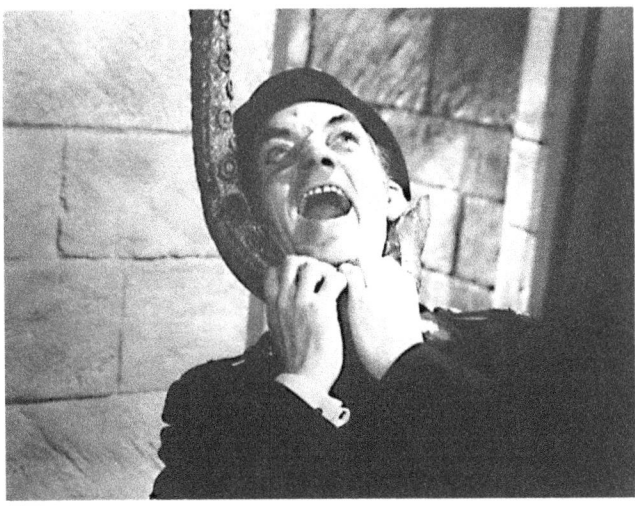

***Island of Terror* was shown November 17, 1984. Sam Kydd gets throttled by one of the terrors.**

04/13/85 *The Mole People* (1956)
04/20/85 *The Leech Woman* (1960)
04/27/85 *When Worlds Collide* (1951)
05/04/85 *The Skull* (1965)
05/11/85 *The Colossus of New York* (1958)
05/18/85 *The Man Who Could Cheat Death* (1959)
05/25/85 *Monster on the Campus* (1958)
06/01/85 *The Black Castle* (1952)
06/08/85 *The Monolith Monsters* (1957)
06/15/85 *The Thing That Couldn't Die* (1958)
06/22/85 *Bride of Vengeance* (1949)
06/29/85 Didn't air
07/06/85 *Creature from the Black Lagoon* (1954)

07/13/85 *The Creature Walks Among Us* (1956)
07/20/85 *Cult of the Cobra* (1955)
07/27/85 *It Came from Outer Space* (1953)
08/03/85 *Crack in the World* (1965)
08/10/85 *The Brotherhood of Satan* (1971)
08/17/85 *The Cat Creature* (1973)
08/24/85 *Tarantula* (1955)
08/31/85 *The Cat Creeps* (1946)
09/07/85 *The Black Cat* (1934); *The Crosby Case* (1934)
09/14/85 *Black Friday* (1940); *Frankenstein* (1931)
09/21/85 *Bride of Frankenstein* (1935); *The Frozen Ghost* (1945)
09/28/85 *The Black Cat* (1941); *Frankenstein Meets the Wolf Man* (1943)
10/05/85 *Calling Dr. Death* (1943); *The Ghost of Frankenstein* (1942)
10/12/85 *Captive Wild Woman* (1943); *The Shadow of the Cat* (1961)
10/19/85 *The Brides of Dracula* (1960); *The Evil of Frankenstein* (1964)
10/26/85 Didn't air
11/02/85 *Frankenstein: The True Story (Pts 1and 2)* (1973)
11/09/85 *Curse of the Fly* (1965); *The Crimson Canary* (1945)
11/16/85 *Theater of Blood* (1973); *Dead Man's Eyes* (1944)
11/23/85 *Night Creatures* (1962); *The Jungle Captive* (1945)

Monster on Campus rampaged on TV screens as a double feature with *The Monolith Monsters*, January 25, 1986.

11/30/85 *The Curse of the Werewolf* (1961); *Jungle Woman* (1944)
12/07/85 *Invisible Agent* (1942); *The Invisible Man* (1933)
12/14/85 *House of Dracula* (1945); *Murders in the Rue Morgue* (1932)
12/21/85 *Mystery of Edwin Drood* (1935); *Night Key* (1937)
12/28/85 *Night Monster* (1942); *The House of Fear* (1939)
01/04/86 *The Colossus of New York* (1958); *Curucu, Beast of the Amazon* (1956)
01/11/86 *Curse of the Undead* (1959); *The Deadly Mantis* (1957)
01/18/86 *The Leech Woman* (1960); *The Mole People* (1956)
01/25/86 *The Monolith Monsters* (1957); *Monster on the Campus* (1958)
02/01/86 *Horror Island* (1941); *House of Horrors* (1946)
02/08/86 *The Ghost of Frankenstein* (1942); *House of Frankenstein* (1944)
02/15/86 *The Invisible Man's Revenge* (1944); *The Invisible Woman* (1940)
02/22/86 *The Invisible Ray* (1936); *The Mad Doctor of Market Street* (1942)
03/01/86 *The Mummy's Tomb* (1942); *Murder in the Blue Room* (1944)
03/08/86 Didn't air
03/15/86 *The Mummy's Curse* (1944); *The Mummy* (1932)
03/22/86 *The Missing Guest* (1938); *The Man Who Reclaimed His Head* (1934)
03/29/86 *The Man Who Cried Wolf* (1937); *Man Made Monster* (1941)
04/05/86 *The Mummy's Hand* (1940); *The Mummy's Ghost* (1944)
04/12/86 *When Worlds Collide* (1951); *The Frozen Ghost* (1945)
04/19/86 *Dracula* (1931); *The Crosby Case* (1934)
04/26/86 *Frankenstein Meets the Wolf Man* (1943); *Mystery of the White Room* (1939)
05/03/86 *Theater of Blood* (1973); *Colossus: The Forbin Project* (1970)
05/10/86 *Mystery on Monster Island* (1981); *The Henderson Monster* (1980)
05/17/86 *The Hound of the Baskervilles* (1959); *Curse of the Fly* (1965)
05/24/86 *The Mad Ghoul* (1943); *Mystery of Marie Roget* (1942)
05/31/86 *Secret of the Blue Room* (1933); *She-Wolf of London* (1946)
06/07/86 *Dr. Jekyll and Mr. Hyde* (1941); *Revenge of the Creature* (1955)
06/14/86 *The Strange Door* (1951); *It Came from Outer Space* (1953)
06/21/86 *Cult of the Cobra* (1955); *The Creature Walks Among Us* (1956)
06/28/86 Didn't air

07/05/86 *Creature from the Black Lagoon* (1954); *The Black Castle* (1952)
07/12/86 *Frankenstein: The True Story (Pts 1 and 2)* (1973)
07/19/86 *Night Monster* (1942); *The Raven* (1935)
07/26/86 *Son of Frankenstein* (1939); *The Wolf Man* (1941)
08/02/86 *The Cat Creeps* (1946); *Captive Wild Woman* (1943)
08/09/86 *Mystery of the Wax Museum* (1933); *Terror on the Beach* (1973)
08/16/86 *The Invisible Man Returns* (1940); *The Crime of Doctor Hallet* (1938)
08/23/86 *Pillow of Death* (1945); *The Mad Ghoul* (1943)
08/30/86 *Rendezvous at Midnight* (1935); *House of Horrors* (1946)
09/06/86 *Secret of the Blue Room* (1933); *She-Wolf of London* (1946)

Airs at 11:30 p.m.
09/13/86 *Son of Dracula* (1943); *Son of Frankenstein* (1939)
09/20/86 *The Spider Woman Strikes Back* (1946)
09/27/86 *Weird Woman* (1944); *The Strange Case of Dr. Rx* (1942)
10/04/86 *Mystery of the Wax Museum* (1933); *Nightmare in Wax* (1969)
10/11/86 *Twisted Brain* (1973); *The Skull* (1965)
10/18/86 *Tarantula* (1955); *Torture Garden* (1967)
10/25/86 *Calling Dr. Death* (1943); *Blood Mania* (1970)
11/01/86 *Dracula* (1931); *Dracula's Castle* (1969)
11/08/86 *Graduation Day* (1981); *The Mummy's Curse* (1944)
11/15/86 *Videodrome* (1983); *The Funhouse* (1981)
11/22/86 *The Black Cat* (1941); *Black Friday* (1940)
11/29/86 *Creature from the Black Lagoon* (1954); *Curucu, Beast of the Amazon* (1956)
12/06/86 *Monster on the Campus* (1958); *Nightmares* (1983)
12/13/86 *The Jungle Captive* (1945)
12/20/86 *The Missing Guest* (1938); *Curse of the Undead* (1959)

Henry Hull in *Werewolf of London*

12/27/86 *Strait-Jacket* (1964); *Berserk* (1967)
01/03/87 *The Blob* (1958); *The Green Slime* (1968)
01/10/87 *Curse of the Fly* (1965); *The Raven* (1935)
01/17/87 *Torture Garden* (1967); *Plan 9 From Outer Space* (1959)
01/24/87 *Dead Man's Eyes* (1944); *The Deadly Mantis* (1957)
01/31/87 *Dracula's Castle* (1969); *Dracula's Daughter* (1936)
02/07/87 *Frankenstein* (1931); *The Ghost of Frankenstein* (1942)
02/14/87 *Graduation Day* (1981); *Rendezvous at Midnight* (1935)
02/21/87 *Kingdom of the Spiders* (1977); *The Mummy's Curse* (1944)
02/28/87 *Revenge of the Creature* (1955); *Plan 9 From Outer Space* (1959)
03/07/87 *The Creeping Terror* (1964) [Airs at 1:00 a.m.]

Airs at 12:30 a.m.
03/14/87 *The Crosby Case* (1934)

03/21/87 *Curse of Bigfoot* (1975)
03/28/87 *Dracula* (1931)
04/04/87 *Psyche 59* (1964)
04/11/87 *The Creature Walks Among Us* (1956)
04/18/87 *The Crime of Doctor Hallet* (1938)
04/25/87 *Cult of the Cobra* (1955)

Airs at Midnight
05/02/87 *The Night Stalker* (1971)
05/09/87 *WereWolf of London* (1935)
05/16/87 *Night Monster* (1942)
05/23/87 *The Mummy* (1932)

Airs at 11:00 p.m.
05/30/87 *Frankenstein Meets the Wolf Man* (1943)
06/06/87 *The Invisible Man* (1933)
06/13/87 *Dracula* (1931)
06/20/87 *House of Fear* (1939)
06/27/87 *Secret of the Blue Room* (1933)
07/04/87 *Curse of the Fly* (1965)

07/11/87 *Frankenstein: The True Story (Pts 1 and 2)* (1973)
07/18/87 *Bride of Frankenstein* (1935)
07/25/87 *Frankenstein and the Monster from Hell* (1974)
08/01/87 *The Wolf Man* (1941)
08/08/87 Didn't air
08/15/87 *House of Dracula* (1945)
08/22/87 *House of Frankenstein* (1944)
08/29/87 *The Invisible Man's Revenge* (1940)
09/05/87 *Revenge of the Creature* (1955)

Sunday Night

Airs around 12:30 a.m.
12/05/71 *Bowery at Midnight* (1942)
12/12/71 *Bury Me Dead* (1947)
12/19/71 *The Brute Man* (1946)
12/26/71 *Bluebeard* (1944)
01/02/72 *Daughter of the Sun God* (1962)
01/09/72 *The Dungeon of Harrow* (1962)
01/16/72 *The Headless Ghost* (1959)
01/23/72 *Strangler of the Swamp* (1946)
01/30/72 *SOS Coast Guard* (1942)
02/06/72 *The Catman of Paris* (1946)

02/13/72 Didn't air
02/20/72 *The Cobra Strikes* (1948)
02/27/72 *Donovan's Brain* (1953)
03/05/72 *The Ape* (1940)
03/12/72 *The Return of Doctor X* (1939)
03/19/72 *Revenge of the Zombies* (1943)
03/26/72 *Woman Who Came Back* (1945)
04/02/72 *The Return of Dracula* (1958)
04/09/72 *Voodoo Island* (1957)
04/16/72 *Curse of the Faceless Man* (1958)
04/23/72 *The Quatermass Xperiment* (1955)
04/30/72 *The Giant Claw* (1957)
05/07/72 *Zombies of Mora Tau* (1957)
05/14/72 *Terror in the Crypt* (1964)

45 Ghost Host Theater. "Night Tide." A mermaid in a side show, who believes herself to be a descendant of a race that must kill when the moon is full, falls in love with a young sailor. Dennis Hopper, Linda Lawson. 1963.

05/21/72 *Konga* (1961)
05/28/72 *Night Tide* (1961)
06/04/72 *The Hideous Sun Demon* (1958)
06/11/72 *Horror Hotel* (1960)
06/18/72 *The Monster of Piedras Blancas* (1959)
06/25/72 *Night Caller from Outer Space* (1965)
07/02/72 *Burn, Witch, Burn* (1962)
07/09/72 *Dr. Orloff's Monster* (1964)
07/16/72 *The Undying Monster* (1942)
07/23/72 *Strangler of the Swamp* (1946)
07/30/72 *Ghidorah, the Three-Headed Monster* (1964)
08/06/72 *The Steel Claw* (1961)
08/13/72 *The H-Man* (1959)
08/20/72 *Attack of the Robots* (1966)
08/27/72 *The Undead* (1957)
09/03/72 *Monster from a Prehistoric Planet* (1967)
09/10/72 *The Spider* (1958)
09/17/72 *Voodoo Woman* (1957)

Friday Night

Various times (Midnight and later)
02/09/73 *Frankenstein Meets the Wolf Man* (1943)
02/16/73 *Voodoo Island* (1957)
02/23/73 *Evil Brain from Outer Space* (1965)
03/02/73 *A Bucket of Blood* (1959)
03/09/73 *Voodoo Man* (1944)
03/16/73 *Ghosts on the Loose* (1943)
03/23/73 *Gallery of Horrors* (1967)
03/30/73 *Frozen Alive* (1964)
04/06/73 *Track of the Vampire* (1966)
04/13/73 *Cat Girl* (1957)
04/20/73 *Strangler of the Swamp* (1946)
04/27/73 *The Undead* (1957)
05/04/73 *The Living Ghost* (1942)
05/11/73 *Curse of the Faceless Man* (1958)
05/18/73 *The Ape* (1940)
05/25/73 *Pharaoh's Curse* (1957)
06/01/73 *The Return of Doctor X* (1939)
06/08/73 *Horror Hotel* (1960)
06/15/73 *Bride of the Monster* (1955)
06/22/73 *Black Sabbath* (1963)

Humphrey Bogart in *The Return of Dr. X*

06/29/73 *Cry of the Bewitched* (1957)
07/06/73 *Black Friday* (1940)
07/13/73 *The Black Cat* (1941)
07/20/73 *Calling Dr. Death* (1943)
07/27/73 *Captive Wild Woman* (1943)
08/03/73 *The Cat Creeps* (1946)
08/10/73 *Dracula* (1931)
08/17/73 *The Frozen Ghost* (1945)
08/24/73 *Frankenstein* (1931)
08/31/73 *The Ghost of Frankenstein* (1942)
09/07/73 *Horror Island* (1941)
09/14/73 *The House of Fear* (1939)
09/21/73 *The Invisible Man's Revenge* (1944)
09/28/73 *The Invisible Woman* (1940)
10/05/73 *The Invisible Ray* (1936)
10/12/73 *House of Horrors* (1946)
10/19/73 *The Invisible Man* (1933)
10/26/73 *The Man Who Reclaimed His Head* (1934)
11/02/73 *The Missing Guest* (1938)
11/09/73 *The Mummy* (1932)
11/16/73 *Mystery of Edwin Drood* (1935)
11/23/73 *Night Key* (1937)
11/30/73 *Night Monster* (1942)
12/07/73 *Murder in the Blue Room* (1944)
12/14/73 *Murders in the Rue Morgue* (1932)
12/21/73 *Pillow of Death* (1945)
12/28/73 *The Raven* (1935)
01/04/74 *She-Wolf of London* (1946)
01/11/74 *The Spider Woman Strikes Back* (1946)
01/18/74 *Creature from the Black Lagoon* (1954)
01/25/74 *Weird Woman* (1944)
02/01/74 *The Thing That Couldn't Die* (1958)
02/08/74 *The Leech Woman* (1960)
02/15/74 *The Mole People* (1956)
02/22/74 *The Monolith Monsters* (1957)
03/01/74 *Monster on the Campus* (1958)
03/08/74 *Cult of the Cobra* (1955)
03/15/74 *The Strange Case of Dr. Rx* (1942)
03/22/74 *Face of Terror* (1962)
03/29/74 *Night Tide* (1961)
04/05/74 Didn't air
04/12/74 *Coast of Skeletons* (1965)
04/19/74 *The Four Skulls of Jonathan Drake* (1959)
04/26/74 *Gog* (1954)

1.45 ㊺ Ghost Host Theater.
"The Invisible Man's Revenge." (1944.) A young man rendered invisible by a scientist trying to obtain an estate kills the scientist for his blood, which will restore physical form. John Carradine, Jon Hall, Gale Sondergaard, Alan Curtis.

Oh boy! Bela Lugosi, lurid sex and a gorilla! Every teenage kid's ideal Saturday night! Lugosi and Arlene Francis in *Murders in the Rue Morgue*

Chapter 6

Count Gore De Vol (1973-1987)

Starting in February 1973, Count Gore De Vol was the host of both *Creature Feature* and the afternoon *Saturday Chiller* for Washington, D.C.'s WDCA Channel 20. He was in appearance the traditional vampire: slicked black hair and widow's peak, flowing black cape, and the expected tuxedo. He spoke with a Transylvanian accent. And like Bela Lugosi's first line in *Dracula*, Gore opened his nighttime show with, "Good evening. I am the Count, Gore De Vol," after rising from his coffin. For two hours, Gore presented classic and not-so-classic horrors, injecting his host segments with deadpan humor, parodies, and satire. He also fancied himself a sex symbol, even having several *Penthouse* pets promote and/or appear on his show. We never were sure how the Count made out after he delivered his closing line, "And may all your blood be warm."

The Count was played by Chicago native Dick Dyszel, who prior to his move to Washington, D.C., had been working in Paducah, Kentucky at independent Channel 29, WDXR-TV, which had begun broadcasting in June of 1971 (it ceased operating in October 1975). While in Paducah, Dyszel created the vampire M.T. Graves, who hosted *Night of Terror* live on Friday nights around 10:30 p.m., right after the news. For his debut as M.T. Graves, Dyszel told Sandy Clark for the book *American Scary*,

> I had eight minutes to go from newscaster—get my microphone off, take off my jacket, *run* into the men's room, put on my cape, try to come up with some kind of makeup, run out to the other corner of the studio—and live, hit the air at 10:30 p.m. with *Night of Terror*!

The show opened with a hand-drawn creepy castle. As the camera quickly approaches the artwork, a door opens, bats fly out, and *Night of Terror* appears on the screen. Red footsteps are seen behind the title as more lettering appears: "From the Deep Dark Dungeons of WDXR 29 TV." We continue along a path of colorful skulls and cobwebs and then, "With our most TER-ROR-ble host M.T. Graves." Organ music plays as we now join that host, seated atop his coffin in near darkness. He speaks. "And a very pleasant good evening. Welcome to another night of terror. I'm your terrible host, M.T. Graves, and tonight we're going to bring you another tremendous tale of terror." M.T. Graves looks and speaks much like Count Gore De Vol, although perhaps with less enthusiasm. Also missing is the playfulness.

In 1972, Dyszel relocated to the Nation's Capital. Now at Channel 20, one of his first duties was playing the role of a famous clown for the weekday afternoon children's programming. "I was hired to play Bozo," Dyszel told the author. "That started June 10, 1972." The station used the set from *Wing Ding*, the show once hosted by Bill "The Great Zucchini" Miller, for *Bozo's Circus*.

It was during the 1972 Halloween episode of *Bozo's Circus* where Dyszel introduced M.T. Graves to a new audience. In bat form, Graves shows up wanting a treat. When Bozo fails to provide one Graves turns the clown's young pals into pumpkins. For the spell to be reversed Bozo must accompany Graves to his haunted castle. A purple-haired Frankenstein monster puppet performs *Monster Mash* while Bozo must learn the secret of Halloween, which is giving a treat before getting a trick. Graves returns Bozo's pals to normal. M.T. Graves morphed into Count Gore De Vol.

"[WDCA President] Milt Grant was hesitant to put a horror host on the air," Dyszel related, "because Sir

WDRX's Halloween Special featured Dick Dyszel as M.T. Graves and Bozo.

Early makeup for Count Gore

Graves was not seen as a success. But I did a demo and in January 1973 Milt gave me the okay."

And the name? "It was Milt who insisted Gore be part of the name," Dyszel continued. "I'm not sure where De Vol came from. Was it because I passed by De Vol Funeral Home every day, or was it because I saw a copy of a Gore Vidal novel sitting on Milt's desk?"

Shortly after Grant gave the newly dubbed Count Gore De Vol his blessing, Gore took over the Saturday night horror movie program *Creature Feature* in February 1973. *Creature Feature* had started airing, sans host, in January 1971 during the early prime time hours. The station moved the show to the more appropriate 11 o'clock hour when Count Gore assumed hosting duties.

However, there was a catch of sorts. Not only did Gore have to host Saturday nights, but he also presented *Saturday Chiller*, which aired in the afternoons. "Milt said *Saturday Chiller* aired monster movies and *Creature Feature* aired horror movies," Dyszel explained. "But I wanted to play the character, so I did both."

Richard E. Dyszel was born March 20, 1947 in Illinois, receiving his radio-TV degree from Southern Illinois University. In June 1972, he was hired as the new Bozo the Clown (and announcer) for WDCA Channel 20, and in September 1972 took over the role of Captain 20, the host of the daily afternoon kids programming. During the 1980s, Dyszel produced two educational children's programs for the station: *W.O.W.* and *Kids Break*, the latter winning a local Emmy in 1984 after several earlier nominations. Dyszel also acted in locally produced horror/science fiction efforts, playing Mayor Wicker in *The Alien Factor* (1978), *Nightbeast* (1982), and *Crawler* (2004), and Dr. William Tracy in *The Galaxy Invader* (1985).

Playing Count Gore, Dyszel stacked up additional accomplishments. On November 15, 1975, Gore presented the first unedited showing of George A. Romero's classic *Night of the Living Dead*. The May 25, 1985 showing of *Zardoz* was Washington, D.C.'s first discrete stereo broadcast. "I sneaked it in because I was friends with the chief engineer," Dyszel explained for *American Scary*, "and I found out we were actually capable of doing stereo. And a week before they were going to have the big premiere, I ran my show in stereo and made a big deal about it. And there was a lot that hit the fan the following Monday. But I said, 'It's too late: I'm already in the history books.'" In July 1998, Count Gore had his greatest "first" yet. He began hosting *Creature Feature: The Weekly Web Program*, which has produced over 1,000 shows to date. Thus, Dyszel was the first person to bring horror hosting to the internet.

Count Gore officially debuted February 3, 1973, first presenting *The Tingler* on *Saturday Chiller*, and then hosting Universal's monster rally *House of Frankenstein* on *Creature Feature*. The shows openings were very different. *Saturday Chiller* began with the drawn image of a purple castle. Bats are gently bobbing up and down. The music is eerie but slightly playful. The program's title appears at a slight angle in yellow letters, as does, "With your host Gore De Vol." Soon we're in a dimly lit cellar with a brick backdrop. A coffin is on the left and a table bearing

One banana, two banana, three banana, four, the Banana Splits visiting Captain 20 in Baltimore! Well, it was really DC but that didn't rhyme.

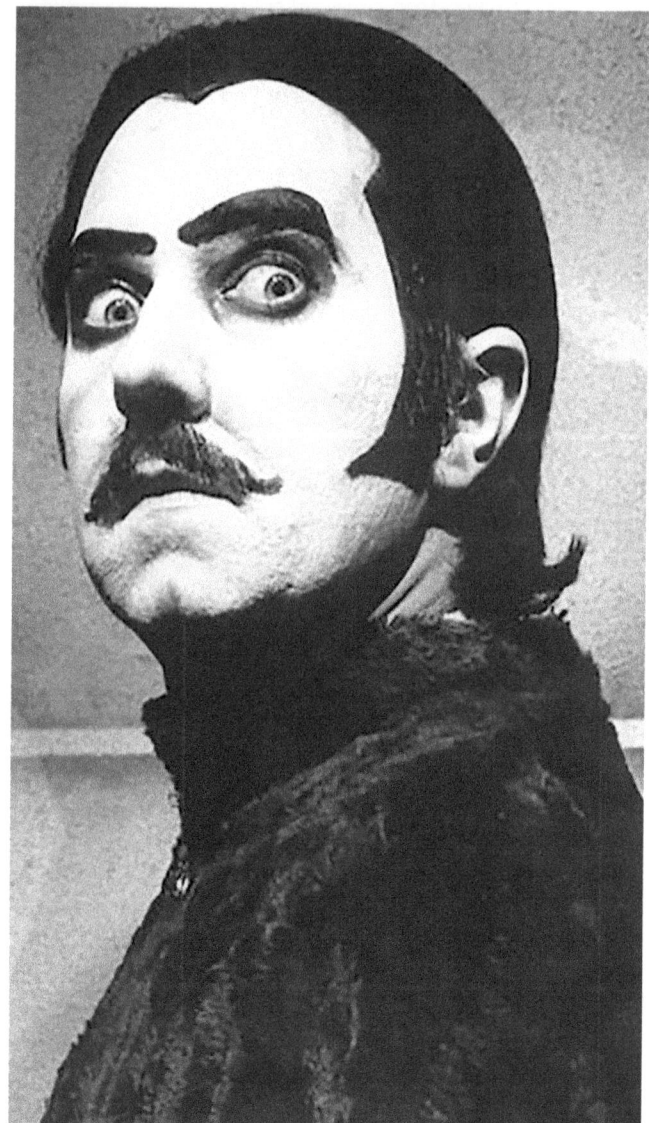

a three-footed candleholder is on the right. It's a minimalist set, just enough to tell the young viewer something creepy is coming.

The *Creature Feature* opening however is a bit more threatening. A candle flame appears slightly off-center towards the left. A scream is heard. In yellow caps, the program title tilts and bobs on the screen, as a second flame appears. Finally, the title flies in and away like a bat. Squeaks are heard as we are told, "With your host Gore De Vol." Ominous organ music starts playing as we are now in a castle basement. The flame is burning from a pumpkin candleholder, which sits next to large bottles of blood of various (fictitious) types. The camera pulls back as a barred window comes into view. A severed hand is clinging to one of the bars! We see skulls adorning a red-clothed table and skull mugs resting on a shelf. The camera continues to pull back as it pans to the right, revealing a coffin. Suddenly thunder crashes as the organ score continues. With the casket now in full view, the lid starts to open, creaking loudly and continuously until upright. It is easy to imagine the child watching in the afternoon might have a different reaction to the later incarnation. The music, the sound effects, and the props combined create the perfect atmosphere for horror, in a Halloween haunted house sort of way.

In 1976, the opening was redone. In this version, a handsomely crafted *Creature Feature* sign hangs and creaks from a cemetery entrance as fog swirls, thunder crashes, and lightning flashes. Soon we see a lone tombstone that reads, Count Gore De Vol: 1800-1847. We then join the Count in his castle. It is the better known of the *Creature Feature* openings.

The tension created by the introductions is typically dissipated thanks to the humor so prevalent in both shows. On *Saturday Chiller*, Count Gore might be knocked over by a man clad only in his undershorts as he swings into view. On *Creature Feature*, he may be in the middle of telling us, "Vampires have no business having sons," as we prepare to watch *Son of Dracula*, when Gore gets a phone call from a former blood donor telling him she's pregnant. In one early program, the Count, with all sincerity, expresses his wish to frighten us.

Count Gore does a comedy bit with the ladies on *Creature Feature*

Good evening and *velcome* to the deepest, darkest, dungeon of your television set. I am the Count, Gore De Vol by name, and it is truly my privilege to bring you classic, tremendous terror. I want to bring it right to you, personally. I want to come closer to you. *Closer to you*…into your living room, your recreation room, your bedroom, wherever you are I want to…

However, as the camera moves closer and closer to Count Gore, there is a sudden cracking effect, as if our TV screen has been broken. Gore is clearly mortified and embarrassed that such a thing could have happened.

Dyszel however did not stop at visual jokes confined to the bowels of his castle. There were commercial parodies, such as the one poking fun at record collections "not sold in stores" and available only through special TV offers. *Count Gore's Treasury of Monstrous Silence* offered such hits as "Silence in the Mummy's Tomb," "Quiet of Dr. Frankenstein's Lab," and "Sounds of the Frozen Blob." An announcer tells us that if we watch *Creature Feature*, we deserve this record.

"We taped once a month," Dyszel offered. "We had anywhere from four to seven host segments depending on who was in charge. Sometimes we had sponsors."

While Count Gore primarily worked alone, he would sometimes receive assistance from both unseen staff and the occasional guest. One gag had Gore being dressed down by the brain he was studying while showing *The Brain from Planet Arous*. Gore was trying to learn why this person died the previous week during the airing of *The Wasp Woman*. Apparently, the viewer couldn't take being sold Bobby Vinton record collections and steak knives that cut glass. He calls Gore stupid several times. Sometimes Gore would be bothered by an unseen visitor (except for maybe his arm) who'd obnoxiously and continuously shout, "Hey Buddy!" until Gore acknowledged him. Then there would be some awful joke told. When showing *The Mummy* on February 12, 1977, Gore is visited by his old friend The Countess, who wants him to make her a mommy, although he thinks she is saying mummy. He is horrified when he realizes what she really wants.

As vampires seem to be the most sexual of all monsters, the Count enjoyed injecting adult humor into his show. One episode had him doing a striptease in a jealous response to Burt Reynold's posing for *Playgirl*. Thankfully, the censors prevent the viewer from seeing too much. During the November 25, 1978 airing of *Island of Lost Souls*, county building inspector Dominique Maure, 1978's *Penthouse* Pet of the Year, arrives to give Gore's castle the onee over. Numerous double entendres ensue, such as Maure asking when the building was erected or, "Where do you plug things in?"

"The Penthouse Pets would go on tour," Dyszel related. "Channel 20 was the only station that would have them on. We had five on our show. Dominique eventually worked *for* Penthouse. She was in charge of all the Penthouse Pets!"

Count Gore also liked to play mad scientist on occasion. To create the ultimate ultra-light beer, Gore invented a process he called heliumination whereby he carbonated the brew with helium. The first attempt results in Gore speaking with a cartoon voice. His second attempt makes him so light that he floats towards the ceiling. When airing *The Mummy*, Gore brews his own herb and spice beverage using lily pads. He croaks.

Entire episodes would sometimes parody then-popular shows. In response to *Saturday Night Live*'s second season beating *Creature Feature* in the ratings, Dyszel counters

with *Saturday Night Dead* with Gore as our host. He plays all the characters: Reverend Oxon Hill, newscaster Silver Spring, and film critic Dean Mallott, a version of Gene Shalit. There is even a musical guest: The Delegates perform *Primary*, a play on the then popular *Convoy* by C.W. McCall.

The Count could not resist having fun with the new comic soap opera *Mary Hartman, Mary Hartman*. In *Gore De Vol, Gore De Vol*, which aired January 31, 1976, Count Gore is pondering how *Creature Feature* was fortunate enough to be showing *Genesis II*, when he learns Grandpa Gore has been arrested for indecent exposure!

Technical difficulties for the sixth anniversary presentation of *House of Dracula* led to an inebriated Gore! When attempting to tape the show that Saturday morning, the tape machines failed to function. To keep the numerous guests happy while technicians worked to fix the problem, Dyszel started serving the champagne early. By the time things were ready to go the bubbly was practically gone. Except for the film crew, the entire party was buzzed during the recording.

A few months later though, the Count seems rather down as he prepares to show us *The Little Shop of Horrors* on September 1, 1979. He explains why by showing us his pink slip—Count Gore is to be taken off the air for 13 weeks for "feetball," which is considered good news by the station's "peasants." They lynch him at show's end, crying out, "No more Gore!" and return him to his coffin, placing a large cross against it. An announcer asks, "Can football kill a vampire?"

Maybe not kill, but certainly stun. The hiatus turns out to be five years, at least on a weekly basis. Gore doesn't truly return until October 1984. However, he hosts Halloween presentations in 1981 and 1982, each time showing the Bela Lugosi classic *Dracula* as well as assorted cartoons and shorts. (The Bugs Bunny cartoon "Broomstick Bunny" and The Little Rascals short "Hide & Shriek" accompany the 1981 program, while *The Twilight Zone* episode "Living Doll" is paired with the 1982 presentation.)

"In 1979, Channel 20 was sold to Taft," Dyszel remembers. "The new program manager was a woman named Stephanie Campbell. I would ask her regularly if we could bring *Creature Feature* back. In 1984, I put together this book of charts and graphs based on Arbitron ratings. She finally agreed to let Gore return, if only because she was tired of me asking her all the time!"

In October 1984, our beloved Count is allowed once again to rise from his coffin, complete with new set. We again see the swaying *Creature Feature* sign and tombstone. Props are sparse but familiar, and the locale is different. A large picture of Bela Lugosi as Dracula is strategically placed above where Gore's coffin will rest. As fog swirls, castle doors swing open and a coffin slowly glides into the room. There is no prize for guessing its occupant. Familiar organ music plays, as do tracks from Disney's *Chilling Thrilling Sounds of the Haunted House*.

The set may be new but it's the same old Count. In order to fill his new dungeon, Gore offers "I sleep

---

11:45 p.m.

Count Gore De Vol, host of Channel 20's "Creature Feature," returns to television with "The Pit and the Pendulum," a thriller starring Vincent Price.

with Count Gore De Vol" nightshirts in exchange for appropriate decorations. One such submission is a propeller-beanie. Gore spins the propeller and suddenly rises, unable to return to solid ground. When showing *Mothra* on May 11, 1985, he builds a giant "moth swatter." It is Gore who is swatted. Commercials for the revived *Creature Feature* include the perfume/cologne "Essence of Evil" (only $9.99) that makes the wearer commit evil acts. "Count Gore De Vol's Alien Creation Kit," inspired by *Dark Star*, is available for anyone to create his or her own alien. The contents are a beach ball, pump, pool repair kit, and monster feet. Act now and you get a can of spray paint, oversized sunglasses, and a blonde wig to help your alien blend in with human folk. Even the closing credits for the show have gags, usually involving the writing credits. Instead of being given a list of names we are told, "They quit!" or "You've got to be kidding."

Since it was now the MTV era, Count Gore made monster music videos. As a tribute to Hugh Marlowe from *Earth vs. the Flying Saucers*, Count Gore composed a song to the theme from *Ghostbusters*. He also pays tribute to *Frankenstein Meets the Wolf Man* with a clip montage set against *Let's Hear It for the Boy* from *Footloose*. When showing *Attack of the Mushroom People*, we're treated to film scenes edited to Terry Noland's *There Was A Fungus Among Us*. The video for *Bride of Frankenstein* cut to the tune of Nick Lowe's performance of *I Knew the Bride When She Used to Rock & Roll* was nominated for a local Emmy.

Count Gore was able to take advantage of new technology. When Gore hosts *Terror of Mechagodzilla*, he does so under protest. He makes no secret that he feels the movie is awful. As a result, he is almost attacked by a wind-up Godzilla apparently sent by Toho studios. Gore gets his own "Godzilla" named Bruno and he watches as the "giants" battle, which is just the two toys walking into each other and then not being able to move further.

During the *Creature Feature* revival, Count Gore hosted live events several times. For Halloween 1985 and 1986, the Count held a party at the Bethesda Cinema & Drafthouse while *Damien: Omen II* played on Channel 20. On February 27, 1986, a *Creature Feature* 13th Anniversary Party was held at AMC Academy 6 in Greenbelt, Maryland. The movie shown was *House*. Admission was a gift for Count Gore or a blood donation to the Red Cross. Attendees in dress-up swarmed the lobby, as Gore put the bite on any female who would let him.

Unfortunately, the February 1987 sale of WDCA to TVX Broadcast Group ultimately led to the cancellation of nearly all local programming in the name of budget cuts and reorganization. Count Gore broadcast his last weekly *Creature Feature* program in May 1987. Gore did return to WDCA in 1999 for a New Year's Eve "Countdown with the Count," which broadcast *Arachnophobia* as the last movie of 1999 and Stephen King's *Graveyard Shift* as the first movie of 2000. However, by that time, he had launched his internet series, and there was no desire to return to conventional television.

Regarding the web series, Dyszel summarized, "In 1998 we had little bandwidth. In 1999, we added audio

interviews. In 2000, we showed Flash Gordon serials. But the website put me in contact with other horror hosts and led to creating the Horror Host Underground."

In terms of longevity, creativity, and commitment, Count Gore De Vol is the Baltimore/D.C. area's most impressive horror host. Gore was (and still is) the real deal: filming new host segments every week (except of course when in need of a break); bringing guests on the show; interacting with viewers via contests and personal appearances; and keeping his legacy alive via DVD-Rs and merchandise available from his website www.countgore.com. His popularity extends well beyond the Tri-State area, which he originally served.

In 2009, Dick Dyszel was the subject of a documentary called *Every Other Day is Halloween*, which focuses on his years both in television and on the internet. In it, he is asked if he'd consider coming back to television. "Why should I?" Dyszel responds. "I'm on the internet; I own the world. Anyone in the world can see me anytime. Why would I want to limit myself to one market?"

Beginning in 2013, he brought Count Gore to the AFI Silver Theatre in Silver Spring, Maryland to begin hosting horror films live. The Count presents three films a year. "We host 400-plus people a show," Dyszel adds

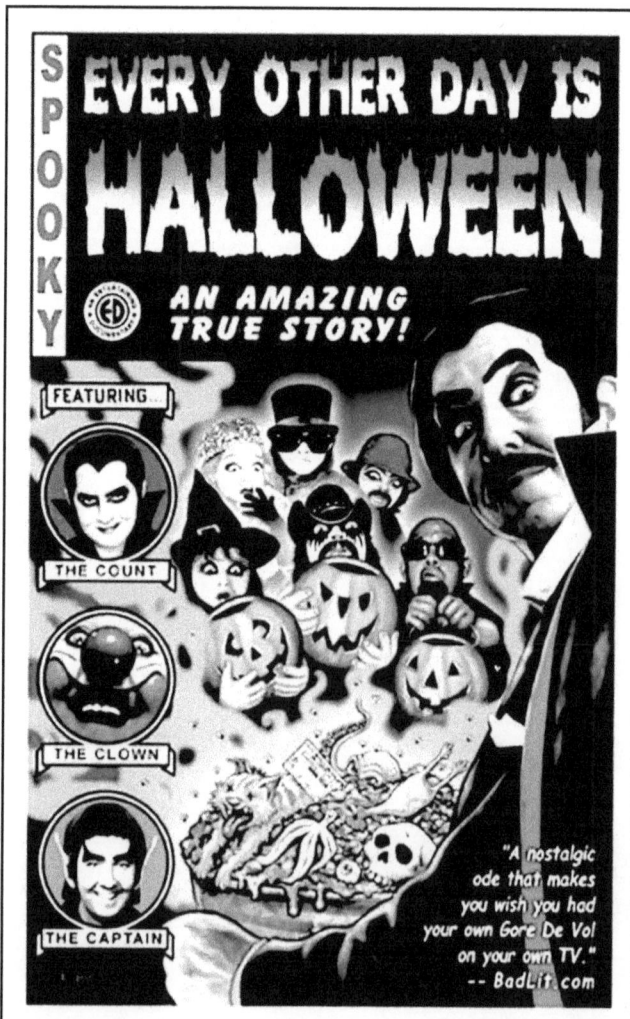

excitedly. "And I get to pick the movies!" This time, however, Gore has some assistance. His co-hosts have included local celebrities such as D.C. media critic (and longtime fan) Arch Campbell; Washington Capitals' arena announcer Wes Johnson; former Fox 5 anchor Tony Perkins; and Good Day DC host Holly Morris, also from Fox 5.

The AFI series is still going strong. Gore and his co-hosts have presented such films as *Frankenstein* (1931), *Bride of Frankenstein*, *Alien*, *King Kong* (1933), *Tarantula*, *House of Frankenstein*, *I Was A Teenage Werewolf*, *Invasion of the Body Snatchers* (1956), *Phantasm*, and *Young Frankenstein*. The 2019 showings included *Son of Frankenstein* (April), *House on Haunted Hill* (August), and *The Exorcist* (October).

But all this still wasn't enough for the Count! In October 2018, Dyszel launched his own Roku channel, *Count Gore De Vol Presents*. "We add 10 new videos a month: four films, four archival interviews, and two short films." Gore hosts all in high definition! He is particularly a fan of the short films, which each run about 20 minutes. He terms them *Creature Feature: The New Blood*.

"My primary focus is the web program," Dyszel explains. "I was at Channel 20 for 15 years but have been on the internet for 20." He does however look fondly upon his time at WDCA. "They were the last days of the

local entertainers. There was a lot of creative freedom. We were doing 'little theater' for television."

Does the Count imagine a future where he isn't hosting? "I see the wall of a dungeon. I see a tiny nail in the wall. And I see a cape on the nail. But…not just yet." He adds, "The horror hosts never go away."

Through his internet presence, live appearances, Roku channel, and convention attendance, Count Gore De Vol continues the great tradition of the horror show host, updated of course for the 21st century. Add to this his many accomplishments noted above, and one can appreciate how fortunate the Baltimore-Washington, D.C. area was to have him. As the *Freaks* would say, we are proud to call Count Gore, "one of us."

Creature Feature
 Saturday

Airs at 11:00 p.m.
02/03/73 *House of Frankenstein* (1944)
02/10/73 *Dracula* (1931)
02/17/73 *Frankenstein* (1931)
02/24/73 *WereWolf of London* (1935)
03/03/73 *The Raven* (1935)
03/10/73 *Bride of Frankenstein* (1935)
03/17/73 *The Mad Doctor of Market Street* (1942)
03/24/73 *The Mad Ghoul* (1943)
03/31/73 *Murders in the Rue Morgue* (1932)
04/07/73 *The Crimson Canary* (1945)
04/14/73 *Captive Wild Woman* (1943)
04/21/73 *The Cat Creeps* (1946)
04/28/73 *The House of Fear* (1939)
05/05/73 *Frankenstein Meets the Wolf Man* (1943)
05/12/73 *Black Friday* (1940)
05/19/73 Didn't Air
05/26/73 *House of Dracula* (1945)

06/02/73 *The Mummy's Tomb* (1942)
06/09/73 *The Human Monster* (1939)
06/16/73 *Calling Dr. Death* (1943)
06/23/73 *The Invisible Woman* (1940)
06/30/73 *The Frozen Ghost* (1945)

07/07/73 *Son of Frankenstein* (1939)
07/14/73 *She-Wolf of London* (1946)
07/21/73 *The Mummy's Curse* (1944)
07/28/73 *The Invisible Man* (1933)
08/04/73 Didn't Air
08/11/73 *Horrors of the Black Museum* (1959)
08/18/73 *Attack of the Giant Leeches* (1959)
08/25/73 *The Giant Gila Monster* (1959)
09/01/73 *The Screaming Skull* (1958)
09/08/73 *Dracula's Daughter* (1936)
09/15/73 *House of Horrors* (1946)
09/22/73 *The Ghost of Frankenstein* (1942)
09/29/73 *The Invisible Man Returns* (1940)
10/06/73 *Dracula* (1931)
10/13/73 *The Mummy* (1932)
10/20/73 *Man Made Monster* (1941)
10/27/73 *House of Frankenstein* (1944)
11/03/73 *Queen of Blood* (1966)
11/10/73 *The Invisible Ray* (1936)
11/17/73 *Frankenstein* (1931)
11/24/73 *Horror Island* (1941)
12/01/73 *Horror Hotel* (1960)
12/08/73 *The Horrible Dr. Hichcock* (1962)
12/15/73 *Invasion of the Body Snatchers* (1956)
12/22/73 *The Crime of Doctor Hallet* (1938)
12/29/73 *The Jungle Captive* (1945)
01/05/74 *The Leech Woman* (1960)

01/12/74 *The Wolf Man* (1941)
01/19/74 *The Creature Walks Among Us* (1956)
01/26/74 *The Thing That Couldn't Die* (1958)
02/02/74 *Bride of Frankenstein* (1935)
02/09/74 *Curse of the Undead* (1959)
02/16/74 *Monster on the Campus* (1958)
02/23/74 *Tarantula* (1955)
03/02/74 *Creature from the Black Lagoon* (1954)
03/09/74 Didn't air
03/16/74 *Cult of the Cobra* (1955)
03/23/74 *The Son of Dr. Jekyll* (1951)
03/30/74 *The Black Castle* (1952)
04/06/74 *The Black Cat* (1934)
04/13/74 *Black Friday* (1940)
04/20/74 *Calling Dr. Death* (1943)
04/27/74 *Frankenstein Meets the Wolf Man* (1943)
05/04/74 *House of Frankenstein* (1944)
05/11/74 *The Invisible Man* (1933)
05/18/74 *House of Dracula* (1945)
05/25/74 *The Mummy's Curse* (1944)
06/01/74 *Revenge of the Creature* (1955)
06/08/74 *The Mummy's Hand* (1940)
06/15/74 *The Mummy's Ghost* (1944)
06/22/74 *The Mummy's Tomb* (1942)
06/29/74 *The Mummy* (1932)
07/06/74 *The Screaming Skull* (1958)
07/13/74 *Ghost of Dragstrip Hollow* (1959)

07/20/74 *The Raven* (1935)
07/27/74 *The Little Shop of Horrors* (1960)
08/03/74 *Castle of Evil* (1966)
08/10/74 *The Unearthly* (1957)
08/17/74 *The Human Monster* (1939)
08/24/74 *Satan's Satellites* (1958)
08/31/74 *Captive Wild Woman* (1943)
09/07/74 *The Man in Half Moon Street* (1942)
09/14/74 *Gorgo* (1961)
09/21/74 *Island of Lost Souls* (1933)
09/28/74 *Murders in the Rue Morgue* (1932)
10/05/74 *Dr. Cyclops* (1940)
10/12/74 *Supernatural* (1933)
10/19/74 *The Monster and the Girl* (1941)
10/26/74 *The Beast with Five Fingers* (1946)
11/02/74 *4D Man* (1959)
11/09/74 *House on Haunted Hill* (1959)
11/16/74 *Queen of Outer Space* (1958)
11/23/74 *Bride of Frankenstein* (1935)
11/30/74 *House of Horrors* (1946)
12/07/74 *From Hell It Came* (1957)
12/14/74 *Not of This Earth* (1957)
12/21/74 Didn't air
12/28/74 *Mesa of Lost Women* (1953)
01/04/75 *The Disembodied* (1957)
01/11/75 *Creature from the Black Lagoon* (1954)

> **20 Creature Feature I.**
> "World Without End." (1956). Hugh Marlowe, Nancy Gates, Rod Taylor. (1½ hours.)

01/18/75 *Frankenstein* (1931)
01/25/75 *Dracula* (1931)
02/01/75 *World Without End* (1956)
02/08/75 *Frankenstein Meets the Wolf Man* (1943)
02/15/75 *Macabre* (1958)
02/22/75 *The Invisible Man* (1933)
03/01/75 *Horror Castle* (1963)
03/08/75 *Creature from the Black Lagoon* (1954)
03/15/75 Didn't air
03/22/75 *The Leech Woman* (1960)
03/29/75 *Tarantula* (1955)
04/05/75 *Curse of the Undead* (1959)
04/12/75 *The Black Cat* (1934)
04/19/75 *Calling Dr. Death* (1943)
04/26/75 *The Terror* (1963)
05/03/75 *The Beast of Hollow Mountain* (1956)
05/10/75 *The Day of the Triffids* (1963)
05/17/75 *The Astro-Zombies* (1968)
05/24/75 *The Castle of the Living Dead* (1964)
05/31/75 *The Creature Walks Among Us* (1956)

Janette Scott meets a triffid in *The Day of the Triffids*.

November 15, 1975: Gore presented the first unedited showing of George A. Romero's classic *Night of the Living Dead*.

06/07/75 *Fearless Frank* (1967)
06/14/75 Didn't air
06/21/75 *Gog* (1954)
06/28/75 *Beast of Blood* (1970)
07/05/75 *Deathmaster* (1972)
07/12/75 *War of the Planets* (1966)
07/19/75 *The Magnetic Monster* (1953)
07/26/75 *Horror Express* (1972)
08/02/75 *The Wasp Woman* (1959)
08/09/75 *The Brain from Planet Arous* (1957)
08/16/75 *Son of Dracula* (1943)
08/23/75 *WereWolf of London* (1935)
08/30/75 *House of Frankenstein* (1944)
09/06/75 Didn't air
09/13/75 *Fiend Without a Face* (1958)
09/20/75 *Corridors of Blood* (1958)
09/27/75 *The Haunted Strangler* (1957)
10/04/75 *Black Sabbath* (1963)
10/11/75 Didn't air
10/18/75 *The Bloody Judge* (1970)
10/25/75 *The Crimson Cult* (1968)
10/31/75 Halloween Special: *Theatre of Death* (1967)
11/01/75 *Horror Express* (1972)
11/08/75 *The Castle of the Living Dead* (1964)
11/15/75 *Night of the Living Dead* (1968)
11/22/75 *The Little Shop of Horrors* (1960)
11/29/75 *The Giant Behemoth* (1959)

12/06/75 *Dracula* (1931)
12/13/75 *Frankenstein* (1931)
12/20/75 *The Invisible Man* (1933)
12/27/75 *The Mummy* (1932)
01/03/76 *House of Frankenstein* (1944)
01/10/76 *The Giant Behemoth* (1959)
01/17/76 *It Came from Outer Space* (1953)
01/24/76 *Torture Chamber of Dr. Sadism* (1967)
01/31/76 Didn't Air
02/07/76 *Genesis II* (1973)
02/14/76 *Terror in the Crypt* (1964)
02/21/76 *The Tingler* (1959)
02/28/76 *The Two Faces of Dr. Jekyll* (1960)
03/06/76 *Circus of Horrors* (1960)
03/13/76 Didn't Air
03/20/76 *Curse of the Swamp Creature* (1966)
03/27/76 *The Mummy's Tomb* (1942)
04/03/76 *Billy the Kid vs. Dracula* (1966)
04/10/76 *The 27th Day* (1957)

㉒ Creature Feature I.
"It Came from Outer Space."
(1953). Richard Carlson. (1½ hours.)

04/17/76 *It! The Terror from Beyond Space* (1958)
04/24/76 *The Uninvited* (1944)
05/01/76 *The Day the Earth Caught Fire* (1961)
05/08/76 *Burn, Witch, Burn* (1962)
05/15/76 *Curse of the Demon* (1957)
05/22/76 *Invasion of the Body Snatchers* (1956)
05/29/76 *Curse of the Vampires* (1966)
06/05/76 *Tarantula* (1955)
06/12/76 *Beast of Blood* (1970)
06/19/76 *The Black Cat* (1934)
06/26/76 *The Snow Devils* (1967)
07/03/76 *Monster on the Campus* (1958)
07/10/76 *Horror Hotel* (1960)
07/17/76 *Snake People* (1971)
07/24/76 *Curse of the Demon* (1957)
07/31/76 *The Invisible Ray* (1936)
08/07/76 *Face of Terror* (1962)
08/14/76 *Dr. Orloff's Monster* (1964)
08/21/76 *The Human Monster* (1939)
08/28/76 *Space Monster* (1965)
09/04/76 *The Human Duplicators* (1965)
09/11/76 Didn't air

> **⑳ Creature Feature.**
> **"Face of Terror." (1960).** A woman's disfigured face, restored by unperfected surgery, reverts in the midst of a romance and the woman seeks re-

09/18/76 *Torture Garden* (1967)
09/25/76 *Curse of the Demon* (1957)
10/02/76 *The Day the Earth Stood Still* (1951)
10/09/76 *Black Sabbath* (1963)
10/16/76 *The Tingler* (1959)
10/23/76 *Night of the Living Dead* (1968)
10/30/76 *Horror Express* (1972)
11/06/76 Didn't air
11/13/76 *The Day of the Triffids* (1963)
11/20/76 *Torture Chamber of Dr. Sadism* (1967)
11/27/76 Didn't air
12/04/76 *Terror in the Crypt* (1964)
12/11/76 *The Crimson Cult* (1968)
12/18/76 *Dracula vs. Frankenstein* (1971)
12/25/76 *Panic in Year Zero* (1962)
01/01/77 *Hatchet for the Honeymoon* (1970)
01/08/77 *The Castle of Fu Manchu* (1969)
01/15/77 *Theatre of Death* (1967)
01/22/77 *The Two Faces of Dr. Jekyll* (1960)
01/29/77 *Island of Lost Souls* (1933)
02/05/77 *The Invisible Man* (1933)

02/12/77 *The Mummy* (1932)
02/19/77 *Frankenstein* (1931)
02/26/77 *Bride of Frankenstein* (1935)
03/05/77 *Brides of Blood* (1968)
03/12/77 *Vampire Men of the Lost Planet* (1970)
03/19/77 *Blood and Black Lace* (1964)
03/26/77 *Castle of Terror* (1964)
04/02/77 *The Terror* (1963)
04/09/77 *Zombies of Mora Tau* (1957)
04/16/77 *Queen of Blood* (1966)
04/23/77 *The Castle of the Living Dead* (1964)
04/30/77 *Countess Dracula* (1971)
05/07/77 *The Mummy's Revenge* (1975)
05/14/77 *Horror Express* (1972)
05/21/77 *The Fury of the Wolfman* (1972)
05/28/77 *The Murder Mansion* (1972)
06/04/77 *Mad Doctor of Blood Island* (1969)
06/11/77 *Konga* (1961)
06/18/77 *Brain of Blood* (1971)
06/25/77 *In the Devil's Garden* (1971)
07/02/77 *The Day the Earth Stood Still* (1951)
07/09/77 *Horror Rises from the Tomb* (1973)
07/16/77 *The Night of the Sorcerers* (1974)
07/23/77 *Black Sabbath* (1963)
07/30/77 *Night of the Living Dead* (1968)
08/06/77 *The Hand of Power* (1968)
08/13/77 *Satanik* (1968)
08/20/77 *The Brain that Wouldn't Die* (1962)
08/27/77 *The Astro-Zombies* (1968)
09/03/77 *The Three Stooges in Orbit* (1962)
Airs at 11:30 p.m.
09/10/77 *Equinox* (1970)
09/17/77 *Dr. Who and the Daleks* (1965)
09/24/77 *Daleks' Invasion Earth 2150 A.D.* (1966)
10/01/77 *Inn of Frightened People* (1971)

November 20, 1976 Count Gore showed the West German film *Torture Chamber of Dr. Sadism* with Carl Lange, Karin Dor and Christopher Lee.

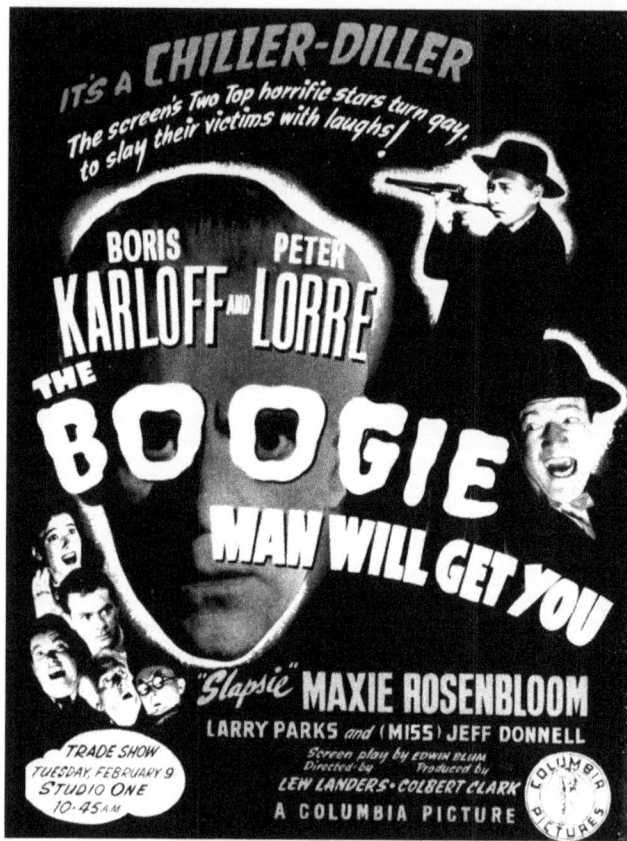

10/08/77 *Curse of the Vampires* (1966)
10/15/77 *Genesis II* (1973)
10/22/77 *Gorgo* (1961)
10/29/77 *The Witches Mountain* (1972)
11/05/77 *Torture Garden* (1967)
11/12/77 *Return of the Fly* (1959)
11/19/77 *The Skull* (1965)
11/26/77 *Inn of Frightened People* (1971)
12/03/77 *Torture Chamber of Dr. Sadism* (1967)
12/10/77 *The Witch* (1966)
12/17/77 *Deathmaster* (1972)
12/24/77 Didn't air
12/31/77 *Crucible of Terror* (1971)
01/07/78 *Theatre of Death* (1967)
01/14/78 *She* (1965)
01/21/78 *The Shuttered Room* (1967)
01/28/78 *Snake People* (1971)
02/04/78 *Vampire Circus* (1972)
02/11/78 *Horror Express* (1972)
02/18/78 *Horrors of the Black Museum* (1959)
02/25/78 *The Incredible 2-Headed Transplant* (1971)
03/04/78 *Supernatural* (1933)
03/11/78 *Frankenstein* (1931)
03/18/78 *Bride of Frankenstein* (1935)
03/25/78 *The Little Shop of Horrors* (1960)
04/01/78 Didn't air
04/08/78 *Beast of Morocco* (1966)
04/15/78 *Carnival of Souls* (1962)
04/22/78 *The Innocents* (1961)
04/29/78 *Doctor Faustus* (1967)
05/06/78 *Dracula* (1931)
05/13/78 *Countess Dracula* (1971)
05/20/78 *The Castle of the Living Dead* (1964)
05/27/78 *Night of the Living Dead* (1968)
06/03/78 *I Was a Teenage Werewolf* (1957)
06/10/78 *The Brides of Fu Manchu* (1966)
06/17/78 *The Horror of Frankenstein* (1970)
06/24/78 *The Mad Doctor* (1940)
07/01/78 *The Boogie Man Will Get You* (1942)
07/08/78 *The Omega Man* (1971)
07/15/78 *Horror Hospital* (1973)
07/22/78 *House of Dracula* (1945)
07/29/78 *The Night of the Sorcerers* (1974)
08/05/78 *In the Devil's Garden* (1971)
08/12/78 *The Sorcerers* (1967)
08/19/78 *Nightmare Castle* (1965)
08/26/78 *Death Curse of Tartu* (1966)
09/02/78 *Rome Against Rome* (1964)
09/09/78 *Horror Castle* (1963)
09/16/78 *Voyage to the End of the Universe* (1963)
09/23/78 *Tarantula* (1955)
09/30/78 *Corridors of Blood* (1958)
10/07/78 *X* (1963)
10/14/78 Didn't air

Airs at 11:00 p.m.
10/21/78 *The Beast with Five Fingers* (1946)
10/28/78 *The Vampire People* (1964)
11/04/78 *The Crimson Cult* (1968)
11/11/78 Didn't air
11/18/78 *Son of Godzilla* (1967)
11/25/78 *Island of Lost Souls* (1933)
12/02/78 *Inn of Frightened People* (1971)

> ⓴ **Creature Feature I.**
> "Son of Godzilla." (1969) Tadao Takashima, Akiro Kubo, Berbay Maeda. (1½ hours.)

12/09/78 Didn't air
12/16/78 *The Mummy* (1932)
12/23/78 *Frankenstein* (1931)
12/30/78 *The Black Cat* (1934)
01/06/79 *The Raven* (1963)
01/13/79 Didn't air
01/20/79 *Scars of Dracula* (1970)
01/27/79 *Carnival of Souls* (1962)
02/03/79 *The Conqueror Worm* (1968)
02/10/79 *Pit and the Pendulum* (1961)
02/17/79 *The Oblong Box* (1969)
02/24/79 *The Masque of the Red Death* (1964)

03/03/79 *House of Dracula* (1945)
03/10/79 *Curse of the Demon* (1957)
03/17/79 *Zombies of Mora Tau* (1957)
03/24/79 Didn't air
03/31/79 *The Invisible Man's Revenge* (1944)
04/07/79 *Horrors of the Black Museum* (1959)
04/14/79 Didn't air
04/21/79 *Crucible of Terror* (1971)
04/28/79 *The Day of the Triffids* (1963)
05/05/79 *Night of the Living Dead* (1968)
05/12/79 *The Frozen Dead* (1966)
05/19/79 *My Blood Runs Cold* (1965)
05/26/79 *Chamber of Horrors* (1966)
06/02/79 *Black Friday* (1940)
06/09/79 *The Mad Ghoul* (1943)
06/16/79 *The Deadly Mantis* (1957)
06/23/79 *The Mole People* (1956)
06/30/79 *Man Made Monster* (1941)
07/07/79 Didn't air
07/14/79 *Corridors of Blood* (1958)
07/21/79 *The Flesh Eaters* (1964)
07/28/79 *Horror Castle* (1963)
08/04/79 *The Beast of Hollow Mountain* (1956)
08/11/79 *Invisible Invaders* (1959)
08/18/79 *Torture Chamber of Dr. Sadism* (1967)
08/25/79 *The Two Faces of Dr. Jekyll* (1960)
09/01/79 *The Little Shop of Horrors* (1960)

Airs at 11:30 p.m.
10/27/84 *Pit and the Pendulum* (1961)
11/03/84 *Earth vs. the Flying Saucers* (1956)
11/10/84 *Theater of Blood* (1973)
11/17/84 *Spirits of the Dead* (1968)
11/24/84 *Frankenstein Meets the Wolf Man* (1943)

WDCA Creature Feature promo for *Dark Star*, long a fan favorite at science fiction conventions

12/01/84 *Monster on the Campus* (1958)
12/08/84 *Terror of Mechagodzilla* (1975)
12/15/84 *Graveyard of Horror* (1971)
12/22/84 *Invaders from Mars* (1953)
12/29/84 *Calling Dr. Death* (1943)
01/05/85 *The Raven* (1935)
01/12/85 Didn't air
01/19/85 *The Thing from Another World* (1951)
01/26/85 *Dark Star* (1974)
02/02/85 *Mystery of the Wax Museum* (1933)
02/09/85 *Them!* (1954)
02/16/85 *The Mummy* (1932)
02/23/85 *The Brides of Dracula* (1960)
03/02/85 *The Crazies* (1973)
03/09/85 *The Wolf Man* (1941)
03/16/85 *The Masque of the Red Death* (1964)
03/23/85 *Son of Frankenstein* (1939)
03/30/85 *Curse of the Demon* (1957)
04/06/85 *Tarantula* (1955)
04/13/85 *The Black Cat* (1934)

> **⓴ Creature Feature I.**
> "Tarantula." (1955). John Agar, Mara Corday, Leo G. Carroll. (1½ hours.)

04/20/85 *Star Pilot* (1966)
04/27/85 *House of Frankenstein* (1944)
05/04/85 *The Beast with Five Fingers* (1946)
05/11/85 *Mothra* (1961)
05/18/85 *Dracula* (1931)
05/25/85 *Zardoz* (1974)
06/01/85 Didn't air
06/08/85 *Phantom of the Rue Morgue* (1954)
06/15/85 *The Incredible 2-Headed Transplant* (1971)
06/22/85 *The Evil of Frankenstein* (1964)

06/29/85 Didn't air
07/06/85 *Attack of the Mushroom People* (1963)
07/13/85 *The Leech Woman* (1960)
07/20/85 *Yog, Monster from Space* (1970)
07/27/85 *The Giant Claw* (1957)
08/03/85 *The Astro-Zombies* (1968)
08/10/85 *The Beach Girls and the Monster* (1965)
08/17/85 *Godzilla vs. the Smog Monster* (1971)
08/24/85 *Zontar, the Thing from Venus* (1966)
08/31/85 *Abbott and Costello Meet Frankenstein* (1948)
09/07/85 *Tales of Terror* (1962)
09/14/85 *The Mole People* (1956)
09/21/85 *The Oblong Box* (1969)
09/28/85 *Bride of Frankenstein* (1935)
10/05/85 *It Came from Outer Space* (1953)
10/12/85 *Tomb of Ligeia* (1965)
10/19/85 *Earth vs. the Flying Saucers* (1956)
10/26/85 Didn't air
10/31/85 Halloween Special: *Damien: Omen II* (1978)
11/02/85 *Son of Dracula* (1943)
11/09/85 *Silent Running* (1972)
11/16/85 *The Crimson Cult* (1968)
11/23/85 *The Shuttered Room* (1967)
11/30/85 *Curse of the Swamp Creature* (1966)
12/07/85 *The Alien Factor* (1978)
12/14/85 *It Came from Beneath the Sea* (1955)
12/21/85 *20 Million Miles to Earth* (1957)
12/28/85 *Man Made Monster* (1941)
01/04/86 *Return of the Fly* (1959)
01/11/86 *Invaders from Mars* (1953)
01/18/86 *The Tingler* (1959)
01/25/86 *Creature from the Black Lagoon* (1954)
02/01/86 *Yor, The Hunter from the Future* (1983)
02/08/86 *Them!* (1954)
02/15/86 *Destroy All Monsters* (1968)

The creepy alien head (Luce Potter) from *Invaders from Mars* (1953) was shown January 11, 1986

02/22/86 *Tarantula* (1955)
03/01/86 *X* (1963)
03/08/86 *The Mysterians* (1957)
03/15/86 *One Million Years B.C.* (1966)
03/22/86 *The Black Castle* (1952)
03/29/86 *The Ghost of Frankenstein* (1942)
04/05/86 *The Mummy's Hand* (1940)
04/12/86 *The Deadly Mantis* (1957)
04/19/86 *The Brain that Wouldn't Die* (1962)
04/26/86 *Assignment Terror* (1970)
05/03/86 *Blood and Lace* (1971)
05/10/86 *Curse of the Undead* (1959)
05/17/86 *Horror House* (1969)
05/24/86 *She-Wolf of London* (1946)
05/31/86 Didn't air
06/07/86 *Frankenstein's Bloody Terror* (1968)
06/14/86 *Dracula vs. Frankenstein* (1971)
06/21/86 *Die, Monster, Die!* (1965)
06/28/86 Didn't air
07/05/86 *The Lucifer Complex* (1978)

10/25/86 *Curse of the Demon* (1957)
10/31/86 Halloween Special: *Damien: Omen II* (1978)
11/01/86 *The Brides of Dracula* (1960)
11/08/86 *Theater of Blood* (1973)
11/15/86 *Earth vs. the Flying Saucers* (1956)
11/22/86 *King Kong* (1933)
11/29/86 *Queen of Blood* (1966)
12/06/86 *The Skull* (1965)
12/13/86 *Atom Age Vampire* (1960)
12/20/86 *Deathmaster* (1972)
12/27/86 *Equinox* (1970)
01/03/87 *Mystery on Monster Island* (1981)
01/10/87 *Two on A Guillotine* (1965)
01/17/87 *The Tingler* (1959)
01/24/87 *My Blood Runs Cold* (1965)
01/31/87 *Creature of Destruction* (1967)
02/07/87 *The Thing from Another World* (1951)
02/14/87 *Godzilla vs. The Thing* (1964)
02/21/87 *The Giant Claw* (1957)
02/28/87 *2 0 Million Miles to Earth* (1957)
03/07/87 *Fearless Frank* (1967)
03/14/87 *The Alien Factor* (1978)
03/21/87 *The Phantom from 10,000 Leagues* (1955)
03/28/87 *Dinosaurus!* (1960)
04/04/87 *Voyage into Space* (1970)
04/11/87 *Where Time Began* (1977)
04/18/87 *Maneater of Hydra* (1967)
04/25/87 *Curse of the Swamp Creature* (1966)
05/02/87 *The Incredible 2-Headed Transplant* (1971)

07/12/86 *The Last Man on Earth* (1964)
07/19/86 *Revenge of the Creature* (1955)
07/26/86 *The Invisible Man Returns* (1940)
08/02/86 *Dracula* (1931)
08/09/86 *Frankenstein* (1931)
08/16/86 *Bride of Frankenstein* (1935)
08/23/86 *The Wolf Man* (1941)
08/30/86 *The Mummy* (1932)
09/06/86 *The Angry Red Planet* (1959)
09/13/86 *The Evil of Frankenstein* (1964)
09/20/86 *Night Creatures* (1962)
09/27/86 *Dark Star* (1974)
10/04/86 *The Curse of the Werewolf* (1961)
10/11/86 *The Manitou* (1977)
10/18/86 *The Crimson Cult* (1968)

Susanne Loret and Alberto Lupo in *Atom Age Vampire*

05/09/87 *The Last Man on Earth* (1964)
05/16/87 *It Came from Outer Space* (1953)
05/23/87 *Invaders from Mars* (1953)

Saturday Chiller

Airs at 2:00 p.m.
02/03/73 *The Tingler* (1959)
02/10/73 *The Killer Shrews* (1959)
02/17/73 *Invasion of the Star Creatures* (1962)
02/24/73 *Voodoo Woman* (1957)
03/03/73 *Son of Dracula* (1943)
03/10/73 *Day the World Ended* (1955)
03/17/73 *The Saga of the Viking Women and Their Voyage to the Waters of the Great Sea Serpent* (1957)
03/24/73 *The Blancheville Monster* (1963)
03/31/73 *Circus of Horrors* (1960)
04/07/73 *Gammera the Invincible* (1966)
04/14/73 *Castle of Evil* (1966)
04/21/73 *The Incredibly Strange Creatures Who Stopped Living and Became Mixed-Up Zombies!!?* (1964)
04/28/73 *The Unearthly* (1957)
05/05/73 *Night of the Blood Beast* (1958)
05/12/73 *Die, Monster, Die!* (1965)
05/19/73 *Blood of Dracula* (1957)
05/26/73 *I Was a Teenage Werewolf* (1957)
06/02/73 *It Conquered the World* (1956)
06/09/73 *The H-Man* (1959)
06/16/73 *The Giant Claw* (1957)
06/23/73 *Battle in Outer Space* (1959)
06/30/73 *Flight to Mars* (1951)
07/07/73 *The Black Cat* (1934)
07/14/73 *Blood of Dracula* (1957)
07/21/73 *The Brain Eaters* (1958)
07/28/73 *How to Make a Monster* (1958)
08/04/73 *Teenage Caveman* (1958)
08/11/73 *The Spider* (1958)
08/18/73 *A Bucket of Blood* (1959)
08/25/73 *The Amazing Colossal Man* (1957)
09/01/73 *The Undead* (1957)
09/08/73 *Journey to the Seventh Planet* (1962)
09/15/73 *Invisible Creature* (1960)
09/22/73 *The Phantom Planet* (1961)
09/29/73 *I Was a Teenage Frankenstein* (1957)

This ultra-modern 1950s TV set from West Germany probably cost more than the entire budget for *The Killer Shrews*.

10/06/73 *The Beast with a Million Eyes* (1955)
10/13/73 *Attack of the Puppet People* (1958)
10/20/73 *Invasion of the Saucer Men* (1957)
10/27/73 *The Killer Shrews* (1959)
11/03/73 *The Brain that Wouldn't Die* (1962)
11/10/73 *Konga* (1961)
11/17/73 *Terror from the Year 5000* (1958)
11/24/73 *Ghost of Dragstrip Hollow* (1959)
12/01/73 *The Bamboo Saucer* (1968)
12/08/73 *Beginning of the End* (1957)
12/15/73 *Lost Planet Airmen* (1951)
12/22/73 *Devil Bat's Daughter* (1946)
12/29/73 *Cat Girl* (1957)

> ⓴ **Saturday Chiller.**
> "Cat Girl." (1957.) A girl inherits a family curse which has her soul enter the body of a leopard that goes on a rampage. Barbara Shelley, Robert Ayres, Kay Ballard.

01/05/74 *Day the World Ended* (1955)
01/12/74 *It Conquered the World* (1956)
01/19/74 *I Was a Teenage Werewolf* (1957)
01/26/74 *The Saga of the Viking Women and Their Voyage to the Waters of the Great Sea Serpent* (1957)
02/02/74 *Planet of the Vampires* (1965)
02/09/74 *Godzilla vs. The Thing* (1964)

Airs at 1:30 p.m.
02/16/74 *The Giant Gila Monster* (1959)
02/23/74 *Die, Monster, Die!* (1965)
03/02/74 *A Bucket of Blood* (1959)
03/09/74 Didn't air
03/16/74 *Abbott and Costello Meet Frankenstein* (1948)
03/23/74 *The She-Creature* (1956)
03/30/74 *War of the Colossal Beast* (1958)
04/06/74 Didn't air
04/13/74 Didn't air
04/20/74 Didn't air
04/27/74 *Mars Needs Women* (1967)
05/04/74 *Dracula's Daughter* (1936)
05/11/74 *The Beast of Hollow Mountain* (1956)
05/18/74 *The Magnetic Monster* (1953)
05/25/74 *The Monster that Challenged the World* (1957)
06/01/74 *Invasion of the Star Creatures* (1962)
06/08/74 *Beyond the Time Barrier* (1960)
06/15/74 *The Beast with a Million Eyes* (1955)
06/22/74 *The Spider* (1958)
06/29/74 *Invasion of the Star Creatures* (1962)
07/06/74 *Monster from a Prehistoric Planet* (1967)

07/13/74 *Attack of the Robots* (1966)
07/20/74 *Beast of Morocco* (1966)
07/27/74 *Majin, Monster of Terror* (1966)
08/03/74 *The Horrible Dr. Hichcock* (1962)
08/10/74 *Horror Hotel* (1960)
08/17/74 *Two Lost Worlds* (1951)
08/24/74 *Beginning of the End* (1957)
08/31/74 *Flight to Mars* (1951)

Chapter 7
Un-hosted Horror Theaters

When it comes to addressing genre movies that aired during the horror host heyday, a discussion of said hosts barely scratches the coffin lid. Many stations ran films in specific time slots dedicated to fright fare, giving these "theaters" appropriate names in the process. Furthermore, this by no means precluded these very same stations from airing horrors under more harmless-sounding banners such as "The Late Show." The following is a list of the horror-specific movie blocks organized by debut date.

HORROR! (WBAL Channel 11)

The popularity of *Shock!* led WBAL to add *Horror!* to its line-up, sans host. Again, mysteries and crime dramas were mixed in with authentic monster movies. The Friday night edition lasted about four months, while the Saturday version continued for almost seven.

Airs Friday night at 1:00 a.m.
11/29/57 *The Mummy* (1932)

> SHOCK — "Frankenstein," starring Boris Karloff and Colin Clive. Channel 11 at 11.15 P.M.
> HORROR — "The Frozen Ghost," starring Lon Chaney and Evelyn Ankers. Channel 11 at 1 A.M.

12/06/57 *Frankenstein* (1931)
12/13/57 *Chamber of Horrors* (1940)
12/20/57 *Dr. Renault's Secret* (1942)
12/27/57 *Horror Island* (1941)
01/03/58 *The Cat Creeps* (1946)
01/10/58 *Dracula* (1931)
01/17/58 *The Frozen Ghost* (1945)
01/24/58 *The Mummy's Hand* (1940)
01/31/58 *Dead Man's Eyes* (1944)
02/07/58 *The Human Monster* (1939)
02/14/58 *Chinatown Squad* (1935)
02/21/58 *Destination Unknown* (1942)
02/28/58 *The Man Who Wouldn't Die* (1942)
03/07/58 *The Black Cat* (1934)
03/14/58 *The Last Warning* (1938)
03/21/58 *The Crime of Helen Stanley* (1934)
03/28/58 *House of Horrors* (1946)

Airs Saturday night at 12:45/1:00 a.m.
11/30/57 *The Undying Monster* (1942)
12/07/57 *The Wolf Man* (1941)
12/14/57 Didn't air
12/21/57 *Weird Woman* (1944)
12/28/57 *The Last Warning* (1938)
01/04/58 *Calling Dr. Death* (1943)
01/11/58 *The Mad Doctor of Market Street* (1942)
01/18/58 *She-Wolf of London* (1946)
01/25/58 *The Witness Vanishes* (1939)
02/01/58 *The Spider Woman Strikes Back* (1946)
02/08/58 *Secret of the Chateau* (1934)
02/15/58 *Mystery of the White Room* (1939)
02/22/58 *Danger Woman* (1946)
03/01/58 *The Invisible Man* (1933)
03/08/58 *Horror Island* (1941)
03/15/58 *The Man Who Cried Wolf* (1937)
03/22/58 *The Mummy* (1932)
03/29/58 *Alibi for Murder* (1936)

> 11.15 P.M.—SHOCK—"She-Wolf of London." A girl insists that she is responsible for a series of murders. June Lockhart. (1946.) Channel 11.
> 1 A.M.—HORROR—"Convicted Woman." Glenn Ford and Bruce Cabot star. Channel 11.

04/05/58 *Before Midnight* (1933)
04/12/58 *The Mummy's Tomb* (1942)
04/19/58 *WereWolf of London* (1935)
04/26/58 *The Strange Case of Dr. Rx* (1942)
05/03/58 *Who Killed Gail Preston?* (1938)
05/10/58 *Frankenstein Meets the Wolf Man* (1943)
05/17/58 *Dead Man's Eyes* (1944)
05/24/58 *When G-Men Step In* (1938)
05/31/58 *Enemy Agent* (1940)
06/07/58 *The Frozen Ghost* (1945)
06/14/58 *Convicted Woman* (1940)

SHOCK! (WTOP Channel 9)

The *Shock!* package came to D.C. without a host just a month after arriving in Baltimore. Incredibly, the nation's capital incarnation lasted for 11 years! For nearly eight years, the program showed primarily the Universal and Columbia films, as well as several Paramount productions Universal owned. In the fall of 1965, the station added Mexican horrors to the rotation. The following description of the *Shock!* opening is taken from Classic Horror Film Board contributor ProfessorWalgate. "[*Shock!*] began with handheld camera shots of gravestones, candles and hands coming out of the ground while the narrator would intone specially written tomes such as, 'Did a wing just touch your cheek? When you wake, will that cheek be pale?...Are you to have a visitor...from the House... of Dracula?' Later the narration went generic with, 'Do not feel so secure in your warm and quiet home... The Invisible Man...The Mummy...The Wolf Man... Frankenstein, etc. is looking for you!'" Author Gregory William Mank remembered that for most films, the opening credits were moved to the end of the film so that the action started right away.

Beginning with the July 23, 1966 airing of *The Revenge of Frankenstein*, local papers started listing this movie slot as *The Late Late Show* but would nevertheless occasionally list it as *Shock!* As the films shown during this time continued to be the same films shown during *Shock!* they are included here for completeness purposes.

Airs Sunday at 11:15 p.m.
12/01/57 *Frankenstein* (1931)
12/08/57 *The Invisible Ray* (1936)
12/15/57 *Man Made Monster* (1941)
12/22/57 *The Cat Creeps* (1946)
12/29/57 *The Mummy* (1932)
01/05/58 *Dracula* (1931)
01/12/58 *Frankenstein Meets the Wolf Man* (1943)
01/19/58 *Dracula's Daughter* (1936)
01/26/58 *Murders in the Rue Morgue* (1932)
02/02/58 *Son of Frankenstein* (1939)
02/09/58 *Night Monster* (1942)
02/16/58 *The Mummy's Tomb* (1942)
02/23/58 *The Mad Ghoul* (1943)
03/02/58 *WereWolf of London* (1935)
03/09/58 *The Frozen Ghost* (1945)
03/16/58 *The Mummy's Hand* (1940)
03/23/58 *Son of Dracula* (1943)
03/30/58 *House of Horrors* (1946)
04/06/58 *The Human Monster* (1939)
04/13/58 *The Wolf Man* (1941)
04/20/58 *Pillow of Death* (1945)
04/27/58 *The Mummy's Ghost* (1944)
05/04/58 *Dead Man's Eyes* (1943)
05/11/58 *The Raven* (1935)
05/18/58 *The Mad Doctor of Market Street* (1942)
05/25/58 *Night Key* (1937)
06/01/58 *Calling Dr. Death* (1943)
06/08/58 *The Invisible Man* (1933)
06/15/58 *Weird Woman* (1944)
06/22/58 *She-Wolf of London* (1946)
06/29/58 *The Invisible Man Returns* (1940)
07/06/58 *Nightmare* (1942)
07/13/58 *The Black Cat* (1934)
07/20/58 *The Strange Case of Dr. Rx* (1942)
07/27/58 *The Spider Woman Strikes Back* (1946)
08/03/58 *Secret of the Blue Room* (1933)
08/10/58 *Horror Island* (1941)
08/17/58 *Mystery of Edwin Drood* (1935)
08/24/58 *The Great Impersonation* (1935)
08/31/58 *Mystery of Marie Roget* (1942)
09/07/58 *House of Dracula* (1945)
09/14/58 *House of Frankenstein* (1944)

Universal's *Shock!* pressbook

Excitement tonight and Saturday for SHOCK and HORROR fans!

TONIGHT
1:00 A.M.
(following Jack Paar)

HORROR!

Boris Karloff in

FRANKENSTEIN

11:15 SATURDAY

SHOCK!

BELA LUGOSI in

DRACULA

followed by

HORROR! 12:45 a.m.

Lon Chaney and Bela Lugosi

FRANKENSTEIN MEETS THE WOLF MAN

09/21/58 *The Invisible Man's Revenge* (1944)
09/28/58 *The Face Behind the Mask* (1941)
10/05/58 *Before I Hang* (1940)
10/12/58 *The Ghost of Frankenstein* (1942)
10/19/58 *The Man Who Lived Twice* (1936)
10/26/58 *Black Friday* (1940)
11/02/58 *Island of Doomed Men* (1940)
11/09/58 *The Man They Could Not Hang* (1939)
11/16/58 *Captive Wild Woman* (1943)
11/23/58 *The Black Room* (1935)
11/30/58 *The Jungle Captive* (1945)
12/07/58 *The Mummy's Curse* (1944)
12/14/58 *Night of Terror* (1933)
12/21/58 *The Devil Commands* (1941)
12/28/58 *The Man with Nine Lives* (1940)
01/04/59 *Behind the Mask* (1932)
01/11/59 *Bride of Frankenstein* (1935)

> 11.15 (9) The Late Show.
> 12.00 (5) Inner Sanctum.
> 12.30 (4) Good Night Show.
> 1.30 (9) The Late Late Show.

Airs Saturday after *The Late Show*
02/07/59 *Frankenstein* (1931)
02/14/59 *The Boogie Man Will Get You* (1942)
02/21/59 *The Cat Creeps* (1946)
02/28/59 *Man Made Monster* (1941)
03/07/59 *Dracula* (1931)
03/14/59 *The Invisible Ray* (1936)
03/21/59 *The Mummy* (1932)
03/28/59 *Dracula's Daughter* (1936)
04/04/59 *Murders in the Rue Morgue* (1932)
04/11/59 *Frankenstein Meets the Wolf Man* (1943)
04/18/59 *Night Monster* (1942)
04/25/59 *The Mummy's Tomb* (1942)
05/02/59 *Son of Frankenstein* (1939)
05/09/59 *The Mad Ghoul* (1943)
05/16/59 *The Frozen Ghost* (1945)
05/23/59 *The Mummy's Hand* (1940)
05/30/59 *Son of Dracula* (1943)
06/06/59 *The Wolf Man* (1941)
06/13/59 *House of Horrors* (1946)
06/20/59 *WereWolf of London* (1935)
06/27/59 *Pillow of Death* (1945)
07/04/59 *The Mummy's Ghost* (1944)
07/11/59 *The Raven* (1935)
07/18/59 *Dead Man's Eyes* (1944)
07/25/59 *The Mad Doctor of Market Street* (1942)
08/01/59 *The Invisible Man* (1933)
08/08/59 *Night Key* (1937)
08/15/59 *Calling Dr. Death* (1943)
08/22/59 *She-Wolf of London* (1946)

What would you watch on TV in 1959?

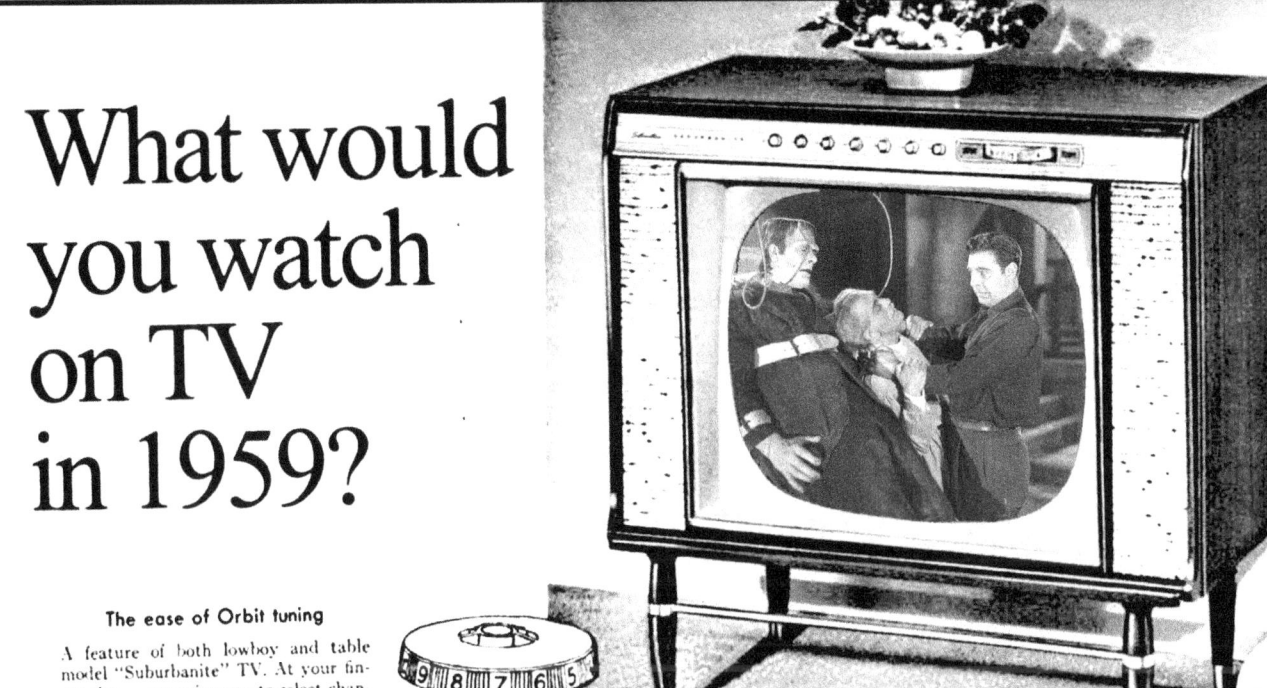

The ease of Orbit tuning
A feature of both lowboy and table model "Suburbanite" TV. At your fingertips... an easier way to select chan-

You would be watching what every monster kid in Baltimore was watching: *The House of Frankenstein* with Glenn Strange, Boris Karloff and Lon Chaney, Jr.

08/29/59 *Weird Woman* (1944)
09/05/59 *Nightmare* (1942)
09/12/59 *The Black Cat* (1934)
09/19/59 *The Strange Case of Dr. Rx* (1942)
09/26/59 *The Spider Woman Strikes Back* (1946)
10/03/59 *Secret of the Blue Room* (1933)
10/10/59 *The Invisible Man Returns* (1940)
10/17/59 *Horror Island* (1941)
10/24/59 *Mystery of Edwin Drood* (1935)
10/31/59 *Bride of Frankenstein* (1935)
11/07/59 *Mystery of Marie Roget* (1942)
11/14/59 *House of Dracula* (1945)
11/21/59 *House of Frankenstein* (1944)
11/28/59 *The Invisible Man's Revenge* (1944)
12/05/59 *The Face Behind the Mask* (1941)
12/12/59 *Before I Hang* (1940)
12/19/59 *The Ghost of Frankenstein* (1942)
12/26/59 *The Man Who Lived Twice* (1936)
01/02/60 *Black Friday* (1940)
01/09/60 *Island of Doomed Men* (1940)
01/16/60 *The Man They Could Not Hang* (1939)
01/23/60 *Captive Wild Woman* (1943)
01/30/60 *The Black Room* (1935)
02/06/60 *The Jungle Captive* (1945)
02/13/60 *The Mummy's Curse* (1944)
02/20/60 *Night of Terror* (1933)
02/27/60 *The Devil Commands* (1941)
03/05/60 *The Man with Nine Lives* (1940)
03/12/60 *Behind the Mask* (1932)
03/19/60 *The Boogie Man Will Get You* (1942)

03/26/60 *The Human Monster* (1939)
04/02/60 *Frankenstein* (1931)
04/09/60 *The Great Impersonation* (1935)
04/16/60 *Island of Lost Souls* (1933)
04/23/60 *The Cat Creeps* (1946)
04/30/60 *Man Made Monster* (1941)
05/07/60 *Dracula* (1931)
05/14/60 *The Invisible Ray* (1936)
05/21/60 *The Mummy* (1932)
05/28/60 *Dracula's Daughter* (1936)
06/04/60 *Murders in the Rue Morgue* (1932)
06/11/60 *Frankenstein Meets the Wolf Man* (1943)
06/18/60 *Night Monster* (1942)
06/25/60 *The Mummy's Tomb* (1942)
07/02/60 *Son of Frankenstein* (1939)
07/09/60 Didn't air
07/16/60 *The Frozen Ghost* (1945)
07/23/60 *The Mummy's Hand* (1940)
07/30/60 *Son of Dracula* (1943)
08/06/60 *The Wolf Man* (1941)
08/13/60 *The Mad Ghoul* (1943)
08/20/60 *House of Horrors* (1946)
08/27/60 Didn't air
09/03/60 Didn't air
09/10/60 Didn't air
09/17/60 *The Mummy's Ghost* (1944)
09/24/60 *The Raven* (1935)
10/01/60 *Dead Man's Eyes* (1944)
10/08/60 *The Devil Doll* (1936)
10/15/60 *Pillow of Death* (1945)

> **11.15 P.M.—SHOCK—"The Mummy's Hand."** A mummy, who has managed to live on for 3,000 years, is determined to keep outsiders from entering his tomb. Dick Foran, Wallace Ford. Channel 11.
>
> **12.30 P.M.—LATE LATE SHOW—"Crimes of Dr. Mabuse."** A mad scientist, through hypnosis, forces his doctor to help him carry out his plan for world domination. Channel 13.
>
> **1 A.M.—HORROR—"Dead Man's Eyes."** A killer is exposed by the eyes of his victim. Lon Chaney, Jr., Jean Parker. Channel 11.

10/22/60 *Secret of the Blue Room* (1933)
10/29/60 *WereWolf of London* (1935)
11/05/60 *The Mad Doctor of Market Street* (1942)
11/12/60 *The Invisible Man* (1933)
11/19/60 *Night Key* (1937)
11/26/60 *Calling Dr. Death* (1943)
12/03/60 *She-Wolf of London* (1946)
12/10/60 *Weird Woman* (1944)
12/17/60 *Nightmare* (1942)
12/24/60 Didn't air
12/31/60 *The Black Cat* (1934)
01/07/61 *The Strange Case of Dr. Rx* (1942)
01/14/61 *The Spider Woman Strikes Back* (1946)
01/21/61 *The Invisible Man Returns* (1940)
01/28/61 *Horror Island* (1941)
02/04/61 *Mystery of Edwin Drood* (1935)
02/11/61 *The Human Monster* (1939)
02/18/61 *Mystery of Marie Roget* (1942)
02/25/61 *The Great Impersonation* (1935)
03/04/61 *Island of Lost Souls* (1933)
03/11/61 *House of Dracula* (1945)
03/18/61 *House of Frankenstein* (1944)
03/25/61 *The Invisible Man's Revenge* (1944)
04/01/61 *The Face Behind the Mask* (1941)
04/08/61 *Before I Hang* (1940)
04/15/61 *The Ghost of Frankenstein* (1942)
04/22/61 *The Man Who Lived Twice* (1936)
04/29/61 *Black Friday* (1940)
05/06/61 *Bride of Frankenstein* (1935)
05/13/61 *Island of Doomed Men* (1940)
05/20/61 *The Man They Could Not Hang* (1939)
05/27/61 *Captive Wild Woman* (1943)
06/03/61 *The Black Room* (1935)
06/10/61 *Dr. Renault's Secret* (1942)
06/17/61 *The Human Monster* (1939)
06/24/61 *The Jungle Captive* (1945)
07/01/61 *The Mummy's Curse* (1944)

07/08/61 *Night of Terror* (1933)
07/15/61 *The Devil Commands* (1941)
07/22/61 *The Man with Nine Lives* (1940)
07/29/61 *Behind the Mask* (1932)
08/05/61 *The Boogie Man Will Get You* (1942)
08/12/61 *Night Monster* (1942)
08/19/61 *The Mummy's Ghost* (1944)
08/26/61 *The Cat Creeps* (1946)
09/02/61 *Dead Man's Eyes* (1944)
09/09/61 *Frankenstein* (1931)
09/16/61 *The Wolf Man* (1941)
09/23/61 *The Invisible Ray* (1936)
09/30/61 *Dracula* (1931)
10/07/61 *Son of Frankenstein* (1939)
10/14/61 *She-Wolf of London* (1946)
10/21/61 *Dracula's Daughter* (1936)
10/28/61 *The Raven* (1935)
11/04/61 *The Mummy* (1932)
11/11/61 *Calling Dr. Death* (1943)
11/18/61 *The Invisible Man* (1933)
11/25/61 *Frankenstein Meets the Wolf Man* (1943)
12/02/61 *Man Made Monster* (1941)
12/09/61 *The Mummy's Tomb* (1942)
12/16/61 *The Frozen Ghost* (1945)
12/23/61 *Son of Dracula* (1943)
12/30/61 *The Black Cat* (1934)
01/06/62 *The Invisible Man Returns* (1940)
01/13/62 *Cry of the Werewolf* (1944)
01/20/62 *The Soul of a Monster* (1944)
01/27/62 *The Return of the Vampire* (1943)
02/03/62 *Pillow of Death* (1945)
02/10/62 *The Mummy's Hand* (1940)
02/17/62 *WereWolf of London* (1935)
02/24/62 *Murders in the Rue Morgue* (1932)
03/03/62 *House of Dracula* (1945)
03/10/62 *Before I Hang* (1940)
03/17/62 *The Mummy's Curse* (1944)

03/24/62 *House of Frankenstein* (1944)
03/31/62 *The Man They Could Not Hang* (1939)
04/07/62 *Bride of Frankenstein* (1935)
04/14/62 *The Invisible Man's Revenge* (1944)
04/21/62 *The Black Room* (1935)
04/28/62 *The Devil Commands* (1941)
05/05/62 *The Ghost of Frankenstein* (1942)
05/12/62 *The Face Behind the Mask* (1941)
05/19/62 *Behind the Mask* (1932)
05/26/62 *Black Friday* (1940)
06/02/62 *The Man Who Lived Twice* (1936)
06/09/62 *Island of Doomed Men* (1940)
06/16/62 *Night of Terror* (1933)
06/23/62 *The Man with Nine Lives* (1940)
06/30/62 *Dr. Cyclops* (1940)
07/07/62 *The Beast with Five Fingers* (1946)
07/14/62 *Night Monster* (1942)
07/21/62 *The Mummy's Ghost* (1944)
07/28/62 *Frankenstein* (1931)
08/04/62 *The Wolf Man* (1941)
08/11/62 *The Invisible Ray* (1936)
08/18/62 *Dracula* (1931)
08/25/62 *She-Wolf of London* (1946)
09/01/62 *Calling Dr. Death* (1943)
09/08/62 *The Cat Creeps* (1946)
09/15/62 *The Raven* (1935)
09/22/62 *Son of Frankenstein* (1939)
09/29/62 *Dead Man's Eyes* (1944)
10/06/62 *Dracula's Daughter* (1936)
10/13/62 *The Mummy* (1932)
10/20/62 *Frankenstein Meets the Wolf Man* (1943)
10/27/62 *The Black Cat* (1934)
11/03/62 *The Invisible Man Returns* (1940)
11/10/62 *Son of Dracula* (1943)
11/17/62 *The Mummy's Tomb* (1942)
11/24/62 *Man Made Monster* (1941)
12/01/62 *WereWolf of London* (1935)
12/08/62 *The Frozen Ghost* (1945)
12/15/62 *House of Dracula* (1945)
12/22/62 *The Return of the Vampire* (1943)
12/29/62 *Cry of the Werewolf* (1944)
01/05/63 *The Soul of a Monster* (1944)
01/12/63 *Pillow of Death* (1945)
01/19/63 *The Mummy's Hand* (1940)
01/26/63 *The Invisible Man* (1933)
02/02/63 *Murders in the Rue Morgue* (1932)
02/09/63 *Before I Hang* (1940)
02/16/63 *The Face Behind the Mask* (1941)

Son of Frankenstein with Boris Karloff, Bela Lugosi and Basil Rathbone

> **The Black Sheep.** Basil Rathbone. 1956. Also: **Neanderthal Man.** Robert Shayne. 1953. ⑤ 11 P.M.
> **Dreamboat.** Clifton Webb. 1952. ⑦ 11.10 P.M.
> **The Road To Singapore.** Bing Crosby. 1940. ⑨ 11.15 P.M.
> **A Face In the Rain.** Rory Calhoun. 1963. ⑪ 11.20 P.M.
> **King Of the Zombies.** Dick Purcell. 1941. ⑬ 11.45 P.M.
> **The Man With Nine Lives.** Boris Karloff. 1940. ⑨ 12.50 A.M.

A great night for horror fiends but oops! That's the *Black SLEEP*!

02/23/63 *The Mummy's Curse* (1944)
03/02/63 *The Black Room* (1935)
03/09/63 *House of Frankenstein* (1944)
03/16/63 *The Invisible Man's Revenge* (1944)
03/23/63 *Bride of Frankenstein* (1935)
03/30/63 *The Man They Could Not Hang* (1939)
04/06/63 *The Ghost of Frankenstein* (1942)
04/13/63 *The Devil Commands* (1941)
04/20/63 *Black Friday* (1940)
04/27/63 *Behind the Mask* (1932)
05/04/63 *The Man Who Lived Twice* (1936)
05/11/63 *Night of Terror* (1933)
05/18/63 *The Man with Nine Lives* (1940)
05/25/63 *Island of Doomed Men* (1940)
06/01/63 *Dr. Cyclops* (1940)
06/08/63 *Island of Lost Souls* (1933)
06/15/63 *Night Monster* (1942)
06/22/63 *The Mummy's Ghost* (1944)
06/29/63 *Frankenstein* (1931)
07/06/63 *The Wolf Man* (1941)
07/13/63 *The Invisible Ray* (1936)
07/20/63 *Dracula* (1931)
07/27/63 *She-Wolf of London* (1946)
08/03/63 *Calling Dr. Death* (1943)
08/10/63 *The Cat Creeps* (1946)
08/17/63 *Son of Frankenstein* (1939)
08/24/63 *The Raven* (1935)
08/31/63 *Dead Man's Eyes* (1944)
09/07/63 *The Frozen Ghost* (1945)
09/14/63 *The Return of the Vampire* (1943)
09/21/63 *Cry of the Werewolf* (1944)
09/28/63 *The Soul of a Monster* (1944)
10/05/63 *Dracula's Daughter* (1936)
10/12/63 *The Mummy* (1932)
10/19/63 *Man Made Monster* (1941)
10/26/63 *The Invisible Man* (1933)
11/02/63 *The Mummy's Tomb* (1942)
11/09/63 *Frankenstein Meets the Wolf Man* (1943)
11/16/63 *The Black Cat* (1934)
11/23/63 *Son of Dracula* (1943)
11/30/63 *The Invisible Man Returns* (1940)
12/07/63 *WereWolf of London* (1935)
12/14/63 *The Mummy's Hand* (1940)
12/21/63 *House of Dracula* (1945)
12/28/63 *Before I Hang* (1940)
01/04/64 *Pillow of Death* (1945)
01/11/64 *The Face Behind the Mask* (1941)
01/18/64 *Murders in the Rue Morgue* (1932)
01/25/64 *Son of Dracula* (1943)
02/01/64 *The Mummy's Curse* (1944)
02/08/64 *The Black Room* (1935)
02/15/64 *Black Friday* (1940)
02/22/64 *The Invisible Man's Revenge* (1944)
02/29/64 *The Man They Could Not Hang* (1939)
03/07/64 *The Devil Commands* (1941)
03/14/64 *House of Frankenstein* (1944)
03/21/64 *Night of Terror* (1933)
03/28/64 *The Man with Nine Lives* (1940)
04/04/64 *The Ghost of Frankenstein* (1942)
04/11/64 *Bride of Frankenstein* (1935)
04/18/64 *Island of Doomed Men* (1940)
04/25/64 *Behind the Mask* (1932)
05/02/64 *The Man Who Lived Twice* (1936)
05/09/64 *The Son of Dr. Jekyll* (1951)
05/16/64 *Dr. Cyclops* (1940)
05/23/64 *The Monster and the Girl* (1941)
05/30/64 *Night Monster* (1942)
06/06/64 *The Mummy's Ghost* (1944)
06/13/64 *Frankenstein* (1931)
06/20/64 *The Wolf Man* (1941)
06/27/64 *The Invisible Ray* (1936)
07/04/64 *Dracula* (1931)
07/11/64 *She-Wolf of London* (1946)
07/18/64 *Calling Dr. Death* (1943)
07/25/64 *The Cat Creeps* (1946)
08/01/64 *Frankenstein* (1931)
08/08/64 *Dead Man's Eyes* (1944)
08/15/64 *Dracula's Daughter* (1936)
08/22/64 *The Mummy's Hand* (1940)
08/29/64 *The Invisible Man* (1933)
09/05/64 *The Soul of a Monster* (1944)
09/12/64 *Before I Hang* (1940)
09/19/64 *Cry of the Werewolf* (1944)
09/26/64 *The Invisible Man Returns* (1940)
10/03/64 *The Return of the Vampire* (1943)
10/10/64 *WereWolf of London* (1935)
10/17/64 *The Mummy* (1932)

10/24/64 *Man Made Monster* (1941)
10/31/64 *Son of Frankenstein* (1939)
11/07/64 *House of Dracula* (1945)
11/14/64 *Island of Lost Souls* (1933)
11/21/64 *The Face Behind the Mask* (1941)
11/28/64 *The Man They Could Not Hang* (1939)
12/05/64 *The Mummy's Tomb* (1942)
12/12/64 *Murders in the Rue Morgue* (1932)
12/19/64 *Son of Dracula* (1943)
12/26/64 *The Raven* (1935)
01/02/65 *House of Dracula* (1945)
01/09/65 *The Black Cat* (1934)
01/16/65 *The Invisible Man's Revenge* (1944)
01/23/65 *The Mummy's Curse* (1944)
01/30/65 *The Black Room* (1935)
02/06/65 *Night of Terror* (1933)
02/13/65 *Island of Doomed Men* (1940)
02/20/65 *Pillow of Death* (1945)
02/27/65 *Black Friday* (1940)
03/06/65 *Dr. Cyclops* (1940)
03/13/65 *The Frozen Ghost* (1945)
03/20/65 *Bride of Frankenstein* (1935)
03/27/65 *The Man Who Lived Twice* (1936)
04/03/65 *The Devil Commands* (1941)
04/10/65 *Behind the Mask* (1932)
04/17/65 *The Man with Nine Lives* (1940)
04/24/65 *Night Monster* (1942)
05/01/65 *Frankenstein Meets the Wolf Man* (1943)
05/08/65 *The Monster and the Girl* (1941)
05/15/65 *Behind the Mask* (1932)
05/22/65 *The Wolf Man* (1941)
05/29/65 *The Invisible Ray* (1936)
06/05/65 *Frankenstein Meets the Wolf Man* (1943)
06/12/65 *WereWolf of London* (1935)
06/19/65 *The Invisible Man Returns* (1940)
06/26/65 *Cry of the Werewolf* (1944)
07/03/65 *The Soul of a Monster* (1944)
07/10/65 *The Mummy's Ghost* (1944)
07/17/65 *Dracula* (1931)
07/24/65 *Island of Lost Souls* (1933)
07/31/65 *She-Wolf of London* (1946)
08/07/65 *Calling Dr. Death* (1943)
08/14/65 *Before I Hang* (1940)
08/21/65 *Son of Frankenstein* (1939)
08/28/65 *The Face Behind the Mask* (1941)
09/04/65 *House of Frankenstein* (1944)
09/11/65 *The Cat Creeps* (1946)
09/18/65 *Dead Man's Eyes* (1944)
09/25/65 *Dracula's Daughter* (1936)
10/02/65 *Frankenstein* (1931)
10/09/65 *House of Dracula* (1945)
10/16/65 *Murders in the Rue Morgue* (1932)
10/23/65 *The Raven* (1935)

10/30/65 *The Witch's Mirror* (1962)
11/06/65 *The Man They Could Not Hang* (1939)
11/13/65 *Pillow of Death* (1945)
11/20/65 *Curse of the Crying Woman* (1963)
11/27/65 *Island of Doomed Men* (1940)
12/04/65 *The Black Cat* (1934)
12/11/65 *El Vampiro* (1957)
12/18/65 *The Man Who Lived Twice* (1936)
12/25/65 *The Devil Commands* (1941)
01/01/66 *Man Made Monster* (1941)
01/08/66 *The Bloody Vampire* (1962)
01/15/66 *Son of Dracula* (1943)
01/22/66 *The Mummy* (1932)
01/29/66 *House of Dracula* (1945)
02/05/66 *The Living Head* (1963)
02/12/66 *Night of Terror* (1933)
02/19/66 *Dracula* (1931)
02/26/66 *The Man with Nine Lives* (1940)
03/05/66 *The Brainiac* (1962)
03/12/66 *The Black Room* (1935)
03/19/66 *The Mummy's Hand* (1940)
03/26/66 *Black Friday* (1940)
04/02/66 *The Invisible Man* (1933)
04/09/66 *The Werewolf* (1956)
04/16/66 *The Robot vs. the Aztec Mummy* (1959)

Bela Lugosi in *The Raven* (1935), shown December 31, 1966. It was a happy New Year for monster fans.

04/23/66 *The Thing That Couldn't Die* (1958)
04/30/66 *The Curse of Nostradamus* (1961)
05/07/66 *The World of the Vampires* (1961)
05/14/66 *The Curse of the Doll People* (1961)
05/21/66 *Doctor of Doom* (1963)
05/28/66 *The Monsters Demolisher* (1962)
06/04/66 *The Genie of Darkness* (1962)
06/11/66 *Samson in the Wax Museum* (1963)
06/18/66 *The Vampire's Coffin* (1958)
06/25/66 *The Man and the Monster* (1959)
07/02/66 *The Curse of the Aztec Mummy* (1957)
07/09/66 *Samson vs. the Vampire Women* (1962)
07/16/66 *The Witch's Mirror* (1962)

07/23/66 *The Revenge of Frankenstein* (1958)
07/30/66 *The Blood of Nostradamus* (1962)
08/06/66 *The Invasion of the Vampires* (1963)
08/13/66 *Calling Dr. Death* (1943)
08/20/66 *Behind the Mask* (1932)
08/27/66 *The Invisible Man's Revenge* (1944)
09/03/66 *The Frozen Ghost* (1945)
09/10/66 *Night Monster* (1942)
09/17/66 *The Bloody Vampire* (1962)
09/24/66 *Curse of the Crying Woman* (1963)
10/01/66 *The Cat Creeps* (1946)
10/08/66 *El Vampiro* (1957)
10/15/66 *The Invisible Ray* (1936)

10/22/66 *The Mummy's Ghost* (1944)
10/29/66 *The Wolf Man* (1941)
11/05/66 *She-Wolf of London* (1946)
11/12/66 *The Monster and the Girl* (1941)
11/19/66 *Bride of Frankenstein* (1935)
11/26/66 *The Devil Commands* (1941)
12/03/66 *The Man Who Lived Twice* (1936)
12/10/66 *Island of Doomed Men* (1940)
12/17/66 *Before I Hang* (1940)
12/24/66 Didn't air
12/31/66 *The Raven* (1935)
01/07/67 *The Wolf Man* (1941)
01/14/67 *Son of Frankenstein* (1939)
01/21/67 *House of Dracula* (1945)
01/28/67 *The Black Room* (1935)
02/04/67 *Dracula* (1931)
02/11/67 *The Werewolf* (1956)
02/18/67 *WereWolf of London* (1935)
02/25/67 *Frankenstein Meets the Wolf Man* (1943)
03/04/67 *Murders in the Rue Morgue* (1932)
03/11/67 *The Black Cat* (1934)
03/18/67 *Night of Terror* (1933)
03/25/67 *The Ghost of Frankenstein* (1942)
04/01/67 *The Invisible Man Returns* (1940)
04/08/67 *Dead Man's Eyes* (1944)
04/15/67 *The Face Behind the Mask* (1941)
04/22/67 *Pillow of Death* (1945)
04/29/67 *The Man They Could Not Hang* (1939)
05/06/67 *The Return of the Vampire* (1943)
05/13/67 *The Son of Dr. Jekyll* (1951)
05/20/67 *The Mummy's Curse* (1944)
05/27/67 *Cry of the Werewolf* (1944)
06/03/67 *Dr. Cyclops* (1940)
06/10/67 *House of Frankenstein* (1944)
06/17/67 *The Soul of a Monster* (1944)
06/24/67 *Dracula's Daughter* (1936)
07/01/67 *Calling Dr. Death* (1943)
07/08/67 *The Mummy's Tomb* (1942)
07/15/67 *House of Frankenstein* (1944)
07/22/67 *The Monster and the Girl* (1941)
07/29/67 *The Man with Nine Lives* (1940)
08/05/67 *The Phantom of the Opera* (1943)
08/12/67 *The Mummy* (1932)
08/19/67 *Island of Doomed Men* (1940)
08/26/67 *The Black Castle* (1952)
09/02/67 *Frankenstein* (1931)
09/09/67 *The Raven* (1935)
09/16/67 *The Devil Commands* (1941)

```
11.15 (9) The Late Show.
12.00 (5) Inner Sanctum.
12.30 (4) Good Night Show.
 1.30 (9) The Late Late Show.
```

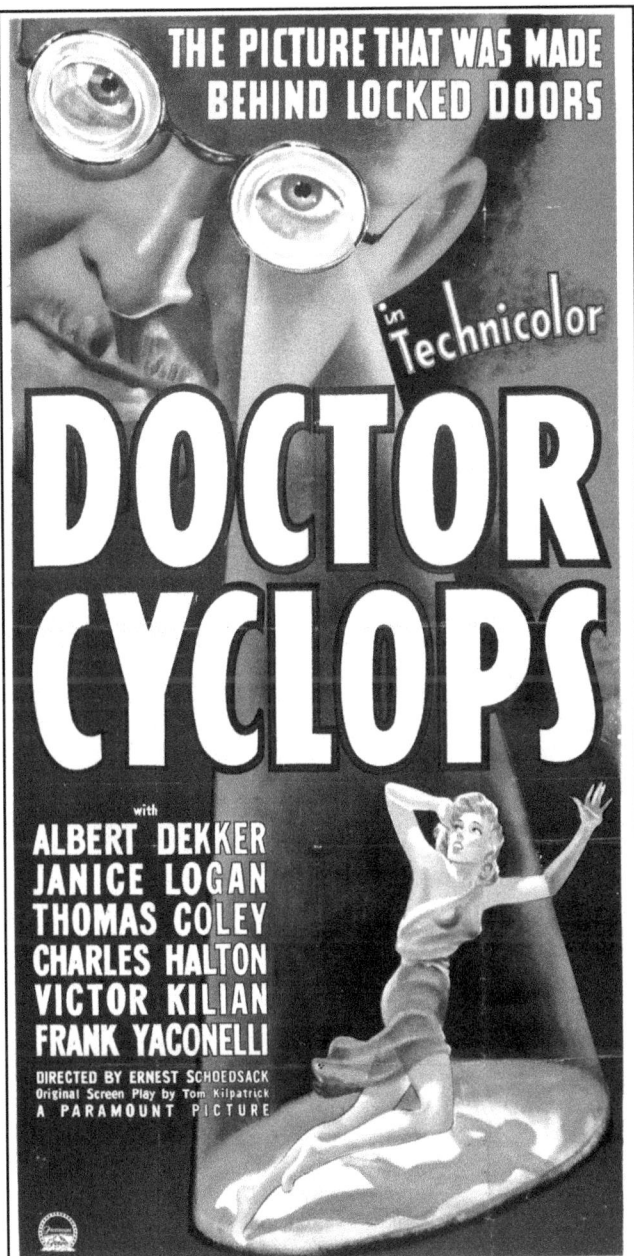

09/23/67 *She-Wolf of London* (1946)
09/30/67 *The Mummy's Hand* (1940)
10/07/67 *Before I Hang* (1940)
10/14/67 *Behind the Mask* (1932)
10/21/67 *Black Friday* (1940)
10/28/67 *Son of Frankenstein* (1939)
11/04/67 *House of Dracula* (1945)
11/11/67 *The Cat Creeps* (1946)
11/18/67 *The Frozen Ghost* (1945)
11/25/67 *The Black Room* (1935)
12/02/67 *The Son of Dr. Jekyll* (1951)
12/09/67 *Unearthly Stranger* (1963)
12/16/67 *The Terror* (1963)
12/23/67 *Attack of the Mushroom People* (1963)
12/30/67 *It Came from Outer Space* (1953)
01/06/68 *Revenge of the Creature* (1955)
01/13/68 *Atragon* (1963)

The Deadly Mantis

01/20/68 *Tarantula* (1955)
01/27/68 *The Deadly Mantis* (1957)
02/03/68 *Burn, Witch, Burn* (1962)
02/10/68 *Murders in the Rue Morgue* (1932)
02/17/68 *WereWolf of London* (1935)
02/24/68 *Dracula* (1931)
03/02/68 *Bride of Frankenstein* (1935)
03/09/68 *The Raven* (1935)
03/16/68 *The Return of the Vampire* (1943)
03/23/68 *The Invisible Man* (1933)
03/30/68 *Son of Dracula* (1943)
04/06/68 *The Mummy* (1932)
04/13/68 *Man Made Monster* (1941)
04/20/68 *House of Frankenstein* (1944)
04/27/68 *The Invisible Man Returns* (1940)
05/04/68 *Frankenstein* (1931)
05/11/68 *The Man Who Lived Twice* (1936)
05/18/68 *Frankenstein Meets the Wolf Man* (1943)
05/25/68 *The Invisible Man's Revenge* (1944)
06/01/68 *The Vampire's Coffin* (1958)
06/08/68 *Cry of the Werewolf* (1944)
06/15/68 *The Witch's Mirror* (1962)
06/22/68 *Before I Hang* (1940)
06/29/68 *Behind the Mask* (1932)
07/06/68 *The Wolf Man* (1941)
07/13/68 *The Cat Creeps* (1946)
07/20/68 *The Devil Commands* (1941)
07/27/68 *The Mummy's Hand* (1940)
08/03/68 *Calling Dr. Death* (1943)
08/10/68 *The Frozen Ghost* (1945)
08/17/68 *Dr. Orloff's Monster* (1964)
08/24/68 *The Brainiac* (1962)
08/31/68 *Dracula's Daughter* (1936)
09/07/68 *The Ghost of Frankenstein* (1942)
09/14/68 *The Face Behind the Mask* (1941)
09/21/68 *El Vampiro* (1957)
09/28/68 *The Black Cat* (1934)
10/05/68 *Attack of the Mushroom People* (1963)
10/12/68 *Son of Frankenstein* (1939)
10/19/68 *The Ghost of Frankenstein* (1942)
10/26/68 *Frankenstein Meets the Wolf Man* (1943)
11/02/68 *The Terror* (1963)
11/09/68 *The Man They Could Not Hang* (1939)
11/16/68 *The Curse of the Aztec Mummy* (1957)
11/23/68 *Cry of the Werewolf* (1944)
11/30/68 *Corridors of Blood* (1958)
12/07/68 *The Black Room* (1935)
12/14/68 *The Gamma People* (1956)
12/21/68 *The Witch's Mirror* (1962)
12/28/68 *The Curse of Nostradamus* (1961)
01/04/69 *The Blood of Nostradamus* (1962)
01/11/69 *Dracula* (1931)
01/18/69 *The Curse of the Doll People* (1961)
01/25/69 *The Living Head* (1963)

Mexican poster for double feature of *Aztec Mummy* and *Curse of the Aztec Mummy*

THE TWILIGHT MOVIE (WMAR Channel 2)

Debuting on September 2, 1963, *The Twilight Movie* offered a mix of comedy, horror, science fiction, and action films that aired weekday afternoons. The following is a list of "monster movies" that aired during the program's run.

Airs at 4:30 p.m.
09/04/63 *The Disembodied* (1957)
09/09/63 *Bride of the Monster* (1955)
09/12/63 *The Snow Creature* (1954)
10/07/63 *The Spaniard's Curse* (1958)
10/18/63 *War of the Satellites* (1958)
10/23/63 *The Cosmic Man* (1959)
10/24/63 *From Hell It Came* (1957)
10/28/63 *The Atomic Submarine* (1959)
10/29/63 *The Cyclops* (1957)
11/06/63 *House of Wax* (1953)
11/11/63 *Abbott and Costello Meet Frankenstein* (1948)
11/14/63 *Phantom from Space* (1953)
11/18/63 *Invasion of the Body Snatchers* (1956)
11/22/63 *The Beast from 20,000 Fathoms* (1953)
11/26/63 *The Invisible Woman* (1940)
12/04/63 *The Atomic Man* (1955)
12/06/63 *The Bowery Boys Meet the Monsters* (1954)
12/11/63 *House on Haunted Hill* (1959)
12/16/63 *Killers from Space* (1954)
01/03/64 *Attack of the Crab Monsters* (1957)
01/08/64 *Attack of the 50 Foot Woman* (1958)
01/24/64 *Daughter of Dr. Jekyll* (1957)
02/06/64 *The Snow Creature* (1954)
02/24/64 *The Disembodied* (1957)
03/04/64 *Beast from Haunted Cave* (1959)
03/06/64 *The Hypnotic Eye* (1960)
03/11/64 *Last Woman on Earth* (1960)
03/16/64 *The Little Shop of Horrors* (1960)
03/17/64 *The Wasp Woman* (1959)
03/24/64 *The Brain from Planet Arous* (1957)
03/26/64 *Daughter of Dr. Jekyll* (1957)
03/27/64 *The Bat* (1959)
03/30/64 *Not of This Earth* (1957)
03/31/64 *Target Earth* (1954)
04/02/64 *The Cosmic Man* (1959)
04/08/64 *The Cyclops* (1957)
04/16/64 *From Hell It Came* (1957)
04/22/64 *Queen of Outer Space* (1958)
04/28/64 *War of the Satellites* (1958)
05/01/64 *Master Minds* (1949)
05/05/64 *Phantom from Space* (1953)
05/14/64 *Creature from the Haunted Sea* (1961)
05/19/64 *The Bride and the Beast* (1958)
05/28/64 *Indestructible Man* (1956)
06/11/64 *House on Haunted Hill* (1959)
06/17/64 *Caltiki, the Immortal Monster* (1959)
06/19/64 *Invasion of the Body Snatchers* (1956)
06/23/64 *The Atomic Submarine* (1959)
06/26/64 *Attack of the Crab Monsters* (1957)
06/30/64 *The Snow Creature* (1954)
07/03/64 *Attack of the 50 Foot Woman* (1958)
07/17/64 *The Brain from Planet Arous* (1957)
08/07/64 *Daughter of Dr. Jekyll* (1957)
08/13/64 *The Invisible Woman* (1940)
08/21/64 *From Hell It Came* (1957)
08/25/64 *Killers from Space* (1954)
09/04/64 *Not of This Earth* (1957)
09/11/64 *Target Earth* (1954)
09/18/64 *Terror in the Haunted House* (1958)
09/23/64 *From Hell It Came* (1957)
09/25/64 *World Without End* (1956)
10/08/64 *The Bowery Boys Meet the Monsters* (1954)
10/16/64 *The H-Man* (1959)
10/22/64 *X the Unknown* (1956)
10/28/64 *The Tingler* (1959)
10/29/64 *The Giant Claw* (1957)
11/06/64 *Earth vs. the Flying Saucers* (1956)
11/12/64 *Gigantis, the Fire Monster* (1959)
11/16/64 *Phantom of the Rue Morgue* (1954)
11/18/64 *The Electronic Monster* (1958)
11/20/64 *The Mermaids of Tiburon* (1962)
11/24/64 *The Stranglers of Bombay* (1959)
12/04/64 *The Bat* (1959)
12/10/64 *The Cosmic Man* (1959)
12/11/64 *Abbott and Costello Meet Frankenstein* (1948)
12/16/64 *The Giant Behemoth* (1959)
12/22/64 *Frankenstein 1970* (1958)
12/28/64 *The Hypnotic Eye* (1960)
01/07/65 *The Atomic Man* (1955)
01/14/65 *The Disembodied* (1957)
01/20/65 *12 to the Moon* (1960)
01/27/65 *The Man Who Turned to Stone* (1957)
02/09/65 *Creature from the Haunted Sea* (1961)
02/11/65 *Hands of A Stranger* (1962)
02/19/65 *Indestructible Man* (1956)
02/22/65 *Queen of Outer Space* (1958)
02/26/65 *House on Haunted Hill* (1959)
03/01/65 *The Invisible Woman* (1940)
03/03/65 *Satellite in the Sky* (1956)

> **TWILIGHT MOVIE**—"Hands of a Stranger." When the hands of a famous musician are damaged in an accident, his physician transplants the hands of a slain man to the piaoist's wrists. John Lukather and Joan Harvey star. Channel 2 at 4.30 P.M.

03/09/65 *20 Million Miles to Earth* (1957)
03/11/65 *Curse of the Demon* (1957)
03/12/65 *X the Unknown* (1956)
03/15/65 *The Werewolf* (1956)
03/17/65 *Mothra* (1961)
03/19/65 *The 27th Day* (1957)
03/23/65 *The Woman Eater* (1958)
03/24/65 *The Black Scorpion* (1957)
03/25/65 *The Beast from 20,000 Fathoms* (1953)
03/26/65 *Beast from Haunted Cave* (1959)
03/29/65 *Zombies of Mora Tau* (1957)
03/31/65 *Teenagers from Outer Space* (1959)
04/08/65 *Attack of the 50 Foot Woman* (1958)
04/15/65 *Daughter of Dr. Jekyll* (1957)
06/23/65 *The Cosmic Man* (1959)
06/25/65 *Gigantis, the Fire Monster* (1959)
06/29/65 *The Giant Behemoth* (1959)
07/09/65 *Attack of the Crab Monsters* (1957)
07/15/65 *The Brain from Planet Arous* (1957)
07/21/65 *Caltiki, the Immortal Monster* (1959)
07/27/65 *Frankenstein 1970* (1958)
08/13/65 *The Hypnotic Eye* (1960)
08/19/65 *Indestructible Man* (1956)
08/25/65 *Queen of Outer Space* (1958)
08/27/65 *Daughter of Dr. Jekyll* (1957)
09/10/65 *World Without End* (1956)
09/16/65 *Target Earth* (1954)
09/22/65 *The Bride and the Beast* (1958)
09/28/65 *Hands of A Stranger* (1962)
09/30/65 *Creature from the Haunted Sea* (1961)
10/06/65 *The Stranglers of Bombay* (1959)
10/18/65 *The Electronic Monster* (1958)
10/28/65 *12 to the Moon* (1960)
11/02/65 *Curse of the Demon* (1957)
11/04/65 *Gorilla at Large* (1954)
11/08/65 *X the Unknown* (1956)
11/10/65 *The Black Scorpion* (1957)
11/18/65 *Phantom of the Rue Morgue* (1954)
11/22/65 *The H-Man* (1959)
12/02/65 *The Mermaids of Tiburon* (1962)
12/07/65 *The Little Shop of Horrors* (1960)
12/10/65 *The Atomic Submarine* (1959)
12/16/65 *Attack of the 50 Foot Woman* (1958)
12/22/65 *The Cosmic Man* (1959)
12/28/65 *House on Haunted Hill* (1959)
01/03/66 *The Revenge of Frankenstein* (1958)
01/07/66 *The Woman Eater* (1958)
01/11/66 *The Werewolf* (1956)
01/13/66 *The 27th Day* (1957)

Airs at 5:00 p.m.
01/19/66 *The Tingler* (1959)
01/20/66 *The Hypnotic Eye* (1960)

01/24/66 *The Atomic Man* (1955)
01/28/66 *Return of the Fly* (1959)
02/01/66 *The Monolith Monsters* (1957)
02/03/66 *Them!* (1954)
02/07/66 *The Incredible Shrinking Man* (1957)
02/11/66 *The Thing That Couldn't Die* (1958)
02/15/66 *This Island Earth* (1955)
02/17/66 *Tarantula* (1955)
02/21/66 *The Mole People* (1956)
03/02/66 *Attack of the Crab Monsters* (1957)
03/08/66 *The Giant Behemoth* (1959)
03/09/66 *Not of This Earth* (1957)
03/15/66 *Last Woman on Earth* (1960)
03/17/66 *From Hell It Came* (1957)
03/21/66 *Terror in the Haunted House* (1958)
03/31/66 *Warning from Space* (1956)
04/01/66 *The Beast from 20,000 Fathoms* (1953)
04/05/66 *Satellite in the Sky* (1956)
04/08/66 *House of Wax* (1953)
04/18/66 *Master Minds* (1949)
06/28/66 *Curse of the Demon* (1957)
07/14/66 *Daughter of Dr. Jekyll* (1957)
07/19/66 *The Brain from Planet Arous* (1957)
07/27/66 *The Atomic Submarine* (1959)
08/03/66 *Queen of Outer Space* (1958)
08/09/66 *Indestructible Man* (1956)
08/15/66 *Frankenstein 1970* (1958)
08/25/66 *War of the Satellites* (1958)
09/02/66 *World Without End* (1956)
09/09/66 *The Black Scorpion* (1957)
09/16/66 *The Mad Magician* (1954)
09/28/66 *Zombies of Mora Tau* (1957)
10/07/66 *Battle in Outer Space* (1959)
10/13/66 *The Electronic Monster* (1958)
10/19/66 *The Giant Claw* (1957)

★**Twilight Movie**
"Giant Claw"

10/21/66 *Teenagers from Outer Space* (1959)
10/25/66 *The Stranglers of Bombay* (1959)
10/31/66 *The Brain from Planet Arous* (1957)
11/11/66 *Curucu, Beast of the Amazon* (1956)
11/17/66 *The Deadly Mantis* (1957)
11/23/66 *The Leech Woman* (1960)
11/29/66 *The H-Man* (1959)
12/05/66 *Target Earth* (1954)
12/13/66 *Hands of A Stranger* (1962)
12/21/66 *Phantom of the Rue Morgue* (1954)
12/29/66 *Gorilla at Large* (1954)
01/02/67 *Satellite in the Sky* (1956)
01/19/67 *Gigantis, the Fire Monster* (1959)
01/27/67 *X the Unknown* (1956)

01/31/67 *The Mole People* (1956)
02/15/67 *Monster on the Campus* (1958)
02/23/67 *The Tingler* (1959)
03/01/67 *The 27th Day* (1957)
03/07/67 *The Woman Eater* (1958)
03/16/67 *The Abominable Snowman* (1957)
04/06/67 *Daughter of Dr. Jekyll* (1957)
04/12/67 *The Beast from 20,000 Fathoms* (1953)
04/18/67 *The Atomic Submarine* (1959)

> **TWILIGHT MOVIE** — "Man Who Turned To Stone," starring Victor Jory, Charlotte Austin and Ann Doran. A group of 18th Century scientists discover a way to prolong their lives. Channel 2 at 4:30 P.M.

05/01/67 *The Man Who Turned to Stone* (1957)
05/03/67 *Attack of the Crab Monsters* (1957)
05/09/67 *Caltiki, the Immortal Monster* (1959)
05/19/67 *From Hell It Came* (1957)
05/22/67 *The Giant Behemoth* (1959)
06/01/67 *Attack of the 50 Foot Woman* (1958)
06/07/67 *Earth vs. the Flying Saucers* (1956)
06/23/67 *Zombies of Mora Tau* (1957)
06/28/67 *Warning from Space* (1956)
07/04/67 *The Atomic Man* (1955)
07/12/67 *Hands of A Stranger* (1962)
07/14/67 *Terror in the Haunted House* (1958)
09/15/67 *The Werewolf* (1956)
10/06/67 *The Brain from Planet Arous* (1957)
10/18/67 *Frankenstein 1970* (1958)
10/24/67 *House on Haunted Hill* (1959)
10/30/67 *The Hypnotic Eye* (1960)
11/09/67 *The Stranglers of Bombay* (1959)

11/15/67 *The Electronic Monster* (1958)
11/21/67 *The Black Scorpion* (1957)
11/27/67 *Satellite in the Sky* (1956)
12/07/67 *Daughter of Dr. Jekyll* (1957)
12/13/67 *Indestructible Man* (1956)
12/19/67 *The Little Shop of Horrors* (1960)
12/27/67 *The Mermaids of Tiburon* (1962)
01/02/68 *The Smiling Ghost* (1941)
01/03/68 *Horror of Dracula* (1958)
01/12/68 *Devil Doll* (1964)
02/06/68 *Return of the Fly* (1959)
02/16/68 *Gorilla at Large* (1954)
02/22/68 *X the Unknown* (1956)
03/05/68 *The Beast with Five Fingers* (1946)
03/11/68 *The Tingler* (1959)
04/15/68 *Master Minds* (1949)
04/19/68 *The Mad Magician* (1954)
04/25/68 *The Land Unknown* (1957)
07/01/68 *The Atomic Submarine* (1959)
07/02/68 *The Bowery Boys Meet the Monsters* (1954)
07/05/68 *Gigantis, the Fire Monster* (1959)
07/11/68 *The Abominable Snowman* (1957)
07/19/68 *The Brain from Planet Arous* (1957)
08/05/68 *The Man Who Turned to Stone* (1957)
08/20/68 *The Giant Behemoth* (1959)
08/28/68 *Not of This Earth* (1957)
09/04/68 *Queen of Outer Space* (1958)
09/10/68 *Target Earth* (1954)

Airs at 4:30 p.m.
09/26/68 *Tormented* (1960)
10/04/68 *Tarantula* (1955)
10/10/68 *The Thing That Couldn't Die* (1958)
10/16/68 *This Island Earth* (1955)
10/21/68 *Devils of Darkness* (1965)
10/22/68 *Return of the Fly* (1959)
10/28/68 *Gigantis, the Fire Monster* (1959)
11/05/68 *Indestructible Man* (1956)
11/08/68 *Village of the Giants* (1965)
11/14/68 *2 0 Million Miles to Earth* (1957)
11/20/68 *Zombies of Mora Tau* (1957)
11/26/68 *1 2 to the Moon* (1960)
12/05/68 *House of Wax* (1953)
12/18/68 *The Smiling Ghost* (1941)
01/09/69 *The 27th Day* (1957)
01/21/69 *The Deadly Mantis* (1957)
01/27/69 *The Leech Woman* (1960)
01/30/69 *This Is Not a Test* (1962)
02/05/69 *Curucu, Beast of the Amazon* (1956)
02/14/69 *The Fly* (1958)
02/17/69 *Curse of the Demon* (1957)
02/26/69 *Teenagers from Outer Space* (1959)
03/06/69 *Curse of the Undead* (1959)

Carol Ohmart in *The House on Haunted Hill*

05/09/69 *The Werewolf* (1956)
05/28/69 *The Mole People* (1956)
06/05/69 *Earth vs. the Flying Saucers* (1956)
07/09/69 *The Bowery Boys Meet the Monsters* (1954)
07/22/69 *Return of the Fly* (1959)
08/27/69 *12 to the Moon* (1960)

Airs at 5:00 p.m.
09/17/69 *The Man Who Turned to Stone* (1957)
10/23/69 *The Beast with Five Fingers* (1946)
11/19/69 *Journey to the Center of Time* (1967)
11/24/69 *Monster on the Campus* (1958)
12/03/69 *20 Million Miles to Earth* (1957)
12/29/69 *The Smiling Ghost* (1941)
12/31/69 *Tarantula* (1955)

Airs at 4:30 p.m.
02/18/70 *Cyborg 2087* (1966)
02/25/70 *Destination Inner Space* (1966)
03/03/70 *20 Million Miles to Earth* (1957)
03/12/70 *World Without End* (1956)
08/06/70 *Them!* (1954)
07/02/71 *The Deadly Mantis* (1957)
07/09/71 *Hands of a Stranger* (1962)
07/16/71 *The Incredible Shrinking Man* (1957)
07/23/71 *Beast from Haunted Cave* (1959)
08/06/71 *World Without End* (1956)
08/10/71 *The Land Unknown* (1957)
08/13/71 *The Monolith Monsters* (1957)
08/16/71 *Last Woman on Earth* (1960)
08/20/71 *Curucu, Beast of the Amazon* (1956)
08/27/71 *Terror in the Haunted House* (1958)
09/03/71 *Curse of the Undead* (1959)
08/08/72 *The Brain from Planet Arous* (1957)
08/15/72 *The Little Shop of Horrors* (1960)
08/22/72 *House on Haunted Hill* (1959)
08/24/72 *The Disembodied* (1957)
08/29/72 *Indestructible Man* (1956)
08/30/72 *The Incredible Shrinking Man* (1957)
09/05/72 *Curse of the Undead* (1959)
09/06/72 *Queen of Outer Space* (1958)
09/07/72 *The Deadly Mantis* (1957)
09/08/72 *The Little Shop of Horrors* (1960)

5.00 ❷ **Twilight Movie.** "The Little Shop of Horrors." Comedy horror film about a simple-minded youth who develops a plant that feeds on people. Jonathan Haze, Mel Welles, Jackie Joseph. 1960.

03/19/69 *Devil Doll* (1964)
04/10/69 *Master Minds* (1949)
04/18/69 *The Mad Magician* (1954)

THE WORLD BEYOND (WTTG Channel 5)

WTTG's first prime time genre program offered mostly science fiction thrillers of the '50s and '60s. The station's previous offerings had consisted mostly of the RKO horror/sci-fi catalogue (the Val Lewton productions, *The Thing*, and *King Kong* each received many airings). Taking advantage of several recent and/or new film packages, WTTG launched *The World Beyond* and *Chiller* less than three weeks apart. Initially airing just on Thursdays starting in October 1963, a Tuesday edition was added in September 1965.

```
7.30  (4) Daniel Boone.
      (5) The World Beyond.
      (7) ★Flintstones.
      (9) The Munsters.
```

Thursdays at 7:30 p.m.
10/17/63 *The Giant Behemoth* (1959)
10/24/63 *It! The Terror from Beyond Space* (1958)
10/31/63 *Attack of the Crab Monsters* (1957)
11/07/63 *The Giant Claw* (1957)
11/14/63 *Mothra* (1961)
11/21/63 *Quatermass 2* (1957)
11/28/63 *Invaders from Mars* (1953)
12/05/63 *Destination Moon* (1950)
12/12/63 *The Man from Planet X* (1951)
12/19/63 *The Magnetic Monster* (1953)
12/26/63 *The Thing from Another World* (1951)
01/02/64 *She Devil* (1957)
01/09/64 *Invisible Invaders* (1959)
01/16/64 *The Lost Missile* (1958)
01/23/64 *The Monster That Challenged the World* (1957)
01/30/64 *The Incredible Petrified World* (1959)
02/06/64 *Terror is A Man* (1959)
02/13/64 *The Cosmic Man* (1959)
02/20/64 *Riders to the Stars* (1954)
02/27/64 *Battle in Outer Space* (1959)
03/05/64 *The Tingler* (1959)
03/12/64 *The Atomic Submarine* (1959)
03/19/64 *U.F.O.* (1956)
03/26/64 *Gog* (1954)
04/02/64 *The Day the Sky Exploded* (1958)
04/09/64 *The Cyclops* (1957)
04/16/64 *From Hell it Came* (1957)

```
THE WORLD BEYOND—"Attack of
the Crab Monster," starring Rich-
ard Garland and Pamela Duncan.
(1957) Channel 5 at 7.30 P.M.
```

How perfect is this for the Bmore horror fan? *Attack of the Crab Monsters*

04/23/64 *The Crawling Eye* (1958)
04/30/64 *Cosmic Monsters* (1958)
05/07/64 *Four Sided Triangle* (1953)
05/14/64 *Queen of Outer Space* (1958)
05/21/64 *Kronos* (1957)
05/28/64 *The Fabulous World of Jules Verne* (1958)
06/04/64 *Quatermass 2* (1957)
06/11/64 *Teenage Zombies* (1958)
06/18/64 *Red Planet Mars* (1952)
06/25/64 *The Bat* (1959)
07/02/64 *It! The Terror from Beyond Space* (1958)
07/09/64 *The Flame Barrier* (1958)
07/16/64 *The Giant Behemoth* (1959)
07/23/64 *Things to Come* (1936)
07/30/64 *House on Haunted Hill* (1959)
08/06/64 *Attack of the Crab Monsters* (1957)
08/13/64 *The Giant Claw* (1957)
08/20/64 *Mothra* (1961)
08/27/64 *The Astounding She-Monster* (1957)
09/03/64 *Attack of the Giant Leeches* (1959)
09/10/64 *The Giant Gila Monster* (1959)
09/17/64 *Attack of the Puppet People* (1958)
09/24/64 *The Beast with a Million Eyes* (1955)
10/01/64 *The Phantom Planet* (1961)
10/08/64 *The Crawling Eye* (1958
10/15/64 *The Cape Canaveral Monsters* (1960)
10/22/64 *Beyond the Time Barrier* (1960)

> THE WORLD BEYOND — "Beyond the Time Barrier," starring Robert Clarke and Darlene Tompkins. (1960) Channel 5 at 7.30 P.M.

10/29/64 *Attack of the 50 Foot Woman* (1958)
11/05/64 *Teenage Monster* (1960)
11/12/64 *Killers from Space* (1954)
11/19/64 *War of the Satellites* (1958)
11/26/64 *The Snow Creature* (1954)
12/03/64 *The Hideous Sun Demon* (1958)
12/10/64 *The Saga of the Viking Women and Their Voyage to the Waters of the Great Sea Serpent* (1957)
12/17/64 *War of the Colossal Beast* (1958)
12/24/64 *Teenage Caveman* (1958)
12/31/64 *It Conquered the World* (1956)
01/07/65 *The Electronic Monster* (1958)
01/14/65 *The H-Man* (1959)
01/21/65 *First Spaceship on Venus* (1960)
01/28/65 *Varan the Unbelievable* (1962)
02/04/65 *Beginning of the End* (1957)
02/11/65 *Missile to the Moon* (1958)
02/18/65 *Phantom from Space* (1953)
02/25/65 *Giant from the Unknown* (1958)
03/04/65 *Not of This Earth* (1957)
03/11/65 *The 27th Day* (1957)
03/18/65 *The Atomic Man* (1955)
03/25/65 *The Brain from Planet Arous* (1957)
04/01/65 *Cat-Women of the Moon* (1953)
04/08/65 *The Cyclops* (1957)
04/15/65 *The Wasp Woman* (1959)
04/22/65 *The Angry Red Planet* (1959)
04/29/65 *Assignment: Outer Space* (1960)
05/06/65 *The Atomic Submarine* (1959)

> THE WORLD BEYOND — "Atomic Submarine," starring Arthur Franz and Dick Foran. (1959) Channel 5 at 7.30 P.M.

05/13/65 *The Bride and the Beast* (1958)
05/20/65 *Beast from Haunted Cave* (1959)
05/27/65 *Invasion of the Star Creatures* (1962)
06/03/65 *Attack of the 50 Foot Woman* (1958)
06/10/65 *Last Woman on Earth* (1960)
06/17/65 *Invasion of the Animal People* (1962)
06/24/65 *Four Sided Triangle* (1953)

07/01/65 *The Man from Planet X* (1951)
07/08/65 *First Spaceship on Venus* (1960)
07/15/65 *Riders to the Stars* (1954)
07/22/65 *The Flame Barrier* (1958)
07/29/65 *Invisible Invaders* (1959)
08/05/65 *It! The Terror from Beyond* Space (1958)
08/12/65 *The Lost Missile* (1958)
08/19/65 *The Magnetic Monster* (1953)
08/26/65 *The Monster That Challenged the World* (1957)
09/02/65 *Red Planet Mars* (1952)
09/09/65 *Donovan's Brain* (1953)
09/16/65 *Kronos* (1957)
09/23/65 *Evil Brain from Outer Space* (1965)
09/30/65 *Planets Against Us* (1962)
10/07/65 *Lost Continent* (1951)
10/14/65 *Spaceways* (1953)
10/21/65 *The Day the Earth Froze* (1959)
10/28/65 *Day the World Ended* (1955)
11/04/65 *12 to the Moon* (1960)
11/11/65 *The Jungle* (1952)
11/18/65 *The Head* (1959)
11/25/65 *The Cape Canaveral Monsters* (1960)
12/02/65 *Frankenstein 1970* (1958)

12/09/65 *The Cosmic Man* (1959)
12/16/65 *From Hell it Came* (1957)
12/23/65 *The Giant Behemoth* (1959)
12/30/65 *The Phantom Planet* (1961)
01/06/66 *The Snow Creature* (1954)
01/13/66 *Invasion of the Body Snatchers* (1956)
01/20/66 *The Unearthly* (1957)
01/27/66 *The Man from Planet X* (1951)
02/03/66 *Red Planet Mars* (1952)
02/10/66 *The Final War* (1960)
02/17/66 *Quatermass 2* (1957)
02/24/66 *The Electronic Monster* (1958)
03/03/66 *Warning from Space* (1956)
03/10/66 *The Amazing Colossal Man* (1957)
03/17/66 *Evil Brain from Outer Space* (1965)

Tuesdays at 7:30 p.m.
09/21/65 *Journey to the Seventh Planet* (1962)
09/28/65 *Attack of the Crab Monsters* (1957)

> THE WORLD BEYOND—"Electronic Monster," starring Rod Cameron, Mary Murphy and Meredith Edwards. Channel 5 at 7.30 P.M.

10/05/65 *Target Earth* (1954)
10/12/65 *Caltiki, the Immortal Monster* (1959)
10/19/65 *Rocketship X-M* (1950)
10/26/65 *The Brain from Planet Arous* (1957)

> **THE WORLD BEYOND** — "Brain from Planet Arous," starring John Agar and Joyce Meadows. (1958) Channel 5 at 7.30 P.M.

11/02/65 *Invasion of the Saucer Men* (1957)
11/09/65 *The Day the Sky Exploded* (1958)
11/16/65 *Destination Moon* (1950)
11/23/65 *The Secret of the Telegian* (1960)
11/30/65 *Battle in Outer Space* (1959)
12/07/65 *Battle Beyond the Sun* (1963)
12/14/65 *Queen of Outer Space* (1958)
12/21/65 *The Atomic Man* (1955)
12/28/65 *Beyond the Time Barrier* (1960)
01/04/66 *Killers from Space* (1954)
01/11/66 *The Disembodied* (1957)
01/18/66 *Not of This Earth* (1957)
01/25/66 *The Hideous Sun Demon* (1958)
02/01/66 *The Wasp Woman* (1959)
02/08/66 *World Without End* (1956)
02/15/66 *Attack of the 50 Foot Woman* (1958)
02/22/66 *Kronos* (1957)
03/01/66 *Attack of the Puppet People* (1958)
03/08/66 *Invasion of the Neptune Men* (1964)
03/15/66 *Missile to the Moon* (1958)
03/22/66 *Invasion of the Neptune Men* (1964)
03/29/66 *Riders to the Stars* (1954)
04/05/66 *Fire Maidens of Outer Space* (1956)
04/12/66 *It Conquered the World* (1956)
04/19/66 *The Giant Claw* (1957)
04/26/66 *War of the Colossal Beast* (1958)
05/03/66 *Terror from the Year 5000* (1958)
05/10/66 *It! The Terror from Beyond Space* (1958)
05/17/66 *The Atomic Submarine* (1959)
05/24/66 *Attack of the Crab Monsters* (1957)
05/31/66 *The Brain from Planet Arous* (1957)
06/07/66 *Journey to the Seventh Planet* (1962)
06/14/66 *Teenage Monster* (1958)
06/21/66 *The Jungle* (1952)
06/28/66 *Spaceways* (1953)
07/05/66 *The Giant Gila Monster* (1959)
07/12/66 *Cosmic Monsters* (1958)
07/19/66 *The Day the Sky Exploded* (1958)
07/26/66 *Destination Moon* (1950)
08/02/66 *The Flame Barrier* (1958)
08/09/66 *Invisible Invaders* (1959)
08/16/66 Didn't air
08/23/66 *First Spaceship on Venus* (1960)
08/30/66 *Varan the Unbelievable* (1962)

CHILLER (WTTG Channel 5)

If *Shock!* on Channel 9 started too late for some viewers (it aired after *The Late Show* and sometimes didn't start until 1:30 a.m.), or if one had seen all the horrors *Shock!* offered, then *Chiller* provided an alternative. Beginning Saturdays in November 1963 and lasting until September 1971, *Chiller* presented a terrific mix of shockers from the 1930s through the 1960s. From classics such as *King Kong* to dreadful efforts like *Teenage Zombies*, the quality of the programming ran the gamut. Nevertheless, the variety *Chiller* offered remains impressive. A Friday *Chiller* was added in June 1968 that lasted until April 1969. Two weekly *Chiller Festivals* also aired in May and July 1970.

Saturdays

Airs at 11:00 p.m.
11/02/63 *The Bat* (1959)
11/09/63 *Frankenstein 1970* (1958)
11/16/63 *The Woman Eater* (1958)
11/23/63 *The Four Skulls of Jonathan Drake* (1959)
11/30/63 *Curse of the Demon* (1957)
12/07/63 *Daughter of Dr. Jekyll* (1957)
12/14/63 *The Little Shop of Horrors* (1960)
12/21/63 *I Bury the Living* (1958)
12/28/63 *The Unknown Terror* (1957)
01/04/64 *The Return of Dracula* (1958)
01/11/64 *Creature from the Haunted Sea* (1961)
01/18/64 *The Vampire* (1957)
01/25/64 *King Kong* (1933)
02/01/64 *Teenage Zombies* (1958)
02/08/64 *Back from the Dead* (1957)
02/15/64 *The Bride and the Beast* (1958)
02/22/64 *The Hypnotic Eye* (1960)
02/29/64 *Dr. Jekyll and Mr. Hyde* (1941)
03/07/64 *Indestructible Man* (1956)
03/14/64 *The Astounding She-Monster* (1957)
03/21/64 *The Hound of the Baskervilles* (1959)
03/28/64 *House on Haunted Hill* (1959)
04/04/64 *The Four Skulls of Jonathan Drake* (1959)
04/11/64 *The Disembodied* (1957); *Destination Moon* (1950)
04/18/64 *Blood of Dracula* (1957); *She Devil* (1957)
04/25/64 *Cat Girl* (1957); *The Unknown Terror* (1957)
05/02/64 *Mill of the Stone Women* (1960)
05/09/64 *The Tell-Tale Heart* (1960); *Invisible Invaders* (1959)
05/16/64 *Trauma* (1962); *The Woman Eater* (1958)
05/23/64 *The Woman in White* (1948); *The Magnetic Monster* (1953)
05/30/64 *Curse of the Faceless Man* (1958); *Curse of the Demon* (1957)
06/06/64 *The Werewolf* (1956); *The Incredible Petrified World* (1959)
06/13/64 *The Undead* (1957); *Creature from the Haunted Sea* (1961)
06/20/64 *The Killer Shrews* (1959); *I Bury the Living* (1958)
06/27/64 *Night of the Blood Beast* (1958); *Back from the Dead* (1957)
07/04/64 *She-Gods of Shark Reef* (1958); *The Hypnotic Eye* (1960)
07/11/64 *The Screaming Skull* (1958); *The Man from Planet X* (1951)
07/18/64 *Daughter of Dr. Jekyll* (1957); *Dr. Jekyll and Mr. Hyde* (1941)
07/25/64 *The Cosmic Man* (1959); *The Body Snatcher* (1945)
08/01/64 *The Little Shop of Horrors* (1960); *Bedlam* (1946)
08/08/64 *The Bride and the Beast* (1958); *The Curse of the Cat People* (1944)
08/15/64 Didn't air
08/22/64 *The Return of Dracula* (1958); *The Leopard Man* (1943)
08/29/64 *From Hell It Came* (1957)
09/05/64 *Pharaoh's Curse* (1957)
09/12/64 *The Vampire* (1957)
09/19/64 *The Monster that Challenged the World* (1957); *The Gorilla Man* (1943)

Washington
CIRCLE 9 WEST—"The Duel At Silver Creek," starring Audie Murphy and Faith Domergue. (1952) Channel 9 at 1.30 P.M.
AMAZING ADVENTURE—"The Man With the X-Ray Eyes," starring Ray Milland and Diana Van Der Vlis. Channel 9 at 3 P.M.
JUNGLE CALL—"Tarzan and the Huntress," starring Johnny Weissmuller and Brenda Joyce. (1947) Channel 5 at 4 P.M.
CHILLER—"Mark of the Vampire," starring John Beal and Coleen Gray. (1957) Second feature — "Curse of Dracula," starring Francis Lederer and Norm Eberhardt. (1958) Channel 5 at 11 P.M.
THE LATE SHOW—"Take the High Ground," starring Richard Widmark and Elaine Stewart. (1953) Channel 9 at 11.15 P.M.
MOVIE 4 SATURDAY—"The Reluctant Spy," starring Genevieve Page and Jean Marals. (1965) Channel 4 at 12 P.M.
THE LATE, LATE SHOW — "The Vampires," starring Abel Salazar and Adriadne Walter. (1960) Channel 9 at 11.15 P.M.

09/26/64 *The Neanderthal Man* (1953); *The Lost Missile* (1958)
10/03/64 *Invisible Creature* (1960); *Terror of the Bloodhunters* (1962)
10/10/64 *The Violent and the Damned* (1963); *The Amazing Transparent Man* (1960)
10/17/64 *The Blancheville Monster* (1963); *The Black Sleep* (1956)
10/24/64 *Cosmic Monsters* (1958); *The Beast of Hollow Mountain* (1956)
10/31/64 *Invasion of the Animal People* (1962); *Terror is A Man* (1959)
11/07/64 *The Quatermass Xperiment* (1955); *The Mad Monster* (1944)
11/14/64 *Horrors of the Black Museum* (1959); *Black Dragons* (1942)
11/21/64 *The Walking Dead* (1936); *The Devil's Hand* (1961)
11/28/64 *Bloodlust!* (1961); *The Beast with Five Fingers* (1946)
12/05/64 *The Headless Ghost* (1959); *Frankenstein 1970* (1958)
12/12/64 *I Was a Teenage Frankenstein* (1957); *Queen of Outer Space* (1958)
12/19/64 *The She-Creature* (1956); *The Cyclops* (1957)
12/26/64 *Voodoo Woman* (1957); *Voodoo Man* (1944)
01/02/65 *Zombies of Mora Tau* (1957); *Invisible Ghost* (1941)
01/09/65 *Fright* (1956); *Indestructible Man* (1956)
01/16/65 *The Man Without a Body* (1957); *The Disembodied* (1957)
01/23/65 *The Tingler* (1959); *The Hand* (1960)
01/30/65 *Terror in the Crypt* (1964); *She Devil* (1957)
02/06/65 *Invasion of the Body Snatchers* (1956); *Attack of the Giant Leeches* (1959)
02/13/65 *Bride of the Monster* (1955); *The Astounding She-Monster* (1957)
02/20/65 *The Monster of Piedras Blancas* (1959); *The Giant Gila Monster* (1959)
02/27/65 *The Unearthly* (1957); *The Beast with a Million Eyes* (1955)
03/06/65 *Hands of A Stranger* (1962); *Dead Men Walk* (1943)
03/13/65 *Donovan's Brain* (1953); *The Crawling Eye* (1958)
03/20/65 *The Horror Chamber of Dr. Faustus* (1959); *Konga* (1961)
03/27/65 *Circus of Horrors* (1960); *The Devil Bat* (1940)
04/03/65 *The Four Skulls of Jonathan Drake* (1959); *Curse of the Faceless Man* (1958)
04/10/65 *The Beast of Hollow Mountain* (1956); *Dr. Jekyll and Mr. Hyde* (1941)
04/17/65 *The Black Sleep* (1956); *The Neanderthal Man* (1953)
04/24/65 *Mothra* (1961)
05/01/65 *Circus of Horrors* (1960)
05/08/65 *Curse of the Demon* (1957); *Black Tide* (1958)
05/15/65 *Mill of the Stone Women* (1960); *Voodoo Man* (1944)

Kiddom heaven: new color and portable TVs! Now showing *The Beast with a Million Eyes* and *Queen of Outer Space*

> **CHILLER** — "I Bury the Living," starring Richard Boone and Theodore Bikel. (1958). Second feature—"Enemy From Space," starring Brian Donlevy and John Longden. (1957) Channel 5 at 11 P.M.
> **BIG MOVIE OF THE WEEK**—"The Lusty Men," starring Robert Mitchum and Susan Hayward. (1952) Channel 7 at 11.30 P.M.
> **THE LATE SHOW** — "Prisoner of Zenda," starring Stewart Granger, Deborah Kerr and Louis Calhern. (1952) Channel 9 at 11.15 P.M.
> **MOVIE 4 SATURDAY**—"The Rains of Ranchipur," starring Richard Burton and Lana Turner. (1955) Channel 4 at 11.45 P.M.
> **THE LATE LATE SHOW**—"Bloody Vampire," starring Jaims Fernandez and Adrias Roel. (1963) Channel 9 at 1.10 A.M.
> **FOREIGN FILM FESTIVAL**—"Trouble In Stone," starring Norman Wisdom and Margaret Rutherford. (British-1956) Channel 4 at

05/22/65 *Night Tide* (1961); *Cat Girl* (1957)
05/29/65 *Terror is a Man* (1959); *Invisible Ghost* (1941)
06/05/65 *The Bat* (1959); *Invisible Creature* (1960)
06/12/65 *Daughter of Dr. Jekyll* (1957); *Terror in the Crypt* (1964)
06/19/65 *The Disembodied* (1957); *The Hand* (1960)
06/26/65 *House on Haunted Hill* (1959); *The Blancheville Monster* (1963)
07/03/65 *Fright* (1956); *The Amazing Transparent Man* (1960)
07/10/65 *The Man Without a Body* (1957); *Spy in the Sky!* (1958)
07/17/65 *The Devil's Hand* (1961); *Bloodlust!* (1961)
07/24/65 *The Tell-Tale Heart* (1960); *Dead Men Walk* (1943)
07/31/65 *Mill of the Stone Women* (1960); *The Walking Dead* (1936)
08/07/65 *Trauma* (1962); *The Devil Bat* (1940)
08/14/65 *The Quatermass Xperiment* (1955); *The Black Raven* (1943)
08/21/65 *The Return of Dracula* (1958); *The Monster Maker* (1944)
08/28/65 *Curse of the Faceless Man* (1958); *The Woman in White* (1948)
09/04/65 *Fright* (1956); *The Vampire* (1957)
09/11/65 *The Man Without a Body* (1957); *I Bury the Living* (1958)
09/18/65 *Pharaoh's Curse* (1957); *The Neanderthal Man* (1953)
09/25/65 *The Hound of the Baskervilles* (1959); *Terror is A Man* (1959)
10/02/65 *Black Sunday* (1960); *Voodoo Island* (1957)
10/09/65 *Konga* (1961); *Bride of the Monster* (1955)
10/16/65 *The Crawling Hand* (1963); *Terror of the Bloodhunters* (1962)
10/23/65 *Curse of the Stone Hand* (1965); *The Violent and the Damned* (1963)

> **CHILLER**—"Unknown Terror," starring John Howard, Mala Powers and May Wynn. (1957) Second Feature—"Horror Chamber of Dr. Faustus," starring Pierre Brasseur and Alida Valli. (1962) Channel 5 at 11 P.M.

10/30/65 *The Slime People* (1963); *Back from the Dead* (1957)
11/06/65 *Carnival of Souls* (1962); *The Unknown Terror* (1957)
11/13/65 *The Creation of the Humanoids* (1962); *Black Dragons* (1942)
11/20/65 *The Devil's Messenger* (1961); *Horrors of the Black Museum* (1959)
11/27/65 *The Beast with Five Fingers* (1946); *Voodoo Man* (1944)
12/04/65 *Mania* (1960); *Zombies of Mora Tau* (1957)
12/11/65 *The Tell-Tale Heart* (1960); *Teenage Zombies* (1958)
12/18/65 *The Hypnotic Eye* (1960); *Beast from Haunted Cave* (1959)
12/25/65 *Black Tide* (1958); *The Gorilla Man* (1943)
01/01/66 *The Bride and the Beast* (1958); *Creature from the Haunted Sea* (1961)
01/08/66 *The Mermaids of Tiburon* (1962); *The Monster of Piedras Blancas* (1959)
01/15/66 *Hands of A Stranger* (1962); *The Stranglers of Bombay* (1959)
01/22/66 *Invasion of the Animal People* (1962); *The Screaming Skull* (1958)
01/29/66 *The Tingler* (1959); *Back from the Dead* (1957)
02/05/66 *The Unknown Terror* (1957); *The Horror Chamber of Dr. Faustus* (1959)
02/12/66 *Dr. Renault's Secret* (1942); *Invisible Ghost* (1941)
02/19/66 *The Devil Bat* (1940); *Devil Bat's Daughter* (1946)
02/26/66 *She Devil* (1957); *The Brute Man* (1946)

> **⑳ Saturday Chiller.**
> "Cat Girl." (1957.) A girl inherits a family curse which has her soul enter the body of a leopard that goes on a rampage. Barbara Shelley, Robert Ayres, Kay Ballard.

03/05/66 *Fright* (1956); *Bury Me Dead* (1947)
03/12/66 *The Mask of Diijon* (1946); *The Monster of Piedras Blancas* (1959)
03/19/66 *The Human Monster* (1939); *Giant from the Unknown* (1958)
03/26/66 *The Undying Monster* (1942); *Cat Girl* (1957)
04/02/66 *The Horrible Dr. Hichcock* (1962); *The Headless Ghost* (1959)
04/09/66 *The Awful Dr. Orlof* (1962); *The Beast with a Million Eyes* (1955)
04/16/66 *The Ape Man* (1943); *The Undead* (1957)
04/23/66 *The Head* (1959); *The Man Without a Body* (1957)
04/30/66 *The Corpse Vanishes* (1942); *Night of the Blood Beast* (1958)
05/07/66 *The Quatermass Xperiment* (1955); *The Woman Eater* (1958)
05/14/66 *The Return of Dracula* (1958); *The Incredible Petrified World* (1959)
05/21/66 *The Black Sleep* (1956); *The Black Raven* (1943)
05/28/66 *The Four Skulls of Jonathan Drake* (1959); *Dead Men Walk* (1943)
06/04/66 *Daughter of Dr. Jekyll* (1957); *The Amazing Transparent Man* (1960)
06/11/66 *The Blancheville Monster* (1963); *The Hand* (1960)
06/18/66 *Circus of Horrors* (1960); *Invisible Creature* (1960)
06/25/66 *Konga* (1961); *Bride of the Monster* (1955)
07/02/66 *The Crawling Hand* (1963)
07/09/66 *Curse of the Stone Hand* (1965)

07/16/66 *The Slime People* (1963)
07/23/66 *Terror of the Bloodhunters* (1962)
07/30/66 *The Violent and the Damned* (1963)
08/06/66 *The Devil's Messenger* (1961)
08/13/66 *Horror Hotel* (1960)
08/20/66 *The Dungeon of Harrow* (1962)
08/27/66 *The She-Creature* (1956)
09/03/66 *The Walking Dead* (1936)
09/10/66 *The Woman in White* (1948); *The Beast of Hollow Mountain* (1956)
09/17/66 *I Bury the Living* (1958); *Quatermass 2* (1957)
09/24/66 *The Hound of the Baskervilles* (1959); *The Magnetic Monster* (1953)
10/01/66 *The Neanderthal Man* (1953); *The Gorilla Man* (1943)
10/08/66 *The Vampire* (1957); *The Return of Dracula* (1958)
10/15/66 *The Monster that Challenged the World* (1957); *Gog* (1954)
10/22/66 *Donovan's Brain* (1953); *Pharaoh's Curse* (1957)
10/29/66 *Riders to the Stars* (1954); *Terror is A Man* (1959)
11/05/66 *Voodoo Island* (1957); *The Beast with Five Fingers* (1946)
11/12/66 Didn't air
11/19/66 *Trauma* (1962); *Bloodlust!* (1961)
11/26/66 *The Tell-Tale Heart* (1960); *The Devil's Hand* (1961)
12/03/66 *The Secret of the Telegian* (1960); *Back from the Dead* (1957)

Diane Webber in *The Mermaids of Tiburon*, shown on *Chiller* February 25, 1967

12/10/66 *Devil Bat's Daughter* (1946); *Bluebeard* (1944)
12/17/66 *Fire Maidens of Outer Space* (1956); *The Brute Man* (1946)
12/24/66 *Bury Me Dead* (1947); *The Flying Serpent* (1946)
12/31/66 *The Human Monster* (1939); *Dr. Renault's Secret* (1942)
01/07/67 *The Mask of Diijon* (1946); *Missiles from Hell* (1958)
01/14/67 *The Missing Corpse* (1945); *She Devil* (1957)
01/21/67 *Strangler of the Swamp* (1946); *The Undying Monster* (1942)
01/28/67 *Attack of the 50 Foot Woman* (1958); *Unknown Island* (1948)
02/04/67 *Caltiki, the Immortal Monster* (1959); *World Without End* (1956)
02/11/67 *Terror in the Haunted House* (1958); *War of the Satellites* (1958)
02/18/67 *Beast from Haunted Cave* (1959); *Target Earth* (1954)
02/25/67 *Creature from the Haunted Sea* (1961); *The Mermaids of Tiburon* (1962)
03/04/67 *Ghost of Dragstrip Hollow* (1959)
03/11/67 *The Spider* (1958)
03/18/67 *Invasion of the Body Snatchers* (1956)
03/25/67 *A Bucket of Blood* (1959)
04/01/67 *King Dinosaur* (1955)
04/08/67 *How to Make a Monster* (1958)
04/15/67 *The Human Monster* (1939)

Airs at Midnight

02/24/68 *Terror of the Bloodhunters* (1962)
03/02/68 *The Crawling Hand* (1963)
03/09/68 *Bury Me Dead* (1947)
03/16/68 *The Unknown Terror* (1957)
03/23/68 *The Devil's Messenger* (1961)
03/30/68 *Back from the Dead* (1957)
04/06/68 *The Horrible Dr. Hichcock* (1962)
04/13/68 *Horror Hotel* (1960)
04/20/68 *The Awful Dr. Orlof* (1962)
04/27/68 *The Dungeon of Harrow* (1962)
05/04/68 *The Missing Corpse* (1945)
05/11/68 *Frankenstein 1970* (1958)
05/18/68 *Caltiki, the Immortal Monster* (1959)
05/25/68 *Teenage Monster* (1958)
06/01/68 *She Devil* (1957)

06/08/68 *I Was a Teenage Werewolf* (1957)
06/15/68 *The She-Creature* (1956)
06/22/68 *The Amazing Colossal Man* (1957)
06/29/68 *Voodoo Woman* (1957)
07/06/68 *Invasion of the Saucer Men* (1957)
07/13/68 *Blood of Dracula* (1957)
07/20/68 *The Beast with a Million Eyes* (1955)
07/27/68 *The Undead* (1957)
08/03/68 *Teenage Zombies* (1958)
08/10/68 *The Mad Monster* (1942)
08/17/68 *Strangler of the Swamp* (1946)
08/24/68 *The Ape Man* (1943)
08/31/68 *She Demons* (1958)
09/07/68 *The Quatermass Xperiment* (1955)
09/14/68 *The Return of Dracula* (1958)
09/21/68 *The Flame Barrier* (1958)
09/28/68 *The Lost Missile* (1958)
10/05/68 *Destination Moon* (1950)
10/12/68 *The Magnetic Monster* (1953)
10/19/68 *I Bury the Living* (1958)
10/26/68 *The Monster that Challenged the World* (1957)

11/02/68 *Voodoo Island* (1957)
11/09/68 *Terror is a Man* (1959)
11/16/68 *Red Planet Mars* (1952)
11/23/68 *Pharaoh's Curse* (1957)
11/30/68 *Missile to the Moon* (1958)
12/07/68 *Lost Continent* (1951)
12/14/68 *Rocketship X-M* (1950)
12/21/68 *Frankenstein's Daughter* (1958)
12/28/68 *The Man Without a Body* (1957)
01/04/69 *The Invisible Woman* (1940)
Airs at 12:30 a.m.
01/11/69 *Curse of the Stone Hand* (1965)
01/18/69 *Evil Brain from Outer Space* (1965)
01/25/69 *Carnival of Souls* (1962)
02/01/69 *Attack from Space* (1965)

02/08/69 *The Final War* (1960)
02/15/69 *The Mad Monster* (1942)
02/22/69 *The Beast of Hollow Mountain* (1956)
03/01/69 *Invaders from Space* (1965)
03/08/69 *The Black Sleep* (1956)
03/15/69 *Planets Against Us* (1962)
03/22/69 *She Devil* (1957)
03/29/69 *The Awful Dr. Orlof* (1962)
04/05/69 *The Day the Earth Froze* (1959)
04/12/69 *The Dungeon of Harrow* (1962)
04/19/69 *Target Earth* (1954)
04/26/69 *Last Woman on Earth* (1960)
05/03/69 *The Disembodied* (1957)
05/10/69 *Frankenstein 1970* (1958)
05/17/69 *Indestructible Man* (1956)
05/24/69 *The Return of Dracula* (1958)
05/31/69 *The Quatermass Xperiment* (1955)
06/07/69 *Invasion of the Star Creatures* (1962)
06/14/69 Didn't air
06/21/69 Didn't air
06/28/69 *Queen of Outer Space* (1958)
07/05/69 *Beyond the Time Barrier* (1960)
07/12/69 *Fright* (1956)
07/19/69 *The Invisible Woman* (1940)
07/26/69 *Teenage Monster* (1958)
Didn't air 08/02/69-08/23/69
08/30/69 *Bury Me Dead* (1947)
09/06/69 *House on Haunted Hill* (1959)
09/13/69 *Terror in the Haunted House* (1958)
09/20/69 *Hands of A Stranger* (1962)
09/27/69 *The Hideous Sun Demon* (1958)
10/04/69 *Curse of the Faceless Man* (1958)
10/11/69 *Gog* (1954)
10/18/69 *The Neanderthal Man* (1953)
10/25/69 *The Beast from 20,000 Fathoms* (1953)
11/01/69 *Invisible Invaders* (1959)
11/08/69 *Voodoo Island* (1957)
11/15/69 *The Man from Planet X* (1951)
11/22/69 *Donovan's Brain* (1953)
11/29/69 *The Walking Dead* (1936)
12/06/69 *World Without End* (1956)
12/13/69 *The Wasp Woman* (1959)
12/20/69 *Curse of the Stone Hand* (1965)
12/27/69 *Back from the Dead* (1957)
01/03/70 *Frankenstein 1970* (1958)
01/10/70 *The Awful Dr. Orlof* (1962)
01/17/70 *The Disembodied* (1957)

CHILLER—"Walking Dead," starring Boris Karloff, Barton MacLane and Ricardo Cortez. (1936) Second feature—"Red Planet Mar," starring Peter Graves and Andrea King. (1952) Channel 5 at 11 P.M.

01/24/70 *The Horrible Dr. Hichcock* (1962)
01/31/70 *Horror Hotel* (1960)
02/07/70 *The Dungeon of Harrow* (1962)
02/14/70 *The Hypnotic Eye* (1960)
02/21/70 *Black Sunday* (1960)
02/28/70 *Creature from the Haunted Sea* (1961)
03/07/70 *Beast from Haunted Cave* (1959)
03/14/70 *The Mermaids of Tiburon* (1962)
03/21/70 *Invasion of the Animal People* (1962)
03/28/70 *The Slime People* (1963)
04/04/70 *Indestructible Man* (1956)
04/11/70 *War of the Satellites* (1958)
04/18/70 *The Gorilla Man* (1943)
04/25/70 *Carnival of Souls* (1962)
05/02/70 *The Giant Behemoth* (1959)
05/09/70 *The Little Shop of Horrors* (1960)
05/16/70 *Queen of Outer Space* (1958)
05/23/70 *Fright* (1956)
05/30/70 *Terror in the Haunted House* (1958)
06/06/70 *Circus of Horrors* (1960)
06/13/70 *House on Haunted Hill* (1959)
06/20/70 *The Man Without a Body* (1957)
06/27/70 *Hands of A Stranger* (1962)

Doesn't air for almost three months; *Today in Your Life* is shown instead.

09/19/70 *Beyond the Time Barrier* (1960)
09/26/70 *The Blancheville Monster* (1963)

Airs at 1:00 a.m.
10/03/70 *Invasion of the Star Creatures* (1962)
10/10/70 *The Beast of Hollow Mountain* (1956)
10/17/70 *The Quatermass Xperiment* (1955)
10/24/70 *The Day the Earth Froze* (1959)
10/31/70 *Battle Beyond the Sun* (1963)
11/07/70 *Curse of the Faceless Man* (1958)
11/14/70 *The Magnetic Monster* (1953)
11/21/70 *Pharaoh's Curse* (1957)
11/28/70 *The Walking Dead* (1936)
12/05/70 *Invisible Creature* (1960)
12/12/70 *Freedom to Die* (1961)
12/19/70 *It! The Terror from Beyond Space* (1958)
12/26/70 *The Man from Planet X* (1951)
01/02/71 *Journey to the Seventh Planet* (1962)
01/09/71 *The Werewolf* (1956)
01/16/71 *Gog* (1954)
01/23/71 *The Monster that Challenged the World* (1957)
01/30/71 Didn't air
02/06/71 *The Revenge of Frankenstein* (1958)
02/13/71 *Voodoo Island* (1957)
02/20/71 *Donovan's Brain* (1953)
02/27/71 *The Beast with Five Fingers* (1946)
03/06/71 *The Last Man on Earth* (1964)
03/13/71 *The Black Sleep* (1956)
03/20/71 *The Quatermass Xperiment* (1955)
03/27/71 *The Return of Dracula* (1958)
04/03/71 *I Bury the Living* (1958)
04/10/71 *Terror is a Man* (1959)
04/17/71 *The Hound of the Baskervilles* (1959)

04/24/71 *The Walking Dead* (1936)
05/01/71 *Battle Beyond the Sun* (1963)
05/08/71 *The Blancheville Monster* (1963)
05/15/71 *Circus of Horrors* (1960)
05/22/71 *The Amazing Transparent Man* (1960)
05/29/71 *The Vampire* (1957)
06/05/71 *Invisible Invaders* (1959)
06/12/71 *The Beast of Hollow Mountain* (1956)
06/19/71 *Curse of the Faceless Man* (1958)
06/26/71 *The Neanderthal Man* (1953)
07/03/71 *The Monster that Challenged the World* (1957)
07/10/71 *It! The Terror from Beyond Space* (1958)
07/17/71 *The Magnetic Monster* (1953)
07/24/71 *The Man from Planet X* (1951)
07/31/71 *The Werewolf* (1956)
08/07/71 *Pharaoh's Curse* (1957)
08/14/71 *The Beast with Five Fingers* (1946)
08/21/71 *The Quatermass Xperiment* (1955)
08/28/71 *The Black Sleep* (1956)
09/04/71 *Invasion of the Star Creatures* (1962)

Fridays (airs at Midnight)

06/21/68 *Black Sunday* (1960)
06/28/68 *Circus of Horrors* (1960)
07/05/68 *Invisible Creature* (1960)
07/12/68 *Terror in the Crypt* (1964)
07/19/68 *The Hideous Sun Demon* (1958)
07/26/68 *The Monster of Piedras Blancas* (1959)
08/02/68 *The Slime People* (1963)
08/09/68 *The Brute Man* (1946)
08/16/68 *Devil Bat's Daughter* (1946)
08/23/68 *The Corpse Vanishes* (1942)
08/30/68 *King Dinosaur* (1955)
09/06/68 *The Black Raven* (1943)
09/13/68 *Curse of the Faceless Man* (1958)
09/20/68 *Gog* (1954)
09/27/68 *The Neanderthal Man* (1953)

10/04/68 *The Beast from 20,000 Fathoms* (1953)
10/11/68 *Phantom of the Rue Morgue* (1954)
10/18/68 *Giant from the Unknown* (1958)
10/25/68 *It! The Terror from Beyond Space* (1958)
11/01/68 *The Man from Planet X* (1951)
11/08/68 *The Four Skulls of Jonathan Drake* (1959)
11/15/68 *Donovan's Brain* (1953)
11/22/68 *Invisible Invaders* (1959)
11/29/68 *The Vampire* (1957)
12/06/68 *The Beast with Five Fingers* (1946)
12/13/68 *One Million B.C.* (1940)
12/20/68 *Spaceways* (1953)
12/27/68 *Fright* (1956)
01/03/69 *The Last Man on Earth* (1964)
01/10/69 *Warning from Space* (1956)
01/17/69 *Invasion of the Animal People* (1962)
01/24/69 *Atomic Rulers of the World* (1965)
01/31/69 *The Creation of the Humanoids* (1962)
02/07/69 *The Horror Chamber of Dr. Faustus* (1959)
02/14/69 *Fire Maidens of Outer Space* (1956)
02/21/69 *The Unknown Terror* (1957)
02/28/69 *Invasion of the Neptune Men* (1964)
03/07/69 *The Walking Dead* (1936)
03/14/69 *Back from the Dead* (1957)
03/21/69 *Devil Bat's Daughter* (1946)
03/28/69 *Horror Hotel* (1960)
04/04/69 *The Atomic Submarine* (1959)
04/11/69 *The Horrible Dr. Hichcock* (1962)

Chiller Festival (airs at 11:00 p.m.)

05/11/70 *Frankenstein 1970* (1958)
05/12/70 *The Black Sleep* (1956)
05/13/70 *The Devil's Messenger* (1961)
05/14/70 *Revenge of Frankenstein* (1958)
05/15/70 *House of Wax* (1953) [Airs at Midnight]
07/13/70 *Phantom of the Rue Morgue* (1954)
07/14/70 *Horror Hotel* (1960)
07/15/70 *The Horrible Dr. Hitchcock* (1962)

> ⑤ **Chiller Festival.**
> "Frankenstein 1970." A scientist allows an American camera crew to use his castle in return for a reactor he can use in his laboratory. Boris Karloff. 1958.

> ⑤ **Chiller Festival.**
> "Devil's Messenger." Lon Chaney, Karen Kadler, John Crawford. 1961.

07/16/70 *The Awful Dr. Orloff* (1962)
07/17/70 *The Return of Dracula* (1958) [Airs at Midnight]

BEYOND THE LIMITS
(Saturday on WJZ Channel 13 at 11:30 p.m.)

Channel 13 had been showing genre fare since the early 1950s on *Early Bird Theater, Morning Movies, Matinee Movies, Mysteries 'Till Midnight,* and *The Late Show. Beyond the Limits* is the station's first "horror" program, and it lasted about a year. For those whose rooftop antennae could not pull in D.C. signals, at least now they had something scary to watch on Saturday nights.

09/19/64 *The Return of Dracula* (1958)

> BEYOND THE LIMITS — "Beast of Hollow Mountain," starring Guy Madison and Patricia Medina. A prehistoric monster terrorizes a western ranch. Channel 13 at 11.30 P.M.

09/26/64 *The Magnetic Monster* (1953)
10/03/64 *Red Planet Mars* (1952)
10/10/64 *The Man from Planet X* (1951)
10/17/64 *The Beast of Hollow Mountain* (1956)
10/24/64 *The Quatermass Xperiment* (1955)
10/31/64 *It! The Terror from Beyond Space* (1958)
11/07/64 *The Monster that Challenged the World* (1957)
11/14/64 *I Bury the Living* (1958)
11/21/64 *Quatermass 2* (1957)
11/28/64 *Creature with the Atom Brain* (1955)
12/05/64 *Son of Kong* (1933)
12/12/64 *The Curse of the Cat People* (1944)
12/19/64 *First Man into Space* (1959)
12/26/64 *Isle of the Dead* (1945)
01/02/65 Didn't air

> BEYOND THE LIMITS — "Voodoo Island," starring Boris Karloff and Beverly Tyler. A famous writer investigates voodoo horrors on a tropical island. Channel 13 at 12.30 A.M.

01/09/65 *The Vampire* (1957)
01/16/65 Didn't air
01/23/65 *The Four Skulls of Jonathan Drake* (1959)
01/30/65 *Voodoo Island* (1957)
02/06/65 *Pharaoh's Curse* (1957)
02/13/65 *The Flame Barrier* (1958)
02/20/65 *Macumbra Love* (1960)
02/27/65 Didn't air

03/06/65 *Pharaoh's Curse* (1957)
03/13/65 *The Neanderthal Man* (1953)
03/20/65 *The Black Sleep* (1956)
03/27/65 *The Face of Marble* (1946)
04/03/65 *U.F.O.* (1956)
04/10/65 *The Return of Dracula* (1958)
04/17/65 *King of the Zombies* (1941)
04/24/65 *The Ape* (1940)
05/01/65 *Curse of the Faceless Man* (1958)
05/08/65 *The Vampire* (1957)
05/15/65 *Gog* (1954)
05/22/65 *Lady of Vengeance* (1957)
05/29/65 *The Strange Mr. Gregory* (1945)
06/05/65 *Terror is A Man* (1959)
06/12/65 *Destination Moon* (1950)
06/19/65 *The Lost Missile* (1958)
06/26/65 *Alias John Preston* (1955)
07/03/65 *Riders to the Stars* (1954)
07/10/65 *Fiend Without a Face* (1958)
07/17/65 *First Man into Space* (1959)
07/24/65 *The Body Snatcher* (1945)
07/31/65 *The Thing from Another World* (1951)
08/07/65 *The Four Skulls of Jonathan Drake* (1959)
08/14/65 *The Beast of Hollow Mountain* (1956)

> BEYOND THE LIMITS—"Donovan's Brain." A scientist experiments with a dead man's brain. Lew Ayers and Gene Evans star. Channel 13 at 11.45 P.M.

Walter Pidgeon and Robby the Robot in *Forbidden Planet*

08/21/65 *The Ape* (1940)
08/28/65 *Forbidden Planet* (1956)
09/04/65 *Donovan's Brain* (1953)
09/11/65 *The Living Ghost* (1942)

OUT OF THIS WORLD
(Saturday on WTOP Channel 9 at 1:30 p.m.)

An unfortunately short-lived creature feature from Channel 9, this program managed to show the Gill-man trilogy during its brief run, albeit in reverse order.

09/11/65 *Creature with the Atom Brain* (1955); *The Monster and the Girl* (1941)
09/18/65 *Flight to Mars* (1951)
09/25/65 *The Beast from 20,000 Fathoms* (1953)
10/02/65 *Dr. Cyclops* (1940)
10/09/65 *The Creature Walks Among Us* (1956)
10/16/65 *The Gamma People* (1956)
10/23/65 *It Came from Beneath the Sea* (1955)
10/30/65 *13 Ghosts* (1960)
11/06/65 *Earth vs. the Flying Saucers* (1956)
11/13/65 *Revenge of the Creature* (1955)

> **WASHINGTON**
> JUNGLE CALL — "Tarzan's Hidden Jungle," starring Gordon Scott and Vera Miles. (1955) Channel 5 at 10 A.M.
> OUT OF THIS WORLD—"The Gamma People," starring Paul Douglas and Eva Bartok. (1956) Channel 9 at 1.30 P.M.
> THE GLADIATORS—"79 A.D." Susan Paget, Brad Harris and Mara Lane star in drama of a gladiator's fight against oppressors of ancient Rome. (1960) Channel 5 at 2.30 P.M.
> JUNGLE—"Devil Goddess," starring Johnny Weissmuller and Angela Stevens. (1955) Channel 9 at 3 P.M.
> EASTSIDE COMEDY — "Clipped Wings," starring the Bowery Boys. (1953) Channel 5 at 4 P.M.
> CHILLER — "The Crawling Hand," starring Peter Breck, Kent Taylor and Rod Lauren. (1963). Second feature — "Terror of the Blood Hunters." (1962) Robert Conte and Steve Conte star in drama of two prisoner's escape from a penal colony with the prison commandant's daughter. Channel 5 at 11 P.M.

> **WASHINGTON**
> OUT OF THIS WORLD — "Earth Versus the Flying Saucers," starring Joan Taylor and Hugh Marlowe. (1956) Channel 9 at 1.30 P.M.
> THE GLADIATORS—"Slave Queen of Babylon," starring John Ericson and Yvonne Furneaux. (1962) Channel 5 at 2.30 P.M.
> JUNGLE—"Voodoo Tiger," starring Johnny Weissmuller and Jean Byron. (1952) Channel 9 at 3 P.M.
> CHILLER—"Carnival of Souls," starring Candace Hilligoss and Sidney Berger (1963). Second feature—"Unknown Terror," starring John Howard and Mala Powers. (1957) Channel 5 at 11 P.M.

11/20/65 *20 Million Miles to Earth* (1957)
11/27/65 *Creature from the Black Lagoon* (1954)
12/04/65 *The Man Who Turned to Stone* (1957)
12/11/65 *It Came from Outer Space* (1953)

HOUSE OF HORRORS (
WDCA Channel 20)

Independent station WDCA began broadcasting Wednesday, April 20, 1966. Before it debuted its first horror host, The Great Zucchini, the following year, Channel 20 offered *House of Horrors* on Saturday and Sunday afternoons. The program was a mix of low-budget horrors, mysteries, and German *krimis* (crime pictures), with a Universal thriller airing occasionally. The Saturday edition of *House of Horrors* ran through January 1970, when it was replaced with *Saturday Chiller*.

> ⑳ **House of Horrors.**
> "House of Horrors." Bill Goodwin and Robert Lowery. 1946.

Airs Saturday at 5:00 p.m.
04/23/66 *Captive Wild Woman* (1943) [Airs at 5:30 p.m.]
04/30/66 *The Living Ghost* (1942)
05/07/66 *Revenge of the Zombies* (1943) [Airs at 5:30 p.m.]
05/14/66 *House of Horrors* (1946)
05/21/66 *The Mad Ghoul* (1943)
05/28/66 *Invaders from Mars* (1953)
06/04/66 *The Carpet of Horror* (1962)
06/11/66 *The Fellowship of the Frog* (1959)
06/18/66 *The Invisible Terror* (1963)

06/25/66 *The Squeaker* (1963)
07/02/66 *The Boogie Man Will Get You* (1942)
07/09/66 *The Mysterious Magician* (1964)
07/16/66 *The Secret of the Black Trunk* (1962)
07/23/66 *Night Key* (1937)
07/30/66 *The Spider Woman Strikes Back* (1946)
08/06/66 *Woman Who Came Back* (1945)
08/13/66 *Fog for a Killer* (1962)
08/20/66 *The Strange Mr. Gregory* (1945)
08/27/66 *The Secret of the Black Widow* (1963)
09/03/66 *The Curse of the Hidden Vault* (1964)
09/10/66 *The Indian Scarf* (1963)
09/17/66 *The Green Archer* (1961)
09/24/66 *Room 13* (1964)

5.00—House of Horrors: Fog For A Killer.

10/01/66 *The Strangler of Blackmoor Castle* (1963)
10/08/66 *Bela Lugosi Meets a Brooklyn Gorilla* (1952)
10/15/66 *The Inn on Dartmoor* (1964)
10/22/66 *The Terrible People* (1960)
10/29/66 *Violent Midnight* (1963)
11/05/66 *The Testament of Dr. Mabuse* (1962)
11/12/66 *Ghost Diver* (1957)
11/19/66 *No Survivors Please.* (1964)
11/26/66 *The Crimes of Stephen Hawke* (1936)
12/03/66 *The Red Circle* (1960)
12/10/66 *The Fellowship of the Frog* (1959)
12/17/66 *The Forger of London* (1961)
12/24/66 *Shadow of Terror* (1945)
12/31/66 *Crimes at the Dark House* (1940)
01/07/67 *The Black Cobra* (1963)
01/14/67 *The Amazing Mr. X* (1948)
01/21/67 *Captive Wild Woman* (1943)
01/28/67 *The Ape* (1940)
02/04/67 *Fog for a Killer* (1962)
02/11/67 *The Crawling Eye* (1958)
02/18/67 *Sky Above Heaven* (1965)
02/25/67 *The Curse of the Hidden Vault* (1964)
03/04/67 *Bride of the Gorilla* (1951)
03/11/67 *The Death Ray Mirror of Doctor Mabuse* (1964)
03/18/67 *The Invisible Dr. Mabuse* (1962)
03/25/67 *The Hooded Terror* (1938)
04/01/67 *House of Horrors* (1946)
04/08/67 *The Vampire Bat* (1933)
04/15/67 *Man in Black* (1949)
04/22/67 *Murder in the Red Barn* (1935)
04/29/67 *The Strangler of Blackmoor Castle* (1963)
05/06/67 *Invisible Agent* (1942)
05/13/67 *Project Moonbase* (1953)
05/20/67 *The Face at the Window* (1939)
05/27/67 *The Secret of the Red Orchid* (1962)
06/03/67 *The Fellowship of the Frog* (1959)

06/10/67 *Teenage Monster* (1958)
06/17/67 *Jack the Ripper* (1959)
06/24/67 *The Secret of the Black Trunk* (1962)
07/01/67 *The Curse of the Hidden Vault* (1964)
07/08/67 *The Terrible People* (1960)
07/15/67 *Robot Monster* (1953)
07/22/67 *The Mad Ghoul* (1943)
07/29/67 *The Testament of Dr. Mabuse* (1962)
08/05/67 *Room 13* (1964)
08/12/67 *The Secret of the Chinese Carnation* (1964)
08/19/67 *The Living Ghost* (1942)
08/26/67 *The Jungle Captive* (1945)

Airs Saturday at 4:00 p.m.
09/21/68 *No Survivors Please.* (1964)
09/28/68 *The Squeaker* (1963)
10/05/68 *The Tingler* (1959)
10/12/68 *Battle in Outer Space* (1959)
10/19/68 *The Time Travelers* (1964)
10/26/68 *The Invisible Dr. Mabuse* (1962)
11/02/68 *The Creeper* (1948)
11/09/68 *Attack of the Robots* (1966)
11/16/68 *Voyage to the End of the Universe* (1963)
11/23/68 *It Came from Beneath the Sea* (1955)
11/30/68 *Invisible Agent* (1942)
12/07/68 *The 27th Day* (1957)

Rondo Hatton in *Jungle Captive*

12/14/68 *The Electronic Monster* (1958)
12/21/68 *Cobra Woman* (1944)
12/28/68 *The Secret of the Red Orchid* (1962)
01/04/69 *The Curse of the Hidden Vault* (1964)
01/11/69 *The Mad Magician* (1954)
01/18/69 *The Son of Dr. Jekyll* (1951)
01/25/69 *12 to the Moon* (1960)
02/01/69 *Rome Against Rome* (1964)
02/08/69 *The Curse of the Yellow Snake* (1963)
02/15/69 *Monster from a Prehistoric Planet* (1967)
02/22/69 *Creature of Destruction* (1967)
03/01/69 *Beast of Morocco* (1966)
03/08/69 *Planet of the Vampires* (1965)
03/15/69 *Project Moonbase* (1953)
03/22/69 *The Ape* (1940)
03/29/69 *King of the Zombies* (1941)
04/05/69 *The Giant Claw* (1957)
04/12/69 *It Came from Beneath the Sea* (1955)
04/19/69 *Curse of the Demon* (1957)
04/26/69 *Mothra* (1961)
05/03/69 *Majin, Monster of Terror* (1966)
05/10/69 *The Time Travelers* (1964)
05/17/69 *Die, Monster, Die!* (1965)
05/24/69 *Creature of Destruction* (1967)
05/31/69 *Cobra Woman* (1944)
06/07/69 *Attack of the Robots* (1966)
06/14/69 *Ghost Ship* (1952)
06/21/69 *Invisible Agent* (1942)
06/28/69 *Invaders from Mars* (1953)
07/05/69 *The Vampire Bat* (1933)
07/12/69 *In the Year 2889* (1967)
07/19/69 *Beast of Morocco* (1966)
07/26/69 *Captive Wild Woman* (1943)
08/02/69 *The Electronic Monster* (1958)
08/09/69 *King of the Zombies* (1941)
08/16/69 *Voyage to the End of the Universe* (1963)
08/23/69 *Night Key* (1937)
08/30/69 *Shadow of Terror* (1945)
09/06/69 *Devil's Island* (1939)
09/13/69 *The 27th Day* (1957)
09/20/69 *The Carpet of Horror* (1962)
09/27/69 *Robot Monster* (1953)
10/04/69 *Ape Man of the Jungle* (1964)
10/11/69 *Majin, Monster of Terror* (1966)
10/18/69 *Mars Needs Women* (1967)
10/25/69 *The Mad Ghoul* (1943)
11/01/69 *War of the Monsters* (1966)
11/08/69 *Godzilla vs. The Thing* (1964)
11/15/69 *Bride of the Gorilla* (1951)
11/22/69 Didn't Air
11/29/69 *Invaders from Mars* (1953)
12/06/69 *Monster from the Ocean Floor* (1954)
12/13/69 *Shadow of Chinatown* (1936)

WDCA-TV, Channel 20

12.00—Movie: "Rockabilly Baby."
1.30—Mystery Movie: "Zanzibar."
3.00—Wresting, from Buffalo.
4.00—Dance Party.
5.00—House of Horrors: "Secret of the Black Trunk."
6.30—Have Gun; Will Travel.
7.00—Invitation to Murder: "Strangler's Web."
8.00—Bullfights from Mexico.
10.00—Ernest Tubbs Show.
10.30—Step This Way.
11.00—Movie: "Bernadette of Lourdes."

Sunday Programs

10.00—Man from Cochise.
10.30—Western Theater: "West of the Divide."
11.30—Shirley Temple Theater
1.00—Alaskan Brown Bear.
1.30—Drag Racing Championships.
2.00—Roller Skating Championships.
3.00—Movie: "Mission of the Seahawk."
5.00—House of Horrors: "The White Spider."
6.30—Award Theater: "Fabiola."
8.30—Play of the Week: "Climate of Eden."
10.30—News Magazine.
11.00—Open End.
12.00—Newsbeat Twenty.

12/20/69 *The Secret of the Black Widow* (1963)
12/27/69 *Planet of the Vampires* (1965)
01/03/70 *Creature of Destruction* (1967)
01/10/70 *Ghidorah, the Three-Headed Monster* (1964)
01/17/70 *Revenge of the Zombies* (1943)
Airs Sunday at 5:00 p.m.
04/24/66 *King of the Zombies* (1941)
05/01/66 *Jack the Ripper* (1959)
05/08/66 *The Ape* (1940)
05/15/66 *The Man Who Changed His Mind* (1936)
05/22/66 *The Face of Marble* (1946)
05/29/66 *Uncle Was A Vampire* (1959)
06/05/66 *No Survivors Please.* (1964)
06/12/66 *The Black Abbot* (1963)
06/19/66 *The Ringer* (1952)
06/26/66 *The Amazing Mr. X* (1948)
07/03/66 *Horror Island* (1941)
07/10/66 *The Inn on the River* (1962)
07/17/66 *The White Spider* (1963)
07/24/66 *The Red Circle* (1960)

07/31/66 *The Mad Doctor of Market Street* (1942)
08/07/66 *The Red Hand* (1960)
08/14/66 *The Forger of London* (1961)
08/21/66 *The Strange Countess* (1961)
08/28/66 *The Secret of the Red Orchid* (1962)
09/04/66 *The Avenger* (1960)
09/11/66 *The Door with Seven Locks* (1962)
09/18/66 *The Curse of the Yellow Snake* (1963)
09/25/66 *The Black Cobra* (1963)
10/02/66 *The Invisible Dr. Mabuse* (1962)
10/09/66 *Man in Black* (1949)
10/16/66 *Elevator to the Gallows* (1958)
10/23/66 *Murder Will Out* (1952)
10/30/66 *The Whip and the Body* (1963)
11/06/66 *Fanny by Gaslight* (1944)
11/13/66 *The Vampire Bat* (1933)
11/20/66 *Invisible Agent* (1942)
11/27/66 *The Squeaker* (1963)
12/04/66 *The Black Abbot* (1963)
12/11/66 *The Invisible Terror* (1963)
12/18/66 *Murder in the Red Barn* (1935)
12/25/66 *House of Horrors* (1946)
01/01/67 *The Secret of the Red Orchid* (1962)
01/08/67 *Room 13* (1964)
01/15/67 *The Mysterious Magician* (1964)
01/22/67 *The Secret of the Black Widow* (1963)
01/29/67 *Teenage Monster* (1958)
02/05/67 *The Secret of the Chinese Carnation* (1964)
02/12/67 *The Testament of Dr. Mabuse* (1962)
02/19/67 *The Curse of the Yellow Snake* (1963)
02/26/67 *The Green Archer* (1961)
03/05/67 *The Terrible People* (1960)
03/12/67 *Monster from the Ocean Floor* (1954)
03/19/67 *The Strange Countess* (1961)
03/26/67 *The Strangler of Blackmoor Castle* (1963)
04/02/67 *The Door with Seven Locks* (1962)
04/09/67 *Murder by Two* (1960)
04/16/67 *The Black Panther of Ratana* (1963)
04/23/67 *The Ringer* (1952)
04/30/67 *Shadow of Chinatown* (1936)
05/07/67 *The Squeaker* (1963)
05/14/67 *The Avenger* (1960)
05/21/67 *The Inn on the River* (1962)
05/28/67 *The Black Abbot* (1963)
06/04/67 *The Crawling Eye* (1958)
06/11/67 *The Carpet of Horror* (1962)
06/18/67 *Fog for A Killer* (1962)
06/25/67 *The Red Circle* (1960)
07/02/67 *The Black Cobra* (1963)
07/09/67 *Bride of the Gorilla* (1951)
07/16/67 *The Invisible Dr. Mabuse* (1962)
07/23/67 *The Vampire Bat* (1933)

07/30/67 *The Green Archer* (1961)
08/06/67 *The Mysterious Magician* (1964)
08/13/67 *Captive Wild Woman* (1943)
08/20/67 *The Face of Marble* (1946)
08/27/67 *The Ape* (1940)

Airs Sunday at 4:30 p.m.
09/03/67 *The Inn on Dartmoor* (1964)
09/10/67 *The Hooded Terror* (1938)
09/17/67 *The Strangler of Blackmoor Castle* (1963)

09/24/67 *The Secret of the Red Orchid* (1962)
10/01/67 *Monster from the Ocean Floor* (1954)
10/08/67 *The Door with Seven Locks* (1962)
10/15/67 *The Whip and the Body* (1963)
10/22/67 *House of Horrors* (1946)
10/29/67 *The Mad Ghoul* (1943)
11/05/67 *The Crawling Eye* (1958)
11/12/67 *No Survivors Please.* (1964)
11/19/67 *The Undying Monster* (1942)
11/26/67 *The Indian Scarf* (1963)

12/03/67 *Invisible Agent* (1942)
12/10/67 *The Secret of the Black Trunk* (1962)
12/17/67 *The Living Ghost* (1942)
12/24/67 *Bela Lugosi Meets a Brooklyn Gorilla* (1952)
12/31/67 *Fog for A Killer* (1962)
01/07/68 *The Ringer* (1952)
01/14/68 *King of the Zombies* (1941)
01/21/68 *The Electronic Monster* (1958)
01/28/68 *The Giant Claw* (1957)
02/04/68 *The Mad Magician* (1954)
02/11/68 *The Gamma People* (1956)
02/18/68 *Battle in Outer Space* (1959)
02/25/68 *Jack the Ripper* (1959)
03/03/68 *1 2 to the Moon* (1960)
03/10/68 *Zombies of Mora Tau* (1957)
03/17/68 *Teenage Monster* (1958)

03/24/68 *The Death Ray Mirror of Doctor Mabuse* (1964)
03/31/68 *Revenge of the Zombies* (1943)
04/07/68 *The Ape* (1940)
04/14/68 *The Terrible People* (1960)
04/21/68 *The Crimes of Stephen Hawke* (1936)
04/28/68 *The Inn on the River* (1962)
05/05/68 *The Mad Magician* (1954)
05/12/68 *The H-Man* (1959)
05/19/68 *Cobra Woman* (1944)
05/26/68 *The Creeper* (1948)
06/02/68 *The Ape* (1940)
06/09/68 *The Jungle Captive* (1945)
06/16/68 *Captive Wild Woman* (1943)
06/23/68 *The Mad Ghoul* (1943)
06/30/68 *The Spider Woman Strikes Back* (1946)
07/07/68 *The Undying Monster* (1942)
07/14/68 *Ghidorah, the Three-Headed Monster* (1964)
07/21/68 *Creature with the Atom Brain* (1955)
07/28/68 *The Tingler* (1959)
08/04/68 *The Son of Dr. Jekyll* (1951)
08/11/68 *The Face of Marble* (1946)
08/18/68 *The Amazing Mr. X* (1948)
08/25/68 *The 27th Day* (1957)
09/01/68 *The Strangler of Blackmoor Castle* (1963)
09/08/68 *The Secret of the Red Orchid* (1962)
09/15/68 *The Night Has Eyes* (1942)
09/22/68 *The Red Cloak* (1955)
09/29/68 *Curse of the Demon* (1957)
10/06/68 *Mars Needs Women* (1967)
10/13/68 *Majin, Monster of Terror* (1966)
10/20/68 *Ape Man of the Jungle* (1964)
10/27/68 *The Testament of Dr. Mabuse* (1962)
11/03/68 *1 2 to the Moon* (1960)
11/10/68 *The Giant Claw* (1957)
11/17/68 *Die, Monster, Die!* (1965)
11/24/68 *Beast of Morocco* (1966)
12/01/68 *The Woman Eater* (1958)
12/08/68 *Room 13* (1964)

12/15/68 *House of Horrors* (1946)
12/22/68 *Fog for A Killer* (1962)
12/29/68 *Teenage Monster* (1960)
01/05/69 *The Inn on Dartmoor* (1964)
01/12/69 *The H-Man* (1959)

Airs Sunday at 5:00 p.m.
01/19/69 *Battle in Outer Space* (1959)
01/26/69 *The Whip and the Body* (1963)
02/02/69 *The Ape* (1940)
02/09/69 *King of the Zombies* (1941)
02/16/69 *Tower of Terror* (1941)
02/23/69 *Die, Monster, Die!* (1965)
03/02/69 *War of the Monsters* (1966)
03/09/69 *In the Year 2889* (1967)
03/16/69 *Bride of the Gorilla* (1951)
03/23/69 *Invaders from Mars* (1953)
03/30/69 *The Mysterious Magician* (1964)
04/06/69 *The Woman Eater* (1958)
04/13/69 *Monster from the Ocean Floor* (1954)
04/20/69 *The Secret of the Black Widow* (1963)
04/27/69 *No Survivors Please.* (1964)
05/04/69 *The 27th Day* (1957)
05/11/69 *Battle in Outer Space* (1959)
05/18/69 *Circus of Fear* (1966)
05/25/69 *12 to the Moon* (1960)
06/01/69 *Ape Man of the Jungle* (1964)
06/08/69 *House of Horrors* (1946)
06/15/69 *The Crawling Eye* (1958)
06/22/69 *Ghost Diver* (1957)
06/29/69 *Room 13* (1964)
07/06/69 *Fame and the Devil* (1949)
07/13/69 *Planet of the Vampires* (1965)
07/20/69 *Maneater of Hydra* (1967)
07/27/69 *The Crawling Eye* (1958)
08/03/69 *Sky Above Heaven* (1965)
08/10/69 *The Tingler* (1959)
08/17/69 *Creature of Destruction* (1967)
08/24/69 *Revenge of the Zombies* (1943)
08/31/69 *The Curse of the Yellow Snake* (1963)
09/07/69 *Battle in Outer Space* (1959)

Airs Sunday at 5:30 p.m.
09/14/69 *The Face of Marble* (1946)
09/21/69 *Teenage Monster* (1958)
09/28/69 *The Secret of the Black Trunk* (1962)
10/05/69 *Circus of Fear* (1966)
10/12/69 *Rome Against Rome* (1964)
10/19/69 *Die, Monster, Die!* (1965)
10/26/69 *Attack of the Robots* (1966)
11/02/69 *Beast of Morocco* (1966)
11/09/69 *The Crawling Eye* (1958)
11/16/69 *The Time Travelers* (1964)

11/23/69 *Project Moonbase* (1953)
11/30/69 *Voyage to the End of the Universe* (1963)
12/07/69 *The Jungle Captive* (1945)

12/14/69 *Robot Monster* (1953)
12/21/69 *The Undying Monster* (1942)
12/28/69 *The Terrible People* (1960)
01/04/70 *Maneater of Hydra* (1967)
01/11/70 *Teenage Monster* (1958)
01/18/70 *Monster from a Prehistoric Planet* (1967)

SCIENCE FICTION THEATER
(WDCA Channel 20)

Sporadically airing during 1969 and 1970, WDCA's *Science Fiction Theater* finally settled into its Saturday afternoon slot in January 1971 and showed more than just what its title suggested. Here one could find AIP '50s fare, Americanized Japanese imports, and the occasional Gothic thriller.

Airs Saturday at 11:00 a.m.
05/03/69 *Teenage Monster* (1958)
05/10/69 *Godzilla vs. The Thing* (1964)
05/17/69 *Voyage to the End of the Universe* (1963)
05/24/69 *Monster from a Prehistoric Planet* (1967)
05/31/69 *Mars Needs Women* (1967)
06/07/69 *The Curse of the Hidden Vault* (1964)

> ⓴ Science Fiction Theater ©
> "The Invisible Terror." Hannes Schmidhauser, Ellen Schwiers, Hans Borosody. 1963.

06/14/69 *The Invisible Terror* (1963)
06/21/69 *Things to Come* (1936)
06/28/69 *Project Moonbase* (1953)
07/05/69 *No Survivors Please.* (1964)
07/12/69 *War of the Monsters* (1966)
07/19/69 *The Man Who Could Work Miracles* (1936)
07/26/69 *Horror Island* (1941)
08/02/69 *The Time Travelers* (1964)
08/09/69 *The H-Man* (1959)
08/16/69 *Things to Come* (1936)
08/23/69 *The Testament of Dr. Mabuse* (1962)
08/30/69 *The Avenger* (1960)
Preempted by *Football Replay*
01/03/70 *Planet of the Vampires* (1965) [Airs at 12:00 p.m.]
01/10/70 *Monster from a Prehistoric Planet* (1967) [Airs at 12:00 p.m.]
01/17/70 *Teenage Monster* (1958) [Airs at 12:00 p.m.]

Italian poster for *Monster from a Prehistoric Planet*, the original title was *Gappa the Triphibian Monsters*

Airs Saturday at 3:30 p.m.
05/23/70 *It Conquered the World* (1956)
05/30/70 *Attack of the Puppet People* (1958)
06/06/70 *The Beast with a Million Eyes* (1955)
06/13/70 *The Saga of the Viking Women and Their Voyage to the Waters of the Great Sea Serpent* (1957)
06/20/70 *The Beast with a Million Eyes* (1955)
06/27/70 *Invaders from Mars* (1953)
07/04/70 *Gammera the Invincible* (1966)
07/11/70 *Beast of Morocco* (1966)
07/18/70 *I Was a Teenage Werewolf* (1957)
07/25/70 *Rome Against Rome* (1964)
08/01/70 *Castle of Evil* (1966)
08/08/70 *Night Caller from Outer Space* (1965)
08/15/70 *The Unearthly* (1957)
08/22/70 *Slaves of the Invisible Monster* (1966)

Airs Saturday at 2:00 p.m.
01/02/71 *Maneater of Hydra* (1967)
01/09/71 *Gamera vs. Monster X* (1970)
01/16/71 *The Time Travelers* (1964)
01/23/71 *How to Make a Monster* (1958)
01/30/71 *Beast of Morocco* (1966)
02/06/71 *Day the World Ended* (1955)
02/13/71 *The X from Outer Space* (1967)

> **㉘ Science Fiction Theater.**
> "Man-Eater of Hydra." After a baron opens his villa on a small island to visitors, an exclusive group of tourists are murdered one by one. Cameron Mitchell, Kai Fischer, George Martin. 1965.

02/20/71 *The She-Creature* (1956)
02/27/71 *Yongary, Monster from the Deep* (1967)
03/06/71 *Gamera vs. Monster X* (1970)
03/13/71 *The Spider* (1958)
03/20/71 *The Saga of the Viking Women and Their Voyage to the Waters of the Great Sea Serpent* (1957)
03/27/71 *In the Year 2889* (1967)
04/03/71 *Kronos* (19957)
04/10/71 *The 27th Day* (1957)
04/17/71 *12 to the Moon* (1960)
04/24/71 *Mothra* (1961)
05/01/71 *The H-Man* (1959)
05/08/71 *Planet of the Vampires* (1965)
05/15/71 *Frankenstein Conquers the World* (1965)
05/22/71 *Die, Monster, Die!* (1965)
05/29/71 *Voyage to the End of the Universe* (1963)

06/05/71 *Mars Needs Women* (1967)
06/12/71 *The Cape Canaveral Monsters* (1960)
06/19/71 *Majin, Monster of Terror* (1966)
06/26/71 *Creature of Destruction* (1967)
07/03/71 *Day the World Ended* (1955)
07/10/71 *Terror from the Year 5000* (1958)
07/17/71 *Godzilla vs. The Thing* (1964)
07/24/71 *The Bamboo Saucer* (1968)
07/31/71 *Missile Monsters* (1958)
08/07/71 *The Human Monster* (1939)
08/14/71 *Fire Maidens of Outer Space* (1956)
08/21/71 *Two Lost Worlds* (1951)
08/28/71 *The Time Travelers* (1964)
09/04/71 *Circus of Fear* (1966)
09/11/71 *Flight to Mars* (1951)
09/18/71 *Attack of the Puppet People* (1958)
09/25/71 *The Mysterians* (1957)
10/02/71 *The Brain that Wouldn't Die* (1962)
10/09/71 *Beyond the Time Barrier* (1960)
10/16/71 *Invisible Creature* (1960)
10/23/71 *The Invisible Man's Revenge* (1944)
10/30/71 *Invasion of the Star Creatures* (1962)
11/06/71 *It's Alive!* (1969)
11/13/71 *Yongary, Monster from the Deep* (1967)
11/20/71 *Attack of the Monsters* (1969)
11/27/71 *The Giant Claw* (1957)
12/04/71 *It Came from Outer Space* (1953)
12/11/71 Didn't air
12/18/71 *The Amazing Colossal Man* (1957)
12/25/71 *Santa Claus Conquers the Martians* (1964)
01/01/72 *The Hideous Sun Demon* (1958)
01/08/72 *Beginning of the End* (1957)
01/15/72 *12 to the Moon* (1960)
01/22/72 *The 27th Day* (1957)
01/29/72 *Attack of the Robots* (1966)
02/05/72 *It Conquered the World* (1956)
02/12/72 *The Giant Gila Monster* (1959)

Santa Claus Conquers the Martians aired Dec. 25, 1971!

Baltimore-Washington Area Horror Hosts and More! (1957-1987)

02/19/72 *The Phantom Planet* (1961)
02/26/72 *The Angry Red Planet* (1959)
03/04/72 *Beast of Morocco* (1966)
03/11/72 *Kronos* (1957)
03/18/72 *The Dungeon of Harrow* (1962)
03/25/72 *The Beast with a Million Eyes* (1955)
04/01/72 *It's Alive!* (1969)
04/08/72 *Night Caller from Outer Space* (1965)
04/15/72 *Attack of the Monsters* (1969)
04/22/72 *Flight to Mars* (1951)

> 11.00 ⑬ ⑦ Journey to the Center of the Earth. ©
> ⑳ Science Fiction Theater "Voyage to the End of the Universe," Dennis Stephens, Frances Sondens. 1964.

04/29/72 *Voyage to the End of the Universe* (1963)
05/06/72 *The She-Creature* (1956)
05/13/72 *The Spider* (1958)
05/20/72 *War of the Colossal Beast* (1958)
05/27/72 *The Saga of the Viking Women and Their Voyage to the Waters of the Great Sea Serpent* (1957)
06/03/72 *Mars Needs Women* (1967)
06/10/72 *Monster from a Prehistoric Planet* (1967)
06/17/72 *The Time Travelers* (1964)
06/24/72 *In the Year 2889* (1967)
07/01/72 *Beyond the Time Barrier* (1960)
07/08/72 *Invasion of the Star Creatures* (1962)
07/15/72 *Journey to the Seventh Planet* (1962)
07/22/72 *The Day the Earth Froze* (1959)
07/29/72 *Terror from the Year 5000* (1958)
08/05/72 *Die, Monster, Die!* (1965)
08/12/72 *Creature of Destruction* (1967)
08/19/72 *The Incredibly Strange Creatures Who Stopped Living and Became Mixed-Up Zombies!!?* (1964)
08/26/72 *Beginning of the End* (1957)
09/02/72 *The Headless Ghost* (1959)
09/09/72 *The Screaming Skull* (1958)

Airs Sunday at 3:00 p.m.
09/13/70 *The Beast with a Million Eyes* (1955)
09/20/70 *The Screaming Skull* (1958)
09/27/70 *Godzilla vs. The Thing* (1964)
10/04/70 *Frankenstein Conquers the World* (1965)
10/11/70 *It's Alive!* (1969)
10/18/70 *Return of the Giant Monsters* (1967)
10/25/70 *Goliath and the Vampires* (1961)
11/01/70 *Attack of the Crab Monsters* (1957)
11/08/70 *Destroy All Monsters* (1968)
11/15/70 *Voyage into Space* (1970)
11/22/70 *Destroy All Planets* (1968)
11/29/70 *In the Year 2889* (1967)
12/06/70 *Attack of the Robots* (1966)
12/13/70 *Creature of Destruction* (1967)
12/20/70 *Planet of the Vampires* (1965)
12/27/70 *Die, Monster, Die!* (1965)
01/03/71 *Majin, Monster of Terror* (1966)
01/10/71 *The Amazing Colossal Man* (1957)
01/17/71 *Rome Against Rome* (1964)
01/24/71 *The Return of Giant Majin* (1966)

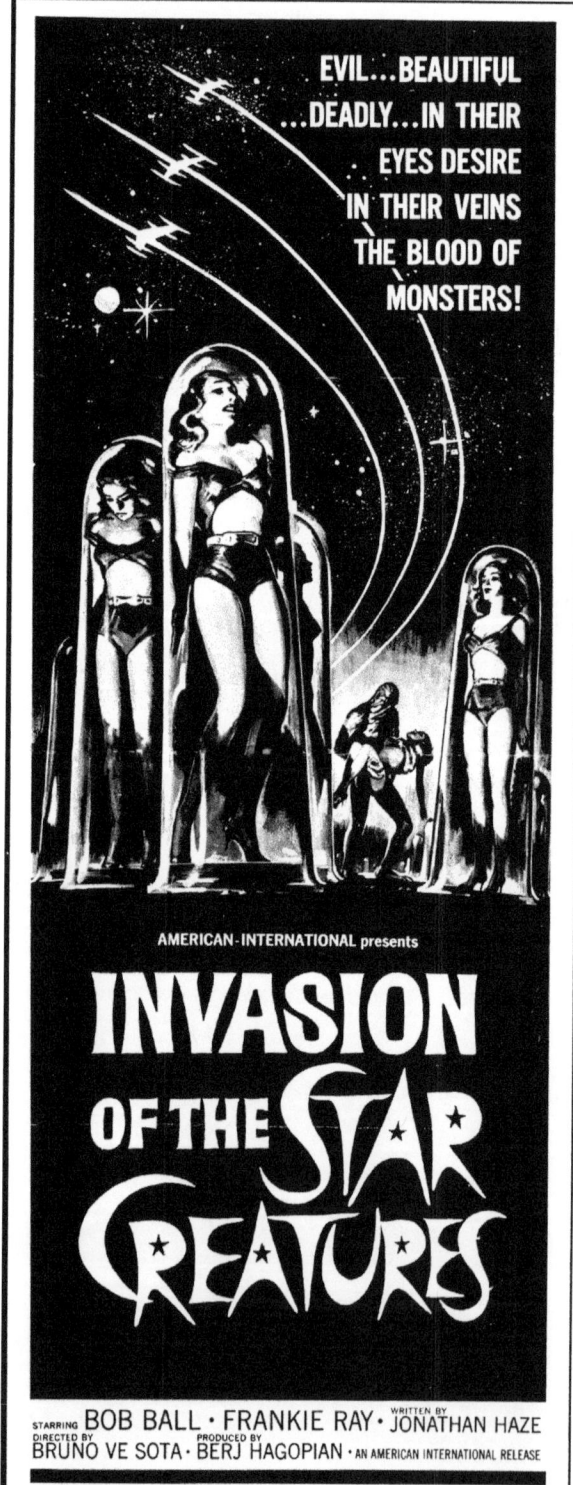

01/31/71 *It Conquered the World* (1956)
02/07/71 *Terror from the Year 5000* (1958)
02/14/71 *Magic Serpent* (1966)
02/21/71 *The Undead* (1957)
02/28/71 *Night of the Blood Beast* (1958)
03/07/71 *War of the Colossal Beast* (1958)
03/14/71 *War of the Monsters* (1966)
03/21/71 *Invasion of the Saucer Men* (1957)
03/28/71 *Voodoo Woman* (1957)
04/04/71 *Flight of the Lost Balloon* (1961)
04/11/71 *Invasion of the Body Snatchers* (1956)
04/18/71 *The Tingler* (1959)
04/25/71 *The Giant Claw* (1957)
05/02/71 *Monster from a Prehistoric Planet* (1967)
05/09/71 *The Screaming Skull* (1958)
05/16/71 *War of the Monsters* (1966)
05/23/71 *The Amazing Colossal Man* (1957)
05/30/71 *How to Make a Monster* (1958)
06/06/71 *Lost Planet Airmen* (1951)
06/13/71 *Slaves of the Invisible Monster* (1966)
06/20/71 *Dr. Satan's Robot* (1966)
06/27/71 *Cyclotrode "X"* (1966)
07/04/71 *Retik, the Moon Menace* (1966)
07/11/71 *D-Day on Mars* (1966)
07/18/71 *The Dungeon of Harrow* (1962)
07/25/71 *Horror Hotel* (1960)
08/01/71 *I Was a Teenage Werewolf* (1957)
08/08/71 *The Saga of the Viking Women and Their Voyage to the Waters of the Great Sea Serpent* (1957); *The Screaming Skull* (1958)
08/15/71 *War of the Colossal Beast* (1958); *She Gods of Shark Reef* (1958)
08/22/71 Didn't air
08/29/71 Didn't air
09/05/71 *Teenage Caveman* (1958); *The Astounding She-Monster* (1957)
09/12/71 *Attack of the Giant Leaches* (1959); *Ghost of Dragstrip Hollow* (1959)
09/19/71 *Pillow of Death* (1945); *The Flying Serpent* (1946)
09/26/71 *The Mummy's Curse* (1944); *Weird Woman* (1944)
10/03/71 *The Raven* (1935); *The Cat Creeps* (1946)
10/10/71 *Lost Battalion* (1960)
10/17/71 *The Blancheville Monster* (1963)
10/24/71 *Terror in the Crypt* (1964)
10/31/71 *The Phantom Planet* (1961)
11/07/71 *Jungle Woman* (1944); *The Amazing Transparent Man* (1960)
11/14/71 *Sombra, the Spider Woman* (1966)
11/21/71 *Voyage into Space* (1970)
11/28/71 *U-238 and the Witch Doctor* (1966)
12/05/71 *Mothra* (1961)

12/12/71 *The H-Man* (1959)
12/19/71 *The Tingler* (1959)
12/26/71 *Curse of the Demon* (1957)
01/02/72 *War of the Monsters* (1966)
01/09/72 Didn't air
01/16/72 *Rome Against Rome* (1964)
01/23/72 *Konga* (1961)
01/30/72 *Warning from Space* (1956)
02/06/72 *The Mysterians* (1957)
02/13/72 *Planet of the Vampires* (1965)
02/20/72 *Majin, Monster of Terror* (1966)
02/27/72 *Godzilla vs. The Thing* (1964)
03/05/72 *Horrors of the Black Museum* (1959)
03/12/72 *Gamera vs. Monster X* (1970)
03/19/72 *The X from Outer Space* (1967)
03/26/72 *The Amazing Colossal Man* (1957)
04/02/72 *Destroy All Planets* (1968)
04/09/72 *The Claw Monsters* (1966)
04/16/72 *Dr. Satan's Robot* (1966)
04/23/72 *Slaves of the Invisible Monster* (1966)
04/30/72 *Sky Above Heaven* (1965)
05/07/72 *Mission Stardust* (1967)
05/14/72 *Mothra* (1961)

05/21/72 *War of the Monsters* (1966)
05/28/72 *Ghidorah, the Three-Headed Monster* (1964)
06/04/72 *Terror in the Crypt* (1964)
06/11/72 *Cyclotrode "X"* (1966)
06/18/72 *D-Day on Mars* (1966)
06/25/72 *Torpedo of Doom* (1966)
07/02/72 *Sharad of Atlantis* (1966)
07/09/72 *Retik, the Moon Menace* (1966)
07/16/72 *Flight of the Lost Balloon* (1961)
07/23/72 *Curse of the Demon* (1957)
07/30/72 *Sombra, the Spider Woman* (1966)
08/06/72 *War of the Monsters* (1966)
08/13/72 *The Angry Red Planet* (1959)
08/20/72 *Rome Against Rome* (1964)
08/27/72 *The Bamboo Saucer* (1968)
09/03/72 *Horrors of the Black Museum* (1959)
09/10/72 *She Gods of Shark Reef* (1958)

SATURDAY CHILLER
(WDCA Channel 20 before hosted by Count Gore De Vol)

In January 1970, Channel 20 replaced its Saturday afternoon airing of *House of Horrors* with *Saturday Chiller*. Despite the title change, the redubbed program offered the same kinds of films as its predecessor. *Saturday Chiller* left the air in August 1970 but returned the following May in a new time slot. The program continued to air Saturday afternoons, eventually hosted by Count Gore De Vol. Hosting two Saturday horror shows however proved too much for the poor Count, so he eventually stopped hosting the afternoon show. There was even a *Sunday Chiller* that ran in December 1972.

Airs at 2:00 p.m.
01/24/70 *Castle of Evil* (1966)
01/31/70 *Gammera the Invincible* (1966)
02/07/70 *In the Year 2889* (1967)
02/14/70 *Night Caller from Outer Space* (1965)
02/21/70 *Sky Above Heaven* (1965)
02/28/70 *Amphibian Man* (1962)
03/07/70 *Castle of Evil* (1966)
03/14/70 *Attack of the Robots* (1966)
03/21/70 *D-Day on Mars* (1966)
03/28/70 *Godzilla vs. The Thing* (1964)
04/04/70 *I Was a Teenage Frankenstein* (1957)
04/11/70 *Planet of the Vampires* (1965)
04/18/70 *The Spider* (1958)
04/25/70 *War of the Monsters* (1966)
05/02/70 *The Amazing Colossal Man* (1957)
05/09/70 *War of the Colossal Beast* (1958)
05/16/70 *How to Make a Monster* (1958)
05/23/70 *The Time Travelers* (1964)
05/30/70 *Attack of the Puppet People* (1958)

> **⑳ Saturday Chiller.**
> "Godzilla vs. The Thing," Akina Takarada, Yuriki Hoshi. 1964.

06/06/70 *Creature of Destruction* (1967)
06/13/70 *Voodoo Woman* (1957)
06/20/70 *No Survivors Please.* (1964)

> **⑳ Saturday Chiller.**
> "War of the Monsters." Kojiro Hongo, Kyoka Enami. 1966.

06/27/70 *Teenage Monster* (1958)
07/04/70 *The Crawling Eye* (1958)
07/11/70 *Maneater of Hydra* (1967)
07/18/70 *Invasion of the Saucer Men* (1957)
07/25/70 *Monster from a Prehistoric Planet* (1967)
08/01/70 *The Incredibly Strange Creatures Who Stopped Living and Became Mixed-Up Zombies!!?* (1964)
08/08/70 *Beginning of the End* (1957)
08/15/70 *Flight to Mars* (1951)
08/22/70 *Amphibian Man* (1962)

Airs at 12:30 p.m.
05/01/71 *Goliath and the Vampires* (1961)
05/08/71 *A Bucket of Blood* (1959)
05/15/71 *Return of the Giant Monsters* (1967)
05/22/71 *Blood of Dracula* (1957)
05/29/71 *Attack of the Robots* (1966)
06/05/71 *It Came from Beneath the Sea* (1955)
06/12/71 *Curse of the Demon* (1957)
06/19/71 *Amphibian Man* (1962)
06/26/71 *Maneater of Hydra* (1967)
07/03/71 *It Conquered the World* (1956)
07/10/71 *Night of the Blood Beast* (1958)
07/17/71 *The Undead* (1957)
07/24/71 *Ghidorah, the Three-Headed Monster* (1964)
07/31/71 *Devil Bat's Daughter* (1946)
08/07/71 *Flight to Mars* (1951)
08/14/71 *The Undying Monster* (1942)
08/21/71 *Horrors of the Black Museum* (1959)
08/28/71 *In the Year 2889* (1967)
09/04/71 *Gammera the Invincible* (1966)
09/11/71 *The Return of Giant Majin* (1966)
09/18/71 *The Incredibly Strange Creatures Who Stopped Living and Became Mixed-Up Zombies!!?* (1964)
09/25/71 *The Beast with a Million Eyes* (1955)
10/02/71 *House of Frankenstein* (1944)
10/09/71 *The Invisible Woman* (1940)
10/16/71 *Night Monster* (1942)
10/23/71 *WereWolf of London* (1935)
10/30/71 *The Wolf Man* (1941)
11/06/71 *Black Friday* (1940)
11/13/71 *Dracula's Daughter* (1936)
11/20/71 *The Invisible Man Returns* (1940)
11/27/71 *Frankenstein Meets the Wolf Man* (1943)
12/04/71 *The Missing Guest* (1938)
12/11/71 Didn't air
12/18/71 *The Spider Woman Strikes Back* (1946)
12/25/71 *The Invisible Ray* (1936)
01/01/72 *The Crime of Doctor Hallet* (1938)
01/08/72 *Cult of the Cobra* (1955)
01/15/72 *The Mad Ghoul* (1943)
01/22/72 *Creature of Destruction* (1967)
01/29/72 *The Strange Door* (1951)

George Zucco in *The Mad Ghoul*, which aired January 15 1972.

02/05/72 *The Black Castle* (1952)
02/12/72 *Die, Monster, Die!* (1965)
02/19/72 *Return of the Giant Monsters* (1967)
02/26/72 *The Unearthly* (1957)
03/04/72 *Circus of Fear* (1966)
03/11/72 *Nightmare Alley* (1947)
03/18/72 *The Devil's Messenger* (1961)
03/25/72 *Horror Hotel* (1960)
04/01/72 *Yongary, Monster from the Deep* (1967)
04/08/72 *Castle of Evil* (1966)
04/15/72 *The Human Monster* (1939)
04/22/72 *Devil Bat's Daughter* (1946)
04/29/72 *Beast of Morocco* (1966)
05/06/72 *Blood of Dracula* (1957)
05/13/72 *How to Make a Monster* (1958)
05/20/72 *I Was a Teenage Frankenstein* (1957)
05/27/72 *Teenage Caveman* (1958)
06/03/72 *Maneater of Hydra* (1967)
06/10/72 *Voodoo Woman* (1957)
06/17/72 *Attack of the Puppet People* (1958)
06/24/72 *The Undead* (1957)
07/01/72 *The Blancheville Monster* (1963)
07/08/72 *Invisible Creature* (1960)
07/15/72 *The Hand* (1960)
07/22/72 *Attack of the Giant Leeches* (1959)
07/29/72 *The Killer Shrews* (1959)
08/05/72 *Cat Girl* (1957)
08/12/72 *The Brain Eaters* (1958)
08/19/72 *Gammera the Invincible* (1966)
08/26/72 *Return of the Ape Man* (1944)
09/02/72 *It Conquered the World* (1956)
09/09/72 *Invasion of the Saucer Men* (1957)

09/16/72 *The Amazing Colossal Man* (1957) [Airs at 1:00 p.m.]
09/23/72 *Circus of Horrors* (1960) [Airs at 1:00 p.m.]

Airs at 12:00 p.m.
09/30/72 *The Mummy's Ghost* (1944); *A Bucket of Blood* (1959)
10/07/72 *Blood of Dracula* (1957); *The Hand* (1960)
10/14/72 *I Was a Teenage Werewolf* (1957); *The Amazing Transparent Man* (1960)
10/21/72 *The Spider* (1945); *The Day the Earth Froze* (1959)
10/28/72 *How to Make a Monster* (1958); *Terror from the Year 5000* (1958)
11/04/72 *The Frozen Ghost* (1945); *I Was a Teenage Frankenstein* (1957)
11/11/72 *The Mummy's Hand* (1940); *War of the Colossal Beast* (1958)
11/18/72 *She-Wolf of London* (1946); *Night of the Blood Beast* (1958)
11/25/72 *Man Made Monster* (1941); *Dead Man's Eyes* (1944)
12/02/72 *12 to the Moon* (1960); *Horror Island* (1941)
12/09/72 *The Human Monster* (1939); *Battle in Outer Space* (1959)
12/16/72 Didn't air

> **⑳ Saturday Chiller.**
> "The Mummy's Hand," Dick Foran, John Carradine. 1940. Also: "War of the Colossal Beast." Sally Fraser, Roger Pace. 1958.

12/23/72 *Missile Monsters* (1958); *The Giant Gila Monster* (1959)
12/30/72 *The She-Creature* (1956); *Attack of the Puppet People* (1958)

> **⑳ Saturday Chiller.**
> "Night of the Blood Beast," Michael Emmet, Angela Greene. 1958.

01/06/73 *Attack of the Giant Leeches* (1959); *The Undead* (1957)
01/13/73 *The Beast with a Million Eyes* (1955); *Invasion of the Star Creatures* (1962)
01/20/73 *The Killer Shrews* (1959); *It Came from Beneath the Sea* (1955)
01/27/73 *The Son of Dr. Jekyll* (1951) [Airs at 2:00 p.m.]

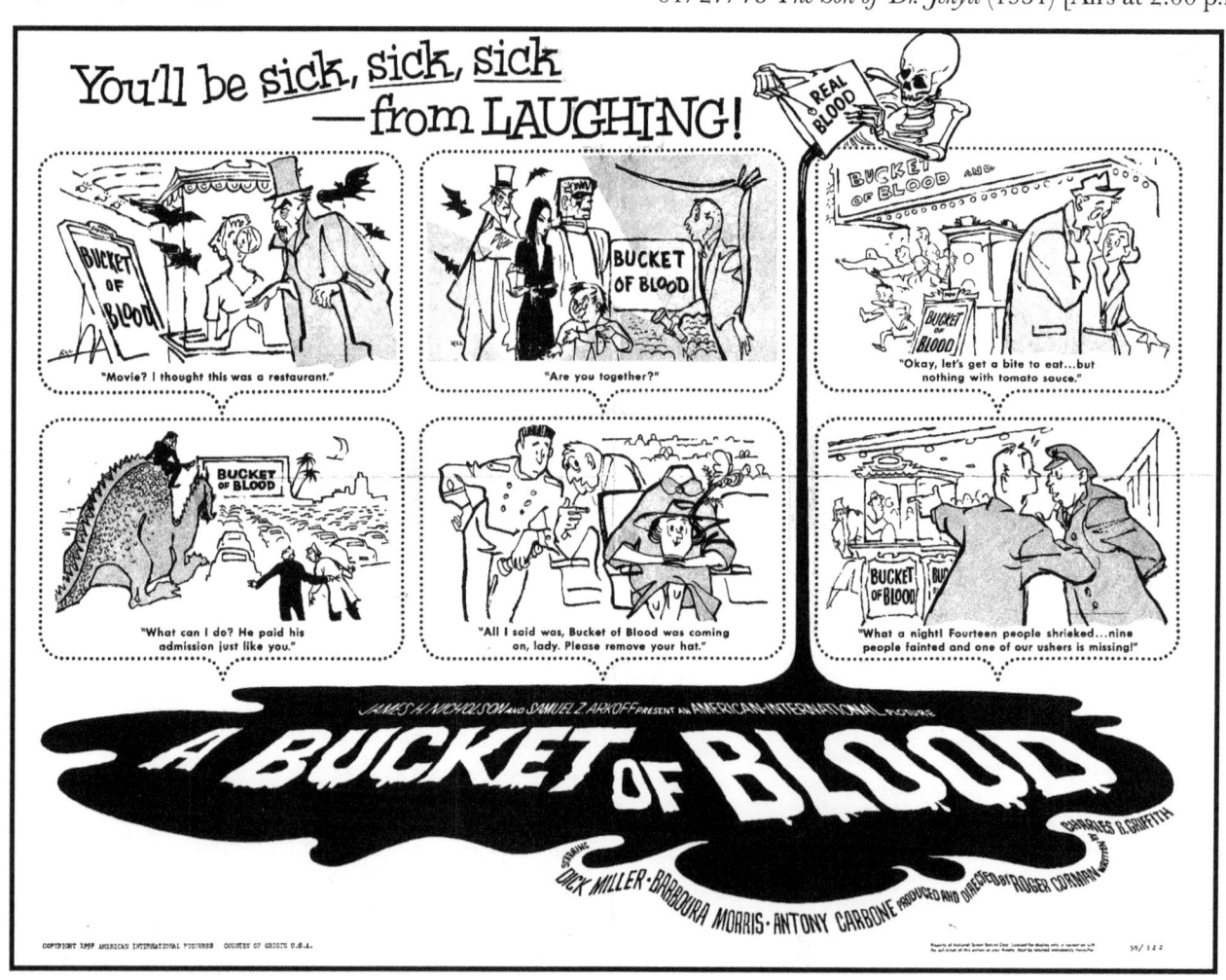

Airs at 12:00 p.m.
04/19/75 *Track of the Vampire* (1966)
04/26/75 *The Crimson Cult* (1968)
05/03/75 *The Bloody Judge* (1970)
05/10/75 *Dracula vs. Frankenstein* (1971)
05/17/75 *Godzilla vs. the Smog Monster* (1971)
05/24/75 *Blood of Dracula* (1957)
05/31/75 *The Headless Ghost* (1959)
06/07/75 *A Bucket of Blood* (1959)
06/14/75 *Dead Eyes of London* (1961)
06/21/75 *How to Make a Monster* (1958)
06/28/75 *Teenage Caveman* (1958)
07/05/75 *Invasion* (1965)
07/12/75 *X* (1963)
07/19/75 *Space Monster* (1965)
07/26/75 *Reptilicus* (1961)
08/02/75 *The Amazing Colossal Man* (1957)
08/09/75 *It Conquered the World* (1956)
08/16/75 *I Was a Teenage Frankenstein* (1957)
08/23/75 *I Was a Teenage Werewolf* (1957)
08/30/75 *War of the Colossal Beast* (1958)
09/06/75 *Cry of the Bewitched* (1957)
09/13/75 *Attack of the Mushroom People* (1963)
09/20/75 *4D Man* (1959)
09/27/75 *Frankenstein Meets the Spacemonster* (1965)
10/04/75 *It's Alive!* (1969)
10/11/75 *The Beach Girls and the Monster* (1965)
10/18/75 *The Terror* (1963)
10/25/75 *Unearthly Stranger* (1963)
11/01/75 *Son of Godzilla* (1967)
11/08/75 *House on Haunted Hill* (1959)
11/15/75 *Ghidorah, the Three-Headed Monster* (1964)

SUNDAY CHILLER
(Airs at 2:30 p.m. on WDCA Channel 20)

11/26/72 *Circus of Fear* (1966)

> 2.30 (7) Apartment C-410.
> (9) The Thrill Seekers.
> (20) Sunday Chiller.

12/03/72 *Mothra* (1961)
12/10/72 *Curse of the Demon* (1957)
12/17/72 *No Survivors Please.* (1964)
12/24/72 *Attack of the Robots* (1966)
12/31/72 *Frankenstein Conquers the World* (1965)

CREATURE FEATURE
(Saturday on WDCA Channel 20
not hosted by Count Gore de Vol)

The Great Zucchini's *Supernatural Theater* ended in September 1970. A few months later WDCA launched its most famous horror program yet. *Creature Feature* debuted the first Saturday night of 1971 with a prime time showing of *The Lodger*. Soon afterwards, the start time was moved up half an hour allowing for frequent double features. It was moved to its more familiar 11:00 p.m. time slot the week before a certain Count would begin hosting duties.

Airs at 9:00 p.m.

01/02/71 *The Lodger* (1944)
01/09/71 *A Bucket of Blood* (1959); *The Killer Shrews* (1959)

Airs at 8:30 p.m.
01/16/71 *The Horrible Dr. Hichcock* (1962)
01/23/71 *The Brain Eaters* (1958); *Blood of Dracula* (1957)
01/30/71 *Jack the Ripper* (1959)
02/06/71 *Horrors of the Black Museum* (1959)
02/13/71 *Shock Treatment* (1964)
02/20/71 *The 10th Victim* (1965)
02/27/71 *Daughter of the Mind* (1969)
03/06/71 *I Was a Teenage Frankenstein* (1957)
03/13/71 *I Was a Teenage Werewolf* (1957)
03/20/71 *Mission Stardust* (1967)
03/27/71 *The Return of Giant Majin* (1966)
04/03/71 *The Astounding She-Monster* (1957); *The Headless Ghost* (1959)
04/10/71 *Attack of the Giant Leeches* (1959); *The Beast with a Million Eyes* (1955)
04/17/71 *Ghost of Dragstrip Hollow* (1959); *She Gods of Shark Reef* (1958)
04/24/71 *Teenage Caveman* (1958); *Attack of the Puppet People* (1958)
05/01/71 *The Mad Magician* (1954); *The Tingler* (1959)
05/08/71 *Murder, Inc.* (1960)
05/15/71 *Phone Call from a Stranger* (1952)
05/22/71 *The Lost World* (1960)
05/29/71 *Nightmare Alley* (1947)
06/05/71 *The Brain Eaters* (1958)
06/12/71 *The Killer Shrews* (1959); *The Vampire Bat* (1933)
06/19/71 *The Hideous Sun Demon* (1958); *Cat Girl* (1957)
06/26/71 *The Horrible Dr. Hichcock* (1962); *The Claw Monsters* (1966)
07/03/71 *The Unearthly* (1957); *Beginning of the End* (1957)
07/10/71 *The Phantom of the Opera* (1943)
07/17/71 *Return of the Ape Man* (1944); *The Son of Dr. Jekyll* (951)
07/24/71 *The Hideous Sun Demon* (1958)
07/31/71 *The Human Monster* (1939); *The Devil's Messenger* (1961)

> ⓴ **Creature Feature.** "The Human Monster." Assigned to investigate five drownings, a Scotland Yard investigator discovers the "monster" responsible. Bela Lugosi, 1940. Also: "The Devil's Messenger." A beautiful murder victim returns to earth as the devil's emissary. Lon Chaney, Jr. 1961.

08/07/71 *The She-Creature* (1956); *The Headless Ghost* (1959)
08/14/71 *The Spider* (1958); *Invasion of the Saucer Men* (1957)

> ⓴ **Creature Feature.** "Daughter of the Mind." A scientist seeks the aid of a psychologist specializing in psychic phenomena when the spirit of his deceased daughter begins appearing and talking to him. Ray Milland, Gene Tierney, Don Murray. 1969.

08/21/71 *Voodoo Woman* (1957); *I Was a Teenage Frankenstein* (1957)
08/28/71 *The X from Outer Space* (1967)
09/04/71 *Dead Man's Eyes* (1944); *The Horrible Dr. Hichcock* (1962)
09/11/71 *Night Key* (1937); *Fog Island* (1945)
09/18/71 *The Invisible Man* (1933); *Lost Planet Airmen* (1951)
09/25/71 *The Black Cat* (1934); *Captive Wild Woman* (1943)
10/02/71 *The Shuttered Room* (1967)
10/09/71 *The Innocents* (1961)
10/16/71 *Frankenstein* (1931); *Bride of Frankenstein* (1935)
10/23/71 *Dracula* (1931); *The Mummy* (1932)
10/30/71 *The Mummy's Hand* (1940); *Horror Island* (1941)

Bette Davis in *Hush...Hush, Sweet Charlotte*

11/06/71 *Hush...Hush, Sweet Charlotte* (1964)
11/13/71 *What Ever Happened to Baby Jane?* (1962)
11/20/71 Didn't air
11/27/71 *The Mummy's Tomb* (1942); *Murder in the Blue Room* (1944)
12/04/71 *Murders in the Rue Morgue* (1932); *The Mummy's Ghost* (1944)
12/11/71 *Bluebeard* (1963)
12/18/71 *Blood of Dracula* (1957) *
12/25/71 *Frankenstein Conquers the World* (1965) *
01/01/72 *The Brain Eaters* (1958); *Night of the Blood Beast* (1958)
01/08/72 *The Ghost of Frankenstein* (1942); *Destroy All Monsters* (1968)
01/15/72 *House of Dracula* (1945); *House of Horrors* (1946)
01/22/72 *Gammera the Invincible* (1966); *The Frozen Ghost* (1945)
01/29/72 *Goliath and the Vampires* (1961); *The Jungle Captive* (1945)
02/05/72 *Revenge of the Creature* (1955); *She-Wolf of London* (1946)
02/12/72 *Son of Frankenstein* (1939); *Calling Dr. Death* (1943)
02/19/72 *The Tingler* (1959) *
02/26/72 *Creature from the Black Lagoon* (1954) *
03/04/72 *Son of Dracula* (1943); *Man Made Monster* (1941)
03/11/72 *A Bucket of Blood* (1959); *Cat Girl* (1957)
03/18/72 *Day the World Ended* (1955); *The Headless Ghost* (1959)
03/25/72 *I Was a Teenage Werewolf* (1957); *Mystery of the White Room* (1939)
04/01/72 *Peeping Tom* (1960); *The Crosby Case* (1934)
04/08/72 *Satan's Satellites* (1958); *The Devil's Messenger* (1961)
04/15/72 *The Son of Dr. Jekyll* (1951); *The Man Who Cried Wolf* (1937)
04/22/72 *Horror Island* (1941); *Mystery of Marie Roget* (1942)
04/29/72 *House of Frankenstein* (1944); *The Mummy's Curse* (1944)
05/06/72 *The Wolf Man* (1941); *The Black Cat* (1934)
05/13/72 *Dracula* (1931); *Dead Man's Eyes* (1944)
05/20/72 *Frankenstein* (1931); *The Ghost of Frankenstein* (1942)
05/27/72 *The Invisible Man* (1933); *Rendezvous at Midnight* (1935)
06/03/72 *Captive Wild Woman* (1943); *Night Key* (1937)
06/10/72 *Pillow of Death* (1945); *Secret of the Chateau* (1934)
06/17/72 *The Strange Case of Dr. Rx* (1942); *Secret of the Blue Room* (1933)
06/24/72 *The Cat Creeps* (1946); *The Crimson Canary* (1945)
07/01/72 *Black Friday* (1940); *Weird Woman* (1944)
07/08/72 *Bride of Frankenstein* (1935); *Murder in the Blue Room* (1944)
07/15/72 *Frankenstein Meets the Wolf Man* (1943); *Murders in the Rue Morgue* (1932)
07/22/72 *The Invisible Man Returns* (1940); *The Raven* (1935)
07/29/72 *The Mummy* (1932); *The Mummy's Hand* (1940)
08/05/72 *Dracula's Daughter* (1936); *House of Horrors* (1946)
08/12/72 *Invisible Agent* (1942); *The Crime of Doctor Hallet* (1938)
08/19/72 *The Invisible Man's Revenge* (1944); *Lost Planet Airmen* (1951)
08/26/72 *WereWolf of London* (1935); *The Unearthly* (1957)
09/02/72 Didn't air
09/09/72 *The Jungle Captive* (1945); *Horror Hotel* (1960)
09/16/72 *The Invisible Ray* (1936; *Devil Bat's Daughter* (1946)
09/23/72 *The Mummy's Tomb* (1942); *Calling Dr. Death* (1943)

09/30/72 House of Dracula (1945)
10/07/72 The Man Who Reclaimed His Head (1934); Jungle Woman (1944)
10/14/72 Revenge of the Creature (1955)
10/21/72 Son of Frankenstein (1939)
10/28/72 Didn't air
11/04/72 Dracula (1931)
11/11/72 Creature from the Black Lagoon (1954)
11/18/72 Frankenstein (1931)
11/25/72 The Mummy's Tomb (1942)
12/02/72 The Black Cat (1934)
12/09/72 The Ghost of Frankenstein (1942)
12/16/72 The Invisible Man (1933)
12/23/72 The Mummy's Ghost (1944)
12/30/72 Didn't air
01/06/73 The Wolf Man (1941)
01/13/73 The Creature Walks Among Us (1956)
01/20/73 The Mummy (1932)
01/27/73 The Invisible Man Returns (1940) [Note: Airs at 11:00 p.m.]

*Delayed until 10:30 p.m. due to sporting event

Count Gore De Vol hosts *Creature Feature* February 3, 1973 through September 1, 1979. Football games preempted the next three shows. When *Creature Feature* resumes in October, there is no host. *Creature Feature* periodically leaves the air at various points during Gore's absence. Count Gore retakes hosting duties when *Creature Feature* returns in October 1984.

Airs at 11:00 p.m.
10/06/79 The Amazing Colossal Man (1957)
10/13/79 Assignment Terror (1970)
10/20/79 Dementia 13 (1963)
10/27/79 Didn't air
11/03/79 Didn't air
11/10/79 Tales of Terror (1962)
11/17/79 Dr. Cyclops (1940)
11/24/79 Didn't air
12/01/79 Castle of Terror (1964)
Doesn't air for four weeks
01/05/80 The Brides of Fu Manchu (1966)
01/12/80 Didn't air
01/19/80 Torture Garden (1967)
01/26/80 The Tingler (1959)
02/02/80 The Castle of Fu Manchu (1969)
02/09/80 Corridors of Blood (1958)
02/16/80 Chamber of Horrors (1940)
02/23/80 Ghidorah, the Three-Headed Monster (1964)
03/01/80 Track of the Vampire (1966)
03/08/80 Dead Eyes of London (1961)
03/15/80 Evil Brain from Outer Space (1965)
03/22/80 Didn't air
03/29/80 The Flesh Eaters (1964)
04/05/80 The Beast from 20,000 Fathoms (1953)
04/12/80 Marooned (1969)
04/19/80 Coast of Skeletons (1965)
04/26/80 Planet of the Vampires (1965)
05/03/80 The Castle of the Living Dead (1964)
05/10/80 Master of the World (1961)
05/17/80 The Crimson Cult (1968)

05/24/80 *Satanik* (1968)
05/31/80 *House on Haunted Hill* (1959)
06/07/80 *Castle of Terror* (1964)
06/14/80 *Curse of the Demon* (1957)
06/21/80 *Track of the Vampire* (1966)

Airs at 11:30 p.m.
06/04/83 *The Invisible Man* (1933)
06/11/83 *The Invisible Man Returns* (1940)
06/18/83 *Earth vs. the Flying Saucers* (1956)
06/25/83 *Panic in Year Zero* (1962)
07/02/83 *X* (1963)
07/09/83 *Dagora, the Space Monster* (1964)
07/16/83 *Frankenstein Meets the Wolf Man* (1943)
07/23/83 *Godzilla: King of the Monsters* (1956)
07/30/83 *The Deadly Mantis* (1957)
08/06/83 *The Mole People* (1956)
08/13/83 *The Black Cat* (1941)
08/20/83 *The Brides of Dracula* (1960)
08/27/83 *The Curse of the Werewolf* (1961)
09/03/83 *Horror House* (1969)
09/10/83 *Curse of the Swamp Creature* (1966)
09/17/83 *Konga* (1961)

Count Gore's last presentation of *Creature Feature* was on May 23, 1987. The following week's show was preempted for sports. When the horror films returned in June, Count Gore was no longer hosting.

Airs at Midnight
06/06/87 *The Time Travelers* (1964)
06/13/87 *The Phantom Planet* (1961)
06/20/87 *The Brain that Wouldn't Die* (1962)
06/27/87 *Horror House* (1969)
07/04/87 *The Night the World Exploded* (1957)
07/11/87 *The Frozen Dead* (1966)
07/18/87 *Kong Island* (1968)
07/25/87 *Race with the Devil* (1975)
08/01/87 *Attack of the Mushroom People* (1963)
08/08/87 *The Last Days of Planet Earth* (1974)
08/15/87 *The Angry Red Planet* (1959)
08/29/87 *Web of Violence* (1966)
09/05/87 *Dracula vs. Frankenstein* (1971)

Saturday Afternoon

Airs at 11:30 a.m.
06/26/76 *Black Friday* (1940)
07/03/76 *The Frozen Ghost* (1945)
07/10/76 *Frankenstein* (1931)
07/17/76 *Bride of Frankenstein* (1935)
07/24/76 *Son of Frankenstein* (1939)
07/31/76 *The Ghost of Frankenstein* (1942)

08/07/76 *Dead Eyes of London* (1961)
08/14/76 *Fire Maidens of Outer Space* (1956)
08/21/76 *Mission Stardust* (1967)
08/28/76 *Zontar, the Thing from Venus* (1966)

Airs at 12:00 p.m.
09/04/76 *Voyage to the Prehistoric Planet* (1965)
09/11/76 *Attack of the Crab Monsters* (1957)
09/18/76 *Man in Outer Space* (1962)
09/25/76 *Yongary, Monster from the Deep* (1967)
10/02/76 *Reptilicus* (1961)
10/09/76 *Godzilla vs. the Sea Monster* (1966)
10/16/76 *Son of Godzilla* (1967)
10/23/76 *Mothra* (1961)
10/30/76 *Battle in Outer Space* (1959)
11/06/76 *Gamera vs. Monster X* (1970)
11/13/76 *Godzilla vs. the Smog Monster* (1971)
11/20/76 *Ghidorah, the Three-Headed Monster* (1964)

Airs at 11:00 a.m.
11/27/76 *Destroy All Monsters* (1968)
12/04/76 *Kronos* (1957)
12/11/76 *Attack of the Mushroom People* (1963)
12/18/76 *Yog, Monster from Space* (1970)
12/25/76 *Santa Claus Conquers the Martians* (1964)

Airs at 12:00 p.m.
01/01/77 *Dagora, the Space Monster* (1964)
01/08/77 *The Giant Behemoth* (1959)
01/15/77 *Attack of the Monsters* (1969)
01/22/77 *The X from Outer Space* (1967)
01/29/77 *Monster from a Prehistoric Planet* (1967)
02/05/77 *Godzilla vs. The Thing* (1964)
02/12/77 *Gorgo* (1961)
02/19/77 *Die, Monster, Die* (1965)
02/26/77 *Curse of the Swamp Creature* (1966)
03/05/77 *Beyond the Time Barrier* (1960)

Airs at 1:30 p.m.
03/12/77 *The Phantom Planet* (1961)
03/19/77 *Journey to the Seventh Planet* (1962)
03/26/77 *Invasion* (1965)
04/02/77 *Night Monster* (1942)
04/09/77 *Frankenstein Meets the Wolf Man* (1943)
04/16/77 *The Invisible Man's Revenge* (1944)
04/23/77 *Dracula* (1931)
04/30/77 *WereWolf of London* (1935)
05/07/77 *Creature from the Black Lagoon* (1954)
05/14/77 *The Wolf Man* (1941)
05/21/77 *Revenge of the Creature* (1955)
05/28/77 *The Black Castle* (1952)
06/04/77 *Night Monster* (1942)
06/11/77 *Son of Dracula* (1943)

Robert Tayman as Count Mitterhaus in Vampire Circus, shown 11/12/77

06/18/77 *Tarantula* (1955)
06/25/77 *Cult of the Cobra* (1955)
07/02/77 *The Invisible Ray* (1936)
07/09/77 *House of Frankenstein* (1944)
07/16/77 *Reptilicus* (1961)
07/23/77 *The Mummy's Tomb* (1942)
07/30/77 *Son of Frankenstein* (1939)
08/06/77 *The Wasp Woman* (1959)
08/13/77 *World Without End* (1956)
08/20/77 Didn't air
08/27/77 *Cry of the Bewitched* (1957)
09/03/77 *House of Horrors* (1946)
09/10/77 *The Ghost of Frankenstein* (1942)
09/17/77 *The Spider Woman Strikes Back* (1946)
09/24/77 *Yog, Monster from Space* (1970)
10/01/77 *Queen of Outer Space* (1958)
10/08/77 *Jesse James Meets Frankenstein's Daughter* (1966)
10/15/77 *Son of Godzilla* (1967)
10/22/77 *Creature from the Haunted Sea* (1961)
10/29/77 *Atragon* (1963)
11/05/77 *The Beast of Hollow Mountain* (1956)
11/12/77 *Vampire Circus* (1972)
11/19/77 *House of Dracula* (1945)
11/26/77 *The Terror* (1963)
12/03/77 *It Came from Outer Space* (1953)

12/10/77 *The Thing That Couldn't Die* (1958)
12/17/77 *She-Wolf of London* (1946)
12/24/77 *The Mummy's Ghost* (1944)
12/31/77 Didn't air
01/07/78 *The Giant Claw* (1957)
01/14/78 *Mothra* (1961)
01/21/78 *Monster from a Prehistoric Planet* (1967)
01/28/78 *War of the Monsters* (1966)
02/04/78 *The Human Duplicators* (1965)
02/11/78 *4D Man* (1959)
Didn't air for several weeks due to pro ice hockey.
04/15/78 *Planets Against Us* (1962)
04/22/78 *The Diabolical Dr. Z* (1966)
04/29/78 *Panic in Year Zero* (1962)
05/06/78 *The Wild, Wild Planet* (1966)
05/13/78 *In the Year 2889* (1967)
05/20/78 *Son of Frankenstein* (1939)
05/27/78 *Battle of the Worlds* (1961)
06/03/78 *The Beast with a Million Eyes* (1955)
06/10/78 *Space Monster* (1965)
06/17/78 *Pyro* (1964)
06/24/78 *The Terror* (1963)
07/01/78 *The Wolf Man* (1941)
07/08/78 *Creature from the Black Lagoon* (1954)
07/15/78 *The Mummy* (1932)

07/22/78 *Revenge of the Creature* (1955)
07/29/78 *Frankenstein* (1931)
08/05/78 *Frankenstein Meets the Wolf Man* (1943)
08/12/78 *She-Wolf of London* (1946)
08/19/78 *The Mummy's Hand* (1940)
08/26/78 *The Ghost of Frankenstein* (1942)
09/02/78 *Cry of the Bewitched* (1957)
09/09/78 *War of the Monsters* (1966)
09/16/78 *Godzilla vs. The Thing* (1964)
09/23/78 *Attack of the Puppet People* (1958)
09/30/78 *The Brain from Planet Arous* (1957)
10/07/78 *Monster from a Prehistoric Planet* (1967)

Airs at 2:00 p.m.
10/14/78 *The Invisible Man* (1933)
10/21/78 *War of the Monsters* (1966)
10/28/78 *The Mummy's Ghost* (1944)
11/04/78 *World Without End* (1956)
11/11/78 *War of the Satellites* (1958)
11/18/78 *Curse of the Fly* (1965)
11/25/78 *Mesa of Lost Women* (1953)
12/02/78 *Planet of the Vampires* (1965)
12/09/78 *Die, Monster, Die* (1965)
12/16/78 Didn't air
12/23/78 *The Beast with a Million Eyes* (1955)
12/30/78 *Invasion of the Saucer Men* (1957)
01/06/79 *They Came from Beyond Space* (1967)
01/13/79 *From the Earth to the Moon* (1958)
01/20/79 *The Atomic Submarine* (1959)
01/27/79 *Creature from the Black Lagoon* (1954)
02/03/79 *War Between the Planets* (1966)
02/10/79 *The Creation of the Humanoids* (1962)
02/17/79 *The Time Travelers* (1964)
02/24/79 *Rome Against Rome* (1964)
03/03/79 *Attack of the Mushroom People* (1963)
Didn't air for several weeks due to pro ice hockey.
05/05/79 *Planet of the Apes* (1968)
05/12/79 *Beneath the Planet of the Apes* (1970)
05/19/79 *Escape from the Planet of the Apes* (1971)
05/26/79 *Conquest of the Planet of the Apes* (1972)
06/02/79 *Voyage to the End of the Universe* (1963)
06/09/79 *Revenge of the Creature* (1955)
06/16/79 Didn't Air
06/23/79 *The Wolf Man* (1941)
06/30/79 *Son of Dracula* (1943)
07/07/79 *Creature of Destruction* (1967)
07/14/79 *Majin, Monster of Terror* (1966)
07/21/79 *Rome Against Rome* (1964)
07/28/79 *Monster from a Prehistoric Planet* (1967)
08/04/79 *The Giant Claw* (1957)
08/11/79 *The Night the World Exploded* (1957)
08/18/79 *The H-Man* (1959)
08/25/79 *12 to the Moon* (1960)

09/01/79 *Indestructible Man* (1956)
09/08/79 Didn't air
09/15/79 *Not of This Earth* (1957)
09/22/79 *House on Haunted Hill* (1959)
09/29/79 *Frankenstein* (1931)
10/06/79 *Man in Outer Space* (1962)

Airs at 1:30 p.m.
10/13/79 *I Was a Teenage Werewolf* (1957)
10/20/79 *Unearthly Stranger* (1963)
10/27/79 *Attack of the Mushroom People* (1963)
11/03/79 *War of the Monsters* (1966)
11/10/79 *Day the World Ended* (1955)
11/17/79 Didn't air
11/24/79 *The Spider* (1958)
12/01/79 Didn't air
12/08/79 *Graveyard of Horror* (1971)
12/15/79 Didn't air
12/22/79 *Horror Castle* (1963)
12/29/79 *The Curse of the Living Corpse* (1964)
01/05/80 *Panic in Year Zero* (1962)
Didn't air for several weeks due to basketball
03/01/80 *The Astro-Zombies* (1968)
03/08/80 *Countess Dracula* (1971)
03/15/80 *Quatermass and the Pit* (1967)

03/22/80 *Graveyard of Horror* (1971)
03/29/80 *Journey to the Unknown* (1969)
04/05/80 *Fiend Without a Face* (1958)

SCI-FI THEATER
(Saturday at 2:00 p.m. on WBFF Channel 45)

With *Ghost Host* airing Saturday nights on the newly launched WBFF-TV, the afternoons featured sci-fi thrillers from the '50s and '60s. However, the program lasted only through October 1971.

04/17/71 *Invaders from Space* (1965)
04/24/71 *Evil Brain from Outer Space* (1965)

> **45 Sci-Fi Theater.**
> "Evil Brain from Outer Space." A group of men try to develop a formula to destroy the brain of a diabolical genius. Harold Kim. 1965.

05/01/71 *The Final War* (1960)
05/08/71 *The Creation of the Humanoids* (1962)
05/15/71 *Invaders from Space* (1965)
05/22/71 *Red Planet Mars* (1952)
05/29/71 *Invasion of the Neptune Men* (1964)
06/05/71 *Curse of the Demon* (1957)
06/12/71 *The Giant Claw* (1957)
06/19/71 *The H-Man* (1959)
06/26/71 *Creature with the Atom Brain* (1955)
07/03/71 *It Came from Outer Space* (1953)
07/10/71 *The Magnetic Monster* (1953)
07/17/71 *The Gamma People* (1956)
07/24/71 *Creature with the Atom Brain* (1955)
07/31/71 *The Lost Missile* (1958)
08/07/71 *The Monster that Challenged the World* (1957)
08/14/71 *The Day the Earth Stood Still* (1951)
08/21/71 *Gog* (1954)
08/28/71 *Two Lost Worlds* (1951)
09/04/71 *Terror is A Man* (1959)
09/11/71 *The Twonky* (1953)
09/18/71 *Daughter of the Sun God* (1962)
09/25/71 *Treasure of the Petrified Forest* (1965)

> **45 Sci-Fi Theater.**
> "The Monster that Challenged the World." Giant radioactive beasts which cause many murders are unearthed by atomic experiments. Tim Holt, Hans Conreid. 1957.

10/02/71 *Captain Blackjack* (1950)
10/09/71 *Planet of the Vampires* (1965)
10/16/71 *The Neanderthal Man* (1953)
10/23/71 *Atragon* (1963)
10/30/71 *Panic in Year Zero* (1962)

WEIRD TALES / WEIRD TALES II
(WTOP Channel 9)

Sir Graves Ghastly presented his last film on May 7, 1971. The following week his Friday night slot was re-dubbed *Weird Tales*. Second features were sometimes shown as *Weird Tales II*. However, not all the second films were genre offerings. Therefore, second features are listed only if they qualify as "monster movies."

Airs Friday at 11:30 p.m.
05/14/71 *The Wolf Man* (1941); *Curse of the Crying Woman* (1963)
05/21/71 *The Invisible Man Returns* (1940)
05/28/71 *The Raven* (1935)
06/04/71 *Son of Frankenstein* (1939); *Dracula's Daughter* (1936)
06/11/71 *Son of Dracula* (1943); *Tarantula* (1955)
06/18/71 *The Ghost of Frankenstein* (1942); *Hunter of the Unknown* (1966)
06/25/71 *House of Frankenstein* (1944)
07/02/71 *Voyage to the Prehistoric Planet* (1965); *The Man and the Monster* (1959)
07/09/71 *Black Sabbath* (1963); *The Curse of the Doll People* (1961)
07/16/71 *The Castle of the Living Dead* (1964); *The Monolith Monsters* (1957)
07/23/71 *Reptilicus* (1961); *Samson in the Wax Museum* (1963)
07/30/71 *Atom Age Vampire* (1960); *Unearthly Stranger* (1963)
08/06/71 *The Curse of Nostradamus* (1961); *The Robot vs. the Aztec Mummy* (1959)
08/13/71 *The Brainiac* (1962); *Samson vs. the Vampire Women* (1962)
08/20/71 *The Curse of the Aztec Mummy* (1957); *The Blood of Nostradamus* (1962)
08/27/71 *Doctor of Doom* (1963); *The Bloody Vampire* (1962)
09/03/71 *Dr. Orloff's Monster* (1964)
09/10/71 *Face of Terror* (1962)
09/17/71 *The Evil Eye* (1963)
09/24/71 *Pyro* (1964)
10/01/71 *Games* (1967)
10/08/71 *Godzilla: King of the Monsters* (1956)
10/15/71 *King Kong vs. Godzilla* (1962)
10/22/71 *Panic in Year Zero* (1962); *It Came from Outer Space* (1953)

10/29/71 *Dementia 13* (1963)
11/05/71 *Psycho* (1960)
11/12/71 *Black Sabbath* (1963)
11/19/71 *The Hunchback of Notre Dame* (1923)
11/26/71 *Queen of Blood* (1966)
12/03/71 *Burn, Witch, Burn* (1962)
12/10/71 *Dr. Orloff's Monster* (1964)
12/17/71 *The Eye Creatures* (1965)
12/24/71 Didn't air
12/31/71 *Track of the Vampire* (1966) [Airs at 1:00 a.m.]
01/07/72 *Bedlam* (1946); *Cry of the Bewitched* (1957)
01/14/72 *Cat People* (1942); *The Mind Benders* (1963)
01/21/72 *Isle of the Dead* (1945); *The Beach Girls and the Monster* (1965)
01/28/72 *The Seventh Victim* (1943); *Curse of the Swamp Creature* (1966)
02/04/72 *The Body Snatcher* (1945); *Portrait in Terror* (1965)
02/11/72 *King Kong* (1933); *Voyage to the Planet of Prehistoric Women* (1968)
02/18/72 *The Black Sleep* (1956); *Zontar, the Thing from Venus* (1966)
02/25/72 *The War of the Gargantuas* (1966); *Hunter of the Unknown* (1966)

> ⑨ **Weird Tales. I.**
> "The Cat People," Tom Conway, Jane Randolph. 1942.
> ⑳ **Cinema 20.**
> "The Bridge of San Luis Rey." Lynn Bari, Francis Lederer. 1944.
> ㉖ **Hatha Yoga.**
> ㊸ **Mystery Playhouse.**
> ⑤ **Midnight Movie.**
> "Ride Lonesome," Randolph Scott, Pernell Roberts. 1959.
> ㊺ **Film Festival Bonus.**
> "Daughters of the Sun God." Explorers search for a lost Inca city of gold. William Holmes, Lisa Montell. 1960.
> ⑪ **News; Devotions.**
> ④ **Starlight Theater.**
> "Los Farantos," Antonio Gades, Sara Lezana. 1963.
> ⑧ **News; Bible Reading.**
> ⑨ **Weird Tales. II.**
> "The Mind Benders," Dick Bogarde. 1963.

> ⑨ **Weird Tales I.**
> "The Four Skulls of Jonathan Drake." Modern science is applied to the mystery of a voodoo curse which has plagued a respected family for centuries. Henry Daniell, Eduard Franz. 1959.
> ⑳ **Cinema 20.**
> "The Trap." Charlie Chan uncovers a murder while vacationing on Malibu Beach with a theatrical troupe. Sidney Toler, Mantan Moreland. 1946.
> ⑤ **Midnight Movie.**
> "Guilty of Treason." Film account of the trial of Cardinal Mindszenty by the Hungarian Communists and of the coverage of the trial by an American reporter. Charles Bickford, Paul Kelly, Bonita Granville. 1950.
> ⑪ **News; Devotions.**
> ④ **Starlight Theater.**
> "Bellissima." An Italian woman in need of money enters her not-so-gifted child in a talent contest hoping that she'll win and put an end to the family's poverty. Anna Magnani, Walter Chiari. 1966.
> ⑧ **News; Bible Reading.**
> ⑨ **Weird Tales II.**
> "Monster from the Surf." A man's driving urge to control his son's life and his jealousy of his young wife's interest in others leads to murder. Jon Hall. 1963.

03/03/72 *The Man They Could Not Hang* (1939); *The Mind Benders* (1963)
03/10/72 *The Four Skulls of Jonathan Drake* (1959); *The Beach Girls and the Monster* (aka *Monster from the Surf*, 1965)

03/17/72 *Rodan* (1957); *Werewolf in a Girl's Dormitory* (1961)
03/24/72 *The Thing That Couldn't Die* (1958)
03/31/72 Didn't air
04/07/72 *The Man with Nine Lives* (1940); *Invasion* (1965)
04/14/72 *Island of the Burning Doomed* (1967); *The Evil Eye* (1963)
04/21/72 *Before I Hang* (1940); *Face of Terror* (1962)
04/28/72 *The Ape* (1940); *Pyro* (1964)
05/05/72 *The Brighton Strangler* (1945); *Dr. Orloff's Monster* (1964)
05/12/72 *The Quatermass Xperiment* (1955)
05/19/72 *Monster Zero* (1965)
05/26/72 *Cry of the Werewolf* (1944)
06/02/72 *Cry of the Bewitched* (1957)
06/09/72 *Curse of the Swamp Creature* (1966)
06/16/72 *The Eye Creatures* (1965)
06/23/72 *The Lost World of Sinbad* (1963); *Track of the Vampire* (1966)
06/30/72 *Voyage to the Prehistoric Planet* (1965)
07/07/72 *Curse of the Undead* (1959); *The Beach Girls and the Monster* (1965)
07/14/72 *The Leech Woman* (1960); *Portrait in Terror* (1965)
07/21/72 *The Mole People* (1956); *Space Monster* (1965)
07/28/72 *The Mind Benders* (1963)
08/04/72 *Panic in Year Zero* (1962); *Atragon* (1963)
08/11/72 *Dementia 13* (1963); *Queen of Blood* (1966)
08/18/72 *Dagora, the Space Monster* (1964)
08/25/72 *Voyage to the Planet of Prehistoric Women* (1968)
09/01/72 *The Black Room* (1935)
09/08/72 *Three Strangers* (1946)
09/15/72 *The Curse of the Cat People* (1944)
09/22/72 *The Unholy Three* (1930); *The Land Unknown* (1955)
09/29/72 *The Mask of Fu Manchu* (1932)
10/06/72 *Mad Love* (1935)
10/13/72 *Games* (1967)
10/20/72 *Mark of the Vampire* (1935)
10/27/72 *The Phantom of the Opera* (1925); *Godzilla: King of the Monsters* (1956)
11/03/72 *Night of Terror* (1933)
11/10/72 *Psycho* (1960)

11/17/72 *The Woman in White* (1948)
11/24/72 *The Day of the Triffids* (1963)
12/01/72 *The Face of Marble* (1946); *Curse of the Undead* (1959)
12/08/72 *The Neanderthal Man* (1953)
12/15/72 *The Return of Dracula* (1958)
12/22/72 *I Walked with A Zombie* (1943)
12/29/72 *The Mysterious Doctor* (1943); *Voyage to the Planet of Prehistoric Women* (1968)

Airs Saturday at 3:30 p.m.
01/06/73 *Before I Hang* (1940)
01/13/73 *The Body Snatcher* (1945)
01/20/73 Didn't air
01/27/73 *The Man with Nine Lives* (1940)
02/03/73 *Godzilla: King of the Monsters* (1956)
02/10/73 *The Man They Could Not Hang* (1939)
02/17/73 *The Return of the Vampire* (1943)
02/24/73 *Mystery of the Wax Museum* (1933)

Airs Friday at 11:30 p.m.
01/03/75 *House of Frankenstein* (1944)
01/10/75 *Journey to the Far Side of the Sun* (1969)
01/17/75 *Pit and the Pendulum* (1961) [Airs at 1:00 a.m.]
01/24/75 *The Face of Marble* (1946)
01/31/75 *Scars of Dracula* (1970)
02/07/75 *The Return of the Vampire* (1943) [Airs at 1:00 a.m.]
02/14/75 *Godzilla: King of the Monsters* (1956)
02/21/75 *The Oblong Box* (1969)
02/28/75 *The Vampire Bat* (1933)
03/07/75 *The Body Snatcher* (1945) [Airs at midnight]
03/14/75 Didn't air
03/21/75 *The Unholy Three* (1930)
03/28/75 *The Man with Nine Lives* (1940) [Airs at 1:00 a.m.]
04/04/75 *The Mask of Fu Manchu* (1932) [Airs at midnight]

> ⑨ **Weird Tales.**
> "The Unholy Three." (1930.) From a sinister circus, a ventriloquist, a strongman and a midget pool their talents to do evil. Lon Chaney, Sr.

04/11/75 *Cry of the Werewolf* (1944)
04/18/75 *Bedlam* (1946)
04/25/75 *Mystery of the Wax Museum* (1933)
05/02/75 *War Gods of the Deep* (1965)
05/09/75 *The Raven* (1963)

Lon Chaney, Sr., Harry Earle and Ivan Linow in the 1930 *The Unholy 3*

05/16/75 *Monster Zero* (1965)
05/23/75 *King Kong Escapes* (1968)
05/30/75 *Eye of the Cat* (1969)
06/06/75 *Svengali* (1931)
06/13/75 *The Ape* (1940)
06/20/75 *The Mad Genius* (1931)
06/27/75 *The Quatermass Xperiment* (1955)
07/04/75 *Rodan* (1957)

07/11/75 *Colossus: The Forbin Project* (1970)
07/18/75 *The Man Who Haunted Himself* (1970)
07/25/75 *Before I Hang* (1940)
08/01/75 *The Devil Commands* (1941)
08/08/75 *Son of Kong* (1933)
08/15/75 *Cat People* (1942)
08/22/75 *The Neanderthal Man* (1953)
08/29/75 *Pharaoh's Curse* (1957)

SCI-FI ACTION THEATER
(WBFF Channel 45)

In November 1971 WBFF-TV's Sunday evening *Action Theater* started featuring sci-fi films, finally re-christened *Sci-Fi Action Theater* in December that same year. The program ended the following January but returned in November 1974 and aired Sunday afternoons.

Airs Sunday at 7:00 p.m.
12/19/71 *Unknown Island* (1948)
12/26/71 *Night Caller from Outer Space* (1965)

> **45 Sci-Fi Action Theater.** "Voyage to the Prehistoric Planet." Pioneers from the first space ship to land on Venus find themselves endangered by dinosaurs and quicksand. Basil Rathbone, Faith Domergue. 1965.

01/02/72 *Voyage to the Planet of Prehistoric Women* (1968)
01/09/72 *Battle Beyond the Sun* (1963)
01/16/72 *Invasion of the Star Creatures* (1962)
01/23/72 *Voyage to the Prehistoric Planet* (1965)

Airs Sunday at 2:00 p.m.
11/03/74 *War of the Monsters* (1966)
11/10/74 *Godzilla vs. The Thing* (1964)
11/17/74 *Ghidorah, the Three-Headed Monster* (1964)
11/24/74 *Yongary, Monster from the Deep* (1967)
12/01/74 *The Deadly Mantis* (1957)
12/08/74 *The Leech Woman* (1960)

Airs Sunday at 1:30 p.m.
12/15/74 *The Mole People* (1956)
12/22/74 *The Monolith Monsters* (1957)
12/29/74 *Monster on the Campus* (1958)

> **45 Sci-Fi Action Theater.** "Invasion of the Star Creatures." Soldiers use love to conquer beautiful lady scientists who have tried to take over the Earth with plant-like creatures they control. Bob Ball, Frankie Ray, Gloria Victor. 1963.

01/05/75 *The Creation of the Humanoids* (1962)
01/12/75 *Atomic Rulers of the World* (1965)
01/19/75 *Invasion of the Neptune Men* (1964)
01/26/75 *Evil Brain from Outer Space* (1965)
02/02/75 *Attack of the Puppet People* (1958)
02/09/75 *The Amazing Colossal Man* (1957)
02/16/75 *I Was a Teenage Frankenstein* (1957)
02/23/75 *The Giant Claw* (1957)
03/02/75 *The Wizard of Mars* (1965)
03/09/75 *Missile to the Moon* (1958)
03/16/75 *The Atomic Brain* (1963)
03/23/75 *Journey to the Seventh Planet* (1962)
03/30/75 *The Angry Red Planet* (1959)
04/06/75 *Two Lost Worlds* (1951)
04/13/75 *The Brain That Wouldn't Die* (1962)
04/20/75 *Ghosts on the Loose* (1943)
04/27/75 *Slaughter of the Vampires* (1964)
05/04/75 *Curse of the Demon* (1957)
05/11/75 *The Maze* (1953)
05/18/75 *Horror Castle* (1963)
05/25/75 *Earth vs. the Flying Saucers* (1956)
06/01/75 *The Phantom Planet* (1961)
06/08/75 *Attack from Space* (1965)
06/15/75 *Planets Against Us* (1962)
06/22/75 *Invaders from Space* (1965)
06/29/75 *Invasion of the Star Creatures* (1962)
07/06/75 *Invisible Creature* (1960)
07/13/75 *The Bamboo Saucer* (1968)
07/20/75 *The Astounding She-Monster* (1957)
07/27/75 *The Magnetic Monster* (1953)
08/03/75 *Attack of the Giant Leeches* (1959)
08/10/75 *The Cape Canaveral Monsters* (1960)
08/17/75 *Satan's Satellites* (1958)

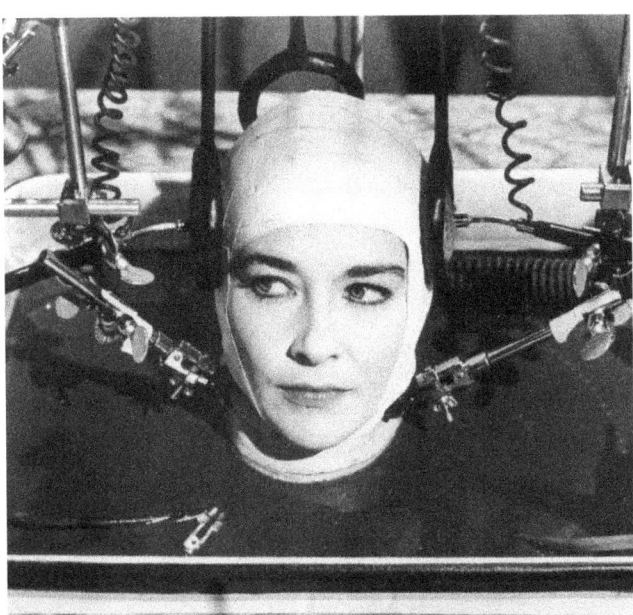
Virginia Leith in *The Brain That Wouldn't Die*

CREATURE FEATURE
(WBFF Channel 45)

Not content with *Ghost Host Theatre* airing its horror programmers Saturday nights, Channel 45 added its own *Creature Feature* in October 1972. (Channel 20 was airing its version of *Creature Feature* on Saturday nights, but Count Gore De Vol did not start hosting until February 1973.) The author vaguely remembers the still image of a fuzzy, scary face with piercing eyes being shown when the featured film came back from commercial breaks.

Airs Sunday at 8:00 p.m.
10/01/72 *The Face of Marble* (1946)
10/08/72 *Doctor X* (1932)
10/15/72 *Gog* (1954)
10/22/72 *The Quatermass Xperiment* (1955)
10/29/72 *The Walking Dead* (1936)
11/05/72 *Unknown Island* (1948)
11/12/72 *The Black Sleep* (1956)
11/19/72 *Chamber of Horrors* (1940)
11/26/72 *The Lady and the Monster* (1944)
12/03/72 Didn't air
12/10/72 *Destination Moon* (1950)

> **45 Creature Feature.** "The Hideous Sun Demon." A physicist who suffered radiation burns turns into a lizard-like creature. Robert Clarke, Nan Peterson. 1955.

12/17/72 *The Hideous Sun Demon* (1958)
12/24/72 Didn't air
12/31/72 *Red Planet Mars* (1952)
01/07/73 *Mothra* (1961)
01/14/73 *Battle in Outer Space* (1959)
01/21/73 *Assignment: Outer Space* (1960)
01/28/73 *Invasion of the Star Creatures* (1962)
02/04/73 *The Eye Creatures* (1965)
02/11/73 *Voyage to the Planet of Prehistoric Women* (1968)
02/18/73 *Voyage to the Prehistoric Planet* (1965)
02/25/73 *One Million B.C.* (1940)
03/04/73 *The Day the Earth Stood Still* (1951)
03/11/73 *The Creation of the Humanoids* (1962)
03/18/73 *The Angry Red Planet* (1959)
03/25/73 *Journey to the Seventh Planet* (1962)
04/01/73 *Gammera the Invincible* (1966)
04/08/73 *Space Monster* (1965)
04/15/73 *Unearthly Stranger* (1963)
04/22/73 Didn't air
04/29/73 *Planet of the Vampires* (1965)

Curse of the Demon; horror fiends had to wait until the very end to see the monster!

05/06/73 *Curse of the Demon* (1957)
05/13/73 Didn't air
05/20/73 *The Revenge of Frankenstein* (1958)
05/27/73 *20 Million Miles to Earth* (1957)
06/03/73 *Queen of Blood* (1966)
06/10/73 Didn't air
06/17/73 *Earth vs. the Flying Saucers* (1956)
06/24/73 *Curse of the Swamp Creature* (1966)
07/01/73 *Beast of Morocco* (1966)
07/08/73 *Creature of Destruction* (1967)
07/15/73 *Horrors of the Black Museum* (1959)
07/22/73 *Voyage to the End of the Universe* (1963)
07/29/73 *Circus of Horrors* (1960)
08/05/73 *The Blancheville Monster* (1963)
08/12/73 *The Brain That Wouldn't Die* (1962)
08/19/73 *In the Year 2889* (1967)
08/26/73 *The Phantom Planet* (1961)

Airs Friday at 8:00 p.m.
10/06/72 *Island of the Lost* (1967)

10/13/72 *The Day the Earth Caught Fire* (1961)
10/20/72 *The Return of Dracula* (1958)
10/27/72 *Castle of Evil* (1966)
11/03/72 *Invasion of the Zombies* (1962)
11/10/72 *The Maze* (1953)
11/17/72 *The Black Cat* (1941)
11/24/72 *Horror Castle* (1963)
12/01/72 Didn't air
12/08/72 *Slaughter of the Vampires* (1964)
12/15/72 *Carnival of Souls* (1962)
12/22/72 *Planets Against Us* (1962)
12/29/72 *Invaders from Space* (1965)

㊺ Creature Feature.
"Planets Against Us." Drama about an interplanetary alliance to destroy Earth. Jany Clair, Michel Lemoine, Maria Pia Luzi. 1961.

GHOUL THEATER
(Weeknights on WBFF Channel 45)

The title suggests horror films of the '30s and '40s; instead, this short-lived program was mostly a way of showing Channel 45's sci-fi library. The nice thing about *Ghoul Theater* though was that it aired nightly on weekdays, at least for the first few months. Toward the end of April 1974, it dropped the Friday night airing. It aired its last film in May 1974.

Airs at 11:00 p.m.
02/04/74 *The Angry Red Planet* (1959)
02/05/74 *Assignment: Outer Space* (1960)
02/06/74 *Journey to the Seventh Planet* (1962)
02/07/74 *Dagora, the Space Monster* (1964)
02/08/74 *Death is a Woman* (1966)

> **45 Ghoul Theater.** "Death Is a Woman." (1967.) An undercover agent sent to the Mediterranean to investigate a drug-smuggling operation becomes the chief suspect in a murder case. Mark Burns, William Dexter, Shawn Curry.

02/11/74 *Atragon* (1963)
02/12/74 *Black Sabbath* (1963)
02/13/74 *Curse of the Swamp Creature* (1966)
02/14/74 *Hunter of the Unknown* (1966)
02/15/74 *Return of the Giant Monsters* (1967)
02/18/74 *Voyage to the Prehistoric Planet* (1965)
02/19/74 *Queen of Blood* (1966)
02/20/74 *Operation Atlantis* (1965)
02/21/74 *The Lost World of Sinbad* (1963)
02/22/74 *Goliath and the Vampires* (1961)
02/25/74 *Mars Needs Women* (1967)
02/26/74 *Planet of the Vampires* (1965)
02/27/74 *Zontar, the Thing from Venus* (1966)
02/28/74 *Voyage to the Planet of Prehistoric Women* (1968)
03/01/74 *The X from Outer Space* (1967)
03/04/74 *The Terror* (1963)
03/05/74 *Die, Monster, Die!* (1965)
03/06/74 *Maneater of Hydra* (1967)
03/07/74 *The Amazing Transparent Man* (1960)
03/08/74 *Forbidden Planet* (1956)
03/11/74 *Beyond the Time Barrier* (1960)
03/12/74 *Invasion of the Star Creatures* (1962)
03/13/74 *Invisible Creature* (1960)
03/14/74 *Dementia 13* (1963)
03/15/74 *The Bamboo Saucer* (1968)
03/18/74 *The Evil Eye* (1963)
03/19/74 *Invasion* (1965)
03/20/74 *The Beach Girls and the Monster* (1965)
03/21/74 *Unearthly Stranger* (1963)
03/22/74 *Man in Outer Space* (1962)
03/25/74 *Attack of the Robots* (1966)
03/26/74 *The Screaming Skull* (1958)
03/27/74 *The Giant Gila Monster* (1959)
03/28/74 *The Beast with a Million Eyes* (1955)
03/29/74 *The Day the Earth Caught Fire* (1961)
04/01/74 *The Brain Eaters* (1958)
04/02/74 *I Was a Teenage Werewolf* (1957)
04/03/74 *The Spider* (1958)
04/04/74 *Blood of Dracula* (1957)
04/05/74 Didn't air

04/08/74 *Monster from a Prehistoric Planet* (1967)
04/09/74 *A Bucket of Blood* (1959)
04/10/74 *The Astounding She-Monster* (1957)
04/11/74 *Godzilla vs. The Thing* (1964)
04/12/74 *The Time Travelers* (1964)
04/15/74 *Majin, Monster of Terror* (1966)
04/16/74 *War of the Monsters* (1966)
04/17/74 *The Undead* (1957)
04/18/74 *Yongary, Monster from the Deep* (1967)
04/19/74 Didn't air
04/22/74 *The She-Creature* (1956)
04/23/74 *How to Make a Monster* (1958)
04/24/74 *Night of the Blood Beast* (1958)
04/25/74 *The Strange Door* (1951)
04/26/74 Didn't air

Airs at midnight (no longer airs Fridays)
04/29/74 *The Undying Monster* (1942)
04/30/74 *The Creation of the Humanoids* (1962)
05/01/74 *The Saga of the Viking Women and Their Voyage to the Waters of the Great Sea Serpent* (1957)
05/02/74 *Horrors of the Black Museum* (1959)
05/06/74 *It's Alive!* (1969)
05/07/74 *Atomic Rulers of the World* (1965)
05/08/74 *The Gamma People* (1956)
05/09/74 *Invasion of the Neptune Men* (1964)
05/13/74 *Evil Brain from Outer Space* (1965)
05/14/74 *Slaughter of the Vampires* (1964)
05/15/74 *Attack from Space* (1965)
05/16/74 *Carnival of Souls* (1962)
05/20/74 *Rome Against Rome* (1964)
05/21/74 *The Final War* (1960)
05/22/74 *The Horrible Dr. Hichcock* (1962)
05/23/74 *Planets Against Us* (1962)
05/27/74 *Invaders from Space* (1965)
05/28/74 *The Werewolf* (1956)
05/29/74 *Earth vs. the Flying Saucers* (1956)
05/30/74 *20 Million Miles to Earth* (1957)

> 12.00 ㊺ Ghoul Theater.
> "Night Star Goddess of Electra." (1965.) Trying to recapture an Armenian treasure stolen from Roman troops before they return to the capital sends a Centurion through strange adventures and dangers which he overcomes with the help of a slave girl whom he marries. John Barrymore, Jr., Susi Andersen.

Night Star Goddess of Electra was the US title for **Rome Against Rome**

CHILLER THEATRE
(WMAR Channel 2)

Mixing quite a few early-to-mid '70s titles with the AIP catalogue, *Chiller Theatre* offered films not seen on other horror presentations. In April 1980, WMAR added a *Chiller Theatre II*, which aired Saturday nights. At times, the station would air a two-part presentation over the two nights. In August 1981, Channel 2 switched network affiliations from CBS to NBC, which had its own Friday late-night programming. Therefore, the Friday *Chiller* ended, and the Saturday edition now aired after *Saturday Night Live*. In May 1982, *Chiller* left the air, but returned in September 1984. The opening to the program showed either the famous still from *The Haunting* where Julie Harris and Claire Bloom are covering their mouths in horror, or original artwork showing the grim reaper and other creepy images. A mildly amused announcer revealed the evening's title. In addition to theatrical horrors and the occasional TV movie, *Chiller* showed episodes of the British TV series *Thriller* during its run; such airings are indicated below with an *.

Friday (airs at 12:30 a.m.)
09/07/79 *The Oblong Box* (1969)
09/14/79 *Planet of the Vampires* (1965)
09/21/79 *Tales of Terror* (1962)
09/28/79 *Die, Monster, Die!* (1965)
10/05/79 *The Severed Arm* (1973)
10/12/79 *The Masque of the Red Death* (1964)
10/19/79 *Doomsday Machine* (1972)
10/26/79 *It Conquered the World* (1956)
11/02/79 *Necromancy* (1972)
11/09/79 *Baron Blood* (1972)
11/16/79 *Dr. Jekyll & Sister Hyde* (1971)
11/23/79 *Beware! The Blob* (1972)
11/30/79 *Legacy of Blood* (1971)
12/07/79 *The Conqueror Worm* (1968)
12/14/79 *Tower of Evil* (1972)
12/21/79 *The Raven* (1963)
12/28/79 *I Was a Teenage Werewolf* (1957)
01/04/80 *The Return of Count Yorga* (1971)
01/11/80 *Tomb of Ligeia* (1965)
01/18/80 *And Now the Screaming Starts* (1973)
01/25/80 *War Gods of the Deep* (1965)
02/01/80 *Maneater of Hydra* (1967)
02/08/80 *Pit and the Pendulum* (1961)
02/15/80 *Grave of the Vampire* (1972)
02/22/80 *Lemora, the Lady Dracula* (1973)
02/29/80 *Blacula* (1972)
03/07/80 *The Human Vapor* (1960)
03/14/80 *The House that Dripped Blood* (1971)
03/21/80 *The Last War* (1961)

This photo of Claire Bloom and Julie Harris from *The Haunting* was sometimes used as the opening for Chiller Theater on channel 2.

03/28/80 *Die Screaming Marianne* (1971)
04/04/80 *The Savage Curse** (1974)
04/11/80 *Island of the Burning Doomed* (1967)
04/18/80 Didn't air
04/25/80 Didn't air
05/02/80 *Screamer** (1974)
05/09/80 *Web of the Spider* (1971)

05/16/80 *Die Sister, Die!* (1978)
05/23/80 *Count Dracula's Great Love* (1972)
05/30/80 *Godzilla vs. the Cosmic Monster* (1974)
06/06/80 *Dead of Night* (1977)
06/13/80 *One Deadly Owner** (1974)
06/20/80 *Come Die with Me* (1974)
06/27/80 *The Eyes Have It** (1973)

> **12:30 ❷ Chiller Theatre**
>
> "The Demon Planet." (1965) A scientist lands on the planet Aura encounters an advanced alien intelligence that is seeking a bodies to escape from the planet. Barry Sullivan, Norma Banguel, Angel Aranda, Evi Marandi and Fernando Villena star. (2 hrs. 10 min.)

07/04/80 *Beware! The Blob* (1972)
07/11/80 *Dr. Jekyll & Sister Hyde* (1971)
07/18/80 *The Severed Arm* (1973)
07/25/80 *Planet of the Vampires* (sks T*he Demon Planet*, 1965)
08/01/80 *Spell of Evil** (1973)
08/08/80 *The Next Victim** (1975)
08/15/80 *The Carnation Killer** (1973)
08/22/80 Didn't air
08/29/80 *Color Him Dead** (1974)
09/05/80 *Godzilla vs. Megalon* (1973)
09/12/80 *Christina* (1974)
09/19/80 *The Double Kill**(1975)
09/26/80 *Gargoyles* (1972)
10/03/80 *Shriek of the Mutilated* (1974)

> **12:30 ❷ Chiller Theatre I**
>
> "Shriek of the Mutilated." (1974) Four college students and their leader search for the elusive Yeti (Abominable Snowman.) Their search sends them down the path of mystery, bloodshed and death. Alan Brock, Jennifer Stock, Michael Harris. (2 hrs.)

10/10/80 *Turn of the Screw* (Part 1) (1974)
10/17/80 *When Every Day Was the Fourth of July* (1978)
10/24/80 *The Picture of Dorian Gray* (Part 1) (1973)
10/31/80 *The Legend of Boggy Creek* (1972)
11/07/80 *The Strange Case of Dr. Jekyll and Mister Hyde* (Part 1) (1968)
11/14/80 *Legacy of Horror* (1978)
11/21/80 *Till Death* (1978)'
11/28/80 *The House that Dripped Blood* (1971)
12/05/80 *Die Screaming Marianne* (1971)
12/12/80 *Grave of the Vampire* (1972)
12/19/80 *Terror from Within** (1975)
12/26/80 Didn't air
01/02/81 *Journey into Fear* (1975)
01/09/81 *Frankenstein: Part 1* (1973)
01/16/81 *Turn of the Screw* (1974)
01/23/81 *The Invasion of Carol Enders* (1974)
01/30/81 *Dracula* (1973)
02/06/81 *Beginning of the End* (1957)
02/13/81 Didn't air
02/20/81 *Disciple of Death* (1972)
02/27/81 *Fortress of the Dead* (1965)
03/06/81 *If It's a Man, Hang Up** (1975)
03/13/81 *Come Out, Come Out, Wherever You Are** (1974)
03/20/81 *Once the Killing Starts** (1974)
03/27/81 *Appointment with A Killer** (1975)
04/03/81 *Warlock Moon* (1973)
04/10/81 *Murder in Mind**(1973)
04/17/81 *The Conqueror Worm* (1968)
04/24/81 *Blacula* (1972)
05/01/81 *Castle of Evil* (1966)
05/08/81 *Cauldron of Blood* (1970)
05/15/81 *Chamber of Horrors* (1940)
05/22/81 *Count Dracula* (1970)
05/29/81 *The Dungeon of Harrow* (1962)
06/05/81 Didn't air
06/12/81 *Death Policy** (1973)
06/19/81 *The Legend of Boggy Creek* (1972)
06/26/81 *Die Sister, Die!* (1978)
07/03/81 *Children Shouldn't Play with Dead Things* (1972)
07/10/81 *Don't Look in the Basement* (1973)
07/17/81 *The Murder Clinic* (1966)
07/24/81 *She Beast* (1966)
07/31/81 *Deathdream* (1974)
08/07/81 *Killer with Two Faces** (1974)
08/14/81 *File It Under Fear** (1973)

Saturday

Airs at 11:30 p.m.
04/05/80 *The Skull* (1965)

> **12:30 ❷ Chiller Theatre II**
>
> "The Strange Case of Dr. Jekyll and Mr. Hyde." (1968) (Part 2 of 2.) Based on the Robert Lewis Stevenson classic, a Victorian research chemist explores the primal nature of good and evil by experimenting with a drug that transforms him into the savage Mr. Hyde who murders young women on his nocturnal rampages. Jack Palance, Leo Genn, Oscar Homolka, Billy Whitelaw, Tessie O'Shea. (2 hrs.)

Monster kids could watch their favorite *Creature Features* on Channel 2—including: *Beginning of the End* (top left), *Children Shouldn't Play with Dead Things* (top right), *Dracula* with Jack Palance (bottom left) and Ingrid Pitt in *The House that Dripped Blood* (bottom right). Pitt was s favorite guest at Baltimore's FANEX 8.

Vincent Price in *The Masque of the Red Death*

04/12/80 *Baron Blood* (1972)
04/19/80 *Atom Age Vampire* (1960)

04/26/80 *The Horror of Frankenstein* (1970)
05/03/80 *Dracula* (1973)

05/10/80 *Warlock Moon* (1973)
05/17/80 *Frankenstein* (1973)
05/24/80 *Peeping Tom* (1960)
05/31/80 *Journey into Fear* (1975)
06/07/80 *Shadow of Fear* (1974)
06/14/80 *Nightmare at 43 Hillcrest* (1974)
06/21/80 *Someone at the Top of the Stairs** (1973)
06/28/80 *A Place to Die** (1973)
07/05/80 *Legacy of Blood* (1971)
07/12/80 *The Masque of the Red Death* (1964)
07/19/80 *Tales of Terror* (1962)
07/26/80 *Tower of Evil* (1972)
08/02/80 *The Killing Game** (1975)
08/09/80 Didn't air
08/16/80 *Only A Scream Away** (1974)
08/23/80 *The Devil's Web** (1975)
08/30/80 *Cry Terror** (1975)

Airs at 12:30 a.m.
09/06/80 *The Skull* (1965)
09/13/80 *Track of the Moon Beast* (1976)
09/20/80 *Godzilla vs. the Cosmic Monster* (1974)
09/27/80 *Murder on the Midnight Express** (1974)
10/04/80 *Count Dracula's Great Love* (1972)
10/11/80 *Turn of the Screw* (Part 2) (1974)
10/18/80 *Creature from Black Lake* (1976)
10/25/80 *The Picture of Dorian Gray* (Part 2) (1973)
11/01/80 *The Return of Count Yorga* (1971)
11/08/80 *The Strange Case of Dr. Jekyll and Mister Hyde* (Part 2) (1968)
11/15/80 *The Oblong Box* (1969)
11/22/80 *And Now the Screaming Starts* (1973)
11/29/80 *Mirror of Deception** (1975)
12/06/80 *Death in Deep Water** (1975)
12/13/80 *Lemora, the Lady Dracula* (1973)
12/20/80 *Necromancy* (1972)
12/27/80 *The Human Vapor* (1960)
01/03/81 *Web of the Spider* (1971)
01/10/81 *Frankenstein: Part 2* (1973)
01/17/81 Didn't air
01/24/81 Didn't air
01/31/81 *Peeping Tom* (1960)
02/07/81 *Terror in the Wax Museum* (1973)
02/14/81 *Octaman* (1971)
02/21/81 *The Thirsty Dead* (1974)
02/28/81 *The Vulture* (1967)
03/07/81 *A Killer in Every Corner** (1975)
03/14/81 *Look Back in Darkness** (1975)
03/21/81 *Sleepwalker** (1975)
03/28/81 *Melody of Hate** (1975)
04/04/81 *Doomsday Machine* (1972)
04/11/81 *Lady in a Cage* (1964)
04/18/81 *Kiss Kiss, Kill Kill** (1974)

04/25/81 *Atom Age Vampire* (1960)
05/02/81 *The Devil's Messenger* (1961)
05/09/81 *Dr. Terror's House of Horrors* (1965)
05/16/81 *Horror Hotel* (1960)
05/23/81 *Gallery of Horrors* (1967)
05/30/81 *The Human Monster* (1939)
06/06/81 Didn't air
06/13/81 *In the Steps of a Dead Man** (1974)
06/20/81 *The Alpha Incident* (1978)
06/27/81 *Die, Monster, Die* (1965)
07/04/81 *Fangs of the Living Dead* (1969)
07/11/81 *The Night Evelyn Came Out of the Grave* (1971)
07/18/81 *The Blood Spattered Bride* (1972)
07/25/81 *A Candle for the Devil* (1973)
08/01/81 *Dial A Deadly Number** (1975)
08/08/81 *Anatomy of Terror** (1973)
08/15/81 *Not Guilty!** (1974)
08/22/81 Didn't air
08/29/81 *Murder Motel** (1975) [Delayed until 1:30 a.m.]

Airs at 1:00 a.m.
09/05/81 *The Vulture* (1967)
09/12/81 Didn't air
09/19/81 *Terror in the Wax Museum* (1973)
09/26/81 *Gargoyles* (1972)
10/03/81 *The Return of Count Yorga* (1971)
10/10/81 *Dr. Jekyll & Sister Hyde* (1971)
10/17/81 *Baron Blood* (1972)
10/24/81 *Tower of Evil* (1972)

10/31/81 *Legacy of Blood* (1971)
11/07/81 *Dead of Night* (1977)
11/14/81 *Come Die with Me* (1974)
11/21/81 *Shadow of Fear* (1974)
11/28/81 *Nightmare at 43 Hillcrest* (1974)
12/05/81 *Beware! The Blob* (1972)
12/12/81 *Die Screaming Marianne* (1971)
12/19/81 *The Severed Arm* (1973)
12/26/81 Didn't air
01/02/82 *Dead of Night* (1977)

01/09/82 *The Boy Who Cried Werewolf* (1973)
01/16/82 *The Andromeda Strain* (1971)
01/23/82 *Dracula* (1973)
01/30/82 *The Deadly Bees* (1967)
02/06/82 *Sssssss* (1973)
02/13/82 *The Man Who Haunted Himself* (1970)
02/20/82 *The Horror of Frankenstein* (1970)
02/27/82 *Grave of the Vampire* (1972)
03/06/82 *Creature from Black Lake* (1976)
03/13/82 *Journey into Fear* (1975)
03/20/82 *Shriek of the Mutilated* (1974)
03/27/82 *Legacy of Horror* (1978)
04/03/82 *Sorry, Wrong Number* (1948)
04/10/82 *Murder!* (1930)
04/17/82 *The Raven* (1963)
04/24/82 *I Was a Teenage Werewolf* (1957)

Airs at 1:00 a.m.
09/24/83 *Baron Blood* (1972)
10/01/83 *The House that Dripped Blood* (1971)
10/08/83 *The Return of Count Yorga* (1971)

> 1:00 ② Movie.
> "Return Of Count Yorga" (1971) Robert Quarry, Mariette Hartley. A bloodthirsty vampire seeks out fresh victims from a nearby orphanage.

10/15/83 *Grave of the Vampire* (1972)
10/22/83 *And Now the Screaming Starts* (1973)
10/29/83 *Legacy of Blood* (1971)
11/05/83 *Die Screaming Marianne* (1971)
11/12/83 *Tower of Evil* (1972)
11/19/83 *The Conqueror Worm* (1968)
11/26/83 *The Oblong Box* (1969)
12/03/83 *Hands of the Ripper* (1971)
12/10/83 *Ssssss* (1973)
12/17/83 *The Vulture* (1967)
12/24/83 Didn't air
12/31/83 *Terror in the Wax Museum* (1973)
01/07/84 *Lady in a Cage* (1964)
01/14/84 *Winter Kill* (1974)

Airs at 2:00 a.m.
01/21/84 *Twins of Evil* (1971)
01/28/84 *Night Gallery* (1969)
02/04/84 *Christina* (1974)
02/11/84 *The Car* (1977)
02/18/84 *Don't Look Now* (1973)
02/25/84 *You'll Like My Mother* (1972)
03/03/84 *Sorry, Wrong Number* (1948)

03/10/84 *The Boy Who Cried Werewolf* (1973)
03/17/84 *The Sentinel* (1977)
03/24/84 *The Severed Arm* (1973)
03/31/84 *Dr. Jekyll & Sister Hyde* (1971)
04/07/84 *The Andromeda Strain* (1971)
04/14/84 *One Deadly Owner** (1974)
04/21/84 *The Next Victim** (1975)
04/28/84 *If It's a Man, Hang Up** (1975)
05/05/84 *The Return of Charlie Chan* (1971)
05/12/84 *King Kong Escapes* (1968)
05/19/84 *Beware! The Blob* (1972)
05/26/84 *The Masque of the Red Death* (1964)
06/02/84 Didn't air
06/09/84 *Dead of Night* (1977)
06/16/84 *The Unearthly* (1957)
06/23/84 *Hands of the Ripper* (1971)
06/30/84 *The Witchmaker* (1969)
07/07/84 *The Human Vapor* (1960)
07/14/84 *Dracula* (1973)
07/21/84 *And Now the Screaming Starts* (1973)
07/28/84 *Doomsday Machine* (1972)
08/04/84 *Come Die with Me* (1974)
08/11/84 *Shadow of Fear* (1974)
08/18/84 *The Picture of Dorian Gray* (1973)
08/25/84 *Frankenstein* (1973)
09/01/84 *Warlock Moon* (1973)
09/08/84 *Peeping Tom* (1960)
09/15/84 Didn't air

Airs at 2:30 a.m.
09/22/84 *The Legend of Boggy Creek* (1972)
09/29/84 *Track of the Moon Beast* (1976)
10/06/84 *Shriek of the Mutilated* (1974)
10/13/84 *Legacy of Horror* (1978)
10/20/84 *Creature from Black Lake* (1976)
10/27/84 *Castle of Evil* (1966)
11/03/84 *Chamber of Horrors* (1940)
11/10/84 *Alien Zone* (1978)
11/17/84 *Land of the Minotaur* (1976)
11/24/84 *The Dungeon of Harrow* (1962)
12/01/84 *The Devil's Messenger* (1961)
12/08/84 *Supersonic Man* (1979)
12/15/84 *Latitude Zero* (1969)
12/22/84 *The Human Monster* (1939)
12/29/84 *Web of the Spider* (1971)
01/05/85 *The Alpha Incident* (1978)
01/12/85 *The Return of Count Yorga* (1971)
01/19/85 *Horror Hotel* (1960)
01/26/85 *Star Odyssey* (1979)
02/02/85 *Count Dracula's Great Love* (1972)
02/09/85 *The War of the Robots* (1978)
02/16/85 *Die Sister, Die!* (1978)
02/23/85 *The Killings at Outpost Zeta* (1980)

03/02/85 *The Cape Canaveral Monsters* (1960)
03/09/85 *The Lady and the Monster* (1944)
03/16/85 *Kiss of the Tarantula* (1976)
03/23/85 *Deathdream* (1974)
03/30/85 *The Invisible Terror* (1963)
04/06/85 *The Blood Spattered Bride* (1972)
04/13/85 *Horror Hotel* (1960)
04/20/85 *Nightmare at 43 Hillcrest* (1974)
04/27/85 *The Electronic Monster* (1958)
05/04/85 *Christina* (1974)
05/11/85 *Blue Sunshine* (1977)
05/18/85 *Don't Look in the Basement* (1973)
05/25/85 *She Beast* (1966)
06/01/85 Didn't air
06/08/85 *Beginning of the End* (1957)
06/15/85 *A Candle for the Devil* (1973)
06/22/85 *Aliens from Spaceship Earth* (1978)
06/29/85 *Buck Rodgers* (1939)
07/06/85 *Children Shouldn't Play with Dead Things* (1972)
07/13/85 *The Murder Clinic* (1966)
07/20/85 *Fangs of the Living Dead* (1969)
07/27/85 *The Night Evelyn Came Out of the Grave* (1971)
08/03/85 *Zombie* (1979)
08/10/85 *Laboratory* (1980)
08/17/85 *The Force on Thunder Mountain* (1978)
08/24/85 Didn't air
08/31/85 *Foes* (1977)
09/07/85 *Captive* (1980)
09/14/85 Didn't air
09/21/85 *The Unearthly* (1957) [Airs at 1:00 a.m.]
09/28/85 *Count Dracula* (1970) [Airs at 2:00 a.m.]
10/05/85 *Death: The Ultimate Mystery* (1979) [Airs at 2:00 a.m.]

Airs at 3:00 a.m.
10/12/85 *Land of the Minotaur* (1976)
10/19/85 *Lifepod* (1981)
10/26/85 *Disciple of Death* (1972)
11/02/85 *Dr. Terror's House of Horrors* (1965)
11/09/85 *Chamber of Horrors* (1940)
11/16/85 *Castle of Evil* (1966)
11/23/85 *The Devil's Messenger* (1961)
11/30/85 *The Dungeon of Harrow* (1962)
12/07/85 *The Invisible Terror* (1963)
12/14/85 *Cauldron of Blood* (1970)
12/21/85 *The Human Monster* (1939)
12/28/85 *Gallery of Horrors* (1967)
01/04/86 *The Cape Canaveral Monsters* (1960)
01/11/86 *The Boy Who Cried Werewolf* (1973)
01/18/86 *The Lady and the Monster* (1944)
01/25/86 *Horror Hotel* (1960)
02/01/86 *Count Dracula* (1970)
02/08/86 *Latitude Zero* (1969)

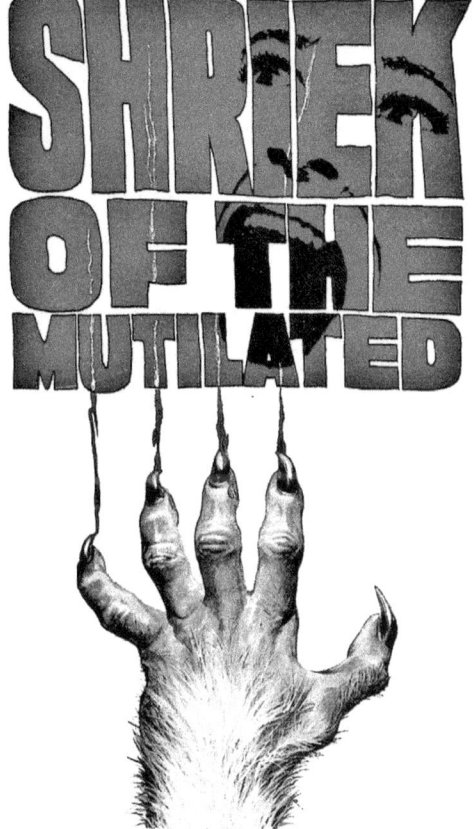

02/15/86 *Dr. Terror's House of Horrors* (1965)
02/22/86 *Warlock Moon* (1973)
03/01/86 *Peeping Tom* (1960)
03/08/86 *Supersonic Man* (1979)
03/15/86 *Castle of Evil* (1966)
03/22/86 *The Dungeon of Harrow* (1962)
03/29/86 *The Devil's Messenger* (1961)
04/05/86 *Web of the Spider* (1971)
04/12/86 *Cauldron of Blood* (1970)
04/19/86 *Alien Zone* (1978)
04/26/86 *Foes* (1977)

Airs at 2:00 a.m.
05/03/86 *The Legend of Boggy Creek* (1972)
05/10/86 *The Killings at Outpost Zeta* (1980)
05/17/86 *Star Odyssey* (1979)
05/24/86 *Shriek of the Mutilated* (1974)
05/31/86 Didn't air
06/07/86 *Creature from Black Lake* (1976)

06/14/86 *The War of the Robots* (1978)
06/21/86 *The Alpha Incident* (1978)
06/28/86 *Count Dracula's Great Love* (1972)
07/05/86 *Godzilla vs. Megalon* (1973)
07/12/86 *The Crater Lake Monster* (1977)
07/19/86 *The War in Space* (1977)
07/26/86 *Track of the Moon Beast* (1976)
08/02/86 *Godzilla vs. the Cosmic Monster* (1974)
08/09/86 *Legacy of Horror* (1978)
08/16/86 *PSI Factor* (1980) [Airs at 3:00 a.m.]
08/23/86 *Laboratory* (1980)
08/30/86 *Captive* (1980)
09/06/86 *Terror in the Wax Museum* (1973)
09/13/86 Didn't air

Airs at 2:30 a.m.
09/20/86 *Land of the Minotaur* (1976)
09/27/86 *Lifepod* (1981) [Airs at 3:00 a.m.]
10/04/86 *Future Woman* (1969)
10/11/86 *Farewell to the Planet of the Apes* (1974)
10/18/86 *Warlock Moon* (1973)

10/25/86 *Blue Sunshine* (1977)
11/01/86 *Till Death* (1978)
11/08/86 *Christina* (1974)
11/15/86 *Die Sister, Die!* (1978)
11/22/86 *Web of the Spider* (1971)
11/29/86 *Beasts* (1983)
12/06/86 *Earth II* (1971)
12/13/86 *Peeping Tom* (1960)
12/20/86 *Supersonic Man* (1979)
12/27/86 *Uncle Was a Vampire* (1959)
01/03/87 *The Legend of Boggy Creek* (1972)

Airs at 1:30 a.m.
01/10/87 *Creature from Black Lake* (1976)
01/17/87 *Shriek of the Mutilated* (1974)
01/24/87 *Journey into Fear* (1975)
01/31/87 *Count Dracula's Great Love* (1972)
02/07/87 *Latitude Zero* (1969)
02/14/87 *The War in Space* (1977)
02/21/87 *PSI Factor* (1980)
02/28/87 *The Crater Lake Monster* (1977)
03/07/87 *Godzilla vs. Megalon* (1973)
03/14/87 *Godzilla vs. the Cosmic Monster* (1974)
03/21/87 *Track of the Moon Beast* (1976)
03/28/87 *The Alpha Incident* (1978)
04/04/87 *Warlock Moon* (1973)
04/11/87 *Web of the Spider* (1971)
04/18/87 *Christina* (1974)
04/25/87 *Laboratory* (1980) [Airs at 2:00 a.m.]
05/02/87 *Star Odyssey* (1979)
05/09/87 *Captive* (1980) [Airs at 2:00 a.m.]
05/16/87 *Future Woman* (1969)
05/23/87 *Back to the Planet of the Apes* (1974)
05/30/87 Didn't air
06/06/87 *Alien Zone* (1978)
06/13/87 *Land of the Minotaur* (1976)
06/20/87 *The War of the Robots* (1978)
06/27/87 *Lifepod* (1981)
07/04/87 *Forgotten City of the Planet of the Apes* (1974)
07/11/87 *Life, Liberty, and Pursuit on the Planet of the Apes* (1974)
07/18/87 *Treachery and Greed on the Planet of the Apes* (1974) [Airs at 2:00 a.m.]
07/25/87 *Farewell to the Planet of the Apes* (1974)
08/01/87 *The War in Space* (1977)
08/08/87 *The Crater Lake Monster* (1977) [Airs at 2:00 a.m.]
08/15/87 *PSI Factor* (1980) [Airs at 2:30 a.m.]
08/22/87 *Satan's Cheerleaders* (1977)
08/29/87 *The Sentinel* (1977) [Airs at 3:00 a.m.]
09/05/87 *2 020 Texas Gladiators* (1982) [Airs at 2:00 a.m.]

SATURDAY MATINEE/ SATURDAY THRILLER THEATER
(WDCA Channel 20)

Beginning in January 1981, Channel 20 changed the title of its Saturday afternoon double features from *Movie I* and *Movie II* to *Saturday Matinee* (1:00 p.m.) and *Saturday Thriller Theater* (2:30 p.m.). The *Saturday Matinee* showings were genre films through January 1982 and are therefore included here.

Saturday Matinee/Saturday Thriller Theater

Airs at 1:00 p.m./2:30 p.m.
01/03/81 *Dagora, the Space Monster* (1964); *Monster from a Prehistoric Planet* (1967)
01/10/81 *Godzilla vs. the Sea Monster* (1966); *Zontar, the Thing from Venus* (1966)
01/17/81 *The Boogie Man Will Get You* (1942); *The Raven* (1963)

> **20 Saturday Matinee**
> "The Boogie Man Will Get You." (1942) While an inn is run upstairs a professor who believes he can create a superman stores a series of corpses in the basement for experiments and an escaped spy adds to the weird events. Boris Karloff, Peter Lorre, Jeff Donnell, Larry Parks, Maxie Rosenbloom. (1 hr. 30 min.)

01/24/81 *Day the World Ended* (1955); *Voyage to the Prehistoric Planet* (1965)
01/31/81 *Planet of the Vampires* (1965); *Curse of the Demon* (1957)
02/07/81 *It Came from Outer Space* (1953); *Frankenstein Meets the Spacemonster* (1965)
02/14/81 *The Castle of Fu Manchu* (1969); *They Came from Beyond Space* (1967)
02/21/81 *The Wolf Man* (1941); *I Was a Teenage Werewolf* (1957)
02/28/81 *The Giant Claw* (1957); *The Night the World Exploded* (1957)
03/07/81 *Voyage to the End of the Universe* (1963); *War Gods of the Deep* (1965)
03/14/81 *Dr. Goldfoot and the Girl Bombs* (1966); *The Million Eyes of Sumuru* (1967)
03/21/81 *The Spider* (1958); *The Pearl of Death* (1944)
03/28/81 *The Wild Racers* (1968); *The Scarlet Claw* (1944)
04/04/81 *The Amazing Colossal Man* (1957); *Cat Girl* (1957)
04/11/81 *The She-Creature* (1956); *Curse of the Swamp Creature* (1966)
04/18/81 *The Black Cat* (1934); Didn't Air
04/25/81 *The Beast with a Million Eyes* (1955); *The Invisible Ray* (1936)
05/02/81 *Godzilla: King of the Monsters* (1956); *Mothra* (1961)
05/09/81 *Atragon* (1963); *The Giant Gila Monster* (1959)
05/16/81 *War of the Monsters* (1966); *Majin, Monster of Terror* (1966)
05/23/81 *Attack of the Puppet People* (1958); *Attack of the Giant Leeches* (1959)
05/30/81 *The H-Man* (1959); *The Skull* (1965)
06/06/81 *War of the Colossal Beast* (1958); *Rome Against Rome* (1964)
06/13/81 *The Time Travelers* (1964); *Voyage to the End of the Universe* (1963)
06/20/81 *In the Year 2889* (1967); *The Killer Shrews* (1959)
06/27/81 Didn't Air; *Battle in Outer Space* (1959) [Airs at 3:00 p.m.]
07/04/81 *Dr. Cyclops* (1940); *The Mole People* (1956)
07/11/81 *Tarantula* (1955); *The Deadly Mantis* (1957)
07/18/81 *Invasion* (1965); *Unearthly Stranger* (1963)
07/25/81 *Creature from the Black Lagoon* (1954); *The Creature Walks Among Us* (1956)
08/01/81 *Curucu, Beast of the Amazon* (1956); *The Alien Factor* (1978)
08/08/81 *Invasion of the Saucer Men* (1957); *It Conquered the World* (1956)
08/15/81 *Ghost of Dragstrip Hollow* (1959); *Mars Needs Women* (1967)
08/22/81 *Star Pilot* (1966); *The Mysterians* (1957)
08/29/81 *Captive Wild Woman* (1943); *Cult of the Cobra* (1955)
09/05/81 *I Was a Teenage Werewolf* (1957); *I Was a Teenage Frankenstein* (1957)

09/12/81 *Attack of the Robots* (1966); *The Amazing Colossal Man* (1957)
09/19/81 *The Brain Eaters* (1958); *The Headless Ghost* (1959)
09/26/81 *Zontar, the Thing from Venus* (1966); *The Giant Claw* (1957)
10/03/81 *The Beast from 20,000 Fathoms* (1953); *Revenge of the Creature* (1955)
10/10/81 *The Monolith Monsters* (1957); *Maneater of Hydra* (1967)
10/17/81 *Battle of the Worlds* (1961); *Day the World Ended* (1955)
10/24/81 *The Invisible Man* (1933); *The Mummy* (1932)
10/31/81 *Frankenstein* (1931); *Bride of Frankenstein* (1935)
11/07/81 *Reptilicus* (1961); *Attack of the Mushroom People* (1963)
11/14/81 *Godzilla vs. The Thing* (1964); *The Thing from Another World* (1951)
11/21/81 *Dagora, the Space Monster* (1964); *Monster from a Prehistoric Planet* (1967)
11/28/81 *The Astounding She-Monster* (1957); *Creature of Destruction* (1967)
12/05/81 *Zombies of Mora Tau* (1957); *Die, Monster, Die* (1965)
12/12/81 *The Invisible Woman* (1940); *Jesse James Meets Frankenstein's Daughter* (1966)
12/19/81 *Monster on the Campus* (1958); *The Fury of the Wolfman* (1972)

> ⑳ Movie.
> "Jesse James Meets Frankenstein's Daughter." (1966) John Lupton, Cal Bolder.

12/26/81 *The Spider Woman Strikes Back* (1946); *The Black Cat* (1934)
01/02/82 *The Stranglers of Bombay* (1959); *The 27th Day* (1957)

Saturday Thriller Theater

Airs at 1:30 p.m.
01/09/82 *Cat Girl* (1957)
01/16/82 *Planet of the Vampires* (1965)
01/23/82 Didn't Air
01/30/82 *The Deadly Mantis* (1957)
02/06/82 *Attack of the Giant Leeches* (1959)
02/13/82 *The Wolf Man* (1941)
02/20/82 *Frankenstein Meets the Spacemonster* (1965)
02/27/82 *It Came from Outer Space* (1953)
03/06/82 *Dracula's Daughter* (1936)
03/13/82 *Dead Man's Eyes* (1944)
03/20/82 *Invaders from Space* (1965)

03/27/82 *Mystery of Edwin Drood* (1935)
04/10/82 *House of Dracula* (1945)
04/17/82 *The Mummy's Hand* (1940)
04/24/82 *Space Monster* (1965)
05/01/82 *Godzilla: King of the Monsters* (1956)
05/08/82 *Terror of Mechagodzilla* (1975)
05/15/82 *Majin, Monster of Terror* (1966)
05/22/82 *Godzilla vs. the Smog Monster* (1971)
05/29/82 *The Bubble* (1966)

Airs at Noon
06/05/82 *The Invisible Man Returns* (1940)
06/12/82 *Son of Dracula* (1943)
06/19/82 *WereWolf of London* (1935)
06/26/82 *Black Friday* (1940)

Airs at Noon and 1:30 p.m.
07/03/82 *The Invisible Ray* (1936); *It Conquered the World* (1956)
07/10/82 *Creature from the Black Lagoon* (1954); *The Beast from 20,000 Fathoms* (1953)
07/17/82 *Frankenstein Meets the Wolf Man* (1943); *Son of Frankenstein* (1939)
07/24/82 *Tarantula* (1955); *The Giant Claw* (1957)
07/31/82 *Curucu, Beast of the Amazon* (1956); *The Monolith Monsters* (1957)
08/07/82 *War of the Colossal Beast* (1958); *Dark Star* (1974)
08/14/82 *The Invisible Woman* (1940); Didn't Air
08/21/82 *The Black Cat* (1934); *The Bubble* (1966)

> ⑳ Movie.
> "It Came From Outer Space." (1953) Richard Carlson, Barbara Rush.

08/28/82 *The Alien Factor* (1978); *No Survivors Please.* (1964)
09/04/82 *The Ghost of Frankenstein* (1942); *The Invisible Man's Revenge* (1944)
09/11/82 Didn't Air

Airs at 1:30 p.m.
09/18/82 *I Was a Teenage Frankenstein* (1957)
09/25/82 *I Was a Teenage Werewolf* (1957)
10/02/82 *The Return of Giant Majin* (1966)
10/09/82 *20 Million Miles to Earth* (1957)
10/16/82 *Monster from a Prehistoric Planet* (1967)
10/23/82 *The Invisible Man* (1933)
10/30/82 *Frankenstein* (1931)
11/06/82 *The Thing from Another World* (1951)
11/13/82 *Attack of the Mushroom People* (1963)
11/20/82 *Reptilicus* (1961)
11/27/82 *Dagora, the Space Monster* (1964)
12/04/82 *The Beast with Five Fingers* (1946)
12/11/82 *Die, Monster, Die* (1965)
12/18/82 *The Strange Door* (1951)

Airs at 2:00 p.m.
10/01/83 *Bride of Frankenstein* (1935)
10/08/83 *Terror Beneath the Sea* (1966)
10/15/83 *The Mummy* (1932)
10/22/83 *Attack of the Puppet People* (1958)
10/29/83 *It Came from Beneath the Sea* (1955)
11/05/83 *Creature from the Black Lagoon* (1954)
11/12/83 *The Tingler* (1959)
11/19/83 *Dracula* (1931)
11/26/83 *Terror of Mechagodzilla* (1975)
12/03/83 *Curucu, Beast of the Amazon* (1956)
12/10/83 *The Deadly Mantis* (1957)
12/17/83 *The Invisible Ray* (1936)
12/24/83 *Tarantula* (1955)
12/31/83 *Mars Needs Women* (1967)
01/07/84 *Return of the Fly* (1959)
01/14/84 *The Million Eyes of Sumuru* (1967)
01/21/84 *Attack of the Mushroom People* (1963)
01/28/84 *Monster from a Prehistoric Planet* (1967)
02/04/84 *Godzilla vs. the Smog Monster* (1971)
02/11/84 *Creature from the Black Lagoon* (1954)

㉓ Movie.
"Beast Of Morocco" (1967) William Sylvester, Diane Clare. Love spells disaster for a beautiful woman because of her predilection for sucking the blood of unsuspecting mortals.

02/18/84 Didn't Air
02/25/84 *It Came from Outer Space* (1953)
03/03/84 *Beast of Morocco* (1966)
03/10/84 *Planet of the Vampires* (1965)
03/17/84 *Atom Age Vampire* (1960)
03/24/84 *Atragon* (1963)
03/31/84 *War of the Monsters* (1966)
04/07/84 *War Gods of the Deep* (1965)
04/14/84 *Master of the World* (1961)
04/21/84 *Destroy All Planets* (1968)
04/28/84 *Yog, Monster from Space* (1970)
05/05/84 *The Thing from Another World* (1951)
05/12/84 *The Beast from 20,000 Fathoms* (1953)
05/19/84 *Godzilla: King of the Monsters* (1956)
05/26/84 *Godzilla vs. The Thing* (1964)

Saturday Night Dead would open with clips from *The Abominable Dr. Phibes* (Vincent Price) conducting his mechanical orchestra.

MOVIE MACABRE/SATURDAY NIGHT DEAD
(WNUV Channel 54)

WNUV began broadcasting July 1, 1982, offering free programming by day, and uncut recent movies via its subscription service (Super TV) by night. However, in April 1986, Channel 54 ended its Super TV and became a more conventional independent station. *Movie Macabre* premiered the first Saturday that April. The opening was a reverse negative of a gated manor house, with a voice-over announcing the evening's title. Eventually redubbed *Saturday Night Dead*, the program now opened with a jazzy, non-horror sounding theme accompanied by clips from *The Abominable Dr. Phibes*, with scenes of the doctor conducting his mechanical orchestra. The intent was apparently to mirror the musical opening of its competition, *Saturday Night Live*.

> **Movie** (54)
> "The Valley Of Gwangi" (1969) James Franciscus, Gila Golan. A prehistoric monster wreaks havoc on a small Mexican town until it is finally destroyed.

Airs at 11:00 p.m.
04/05/86 *THX 1138* (1971)
04/12/86 *The Valley of Gwangi* (1969)
04/19/86 *The Fly* (1958)
04/26/86 *The Mummy* (1959)
05/03/86 *The Curse of Frankenstein* (1957)
05/10/86 *Invasion of the Bee Girls* (1973)
05/17/86 *Taste the Blood of Dracula* (1969)
05/24/86 *The Abominable Dr. Phibes* (1971)
05/31/86 *The Devil Doll* (1936)
06/07/86 *Dark Star* (1974)
06/14/86 *It!* (1967)

Airs at 11:30 p.m.
06/21/86 *The Witches* (1966)
06/28/86 *The Plague of the Zombies* (1966)
07/05/86 *Trog* (1970)
07/12/86 *Frankenstein Created Woman* (1967)
07/19/86 *The Reptile* (1966)
07/26/86 *Invaders from Mars* (1953)
08/02/86 *The Lost Continent* (1968)
08/09/86 *Thirst* (1979)
08/16/86 *The Day Time Ended* (1979)
08/23/86 *Horror Planet* (1981)
08/30/86 *Naked Space* (1983)
09/06/86 *Legend of the 7 Golden Vampires* (1974)
09/13/86 *The Fly* (1958)
09/20/86 *From the Earth to the Moon* (1958)
09/27/86 *The Mummy's Shroud* (1967)
10/04/86 *Frankenstein Must Be Destroyed* (1969)
10/11/86 *Dracula: Prince of Darkness* (1966)
10/18/86 *The Face of Fu Manchu* (1965)
10/25/86 *The Satanic Rites of Dracula* (1973)
11/01/86 *Prehistoric Women* (1967)
11/08/86 *Night of the Living Dead* (1968)
11/15/86 *From Beyond the Grave* (1973)
11/22/86 *Dracula Has Risen from the Grave* (1968)

Movie
"Taste The Blood Of Dracula" (1970) Christopher Lee, Geoffrey Keene. In Victorian London, three middle-aged lechers dabble in black rituals and wind up killing the disciple of a powerful vampire.

11/29/86 *The Devil Rides Out* (1968)
12/06/86 *Dr. Cyclops* (1940)
12/13/86 *Godzilla 1985* (1984)
12/20/86 *The Mummy* (1959)
12/27/86 *The Valley of Gwangi* (1969)
01/03/87 *The Curse of Frankenstein* (1957)

Airs at 11:00 p.m.
01/10/87 *The Devil Rides Out* (1968)
01/17/87 *Taste the Blood of Dracula* (1969)
01/24/87 *The Vengeance of She* (1968)
01/31/87 *It!* (1967)
02/07/87 *The Premature Burial* (1962)
02/14/87 *Dark Star* (1974)
02/21/87 *The Attic* (1980)
02/28/87 *Naked Space* (1983)
03/07/87 *Island of Lost Souls* (1933)
03/14/87 *The Lost Continent* (1968)
03/21/87 *Trog* (1970)
03/28/87 *The Vengeance of Fu Manchu* (1967)

Airs at 11:30 p.m.
04/04/87 *The Plague of the Zombies* (1966)
04/11/87 *Devil Bat's Daughter* (1946)
04/18/87 *Horror Hotel* (1960)
04/25/87 *Night Caller from Outer Space* (1965)
05/02/87 *Frogs* (1972)
05/09/87 *Invasion of the Bee Girls* (1973)
05/16/87 *Laserblast* (1978)
05/23/87 *Dr. Phibes Rises Again* (1972)
05/30/87 Didn't air
06/06/87 *The "Human" Factor* (1975)
06/13/87 *Strangler of the Swamp* (1946)
06/20/87 *The Flying Serpent* (1946)
06/27/87 *The Devil's Messenger* (1961)
07/04/87 *The Dungeons of Harrow* (1962)
07/11/87 *Forbidden Planet* (1956)
07/18/87 *Tarantulas: The Deadly Cargo* (1977)
07/25/87 *Student Bodies* (1981)
08/01/87 *Ghoulies* (1984)
08/08/87 *White Pongo* (1945)
08/15/87 *Rasputin: The Mad Monk* (1966)
08/22/87 *A Boy and His Dog* (1975)
08/29/87 *The Visitor* (1979)
09/05/87 *Tourist Trap* (1979)

SHOCKING THEATER
(WFTY Channel 50)

WFTY-50 launched as a full-time independent station Monday, March 31, 1986. One of its earliest features was *Shocking Theater*, which aired initially on Saturday nights. The creepy opening consisted of an electronic organ and thunderstorm sound effects accompanied by images of a broken window and flashes of lightning. With each flash, one could make out a dark, capped figure brandishing a knife. The announcer's voice was slowed down for spooky effect. (When the station added a weekday afternoon incarnation, their tag line was something akin to "movies too scary to be shown at night.") Unfortunately, Channel 50 was notorious for last-minute programming changes. The following list should be taken with a pound of salt.

Airs Saturday at 9:00 p.m.
04/05/86 *Island Claws* (1980)
04/12/86 *The Great Alligator* (1979)
04/19/86 *Terror Train* (1980)
04/26/86 *Blood from the Mummy's Tomb* (1971)
05/03/86 *Madhouse* (1974)
05/10/86 *Mark of the Devil* (1970)
05/17/86 *Pit and the Pendulum* (1961)
05/24/86 *Murders in the Rue Morgue* (1971)
05/31/86 *Crowhaven Farm* (1970)
06/07/86 Didn't air
06/14/86 *Godzilla 1985* (1984)
06/21/86 *Frankenstein Conquers the World* (1965)
Didn't air 06/28/86-07/19/86
07/26/86 *The Conqueror Worm* (1968)
08/02/86 *The Bat People* (1974)
08/09/86 *Devil Dog: The Hound of Hell* (1978)
08/16/86 *Kingdom of the Spiders* (1977)
08/23/86 Didn't air
08/30/86 *The Dunwich Horror* (1970)

09/06/86 *Dawn of the Mummy* (1981)
09/13/86 *Blood Song* (1982)
09/20/86 *Willard* (1971)
09/27/86 *Monster Zero* (1965)
10/04/86 *Sugar Hill* (1974)
10/11/86 *Welcome to Arrow Beach* (1974)
10/18/86 *Demonoid* (1980)
10/25/86 *The Mafu Cage* (1978)
11/01/86 *Halloween II* (1981)
11/08/86 *Blood from the Mummy's Tomb* (1971)
11/15/86 *Ghost Story* (1981)
11/22/86 *The Demon Murder Case* (1983)
11/29/86 Didn't Air
12/06/86 *Island of the Burning Doomed* (1967)
12/13/86 *KISS Meets the Phantom of the Park* (1978)
12/20/86 Didn't air
12/27/86 *Snowbeast* (1977)
01/03/87 *Legacy of Horror* (1978)

| 13 | Twilight Zone | Movie: "Legacy Of Horror" |

01/10/87 Didn't air
01/17/87 *Ruby* (1977)
01/24/87 Didn't Air
01/31/87 *The Incredible Melting Man* (1978)
02/07/87 *The Comedy of Terrors* (1963)
02/14/87 *Stranger in Our House* (1978)
02/21/87 *Sugar Hill* (1974)
02/28/87 *Madhouse* (1974)
03/07/87 *Uncle Was a Vampire* (1959)
03/14/87 *Breaking Point* (1976)
03/21/87 *The Dunwich Horror* (1970)
03/28/87 *Trick or Treats* (1982)
04/04/87 *The Bat People* (1974)
04/11/87 *Spirits of the Dead* (1968)
04/18/87 *Dawn of the Mummy* (1981)
04/25/87 *Night Watch* (1973)
05/02/87 *The Devil Within Her* (1975)
05/09/87 *The Lady Vanishes* (1979)
05/16/87 *Kingdom of the Spiders* (1977)

05/23/87 *Count Dracula* (1970)
05/30/87 *Terror Train* (1980)
06/06/87 *The Fly* (1958)
06/13/87 *Alligator* (1980)
06/20/87 *The Inheritance* (1947)
06/27/87 *The Legend of Boggy Creek* (1972)
07/04/87 *The Innocents* (1961)
07/11/87 *Cry of the Banshee* (1970)
07/18/87 *Scared to Death* (1980)
07/25/87 *Trick or Treats* (1982)
08/01/87 *Gamera Super Monster* (1980)
08/08/87 *Count Dracula* (1970)
08/15/87 *The Masque of the Red Death* (1964)
08/22/87 *The Oblong Box* (1969)
08/29/87 *The Bat People* (1974)
09/05/87 *Madhouse* (1974)

| 50 | Secret Agent | Movie: "Count Dracula" |

Chapter 8

And the Rest: Additional Local Airings

Local stations did not restrict the airing of monster movies to horror-themed theaters. Terror flicks frequently turned up on *The Late Show* and their generically titled ilk, most having bypassed an official network premiere or prime time airing. Below is a chronological list of such films, by station, that aired during the horror host era, with information on broadcast times provided for each.

Channel 2

Date   Time   Title   Year
03/02/58 1:30 PM *The Lodger* (1944)
03/20/58 11:15 PM *Ghost Catchers* (1944)
05/02/58 11:15 PM *The Spiral Staircase* (1946)
10/06/58 11:15 PM *Ghost Catchers* (1944)
10/07/58 11:15 PM *The Lodger* (1944)
11/23/58 11:15 PM *The Spiral Staircase* (1946)
02/06/59 11:15 PM *Godzilla: King of the Monsters* (1956)
04/20/59 11:15 PM *The Creeper* (1948)
05/23/59 12:45 PM *Ghost Catchers* (1944)
05/24/59 1:00 PM *The Spiral Staircase* (1946)
08/05/59 11:20 PM *Godzilla: King of the Monsters* (1956)
07/30/60 10:30 PM *Cat-Women of the Moon* (1953)
11/04/60 11:20 PM *The Lodger* (1944)
12/27/60 11:20 PM *The Creeper* (1948)
05/07/61 2:45 PM *Abbott and Costello Meet Frankenstein* (1948)
09/26/61 11:20 PM *Invasion of the Body Snatchers* (1956)
09/29/61 11:20 PM *The Beast from 20,000 Fathoms* (1953)
11/07/61 11:20 PM *Godzilla: King of the Monsters* (1956)
01/20/62 12:45 AM *Phantom from Space* (1953)
01/27/62 12:55 AM *Killers from Space* (1954)
03/24/62 1:00 AM *The Snow Creature* (1954)
04/18/62 11:25 PM *Killers from Space* (1954)
05/08/62 11:25 PM *Godzilla: King of the Monsters* (1956)
07/08/62 2:45 PM *Abbott and Costello Meet Frankenstein* (1948)
09/13/62 11:20 PM *Invasion of the Body Snatchers* (1956)
10/19/62 1:20 AM *The Snow Creature* (1954)
10/26/62 1:20 AM *Phantom from Space* (1953)
10/31/62 1:10 AM *The Spaniard's Curse* (1958)
11/02/62 1:05 AM *Killers from Space* (1954)
11/21/62 1:05 AM *The Invisible Woman* (1940)
12/14/62 1:05 AM *Bride of the Monster* (1955)
04/19/63 11:20 PM *The Beast from 20,000 Fathoms* (1953)
06/15/63 11:00 PM *House of Wax* (1953)
10/19/63 1:30 AM *Queen of Outer Space* (1958)
11/02/63 1:45 AM *Caltiki, the Immortal Monster* (1959)
11/09/63 1:00 AM *Indestructible Man* (1956)
11/16/63 1:20 AM *Creature from the Haunted Sea* (1961)
11/23/63 12:55 AM *Attack of the Crab Monsters* (1957)
03/28/64 11:00 PM *The Day the Earth Stood Still* (1951)
04/12/64 12:00 PM *Things to Come* (1936)
10/01/64 11:20 PM *Invasion of the Body Snatchers* (1956)
10/21/64 11:20 PM *The Snow Creature* (1954)
10/31/64 1:00 AM *Phantom from Space* (1953)
11/03/64 1:00 AM *Killers from Space* (1954)
11/06/64 11:20 PM *Them!* (1954)
11/11/64 11:20 PM *House of Wax* (1953)
12/12/64 1:00 AM *The Invisible Woman* (1940)
01/01/65 1:10 AM *Invasion of the Body Snatchers* (1956)
01/15/65 6:00 PM *The Day the Earth Stood Still* (1951)
01/16/65 12:45 AM *The Brain from Planet Arous* (1957)
01/29/65 1:30 AM *Beast from Haunted Cave* (1959)
01/30/65 12:45 AM *The Wasp Woman* (1959)
02/01/65 11:20 PM *Phantom of the Rue Morgue* (1954)
02/03/65 11:20 PM *The Electronic Monster* (1958)
02/06/65 12:50 AM *Attack of the Crab Monsters* (1957)
02/10/65 11:20 PM *Warning from Space* (1956)
02/20/65 12:50 AM *Caltiki, the Immortal Monster* (1959)
02/25/65 11:20 PM *The Revenge of Frankenstein* (1958)
02/27/65 6:00 PM *Gorilla at Large* (1954)
03/20/65 1:10 AM *Target Earth* (1954)
04/03/65 1:20 AM *Them!* (1954)
05/25/65 11:20 PM *The Day the Earth Stood Still* (1951)
06/19/65 6:00 PM *Battle in Outer Space* (1959)
06/23/65 11:20 PM *The Tingler* (1959)
06/27/65 11:20 PM *House of Wax* (1953)
07/03/65 6:00 PM *Earth vs. the Flying Saucers* (1956)
07/26/65 11:20 PM *Satellite in the Sky* (1956)
08/01/65 11:20 PM *Teenagers from Outer Space* (1959)
08/15/65 11:20 PM *Things to Come* (1936)
09/13/65 11:20 PM *The Beast from 20,000 Fathoms* (1953)
09/26/65 12:00 PM *The Disembodied* (1957)
01/23/66 12:00 PM *Gorilla at Large* (1954)
01/29/66 6:00 PM *Earth vs. the Flying Saucers* (1956)
02/07/66 11:20 PM *The Black Scorpion* (1957)

02/23/66 11:20 PM *20 Million Miles to Earth* (1957)
02/27/66 12:00 PM *X the Unknown* (1956)
02/28/66 11:20 PM *Phantom of the Rue Morgue* (1954)
03/14/66 12:40 AM *The Giant Claw* (1957)
03/20/66 12:00 PM *Teenagers from Outer Space* (1959)
04/23/66 11:00 PM *Tower of London* (1939)
05/06/66 11:20 PM *Mothra* (1961)
06/09/66 11:20 PM *Battle in Outer Space* (1959)
06/13/66 1:25 AM *The Hypnotic Eye* (1960)
06/18/66 6:00 PM *The Man Who Turned to Stone* (1957)
08/17/66 11:20 PM *Things to Come* (1936)
09/06/66 1:10 AM *The Wasp Woman* (1959)
09/11/66 12:50 AM *Not of This Earth* (1957)
09/26/66 11:20 PM *The Revenge of Frankenstein* (1958)
10/04/66 11:20 PM *The Werewolf* (1956)
10/08/66 6:00 PM *12 to the Moon* (1960)
10/09/66 12:50 AM *Terror in the Haunted House* (1958)
10/22/66 6:00 PM *Curse of the Undead* (1959)
11/19/66 6:00 PM *The Land Unknown* (1957)
11/24/66 11:20 PM *Return of the Fly* (1959)
01/07/67 6:00 PM *Tower of London* (1939)
02/26/67 12:00 PM *This Island Earth* (1955)
03/04/67 6:00 PM *The Incredible Shrinking Man* (1957)
03/20/67 11:20 PM *Things to Come* (1936)
04/02/67 11:30 PM *Horror of Dracula* (1958)
04/26/67 11:20 PM *The Mad Magician* (1954)
04/30/67 12:00 PM *Master Minds* (1949)
05/11/67 11:20 PM *The Monolith Monsters* (1957)
06/20/67 11:20 PM *Tarantula* (1955)
07/10/67 11:20 PM *The Thing That Couldn't Die* (1958)
07/22/67 6:00 PM *20 Million Miles to Earth* (1957)
08/09/67 11:20 PM *Them!* (1954)
08/18/67 11:35 PM *The Revenge of Frankenstein* (1958)
08/19/67 1:30 AM *The Bowery Boys Meet the Monsters* (1954)
08/23/67 11:20 PM *Curse of the Undead* (1959)
08/30/67 11:20 PM *The Incredible Shrinking Man* (1957)
09/30/67 6:00 PM *Teenagers from Outer Space* (1959)
10/24/67 11:20 PM *The Man Who Turned to Stone* (1957)
10/28/67 6:00 PM *Phantom of the Rue Morgue* (1954)
10/29/67 11:20 PM *The Hands of Orlac* (1960)
11/11/67 6:00 PM *The Day the Earth Stood Still* (1951)
11/27/67 1:00 AM *The Mad Magician* (1954)
12/28/67 11:25 PM *The Abominable Snowman* (1957)
02/04/68 12:00 PM *Earth vs. the Flying Saucers* (1956)
02/05/68 11:25 PM *Curucu, Beast of the Amazon* (1956)
02/20/68 11:25 PM *The Fly* (1958)
02/23/68 1:20 AM *Curse of the Demon* (1957)
02/29/68 11:25 PM *Curse of the Undead* (1959)
03/03/68 12:00 PM *Monster on the Campus* (1958)
03/11/68 11:25 PM *The Leech Woman* (1960)
03/24/68 12:00 PM *Tower of London* (1939)
04/07/68 12:00 PM *The Mole People* (1956)
06/23/68 11:25 PM *Battle in Outer Space* (1959)
07/02/68 11:25 PM *The Werewolf* (1956)
08/05/68 11:25 PM *The Black Scorpion* (1957)
08/08/68 11:25 PM *Them!* (1954)
08/18/68 11:25 PM *The Hands of Orlac* (1960)
09/21/68 6:00 PM *Satellite in the Sky* (1956)

10/18/68 1:25 AM *Not of This Earth* (1957)
11/23/68 12:45 AM *Warning from Space* (1956)
01/04/69 1:00 AM *Daughter of Dr. Jekyll* (1957)
01/18/69 1:00 AM *Attack of the Crab Monsters* (1957)
01/29/69 11:25 PM *The Man Who Turned to Stone* (1957)
02/01/69 11:00 PM *Blood and Black Lace* (1964)
02/27/69 11:25 PM *The Day of the Triffids* (1963)
03/02/69 12:00 PM *The Incredible Shrinking Man* (1957)
03/16/69 11:25 PM *The Beast with Five Fingers* (1946)
03/22/69 1:10 AM *Phantom of the Rue Morgue* (1954)
04/05/69 1:10 AM *Attack of the Crab Monsters* (1957)
04/06/69 11:25 PM *Things to Come* (1936)
04/19/69 1:10 AM *The Giant Behemoth* (1959)
04/27/69 12:00 PM *Tormented* (1960)
05/03/69 1:10 AM *The Atomic Submarine* (1959)
05/13/69 11:25 PM *The Revenge of Frankenstein* (1958)
05/17/69 1:10 AM *House on Haunted Hill* (1959)
06/07/69 1:00 AM *The Hypnotic Eye* (1960)
06/19/69 11:25 PM *The Land Unknown* (1957)
06/21/69 12:50 AM *Frankenstein 1970* (1958)
06/21/69 5:30 PM *The Abominable Snowman* (1957)
06/28/69 12:55 AM *War of the Satellites* (1958)
07/02/69 11:25 PM *Horror of Dracula* (1958)
07/05/69 1:00 AM *Warning from Space* (1956)
07/12/69 12:50 AM *Terror in the Haunted House* (1958)
08/02/69 12:50 AM *World Without End* (1956)
09/20/69 1:35 AM *World Without End* (1956)
09/27/69 1:30 AM *Caltiki, the Immortal Monster* (1959)
11/15/69 1:15 AM *Zombies of Mora Tau* (1957)
11/28/69 1:25 AM *Devil Doll* (1964)
12/26/69 2:00 AM *The Black Scorpion* (1957)
12/27/69 1:20 AM *The Fly* (1958)
01/02/70 1:15 AM *Earth vs. the Flying Saucers* (1956)
01/03/70 1:15 AM *Bluebeards Ten Honeymoons* (1960)
01/04/70 12:00 PM *The Land Unknown* (1957)
01/23/70 1:20 AM *Horror of Dracula* (1958)
01/30/70 1:15 AM *The Hands of Orlac* (1960)
01/30/70 11:30 PM *They Came from Beyond Space* (1967)
02/07/70 1:40 AM *War of the Satellites* (1956)
03/14/70 1:30 AM *Frankenstein 1970* (1958)
03/28/70 5:30 PM *The Incredible Shrinking Man* (1957)
04/19/70 12:00 PM *20 Million Miles to Earth* (1957)
04/24/70 1:35 AM *Zombies of Mora Tau* (1957)
05/01/70 11:30 PM *The Day of the Triffids* (1963)
05/16/70 2:40 AM *The Thing That Couldn't Die* (1958)
06/07/70 12:00 PM *The Abominable Snowman* (1957)
06/26/70 1:15 AM *Satellite in the Sky* (1956)
06/28/70 12:00 PM *X the Unknown* (1956)
06/28/70 1:30 PM *The Brain from Planet Arous* (1957)
07/31/70 1:15 AM *Gorilla at Large* (1954)
08/08/70 1:15 AM *House of Wax* (1953)
10/30/70 1:15 AM *Tower of London* (1939)
11/08/70 12:00 PM *Cyborg 2087* (1966)
11/15/70 4:00 PM *The Incredible Shrinking Man* (1957)
11/21/70 1:45 AM *Creature from the Haunted Sea* (1961)
01/16/71 5:30 PM *The Day of the Triffids* (1963)
02/14/71 12:00 PM *This Island Earth* (1955)
02/20/71 1:30 AM *Return of the Fly* (1959)

03/07/71 12:00 PM *They Came from Beyond Space* (1967)
04/18/71 12:00 PM *Curucu, Beast of the Amazon* (1956)
04/24/71 1:50 AM *This Is Not a Test* (1962)
05/07/71 1:35 AM *Monster on the Campus* (1958)
05/15/71 1:25 AM *Horror of Dracula* (1958)
05/22/71 2:05 AM *Tormented* (1960)
07/24/71 1:40 AM *The Beast with Five Fingers* (1946)
08/06/71 1:35 AM *The Leech Woman* (1960)
09/17/71 11:30 PM *Tower of London* (1939)
10/02/71 11:30 PM *Die! Die! My Darling* (1965)
01/30/72 12:00 PM *They Came from Beyond Space* (1967)
02/13/72 12:00 PM *4D Man* (1959)
02/20/72 12:00 PM *The Blob* (1958)
04/21/72 9:00 PM *First Men in the Moon* (1964)
05/21/72 12:00 PM *Picture Mommy Dead* (1966)
05/28/72 12:00 PM *Journey to the Center of Time* (1967)
08/27/72 12:00 PM *Destination Inner Space* (1966)
10/01/72 11:30 PM *This Island Earth* (1955)
10/14/72 6:00 PM *The Day of the Triffids* (1963)
01/14/73 3:00 PM *Tarantula* (1955)
03/31/73 6:00 PM *The Fly* (1958)
05/18/73 9:00 PM *Psycho* (1960)
06/10/73 11:15 PM *Blood and Black Lace* (1964)
07/29/73 11:15 PM *The Hands of Orlac* (1960)
08/18/73 3:00 PM *Devil Doll* (1964)
08/19/73 11:15 PM *Devils of Darkness* (1965)
09/29/73 11:30 PM *Journey to the Far Side of the Sun* (1969)
10/20/73 6:00 PM *Die! Die! My Darling* (1965)
11/02/73 11:30 PM *Eye of the Cat* (1969)
11/24/73 12:00 AM *The Fly* (1958)
12/07/73 9:30 PM *The Blob* (1958)
03/14/74 12:30 AM *Picture Mommy Dead* (1966)
03/23/74 11:30 PM *The Hands of Orlac* (1960)
04/21/74 12:00 PM *Journey to the Center of Time* (1967)
05/04/74 11:30 PM *Psycho* (1960)
06/09/74 12:00 PM *Cyborg 2087* (1966)
06/22/74 6:00 PM *First Men in the Moon* (1964)
07/19/74 9:00 PM *The Collector* (1965)
08/30/74 11:45 PM *Devils of Darkness* (1965)
09/07/74 6:00 PM *Colossus: The Forbin Project* (1970)
11/30/74 6:00 PM *Crack in the World* (1965)
12/27/74 9:00 PM *Eye of the Cat* (1969)
01/11/75 4:30 PM *The Blob* (1958)
02/09/75 12:00 PM *Cyborg 2087* (1966)
02/16/75 12:00 PM *Destination Inner Space* (1966)
04/26/75 6:30 PM *When Worlds Collide* (1951)
05/10/75 3:30 PM *They Came from Beyond Space* (1967)
05/17/75 2:30 PM *Destination Inner Space* (1966)
05/30/75 9:00 PM *Die! Die! My Darling* (1965)
07/20/75 12:00 PM *Journey to the Center of Time* (1967)
08/15/75 9:00 PM *Colossus: The Forbin Project* (1970)
08/23/75 6:30 PM *4D Man* (1959)
08/28/75 11:30 PM *Psycho* (1960)
10/31/75 1:30 AM *Abbott and Costello Meet Frankenstein* (1948)
10/31/75 3:00 AM *Abbott and Costello Meet Dr. Jekyll and Mr. Hyde* (1953)
11/08/75 2:30 PM *First Men in the Moon* (1964)
11/30/75 12:00 PM *Journey to the Far Side of the Sun* (1969)
11/30/75 11:30 PM *Picture Mommy Dead* (1966)
01/11/76 12:00 PM *Crack in the World* (1965)
03/13/76 3:00 PM *The War of the Worlds* (1953)
04/16/76 9:30 PM *When Worlds Collide* (1951)
04/17/76 3:00 PM *The Man Who Could Cheat Death* (1959)
05/15/76 2:30 PM *The Skull* (1965)
05/30/76 12:00 PM *The Man Who Could Cheat Death* (1959)
06/19/76 11:30 PM *Die! Die! My Darling* (1965)
07/02/76 1:55 AM *Journey to the Far Side of the Sun* (1969)
10/16/76 11:30 PM *Psycho* (1960)
11/20/76 2:30 PM *Journey to the Far Side of the Sun* (1969)
12/12/76 1:30 PM *Crack in the World* (1965)
03/18/77 11:30 PM *Colossus: The Forbin Project* (1970)
05/01/77 11:30 PM *Terror in the Wax Museum* (1973)
05/29/77 11:30 PM *The Collector* (1965)
07/31/77 12:00 PM *First Men in the Moon* (1964)
08/14/77 12:00 PM *The Deadly Bees* (1967)
08/28/77 11:30 PM *Die! Die! My Darling* (1965)
10/09/77 11:30 PM *The War of the Worlds* (1953)
10/29/77 11:30 PM *The Haunting* (1963)
10/30/77 11:30 PM *The Skull* (1965)
01/14/78 12:00 AM *Battle of the Worlds* (1961)
01/15/78 11:30 PM *Monster Zero* (1965)
02/18/78 11:30 PM *Godzilla: King of the Monsters* (1956)
02/18/78 1:30 AM *Atom Age Vampire* (1960)
02/19/78 11:30 PM *Rodan* (1957)
02/19/78 1:30 AM *Island of the Burning Doomed* (1967)
04/23/78 8:30 AM *Colossus: The Forbin Project* (1970)
04/29/78 2:30 PM *Crack in the World* (1965)
05/21/78 11:30 PM *Psycho* (1960)
08/13/78 8:30 AM *The War of the Gargantuas* (1966)
09/03/78 8:30 AM *Godzilla's Revenge* (1971)
11/05/78 11:30 PM *King Kong Escapes* (1968)
11/12/78 11:30 PM *The Andromeda Strain* (1971)
01/13/79 12:30 AM *Godzilla: King of the Monsters* (1956)
02/11/79 11:30 PM *You'll Like My Mother* (1972)
05/19/79 12:30 AM *Psycho* (1960)
06/12/79 11:30 PM *The Horror of Frankenstein* (1970)
07/21/79 11:30 PM *Silent Running* (1972)
08/05/79 11:30 PM *Battle of the Worlds* (1961)
08/12/79 12:00 PM *Colossus: The Forbin Project* (1970)
08/18/79 11:30 PM *The Collector* (1965)
08/26/79 11:30 PM *Monster Zero* (1965)
12/01/79 11:30 PM *King Kong Escapes* (1968)
01/18/81 12:00 PM *King Kong Escapes* (1968)
09/13/81 9:00 AM *The Oblong Box* (1969)
09/13/81 11:00 AM *The War in Space* (1977)
09/20/81 11:00 AM *Star Odyssey* (1979)
09/25/81 12:30 AM *You'll Like My Mother* (1972)
09/27/81 9:00 AM *King Kong Escapes* (1968)
11/07/81 2:00 PM *Aliens from Spaceship Earth* (1978)
01/31/82 11:00 AM *Scared Stiff* (1953)
02/07/82 9:00 AM *King Kong Escapes* (1968)
03/14/82 9:00 AM *Monster Zero* (1965)
07/16/82 8:00 PM *Gorilla at Large* (1954)
07/18/82 11:00 AM *Gorilla at Large* (1954)
10/09/82 1:00 AM *Hands of the Ripper* (1971)
08/21/83 9:00 AM *King Kong Escapes* (1968)

12/09/83 3:00 AM *Scared Stiff* (1953)
05/17/84 2:30 AM *Scared Stiff* (1953)
05/18/84 3:00 AM *Silent Running* (1972)
07/20/84 3:00 AM *Lemora, the Lady Dracula* (1973)
08/25/84 1:30 PM *Ssssss* (1973)
10/14/84 12:45 AM *The Hound of the Baskervilles* (1978)
11/24/84 4:00 PM *The Car* (1977)
12/07/84 3:00 AM *Lifepod* (1981)
01/11/85 3:00 AM *Terror in the Wax Museum* (1973)
01/20/85 4:00 PM *The Sentinel* (1977)
01/25/85 3:00 AM *Don't Look Now* (1973)
01/27/85 9:00 AM *Silent Running* (1972)
02/01/85 3:00 AM *The War in Space* (1977)
02/08/85 3:00 AM *Cauldron of Blood* (1970)
02/10/85 12:45 AM *Godzilla vs. Megalon* (1973)
03/31/85 9:00 AM *You'll Like My Mother* (1972)
05/12/85 9:00 AM *The Car* (1977)
05/31/85 2:30 AM *The Ghost Breakers* (1940)
06/14/85 2:30 AM *The Crater Lake Monster* (1977)
06/21/85 2:30 AM *PSI Factor* (1980)
07/21/85 2:00 AM *What the Peeper Saw* (1972)
08/09/85 2:30 AM *Gorath* (1962)
08/16/85 2:30 AM *Terror in the Wax Museum* (1973)
08/23/85 2:00 AM *Octaman* (1971)
08/30/85 2:30 AM *Psychopath* (1973)
09/15/85 9:00 AM *Don't Look Now* (1973)
09/20/85 2:30 AM *Ssssss* (1973)
10/11/85 2:30 AM *The Hound of the Baskervilles* (1978)
10/13/85 9:00 AM *The Sentinel* (1977)
12/05/85 2:00 AM *Kiss of the Tarantula* (1976)
12/06/85 3:00 AM *The Electronic Monster* (1958)
12/08/85 2:30 AM *Deathdream* (1974)
12/19/85 2:00 AM *A Candle for the Devil* (1973)
12/20/85 3:00 AM *Aliens from Spaceship Earth* (1978)
12/22/85 2:30 AM *Fangs of the Living Dead* (1969)
12/27/85 3:00 AM *She Beast* (1966)
03/14/86 3:00 AM *Don't Look Now* (1973)
04/10/86 2:00 AM *Gallery of Horrors* (1967)
04/11/86 3:00 AM *Till Death* (1978)
04/17/86 2:00 AM *The Lady and the Monster* (1944)
04/18/86 3:00 AM *Chamber of Horrors* (1940)
04/24/86 2:00 AM *The Cape Canaveral Monsters* (1960)
04/25/86 3:00 AM *The Human Monster* (1939)
06/12/86 2:00 AM *The Ghost Breakers* (1940)
06/27/86 2:30 AM *Beasts* (1983)
12/07/86 2:00 AM *Alien Zone* (1978)
12/12/86 2:30 AM *Track of the Moon Beast* (1976)
12/18/86 2:00 AM *The Killings Killing at Outpost Zeta* (1980)
12/19/86 2:30 AM *The War of the Robots* (1978)
01/01/87 2:30 AM *Godzilla vs. the Cosmic Monster* (1974)
01/04/87 9:00 AM *The Sentinel* (1977)
02/06/87 2:30 AM *Blue Sunshine* (1977)
02/08/87 1:00 AM *Till Death* (1978)
02/22/87 1:00 AM *Legacy of Horror* (1978)
03/06/87 2:30 AM *Die Sister, Die!* (1978)
03/13/87 2:30 AM *Peeping Tom* (1960)
04/09/87 2:00 AM *Till Death* (1978)
04/16/87 2:00 AM *Legacy of Horror* (1978)

04/17/87 2:30 AM *Godzilla vs. Megalon* (1973)
04/23/87 2:00 AM *Track of the Moon Beast* (1976)
04/24/87 2:30 AM *Count Dracula's Great Love* (1972)
04/26/87 1:30 AM *Die Sister, Die!* (1978)
05/31/87 8:00 PM *The Shining* (1980)
06/07/87 1:00 AM *The Hound of the Baskervilles* (1978)
07/10/87 2:30 AM *Foes* (1977)
07/12/87 9:00 AM *The Car* (1977)
08/28/87 2:30 AM *Alien Zone* (1978)

Channel 4

Date   Time   Title   Year
12/08/57 11:15 PM *The Spiral Staircase* (1946)
02/02/58 11:20 PM *The Hound of the Baskervilles* (1939)
03/05/58 1:00 PM *The Spiral Staircase* (1946)
03/24/58 1:00 PM *The Hound of the Baskervilles* (1939)
05/09/59 3:00 PM *Tobor the Great* (1954)
04/23/60 2:00 PM *Tobor the Great* (1954)
06/19/60 2:00 PM *The Spaniard's Curse* (1958)
05/19/62 1:00 AM *Kronos* (1957)
03/24/63 11:10 PM *Phantom of the Rue Morgue* (1954)
09/07/63 12:30 PM *The Spaniard's Curse* (1958)
09/21/63 2:00 PM *The Spaniard's Curse* (1958)
10/18/63 1:00 AM *House of Wax* (1953)
10/25/63 1:00 AM *Phantom of the Rue Morgue* (1954)
01/24/64 1:00 AM *The Spaniard's Curse* (1958)
11/30/64 4:30 PM *Satellite in the Sky* (1956)
02/20/65 1:15 AM *Gorilla at Large* (1954)
03/19/65 4:30 PM *The Abominable Snowman* (1957)
05/15/65 1:00 AM *Phantom of the Rue Morgue* (1954)
05/22/65 12:30 PM *The Lodger* (1944)
06/02/65 4:30 PM *Satellite in the Sky* (1956)
06/23/65 4:30 PM *House of Wax* (1953)
10/02/65 1:30 AM *X the Unknown* (1956)
10/13/65 4:30 PM *The Lost World* (1960)
01/04/66 4:30 PM *Gorilla at Large* (1954)
02/14/66 4:30 PM *The Abominable Snowman* (1957)
06/23/66 4:30 PM *Teenagers from Outer Space* (1959)
07/20/66 4:30 PM *Phantom of the Rue Morgue* (1954)
10/04/66 4:30 PM *The Picture of Dorian Gray* (PT 1) (1945)
10/05/66 4:30 PM *The Picture of Dorian Gray* (PT 2) (1945)
10/10/66 4:30 PM *The Lost World* (1960)
10/27/66 4:30 PM *X the Unknown* (1956)
10/29/66 2:30 PM *The Lodger* (1944)
11/29/66 4:30 PM *Satellite in the Sky* (1956)
12/03/66 12:00 AM *The Black Scorpion* (1957)
06/26/67 4:30 PM *The Abominable Snowman* (1957)
07/19/67 4:30 PM *The Lost World* (1960)
08/05/67 12:15 AM *Paranoiac* (1963)
08/07/67 4:30 PM *Gorilla at Large* (1954)
08/19/67 12:00 AM *Night Creatures* (1962)
08/21/67 4:30 PM *The Ghost Breakers* (1940)
10/19/67 4:30 PM *The Black Scorpion* (1957)
11/11/67 11:30 PM *Psycho* (1960)
11/18/67 2:30 PM *House of Wax* (1953)
03/09/68 11:45 PM *Psycho* (1960)
06/16/68 2:30 PM *Satellite in the Sky* (1956)
06/26/68 4:30 PM *Psycho* (1960)

06/28/68 1:00 AM *The Picture of Dorian Gray* (1945)
07/02/68 4:30 PM *Gorilla at Large* (1954)
07/13/68 11:30 PM *Psycho* (1960)
08/09/68 1:00 AM *Paranoiac* (1963)
09/06/68 1:00 AM *The Lodger* (1944)
10/01/68 4:30 PM *Conquest of Space* (1955)
10/07/68 4:30 PM *When Worlds Collide* (1951)
01/24/69 1:00 AM *The Picture of Dorian Gray* (1945)
05/14/70 4:30 PM *The Time Machine* (1960)
08/09/70 4:30 PM *The Picture of Dorian Gray* (1945)
09/25/70 1:00 AM *Dr. Jekyll and Mr. Hyde* (1941)
02/04/71 4:30 PM *The Time Machine* (1960)
10/02/71 11:30 PM *The Birds* (1963)
11/19/71 1:00 AM *A Study in Terror* (1965)
12/10/71 1:00 AM *The War of the Worlds* (1953)
01/31/72 9:00 AM *The Time Machine* (1960)
10/28/72 11:30 PM *The Birds* (1963)
03/03/73 2:00 PM *When Worlds Collide* (1951)
03/17/73 1:05 AM *Kiss of the Vampire* (1963)
04/07/73 12:00 AM *The War of the Worlds* (1953)
04/21/73 12:00 AM *The Phantom of the Opera* (1962)
06/17/73 2:30 PM *The Old Dark House* (1963)
09/01/73 11:30 PM *The Man Who Could Cheat Death* (1959)
11/17/73 1:40 AM *They Came from Beyond Space* (1967)
12/01/73 1:30 AM *The Evil of Frankenstein* (1964)
02/23/74 2:30 PM *The Time Machine* (1960)
03/23/74 1:00 AM *The Night Walker* (1964)
05/04/74 1:00 AM *The Birds* (1963)
11/02/74 3:30 PM *The War of the Worlds* (1953)
11/24/74 1:30 PM *The War of the Worlds* (1953)
12/15/74 1:30 PM *The Phantom of the Opera* (1962)
02/16/75 1:30 PM *The War of the Worlds* (1953)
02/22/75 2:30 PM *The Phantom of the Opera* (1962)
02/28/76 9:00 PM *Westworld* (1973)
07/11/76 3:30 PM *The War of the Worlds* (1953)
10/09/76 1:00 AM *The Birds* (1963)

Channel 5

<u>Date   Time   Title   Year</u>
11/09/57 10:30 PM *The Thing from Another World* (1951)
11/16/57 10:00 PM *I Walked with A Zombie* (1943)
11/23/57 5:00 PM *Ghosts on the Loose* (1943)
12/07/57 10:00 PM *Son of Kong* (1933)
12/12/57 10:00 AM *Thirteen Women* (1932)
12/15/57 10:30 PM *The Leopard Man* (1943)
12/21/57 10:00 PM *The Ghost Ship* (1943)
12/26/57 11:00 PM *Genius at Work* (1946)
12/28/57 5:00 PM *Spooks Run Wild* (1941)
12/29/57 7:30 PM *Cat People* (1942)
01/05/58 7:30 PM *The Body Snatcher* (1945)
01/19/58 7:30 PM *Zombies on Broadway* (1945)
01/26/58 7:30 PM *Bedlam* (1946)
01/29/58 8:00 PM *You'll Find Out* (1940)
01/31/58 11:00 PM *The Whip Hand* (1951)
02/09/58 7:30 PM *The Curse of the Cat People* (1944)
02/26/58 11:00 PM *Woman Who Came Back* (1945)
03/02/58 7:30 PM *The Thing from Another World* (1951)
03/16/58 7:30 PM *Bluebeard* (1944)

03/23/58 7:30 PM *The Brute Man* (1946)
03/30/58 7:30 PM *Devil Bat's Daughter* (1946)
04/05/58 6:00 PM *Ghosts on the Loose* (1943)
04/13/58 7:30 PM *Son of Kong* (1933)
04/20/58 7:30 PM *Strangler of the Swamp* (1946)
04/26/58 2:00 PM *Spooks Run Wild* (1941)
04/27/58 10:30 PM *Things to Come* (1936)
05/11/58 7:30 PM *Bedlam* (1946)
05/16/58 8:00 PM *The Seventh Victim* (1943)
05/16/58 11:20 PM *Genius at Work* (1946)
05/18/58 4:00 PM *The Seventh Victim* (1943)
05/18/58 7:30 PM *Woman Who Came Back* (1945)
05/20/58 11:20 PM *Bluebeard* (1944)
06/22/58 8:00 PM *The Whip Hand* (1951)
06/26/58 11:20 PM *The Leopard Man* (1943)
07/06/58 8:00 PM *The Body Snatcher* (1945)
07/24/58 11:20 PM *You'll Find Out* (1940)
07/29/58 10:55 PM *I Walked with A Zombie* (1943)
07/30/58 11:20 PM *Cat People* (1942)
08/06/58 10:55 PM *The Thing from Another World* (1951)
08/11/58 11:20 PM *Zombies on Broadway* (1945)
08/15/58 10:55 PM *Son of Kong* (1933)
08/22/58 11:20 PM *Isle of the Dead* (1945)
08/29/58 11:20 PM *The Curse of the Cat People* (1944)
08/31/58 11:15 PM *The Whip Hand* (1951)
09/08/58 11:20 PM *The Thing from Another World* (1951)
09/13/58 2:00 PM *Ghosts on the Loose* (1943)
10/05/58 4:00 PM *Bedlam* (1946)
10/18/58 2:00 PM *Spooks Run Wild* (1941)
10/23/58 11:05 PM *The Body Snatcher* (1945)
10/24/58 8:00 PM *Cat People* (1942)

10/30/58 8:00 PM *The Leopard Man* (1943)
11/16/58 11:00 PM *Genius at Work* (1946)
11/26/58 11:05 PM *Thirteen Women* (1932)
01/02/59 8:00 PM *The Ghost Ship* (1943)
01/08/59 8:00 PM *The Seventh Victim* (1943)
01/09/59 8:00 PM *The Whip Hand* (1951)
01/09/59 11:05 PM *King Kong* (1933)
01/22/59 8:00 PM *Son of Kong* (1933)
01/22/59 11:05 PM *Cat People* (1942)
01/29/59 10:00 AM *The Leopard Man* (1943)
02/01/59 4:00 PM *The Thing from Another World* (1951)
02/28/59 10:30 PM *The Hunchback of Notre Dame* (1939)
03/04/59 8:00 PM *King Kong* (1933)
03/16/59 8:00 PM *Isle of the Dead* (1945)
03/30/59 8:00 PM *I Walked with A Zombie* (1943)
04/05/59 2:00 PM *The Curse of the Cat People* (1944)
04/05/59 6:00 PM *Spaceways* (1953)
04/19/59 2:00 PM *The Ghost Ship* (1943)
04/28/59 11:00 PM *Zombies on Broadway* (1945)
05/31/59 10:00 PM *Rocketship X-M* (1950)
06/08/59 11:00 PM *Things to Come* (1936)
06/13/59 2:00 PM *Monster from the Ocean Floor* (1954)
06/17/59 8:00 PM *The Thing from Another World* (1951)
07/11/59 2:00 PM *The Body Snatcher* (1945)
08/05/59 8:00 PM *The Hunchback of Notre Dame* (1939)
08/16/59 8:00 PM *Isle of the Dead* (1945)
08/19/59 8:00 PM *Son of Kong* (1933)
08/19/59 9:30 PM *I Walked with A Zombie* (1943)
08/21/59 1:00 PM *The Seventh Victim* (1943)
08/31/59 8:00 PM *The Whip Hand* (1951)
09/09/59 8:00 PM *Mighty Joe Young* (1949)
10/04/59 3:30 PM *Bedlam* (1946)
10/11/59 2:00 PM *Ghosts on the Loose* (1943)
10/18/59 2:00 PM *Spooks Run Wild* (1941)
10/19/59 8:00 PM *The Thing from Another World* (1951)
10/30/59 8:00 PM *King Kong* (1933)
10/31/59 10:30 PM *The Lodger* (1944)
11/04/59 10:00 AM *The Ghost Ship* (1943)
11/11/59 8:00 PM *Monster from the Ocean Floor* (1954)
11/11/59 9:30 PM *King Dinosaur* (1955)
11/23/59 11:00 PM *The Seventh Victim* (1943)
11/29/59 8:00 PM *The Stolen Face* (1952)
12/01/59 11:00 PM *Isle of the Dead* (1945)
12/09/59 8:00 PM *Rocketship X-M* (1950)
12/09/59 9:30 PM *Project Moonbase* (1953)
12/11/59 8:00 PM *Lost Continent* (1951)
01/05/60 11:00 PM *Cat People* (1942)
01/25/60 11:00 PM *The Curse of the Cat People* (1944)
01/29/60 1:00 PM *The Stolen Face* (1952)
02/24/60 8:00 PM *Voodoo Man* (1944)
02/24/60 9:30 PM *Isle of the Dead* (1945)
03/06/60 4:00 PM *King Kong* (1933)
03/09/60 11:00 PM *The Ghost Ship* (1943)
03/18/60 8:00 PM *The Lodger* (1944)
03/27/60 1:00 PM *Bedlam* (1946)
04/08/60 8:00 PM *Mighty Joe Young* (1949)
04/08/60 11:00 PM *The Stolen Face* (1952)
04/10/60 4:00 PM *Son of Kong* (1933)

04/22/60 8:00 PM *Rocketship X-M* (1950)
04/24/60 1:00 PM *Monster from the Ocean Floor* (1954)
04/30/60 1:00 PM *You'll Find Out* (1940)
05/01/60 10:00 PM *Genius at Work* (1946)
05/07/60 10:30 PM *Genius at Work* (1946)
05/08/60 1:00 PM *The Thing from Another World* (1951)
05/18/60 8:00 PM *Bowery at Midnight* (1942)
05/18/60 9:30 PM *Invisible Ghost* (1941)
05/28/60 11:00 AM *Spaceways* (1953)
06/04/60 1:00 PM *The Body Snatcher* (1945)
06/19/60 1:00 PM *Scared to Death* (1947)
06/24/60 11:00 PM *The Hunchback of Notre Dame* (1939)
06/25/60 11:00 AM *The Seventh Victim* (1943)
06/26/60 1:00 PM *Cat People* (1942)
07/03/60 1:00 PM *The Ghost Ship* (1943)
07/10/60 1:00 PM *The Curse of the Cat People* (1944)
07/10/60 4:00 PM *Rocketship X-M* (1950)
07/15/60 11:00 PM *The Lodger* (1944)
07/20/60 1:00 PM *Spaceways* (1953)
07/24/60 1:00 PM *Lost Continent* (1951)
08/06/60 1:00 PM *The Thing from Another World* (1951)
08/09/60 1:00 PM *The Hunchback of Notre Dame* (1939) Part 1
08/10/60 1:00 PM *The Hunchback of Notre Dame* (1939) Part 2
08/15/60 1:00 PM *Cat People* (1942)
08/17/60 1:00 PM *Bedlam* (1946)
08/23/60 1:00 PM *Scared to Death* (1947)
10/01/60 11:00 AM *Lost Continent* (1951)
10/06/60 1:00 PM *The Curse of the Cat People* (1944)
10/15/60 1:00 PM *Isle of the Dead* (1945)
10/16/60 1:00 PM *Rocketship X-M* (1950)
10/29/60 1:00 PM *I Walked with A Zombie* (1943)
10/30/60 4:00 PM *The Stolen Face* (1952)
11/13/60 1:00 PM *Black Dragons* (1942)
11/18/60 11:00 PM *The Hunchback of Notre Dame* (1939)
11/19/60 1:00 PM *Son of Kong* (1933)
11/20/60 1:00 PM *Ghosts on the Loose* (1943)
11/30/60 1:00 PM *The Seventh Victim* (1943)
12/04/60 1:00 PM *Bowery at Midnight* (1942)
12/14/60 8:00 PM *Mighty Joe Young* (1949)
12/16/60 1:00 PM *The Lodger* (1944)
12/30/60 11:00 PM *The Stolen Face* (1952)
01/29/61 1:00 PM *Spaceways* (1953)
02/04/61 1:00 PM *Rocketship X-M* (1950)
02/05/61 1:00 PM *Spooks Run Wild* (1941)
02/26/61 1:00 PM *Voodoo Man* (1944)
03/05/61 1:00 PM *Scared to Death* (1947)
03/15/61 1:00 PM *The Whip Hand* (1951)
04/02/61 4:00 PM *Mighty Joe Young* (1949)
04/07/61 11:00 PM *The Hunchback of Notre Dame* (1939)
04/09/61 1:00 PM *Fire Maidens of Outer Space* (1956)
04/15/61 1:00 PM *The Thing from Another World* (1951)
04/16/61 1:00 PM *Invaders from Mars* (1953)
04/23/61 1:00 PM *I Walked with A Zombie* (1943)
04/29/61 1:00 PM *Cat People* (1942)
06/10/61 11:00 AM *Ghosts on the Loose* (1943)
06/24/61 11:00 AM *Voodoo Man* (1944)
06/24/61 1:00 PM *The Curse of the Cat People* (1944)
06/25/61 1:00 PM *Invisible Ghost* (1941)

07/01/61 11:00 AM *Spooks Run Wild* (1941)
07/08/61 11:00 AM *Bowery at Midnight* (1942)
07/15/61 11:00 AM *The Body Snatcher* (1945)
07/22/61 11:00 AM *Genius at Work* (1946)
07/29/61 11:00 AM *Black Dragons* (1942)
07/30/61 1:00 PM *The Leopard Man* (1943)
08/05/61 11:00 AM *Zombies on Broadway* (1945)
09/03/61 1:00 PM *Spooks Run Wild* (1941)
09/11/61 9:00 PM *Dr. Jekyll and Mr. Hyde* (1941)
09/17/61 1:00 PM *Ghosts on the Loose* (1943)
09/22/61 9:00 PM *Invisible Ghost* (1941)
09/24/61 1:00 PM *Bowery at Midnight* (1942)
10/01/61 1:00 PM *Black Dragons* (1942)
11/18/61 1:00 PM *Spooks Run Wild* (1941)
11/25/61 1:00 PM *The Thing from Another World* (1951)
11/26/61 1:00 PM *Invisible Ghost* (1941)
12/02/61 1:00 PM *Ghosts on the Loose* (1943)
12/04/61 9:00 PM *The Picture of Dorian Gray* (1945)
12/09/61 1:00 PM *Bowery at Midnight* (1942)
12/10/61 1:00 PM *Voodoo Man* (1944)
01/11/62 1:00 PM *The Seventh Victim* (1943)
01/13/62 11:15 AM *Bowery at Midnight* (1942)
01/20/62 11:00 AM *The Curse of the Cat People* (1944)
01/27/62 1:00 PM *Voodoo Man* (1944)
02/03/62 1:00 PM *The Whip Hand* (1951)
02/25/62 1:00 PM *Chandu the Magician* (1932)
03/10/62 1:00 PM *You'll Find Out* (1940)
03/11/62 1:00 PM *Son of Kong* (1933)
03/24/62 1:00 PM *The Seventh Victim* (1943)
04/01/62 1:00 PM *Fire Maidens of Outer Space* (1956)
05/06/62 9:00 PM *The Hunchback of Notre Dame* (1939)
05/12/62 1:00 PM *Mummy's Boys* (1936)
05/13/62 1:00 PM *Mighty Joe Young* (1949)
05/13/62 4:00 PM *Invaders from Mars* (1953)
06/09/62 1:00 PM *I Walked with A Zombie* (1943)
06/23/62 1:00 PM *The Leopard Man* (1943)
07/08/62 4:00 PM *The Thing from Another World* (1951)
08/11/62 1:00 PM *Cat People* (1942)
08/18/62 1:00 PM *The Body Snatcher* (1945)
09/01/62 1:00 PM *Bedlam* (1946)
09/22/62 1:00 PM *Isle of the Dead* (1945)
09/23/62 3:30 PM *Mighty Joe Young* (1949)
10/16/62 1:00 PM *Zombies on Broadway* (1945)
11/17/62 1:00 PM *Fire Maidens of Outer Space* (1956)
12/29/62 1:00 PM *The Curse of the Cat People* (1944)
01/06/63 3:00 PM *The Picture of Dorian Gray* (1945)
01/19/63 1:00 PM *Invaders from Mars* (1953)
02/17/63 3:00 PM *Dr. Jekyll and Mr. Hyde* (1941)
03/02/63 1:00 PM *Genius at Work* (1946)
03/02/63 10:30 PM *The Spiral Staircase* (1946)
03/08/63 9:00 PM *King Kong* (1933)
03/08/63 11:10 PM *The Thing from Another World* (1951)
03/18/63 11:10 PM *Hangover Square* (1945)
06/08/63 1:00 PM *Fire Maidens of Outer Space* (1956)
07/13/63 11:00 AM *The Leopard Man* (1943)
07/20/63 2:30 PM *The Curse of the Cat People* (1944)
07/22/63 10:00 AM *The Seventh Victim* (1943)
07/22/63 10:00 AM *The Body Snatcher* (1945)

07/27/63 1:00 PM *Cat People* (1942)
07/30/63 1:00 PM *I Walked with A Zombie* (1943)
08/11/63 1:00 PM *You'll Find Out* (1940)
08/16/63 9:00 PM *The Hunchback of Notre Dame* (1939)
09/17/63 10:00 AM *Isle of the Dead* (1945)
09/29/63 1:00 PM *Things to Come* (1936)
11/01/63 11:10 PM *The Picture of Dorian Gray* (1945)
12/24/63 10:00 AM *The Leopard Man* (1943)
02/02/64 11:30 PM *Hangover Square* (1945)
02/08/64 4:30 PM *The Bowery Boys Meet the Monsters* (1954)
03/19/64 11:10 PM *Things to Come* (1936)
03/20/64 9:00 PM *The Fabulous World of Jules Verne* (1958)
04/04/64 10:00 AM *Hangover Square* (1945)
05/05/64 12:30 PM *Hangover Square* (1945)
07/16/64 10:00 AM *The Seventh Victim* (1943)
08/31/64 12:30 PM *You'll Find Out* (1940)
09/25/64 11:10 PM *The Bat* (1959)
10/08/64 10:00 AM *Things to Come* (1936)
10/24/64 4:30 PM *Master Minds* (1949)
11/05/64 10:00 AM *Four Sided Triangle* (1953)
11/13/64 12:30 PM *The Spiral Staircase* (1946)
11/22/64 11:30 AM *Battle in Outer Space* (1959)
12/04/64 9:00 PM *The Picture of Dorian Gray* (1945)
01/05/65 11:10 PM *The Woman in White* (1948)
01/10/65 1:00 PM *U.F.O.* (1956)
01/14/65 10:00 AM *The Whip Hand* (1951)
01/24/65 1:00 PM *Mighty Joe Young* (1949)
02/01/65 11:10 PM *Back from the Dead* (1957)
02/05/65 10:00 AM *Hangover Square* (1945)
02/10/65 11:10 PM *Trauma* (1962)
02/17/65 11:10 PM *The Little Shop of Horrors* (1960)
02/22/65 11:10 PM *The Unknown Terror* (1957)
02/28/65 11:30 AM *The Man from Planet X* (1951)
03/14/65 11:30 AM *Cosmic Monsters* (1958)
03/14/65 3:00 PM *Destination Moon* (1950)
03/20/65 4:30 PM *Spooks Run Wild* (1941)
03/21/65 11:30 AM *It! The Terror from Beyond Space* (1958)
03/23/65 10:00 AM *The Picture of Dorian Gray* (1945)
03/28/65 11:30 AM *The Lost Missile* (1958)
04/18/65 11:30 AM *The Crawling Eye* (1958)
04/24/65 4:30 PM *Bowery at Midnight* (1942)
05/01/65 5:00 PM *Ghosts on the Loose* (1943)
05/09/65 11:30 AM *The Cyclops* (1957)
05/23/65 11:30 AM *First Spaceship on Venus* (1960)
05/23/65 1:00 PM *Gog* (1954)
06/27/65 11:30 AM *Invisible Invaders* (1959)
07/05/65 11:10 PM *The Cyclops* (1957)
07/07/65 11:10 PM *The Unknown Terror* (1957)
08/01/65 3:00 PM *U.F.O.* (1956)
08/06/65 9:00 PM *The Spiral Staircase* (1946)
08/08/65 1:00 PM *Quatermass 2* (1957)
08/24/65 11:10 PM *She Devil* (1957)
09/02/65 11:10 PM *The Beast of Hollow Mountain* (1956)
09/12/65 11:30 AM *Varan the Unbelievable* (1962)
10/10/65 11:30 AM *The Atomic Submarine* (1959)
10/18/65 12:30 PM *Things to Come* (1936)
10/19/65 11:10 PM *The Angry Red Planet* (1959)
10/22/65 10:00 AM *Four Sided Triangle* (1953)

10/24/65 11:30 AM *Teenage Monster* (1958)
10/31/65 11:30 AM *The Saga of the Viking Women and Their Voyage to the Waters of the Great Sea Serpent* (1957)
11/21/65 11:30 AM *Beginning of the End* (1957)
12/05/65 11:30 AM *Phantom from Space* (1953)
12/15/65 11:10 PM *The Hands of Orlac* (1960)
01/02/66 11:30 AM *The Fabulous World of Jules Verne* (1958)
01/04/66 11:10 PM *Last Woman on Earth* (1960)
01/09/66 1:00 PM *The Woman in White* (1948)
01/20/66 11:10 PM *One Million B.C.* (1940)
01/23/66 1:00 PM *Curse of the Demon* (1957)
02/01/66 11:10 PM *The Little Shop of Horrors* (1960)
02/05/66 4:30 PM *The Bowery Boys Meet the Monsters* (1954)
02/13/66 11:30 AM *Bluebeard* (1944)
03/01/66 12:30 PM *Things to Come* (1936)
03/02/66 11:10 PM *Hangover Square* (1945)
03/15/66 11:10 PM *Planets Against Us* (1962)
03/27/66 11:30 AM *The Witch's Curse* (1962)
04/15/66 12:10 AM *The Spiral Staircase* (1946)
05/08/66 1 0:00 AM *The Saga of the Viking Women and Their Voyage to the Waters of the Great Sea Serpent* (1957)
05/27/66 12:10 AM *The Hands of Orlac* (1960)
05/29/66 11:30 AM *Invasion of the Star Creatures* (1962)
05/29/66 1:00 PM *Battle in Outer Space* (1959)
06/05/66 11:30 AM *Night Tide* (1961)
06/11/66 4:30 PM *Spooks Run Wild* (1941)
06/12/66 1 0:00 AM *Hercules in the Haunted World* (1961)
07/03/66 11:30 AM *Cat-Women of the Moon* (1953)
09/01/66 12:00 PM *You'll Find Out* (1940)
09/02/66 12:00 PM *Things to Come* (1936)
09/09/66 9:30 PM *The Spiral Staircase* (1946)
02/15/67 9:30 AM *Four Sided Triangle* (1953)
04/23/67 1:00 PM *Two Lost Worlds* (1951)
04/23/67 1:00 PM *The Undying Monster* (1942)
05/21/67 3:00 PM *The Black Pit of Dr. M* (1958)
06/12/67 8:00 PM *The Hunchback of Notre Dame* (1939)
07/09/67 1:00 PM *King Kong* (1933)
08/13/67 1:00 PM *Mighty Joe Young* (1949)
09/24/67 1:30 PM *The Beast of Hollow Mountain* (1956)
10/01/67 1:30 PM *The Day the Earth Caught Fire* (1961)
10/11/67 9:30 AM *Bluebeard* (1944)
10/13/67 9:30 AM *Fog Island* (1945)
10/22/67 1:30 PM *The Black Sleep* (1956)
10/28/67 4:30 PM *The Bowery Boys Meet the Monsters* (1954)
10/31/67 9:30 AM *Unknown Island* (1948)
12/12/67 9:30 AM *The Tell-Tale Heart* (1960)
12/13/67 9:30 AM *First Spaceship on Venus* (1960)
01/11/68 9:30 AM *Four Sided Triangle* (1953)
01/16/68 9:30 AM *Hangover Square* (1945)
02/08/68 9:30 AM *The Mask of Diijon* (1946)
02/15/68 9:30 AM *The Day the Sky Exploded* (1958)
05/13/68 10:30 AM *Bluebeard* (1944)
05/31/68 10:30 AM *Unknown Island* (1948)
06/04/68 10:30 AM *The Day the Earth Froze* (1959)
06/08/68 2:00 PM *Kronos* (1957)
06/22/68 2:00 PM *I Was a Teenage Frankenstein* (1957)
07/11/68 10:30 AM *The Spiral Staircase* (1946)
08/08/68 10:30 AM *Fog Island* (1945)

08/10/68 2:00 PM *Day the World Ended* (1955)
08/14/68 10:30 AM *The Mask of Diijon* (1946)
08/17/68 2:00 PM *Riders to the Stars* (1954)
08/18/68 1:00 PM *The Head* (1959)
08/19/68 10:30 AM *The Day the Sky Exploded* (1958)
08/25/68 1:00 PM *U.F.O.* (1956)
08/29/68 10:30 AM *The Incredible Petrified World* (1959)
09/10/68 10:30 AM *The Hands of Orlac* (1960)
09/15/68 1:30 PM *The Hound of the Baskervilles* (1959)
11/24/68 1:30 PM *House of Wax* (1953)
12/29/68 1:00 PM *Them!* (1954)
12/31/68 10:00 AM *Kronos* (1957)
01/20/69 10:00 AM *Bluebeard* (1944)
02/06/69 10:00 AM *Unknown Island* (1948)
04/02/69 10:00 AM *The Mask of Diijon* (1946)
06/13/69 10:00 AM *House of Wax* (1953)
06/21/69 3:00 PM *The Black Pit of Dr. M* (1959)
07/27/69 3:00 PM *The Hound of the Baskervilles* (1959)
09/20/69 1:00 PM *Them!* (1954)
11/14/69 11:00 PM *Destination Moon* (1950)
12/11/69 11:00 PM *Things to Come* (1936)
12/27/69 1:00 PM *U.F.O.* (1956)
12/29/69 10:30 AM *Phantom of the Rue Morgue* (1954)
12/31/69 10:30 AM *House of Wax* (1953)
04/18/70 1:00 PM *Them!* (1954)
06/19/70 12:00 AM *13 Ghosts* (1960)
09/04/70 12:00 AM *The Hound of the Baskervilles* (1959)
10/08/70 10:00 AM *Last Woman on Earth* (1960)
10/24/70 1:00 PM *The Day the Earth Caught Fire* (1961)
12/07/70 10:00 AM *Night Tide* (1961)
12/14/70 10:00 AM *The Invisible Woman* (1940)
12/18/70 10:00 AM *The Flame Barrier* (1958)
12/23/70 10:00 AM *Riders to the Stars* (1954)
12/30/70 10:00 AM *13 Ghosts* (1960)
01/05/71 2:00 PM *Red Planet Mars* (1952)
01/19/71 2:00 PM *The Lost Missile* (1958)
03/28/71 5:00 PM *The Woman in White* (1948)
04/09/71 2:00 PM *Destination Moon* (1950)
04/24/71 12:30 PM *She Devil* (1957)
07/28/71 2:00 PM *13 Ghosts* (1960)
08/19/71 2:00 PM *Red Planet Mars* (1952)
08/23/71 2:00 PM *The Flame Barrier* (1958)
09/25/71 2:30 PM *The Woman in White* (1948)
09/25/71 12:30 AM *The Return of Dracula* (1958)
10/18/71 12:00 AM *The Last Man on Earth* (1964)
10/30/71 12:30 AM *The Walking Dead* (1936)
11/03/71 12:00 AM *The Quatermass Xperiment* (1955)
11/05/71 12:00 AM *Gog* (1954)
11/09/71 12:00 AM *Curse of the Faceless Man* (1958)
11/13/71 8:00 PM *Dr. Jekyll and Mr. Hyde* (1941)
11/14/71 3:00 PM *Dr. Jekyll and Mr. Hyde* (1941)
11/15/71 12:00 AM *The Flame Barrier* (1958)
11/16/71 12:00 AM *The Neanderthal Man* (1953)
11/22/71 12:00 AM *The Man from Planet X* (1951)
11/23/71 12:00 AM *I Bury the Living* (1958)
11/30/71 12:00 AM *Invisible Invaders* (1959)
12/02/71 12:00 AM *Red Planet Mars* (1952)
12/07/71 12:00 AM *The Magnetic Monster* (1953)

12/09/71 12:00 AM *The Werewolf* (1956)
12/12/71 11:30 AM *Destination Moon* (1950)
12/13/71 12:00 AM *The Monster that Challenged the World* (1957)
12/15/71 12:00 AM *Donovan's Brain* (1953)
12/17/71 12:00 AM *The Vampire* (1957)
12/20/71 12:00 AM *The Lost Missile* (1958)
12/21/71 12:00 AM *Pharaoh's Curse* (1957)
12/28/71 12:00 AM *The Day the Earth Caught Fire* (1961)
01/05/72 12:00 AM *Voodoo Island* (1957)
01/07/72 12:00 AM *The Hound of the Baskervilles* (1959)
01/11/72 12:00 AM *The Beast with Five Fingers* (1946)
01/13/72 12:00 AM *It! The Terror from Beyond Space* (1958)
01/16/72 3:00 PM *The Picture of Dorian Gray* (1945)
01/18/72 12:00 AM *Terror is a Man* (1959)
01/21/72 12:00 AM *Riders to the Stars* (1954)
02/02/72 12:00 AM *The Revenge of Frankenstein* (1958)
04/01/72 12:30 AM *The Devil Doll* (1936)
06/01/72 12:00 AM *The Last Man on Earth* (1964)
06/03/72 12:30 PM *The Day the Earth Caught Fire* (1961)
06/17/72 12:30 AM *The Last Man on Earth* (1964)
06/23/72 12:00 AM *The Devil Doll* (1936)
06/26/72 10:30 AM *The Devil Doll* (1936)
06/29/72 7:30 PM *Dr. Jekyll and Mr. Hyde* (1941)
07/06/72 12:00 AM *The Werewolf* (1956)
07/07/72 10:30 AM *The Werewolf* (1956)
07/08/72 12:30 AM *Donovan's Brain* (1953)
07/15/72 12:30 PM *13 Ghosts* (1960)
07/15/72 12:30 AM *The Beast with Five Fingers* (1946)
07/22/72 12:30 AM *The Revenge of Frankenstein* (1958)
09/04/72 12:30 PM *The Day the Earth Caught Fire* (1961)
09/15/72 12:30 PM *The Picture of Dorian Gray* (1945)
10/25/72 12:30 PM *The Last Man on Earth* (1964)
12/13/72 12:30 AM *The Beast with Five Fingers* (1946)
01/18/73 12:30 AM *The Revenge of Frankenstein* (1958)
03/07/73 12:30 AM *Devil Doll* (1964)
04/02/73 12:30 AM *The Hands of Orlac* (1960)
05/03/73 12:30 AM *The Picture of Dorian Gray* (1945)
05/31/73 12:30 AM *13 Ghosts* (1960)
08/09/73 12:30 AM *The Werewolf* (1956)
09/20/73 12:30 AM *The Day the Earth Caught Fire* (1961)
10/05/73 12:30 AM *The Deadly Bees* (1967)
10/26/73 12:30 AM *The Thing from Another World* (1951)
10/31/73 12:30 AM *The Devil Doll* (1936)
11/18/73 11:00 AM *The Hunchback of Notre Dame* (1939)
01/19/74 3:00 PM *The Picture of Dorian Gray* (1945)
01/25/74 5:15 AM *The Werewolf* (1956)
02/03/74 6:30 PM *Mighty Joe Young* (1949)
02/08/74 5:10 AM *13 Ghosts* (1960)
03/02/74 8:00 PM *Dr. Jekyll and Mr. Hyde* (1941)
03/03/74 4:00 PM *Dr. Jekyll and Mr. Hyde* (1941)
05/04/74 11:30 AM *The Abominable Snowman* (1957)
05/17/74 12:30 AM *The Deadly Bees* (1967)
05/26/74 11:30 AM *Gorilla at Large* (1954)
08/24/74 11:30 AM *The Hunchback of Notre Dame* (1939)
09/29/74 5:00 PM *King Kong* (1933)
10/04/74 2:35 AM *The Devil Doll* (1936)
10/25/74 12:30 AM *The Thing from Another World* (1951)
11/01/74 12:30 AM *Mighty Joe Young* (1949)

11/08/74 12:30 AM *Dr. Jekyll and Mr. Hyde* (1941)
11/15/74 12:30 AM *The Picture of Dorian Gray* (1945)
04/24/75 12:30 AM *The Deadly Bees* (1967)
04/26/75 3:00 PM *Gorilla at Large* (1954)
05/02/75 12:30 AM *X the Unknown* (1956)
05/16/75 12:30 AM *The Abominable Snowman* (1957)
06/08/75 11:00 AM *The Hunchback of Notre Dame* (1939)
09/27/75 11:00 PM *King Kong* (1933)
09/28/75 2:30 PM *King Kong* (1933)
10/11/75 1:30 AM *Gorilla At Large* (1954)
10/31/75 12:30 AM *Dr. Jekyll and Mr. Hyde* (1941)
11/01/75 11:00 AM *Mighty Joe Young* (1949)
11/01/75 3:00 PM *The Thing from Another World* (1951)
11/20/75 12:30 AM *The Picture of Dorian Gray* (1945)
01/31/76 3:00 PM *The Deadly Bees* (1967)
03/20/76 5:00 AM *The Devil Doll* (1936)
07/01/76 12:30 AM *The Hunchback of Notre Dame* (1939)
09/10/76 1:00 AM *The Picture of Dorian Gray* (1945)
10/01/76 1:00 AM *The Vengeance of Fu Manchu* (1967)
10/08/76 1:00 AM *Trog* (1970)
10/23/76 3:00 PM *The Thing from Another World* (1951)
10/23/76 2:00 AM *The Deadly Bees* (1967)
10/29/76 1:00 AM *The Phantom of the Opera* (1962)
11/05/76 1:00 AM *The Evil of Frankenstein* (1964)
11/12/76 1:00 AM *Dracula Has Risen from the Grave* (1968)
11/13/76 3:00 PM *The Lost Continent* (1968)
11/19/76 1:00 AM *The Mummy* (1959)
11/26/76 1:00 AM *Frankenstein Must Be Destroyed* (1969)
11/27/76 3:00 PM *THX 1138* (1971)
01/07/77 12:30 AM *I Walked with A Zombie* (1943)
01/08/77 3:00 PM *I Saw What You Did* (1965)
01/15/77 1:00 PM *The Haunting* (1963)
01/21/77 8:00 PM *King Kong* (1933)
01/21/77 12:30 AM *The Leopard Man* (1943)
01/22/77 3:00 PM *The Night Walker* (1964)
01/28/77 12:30 AM *The Seventh Victim* (1943)
01/29/77 3:00 PM *The Body Snatcher* (1945)
02/04/77 12:30 AM *Theater of Blood* (1973)
02/05/77 11:00 AM *Mighty Joe Young* (1949)
02/11/77 12:30 AM *Cat People* (1942)
02/12/77 2:30 PM *The Power* (1968)
02/18/77 12:30 AM *Isle of the Dead* (1945)
02/25/77 12:30 AM *Bedlam* (1946)
02/26/77 3:00 PM *Son of Kong* (1933)
02/26/77 11:30 PM *The Birds* (1963)
02/27/77 3:00 PM *The Birds* (1963)
03/04/77 12:30 AM *The Devil Doll* (1936)
06/04/77 3:00 PM *Frankenstein Created Woman* (1967)
06/25/77 3:00 PM *X the Unknown* (1956)
07/15/77 12:30 AM *Dr. Jekyll and Mr. Hyde* (1941)
07/30/77 12:30 AM *The Face of Fu Manchu* (1965)
09/16/77 2:30 AM *The Picture of Dorian Gray* (1945)
10/02/77 1:00 PM *The Other* (1972)
10/03/77 12:30 AM *The Seventh Victim* (1943)
10/07/77 12:30 AM *The Thing from Another World* (1951)
11/05/77 3:00 PM *The Legend of Hell House* (1973)
11/12/77 3:00 PM *The Lost Continent* (1968)
11/20/77 11:00 PM *King Kong* (1933)

11/26/77 3:00 PM *The Mummy* (1959)
11/26/77 1:30 AM *The Evil of Frankenstein* (1964)
12/09/77 12:30 AM *The Phantom of the Opera* (1962)
12/16/77 12:30 AM *Dracula Has Risen from the Grave* (1968)
12/17/77 3:00 PM *The Witches* (1966)
12/23/77 12:30 AM *The Valley of Gwangi* (1969)
01/06/78 12:30 AM *Night Must Fall* (1964)
01/07/78 3:00 PM *I Saw What You Did* (1965)
01/07/78 1:30 AM *The Vengeance of Fu Manchu* (1967)
01/14/78 3:40 AM *I Walked with A Zombie* (1943)
01/27/78 12:30 AM *Mighty Joe Young* (1949)
01/28/78 2:00 PM *The Night Walker* (1964)
01/28/78 1:30 AM *The Body Snatcher* (1945)
02/03/78 12:30 AM *The Night Digger* (1971)
02/04/78 2:00 PM *Theater of Blood* (1973)
02/04/78 1:30 AM *Trog* (1970)
02/11/78 2:00 PM *Son of Kong* (1933)
02/11/78 1:30 AM *The Deadly Bees* (1967)
02/18/78 1:30 PM *The Power* (1968)
02/18/78 1:00 AM *Frankenstein Must Be Destroyed* (1969)
02/19/78 4:30 PM *The Birds* (1963)
02/23/78 12:30 AM *Battle Beneath the Earth* (1967)
02/25/78 2:00 PM *Village of the Damned* (1960)
02/27/78 12:30 AM *Eye of the Devil* (1966)
03/03/78 12:30 AM *THX 1138* (1971)
03/04/78 2:00 PM *Children of the Damned* (1964)
03/04/78 11:30 PM *The Mephisto Waltz* (1971)
03/05/78 2:30 PM *The Mephisto Waltz* (1971)
03/10/78 3:05 AM *Isle of the Dead* (1945)
03/17/78 4:30 AM *The Leopard Man* (1943)
03/25/78 3:35 AM *Bedlam* (1946)
04/22/78 1:30 AM *Dracula: Prince of Darkness* (1966)
05/06/78 1:30 AM *The Curse of Frankenstein* (1957)
05/13/78 1:30 PM *The Haunting* (1963)
06/03/78 2:00 AM *Frankenstein Created Woman* (1967)
06/16/78 5:00 AM *The Devil Doll* (1936)
06/24/78 2:00 PM *X the Unknown* (1956)
07/14/78 12:30 AM *Dr. Jekyll and Mr. Hyde* (1941)
07/15/78 2:00 PM *The Thing from Another World* (1951)
07/21/78 3:00 PM *The Picture of Dorian Gray* (1945)
08/05/78 2:00 PM *The Horror of Frankenstein* (1970)
08/19/78 2:30 AM *The Evil of Frankenstein* (1964)
09/02/78 3:20 AM *Cat People* (1942)
09/16/78 10:00 AM *The Hunchback of Notre Dame* (1939)
09/23/78 2:00 PM *The Witches* (1966)
09/30/78 1:30 AM *The Face of Fu Manchu* (1965)
10/07/78 2:00 PM *The Green Slime* (1968)
10/14/78 2:00 PM *Soylent Green* (1973)
10/14/78 11:30 PM *Westworld* (1973)
10/15/78 3:00 PM *Westworld* (1973)
10/31/78 1:00 AM *Dracula Has Risen from the Grave* (1968)
11/10/78 1:00 AM *Dr. Terror's House of Horrors* (1965)
11/18/78 8:00 PM *King Kong* (1933)
12/02/78 5:00 AM *The Seventh Victim* (1943)
01/12/79 12:30 AM *The Mummy* (1959)
01/20/79 12:30 PM *Journey to the Center of Time* (1967)
01/25/79 12:30 AM *The Vengeance of Fu Manchu* (1967)
02/01/79 12:30 AM *Battle Beneath the Earth* (1967)

02/02/79 12:30 AM *I Saw What You Did* (1965)
02/03/79 2:00 PM *Son of Kong* (1933)
02/06/79 12:30 AM *Night Must Fall* (1964)
02/08/79 12:30 AM *Eye of the Devil* (1966)
02/10/79 1:00 PM *The Legend of Hell House* (1973)
02/10/79 11:30 PM *The Birds* (1963)
02/11/79 2:30 PM *The Birds* (1963)
02/12/79 12:30 AM *The Night Walker* (1964)
02/16/79 12:30 AM *The Lost Continent* (1968)
02/19/79 12:30 AM *Trog* (1970)
02/24/79 12:30 PM *Village of the Damned* (1960)
02/28/79 12:30 AM *The Valley of Gwangi* (1969)
03/03/79 1:00 PM *The Mephisto Waltz* (1971)
03/17/79 3:00 PM *Bluebeard* (1944)
03/30/79 2:25 AM *The Phantom of the Opera* (1962)
03/31/79 11:30 PM *The Night Digger* (1971)
04/01/79 3:00 PM *The Night Digger* (1971)
04/07/79 1:00 PM *Soylent Green* (1973)
04/08/79 11:00 PM *Soylent Green* (1973)
04/20/79 12:30 AM *Bedlam* (1946)
04/27/79 2:30 AM *Isle of the Dead* (1945)
04/28/79 11:00 AM *The Power* (1968)
04/28/79 3:00 PM *The Thing from Another World* (1951)
05/04/79 12:30 AM *Frankenstein Must Be Destroyed* (1969)
05/25/79 12:30 AM *Dr. Jekyll and Mr. Hyde* (1941)
05/31/79 12:30 AM *The Body Snatcher* (1945)
06/02/79 4:30 AM *I Walked with A Zombie* (1943)
06/08/79 12:30 AM *The Picture of Dorian Gray* (1945)
06/08/79 2:45 AM *Cat People* (1942)
06/16/79 11:00 AM *Mighty Joe Young* (1949)
06/16/79 11:30 PM *Theater of Blood* (1973)
06/17/79 3:00 PM *Theater of Blood* (1973)
07/07/79 1:30 AM *X the Unknown* (1956)
07/21/79 1:00 AM *The Curse of Frankenstein* (1957)
07/28/79 1:00 AM *Dracula: Prince of Darkness* (1966)
08/04/74 1:30 AM *Frankenstein Created Woman* (1967)
09/15/79 1:30 AM *Dr. Terror's House of Horrors* (1965)
10/07/79 10:30 AM *King Kong* (1933)
10/13/79 2:55 AM *Children of the Damned* (1964)
10/27/79 11:00 AM *Ben* (1972)
10/27/79 1:00 PM *The Reincarnation of Peter Proud* (1975)
10/27/79 3:00 PM *The Other* (1972)
10/28/79 12:00 AM *The Reincarnation of Peter Proud* (1975)
11/02/79 1:00 AM *The Hunchback of Notre Dame* (1939)
11/03/79 3:00 PM *Westworld* (1973)
11/03/79 8:00 PM *Dracula Has Risen from the Grave* (1968)
11/10/79 8:00 PM *The Mummy* (1959)
11/17/79 8:00 PM *The Thing from Another World* (1951)
11/24/79 8:00 PM *Frankenstein Must Be Destroyed* (1969)
12/01/79 1:30 AM *The Green Slime* (1968)
03/28/80 5:00 AM *I Walked with A Zombie* (1943)
04/11/80 5:00 AM *The Lost Continent* (1968)
04/12/80 1:30 AM *The Evil of Frankenstein* (1964)
04/26/80 3:00 PM *Soylent Green* (1973)
04/26/80 11:30 PM *The Phantom of the Opera* (1962)
04/27/80 3:00 PM *The Phantom of the Opera* (1962)
05/03/80 1:30 AM *The Thing from Another World* (1951)
05/10/80 8:00 PM *The Birds* (1963)

05/31/80 8:00 PM *The Picture of Dorian Gray* (1945)
06/27/80 3:00 AM *The Night Digger* (1971)
07/20/80 5:00 PM *The Day the Earth Stood Still* (1951)
09/13/80 3:00 PM *The Mephisto Waltz* (1971)
10/04/80 3:00 AM *Bluebeard* (1944)
10/11/80 3:00 AM *The Seventh Victim* (1943)
10/12/80 2:30 PM *Westworld* (1973)
10/18/80 1:00 PM *King Kong* (1933)
10/19/80 11:00 PM *King Kong* (1933)
10/24/80 1:00 AM *THX 1138* (1971)
10/26/80 4:00 PM *The Other* (1972)
10/31/80 2:30 AM *Frankenstein Must Be Destroyed* (1969)
10/31/80 4:30 AM *The Face of Fu Manchu* (1965)
11/01/80 3:00 PM *Invasion of the Body Snatchers* (1956)
11/01/80 1:30 AM *Dr. Terror's House of Horrors* (1965)
11/01/80 3:00 AM *Isle of the Dead* (1945)
11/01/80 4:30 AM *Cat People* (1942)
11/15/80 1:00 PM *Ben* (1972)
11/16/80 11:00 PM *Ben* (1972)
11/29/80 12:30 PM *Soylent Green* (1973)
11/30/80 11:00 PM *Soylent Green* (1973)
01/10/81 10:30 AM *First Men in the Moon* (1964)
01/10/81 3:30 PM *Old Dracula* (1974)
01/16/81 4:45 AM *Eye of the Devil* (1966)
01/24/81 3:00 PM *The Phantom of the Opera* (1962)
02/06/81 2:55 AM *Frankenstein Created Woman* (1967)
02/07/81 3:30 PM *The Blob* (1958)
02/13/81 5:00 AM *X the Unknown* (1956)
02/21/81 3:30 PM *Frogs* (1972)
02/27/81 5:00 AM *The Night Walker* (1964)
03/06/81 5:00 AM *Theater of Blood* (1973)
03/07/81 3:30 AM *Night Must Fall* (1964)
03/13/81 2:30 AM *The Power* (1968)
03/27/81 4:30 AM *The Valley of Gwangi* (1969)
03/28/81 4:30 AM *The Leopard Man* (1943)
04/04/81 1:30 AM *I Saw What You Did* (1965)
04/04/81 3:00 AM *The Curse of Frankenstein* (1957)
04/09/81 8:00 PM *The Birds* (1963)
04/12/81 6:00 PM *The Reincarnation of Peter Proud* (1975)
04/17/81 3:00 AM *Trog* (1970)
04/17/81 5:00 AM *Bedlam* (1946)
05/01/81 4:30 AM *The Face of Fu Manchu* (1965)
05/02/81 4:30 AM *The Body Snatcher* (1945)
05/09/81 3:00 PM *Mysterious Island* (1961)
05/22/81 4:45 AM *Journey to the Center of Time* (1967)
06/05/81 1:00 AM *The Legend of Hell House* (1973)
06/05/81 5:00 AM *Battle Beneath the Earth* (1967)
06/06/81 11:00 AM *Children of the Damned* (1964)
06/13/81 2:40 AM *Village of the Damned* (1960)
06/13/81 4:15 AM *The Night Walker* (1964)
06/19/81 3:30 AM *The Green Slime* (1968)
06/20/81 12:30 PM *THX 1138* (1971)
06/20/81 3:30 AM *The Evil of Frankenstein* (1964)
06/26/81 3:30 AM *The Mummy* (1959)
07/10/81 5:00 AM *X the Unknown* (1956)
07/12/81 6:00 PM *King Kong* (1933)
07/17/81 12:00 AM *The Blob* (1958)
07/18/81 3:00 PM *The Phantom of the Opera* (1962)

07/24/81 3:00 AM *Old Dracula* (1974)
07/24/81 4:30 AM *The Abominable Dr. Phibes* (1971)
08/01/81 4:00 AM *The Picture of Dorian Gray* (1945)
08/22/81 2:00 AM *I Saw What You Did* (1965)
09/05/81 4:30 AM *Bluebeard* (1944)
09/18/81 4:00 AM *The Other* (1972)
10/02/81 1:00 AM *Dr. Phibes Rises Again* (1972)
10/09/81 1:00 AM *House of Wax* (1953)
10/11/81 11:00 PM *Westworld* (1973)
10/16/81 1:00 AM *Sisters* (1973)
10/24/81 1:00 AM *The Valley of Gwangi* (1969)
10/31/81 1:00 PM *Dracula Has Risen from the Grave* (1968)
10/31/81 3:00 PM *The Blob* (1958)
11/06/81 2:50 AM *The Land That Time Forgot* (1974)
11/07/81 1:00 PM *Invasion of the Body Snatchers* (1956)
11/13/81 3:00 AM *The Food of the Gods* (1976)
11/13/81 5:00 AM *The People That Time Forgot* (1977)
11/15/81 11:00 PM *Don't Look Now* (1973)
11/20/81 1:00 AM *Empire of the Ants* (1977)
11/20/81 2:55 AM *Asylum* (1972)
11/20/81 4:50 AM *The Premature Burial* (1962)
11/21/81 11:00 AM *Tentacles* (1977)
11/27/81 4:30 AM *The Beast Must Die!* (1974)
11/28/81 1:30 AM *The Power* (1968)
12/13/81 11:00 PM *Night Must Fall* (1964)
12/18/81 4:30 AM *Eye of the Devil* (1966)
01/16/82 3:00 PM *First Men in the Moon* (1964)
01/17/82 11:00 PM *The Mephisto Waltz* (1971)
02/12/82 4:40 AM *The Night Digger* (1971)
02/19/82 1:00 AM *Dr. Terror's House of Horrors* (1965)
02/20/82 1:00 PM *Soylent Green* (1973)
02/21/82 11:30 PM *The Reincarnation of Peter Proud* (1975)
02/27/82 1:00 PM *The Abominable Dr. Phibes* (1971)
02/27/82 3:00 PM *Frogs* (1972)
02/27/82 1:30 AM *The Mad Room* (1969)
03/13/82 1:30 AM *Son of Kong* (1933)
03/20/82 1:30 AM *At the Earth's Core* (1976)
04/02/82 3:15 AM *Village of the Damned* (1960)
04/09/82 3:00 AM *Children of the Damned* (1964)
04/10/82 1:30 AM *The Legend of Hell House* (1973)
04/16/82 1:00 AM *Battle Beneath the Earth* (1967)
04/18/82 11:00 PM *Theater of Blood* (1973)
04/30/82 4:30 AM *X the Unknown* (1956)
05/02/82 6:00 PM *Mysterious Island* (1961)
05/07/82 1:00 PM *Bluebeard* (1944)
05/07/82 1:00 AM *Frankenstein Must Be Destroyed* (1969)
05/07/82 3:00 AM *Sisters* (1973)
05/08/82 11:00 AM *Tentacles* (1977)
05/08/82 1:30 AM *The Valley of Gwangi* (1969)
05/14/82 1:00 AM *Dracula: Prince of Darkness* (1966)
05/22/82 11:00 AM *Dracula Has Risen from the Grave* (1968)
05/22/82 1:00 PM *The Blob* (1958)
06/04/82 1:00 AM *Old Dracula* (1974)
06/19/82 8:00 PM *The Picture of Dorian Gray* (1945)
07/03/82 11:30 PM *Shadow of the Hawk* (1976)
07/04/82 4:00 PM *Shadow of the Hawk* (1976)
07/10/82 3:30 PM *Empire of the Ants* (1977)
07/16/82 1:00 AM *THX 1138* (1971)

07/23/82 1:00 AM *Eye of the Devil* (1966)
07/31/82 11:00 AM *The Body Snatcher* (1945)
07/31/82 3:00 PM *The War of the Worlds* (1953)
08/07/82 4:00 AM *The Other* (1972)
08/08/82 11:30 PM *Night Must Fall* (1964)
08/27/82 4:30 AM *Cat People* (1942)
09/03/82 1:00 AM *The Witches* (1966)
09/03/82 2:30 AM *The Lost Continent* (1968)
09/11/82 1:00 PM *The Power* (1968)
09/11/82 11:30 PM *Don't Look Now* (1973)
09/12/82 4:00 PM *Don't Look Now* (1973)
09/17/82 1:00 AM *Journey to the Center of Time* (1967)
09/17/82 2:30 AM *The Seventh Victim* (1943)
09/24/82 2:15 AM *Trog* (1970)
09/25/82 3:00 PM *Frankenstein Created Woman* (1967)
10/01/82 12:30 AM *The Beast Must Die!* (1974)
10/02/82 3:00 PM *Tentacles* (1977)
10/02/82 1:30 AM *At the Earth's Core* (1976)
10/08/82 12:30 AM *Son of Kong* (1933)
10/17/82 11:30 PM *The Mephisto Waltz* (1971)
10/22/82 12:30 AM *Battle Beneath the Earth* (1967)
10/23/82 3:00 PM *Futureworld* (1976)
10/30/82 1:00 PM *The Land that Time Forgot* (1974)
11/05/82 12:30 AM *The Abominable Dr. Phibes* (1971)
11/05/82 4:30 AM *The Night Digger* (1971)
11/06/82 3:00 PM *Frogs* (1972)
11/12/82 11:30 PM *Friday the 13th* (1980)
11/12/82 1:30 AM *Dr. Phibes Rises Again* (1972)
11/13/82 2:00 PM *The Mummy* (1959)
11/14/82 6:00 PM *The Medusa Touch* (1978)
11/19/82 12:30 AM *Dr. Terror's House of Horrors* (1965)
11/20/82 1:00 PM *Ben* (1972)
11/27/82 3:00 PM *The Blob* (1958)
11/28/82 11:30 PM *Theater of Blood* (1973)
12/04/82 3:00 PM *The Green Slime* (1968)
12/10/82 12:30 AM *Dr. Jekyll and Mr. Hyde* (1941)
12/11/82 3:00 PM *The People That Time Forgot* (1977)
12/18/82 3:00 PM *The Vengeance of Fu Manchu* (1967)
12/24/82 4:30 AM *The Legend of Hell House* (1973)
12/26/82 11:30 PM *Westworld* (1973)
01/07/83 12:30 AM *Dracula: Prince of Darkness* (1966)
01/14/83 12:30 AM *Frankenstein Must Be Destroyed* (1969)
01/14/83 4:30 AM *Night Must Fall* (1964)
01/19/83 1:00 PM *The Power* (1968)
01/21/83 12:30 AM *The Valley of Gwangi* (1969)
01/22/83 1:00 PM *Soylent Green* (1973)
01/28/83 2:30 AM *Village of the Damned* (1960)
02/05/83 3:00 PM *The Bees* (1978)
02/11/83 12:30 AM *The Other* (1972)
02/12/83 11:00 AM *Night of the Cobra Woman* (1972)
02/15/83 1:00 PM *The Picture of Dorian Gray* (1945)
02/18/83 1:00 PM *Bluebeard* (1944)
02/18/83 12:30 AM *Isle of the Dead* (1945)
02/25/83 12:30 AM *Trog* (1970)
02/26/83 1:00 PM *Dracula Has Risen from the Grave* (1968)
03/04/83 2:20 AM *The Seventh Victim* (1943)
03/11/83 1:00 AM *Frankenstein Created Woman* (1967)
03/26/83 3:00 PM *House of Wax* (1953)

03/26/83 1:30 AM *The Mad Room* (1969)
04/01/83 12:30 AM *Old Dracula* (1974)
04/08/83 2:10 AM *Sisters* (1973)
04/10/83 4:00 PM *Rosemary's Baby* (1968)
04/16/83 3:00 PM *Dr. Terror's House of Horrors* (1965)
04/23/83 3:00 PM *The Power* (1968)
04/29/83 1:00 AM *Eye of the Devil* (1966)
05/13/83 12:30 AM *Invasion of the Body Snatchers* (1956)
05/13/83 2:00 AM *Asylum* (1972)
05/14/83 1:00 PM *The Abominable Dr. Phibes* (1971)
05/18/83 8:00 PM *Piranha* (1978)
05/20/83 2:30 AM *The Premature Burial* (1962)
05/21/83 1:00 PM *Tentacles* (1977)
05/21/83 3:00 PM *Dr. Phibes Rises Again* (1972)
05/22/83 11:00 PM *The Reincarnation of Peter Proud* (1975)
05/23/83 1:00 PM *First Men in the Moon* (1964)
05/27/83 3:00 AM *The Food of the Gods* (1976)
06/04/83 3:00 PM *The Face of Fu Manchu* (1965)
06/05/83 12:00 AM *The Mephisto Waltz* (1971)
06/10/83 12:30 AM *Empire of the Ants* (1977)
06/18/83 1:00 PM *Shadow of the Hawk* (1976)
07/01/83 2:30 AM *Journey to the Center of Time* (1967)
07/09/83 1:30 AM *Theater of Blood* (1973)
07/15/83 2:30 AM *Battle Beneath the Earth* (1967)
07/16/83 1:00 PM *Dracula: Prince of Darkness* (1966)
07/16/83 3:00 PM *Frogs* (1972)
07/16/83 11:30 PM *Mysterious Island* (1961)
07/16/83 1:30 AM *Dr. Jekyll and Mr. Hyde* (1941)
07/17/83 4:00 PM *Mysterious Island* (1961)
07/22/83 4:30 AM *The Beast Must Die!* (1974)
07/23/83 1:30 AM *The Valley of Gwangi* (1969)
07/29/83 4:30 AM *Night Must Fall* (1964)
07/31/58 12:00 PM *The Blob* (1958)
07/31/83 11:00 PM *The Medusa Touch* (1978)
08/06/83 3:00 PM *The Green Slime* (1968)
08/20/83 1:00 PM *Soylent Green* (1973)
08/20/83 3:00 PM *Westworld* (1973)
08/26/83 3:00 AM *The Mummy* (1959)
08/27/83 1:30 AM *The Vengeance of Fu Manchu* (1967)
09/10/83 4:00 AM *Scream of the Demon Lover* (1970)
09/16/83 1:00 AM *The Other* (1972)
09/16/83 3:00 AM *Night of the Cobra Woman* (1972)
09/17/83 11:00 AM *The People That Time Forgot* (1977)
09/23/83 1:00 AM *The Land that Time Forgot* (1974)
09/24/83 3:00 PM *Futureworld* (1976)
09/30/83 1:00 AM *Dracula Has Risen from the Grave* (1968)
10/07/83 1:00 AM *The Legend of Hell House* (1973)
10/14/83 4:30 AM *THX 1138* (1971)
10/21/83 1:00 AM *Lady Frankenstein* (1971)
10/21/83 4:00 AM *At the Earth's Core* (1976)
10/28/83 3:00 AM *Screamers* (1979)
10/29/83 1:30 AM *The Witches* (1966)
11/04/83 1:00 AM *The Body Snatcher* (1945)
11/04/83 2:30 AM *Cat People* (1942)
11/04/83 4:00 AM *Children of the Damned* (1964)
11/09/83 8:30 PM *Eyes of Laura Mars* (1978)
11/11/83 1:00 AM *Theater of Blood* (1973)
11/11/83 4:30 AM *Bluebeard* (1944)

11/12/83 1:00 PM *Ben* (1972)
11/13/83 12:00 PM *The War of the Worlds* (1953)
11/18/83 1:00 AM *The Curse of Frankenstein* (1957)
11/18/83 2:30 AM *The Lost Continent* (1968)
11/18/83 4:30 AM *Trog* (1970)
11/19/83 11:00 AM *Crack in the World* (1965)
11/25/83 8:30 PM *Friday the 13th Part 2* (1981)
11/25/83 2:30 AM *Son of Kong* (1933)
11/26/83 3:00 PM *The Bees* (1978)
11/27/83 6:00 PM *Invasion of the Body Snatchers* (1956)
11/27/83 11:00 PM *Friday the 13th Part 2* (1981)
12/23/83 1:00 AM *Frankenstein Created Woman* (1967)
12/23/83 3:00 AM *Bedlam* (1946)
12/23/83 4:30 AM *The Leopard Man* (1943)
12/30/83 1:00 AM *Isle of the Dead* (1945)
12/30/83 4:00 AM *Sisters* (1973)
01/01/84 11:00 PM *The Mad Room* (1969)
01/06/84 4:30 AM *Asylum* (1972)
01/13/84 1:00 AM *Westworld* (1973)
01/20/84 3:00 AM *Village of the Damned* (1960)
01/21/84 1:30 AM *The Mummy* (1959)
01/25/84 5:00 PM *The Innocents* (1961)
01/27/84 1:00 AM *Eye of the Devil* (1966)
02/03/84 1:00 AM *The Abominable Dr. Phibes* (1971)
02/03/84 3:00 AM *The Food of the Gods* (1976)
02/03/84 4:30 AM *The Premature Burial* (1962)
02/10/84 1:00 AM *House of Wax* (1953)
02/10/84 2:30 AM *Empire of the Ants* (1977)
02/11/84 1:00 PM *Dracula: Prince of Darkness* (1966)
02/11/84 3:00 PM *Dr. Phibes Rises Again* (1972)
02/17/84 1:00 AM *Dracula Has Risen from the Grave* (1968)
02/18/84 3:00 PM *Tentacles* (1977)
02/19/84 12:00 PM *Piranha* (1978)
02/24/84 1:00 AM *The Vengeance of Fu Manchu* (1967)
02/26/84 11:00 PM *The Howling* (1981)
03/02/84 4:30 AM *Journey to the Center of Time* (1967)
03/17/84 1:30 AM *The Night Digger* (1971)
03/24/84 3:00 PM *Battle Beneath the Earth* (1967)
03/24/84 3:30 AM *The Other* (1972)
04/07/84 1:30 AM *The Reincarnation of Peter Proud* (1975)
04/14/84 1:00 PM *First Men in the Moon* (1964)
04/20/84 2:00 AM *Lady Frankenstein* (1971)
04/28/84 1:30 AM *The Witches* (1966)
05/04/84 2:00 AM *Old Dracula* (1974)
05/06/84 6:00 PM *Mysterious Island* (1961)
05/12/84 11:00 AM *The Blob* (1958)
05/12/84 1:30 AM *Futureworld* (1976)
05/19/84 3:00 PM *Frogs* (1972)
05/23/84 8:30 PM *Invasion of the Body Snatchers* (1956)
05/25/84 2:00 AM *Frankenstein Must Be Destroyed* (1969)
05/26/84 11:00 AM *The Cremators* (1972)
05/26/84 3:00 PM *The Face of Fu Manchu* (1965)
06/01/84 4:30 AM *Sisters* (1973)
06/02/84 3:00 PM *Soylent Green* (1973)
06/02/84 1:30 AM *The Legend of Hell House* (1973)
06/23/84 1:30 AM *The Brain* (1962)
06/29/84 2:00 AM *Children of the Damned* (1964)
07/06/84 4:00 AM *At the Earth's Core* (1976)

07/13/84 2:00 AM *The Land that Time Forgot* (1974)
07/17/84 8:30 PM *The War of the Worlds* (1953)
07/20/84 2:00 AM *The Lost Continent* (1968)
07/21/84 1:30 AM *The Curse of Frankenstein* (1957)
07/27/84 2:00 AM *Trog* (1970)
07/27/84 4:00 AM *Frankenstein Created Woman* (1967)
07/28/84 1:00 PM *Killer Fish* (1979)
07/28/84 3:00 PM *Ben* (1972)
08/03/84 2:00 AM *The Valley of Gwangi* (1969)
08/03/84 4:00 AM *The Mephisto Waltz* (1971)
08/04/84 11:00 AM *The Abominable Dr. Phibes* (1971)
08/04/84 1:00 PM *Dr. Phibes Rises Again* (1972)
08/10/84 2:00 AM *The Beast Must Die!* (1974)
08/10/84 4:00 AM *The Other* (1972)
08/11/84 3:00 PM *Crack in the World* (1965)
08/18/84 3:00 PM *The People That Time Forgot* (1977)
08/31/84 2:00 AM *Dracula: Prince of Darkness* (1966)
08/31/84 4:00 AM *Night Must Fall* (1964)
09/01/84 1:00 PM *The Green Slime* (1968)
09/01/84 3:00 PM *Empire of the Ants* (1977)
09/07/84 2:00 AM *The Reincarnation of Peter Proud* (1975)
09/23/84 6:00 PM *The Medusa Touch* (1978)
10/03/84 8:30 PM *Let's Scare Jessica to Death* (1971)
10/05/84 3:00 AM *Asylum* (1972)
10/11/84 8:30 PM *Magic* (1978)
10/12/84 1:30 AM *Screamers* (1979)
10/13/84 11:30 PM *Piranha* (1978)
10/14/84 4:00 PM *Piranha* (1978)
10/17/84 8:00 PM *The Exorcist* (1973)
10/19/84 1:30 AM *House of Wax* (1953)
10/19/84 3:00 AM *Scream of the Demon Lover* (1970)
10/20/84 11:00 AM *The Island of Dr. Moreau* (1977)
10/24/84 8:30 PM *Exorcist II: The Heretic* (1977)
10/28/84 6:00 PM *Rosemary's Baby* (1968)
11/02/84 1:30 AM *The Mummy* (1959)
11/09/84 1:30 AM *THX 1138* (1971)
11/09/84 3:00 AM *Night of the Cobra Woman* (1972)
11/10/84 11:00 AM *The Time Machine* (1960)
11/10/84 1:00 PM *The Swarm* (1978)
11/10/84 3:00 PM *The Bees* (1978)
11/10/84 1:30 AM *The Vengeance of Fu Manchu* (1967)
11/13/84 8:00 PM *Love at First Bite* (1979)
11/18/84 6:00 PM *Hell Night* (1981)
11/21/84 8:30 PM *The Attic* (1980)
11/23/84 1:30 AM *Phase IV* (1974)
12/02/84 4:00 PM *Time After Time* (1979)
12/02/84 6:00 PM *The Legacy* (1978)
12/15/84 3:00 PM *First Men in the Moon* (1964)
12/15/84 1:30 AM *Shadow of the Hawk* (1976)
12/21/84 1:30 AM *The Witches* (1966)
12/29/84 1:30 AM *Dominique* (1979)
01/04/85 1:30 AM *The Reincarnation of Peter Proud* (1975)
01/11/85 1:30 AM *Frankenstein Must Be Destroyed* (1969)
01/23/85 8:30 PM *The Return* (1980)
01/25/85 1:30 AM *Trog* (1970)
02/01/85 1:30 AM *Soylent Green* (1973)
02/03/85 12:00 PM *Mysterious Island* (1961)
02/09/85 1:00 PM *Futureworld* (1976)

02/09/85 1:30 AM *The Thing from Another World* (1951)
02/13/85 8:30 PM *Invasion of the Body Snatchers* (1956)
02/20/85 8:30 PM *Young Frankenstein* (1974)
03/09/85 1:30 AM *Sisters* (1973)
03/10/85 11:30 PM *The Mad Room* (1969)
03/24/85 2:00 PM *Rosemary's Baby* (1968)
03/30/85 11:30 PM *Don't Look Now* (1973)
03/31/85 4:00 PM *Don't Look Now* (1973)
04/12/85 1:30 AM *The Beast Must Die!* (1974)
04/17/85 1:00 PM *Old Dracula* (1974)
04/26/85 1:30 AM *The People That Time Forgot* (1977)
05/03/85 1:30 AM *The Abominable Dr. Phibes* (1971)
05/04/85 1:30 AM *Dr. Phibes Rises Again* (1972)
05/10/85 1:30 AM *The Valley of Gwangi* (1969)
05/11/85 11:00 AM *Dracula Has Risen from the Grave* (1968)
05/11/85 1:00 PM *Killer Fish* (1979)
05/11/85 3:00 PM *Ben* (1972)
05/11/85 1:30 AM *Crack in the World* (1965)
05/15/85 8:30 PM *Dressed to Kill* (1980)
05/17/85 1:30 AM *Dracula: Prince of Darkness* (1966)
05/19/85 12:00 PM *The Blob* (1958)
05/24/85 1:30 AM *The Face of Fu Manchu* (1965)
05/25/85 3:00 PM *Tentacles* (1977)
05/26/85 10:30 AM *Ghosts on the Loose* (1943)
06/07/85 2:00 AM *The Lost Continent* (1968)
07/03/85 8:30 PM *Westworld* (1973)
07/06/85 11:30 PM *The Little Girl Who Lives Down the Lane* (1976)
07/07/85 4:00 PM *The Little Girl Who Lives Down the Lane* (1976)
07/10/85 8:30 PM *The Attic* (1980)
07/11/85 8:30 PM *Dracula* (1979)
07/12/85 1:30 AM *Frankenstein Must Be Destroyed* (1969)
07/19/85 4:45 AM *Asylum* (1972)
07/20/85 1:00 PM *Futureworld* (1976)
07/20/85 3:00 PM *Empire of the Ants* (1977)
07/20/85 1:30 AM *The Curse of Frankenstein* (1957)
07/22/85 1:30 AM *The Valley of Gwangi* (1969)
07/26/85 1:30 AM *Screamers* (1979)
07/27/85 1:00 PM *The Green Slime* (1968)
07/31/85 8:00 PM *The Haunting of Julia* (1977)
08/02/85 3:30 AM *The Reincarnation of Peter Proud* (1975)
08/03/85 11:30 PM *The Haunting of Julia* (1977)
08/09/85 1:30 AM *THX 1138* (1971)
08/10/85 3:00 PM *The Land that Time Forgot* (1974)
08/13/85 1:30 AM *Trog* (1970)
08/16/85 1:30 AM *The Witches* (1966)
08/17/85 3:00 PM *Frogs* (1972)
08/17/85 1:30 AM *Soylent Green* (1973)
08/19/85 1:30 AM *Frankenstein Created Woman* (1967)
08/27/85 1:30 AM *The Mummy* (1959)
08/31/85 1:00 PM *The Island of Dr. Moreau* (1977)
09/04/85 8:30 PM *Let's Scare Jessica to Death* (1971)
09/13/85 1:30 AM *Sisters* (1973)
09/14/85 4:30 AM *The Premature Burial* (1962)
09/19/85 1:30 AM *The Beast Must Die!* (1974)
09/25/85 8:30 PM *The Return* (1980)
10/04/85 1:30 AM *Dr. Phibes Rises Again* (1972)

10/06/85 2:00 PM *Love at First Bite* (1979)
10/19/85 8:00 PM *Halloween II* (1981)
10/19/85 11:00 PM *Rosemary's Baby* (1968)
10/19/85 1:30 AM *The Abominable Dr. Phibes* (1971)
10/20/85 4:00 PM *Young Frankenstein* (1974)
10/20/85 6:00 PM *The Exorcist* (1973)
10/20/85 11:30 PM *Halloween II* (1981)
10/26/85 1:00 PM *Beasts* (1983)
10/27/85 10:30 AM *Spooks Run Wild* (1941)
10/27/85 4:00 PM *Time After Time* (1979)
10/27/85 6:00 PM *Exorcist II: The Heretic* (1977)
11/03/85 2:00 PM *Piranha* (1978)
11/09/85 11:00 AM *The War of the Worlds* (1953)
11/09/85 3:00 PM *The Bees* (1978)
11/10/85 4:00 PM *Magic* (1978)
11/10/85 6:00 PM *Hell Night* (1981)
11/15/85 1:30 AM *House of Wax* (1953)
11/17/85 12:00 PM *Mysterious Island* (1961)
11/23/85 11:00 AM *The Swarm* (1978)
11/29/85 1:30 AM *Shadow of the Hawk* (1976)
12/22/85 11:30 PM *Eyes of Laura Mars* (1978)
12/27/85 1:30 AM *Old Dracula* (1974)
01/03/86 1:30 AM *Dominique* (1979)
01/05/86 4:00 PM *Killer Fish* (1979)
02/08/86 3:00 PM *Saturn 3* (1980)
02/08/86 1:30 AM *Terror in the Wax Museum* (1973)
02/23/86 6:00 PM *Dressed to Kill* (1980)
02/26/86 8:30 PM *The Attic* (1980)
03/01/86 3:00 PM *First Men in the Moon* (1964)
03/01/86 8:00 PM *Scanners* (1981)
03/02/86 11:30 PM *Scanners* (1981)
03/07/86 3:30 AM *Dr. Jekyll and Mr. Hyde* (1941)
03/29/86 8:00 PM *Strange Invaders* (1983)
03/30/86 11:30 PM *Strange Invaders* (1983)
04/06/86 6:00 PM *The Medusa Touch* (1978)
04/06/86 11:30 PM *The Little Girl Who Lives Down the Lane* (1976)
04/11/86 3:30 AM *Rosemary's Baby* (1968)
04/12/86 8:00 PM *Ghost Story* (1981)
04/13/86 11:30 PM *Ghost Story* (1981)
04/26/86 11:00 AM *Crack in the World* (1965)
05/02/86 1:30 AM *Turkey Shoot* (1982)
05/03/86 3:00 PM *Ben* (1972)
05/17/86 3:00 PM *Tentacles* (1977)
05/23/86 1:30 AM *The Cremators* (1972)
05/23/86 3:00 AM *Lady Frankenstein* (1971)
05/25/86 4:00 PM *Dracula* (1979)
06/06/86 1:30 AM *Screamers* (1979)
06/06/86 4:30 AM *Night of the Cobra Woman* (1972)
06/07/86 1:00 PM *Futureworld* (1976)
06/07/86 3:00 PM *The Island of Dr. Moreau* (1977)
06/08/86 12:00 PM *The Legacy* (1978)
06/13/86 1:30 AM *The People That Time Forgot* (1977)
06/15/86 4:00 PM *Don't Look Now* (1973)
06/19/86 8:00 PM *Eyes of Laura Mars* (1978)
06/20/86 1:30 AM *The Reincarnation of Peter Proud* (1975)
06/28/86 8:00 PM *Bluebeard* (1972)
06/29/86 6:00 PM *The Entity* (1982)

06/29/86 11:30 PM *Bluebeard* (1972)
07/05/86 3:00 PM *Empire of the Ants* (1977)
07/05/86 8:00 PM *Cat People* (1982)
07/06/86 11:30 PM *Cat People* (1982)
07/09/86 8:30 PM *Let's Scare Jessica to Death* (1971)
07/12/86 8:00 PM *Piranha II: The Spawning* (1981)
07/13/86 11:30 PM *Piranha II: The Spawning* (1981)
07/18/86 12:30 AM *The Abominable Dr. Phibes* (1971)
07/18/86 2:30 AM *Old Dracula* (1974)
07/20/86 2:00 PM *Mysterious Island* (1961)
07/20/86 6:00 PM *Piranha* (1978)
07/24/86 8:00 PM *Magic* (1978)
07/25/86 12:30 AM *Dr. Phibes Rises Again* (1972)
07/27/86 4:00 PM *Love at First Bite* (1979)
08/03/86 12:00 PM *The Blob* (1958)
08/03/86 1:30 PM *Journey to the Center of the Earth* (1959)
08/08/86 4:30 AM *Asylum* (1972)
08/13/86 8:30 PM *Phase IV* (1974)
08/15/86 2:30 AM *At the Earth's Core* (1976)
09/10/86 8:30 PM *The Hound of the Baskervilles* (1939)
09/12/86 12:30 AM *Beasts* (1983)
09/26/86 1:30 AM *The Swarm* (1978)
09/28/86 2:00 PM *Time After Time* (1979)
10/07/86 8:00 PM *The Exorcist* (1973)
10/08/86 8:00 PM *Exorcist II: The Heretic* (1977)
10/09/86 8:00 PM *Friday the 13th* (1980)
10/10/86 8:00 PM *Friday the 13th: Part 2* (1981)
10/11/86 3:00 PM *The Bees* (1978)
10/17/86 4:00 AM *Dominique* (1979)
10/18/86 11:30 PM *Frankenstein Must Be Destroyed* (1969)
10/30/86 8:00 PM *Night of the Living Dead* (1968)
10/31/86 8:00 PM *Halloween* (1978)
11/02/86 4:00 PM *Strange Invaders* (1983)
11/03/86 8:30 PM *The War of the Worlds* (1953)
11/15/86 8:00 PM *Amityville: The Demon* (1983)
11/15/86 11:30 PM *Dracula Has Risen from the Grave* (1968)
11/16/86 11:30 PM *Amityville: The Demon* (1983)
11/21/86 8:00 PM *Young Frankenstein* (1974)
12/06/86 4:00 AM *The Mad Room* (1969)
12/28/86 12:00 PM *The Return* (1980)
01/10/87 1:30 AM *The Valley of Gwangi* (1969)
01/15/87 8:00 PM *The Little Girl Who Lives Down the Lane* (1976)
01/16/87 1:30 AM *Let's Scare Jessica To Death* (1971)
01/16/87 3:00 AM *The Cremators* (1972)
01/30/87 3:00 AM *Lady Frankenstein* (1971)
02/06/87 1:30 AM *Phase IV* (1974)
02/16/87 8:00 PM *Dressed to Kill* (1980)
02/21/87 3:00 PM *Saturn 3* (1980)
02/21/87 8:00 PM *Swamp Thing* (1982)
02/22/87 11:30 PM *Swamp Thing* (1982)
02/26/87 8:00 PM *Hell Night* (1981)
02/27/87 1:30 AM *House of Wax* (1953)
02/27/87 4:30 AM *Screamers* (1979)
03/01/87 6:00 PM *The Medusa Touch* (1978)
03/06/87 1:30 AM *The Curse of Frankenstein* (1957)
03/06/87 4:30 AM *The Premature Burial* (1962)
03/20/87 3:00 AM *Night of the Cobra Woman* (1972)

03/28/87 11:30 PM *Dracula* (1979)
03/29/87 11:30 PM *Rosemary's Baby* (1968)
04/03/87 1:30 AM *Old Dracula* (1974)
04/29/87 8:00 PM *Student Bodies* (1981)
04/30/87 2:30 AM *Tales That Witness Madness* (1973)
05/09/87 2:30 AM *Journey to the Center of the Earth* (1959)
05/16/87 3:00 PM *The Land That Time Forgot* (1974)
05/17/87 11:30 PM *The Fan* (1981)
05/18/87 8:00 PM *Jaws* (1975)
05/19/87 8:00 PM *My Bloody Valentine* (1981)
05/21/87 8:00 PM *Happy Birthday to Me* (1981)
05/24/87 12:00 PM *Ben* (1972)
05/24/87 2:00 PM *Mysterious Island* (1961)
05/24/87 4:00 PM *Killer Fish* (1979)
05/24/87 11:30 PM *Fortress* (1985)
05/26/87 8:00 PM *Piranha* (1978)
05/27/87 8:00 PM *Bug* (1975)
06/13/87 4:30 AM *The Cremators* (1972)
06/26/87 8:00 PM *Dominique* (1979)
06/27/87 3:00 PM *Futureworld* (1976)
06/27/87 4:30 AM *Lady Frankenstein* (1971)
07/09/87 8:00 PM *Terror in the Wax Museum* (1973)
07/10/87 8:00 PM *Firestarter* (1984)
07/12/87 11:30 PM *Firestarter* (1984)
07/17/87 3:30 AM *The Legacy* (1978)
07/30/87 3:00 AM *Shadow of the Hawk* (1976)
08/08/87 3:00 PM *Frogs* (1972)
09/03/87 2:30 AM *Tentacles* (1977)

Channel 7
Date Time Title Year
01/21/58 11:20 PM *Cry of the Werewolf* (1944)
07/20/58 11:00 PM *The Return of the Vampire* (1943)
08/24/58 11:00 PM *The Soul of a Monster* (1944)
03/07/59 10:30 PM *Invaders from Mars* (1953)
07/19/59 11:25 PM *Cry of the Werewolf* (1944)
08/09/59 2:00 PM *Invaders from Mars* (1953)
09/26/59 4:00 PM *Cry of the Werewolf* (1944)
11/14/59 11:00 PM *Destination Moon* (1950)
11/21/59 12:30 AM *The Soul of a Monster* (1944)
12/12/59 12:30 AM *The Return of the Vampire* (1943)
01/03/60 1:30 PM *Fire Maidens of Outer Space* (1956)
07/24/60 1:30 PM *Invaders from Mars* (1953)
07/30/60 1:30 PM *Fire Maidens of Outer Space* (1956)
10/01/60 11:00 PM *Destination Moon* (1950)
12/05/60 11:30 PM *Beginning of the End* (1957)
12/13/60 11:30 PM *Sh! The Octopus* (1937)
12/19/60 11:30 PM *The Unearthly* (1957)
01/13/61 11:30 PM *The Phantom from 10,000 Leagues* (1955)
04/09/61 2:00 PM *Godzilla: King of the Monsters* (1956)
04/19/61 11:31 PM *Destination Moon* (1950)
05/14/61 1:30 PM *The Phantom from 10,000 Leagues* (1955)
06/10/61 11:00 PM *The Phantom of the Opera* (1925)
06/14/61 11:31 PM *Sh! The Octopus* (1937)
06/20/61 11:31 PM *The Unearthly* (1957)
08/01/61 11:31 PM *Godzilla: King of the Monsters* (1956)
08/08/61 11:31 PM *Beginning of the End* (1957)
09/19/61 11:31 PM *Destination Moon* (1950)

11/01/61 11:31PM *Invisible Agent* (1942)
11/21/61 11:31PM *The Phantom from 10,000 Leagues* (1955)
12/13/61 11:31PM *Phantom from Space* (1953)
01/03/62 11:31PM *The Phantom of the Opera* (1925)
01/16/62 11:31PM *Sh! The Octopus* (1937)
02/16/62 11:31PM *Flesh and Fantasy* (1943)
02/21/62 11:31PM *Metropolis* (1927)
02/26/62 11:31PM *The Unearthly* (1957)
05/10/62 11:31PM *Invisible Agent* (1942)
06/04/62 11:31PM *The Undying Monster* (1942)
06/14/62 11:31PM *Phantom from Space* (1953)
08/12/62 11:31PM *The Hunchback of Notre Dame* (1939)
09/18/62 11:30 PM *Invisible Agent* (1942)
09/28/62 11:30 PM *Mark of the Vampire* (1935)
10/06/62 11:15 PM *Forbidden Planet* (1956)
01/25/63 11:30 PM *Flesh and Fantasy* (1943)
01/26/63 11:15 PM *Phantom from Space* (1953)
04/26/63 11:30 PM *Forbidden Planet* (1956)
07/13/63 11:15 PM *Invisible Agent* (1942)
09/21/63 12:35 AM *Phantom from Space* (1953)
10/19/63 12:35 AM *Flesh and Fantasy* (1943)
11/16/63 12:35 AM *Forbidden Planet* (1956)
11/22/63 11:30 PM *First Man into Space* (1959)
12/13/63 11:30 PM *The Haunted Strangler* (1958)
01/31/64 11:30 PM *First Man into Space* (1959)
03/07/64 11:30 PM *Mark of the Vampire* (1935)
05/08/64 11:30 PM *Forbidden Planet* (1956)
05/16/64 11:35 PM *The Haunted Strangler* (1958)
07/04/64 12:05 AM *First Man into Space* (1959)
09/01/64 11:30 PM *Battle of the Worlds* (1961)
09/17/64 11:30 PM *Fiend Without a Face* (1958)
09/28/64 11:30 PM *Mark of the Vampire* (1935)
10/19/64 11:30 PM *Atom Age Vampire* (1960)
10/29/64 11:30 PM *The Haunted Strangler* (1958)
12/08/64 1:00 PM *First Man into Space* (1959)
01/30/65 11:10 PM *Return of the Fly* (1959)
04/10/65 11:10 PM *The Day the Earth Stood Still* (1951)
11/16/65 11:30 PM *Gorgo* (1961)
12/14/65 11:30 PM *Battle of the Worlds* (1961)
01/20/66 11:30 PM *The Mysterians* (1957)
01/25/66 11:30 PM *Return of the Fly* (1959)
02/25/66 11:30 PM *From the Earth to the Moon* (1958)
03/23/66 11:30 PM *The Day the Earth Stood Still* (1951)
04/05/66 11:30 PM *Port Sinister* (1953)
04/21/66 11:30 PM *Abbott and Costello Meet Frankenstein* (1948)
05/12/66 11:30 PM *Gorgo* (1961)
06/13/66 11:30 PM *Battle of the Worlds* (1961)
08/19/66 11:30 PM *The Mysterians* (1957)
08/22/66 11:30 PM *Fiend Without a Face* (1958)
08/29/66 11:30 PM *First Man into Space* (1959)
10/08/66 11:15 PM *The Fly* (1958)
10/10/66 11:30 PM *From the Earth to the Moon* (1958)
11/04/66 11:30 PM *Horror of Dracula* (1958)
12/05/66 11:30 PM *Port Sinister* (1953)
01/27/67 11:30 PM *Devil Doll* (1964)
02/13/67 11:30 PM *The Day the Earth Stood Still* (1951)
02/22/67 11:30 PM *From the Earth to the Moon* (1958)
02/24/67 11:30 PM *The Fly* (1958)

04/21/67 1:00 AM *The Haunted Strangler* (1958)
04/28/67 1:00 AM *Fiend Without a Face* (1958)
06/02/67 1:00 AM *Return of the Fly* (1959)
06/09/67 1:00 AM *The Mysterians* (1957)
06/23/67 1:00 AM *Port Sinister* (1953)
10/06/67 1:00 AM *Devil Doll* (1964)
10/13/67 1:00 AM *Horror of Dracula* (1958)
10/20/67 1:00 AM *The Fly* (1958)
11/03/67 1:00 AM *Frozen Alive* (1964)
01/12/68 1:00 AM *Abbott and Costello Meet Frankenstein* (1948)
03/02/68 11:15 PM *Cyborg 2087* (1966)
03/10/68 11:30 PM *Destination Inner Space* (1966)
05/18/68 11:15 PM *Blood of the Vampire* (1958)
07/20/68 2:00 PM *Abbott and Costello Meet Frankenstein* (1948)
08/24/68 11:15 PM *Devil Doll* (1964)
09/29/68 11:45 PM *Cyborg 2087* (1966)
10/26/68 1:00 AM *Blood of the Vampire* (1958)
11/02/68 11:15 PM *Destination Inner Space* (1966)
01/19/69 11:15 PM *Dark Intruder* (1965)
02/08/69 11:15 PM *This Is Not a Test* (1962)
05/10/69 3:30 PM *Munster, Go Home!* (1966)
05/17/69 11:15 PM *Journey to the Center of Time* (1967)
06/06/69 1:00 AM *Blood of the Vampire* (1958)
06/21/69 11:20 PM *Frozen Alive* (1964)
06/27/69 1:00 AM *Gorgo* (1961)
07/12/69 1:00 AM *Nightmare* (1964)
07/25/69 1:00 AM *Return of the Fly* (1959)
08/08/69 1:00 AM *The Day the Earth Stood Still* (1951)
08/16/69 1:00 AM *From the Earth to the Moon* (1958)
09/28/69 11:35 PM *Cyborg 2087* (1966)
10/24/69 1:00 AM *Port Sinister* (1953)
10/26/69 12:20 AM *Scream of Fear* (1961)
10/31/69 1:00 AM *The Gorgon* (1964)
11/07/69 1:00 AM *Homicidal* (1961)
11/08/69 1:00 AM *The Blob* (1958)
11/09/69 4:00 PM *Mysterious Island* (1961)
11/14/69 1:00 AM *Mr. Sardonicus* (1961)
11/21/69 1:00 AM *Maniac* (1963)
11/22/69 12:50 AM *The Curse of the Mummy's Tomb* (1964)
12/05/69 1:00 AM *Maniac* (1963)
01/09/70 1:00 AM *Horror of Dracula* (1958)
01/31/70 11:15 PM *The Birds* (1963)
01/31/70 1:30 AM *Blood of the Vampire* (1958)
02/21/70 11:20 PM *Die! Die! My Darling* (1965)
02/21/70 1:20 AM *First Men in the Moon* (1964)
02/27/70 1:00 AM *Journey to the Center of Time* (1967)
02/28/70 1:20 AM *Nightmare* (1964)
03/13/70 1:00 AM *Dark Intruder* (1965)
04/11/70 1:30 AM *This Is Not a Test* (1962)
04/25/70 11:20 PM *Cyborg 2087* (1966)
07/12/70 11:50 PM *Scream of Fear* (1961)
10/03/70 12:50 AM *Destination Inner Space* (1966)
10/09/70 1:00 AM *The Curse of the Mummy's Tomb* (1964)
10/18/70 4:00 PM *First Men in the Moon* (1964)
10/23/70 1:00 AM *Nightmare* (1964)
11/06/70 1:00 AM *Frozen Alive* (1964)
11/13/70 1:00 AM *Mr. Sardonicus* (1961)
11/14/70 1:20 AM *Island of Terror* (1966)

11/20/70 1:00 AM *Blood of the Vampire* (1958)
11/21/70 11:20 AM *Die! Die! My Darling* (1965)
11/29/70 4:00 PM *Mysterious Island* (1961)
01/08/71 1:00 AM *The Invisible Boy* (1957)
01/23/71 1:30 AM *The Gorgon* (1964)
02/20/71 1:30 AM *Strait-Jacket* (1964)
02/27/71 1:30 AM *Dinosaurus!* (1960)
03/06/71 1:30 AM *Cyborg 2087* (1966)
05/16/71 12:00 AM *Die! Die! My Darling* (1965)
05/29/71 11:00 PM *Mysterious Island* (1961)
07/03/71 3:00 PM *Munster, Go Home!* (1966)
07/23/71 11:30 PM *Island of Terror* (1966)
08/13/71 11:30 PM *Frozen Alive* (1964)
08/20/71 11:30 PM *Nightmare* (1964)
08/28/71 3:00 PM *First Men in the Moon* (1964)
09/10/71 4:00 PM *Dr. Terror's House of Horrors* (1965)
09/16/71 4:00 PM *Mr. Sardonicus* (1961)
11/04/71 4:00 PM *The Nutty Professor* (1963)
11/05/71 4:00 PM *Forbidden Planet* (1956)
12/01/71 4:00 PM *First Men in the Moon* (1964)
12/11/71 11:30 PM *The Curse of the Mummy's Tomb* (1964)
01/22/72 11:30 PM *Diary of a Madman* (1963)
02/26/72 11:30 PM *Doctor Blood's Coffin* (1961)
03/04/72 11:30 PM *The Skull* (1965)
03/07/72 4:00 PM *Die! Die! My Darling* (1965)
03/16/72 4:00 PM *Munster, Go Home!* (1966)
04/20/72 4:00 PM *Journey to the Center of Time* (1967)
04/23/72 12:30 AM *Dark Intruder* (1965)
05/15/72 9:00 PM *Fantastic Voyage* (1966)
06/11/72 11:45 PM *The Projected Man* (1966)
08/26/72 11:30 PM *Strait-Jacket* (1964)
09/27/72 4:00 PM *The Blob* (1958)
10/07/72 11:30 PM *Blood of the Vampire* (1958)
10/17/72 4:00 PM *The Haunting* (1963)
11/02/72 4:00 PM *Phantom of the Rue Morgue* (1954)
12/02/72 11:30 PM *The Gorgon* (1964)
12/16/72 11:30 PM *Diary of a Madman* (1963)
12/21/72 4:00 PM *First Men in the Moon* (1964)
01/15/73 4:00 PM *The Nutty Professor* (1963)
02/22/73 4:00 PM *House of Wax* (1953)
02/28/73 4:00 PM *The Skull* (1965)
03/08/73 4:00 PM *Forbidden Planet* (1956)
03/17/73 11:30 PM *Them!* (1954)
04/07/73 2:30 PM *Mysterious Island* (1961)
05/09/73 4:00 PM *The Nanny* (1965)
07/19/73 4:00 PM *Doctor Blood's Coffin* (1961)
08/10/73 4:00 PM *Nightmare* (1964)
08/11/73 11:30 PM *Scream of Fear* (1961)
10/13/73 11:30 PM *The Brides of Fu Manchu* (1966)
10/15/73 4:00 PM *Phantom of the Rue Morgue* (1954)
10/16/73 4:00 PM *Chamber of Horrors* (1966)
10/17/73 4:00 PM *House of Wax* (1953)
10/18/73 4:00 PM *Die! Die! My Darling* (1965)
10/19/73 4:00 PM *Two on a Guillotine* (1965)
01/26/74 11:30 PM *The Frozen Dead* (1966)
01/27/74 11:30 PM *Dark Intruder* (1965)
02/11/74 4:00 PM *Forbidden Planet* (1956)
02/12/74 4:00 PM *Quatermass and the Pit* (1967)

02/13/74 4:00 PM *The Beast from 20,000 Fathoms* (1953)
02/14/74 4:00 PM *One Million Years B.C.* (1966)
02/17/74 11:30 PM *Strait-Jacket* (1964)
02/23/74 11:30 PM *My Blood Runs Cold* (1965)
03/03/74 11:30 PM *Island of Terror* (1966)
05/11/74 11:30 PM *The Nanny* (1965)
07/29/74 4:00 PM *The Haunting* (1963)
07/30/74 4:00 PM *Cauldron of Blood* (1970)
07/31/74 4:00 PM *Them!* (1954)
08/01/74 4:00 PM *Count Dracula* (1970)
08/02/74 4:00 PM *The Skull* (1965)
10/08/74 4:00 PM *Scared Stiff* (1953)
10/28/74 4:00 PM *Horror of Dracula* (1958)
10/29/74 4:00 PM *The Frozen Dead* (1966)
10/30/74 4:00 PM *The Fly* (1958)
10/31/74 4:00 PM *Return of the Fly* (1959)
11/01/74 4:00 PM *House of Wax* (1953)
11/03/74 4:00 PM *Them!* (1954)
11/03/74 11:30 PM *Phantom of the Rue Morgue* (1954)
01/26/75 11:30 PM *Fantastic Voyage* (1966)
02/03/75 4:00 PM *The Skull* (1965)
02/04/75 4:00 PM *Die! Die! My Darling* (1965)
02/05/75 4:00 PM *I, Monster* (1971)
02/06/75 4:00 PM *Count Dracula* (1970)
02/07/75 4:00 PM *Chamber of Horrors* (1966)
02/16/75 11:15 PM *Tower of London* (1962)
02/26/75 4:00 PM *The Nutty Professor* (1963)
04/05/75 11:30 PM *The Illustrated Man* (1969)
04/20/75 11:15 PM *The Beast from 20,000 Fathoms* (1953)
05/19/75 4:00 PM *One Million Years B.C.* (1966)
05/20/75 4:00 PM *Forbidden Planet* (1956)
05/21/75 4:00 PM *Quatermass and the Pit* (1967)
05/25/75 11:15 PM *Scream of Fear* (1961)
06/15/75 3:00 PM *The Gorgon* (1964)
06/18/75 4:00 PM *The Nanny* (1965)
06/21/75 2:00 PM *Strait-Jacket* (1964)
07/07/75 4:00 PM *Diary of a Madman* (1963)
07/09/75 4:00 PM *Two on a Guillotine* (1965)
07/10/75 4:00 PM *The Haunting* (1963)
07/11/75 4:00 PM *The Vulture* (1967)
07/16/75 4:00 PM *My Blood Runs Cold* (1965)
07/20/75 11:15 PM *When Worlds Collide* (1951)
08/03/75 3:00 PM *Mr. Sardonicus* (1961)
08/10/75 11:15 PM *The Colossus of New York* (1958)
08/31/75 2:30 PM *Homicidal* (1961)
08/31/75 11:15 PM *The Blob* (1958)
10/27/75 4:00 PM *Nightmare in Wax* (1969)
10/28/75 4:00 PM *Theatre of Death* (1967)
10/29/75 4:00 PM *Dracula's Castle* (1969)
10/30/75 4:00 PM *Horror of Dracula* (1958)
10/31/75 4:00 PM *Count Dracula* (1970)
11/25/75 4:00 PM *This Island Earth* (1955)
11/26/75 4:00 PM *The Incredible Shrinking Man* (1957)
11/27/75 4:00 PM *When Worlds Collide* (1951)
01/04/76 4:30 PM *The Colossus of New York* (1958)
01/09/76 4:00 PM *The Nanny* (1965)
01/12/76 4:00 PM *Cauldron of Blood* (1970)
01/13/76 4:00 PM *Chamber of Horrors* (1966)

01/14/76 4:00 PM *House of Wax* (1953)
01/15/76 4:00 PM *The Creeping Terror* (1964)
01/16/76 4:00 PM *Phantom of the Rue Morgue* (1954)
01/25/76 11:30 PM *Tower of London* (1962)
03/01/76 4:00 PM *One Million Years B.C.* (1966)
03/02/76 4:00 PM *Quatermass and the Pit* (1967)
03/03/76 4:00 PM *Them!* (1954)
03/04/76 4:00 PM *Plan 9 From Outer Space* (1959)
03/05/76 4:00 PM *First Spaceship on Venus* (1960)
04/25/76 11:55 PM *The Beast from 20,000 Fathoms* (1953)
05/18/76 4:00 PM *The Nutty Professor* (1963)
05/19/76 4:00 PM *Scared Stiff* (1953)
05/24/76 4:00 PM *The Fly* (1958)
05/25/76 4:00 PM *Two on a Guillotine* (1965)
05/26/76 4:00 PM *The Colossus of New York* (1958)
05/27/76 4:00 PM *The Phantom of the Opera* (1943)
05/28/76 4:00 PM *My Blood Runs Cold* (1965)
05/30/76 11:30 PM *The Haunting* (1963)
07/12/76 4:00 PM *Doctor Blood's Coffin* (1961)
07/14/76 4:00 PM *The Frozen Dead* (1966)
07/15/76 4:00 PM *Blood Mania* (1970)
07/16/76 4:00 PM *They Saved Hitler's Brain* (1963)
07/31/76 11:30 PM *The Illustrated Man* (1969)
09/20/76 4:00 PM *Quatermass and the Pit* (1967)
09/21/76 4:00 PM *Plan 9 From Outer Space* (1959)
09/23/76 4:00 PM *First Spaceship on Venus* (1960)
10/07/76 4:00 PM *My Blood Runs Cold* (1965)
10/31/76 11:30 PM *Two on a Guillotine* (1965)
11/08/76 4:00 PM *Them!* (1954)
11/09/76 4:00 PM *The Beast from 20,000 Fathoms* (1953)
11/11/76 4:00 PM *The Fly* (1958)
11/12/76 4:00 PM *The Creeping Terror* (1964)
11/13/76 11:30 PM *One Million Years B.C.* (1966)
11/14/76 11:55 PM *Stanley* (1972)
01/08/77 11:30 PM *Blood Mania* (1970)
02/12/77 11:30 PM *Terrified* (1963)
02/20/77 11:30 PM *The Nanny* (1965)
02/21/77 4:00 PM *Chamber of Horrors* (1966)
02/22/77 4:00 PM *Phantom of the Rue Morgue* (1954)
02/23/77 4:00 PM *The Vulture* (1966)
02/24/77 4:00 PM *House of Wax* (1953)
02/25/77 4:00 PM *Nightmare in Wax* (1969)
02/26/77 11:30 PM *Curse of Bigfoot* (1975)
04/11/77 4:00 PM *The War of the Worlds* (1953)
04/12/77 4:00 PM *This Island Earth* (1955)
04/13/77 4:00 PM *Crack in the World* (1965)
04/14/77 4:00 PM *When Worlds Collide* (1951)
05/02/77 4:00 PM *Doctor Blood's Coffin* (1961)
05/03/77 4:00 PM *I. Monster* (1972)
05/04/77 4:00 PM *Count Dracula* (1970)
05/05/77 4:00 PM *Dracula's Castle* (1969)
05/06/77 4:00 PM *Horror of Dracula* (1958)
05/14/77 11:30 PM *Rosemary's Baby* (1968)
07/09/77 11:30 PM *The Brides of Fu Manchu* (1966)
07/11/77 4:00 PM *The War of the Gargantuas* (1966)
07/12/77 4:00 PM *Island of the Burning Doomed* (1967)
07/13/77 4:00 PM *Monster Zero* (1965)
07/14/77 4:00 PM *Godzilla's Revenge* (1971)

07/15/77 4:00 PM *Rodan* (1957)
07/16/77 11:30 PM *Cauldron of Blood* (1970)
09/03/77 2:30 PM *Tower of London* (1962)
09/04/77 11:30 PM *The Incredible Shrinking Man* (1957)
09/12/77 4:00 PM *The War of the Worlds* (1953)
09/13/77 4:00 PM *This Island Earth* (1955)
09/14/77 4:00 PM *When Worlds Collide* (1951)
09/15/77 4:00 PM *Quatermass and the Pit* (1967)
09/16/77 4:00 PM *Crack in the World* (1965)
10/14/77 4:00 PM *House of Wax* (1953)
10/23/77 11:30 PM *Two on a Guillotine* (1965)
10/30/77 11:30 PM *The Boy Who Cried Werewolf* (1973)
10/31/77 4:00 PM *Phantom of the Rue Morgue* (1954)
11/01/77 4:00 PM *The Devil's Hand* (1961)
11/02/77 4:00 PM *The Creeping Flesh* (1973)
11/03/77 4:00 PM *The Beast from 20,000 Fathoms* (1953)
11/04/77 4:00 PM *Them!* (1954)
11/06/77 11:30 PM *A Study in Terror* (1965)
11/11/77 4:00 PM *Rosemary's Baby* (1968)
11/27/77 11:30 PM *Stanley* (1972)
01/23/78 4:00 PM *Count Dracula* (1970)
01/24/78 4:00 PM *Dracula's Castle* (1969)
01/26/78 4:00 PM *Horror of Dracula* (1958)
01/27/78 4:00 PM *Chamber of Horrors* (1966)
02/19/78 11:30 PM *One Million Years B.C.* (1966)
03/14/78 4:00 PM *I, Monster* (1971)
03/15/78 4:00 PM *Curse of Bigfoot* (1975)
03/16/78 4:00 PM *The Fly* (1958)
03/17/78 4:00 PM *King Kong vs. Godzilla* (1962)
05/28/78 11:30 PM *Willard* (1971)
07/02/78 12:20 AM *The House That Screamed* (1970)
07/11/78 4:00 PM *The Dunwich Horror* (1970)
07/12/78 4:00 PM *The Nanny* (1965)
07/13/78 4:00 PM *Whoever Slew Auntie Roo?* (1972)
07/14/78 4:00 PM *The Vulture* (1967)
07/24/78 4:00 PM *Godzilla's Revenge* (1971)
07/25/78 4:00 PM *Monster Zero* (1965)
07/26/78 4:00 PM *Rodan* (1957)
07/27/78 4:00 PM *The War of the Gargantuas* (1966)
07/28/78 4:00 PM *Varan the Unbelievable* (1962)
07/29/78 11:30 PM *Blood Mania* (1970)
08/22/75 12:35 AM *Let's Scare Jessica to Death* (1971)
08/26/78 11:30 PM *Psycho* (1960)
09/14/78 4:00 PM *Scared Stiff* (1953)
10/08/78 11:30 PM *Sssssss* (1973)
10/16/78 4:00 PM *The War of the Worlds* (1953)
10/17/78 4:00 PM *This Island Earth* (1955)
10/18/78 4:00 PM *When Worlds Collide* (1951)
10/19/78 4:00 PM *Quatermass and the Pit* (1967)
10/20/78 4:00 PM *Crack in the World* (1965)
10/22/78 11:30 PM *One Million Years B.C.* (1966)
10/29/78 11:30 PM *Two on A Guillotine* (1965)
10/31/78 4:00 PM *Cry of the Banshee* (1970)
11/01/78 4:00 PM *Hands of the Ripper* (1971)
01/29/79 4:00 PM *Games* (1967)
02/11/79 12:30 PM *Cyborg 2087* (1966)
03/11/79 11:30 PM *Fahrenheit 451* (1966)
04/07/79 11:30 PM *The Nanny* (1965)

04/08/79 11:45 PM *Fahrenheit 451* (1966)
04/28/79 11:30 PM *Journey to the Far Side of the Sun* (1969)
05/12/79 11:30 PM *Willard* (1971)
05/14/79 4:00 PM *Let's Scare Jessica to Death* (1971)
05/17/79 4:00 PM *Whoever Slew Auntie Roo?* (1972)
06/04/79 4:00 PM *The Beast from 20,000 Fathoms* (1953)
06/06/79 4:00 PM *King Kong Escapes* (1968)
06/08/79 4:00 PM *The Fly* (1958)
07/21/79 11:30 PM *King Kong Escapes* (1968)
07/22/79 11:30 PM *The Beast in the Cellar* (1971)
08/05/79 11:30 PM *Psycho* (1960)
08/11/79 1:00 AM *The Creeping Flesh* (1973)
08/20/79 4:00 PM *Count Yorga, Vampire* (1970)
08/21/79 4:00 PM *Them!* (1954)
08/22/79 4:00 PM *House of Usher* (1960)
08/23/79 4:00 PM *The Haunted Palace* (1963)
08/24/79 4:00 PM *Murders in the Rue Morgue* (1971)
09/02/79 12:00 AM *The Comedy of Terrors* (1963)
09/30/79 11:35 PM *The War of the Worlds* (1953)
10/07/79 11:35 PM *Dead of Night* (1945)
11/02/79 4:00 PM *Hands of the Ripper* (1971)
01/30/80 4:00 PM *A Study in Terror* (1965)
03/17/80 4:00 PM *House of Usher* (1960)
03/18/80 4:00 PM *The House That Screamed* (Part 1) (1970)
03/19/80 4:00 PM *The House That Screamed* (Part 2) (1970)
03/20/80 4:00 PM *Dracula's Castle* (1969)
03/21/80 4:00 PM *The Haunted Palace* (1963)
04/19/80 11:45 PM *Phase IV* (1974)
04/20/80 11:45 PM *It's Alive!* (1969)
04/28/80 4:00 PM *Twins of Evil* (1971)
04/29/80 4:00 PM *The Dunwich Horror* (1970)
05/20/80 4:00 PM *The Stepford Wives* (1975)
05/21/80 4:00 PM *Let's Scare Jessica to Death* (1971)
05/22/80 4:00 PM *Rosemary's Baby* (Part 1) (1968)
05/23/80 4:00 PM *Rosemary's Baby* (Part 2) (1968)
05/31/80 2:00 PM *Crack in the World* (1965)
06/07/80 11:45 PM *Fahrenheit 451* (1966)
06/08/80 11:45 PM *Cyborg 2087* (1966)
06/16/80 4:00 PM *Rodan* (1957)
06/18/80 4:00 PM *King Kong vs. Godzilla* (1962)
06/19/80 4:00 PM *Return of the Giant Monsters* (1967)
06/20/80 4:00 PM *Godzilla's Revenge* (1971)
07/26/80 12:45 AM *Sasquatch: The Legend of Bigfoot* (1976)
07/27/80 12:00 AM *Willard* (1971)
08/02/80 2:00 PM *When Worlds Collide* (1951)
08/02/80 11:45 PM *Psycho* (1960)
08/12/80 4:00 PM *Stanley* (1972)
08/14/80 4:00 PM *Sssssss* (1973)
08/15/80 4:00 PM *The Deadly Bees* (1967)
10/31/80 12:41 AM *Terror in the Wax Museum* (1973)
11/16/80 11:45 PM *The Sentinel* (1977)
12/31/80 1:00 AM *Goliath and the Vampires* (1961)
01/12/81 4:00 PM *Godzilla's Revenge* (1971)
01/13/81 4:00 PM *Monster Zero* (1965)
01/14/81 4:00 PM *Rodan* (1957)
01/15/81 4:00 PM *The War of the Gargantuas* (1966)
01/16/81 4:00 PM *Return of the Giant Monsters* (1967)
03/21/81 12:45 AM *Cry of the Banshee* (1970)

05/07/81 4:00 PM *Hands of the Ripper* (1971)
05/08/81 4:00 PM *Let's Scare Jessica to Death* (1971)
05/18/81 4:00 PM *King Kong vs. Godzilla* (1962)
05/19/81 4:00 PM *Godzilla vs. Megalon* (1973)
05/20/81 4:00 PM *Godzilla vs. the Cosmic Monster* (1974)
05/21/81 4:00 PM *Godzilla on Monster Island* (1972)
05/22/81 4:00 PM *King Kong Escapes* (1968)
07/31/81 1:10 AM *I Married a Monster from Outer Space* (1958)
09/25/81 1:30 AM *A Study in Terror* (1965)
09/26/81 11:45 PM *Corruption* (1968)
10/23/81 1:45 AM *The Devil's Hand* (1961)
10/24/81 12:45 AM *Point of Terror* (1971)
10/26/81 4:00 PM *House of Usher* (1960)
10/28/81 4:00 PM *Rosemary's Baby* (Part 1) (1968)
10/29/81 4:00 PM *Rosemary's Baby* (Part 2) (1968)
10/30/81 1:30 AM *The Devil's Rain* (1975)
10/31/81 12:45 AM *The Haunted Palace* (1963)
10/31/81 2:10 AM *The House That Screamed* (1970)
10/31/81 3:50 AM *Goliath and the Vampires* (1961)
11/15/81 11:45 PM *Psycho* (1960)
11/27/81 1:30 AM *They Saved Hitler's Brain* (1963)
12/04/81 2:00 AM *The X from Outer Space* (1967)
12/05/81 12:45 AM *Frankenstein Conquers the World* (1965)
12/11/81 1:30 AM *The Comedy of Terrors* (1963)
12/12/81 12:45 AM *Whoever Slew Auntie Roo?* (1972)
12/15/81 4:00 PM *The Boy Who Cried Werewolf* (1973)
01/01/82 1:30 AM *Fright* (1971)
01/09/82 5:00 PM *Terror in the Wax Museum* (1973)
02/04/82 4:00 PM *Satan's Cheerleaders* (1977)
02/24/82 4:00 PM *Let's Scare Jessica to Death* (1971)
02/25/82 4:00 PM *Terror in the Wax Museum* (1973)
02/26/82 4:00 PM *Dead of Night* (1945)
02/26/82 1:03 AM *I, Monster* (1971)
03/10/82 4:00 PM *Murders in the Rue Morgue* (1971)
03/30/82 4:00 PM *Crack in the World* (1965)
04/19/82 4:00 PM *Frankenstein Conquers the World* (1965)
04/20/82 4:00 PM *The Creeping Flesh* (1973)
04/21/82 4:00 PM *The Colossus of New York* (1958)
04/22/82 4:00 PM *It's Alive!* (1969)
04/23/82 4:00 PM *Count Yorga, Vampire* (1970)
05/04/82 4:00 PM *The Uncanny* (1977)
05/05/82 4:00 PM *Willard* (1971)
05/06/82 4:00 PM *Grizzly* (1976)
05/07/82 1:30 AM *What Ever Happened to Aunt Alice?* (1969)
05/14/82 1:30 AM *Sssssss* (1973)
05/17/82 4:00 PM *Godzilla vs. the Cosmic Monster* (1974)
05/18/82 4:00 PM *Rodan* (1957)
05/19/82 4:00 PM *Godzilla vs. Megalon* (1973)
05/20/82 4:00 PM *The War of the Gargantuas* (1966)
05/21/82 4:00 PM *Godzilla's Revenge* (1971)
05/28/82 1:30 AM *Cyborg 2087* (1966)
06/25/82 4:00 PM *I Married a Monster from Outer Space* (1958)
07/12/82 4:00 PM *Cry of the Banshee* (1970)
07/13/82 4:00 PM *Scream and Scream Again* (1969)
07/14/82 4:00 PM *Creature from Black Lake* (1976)
07/15/82 4:00 PM *The Dunwich Horror* (1970)
07/16/82 4:00 PM *I, Monster* (1971)
07/16/82 1:30 AM *The Creeping Terror* (1964)

07/23/82 1:30 AM *Curse of Bigfoot* (1975)
07/25/82 12:15 AM *Stanley* (1972)
07/30/82 1:30 AM *Dracula's Castle* (1969)
07/31/82 12:45 AM *Enter the Devil* (1972)
08/01/82 12:15 AM *The Phantom of the Opera* (1943)
08/06/82 12:30 AM *Nightmare in Wax* (1969)
08/08/82 12:40 AM *The Incredible Shrinking Man* (1957)
08/13/82 1:30 AM *Point of Terror* (1971)
08/20/82 12:30 AM *Twisted Brain* (1973)
08/21/82 12:45 AM *Terrified* (1963)
08/28/82 12:45 AM *The Devil's Hand* (1961)
10/01/82 2:00 AM *Phase IV* (1974)
10/15/82 2:00 AM *Evil of Dracula* (1974)
10/16/82 1:45 AM *The Colossus of New York* (1958)
10/22/82 2:00 AM *Lake of Dracula* (1971)
10/23/82 1:45 AM *Conquest of Space* (1955)
10/28/82 4:00 PM *The Haunted Palace* (1963)
10/29/82 4:00 PM *House of Usher* (1960)
10/29/82 2:00 AM *Psycho* (1960)
10/31/82 12:15 AM *Terror in the Wax Museum* (1973)
11/13/82 1:45 AM *Fright* (1956)
11/19/82 2:00 AM *Killers from Space* (1954)
11/22/82 4:00 PM *Twins of Evil* (1971)
11/23/82 4:00 PM *The Sentinel* (1977)
11/24/82 4:00 PM *Demon Seed* (1977)
11/26/82 4:00 PM *Hands of the Ripper* (1971)
12/11/82 1:45 AM *Phantom from Space* (1953)
01/17/83 4:00 PM *Psycho* (1960)
01/18/83 4:00 PM *The Stepford Wives* (1975)
01/21/83 2:00 AM *The Vulture* (1967)
02/18/83 2:00 AM *Corruption* (1968)
03/23/83 4:00 PM *Sasquatch: The Legend of Bigfoot* (1976)
04/01/83 2:00 AM *The Snow Creature* (1954)
04/29/83 4:00 PM *What Ever Happened to Aunt Alice?* (1969)
05/16/83 4:00 PM *The Car* (1977)
05/20/83 4:00 PM *Sssssss* (1973)
06/02/83 4:00 PM *Scared Stiff* (1953)
06/03/83 4:00 PM *Dark Star* (1974)
06/23/83 12:30 AM *The Day of the Triffids* (1963)
07/06/83 4:00 PM *Day of the Animals* (1977)
07/08/83 4:00 PM *Beginning of the End* (1957)
07/09/83 12:45 AM *The Deadly Bees* (1967)
07/10/83 1:05 AM *The Devil's Rain* (1975)
07/15/83 12:30 AM *Phase IV* (1974)
07/22/83 12:30 AM *Psycho* (1960)
07/25/83 4:00 PM *Let's Scare Jessica to Death* (1971)
10/21/83 12:30 AM *Fahrenheit 451* (1966)
10/29/83 1:45 AM *Terror in the Wax Museum* (1973)
10/29/83 3:20 AM *Murders in the Rue Morgue* (1971)
11/04/83 12:30 AM *The Stepford Wives* (1975)
11/08/83 12:30 AM *Satan's Cheerleaders* (1977)
11/15/83 12:30 AM *The Comedy of Terrors* (1963)
11/16/83 12:30 AM *The Dunwich Horror* (1970)
11/17/83 12:30 AM *The House That Screamed* (1970)
11/18/83 12:30 AM *The Sentinel* (1977)
11/19/83 11:45 PM *Scream and Scream Again* (1969)
01/01/84 12:10 AM *Whoever Slew Auntie Roo?* (1972)
01/10/84 12:30 AM *Games* (1967)

01/27/84 12:30 AM *The Colossus of New York* (1958)
02/02/84 12:30 AM *Hands of the Ripper* (1971)
03/09/84 12:00 AM *A Study in Terror* (1965)
03/24/84 11:45 PM *Cyborg 2087* (1966)
05/12/84 11:45 PM *Psycho* (1960)
06/16/84 11:45 PM *Demon Seed* (1977)
07/21/84 11:45 PM *The Devil's Rain* (1975)
08/25/84 11:45 PM *Horror Express* (1972)
10/30/84 1:00 AM *The Haunted Palace* (1963)
10/31/84 1:00 AM *Cry of the Banshee* (1970)
12/12/84 1:00 AM *The House That Screamed* (1970)
12/26/84 1:00 AM *Return of the Giant Monsters* (1967)
12/29/84 3:00 PM *King Kong vs. Godzilla* (1962)
01/02/85 12:00 AM *It's Alive!* (1969)
01/10/85 12:00 AM *The Car* (1977)
02/06/85 12:00 AM *The Dunwich Horror* (1970)
02/14/85 12:00 AM *The Sentinel* (1977)
02/25/85 12:00 AM *The Stepford Wives* (1975)
04/12/85 12:00 AM *Creature from Black Lake* (1976)
04/15/85 12:00 AM *Satan's Cheerleaders* (1977)
05/29/85 12:00 AM *Demon Seed* (1977)
05/31/85 12:00 AM *The Deadly Bees* (1967)
07/17/85 12:00 AM *I, Monster* (1971)
09/16/85 1:00 AM *I Married a Monster from Outer Space* (1958)
10/07/85 1:00 AM *Deathdream* (1974)
10/14/85 1:00 AM *The Car* (1977)
10/30/85 12:00 AM *Beginning of the End* (1957)
10/31/85 12:00 AM *The Day of the Triffids* (1963)
11/12/85 12:00 PM *The Stepford Wives* (1975)
12/16/85 1:00 AM *Phase IV* (1974)
01/17/86 12:00 AM *Grizzly* (1976)
01/30/86 12:00 AM *The Sentinel* (1977)
02/04/86 12:00 AM *What Ever Happened to Aunt Alice?* (1969)
03/07/86 12:00 AM *Creature from Black Lake* (1976)
03/27/86 12:00 AM *Day of the Animals* (1977)
04/25/86 9:00 PM *King Kong* (1976)
05/01/86 12:30 AM *Orca* (1977)
05/27/86 12:30 AM *The Sentinel* (1977)
06/08/86 11:45 PM *The Car* (1977)
07/27/86 4:00 PM *Day of the Animals* (1977)
08/01/86 12:30 AM *Creature from Black Lake* (1976)
08/30/86 2:00 PM *Godzilla vs. Megalon* (1973)
10/10/86 1:30 AM *Beginning of the End* (1957)
10/31/86 1:00 AM *The Devil's Rain* (1975)
12/05/86 1:00 AM *Orca* (1977)
01/05/87 12:30 AM *Creature from Black Lake* (1976)
01/12/87 12:30 AM *Horror Express* (1972)
01/19/87 12:30 AM *The Day of the Triffids* (1963)
01/23/87 1:00 AM *The Car* (1977)
01/26/87 12:30 AM *Demon Seed* (1977)
02/13/87 1:00 AM *Beginning of the End* (1957)
02/20/87 1:00 AM *Orca* (1977)
02/27/87 1:00 AM *King Kong* (1976)
04/17/87 1:00 AM *Godzilla vs. Megalon* (1973)
04/24/87 1:00 AM *The Uncanny* (1977)
05/27/87 12:00 AM *Day of the Animals* (1977)
06/14/87 3:00 PM *King Kong* (1976)
06/18/87 12:45 AM *Godzilla on Monster Island* (1972)

07/09/87 12:30 AM *Horror Express* (1972)
08/07/87 1:30 AM *Day of the Triffids* (1963)
08/21/87 1:00 AM *The Car* (1977)
08/28/87 1:00 AM *Satan's Cheerleaders* (1977)

Channel 9

Date Time Title Year
11/09/57 12:30 AM *The Undying Monster* (1942)
11/12/57 11:15 PM *Dr. Jekyll and Mr. Hyde* (1941)
11/17/57 11:30 PM *The Human Monster* (1939)
11/22/57 12:30 AM *Monster from the Ocean Floor* (1954)
01/30/58 5:00 PM *Magnetic Monster* (1953)
03/27/58 5:00 PM *The Devil Doll* (1936)
04/08/58 5:00 PM *The Picture of Dorian Gray* (1945)
04/19/58 11:15 PM *Dr. Jekyll and Mr. Hyde* (1941)
04/21/58 11:15 PM *The Mysterious Doctor* (1943)
05/28/58 11:15 PM *King Dinosaur* (1955)
05/30/58 11:15 PM *The Beast with Five Fingers* (1946)
09/25/58 11:15 PM *Chamber of Horrors* (1940)
09/30/58 11:15 PM *The Devil Doll* (1936)
10/01/58 11:15 PM *Riders to the Stars* (1954)
10/04/58 11:50 PM *The Picture of Dorian Gray* (1945)
10/08/58 11:15 PM *Gog* (1954)
10/16/58 11:15 PM *Hangover Square* (1945)
10/18/58 1:45 AM *Magnetic Monster* (1953)
10/25/58 1:15 AM *Monster from the Ocean Floor* (1954)
02/24/59 5:00 PM *Riders to the Stars* (1954)
03/19/59 5:00 PM *The Magnetic Monster* (1953)
04/08/59 5:00 PM *Hangover Square* (1945)
05/03/59 11:15 PM *Dr. Jekyll & Mr. Hyde* (1941)
05/21/59 5:00 PM *The Beast with Five Fingers* (1946)
08/02/59 2:45 PM *Hangover Square* (1945)
11/14/59 10:30 PM *The Uninvited* (1944)
02/24/60 11:30 PM *Dr. Renault's Secret* (1942)
05/12/60 11:15 PM *Chamber of Horrors* (1940)
05/30/60 9:00 AM *The Picture of Dorian Gray* (1945)
06/19/60 11:15 PM *Hangover Square* (1945)
06/22/60 11:15 PM *The Devil Doll* (1936)
07/08/60 12:55 AM *The Undying Monster* (1942)
07/29/60 11:15 PM *The Uninvited* (1944)
08/05/60 11:15 PM *Dr. Jekyll and Mr. Hyde* (1941)
09/21/60 5:00 PM *The Picture of Dorian Gray* (1945)
11/10/60 11:15 PM *Dr. Jekyll and Mr. Hyde* (1941)

11/22/60 9:00 AM *The Picture of Dorian Gray* (1945)
01/15/61 11:15 PM *The Picture of Dorian Gray* (1945)
02/28/61 1:15 AM *The Undying Monster* (1942)
03/02/61 12:50 AM *Dr. Renault's Secret* (1942)
03/21/61 5:00 PM *Chamber of Horrors* (1940)
03/27/61 5:00 PM *Hangover Square* (1945)
04/13/61 12:55 AM *The Human Monster* (1939)
04/14/61 11:15 PM *The Beast from 20,000 Fathoms* (1953)
05/17/61 12:50 AM *Dr. Renault's Secret* (1942)
05/24/61 1:00 AM *Chamber of Horrors* (1940)
05/31/61 12:50 AM *The Undying Monster* (1942)
07/30/61 11:20 PM *The Uninvited* (1944)
08/02/61 12:50 AM *The Undying Monster* (1942)
08/07/61 5:00 PM *Chamber of Horrors* (1940)
08/21/61 1:00 AM *Dr. Renault's Secret* (1942)
10/13/61 12:50 AM *The Beast with Five Fingers* (1946)
11/13/61 11:20 PM *The Mysterious Doctor* (1943)
01/23/62 5:00 PM *Rodan* (1957)
04/13/62 11:25 PM *It Came from Beneath the Sea* (1955)
05/22/62 1:10 AM *The Mysterious Doctor* (1943)
06/11/62 5:00 PM *The Beast from 20,000 Fathoms* (1953)
06/21/62 11:25 PM *The Uninvited* (1944)
08/07/62 5:00 PM *Rodan* (1957)
10/30/62 12:55 AM *Island of Lost Souls* (1933)
11/02/62 12:55 AM *Flight to Mars* (1951)
01/16/63 5:00 PM *The Beast with Five Fingers* (1946)
01/30/63 5:00 PM *The Ghost Breakers* (1940)
02/07/63 12:55 AM *The Mysterious Doctor* (1943)
03/17/63 11:20 PM *The Hunchback of Notre Dame* (1956)
03/27/63 5:00 PM *The Maze* (1953)
05/01/63 12:55 AM *The Uninvited* (1944)
05/17/63 12:55 AM *The Beast from 20,000 Fathoms* (1953)
07/02/63 5:00 PM *Flight to Mars* (1951)
08/12/63 5:00 PM *The Ghost Breakers* (1940)
09/20/63 12:55 AM *Rodan* (1957)
09/28/63 1:00 PM *The Beast from 20,000 Fathoms* (1953)
10/18/63 12:55 AM *The Climax* (1944)
11/01/63 12:55 AM *The Mad Magician* (1954)
11/07/63 5:00 PM *The Hunchback of Notre Dame* (1956)
01/07/64 5:00 PM *The Man in Half Moon Street* (1944)
02/07/64 5:00 PM *Rodan* (1957)
03/13/64 5:00 PM *The Climax* (1944)
06/27/64 11:15 PM *The Uninvited* (1944)
06/30/64 5:00 PM *The Mad Doctor* (1940)
07/25/64 12:30 PM *The Ghost Breakers* (1940)
07/25/64 11:15 PM *The Hunchback of Notre Dame* (1956)
08/11/64 12:55 AM *The Beast from 20,000 Fathoms* (1953)
08/13/64 5:00 PM *It Came from Beneath the Sea* (1955)
10/23/64 12:55 AM *The Maze* (1953)
10/30/64 11:25 PM *The Strange Door* (1951)
12/17/64 11:25 PM *It Came from Outer Space* (1953)
01/11/65 11:25 PM *The Black Castle* (1952)
01/19/65 5:00 PM *Abbott and Costello Meet the Invisible Man* (1951)
01/25/65 5:00 PM *The Creature Walks Among Us* (1956)
01/28/65 11:25 PM *Cult of the Cobra* (1955)
02/11/65 4:30 PM *Earth vs. the Flying Saucers* (1956)
02/11/65 11:25 PM *Creature from the Black Lagoon* (1954)

03/04/65 1:15 AM *The Man in Half Moon Street* (1944)
03/30/65 4:30 PM *20 Million Miles to Earth* (1957)
04/24/65 5:00 PM *The Beast from 20,000 Fathoms* (1953)
04/26/65 11:25 PM *It Came from Beneath the Sea* (1955)
05/07/65 4:30 PM *The Strange Door* (1951)
05/22/65 5:00 PM *Revenge of the Creature* (1955)
06/26/65 5:00 PM *13 Ghosts* (1960)
07/11/65 11:00 AM *Abbott and Costello Meet the Invisible Man* (1951)
07/14/65 11:25 PM *The Hunchback of Notre Dame* (1956)
07/19/65 11:25 PM *It Came from Outer Space* (1953)
07/27/65 11:25 PM *The Climax* (1944)
08/04/65 4:30 PM *The Mad Magician* (1954)
10/25/65 4:30 PM *Abbott and Costello Meet Dr. Jekyll and Mr. Hyde* (1953)
01/17/66 11:25 PM *The Mad Doctor* (1940)
01/19/66 4:30 PM *Cult of the Cobra* (1955)
02/08/66 11:25 PM *This Island Earth* (1955)
02/09/66 4:30 PM *The Lost World* (1960)
02/16/66 4:30 PM *The Mole People* (1956)
03/04/66 4:30 PM *The Monolith Monsters* (1957)
03/18/66 1:35 AM *The Phantom of the Opera* (1943)
03/21/66 11:25 PM *The Incredible Shrinking Man* (1957)
03/30/66 4:30 PM *The Invisible Boy* (1957)
04/15/66 4:30 PM *The Deadly Mantis* (1957)
04/29/66 11:25 PM *This Island Earth* (1955)
05/08/66 11:00 AM *Abbott and Costello Meet the Mummy* (1955)
05/15/66 11:00 AM *Abbott and Costello Meet Dr. Jekyll and Mr. Hyde* (1953)
05/20/66 11:25 PM *The Creature Walks Among Us* (1956)
06/08/66 4:30 PM *The Strange Door* (1951)
06/17/66 11:25 PM *13 Ghosts* (1960)
06/20/66 4:30 PM *It Came from Outer Space* (1953)
07/08/66 1:25 AM *Tower of London* (1939)
07/19/66 4:30 PM *Tarantula* (1955)
07/26/66 4:30 PM *20 Million Miles to Earth* (1957)
08/03/66 11:25 PM *It Came from Beneath the Sea* (1955)
08/13/66 11:15 PM *The Hunchback of Notre Dame* (1956)
08/26/66 12:30 AM *Monster on the Campus* (1958)
09/03/66 3:00 PM *The Beast from 20,000 Fathoms* (1953)
09/10/66 3:00 PM *Curucu, Beast of the Amazon* (1956)
09/17/66 3:00 PM *Reptilicus* (1961)
09/25/66 11:00 AM *Abbott and Costello Meet the Invisible Man* (1951)
10/01/66 3:00 PM *This Island Earth* (1955)
10/08/66 3:00 PM *X* (1963)
10/15/66 3:00 PM *Dagora, the Space Monster* (1964)
10/29/66 3:00 PM *Flight to Mars* (1951)
10/31/66 12:30 AM *Corridors of Blood* (1958)
11/12/66 3:00 PM *The Terror* (1963)
11/19/66 3:00 PM *Attack of the Mushroom People* (1963)
11/25/66 2:10 AM *The Mad Magician* (1954)
11/26/66 3:00 PM *Earth vs. the Flying Saucers* (1956)
12/03/66 3:00 PM *The Beach Girls and the Monster* (1965)
12/09/66 2:05 AM *The Black Castle* (1952)
12/31/66 5:00 PM *The Man Who Turned to Stone* (1957)
01/14/67 5:00 PM *The Deadly Mantis* (1957)
01/28/67 5:00 PM *Tarantula* (1955)

02/02/67 11:40 PM *Werewolf in a Girl's Dormitory* (1963)
02/04/67 5:00 PM *Unearthly Stranger* (1963)
02/11/67 5:00 PM *Invasion* (1965)
02/12/67 11:00 AM *Abbott and Costello Meet the Mummy* (1955)
02/18/67 5:00 PM *Cult of the Cobra* (1955)
02/19/67 11:00 AM *Abbott and Costello Meet Dr. Jekyll and Mr. Hyde* (1953)
02/25/67 5:00 PM *Curucu, Beast of the Amazon* (1956)
03/04/67 5:00 PM *Cry of the Bewitched* (1957)
03/11/67 5:00 PM *The Land Unknown* (1957)
03/17/67 1:10 AM *Pyro* (1964)
03/18/67 5:00 PM *Man in Outer Space* (1962)
03/25/67 5:00 PM *The Invisible Boy* (1957)
04/01/67 5:00 PM *The Gamma People* (1956)
04/07/67 4:30 PM *Reptilicus* (1961)
04/17/67 11:25 PM *Five* (1951)
04/29/67 5:00 PM *The Thing That Couldn't Die* (1958)
04/29/67 11:15 PM *This Island Earth* (1955)
05/05/67 1:45 AM *Burn, Witch, Burn* (1962)
05/06/67 3:30 PM *Dagora, the Space Monster* (1964)
05/13/67 5:00 PM *Space Monster* (1965)
05/16/67 4:30 PM *13 Ghosts* (1960)
05/18/67 11:25 PM *The Strange Door* (1951)
05/19/67 1:45 AM *The Terror* (1963)
05/20/67 3:00 PM *Atragon* (1963)
05/26/67 4:30 PM *X* (1963)
06/03/67 3:00 PM *Dementia 13* (1963)
06/03/67 3:00 PM *The Beast from 20,000 Fathoms* (1953)
06/13/67 11:25 PM *The Thing That Couldn't Die* (1958)
06/24/67 4:00 PM *The Monolith Monsters* (1957)
06/30/67 11:40 PM *This Island Earth* (1955)
07/22/67 3:30 PM *Attack of the Mushroom People* (1963)
07/29/67 3:00 PM *The Castle of the Living Dead* (1964)
08/02/67 4:30 PM *Monster on the Campus* (1958)
08/05/67 3:00 PM *The Incredible Shrinking Man* (1957)
08/18/67 1:35 AM *The Man in Half Moon Street* (1944)
08/19/67 3:00 PM *20 Million Miles to Earth* (1957)
09/02/67 3:00 PM *Queen of Blood* (1966)
09/08/67 4:30 PM *Werewolf in a Girl's Dormitory* (1963)
09/08/67 1:05 AM *The Beach Girls and the Monster* (1965)
09/18/67 11:30 PM *Corridors of Blood* (1958)
10/08/67 10:30 AM *Abbott and Costello Meet the Invisible Man* (1951)
10/29/67 10:30 AM *Abbott and Costello Meet the Mummy* (1955)
11/03/67 1:35 AM *Hunter of the Unknown* (1966)
11/04/67 11:15 PM *Master of the World* (1961)
11/13/67 11:30 PM *Curucu, Beast of the Amazon* (1956)
01/25/68 11:30 PM *Creature from the Black Lagoon* (1954)
02/23/68 11:30 PM *X* (1963)
03/15/68 11:30 PM *13 Ghosts* (1960)
04/11/68 11:30 PM *This Island Earth* (1955)
05/10/68 11:30 PM *The Strange Door* (1951)
06/14/68 11:30 PM *Master of the World* (1961)
06/14/68 1:10 AM *Dementia 13* (1963)
06/17/68 11:30 PM *The Thing That Couldn't Die* (1958)
07/07/68 11:00 AM *Abbott and Costello Meet the Mummy* (1955)
07/12/68 1:25 AM *Queen of Blood* (1966)
08/15/68 11:30 PM *The Incredible Shrinking Man* (1957)

08/23/68 1:20 AM *Panic in Year Zero* (1962)
08/30/68 1:50 AM *Behind the Mask* (1932)
08/31/68 2:00 PM *The Deadly Mantis* (1957)
09/06/68 11:30 PM *Curucu, Beast of the Amazon* (1956)
09/24/68 11:30 PM *The Creature Walks Among Us* (1956)
09/27/68 1:10 AM *The Monster and the Girl* (1941)
10/04/68 1:50 AM *Unearthly Stranger* (1963)
10/25/68 1:30 AM *X* (1963)
10/29/68 11:30 PM *Creature from the Black Lagoon* (1954)
11/01/68 1:10 AM *Doctor of Doom* (1963)
11/08/68 2:10 AM *Atragon* (1963)
11/29/68 2:40 AM *Monster on the Campus* (1958)
02/15/69 12:35 AM *The Incredible Shrinking Man* (1957)
03/22/69 12:25 AM *Cult of the Cobra* (1955)
04/04/69 1:45 AM *The Mole People* (1956)
04/05/69 12:15 AM *The Invisible Boy* (1957)
04/12/69 12:20 AM *The Land Unknown* (1957)
04/18/69 1:35 AM *The Monolith Monsters* (1957)
04/25/69 2:05 AM *Monster on the Campus* (1958)
04/28/69 4:30 PM *Master of the World* (1961)
04/30/69 4:30 PM *The Black Castle* (1952)
05/02/69 4:30 PM *The Thing That Couldn't Die* (1958)
05/06/69 4:30 PM *The Deadly Mantis* (1957)
05/08/69 4:30 PM *Reptilicus* (1961)
05/12/69 4:30 PM *Voyage to the Prehistoric Planet* (1965)
05/14/69 4:30 PM *Dagora, the Space Monster* (1964)
05/16/69 4:30 PM *Unearthly Stranger* (1963)
05/22/69 4:30 PM *Revenge of the Creature* (1955)
05/26/69 4:30 PM *Man in Outer Space* (1962)
05/28/69 4:30 PM *Space Monster* (1965)
05/30/69 4:30 PM *The Incredible Shrinking Man* (1957)
06/03/69 4:30 PM *Cult of the Cobra* (1955)
06/05/69 4:30 PM *Abbott and Costello Meet the Invisible Man* (1951)
06/07/69 1:00 AM *The Terror* (1963)
07/05/69 1:00 AM *This Island Earth* (1955)
07/12/69 1:10 AM *Revenge of the Creature* (1955)
07/26/69 1:10 AM *The Witch's Mirror* (1962)
08/23/69 1:05 AM *The Strange Door* (1951)
12/05/69 1:10 AM *El Vampiro* (1957)
02/13/70 4:00 PM *Abbott and Costello Meet Frankenstein* (1948)
03/07/70 2:30 PM *Attack of the Mushroom People* (1963)
04/10/70 1:00 AM *The Monsters Demolisher* (1962)
04/17/70 1:00 AM *The Witch's Mirror* (1962)
04/24/70 1:00 AM *The Vampire's Coffin* (1958)
05/01/70 1:00 AM *Face of Terror* (1962)
05/06/70 11:30 PM *The Strange Door* (1951)
05/08/70 1:00 AM *Curse of the Crying Woman* (1963)
05/13/70 9:00 PM *Fahrenheit 451* (1966)
05/15/70 1:00 AM *The Man and the Monster* (1959)
05/22/70 1:00 AM *Unearthly Stranger* (1963)
05/29/70 1:00 AM *Dementia 13* (1963)
06/05/70 1:00 AM *Dr. Orloff's Monster* (1964)
06/08/70 11:30 PM *Portrait in Terror* (1965)
06/10/70 11:30 PM *The Invasion of the Vampires* (1963)
06/12/70 1:00 AM *Burn, Witch, Burn* (1962)
06/15/70 11:30 PM *The Brainiac* (1962)
06/16/70 11:30 PM *The Bloody Vampire* (1962)

06/19/70 1:00 AM *Space Monster* (1965)
06/22/70 11:30 PM *Samson in the Wax Museum* (1963)
06/26/70 1:00 AM *Invasion* (1965)
07/03/70 1:00 AM *Cry of the Bewitched* (1957)
07/10/70 1:00 AM *Doctor of Doom* (1963)
07/17/70 1:00 AM *The Curse of Nostradamus* (1961)
07/22/70 11:30 PM *It Came from Outer Space* (1953)
07/24/70 1:00 AM *The Robot vs. the Aztec Mummy* (1959)
07/31/70 1:00 AM *Samson vs. the Vampire Women* (1962)
08/01/70 2:00 PM *Curucu, Beast of the Amazon* (1956)
08/07/70 1:00 AM *Monster on the Campus* (1958)
08/14/70 1:30 AM *Man in Outer Space* (1962)
08/17/70 11:30 PM *El Vampiro* (1957)
08/18/70 11:30 PM *The Living Head* (1963)
08/19/70 11:30 PM *The Vampire's Coffin* (1958)
08/20/70 11:30 PM *The Man and the Monster* (1959)
08/29/70 2:00 PM *Voyage to the Prehistoric Planet* (1965)
10/09/70 1:00 AM *The Thing That Couldn't Die* (1958)
10/23/70 1:00 AM *Atragon* (1963)
11/13/70 1:10 AM *Zontar, the Thing from Venus* (1966)
11/27/70 1:00 AM *The Genie of Darkness* (1962)
12/04/70 1:00 AM *The Land Unknown* (1957)
01/01/71 1:00 AM *Face of Terror* (1962)
03/05/71 1:00 AM *The Monsters Demolisher* (1962)
03/25/71 11:30 PM *The Mummy's Ghost* (1944)
03/31/71 11:30 PM *The Invisible Boy* (1936)
04/02/71 1:00 AM *The Invasion of the Vampires* (1963)
04/28/71 9:00 PM *Fahrenheit 451* (1966)
05/12/71 9:00 PM *King Kong* (1933)
06/10/71 11:30 PM *House of Dracula* (1945)
06/12/71 2:30 PM *Abbott and Costello Meet Frankenstein* (1948)
01/15/72 11:30 PM *Mystery of the Wax Museum* (1933)
02/09/72 11:30 PM *King Kong vs. Godzilla* (1962)
02/10/72 11:30 PM *Son of Kong* (1933)
03/04/72 11:30 PM *Chandu the Magician* (1932)
04/08/72 11:30 PM *Svengali* (1931)
09/16/72 1:00 AM *Chandu the Magician* (1932)
11/11/72 2:00 PM *Colossus: The Forbin Project* (1970)
01/20/73 11:30 PM *The Monster* (1925)
03/08/73 9:00 PM *Journey to the Far Side of the Sun* (1969)
03/22/73 9:00 PM *The Oblong Box* (1969)
04/15/73 1:00 PM *The Day of the Triffids* (1963)
05/19/73 1:00 AM *Chandu the Magician* (1932)
06/09/73 2:30 PM *Bedlam* (1946)
06/15/73 1:00 AM *Curse of the Undead* (1959)
07/06/73 1:00 AM *The Eye Creatures* (1965)
07/28/73 11:30 PM *The Monster* (1925)
08/11/73 2:30 PM *Fahrenheit 451* (1966)
09/29/73 2:30 PM *Mystery of the Wax Museum* (1933)
10/13/73 11:30 PM *Things to Come* (1936)
10/21/73 5:00 PM *King Kong* (1933)
10/27/73 11:30 PM *Dr. Jekyll and Mr. Hyde* (1931)
10/27/73 1:30 AM *The Vampire Bat* (1933)
12/08/73 11:30 PM *Vampyr* (1932)
01/05/74 2:00 PM *King Kong vs. Godzilla* (1962)
01/26/74 12:00 AM *West of Zanzibar* (1929)
02/02/74 11:30 PM *The Mad Genius* (1931)
02/09/74 11:30 PM *Doctor X* (1932)

02/16/74 2:00 PM *Colossus: The Forbin Project* (1970)
03/23/74 11:30 PM *The Unholy Three* (1925)
08/10/74 1:00 PM *Voyage to the Planet of Prehistoric Women* (1968)
08/31/74 1:00 PM *Curse of the Swamp Creature* (1966)
11/02/74 11:30 PM *Psycho* (1960)
11/09/74 3:30 PM *King Kong vs. Godzilla* (1962)
11/29/74 1:30 AM *Before I Hang* (1940)
11/30/74 12:00 AM *Games* (1967)
12/06/74 12:30 AM *The Return of Dracula* (1958)
12/13/74 12:30 AM *The Quatermass Xperiment* (1955)
12/14/74 11:30 PM *Fahrenheit 451* (1966)
12/20/74 12:30 AM *The Four Skulls of Jonathan Drake* (1959)
12/27/74 12:30 AM *The Curse of the Cat People* (1944)
01/30/75 12:30 AM *Son of Kong* (1933)
09/21/75 4:00 PM *Journey to the Far Side of the Sun* (1969)
10/25/75 2:00 PM *Godzilla: King of the Monsters* (1956)
11/08/75 2:00 PM *Godzilla's Revenge* (1971)
02/07/76 2:00 PM *King Kong Escapes* (1968)
02/14/76 2:00 PM *The Crawling Eye* (1958)
02/20/76 11:30 PM *Pit and the Pendulum* (1961)
04/16/76 11:30 PM *Colossus: The Forbin Project* (1970)
05/08/76 2:00 PM *The Horror of Frankenstein* (1970)
05/16/76 12:30 PM *Godzilla: King of the Monsters* (1956)
05/22/76 2:00 PM *Journey to the Far Side of the Sun* (1969)
05/23/76 12:30 PM *Mystery of the Wax Museum* (1933)
06/05/76 2:30 PM *Eye of the Cat* (1969)
06/12/76 2:30 PM *The Mad Genius* (1931)
06/13/76 1:00 PM *The Man Who Haunted Himself* (1970)
07/11/76 12:30 PM *The Man with Nine Lives* (1940)
08/07/76 1:00 AM *Mark of the Vampire* (1935)
08/14/76 2:00 PM *King Kong Escapes* (1968)
09/17/76 12:00 AM *Scars of Dracula* (1970)
10/15/76 11:30 PM *Tales of Terror* (1962)
10/29/76 12:20 AM *Colossus: The Forbin Project* (1970)
10/31/76 12:00 PM *Journey to the Far Side of the Sun* (1969)
11/19/76 11:30 PM *War Gods of the Deep* (1965)
01/07/77 11:30 PM *King Kong Escapes* (1968)
01/08/77 2:30 PM *Godzilla: King of the Monsters* (1956)
02/11/77 11:30 PM *The Brotherhood of Satan* (1971)
02/26/77 2:30 PM *The Raven* (1963)
03/04/77 11:30 PM *The Man Who Haunted Himself* (1970)
05/27/77 11:30 PM *Eye of the Cat* (1969)
06/11/77 11:30 PM *The Oblong Box* (1969)
06/17/77 11:30 PM *The Horror of Frankenstein* (1970)
11/24/77 11:30 PM *Pit and the Pendulum* (1961)
12/29/77 11:30 PM *The Oblong Box* (1969)
04/20/78 11:30 PM *Scars of Dracula* (1970)
04/22/78 11:30 PM *The Raven* (1963)
04/29/78 11:30 PM *Pit and the Pendulum* (1961)
06/03/78 11:30 PM *Tales of Terror* (1962)
06/17/78 11:30 PM *Tomb of Ligeia* (1965)
07/09/78 12:00 PM *The Man Who Haunted Himself* (1970)
08/20/78 12:00 PM *Lust for a Vampire* (1971)
05/09/81 8:30 PM *The Exorcist* (1973)
04/09/83 1:30 PM *The Fly* (1958)
02/17/84 1:00 AM *The Fly* (1958)
05/19/84 12:15 AM *Race with the Devil* (1975)
03/01/86 12:30 AM *Ghosts That Still Walk* (1977)

Channel 11
Date Time Title Year
05/22/58 1:35 PM *Dr. Renault's Secret* (1942)
06/15/58 1:00 PM *Hangover Square* (1945)
07/12/58 5:00 PM *King Dinosaur* (1955)
08/05/58 5:00 PM *Lost Continent* (1951)
09/15/58 5:00 PM *Rocketship X-M* (1950)
09/16/58 5:00 PM *The Stolen Face* (1952)
11/03/58 5:00 PM *Hangover Square* (1945)
12/08/58 5:00 PM *Dr. Renault's Secret* (1942)
01/03/59 1:00 PM *Project Moonbase* (1953)
01/05/59 5:00 PM *Lost Continent* (1951)
01/08/59 5:00 PM *Monster from the Ocean Floor* (1954)
01/10/59 2:30 PM *The Invisible Man* (1933)
01/10/59 5:00 PM *King Dinosaur* (1955)
03/07/59 2:30 PM *Monster from the Ocean Floor* (1954)
03/07/59 4:30 PM *Spaceways* (1953)
04/11/59 2:30 PM *Rocketship X-M* (1950)
06/09/59 5:00 PM *Dr. Renault's Secret* (1942)
06/13/59 1:00 PM *The Stolen Face* (1952)
07/26/59 3:30 PM *Spaceways* (1953)
08/01/59 11:30 PM *Rocketship X-M* (1950)
08/22/59 11:30 PM *Scared to Death* (1947)
09/05/59 11:30 PM *The Frozen Ghost* (1945)
09/08/59 5:00 PM *Lost Continent* (1951)
09/12/59 11:30 PM *House of Horrors* (1946)
09/26/59 11:30 PM *The Mummy* (1932)
10/10/59 11:30 PM *Dracula's Daughter* (1936)
10/24/59 11:30 PM *Frankenstein Meets the Wolf Man* (1943)
10/31/59 11:30 PM *The Mad Ghoul* (1943)
11/21/59 11:30 PM *The Invisible Man* (1933)
11/28/59 11:30 PM *The Mummy's Tomb* (1942)
12/05/59 11:30 PM *Murders in the Rue Morgue* (1932)
02/06/60 12:45 AM *The Invisible Man Returns* (1940)
02/26/60 5:00 PM *King Dinosaur* (1955)
03/05/60 1:00 AM *Son of Frankenstein* (1939)
03/26/60 1:00 AM *Fire Maidens of Outer Space* (1956)
04/02/60 11:45 PM *WereWolf of London* (1935)
04/06/60 5:00 PM *The Invisible Man Returns* (1940)
04/09/60 12:45 AM *The Beast with Five Fingers* (1946)
04/18/60 5:00 PM *Invaders from Mars* (1953)
04/23/60 12:30 AM *Calling Dr. Death* (1943)
04/30/60 3:00 PM *Spaceways* (1953)
05/07/60 12:45 AM *The Mummy's Ghost* (1944)
05/21/60 12:30 AM *The Raven* (1935)
05/28/60 11:45 PM *The Walking Dead* (1936)
06/04/60 11:45 PM *The Wolf Man* (1941)
06/11/60 12:45 AM *The Spider Woman Strikes Back* (1946)
06/18/60 12:45 AM *Mystery of Marie Roget* (1942)
06/24/60 5:00 PM *Rocketship X-M* (1950)
06/25/60 12:45 AM *The Black Cat* (1934)
07/02/60 12:45 AM *The Undying Monster* (1942)
07/08/60 5:00 PM *The Stolen Face* (1952)
07/20/60 5:00 PM *Lost Continent* (1951)
07/23/60 12:45 AM *Frankenstein Meets the Wolf Man* (1943)
08/05/60 5:00 PM *Invaders from Mars* (1953)
08/06/60 11:45 PM *Man Made Monster* (1941)
08/10/60 5:00 PM *Night Key* (1937)

08/18/60 5:00 PM *The Last Warning* (1938)
01/01/61 11:20 PM *The Woman in White* (1948)
08/13/61 12:00 PM *Invaders from Mars* (1953)
08/16/61 9:00 PM *House of Mystery* (1961)
10/20/61 7:00 PM *The Ghost Breakers* (1940)
11/24/61 7:00 PM *The Invisible Man* (1933)
03/03/62 9:00 PM *The Day the Earth Stood Still* (1951)
04/07/62 11:05 PM *Dr. Cyclops* (1940)
06/09/62 11:05 PM *The Uninvited* (1944)
06/24/62 12:00 PM *The Ghost Breakers* (1940)
08/04/62 9:00 PM *The Day the Earth Stood Still* (1951)
09/08/62 11:05 PM *The Invisible Man* (1933)
10/11/62 5:30 PM *The Ghost Breakers* (1940)
03/24/63 11:20 PM *The Uninvited* (1944)
04/06/63 11:05 PM *The Fabulous World of Jules Verne* (1958)
09/08/63 11:20 PM *Island of Lost Souls* (1933)
09/16/63 5:00 PM *The Fabulous World of Jules Verne* (1958)
09/21/63 11:15 PM *Jack the Ripper* (1959)
10/21/63 5:00 PM *The Ghost Breakers* (1940)
12/09/63 5:00 PM *The Fabulous World of Jules Verne* (1958)
12/16/63 7:30 PM *The Lost World* (1960)
02/24/64 5:00 PM *Dr. Cyclops* (1940)
02/28/64 5:00 PM *Invaders from Mars* (1953)
03/06/64 5:55 AM *The Beast with Five Fingers* (1946)
03/06/64 1:00 AM *The Beast with Five Fingers* (1946)
03/13/64 5:55 AM *The Body Disappears* (1941)
03/13/64 1:00 AM *The Body Disappears* (1941)
03/20/64 5:55 AM *Gorilla Man* (1943)
03/20/64 1:00 AM *Gorilla Man* (1943)
03/30/64 5:00 PM *The Ghost Breakers* (1940)
04/10/64 5:55 AM *Doctor X* (1932)
04/10/64 1:00 AM *Doctor X* (1932)
05/27/64 5:00 PM *Invaders from Mars* (1953)
06/19/64 5:00 PM *Fire Maidens of Outer Space* (1956)
08/10/64 6:00 AM *The Mysterious Doctor* (1943)
08/10/64 1:00 AM *The Mysterious Doctor* (1943)
09/18/64 6:00 AM *The Return of Doctor X* (1939)
09/18/64 1:00 AM *The Return of Doctor X* (1939)
10/17/64 11:35 PM *Jack the Ripper* (1959)
11/02/64 1:00 AM *Invaders from Mars* (1953)
12/09/64 6:00 AM *Sh! The Octopus* (1937)
12/09/64 1:00 AM *Sh! The Octopus* (1937)
03/02/65 6:00 AM *The Walking Dead* (1936)
03/02/65 1:00 AM *The Walking Dead* (1936)
03/25/65 6:00 AM *The Smiling Ghost* (1941)
03/25/65 1:00 AM *The Smiling Ghost* (1941)
07/05/65 6:00 AM *Murders in the Zoo* (1933)
07/05/65 1:00 AM *Murders in the Zoo* (1933)
09/24/65 5:50 AM *Supernatural* (1933)
09/24/65 1:00 AM *Supernatural* (1933)
10/09/65 11:35 PM *The Hunchback of Notre Dame* (1956)
10/23/65 11:35 PM *From the Earth to the Moon* (1958)
12/31/65 1:00 AM *The Man in Half Moon Street* (1944)
01/11/66 1:00 AM *Murder by the Clock* (1931)
02/11/66 1:00 AM *The Monster and the Girl* (1941)
02/27/66 11:30 PM *From the Earth to the Moon* (1958)
03/13/66 12:00 PM *The Lost World* (1960)
03/20/66 12:00 PM *The Uninvited* (1944)

05/28/66 12:00 PM *The Ghost Breakers* (1940)
09/25/66 12:00 PM *The Hunchback of Notre Dame* (1956)
12/16/66 1:00 AM *Dr. Cyclops* (1940)
05/17/67 1:00 AM *Island of Lost Souls* (1933)
06/17/67 1:00 AM *The Lost World* (1960)
11/11/67 4:00 PM *From the Earth to the Moon* (1958)
03/09/68 4:00 PM *The Lost World* (1960)
03/24/68 12:00 PM *Master of the World* (1961)
11/17/68 12:00 PM *X* (1963)
11/21/68 1:00 AM *The Monster and the Girl* (1941)
12/12/68 1:00 AM *Dr. Cyclops* (1940)
02/23/69 12:00 PM *Master of the World* (1961)
04/27/69 12:00 PM *The Lost World* (1960)
08/03/69 12:00 PM *X* (1963)
11/14/69 1:05 AM *The Lost World* (1960)
01/02/70 1:05 AM *Pyro* (1964)
01/04/70 12:00 PM *From the Earth to the Moon* (1958)
04/02/70 1:05 AM *Master of the World* (1961)
06/21/70 10:00 AM *The Lost World* (1960)
08/16/70 12:00 PM *X* (1963)
08/23/70 10:00 AM *From the Earth to the Moon* (1958)
09/06/70 12:00 PM *Master of the World* (1961)
08/01/71 10:00 AM *X* (1963)
09/10/71 8:30 PM *The Hunchback of Notre Dame* (1923)
10/17/71 10:00 AM *Journey to the Center of the Earth* (1959)
02/27/72 10:00 AM *Master of the World* (1961)
02/27/72 12:00 PM *Voyage to the Bottom of the Sea* (1961)
05/07/72 12:00 PM *Hush...Hush, Sweet Charlotte* (1964)
05/27/72 7:30 PM *Dr. Jekyll and Mr. Hyde* (1920)
07/21/72 8:30 PM *Journey to the Center of the Earth* (1959)
07/30/72 10:00 AM *X* (1963)
09/12/72 8:30 PM *The Phantom of the Opera* (1925)
10/15/72 10:00 AM *What Ever Happened to Baby Jane?* (1962)
02/25/73 12:00 PM *Hush...Hush, Sweet Charlotte* (1964)
12/28/72 10:30 AM *The Innocents* (1961)
01/24/76 11:30 PM *The Shuttered Room* (1967)
07/29/73 12:00 PM *Journey to the Center of the Earth* (1959)
01/20/74 12:00 PM *The Innocents* (1961)
03/03/74 12:00 PM *The Shuttered Room* (1967)
09/08/74 12:00 PM *Voyage to the Bottom of the Sea* (1961)
10/06/74 10:30 AM *The Nanny* (1965)
10/27/74 10:30 AM *One Million Years B.C.* (1966)
11/23/74 1:00 AM *Dr. Jekyll and Mr. Hyde* (1920)
12/01/74 10:30 AM *What Ever Happened to Baby Jane?* (1962)
02/22/75 2:00 AM *The Hunchback of Notre Dame* (1923)
06/07/75 11:30 PM *Hush...Hush, Sweet Charlotte* (1964)
06/12/75 9:00 PM *The Shuttered Room* (1967)
06/28/75 11:30 PM *Voyage to the Bottom of the Sea* (1961)
08/17/75 12:00 PM *Journey to the Center of the Earth* (1959)
09/28/75 12:00 PM *Quatermass and the Pit* (1967)
10/12/75 10:30 AM *Two on a Guillotine* (1965)
10/26/75 10:30 AM *The Nanny* (1965)
11/15/75 12:00 AM *What Ever Happened to Baby Jane?* (1962)
02/21/76 11:30 PM *Voyage to the Bottom of the Sea* (1961)
03/28/76 12:00 PM *Hush...Hush, Sweet Charlotte* (1964)
05/15/76 11:30 PM *Quatermass and the Pit* (1967)
08/08/76 12:00 PM *What Ever Happened to Baby Jane?* (1962)
08/15/76 12:00 PM *The Innocents* (1961)

08/22/76 12:00 PM *Journey to the Center of the Earth* (1959)
09/12/76 10:30 AM *One Million Years B.C.* (1966)
10/03/76 9:00 AM *Abbott and Costello Meet Dr. Jekyll and Mr. Hyde* (1953)
10/09/76 2:00 PM *Journey to the Center of the Earth* (1959)
10/17/76 12:00 AM *The Shuttered Room* (1967)
10/31/76 9:00 AM *Abbott and Costello Meet Frankenstein* (1948)
10/31/76 10:30 AM *The Brides of Fu Manchu* (1966)
11/07/76 11:30 PM *Quatermass and the Pit* (1967)
11/28/76 9:00 AM *Abbott and Costello Meet the Mummy* (1955)
01/16/77 12:00 PM *My Blood Runs Cold* (1965)
01/23/77 10:30 AM *Abbott and Costello Meet the Invisible Man* (1951)
03/06/77 12:00 PM *The Innocents* (1961)
04/24/77 12:00 PM *What's the Matter with Helen?* (1971)
04/24/77 11:30 PM *The Illustrated Man* (1969)
05/01/77 11:30 PM *Two on a Guillotine* (1965)
05/08/77 12:00 PM *The Omega Man* (1971)
06/26/77 12:00 PM *The Nanny* (1965)
09/18/77 12:00 PM *One Million Years B.C.* (1966)
10/09/77 9:00 AM *Abbott and Costello Meet the Mummy* (1955)
10/16/77 9:00 AM *Ghosts on the Loose* (1943)
11/13/77 9:00 AM *Abbott and Costello Meet Dr. Jekyll and Mr. Hyde* (1953)
11/20/77 9:00 AM *Spooks Run Wild* (1941)
12/04/77 10:30 AM *The Brides of Fu Manchu* (1966)
01/08/78 11:30 PM *The Shuttered Room* (1967)
01/22/78 11:30 PM *Chamber of Horrors* (1966)
02/26/78 10:30 AM *Abbott and Costello Meet the Invisible Man* (1951)
04/02/78 11:30 PM *The Frozen Dead* (1966)
04/16/78 12:00 PM *Quatermass and the Pit* (1967)
04/16/78 11:30 PM *Two on a Guillotine* (1965)
06/04/78 10:30 AM *Abbott and Costello Meet the Mummy* (1955)
06/18/78 10:30 AM *Ghosts on the Loose* (1943)
07/02/78 12:00 PM *The Brides of Fu Manchu* (1966)
07/23/78 10:30 AM *Spooks Run Wild* (1941)
07/23/78 12:00 PM *One Million Years B.C.* (1966)
07/30/78 10:30 AM *Abbott and Costello Meet Dr. Jekyll and Mr. Hyde* (1953)
10/22/78 9:00 AM *Abbott and Costello Meet Frankenstein* (1948)
10/22/78 11:30 PM *The Curse of Frankenstein* (1957)
10/29/78 11:30 PM *My Blood Runs Cold* (1965)
11/05/78 11:30 PM *Dracula: Prince of Darkness* (1966)
11/26/78 11:30 PM *The Mummy* (1959)
01/07/79 11:30 PM *THX 1138* (1971)
01/28/79 9:00 AM *Abbott and Costello Meet the Invisible Man* (1951)
01/28/79 11:30 PM *The Illustrated Man* (1969)
02/04/79 11:30 PM *Frankenstein Created Woman* (1967)
02/18/79 11:30 PM *The Valley of Gwangi* (1969)
04/29/79 11:30 PM *The Brides of Fu Manchu* (1966)
05/27/79 11:30 PM *The Lost Continent* (1968)
06/24/79 10:30 AM *Ghosts on the Loose* (1943)
07/01/79 12:00 PM *The Nanny* (1965)
07/29/79 9:00 AM *Abbott and Costello Meet Frankenstein* (1948)
08/12/79 11:30 PM *The Innocents* (1961)
08/19/79 10:30 AM *Spooks Run Wild* (1941)

12/02/79 10:30 AM *My Blood Runs Cold* (1965)
12/16/79 10:30 AM *The Illustrated Man* (1969)
12/16/79 1:30 AM *The Frozen Dead* (1966)
12/30/79 11:30 PM *The Omega Man* (1971)
02/17/80 11:30 PM *The Power* (1968)
03/02/80 10:30 AM *The Witches* (1966)
03/09/80 11:30 PM *I, Monster* (1971)
04/20/80 11:30 PM *Trog* (1970)
04/27/80 12:30 PM *Two on A Guillotine* (1965)
05/11/80 9:00 AM *It's Alive!* (1969)
05/11/80 11:30 PM *The Vengeance of Fu Manchu* (1967)
05/18/80 11:30 PM *Destroy All Monsters* (1968)
05/18/80 11:30 PM *The Mummy* (1959)
05/25/80 9:00 AM *Gamera vs. Monster X* (1970)
06/22/80 9:00 AM *Spooks Run Wild* (1941)
06/22/80 10:30 AM *The Curse of Frankenstein* (1957)
07/13/80 10:30 AM *Dracula: Prince of Darkness* (1966)
07/20/80 10:30 AM *Chamber of Horrors* (1966)
07/27/80 10:30 AM *Dracula Has Risen from the Grave* (1968)
08/03/80 10:30 AM *What's the Matter with Helen?* (1971)
08/10/80 10:30 AM *Frankenstein Must Be Destroyed* (1969)
08/21/80 9:30 PM *The Omega Man* (1971)
08/24/80 10:30 AM *The Frozen Dead* (1966)
09/28/80 11:00 AM *Attack of the Puppet People* (1958)
11/09/80 10:30 AM *Master of the World* (1961)
11/23/80 9:00 AM *X* (1963)
12/21/80 12:30 PM *The Face of Fu Manchu* (1965)
12/28/80 10:30 AM *Frankenstein Conquers the World* (1965)
12/31/80 2:00 AM *The Omega Man* (1971)
01/04/81 12:00 AM *The Eye Creatures* (1965)
01/25/81 9:00 AM *I Was a Teenage Frankenstein* (1957)
01/25/81 10:30 AM *The Power* (1968)
02/08/81 12:00 AM *Queen of Blood* (1966)
02/15/81 9:00 AM *Westworld* (1973)
03/15/81 10:30 AM *Return of the Giant Monsters* (1967)
04/26/81 10:30 AM *Curse of the Swamp Creature* (1966)
08/09/81 10:30 AM *The Omega Man* (1971)
09/05/81 2:00 AM *The Phantom Planet* (1961)
09/12/81 1:00 AM *Reptilicus* (1961)
09/26/81 11:30 PM *The Stepford Wives* (1975)
09/26/81 1:00 AM *Day the World Ended* (1955)
10/03/81 1:15 AM *Invasion of the Star Creatures* (1962)
10/10/81 1:00 AM *Terror from the Year 5000* (1958)
10/17/81 11:30 PM *J.D.'s Revenge* (1976)
10/17/81 1:00 AM *The Brain That Wouldn't Die* (1962)
10/24/81 1:00 AM *Yongary, Monster from the Deep* (1967)
10/31/81 1:00 AM *The Angry Red Planet* (1959)
11/07/81 11:30 PM *Grizzly* (1976)
11/07/81 1:00 AM *The Beast with a Million Eyes* (1955)
11/14/81 1:00 AM *The Phantom from 10,000 Leagues* (1955)
11/21/81 1:15 AM *The Killer Shrews* (1959)
11/28/81 1:15 AM *Magic Serpent* (1966)
12/05/81 1:15 AM *Majin, Monster of Terror* (1966)
12/12/81 1:15 AM *Konga* (1961)
12/19/81 1:15 AM *Voyage into Space* (1970)
12/26/81 1:00 AM *Creature of Destruction* (1967)
01/09/82 11:30 PM *Soylent Green* (1973)
03/28/82 10:30 AM *Journey to the Seventh Planet* (1962)

06/12/82 11:30 PM *What's the Matter with Helen?* (1971)
07/25/82 10:30 AM *Dracula Has Risen from the Grave* (1968)
09/11/82 11:30 PM *The Power* (1968)
10/30/82 12:00 AM *Spirits of the Dead* (1968)
10/31/82 10:30 AM *Master of the World* (1961)
10/31/82 12:30 PM *Queen of Blood* (1966)
10/31/82 2:00 PM *X* (1963)
11/13/82 12:30 AM *Audrey Rose* (1977)
12/26/82 10:30 AM *Zontar, the Thing from Venus* (1966)
03/20/83 10:30 AM *What's the Matter with Helen?* (1971)
04/16/83 11:30 PM *Soylent Green* (1973)
05/27/83 12:00 AM *I, Monster* (1971)
01/29/84 10:30 AM *Westworld* (1973)
03/03/84 12:30 AM *Attack of the Puppet People* (1958)
04/07/84 12:30 AM *The Power* (1968)
04/21/84 12:30 AM *Spirits of the Dead* (1968)
05/05/84 12:30 AM *Master of the World* (1961)
05/19/84 12:45 AM *Race with the Devil* (1975)
05/26/84 12:30 AM *Soylent Green* (1973)
06/16/84 12:30 AM *It's Alive!* (1969)
07/14/84 12:30 AM *X* (1963)
07/21/84 12:30 AM *The Green Slime* (1968)
08/25/84 1:30 AM *Zontar, the Thing from Venus* (1966)
08/26/84 10:30 AM *Burnt Offerings* (1976)
09/19/84 1:00 AM *Invasion* (1965)
10/27/84 11:30 PM *Carrie* (1976)
04/21/85 10:30 AM *Day of the Animals* (1977)
06/09/85 10:30 AM *Audrey Rose* (1977)
07/06/85 11:30 PM *Soylent Green* (1973)
07/14/85 12:30 PM *The Stepford Wives* (1975)
08/24/85 11:30 PM *I. Monster* (1970)
08/31/85 1:30 AM *The Power* (1968)
02/16/86 10:30 AM *Westworld* (1973)
03/01/86 12:30 AM *Spirits of the Dead* (1968)
03/02/86 9:00 PM *Scanners* (1981)
05/03/86 12:30 AM *Master of the World* (1961)
05/24/86 2:00 PM *Burnt Offerings* (1976)
06/01/86 10:30 AM *Orca* (1977)
08/09/86 12:30 AM *Soylent Green* (1973)
08/23/86 1:30 AM *Reptilicus* (1961)
08/30/86 1:30 AM *Zontar, the Thing from Venus* (1966)
10/04/86 12:30 AM *Westworld* (1973)
10/26/86 1:30 PM *The Green Slime* (1968)
10/28/86 9:00 PM *Carrie* (1976)
03/07/87 12:30 AM *Panic in Year Zero* (1962)
04/25/87 12:30 AM *Spirits of the Dead* (1968)
05/30/87 1:00 PM *Audrey Rose* (1977)
06/13/87 1:30 PM *Burnt Offerings* (1976)
07/12/87 12:30 PM *Orca* (1977)

Channel 13

Date Time Title Year
11/09/57 12:20 AM *Mark of the Vampire* (1935)
11/10/57 6:00 PM *Son of Kong* (1933)
11/29/57 11:50 PM *The Magnetic Monster* (1953)
12/03/57 10:30 PM *The Picture of Dorian Gray* (1945)
12/07/57 12:50 AM *Isle of the Dead* (1945)
01/01/58 6:00 PM *Red Planet Mars* (1952)
01/12/58 6:00 PM *Devil Girl from Mars* (1954)
01/17/58 1:00 PM *Thirteen Women* (1932)
01/18/58 6:00 PM *Riders to the Stars* (1954)
02/01/58 10:40 PM *Dr. Jekyll and Mr. Hyde* (1941)
02/01/58 1:00 AM *The Curse of the Cat People* (1944)
02/07/58 12:45 AM *The Thing from Another World* (1951)
02/08/58 6:00 PM *Spaceways* (1953)
02/17/58 6:00 PM *Unknown World* (1951)
03/12/58 1:00 PM *Alias John Preston* (1955)
03/27/58 10:40 PM *Three Cases of Murder* (1954)
03/30/58 6:00 PM *The Man from Planet X* (1951)
04/05/58 12:55 AM *Gog* (1954)
04/11/58 1:00 AM *The Mask of Fu Manchu* (1932)
04/13/58 10:40 PM *King Kong* (1933)
04/25/58 1:00 PM *Four Sided Triangle* (1953)
05/06/58 6:00 PM *The Seventh Victim* (1943)
05/10/58 12:45 AM *The Body Snatcher* (1945)
05/15/58 11:00 AM *You'll Find Out* (1940)
05/24/58 12:40 AM *Donovan's Brain* (1953)
06/02/58 6:00 PM *The Whip Hand* (1951)
07/02/58 10:40 PM *The Picture of Dorian Gray* (1945)
07/04/58 12:45 AM *The Leopard Man* (1943)
07/11/58 1:20 AM *The Devil Doll* (1936)
07/12/58 6:00 PM *Son of Kong* (1933)
07/18/58 12:45 AM *Devil Girl from Mars* (1954)
07/23/58 11:00 AM *Zombies on Broadway* (1945)
08/02/58 12:30 AM *Red Planet Mars* (1952)
09/06/58 6:00 PM *The Thing from Another World* (1951)
09/23/58 6:00 PM *The Magnetic Monster* (1953)
09/30/58 6:00 PM *Riders to the Stars* (1954)
10/01/58 11:00 AM *Mummy's Boys* (1936)
10/05/58 6:00 PM *Gog* (1954)
10/06/58 6:00 PM *Alias John Preston* (1955)
11/23/58 6:00 PM *Unknown World* (1951)
11/26/58 11:50 PM *The Whip Hand* (1951)
11/30/58 6:00 PM *Red Planet Mars* (1952)
12/13/58 6:00 PM *The Man from Planet X* (1951)
01/05/59 11:50 PM *The Seventh Victim* (1943)
01/11/59 10:40 PM *Son of Kong* (1933)
01/17/59 1:00 PM *You'll Find Out* (1940)
02/17/59 10:40 PM *Donovan's Brain* (1953)
03/02/59 10:40 PM *Bedlam* (1946)
03/09/59 1:30 PM *Four Sided Triangle* (1953)
03/24/59 10:45 PM *The Magnetic Monster* (1953)
04/05/59 6:00 PM *Riders to the Stars* (1954)
04/11/59 1:00 PM *The Thing from Another World* (1951)
04/20/59 10:50 PM *Three Cases of Murder* (1954)
04/28/59 12:00 AM *Gog* (1954)
05/05/59 10:45 PM *Dr. Jekyll and Mr. Hyde* (1941)
05/11/59 1:00 AM *The Body Snatcher* (1945)
05/23/59 6:00 PM *Zombies on Broadway* (1945)
06/09/59 1:30 PM *The Whip Hand* (1951)
06/09/59 1:00 AM *The Curse of the Cat People* (1944)
08/20/59 11:00 PM *The Unholy Three* (1930)
08/22/59 6:00 PM *Cat People* (1942)
08/26/59 12:30 PM *The Devil Doll* (1936)
09/09/59 12:30 PM *The Seventh Victim* (1943)
09/15/59 11:15 PM *The Picture of Dorian Gray* (1945)

09/19/59 12:30 PM *Isle of the Dead* (1945)
10/10/59 12:30 PM *I Walked with A Zombie* (1943)
10/18/59 11:00 PM *Mighty Joe Young* (1949)
10/19/59 12:30 PM *Mummy's Boys* (1936)
10/24/59 12:30 PM *The Body Snatcher* (1945)
10/24/59 6:00 PM *You'll Find Out* (1940)
10/24/59 11:00 PM *Destination Moon* (1950)
10/29/59 12:30 PM *Bedlam* (1946)
10/31/59 6:00 PM *The Magnetic Monster* (1953)
11/14/59 12:30 PM *Gog* (1954)
11/14/59 6:00 PM *Lost Planet Airmen* (1951)
11/30/59 11:00 PM *Dr. Jekyll and Mr. Hyde* (1941)
12/05/59 12:45 AM *The Mask of Fu Manchu* (1932)
12/12/59 6:00 PM *The Thing from Another World* (1951)
03/16/60 6:00 PM *The Seventh Victim* (1943)
03/27/60 11:00 PM *Destination Moon* (1950)
04/03/60 12:30 PM *The Picture of Dorian Gray* (1945)
04/22/60 12:30 PM *Zombies on Broadway* (1945)
05/19/60 6:00 PM *Gog* (1954)
06/04/60 11:00 PM *Mighty Joe Young* (1949)
06/12/60 6:00 PM *Son of Kong* (1933)
06/23/60 11:00 PM *You'll Find Out* (1940)
07/28/60 11:00 PM *Dr. Jekyll and Mr. Hyde* (1941)
08/17/60 6:00 PM *Destination Moon* (1950)
09/11/60 1:30 PM *The Whip Hand* (1951)
09/25/60 6:00 PM *Lost Planet Airmen* (1951)
10/21/60 6:00 PM *The Thing from Another World* (1951)
11/12/60 11:15 PM *The Picture of Dorian Gray* (1945)
12/20/60 6:00 PM *The Black Sleep* (1956)
12/28/60 6:00 PM *The Twonky* (1953)
01/13/61 11:15 PM *The Hunchback of Notre Dame* (1939)
01/17/61 6:00 PM *Untamed Women* (1952)
02/23/61 6:00 PM *Dr. Jekyll and Mr. Hyde* (Part 1) (1941)
02/24/61 6:00 PM *Dr. Jekyll and Mr. Hyde* (Part 2) (1941)
02/27/61 11:15 PM *Mighty Joe Young* (1949)
03/16/61 6:00 PM *U.F.O.* (1956)
03/31/61 11:20 PM *The Quatermass Xperiment* (1955)
04/09/61 11:15 PM *Destination Moon* (1950)
04/18/61 11:15 PM *The Black Sleep* (1956)
04/30/61 6:00 PM *Son of Kong* (1933)
06/10/61 12:30 PM *The Thing from Another World* (1951)
07/02/61 11:15 AM *The Curse of the Cat People* (1944)
07/21/61 1:15 AM *The Neanderthal Man* (1953)
08/06/61 10:00 AM *Mummy's Boys* (1936)
08/06/61 11:15 PM *The Hunchback of Notre Dame* (1939)
08/11/61 12:45 AM *Bedlam* (1946)
08/12/61 10:40 AM *Cat People* (1942)
08/25/61 10:00 AM *Genius at Work* (1946)
08/25/61 1:15 AM *The Body Snatcher* (1945)
08/29/61 5:30 PM *Mighty Joe Young* (1949)
09/07/61 5:30 PM *Destination Moon* (1950)
09/08/61 12:45 AM *Tobor the Great* (1954)
09/12/61 10:00 AM *The Twonky* (1953)
09/15/61 12:45 AM *The Mask of Fu Manchu* (1932)
09/22/61 1:15 AM *The Neanderthal Man* (1953)
09/29/61 12:45 AM *Mark of the Vampire* (1935)
10/06/61 12:45 AM *Isle of the Dead* (1945)
10/20/61 12:45 AM *You'll Find Out* (1940)

10/24/61 5:30 PM *The Leopard Man* (1943)
10/27/61 12:45 AM *I Walked with A Zombie* (1943)
11/03/61 12:45 AM *Dr. Jekyll and Mr. Hyde* (1941)
11/10/61 12:45 AM *The Seventh Victim* (1943)
11/24/61 12:45 AM *The Black Sleep* (1956)
12/01/61 12:45 AM *The Body Snatcher* (1945)
12/22/61 12:45 AM *The Quatermass Xperiment* (1955)
03/02/62 12:45 AM *Bedlam* (1946)
03/03/62 12:15 AM *The Hunchback of Notre Dame* (1939)
04/08/62 1:30 PM *Forbidden Planet* (1956)
04/13/62 12:45 AM *Isle of the Dead* (1945)
06/06/62 1:00 PM *The Picture of Dorian Gray* (1945)
10/28/62 8:00 PM *I Bury the Living* (1958)
12/30/62 11:15 PM *Forbidden Planet* (1956)
01/12/63 12:00 AM *The Black Sleep* (1956)
01/13/63 5:00 PM *King Kong* (1933)
02/24/63 5:00 PM *Mighty Joe Young* (1949)
04/21/63 11:15 PM *First Man into Space* (1959)
06/01/63 12:00 AM *Dr. Jekyll and Mr. Hyde* (1941)
07/06/63 12:00 AM *The Whip Hand* (1951)
07/19/63 12:55 AM *The Curse of the Cat People* (1944)
07/20/63 12:00 AM *Cat People* (1942)
08/06/63 1:00 PM *The Mask of Fu Manchu* (1932)
08/10/63 12:00 AM *The Body Snatcher* (1945)
08/17/63 12:00 AM *Isle of the Dead* (1945)
08/31/63 12:00 AM *The Seventh Victim* (1943)
10/09/63 1:00 PM *Hangover Square* (1945)
11/02/63 11:40 PM *The Spiral Staircase* (1946)
12/06/63 12:55 AM *Bedlam* (1946)
01/04/64 11:30 PM *The Haunted Strangler* (1958)
01/11/64 11:15 PM *Forbidden Planet* (1956)
01/18/64 11:15 PM *It Came from Beneath the Sea* (1955)
01/25/64 11:15 PM *The Thing from Another World* (1951)
02/01/64 11:15 PM *King Kong* (1933)
02/01/64 1:00 AM *Son of Kong* (1933)
02/08/64 11:15 PM *Cat People* (1942)
02/08/64 12:45 AM *The Curse of the Cat People* (1944)
02/15/64 11:15 PM *Mighty Joe Young* (1949)
02/22/64 11:15 PM *The Son of Dr. Jekyll* (1951)
02/22/64 12:45 AM *I Walked with A Zombie* (1943)
02/29/64 11:15 PM *First Man into Space* (1959)
02/29/64 12:45 AM *The Leopard Man* (1943)
03/07/64 11:15 PM *Creature with the Atom Brain* (1955)
03/21/64 11:15 PM *The Gamma People* (1956)
03/28/64 11:15 PM *Fiend Without a Face* (1958)
04/04/64 11:15 PM *The Hunchback of Notre Dame* (1939)
04/04/64 1:10 AM *The Whip Hand* (1951)
04/11/64 11:15 PM *Isle of the Dead* (1945)
04/18/64 11:15 PM *The Lodger* (1944)
04/18/64 12:50 AM *The Seventh Victim* (1943)
04/25/64 11:15 PM *The Body Snatcher* (1945)
04/29/64 12:45 AM *Bedlam* (1946)
05/09/64 12:45 AM *The Black Cat* (1941)
06/20/64 11:15 PM *The Phantom of the Opera* (1943)
07/11/64 12:50 AM *The Great Impersonation* (1935)
09/12/64 11:20 PM *The Gamma People* (1956)
09/24/64 11:15 PM *The Haunted Strangler* (1958)
09/21/64 11:15 PM *The Thing from Another World* (1951)

10/01/64 11:15 PM *Cat People* (1942)
10/01/64 11:15 PM *The Son of Dr. Jekyll* (1951)
10/08/64 11:15 PM *It Came from Beneath the Sea* (1955)
10/08/64 11:15 PM *Fiend Without a Face* (1958)
10/15/64 1:00 PM *The Spiral Staircase* (1946)
10/27/64 5:30 PM *Forbidden Planet* (1956)
10/30/64 1:00 PM *The Lodger* (1944)
10/30/64 5:30 PM *King Kong* (1933)
11/11/64 1:00 PM *Flesh and Fantasy* (1943)
01/05/65 5:30 PM *Destination Moon* (1950)
01/12/65 5:30 PM *Mark of the Vampire* (1935)
01/19/65 5:30 PM *Gog* (1954)
01/20/65 5:30 PM *The Hound of the Baskervilles* (1959)
01/26/65 5:30 PM *The Lost Missile* (1958)
01/29/65 1:00 AM *The Seventh Victim* (1943)
02/02/65 5:30 PM *Donovan's Brain* (1953)
02/09/65 5:30 PM *The Magnetic Monster* (1953)
02/16/65 5:00 PM *Riders to the Stars* (1954)
02/23/65 5:00 PM *Terror is a Man* (1959)
03/02/65 5:00 PM *The Man from Planet X* (1951)
03/09/65 5:00 PM *It Came from Beneath the Sea* (1955)
03/16/65 5:00 PM *It! The Terror from Beyond Space* (1958)
03/23/65 5:00 PM *The Monster that Challenged the World* (1957)
03/24/65 1:00 PM *The Whip Hand* (1951)
03/30/65 5:00 PM *I Bury the Living* (1958)
04/13/65 5:00 PM *Red Planet Mars* (1952)
04/23/65 5:00 PM *The Phantom of the Opera* (1943)
04/27/65 5:00 PM *The Quatermass Xperiment* (1955)
05/04/65 5:00 PM *Invisible Invaders* (1959)
05/11/65 5:00 PM *Voodoo Island* (1957)
05/18/65 5:00 PM *The Gamma People* (1956)
05/25/65 5:00 PM *Creature with the Atom Brain* (1955)
06/01/65 5:00 PM *Mighty Joe Young* (1949)
06/08/65 5:00 PM *The Flame Barrier* (1958)
06/15/65 5:00 PM *The Black Sleep* (1956)
06/22/65 5:00 PM *The Hound of the Baskervilles* (1959)
06/27/65 11:20 PM *The Haunted Strangler* (1958)
06/29/65 5:00 PM *Pharaoh's Curse* (1957)
07/03/65 1:15 AM *Macumbra Love* (1960)
07/06/65 5:00 PM *U.F.O.* (1956)
07/13/65 5:00 PM *The Black Cat* (1941)
07/17/65 1:15 AM *The Leopard Man* (1943)
07/21/65 5:00 PM *The Return of Dracula* (1958)
07/24/65 1:15 AM *Cat People* (1942)
07/27/65 5:00 PM *The Son of Dr. Jekyll* (1951)
07/30/65 1:00 AM *I Walked with A Zombie* (1943)
07/31/65 1:15 AM *The Curse of the Cat People* (1944)
08/13/65 1:00 PM *Hangover Square* (1945)
09/10/65 1:00 PM *The Spiral Staircase* (1946)
09/16/65 5:00 PM *Flesh and Fantasy* (1943)
12/09/65 5:00 PM *The Invisible Boy* (1957)
01/21/66 1:10 AM *The Lodger* (1944)
02/14/66 7:30 PM *Five* (1951)
04/08/66 1:10 AM *The Hunchback of Notre Dame* (1939)
08/05/66 12:45 PM *Creature with the Atom Brain* (1955)
08/09/66 12:00 AM *Riders to the Stars* (1954)
08/19/66 5:00 PM *Hangover Square* (1945)
08/19/66 12:00 AM *The Thing from Another World* (1951)

09/04/66 11:35 PM *The Spiral Staircase* (1946)
09/13/66 11:30 PM *The Gamma People* (1956)
11/01/66 5:00 PM *Cult of the Cobra* (1955)
11/10/66 11:30 PM *It Came from Outer Space* (1953)
11/11/66 5:00 PM *Creature from the Black Lagoon* (1954)
11/28/66 11:30 PM *Invisible Invaders* (1959)
12/15/66 11:30 PM *The Hound of the Baskervilles* (1959)
12/27/66 5:00 PM *Mighty Joe Young* (1949)
01/12/67 4:30 PM *Godzilla: King of the Monsters* (1956)
01/12/67 11:30 PM *Battle of the Worlds* (1961)
01/19/67 11:30 PM *The Strange Door* (1951)
01/26/67 4:30 PM *The Creature Walks Among Us* (1956)
02/01/67 4:30 PM *Gog* (1954)
02/08/67 11:30 PM *The Quatermass Xperiment* (1955)
02/09/67 4:30 PM *The Black Sleep* (1956)
02/10/67 1:00 AM *The Leopard Man* (1943)
02/15/67 4:30 PM *Gorgo* (1961)
02/16/67 11:30 PM *The Manster* (1959)
02/28/67 11:30 PM *The Black Castle* (1952)
03/02/67 11:30 PM *I Bury the Living* (1958)
03/09/67 4:30 PM *King Kong* (1933)
03/09/67 11:30 PM *The Thing from Another World* (1951)
03/14/67 11:30 PM *The Phantom of the Opera* (1943)
03/19/67 1:30 AM *Genius at Work* (1946)
03/20/67 4:30 PM *The Son of Dr. Jekyll* (1951)
03/22/67 11:30 PM *Red Planet Mars* (1952)
03/30/67 11:30 PM *The Body Snatcher* (1945)
03/31/67 4:30 PM *Destination Moon* (1950)
04/06/67 11:30 PM *The Monster that Challenged the World* (1957)
04/13/67 11:30 PM *Voodoo Island* (1957)
04/20/67 11:30 PM *The Magnetic Monster* (1953)
04/27/67 11:30 PM *Alias John Preston* (1955)
05/04/67 11:30 PM *Fiend Without a Face* (1958)
05/06/67 1:45 AM *The Seventh Victim* (1943)
05/11/67 11:30 PM *The Vampire* (1957)
05/18/67 11:30 PM *The Neanderthal Man* (1953)
05/25/67 11:30 PM *The Beast of Hollow Mountain* (1956)
06/01/67 11:30 PM *The Terror of the Tongs* (1961)
06/08/67 11:30 PM *Revenge of the Creature* (1955)
06/22/67 11:30 PM *Bedlam* (1946)
06/29/67 11:30 PM *Isle of the Dead* (1945)
07/06/67 11:30 PM *Curse of the Faceless Man* (1958)
07/13/67 11:30 PM *Terror is a Man* (1959)
07/15/67 8:00 AM *Abbott and Costello Meet the Mummy* (1955)
07/20/67 11:30 PM *The Face of Marble* (1946)
07/27/67 11:30 PM *Donovan's Brain* (1953)
08/03/67 11:30 PM *The Haunted Strangler* (1958)
08/10/67 11:30 PM *Macumba Love* (1960)
08/17/67 11:30 PM *The Flame Barrier* (1958)
08/24/67 11:30 PM *U.F.O.* (1956)
08/31/67 11:30 PM *First Man into Space* (1959)
09/07/67 11:30 PM *The Gamma People* (1956)
09/14/67 11:30 PM *The Return of Dracula* (1958)
09/20/67 11:30 PM *Flesh and Fantasy* (1943)
09/21/67 11:30 PM *Isle of the Dead* (1945)
09/28/67 11:30 PM *Cat People* (1942)
10/05/67 11:30 PM *Homicidal* (1961)
10/12/67 11:30 PM *Maniac* (1963)

10/15/67 12:00 AM *Scream of Fear* (1961)
10/19/67 11:30 PM *Hangover Square* (1945)
10/22/67 8:00 AM *The Invisible Boy* (1957)
10/22/67 5:00 PM *Mysterious Island* (1961)
10/24/67 11:30 PM *Five* (1951)
10/26/67 11:30 PM *The Four Skulls of Jonathan Drake* (1959)
11/02/67 11:30 PM *Mr. Sardonicus* (1961)
11/10/67 1:45 AM *The Ape* (1940)
11/16/67 11:30 PM *Riders to the Stars* (1954)
11/25/67 11:30 PM *Strait-Jacket* (1964)
12/08/67 1:00 AM *I Walked with A Zombie* (1943)
12/28/67 11:30 PM *Cult of the Cobra* (1955)
12/29/67 1:00 PM *Mighty Joe Young* (1949)
01/04/68 11:30 PM *The Hound of the Baskervilles* (1959)
01/19/68 1:30 AM *The Curse of the Cat People* (1944)
01/28/68 8:00 AM *Abbott and Costello Meet Dr. Jekyll and Mr. Hyde* (1953)
02/01/68 11:30 PM *The Haunted Strangler* (1958)
02/19/68 11:30 PM *The Old Dark House* (1963)
02/23/68 1:30 AM *The Leopard Man* (1943)
03/14/68 1:00 PM *The Whip Hand* (1951)
03/28/68 11:30 PM *Destination Moon* (1950)
04/04/68 11:30 PM *The Lodger* (1944)
04/11/68 11:30 PM *It Came from Outer Space* (1953)
04/18/68 11:30 PM *The Thing from Another World* (1951)
04/25/68 11:30 PM *Godzilla: King of the Monsters* (1956)
05/02/68 1:00 PM *Most Dangerous Man Alive* (1961)
05/08/68 1:00 PM *The Spiral Staircase* (1946)
06/02/68 8:00 AM *Abbott and Costello Meet the Invisible Man* (1951)
06/13/68 11:30 PM *The Phantom of the Opera* (1943)
06/20/68 11:30 PM *The Black Castle* (1952)
07/11/68 11:30 PM *Red Planet Mars* (1952)
07/14/68 8:00 AM *Abbott and Costello Meet the Mummy* (1955)
08/08/68 11:30 PM *Terror is a Man* (1959)
08/15/68 12:30 AM *The Beast of Hollow Mountain* (1956)
10/18/68 1:00 AM *The Hunchback of Notre Dame* (1939)
10/27/68 4:00 PM *Mysterious Island* (1961)
11/08/68 1:00 AM *Strait-Jacket* (1964)
12/01/68 2:00 PM *The Whip Hand* (1951)
12/06/68 1:00 AM *Bedlam* (1946)
12/30/68 2:30 PM *Mighty Joe Young* (1949)
01/04/69 1:30 AM *The Body Snatcher* (1945)
01/26/69 8:00 AM *The Invisible Boy* (1957)
01/31/69 1:00 AM *The Hound of the Baskervilles* (1959)
02/01/69 1:30 AM *Invisible Invaders* (1959)
02/02/69 8:00 AM *Abbott and Costello Meet Dr. Jekyll and Mr. Hyde* (1953)
02/08/69 1:30 AM *It! The Terror from Beyond Space* (1958)
02/15/69 1:30 AM *Voodoo Island* (1957)
02/22/69 1:30 AM *The Quatermass Xperiment* (1955)
03/07/69 1:00 AM *The Brides of Dracula* (1960)
03/14/69 1:00 AM *The Phantom of the Opera* (1943)
03/21/69 1:00 AM *U.F.O.* (1956)
03/28/69 1:00 AM *The Thing from Another World* (1951)
04/04/69 1:00 AM *King Kong* (1933)
04/11/69 1:00 AM *The Black Castle* (1952)
04/12/69 1:30 AM *The Leopard Man* (1943)

04/13/89 11:15 PM *The Woman in White* (1948)
04/18/69 1:00 AM *Battle of the Worlds* (1961)
04/25/69 1:00 AM *The Body Snatcher* (1945)
05/02/69 1:00 AM *The Return of Dracula* (1958)
05/09/69 1:00 AM *Creature with the Atom Brain* (1955)
05/10/69 11:30 PM *Five* (1951)
05/16/69 1:00 AM *I Bury the Living* (1958)
05/17/69 1:30 AM *The Man from Planet X* (1951)
05/23/69 1:00 AM *The Lost Missile* (1958)
06/06/69 1:00 AM *The Son of Dr. Jekyll* (1951)
06/13/69 1:00 AM *It Came from Beneath the Sea* (1955)
06/20/69 1:00 AM *The Monster that Challenged the World* (1957)
06/27/69 1:00 AM *The Black Sleep* (1956)
07/04/69 1:00 AM *The Vampire* (1957)
07/06/69 5:00 PM *The Old Dark House* (1963)
07/11/69 1:00 AM *Pharaoh's Curse* (1957)
07/18/69 1:00 AM *Terror is a Man* (1959)
07/25/69 1:00 AM *Gog* (1954)
08/01/69 12:45 AM *The Magnetic Monster* (1953)
08/08/69 1:00 AM *The Neanderthal Man* (1953)
08/15/69 1:00 AM *Riders to the Stars* (1954)
08/22/69 1:00 AM *Donovan's Brain* (1953)
08/27/69 10:00 AM *Red Planet Mars* (1952)
08/29/69 1:00 AM *The Face of Marble* (1946)
09/05/69 1:00 AM *The Beast of Hollow Mountain* (1956)
09/12/69 1:00 AM *Curse of the Faceless Man* (1958)
09/19/69 1:00 AM *U.F.O.* (1956)
09/26/69 1:00 AM *Destination Moon* (1950)
10/03/69 1:00 AM *The Flame Barrier* (1958)
10/10/69 1:00 AM *The Four Skulls of Jonathan Drake* (1959)
10/12/69 8:00 AM *Abbott and Costello Meet the Invisible Man* (1951)
10/17/69 1:00 AM *Macumba Love* (1960)
10/24/69 1:00 AM *The Gamma People* (1956)
10/31/69 1:00 AM *The Thing from Another World* (1951)
11/07/69 1:00 AM *Kronos* (1957)
11/14/69 1:00 AM *The Unknown Terror* (1957)
11/21/69 1:00 AM *Battle of the Worlds* (1961)
11/28/69 1:00 AM *Mighty Joe Young* (1949)
12/12/69 1:00 AM *Five* (1951)
12/26/69 1:00 AM *Creature with the Atom Brain* (1955)
12/27/69 1:45 AM *U.F.O.* (1956)
01/04/70 8:00 AM *Abbott and Costello Meet the Mummy* (1955)
01/23/70 1:00 AM *Creature from the Black Lagoon* (1954)
01/30/70 1:00 AM *Godzilla: King of the Monsters* (1956)
02/06/70 1:00 AM *The Curse of the Cat People* (1944)
02/13/70 1:00 AM *It Came from Outer Space* (1953)
02/20/70 10:00 AM *Most Dangerous Man Alive* (1961)
02/20/70 1:00 AM *Revenge of the Creature* (1955)
02/21/70 11:30 PM *Games* (1967)
02/27/70 1:00 AM *Back from the Dead* (1957)
03/20/70 1:00 AM *Scream of Fear* (1961)
03/27/70 1:00 AM *The Creature Walks Among Us* (1956)
04/19/70 12:15 AM *The Hunchback of Notre Dame* (1939)
05/08/70 10:00 AM *She Devil* (1957)
05/09/70 1:45 AM *The Black Castle* (1952)
06/02/70 10:00 AM *The Invisible Boy* (1957)
06/20/70 11:30 PM *King Kong* (1933)

07/08/70 10:00 AM *Cult of the Cobra* (1955)
07/17/70 1:05 AM *Hangover Square* (1945)
07/18/70 7:00 PM *Battle of the Worlds* (1961)
08/14/70 8:00 PM *Mysterious Island* (1961)
08/28/70 1:05 AM *Cat People* (1942)
09/05/70 1:45 AM *Homicidal* (1961)
09/06/70 5:00 PM *The Old Dark House* (1963)
10/11/70 8:00 AM *Abbott and Costello Meet the Invisible Man* (1951)
10/29/70 11:30 PM *Scream of Fear* (1961)
12/01/70 10:15 AM *Hangover Square* (1945)
12/06/70 5:00 PM *The Whip Hand* (1951)
12/17/70 11:30 PM *Back from the Dead* (1957)
12/19/70 1:45 AM *Gorgo* (1961)
12/31/70 11:30 PM *Battle of the Worlds* (1961)
01/02/71 1:45 AM *The Body Snatcher* (1945)
01/05/71 11:30 PM *Godzilla: King of the Monsters* (1956)
01/07/71 11:30 PM *I Saw What You Did* (1965)
01/26/71 11:30 PM *Homicidal* (1961)
01/27/71 9:00 PM *Mysterious Island* (1961)
02/09/71 11:30 PM *Strait-Jacket* (1964)
02/22/71 11:30 PM *The Beast from 20,000 Fathoms* (1953)
03/04/71 11:30 PM *Them!* (1954)
03/06/71 11:30 PM *Fahrenheit 451* (1966)
03/12/71 10:15 AM *Battle of the Worlds* (1961)
03/15/71 10:15 AM *Godzilla: King of the Monsters* (1956)
04/03/71 2:15 AM *Genius at Work* (1946)
04/17/71 1:45 AM *Bedlam* (1946)
05/21/71 10:15 AM *The Strange Door* (1951)
05/22/71 11:30 PM *The Evil of Frankenstein* (1964)
05/24/71 11:30 PM *The Thing from Another World* (1951)
05/25/71 10:15 AM *The Seventh Victim* (1943)
05/25/71 11:30 PM *The Curse of the Werewolf* (1961)
05/26/71 11:30 PM *Strait-Jacket* (1964)
05/27/71 11:30 PM *The Black Castle* (1952)
05/28/71 12:00 AM *King Kong* (1933)
06/10/71 11:30 PM *Kronos* (1957)
07/14/71 10:15 AM *Hangover Square* (1945)
07/23/71 10:15 AM *The Old Dark House* (1963)
07/29/71 10:15 AM *Most Dangerous Man Alive* (1961)
08/14/71 2:00 AM *The Unknown Terror* (1957)
08/17/71 11:30 PM *Mighty Joe Young* (1949)
08/21/71 1:30 AM *Revenge of the Creature* (1955)
08/27/71 11:30 PM *Circus of Fear* (1966)
09/04/71 11:30 PM *She Devil* (1957)
09/10/71 11:30 PM *The Terror of the Tongs* (1961)
09/14/71 11:30 PM *The Night Walker* (1964)
09/19/71 8:00 AM *Abbott and Costello Meet the Mummy* (1955)
09/23/71 11:30 PM *The Whip Hand* (1951)
09/24/71 11:30 PM *Back from the Dead* (1957)
10/01/71 11:30 PM *Paranoiac* (1963)
10/07/71 11:30 PM *Phantom of the Rue Morgue* (1954)
10/16/71 11:30 PM *Kiss of the Vampire* (1963)
10/23/71 1:15 AM *Creature from the Black Lagoon* (1954)
10/30/71 1:45 AM *Blood of the Vampire* (1958)
10/31/71 8:30 AM *Abbott and Costello Meet the Invisible Man* (1951)
11/13/71 1:30 AM *Dark Intruder* (1965)

11/20/71 11:30 PM *The Phantom of the Opera* (1962)
11/20/71 1:30 AM *The Shadow of the Cat* (1961)
11/27/71 1:15 AM *The Creature Walks Among Us* (1956)
11/28/71 3:00 PM *Mysterious Island* (1961)
12/01/71 9:30 PM *Games* (1967)
12/05/71 8:30 AM *Abbott and Costello Meet Dr. Jekyll and Mr. Hyde* (1953)
12/27/71 12:15 AM *The Lodger* (1944)
12/29/71 11:30 PM *The Evil of Frankenstein* (1964)
01/05/74 11:30 PM *Bedlam* (1946)
12/31/71 11:30 PM *The Hunchback of Notre Dame* (1939)
01/01/72 1:45 AM *It Came from Outer Space* (1953)
01/08/72 11:30 PM *Island of Terror* (1966)
01/08/72 1:30 AM *Cult of the Cobra* (1955)
01/15/72 1:45 AM *Mr. Sardonicus* (1961)
01/18/72 12:30 AM *Night Creatures* (1962)
01/22/72 1:45 AM *Maniac* (1963)
02/05/72 1:45 AM *Them!* (1954)
02/09/72 11:30 PM *Diary of a Madman* (1963)
02/12/72 2:00 AM *The Curse of the Werewolf* (1961)
02/14/72 11:30 PM *Monster Zero* (1965)
02/15/72 11:30 PM *The Beast from 20,000 Fathoms* (1953)
02/16/72 11:30 PM *Rodan* (1957)
02/17/72 11:30 PM *Return of the Fly* (1959)
02/18/72 11:30 PM *The War of the Gargantuas* (1966)
02/19/72 2:00 AM *The Brides of Dracula* (1960)
02/20/72 8:30 AM *Munster, Go Home!* (1966)
02/23/72 8:30 PM *The Birds* (1963)
02/26/72 1:45 AM *The Brides of Dracula* (1960)
03/04/72 2:15 AM *Isle of the Dead* (1945)
03/07/72 11:30 PM *Theatre of Death* (1967)
03/09/72 11:30 PM *Homicidal* (1961)
03/11/72 1:30 AM *The Body Snatcher* (1945)
03/15/72 10:00 AM *Cat People* (1942)
03/30/72 11:30 PM *Fahrenheit 451* (1966)
04/05/72 11:30 PM *Nightmare* (1964)
04/08/72 2:00 AM *The Body Snatcher* (1945)
05/03/72 9:55 AM *She Devil* (1957)
05/05/72 11:30 PM *Circus of Fear* (1966)
05/06/72 1:45 AM *The Leopard Man* (1943)
05/08/72 11:30 PM *The Curse of the Werewolf* (1961)
05/09/72 11:30 PM *Strait-Jacket* (1964)
05/10/72 11:30 PM *The Projected Man* (1966)
05/11/72 11:30 PM *The Evil of Frankenstein* (1964)
05/12/72 12:00 AM *The Brides of Dracula* (1960)
05/13/72 2:30 AM *The Curse of the Cat People* (1944)
05/15/72 11:30 PM *King Kong* (1933)
05/16/72 11:45 PM *Son of Kong* (1933)
05/17/72 12:00 AM *The Creature Walks Among Us* (1956)
05/18/72 11:30 PM *Kronos* (1957)
05/19/72 11:30 PM *Godzilla's Revenge* (1971)
05/20/72 11:30 PM *Blood of the Vampire* (1958)
05/20/72 1:30 AM *Doctor Blood's Coffin* (1961)
05/25/72 11:30 PM *Island of the Burning Doomed* (1967)
06/05/72 11:30 PM *It Came from Outer Space* (1953)
06/07/72 11:30 PM *The Black Castle* (1952)
06/16/72 11:30 PM *The Thing from Another World* (1951)
06/27/72 11:30 PM *Revenge of the Creature* (1955)

07/01/72 1:45 AM *Bedlam* (1946)
07/05/72 11:30 PM *I Saw What You Did* (1965)
07/22/72 1:30 AM *The Seventh Victim* (1943)
07/27/72 4:00 PM *Warning from Space* (1956)
07/27/72 11:30 PM *The Shadow of the Cat* (1961)
07/31/72 11:30 PM *Most Dangerous Man Alive* (1961)
08/01/72 4:00 PM *The Old Dark House* (1963)
08/04/72 11:30 PM *The Night Walker* (1964)
08/11/72 11:30 PM *Back from the Dead* (1957)
08/13/72 8:30 AM *Abbott and Costello Meet the Invisible Man* (1951)
08/18/72 4:00 PM *Mighty Joe Young* (1949)
08/22/72 9:55 AM *The Whip Hand* (1951)
08/23/72 4:00 PM *Mysterious Island* (1961)
08/23/72 11:30 PM *The Strange Door* (1951)
09/01/72 4:00 PM *Attack of the Monsters* (1969)
09/05/72 11:30 PM *Scream of Fear* (1961)
09/12/72 4:00 PM *Destroy All Planets* (1968)
09/12/72 11:30 PM *Nightmare* (1964)
09/16/72 9:00 PM *Phantom of the Rue Morgue* (1954)
09/16/72 11:30 PM *The Terror of the Tongs* (1961)
09/19/72 11:30 PM *The Phantom of the Opera* (1962)
09/23/72 9:00 PM *Diary of a Madman* (1963)
09/27/72 4:00 PM *Munster, Go Home!* (1966)
10/07/72 9:00 PM *The Masque of the Red Death* (1964)
10/12/72 11:30 PM *Paranoiac* (1963)
10/14/72 9:00 PM *War Gods of the Deep* (1965)
10/21/72 9:00 PM *Kiss of the Vampire* (1963)
10/28/71 9:00 PM *Tomb of Ligeia* (1965)
10/30/72 4:00 PM *Magic Serpent* (1966)
10/30/72 12:15 AM *Gamera vs. Monster X* (1970)
10/31/72 11:30 PM *Frankenstein Conquers the World* (1965)
11/01/72 11:30 PM *Dinosaurus!* (1960)
11/02/72 11:30 PM *The Gorgon* (1964)
11/03/72 11:30 PM *Destroy All Monsters* (1968)
11/04/72 9:00 PM *The Conqueror Worm* (1968)
11/09/72 11:30 PM *Corruption* (1968)
11/11/72 9:00 PM *The Oblong Box* (1969)
11/18/72 9:00 PM *Pit and the Pendulum* (1961)
11/22/72 4:00 PM *Godzilla's Revenge* (1971)
11/25/72 9:00 PM *Games* (1967)
12/04/72 12:15 AM *Night of the Witches* (1970)
12/09/72 9:00 PM *The Evil of Frankenstein* (1964)
12/15/72 4:00 PM *Voyage into Space* (1970)
12/15/72 11:30 PM *Creature from the Black Lagoon* (1954)
12/16/72 9:00 PM *Kiss of the Vampire* (1963)
12/19/72 11:30 PM *The Unknown Terror* (1957)
12/29/72 9:55 AM *Abbott and Costello Meet Dr. Jekyll and Mr. Hyde* (1953)
12/29/72 4:00 PM *The Return of Giant Majin* (1966)
12/30/72 9:00 PM *Blood of the Vampire* (1958)
01/02/73 9:55 AM *I Saw What You Did* (1965)
01/02/73 4:00 PM *The Night Walker* (1964)
01/12/73 4:00 PM *The War of the Gargantuas* (1966)
01/20/73 11:30 PM *The Birds* (1963)
01/22/73 4:00 PM *Monster Zero* (1965)
01/23/73 4:00 PM *The Beast from 20,000 Fathoms* (1953)
01/23/73 11:30 PM *Curse of the Voodoo* (1965)
01/24/73 4:00 PM *Return of the Fly* (1959)

01/25/73 4:00 PM *The Curse of the Mummy's Tomb* (1964)
01/25/73 11:30 PM *Godzilla: King of the Monsters* (1956)
01/26/73 4:00 PM *Frankenstein Meets the Spacemonster* (1965)
01/27/73 11:30 PM *Homicidal* (1961)
02/01/73 11:30 PM *The Phantom of Soho* (1964)
02/03/73 11:30 PM *Island of Terror* (1966)
02/11/73 5:00 PM *Fantastic Voyage* (1966)
02/16/73 4:00 PM *Pit and the Pendulum* (1961)
02/19/73 4:00 PM *The Curse of the Mummy's Tomb* (1964)
02/27/73 4:00 PM *Mutiny in Outer Space* (1965)
02/28/73 11:30 PM *Berserk* (1967)
03/01/73 11:30 PM *Snake People* (1971)
03/08/73 11:30 PM *Maniac* (1963)
03/12/73 11:30 PM *Mr. Sardonicus* (1961)
03/13/73 4:00 PM *The Creature Walks Among Us* (1956)
03/16/73 4:00 PM *Island of the Burning Doomed* (1967)
03/16/73 11:30 PM *The Brides of Dracula* (1960)
03/21/73 4:00 PM *Cult of the Cobra* (1955)
03/29/73 11:30 PM *Fahrenheit 451* (1966)
03/30/73 11:30 PM *Theatre of Death* (1967)
04/13/73 9:55 AM *Nightmare* (1964)
04/16/73 11:30 PM *The Old Dark House* (1963)
04/26/73 4:00 PM *The Curse of the Werewolf* (1961)
05/14/73 10:00 PM *Dark Intruder* (1965)
05/15/73 11:30 PM *Scream of Fear* (1961)
05/23/73 8:30 PM *The Spiral Staircase* (1946)
05/23/73 11:30 PM *Strait-Jacket* (1964)
05/24/73 1:00 AM *A Study in Terror* (1965)
06/08/73 11:30 PM *It Came from Outer Space* (1953)
06/09/73 11:30 PM *The Crawling Eye* (1958)
06/16/73 11:30 PM *Doctor Blood's Coffin* (1961)
06/18/73 4:00 PM *Kronos* (1957)
06/27/73 9:55 AM *She Devil* (1957)
06/30/73 11:30 PM *Circus of Fear* (1966)
07/09/73 4:00 PM *Back from the Dead* (1957)
07/16/73 4:00 PM *Night Creatures* (1962)
07/18/73 11:30 PM *Cat People* (1942)
07/20/73 4:00 PM *The Whip Hand* (1951)
07/22/73 2:00 PM *Mighty Joe Young* (1949)
07/27/73 4:00 PM *The Phantom of the Opera* (1962)
07/27/73 11:40 PM *The Terror of the Tongs* (1961)
08/10/73 4:00 PM *Hangover Square* (1945)
08/13/73 11:30 PM *Diary of a Madman* (1963)
08/17/73 4:00 PM *Kiss of the Vampire* (1963)
08/20/73 4:00 PM *She Devil* (1957)
08/21/73 4:00 PM *The Lodger* (1944)
08/22/73 4:00 PM *Corruption* (1968)
08/24/73 11:30 PM *The Unknown Terror* (1957)
08/25/73 11:30 PM *The Hunchback of Notre Dame* (1939)
08/29/73 4:00 PM *I Saw What You Did* (1965)
09/21/73 11:30 PM *The Curse of the Mummy's Tomb* (1964)
09/24/73 4:00 PM *Godzilla: King of the Monsters* (1956)
09/25/73 4:00 PM *Magic Serpent* (1966)
09/26/73 4:00 PM *Frankenstein Meets the Spacemonster* (1965)
09/27/63 4:00 PM *Attack of the Monsters* (1969)
09/28/73 4:00 PM *King Kong* (1933)
10/05/73 4:00 PM *Curse of the Fly* (1965)
10/19/73 11:30 PM *The Thing from Another World* (1951)
10/20/73 11:30 PM *Mr. Sardonicus* (1961)

10/26/73 11:30 PM *The Thing from Another World* (1951)
10/30/73 4:00 PM *Godzilla: King of the Monsters* (1956)
11/12/73 12:30 AM *The Raven* (1963)
11/13/73 11:30 PM *Tomb of Ligeia* (1965)
11/14/73 11:30 PM *War Gods of the Deep* (1965)
11/15/73 11:30 PM *The Masque of the Red Death* (1964)
11/16/73 11:30 PM *Pit and the Pendulum* (1961)
11/20/73 11:30 PM *The Night Walker* (1964)
11/26/73 12:30 AM *The Seventh Victim* (1943)
12/26/73 4:00 PM *Munster, Go Home!* (1966)
01/12/74 11:30 PM *The Beast from 20,000 Fathoms* (1953)
01/13/74 3:30 PM *Voyage into Space* (1970)
01/26/74 11:30 PM *Night of the Witches* (1970)
02/09/74 11:30 PM *Curse of the Fly* (1965)
02/23/74 11:30 PM *Blood of the Vampire* (1958)
03/02/74 11:30 PM *Circus of Fear* (1966)
03/09/74 11:30 PM *The Crawling Eye* (1958)
03/19/74 11:30 PM *Fahrenheit 451* (1966)
03/23/74 11:30 PM *Kiss of the Vampire* (1963)
04/13/74 11:30 PM *Homicidal* (1961)
04/18/74 11:30 PM *Games* (1967)
04/20/74 11:30 PM *Berserk* (1967)
04/27/74 11:30 PM *The Mad Room* (1969)
05/04/74 11:30 PM *Frankenstein Conquers the World* (1965)
05/07/74 11:30 PM *Phantom of the Rue Morgue* (1954)
05/11/74 11:30 PM *Spirits of the Dead* (1968)
05/18/74 11:30 PM *A Study in Terror* (1965)
05/25/74 11:30 PM *Curse of the Voodoo* (1965)
06/01/74 12:00 AM *Destroy All Monsters* (1968)
06/05/74 1:05 AM *I Saw What You Did* (1965)
06/08/74 11:30 PM *Gamera vs. Monster X* (1970)
06/12/74 1:05 AM *The Projected Man* (1966)
06/15/74 12:30 AM *Warning from Space* (1956)
06/22/74 12:00 AM *Destroy All Planets* (1968)
06/29/74 11:30 PM *Mission Stardust* (1967)
06/30/74 12:00 PM *Genius at Work* (1946)
07/06/74 11:30 PM *Night of the Witches* (1970)
07/13/74 12:00 AM *The War of the Gargantuas* (1966)
07/20/74 11:30 PM *Rodan* (1957)
07/27/74 11:30 PM *Theatre of Death* (1967)
08/03/74 11:30 PM *Magic Serpent* (1966)
08/10/74 11:30 PM *Attack of the Monsters* (1969)
08/11/74 12:00 PM *Son of Kong* (1933)
08/24/74 11:30 PM *The Return of Giant Majin* (1966)
08/31/74 11:30 PM *Voyage into Space* (1970)
09/28/74 11:30 PM *The Birds* (1963)
10/17/74 1:05 AM *The Curse of the Mummy's Tomb* (1964)
10/26/74 11:30 PM *I. Monster* (1972)
10/28/74 12:30 AM *Diary of a Madman* (1963)
10/31/74 1:05 AM *Pit and the Pendulum* (1961)
11/03/74 2:30 PM *Dark Intruder* (1965)
11/10/74 2:00 PM *Dinosaurus!* (1960)
11/23/74 11:30 PM *Mr. Sardonicus* (1961)
11/30/74 12:00 AM *The Evil of Frankenstein* (1964)
12/07/74 11:30 PM *The Raven* (1963)
12/14/74 12:15 AM *War Gods of the Deep* (1965)
12/21/74 11:30 PM *The Brides of Dracula* (1960)
12/28/74 11:30 PM *The Curse of the Werewolf* (1961)
01/02/75 1:05 AM *Them!* (1954)

01/04/75 11:30 PM *The Body Snatcher* (1945)
01/11/75 11:30 PM *King Kong* (1933)
01/15/75 1:10 AM *Phantom of the Rue Morgue* (1954)
01/18/75 11:45 PM *Mighty Joe Young* (1949)
02/01/75 11:45 PM *The Oblong Box* (1969)
02/06/75 1:10 AM *Circus of Fear* (1966)
02/08/75 1:15 AM *Tales of Terror* (1962)
03/01/75 11:45 PM *The Masque of the Red Death* (1964)
03/05/75 1:10 AM *Fahrenheit 451* (1966)
04/05/75 11:30 PM *The Gorgon* (1964)
04/12/75 11:45 PM *The Human Duplicators* (1965)
04/19/75 11:30 PM *Frankenstein Meets the Spacemonster* (1965)
05/13/75 1:10 AM *Games* (1967)
05/20/75 12:00 AM *The Mad Room* (1969)
05/22/75 1:10 AM *Berserk* (1967)
05/31/75 11:30 PM *Theatre of Death* (1967)
06/07/75 12:00 AM *The Birds* (1963)
06/21/75 12:30 AM *Snake People* (1971)
10/29/75 1:10 AM *Kiss of the Vampire* (1963)
11/19/75 1:40 AM *Phantom of the Rue Morgue* (1954)
12/18/75 1:40 AM *I Saw What You Did* (1965)
12/25/75 1:00 PM *Munster, Go Home!* (1966)
12/31/75 4:30 AM *Blood of the Vampire* (1958)
01/03/76 11:30 PM *The Phantom of the Opera* (1962)
02/04/76 1:20 AM *Fahrenheit 451* (1966)
02/26/76 1:55 AM *Doctor Faustus* (1967)
04/18/76 12:55 AM *Fantastic Voyage* (1966)
05/02/76 12:55 AM *Berserk* (1967)
05/06/76 1:55 AM *The Curse of the Werewolf* (1961)
05/10/76 1:10 AM *Curse of the Fly* (1965)
05/13/76 1:55 AM *Island of Terror* (1966)
05/16/76 12:30 AM *The Mad Room* (1969)
05/20/76 1:55 AM *Night Creatures* (1962)
05/27/76 1:55 AM *The Night Walker* (1964)
06/04/76 1:00 AM *Kiss of the Vampire* (1963)
06/11/76 12:45 AM *I Saw What You Did* (1965)
06/30/76 1:20 AM *Tower of London* (1962)
08/08/76 12:30 PM *I, Monster* (1971)
08/08/76 1:45 AM *Corruption* (1968)
09/12/76 12:55 AM *Diary of a Madman* (1963)
09/30/76 1:45 AM *Fantastic Voyage* (1966)
10/18/76 12:30 AM *Nightmare* (1964)
10/29/76 12:40 AM *Paranoiac* (1963)
11/21/76 2:00 PM *The Nutty Professor* (1963)
12/10/76 12:45 AM *Son of Kong* (1933)
12/10/76 3:45 AM *Mighty Joe Young* (1949)
12/12/76 4:30 PM *King Kong* (1933)
12/26/76 2:00 PM *The Hunchback of Notre Dame* (1939)
01/17/77 12:15 AM *Tomb of Ligeia* (1965)
01/18/77 1:10 AM *The Masque of the Red Death* (1964)
01/19/77 1:10 AM *The Raven* (1963)
01/20/77 1:10 AM *The Oblong Box* (1969)
01/21/77 12:45 AM *Pit and the Pendulum* (1961)
01/21/77 3:45 AM *Spirits of the Dead* (1968)
01/24/77 1:10 AM *Bedlam* (1946)
03/11/77 3:45 AM *Theatre of Death* (1967)
03/19/77 3:00 AM *The Body Snatcher* (1945)
04/02/77 3:50 AM *The Curse of the Mummy's Tomb* (1964)
04/09/77 2:30 AM *The Beast from 20,000 Fathoms* (1953)

04/16/77 2:30 AM *Frankenstein Conquers the World* (1965)
04/23/77 3:15 AM *Destroy All Monsters* (1968)
04/30/77 1:45 AM *Attack of the Monsters* (1969)
05/07/77 3:20 AM *Gamera vs. Monster X* (1970)
05/14/77 2:15 AM *The Gorgon* (1964)
05/21/77 2:30 AM *Curse of the Fly* (1965)
05/27/77 12:30 AM *Berserk* (1967)
06/04/77 1:50 AM *Dinosaurus!* (1960)
06/11/77 1:55 AM *The Human Duplicators* (1965)
06/18/77 1:45 AM *Phantom of the Rue Morgue* (1954)
07/17/77 12:30 PM *Fantastic Voyage* (1966)
07/29/77 3:40 AM *Them!* (1954)
08/26/77 4:55 AM *The Beast from 20,000 Fathoms* (1953)
08/29/77 1:55 AM *Snake People* (1971)
09/02/77 12:45 AM *The Mad Room* (1969)
09/03/77 3:05 AM *The Beast from 20,000 Fathoms* (1953)
09/09/77 4:15 AM *Back from the Dead* (1957)
11/05/77 3:10 AM *Kronos* (1957)
11/25/77 1:30 AM *Mighty Joe Young* (1949)
11/25/77 3:20 AM *Son of Kong* (1933)
11/26/77 2:50 AM *She Devil* (1957)
11/27/77 2:00 PM *King Kong* (1933)
12/31/77 3:40 AM *The Hunchback of Notre Dame* (1939)
01/20/78 9:00 AM *Berserk* (1967)
01/20/78 3:00 AM *Cat People* (1942)
01/24/78 1:15 AM *Berserk* (1967)
01/30/78 12:45 AM *The Mad Room* (1969)
02/03/78 12:45 AM *You'll Find Out* (1940)
02/09/78 9:00 AM *The Two Faces of Dr. Jekyll* (1960)
02/25/78 3:20 AM *The Curse of the Cat People* (1944)
03/14/78 1:25 AM *The Leopard Man* (1943)
03/18/78 11:30 PM *Fantastic Voyage* (1966)
04/14/78 12:45 AM *The Thing from Another World* (1951)
05/05/78 2:40 AM *Genius at Work* (1946)
06/09/78 2:25 AM *The Seventh Victim* (1943)
07/18/78 11:30 PM *The Giant Spider Invasion* (1975)
08/17/78 2:00 AM *The Whip Hand* (1951)
11/18/78 2:15 AM *The Body Snatcher* (1945)
11/24/78 1:25 AM *Mighty Joe Young* (1949)
11/24/78 3:15 AM *Son of Kong* (1933)
11/26/78 2:00 PM *King Kong* (1933)
12/11/78 12:50 AM *Curse of the Fly* (1965)
12/17/78 2:00 PM *Fantastic Voyage* (1966)
12/31/78 4:30 AM *I, Monster* (1971)
02/05/79 12:50 AM *Homicidal* (1961)
03/02/79 9:00 PM *The Little Girl Who Lives Down the Lane* (1976)
03/02/79 4:10 AM *The Creeping Flesh* (1973)
03/31/79 2:20 AM *A Reflection of Fear* (1972)
04/27/79 4:10 AM *Scream of Fear* (1961)
05/04/79 3:10 AM *Mysterious Island* (1961)
05/12/79 4:55 AM *Homicidal* (1961)
05/19/79 1:40 AM *The Thing from Another World* (1951)
05/26/79 2:00 PM *The Nutty Professor* (1963)
06/22/79 3:50 AM *Tower of London* (1962)
07/04/79 1:55 AM *Doctor Faustus* (1967)
07/06/79 1:40 AM *I, Monster* (1971)
07/23/79 1:48 AM *Sasquatch: The Legend of Bigfoot* (1976)

07/26/79 1:55 AM *The Curse of the Cat People* (1944)
08/13/79 1:48 AM *Thirteen Women* (1932)
10/05/79 3:00 AM *The Two Faces of Dr. Jekyll* (1960)
10/22/79 1:00 AM *The Terror of the Tongs* (1961)
11/02/79 12:37 AM *Mighty Joe Young* (1949)
11/20/79 2:13 AM *Bedlam* (1946)
01/09/80 2:10 AM *Mr. Sardonicus* (1961)
01/31/80 2:14 AM *Corruption* (1968)
02/29/80 4:25 AM *You'll Find Out* (1940)
03/07/80 12:55 AM *Lisa and the Devil* (1973)
03/17/80 2:35 AM *The Whip Hand* (1951)
04/03/80 2:14 AM *A Reflection of Fear* (1972)
04/14/80 2:05 AM *Isle of the Dead* (1945)
04/19/80 1:30 PM *The Hunchback of Notre Dame* (1939)
04/19/80 3:55 AM *The Leopard Man* (1943)
04/27/80 11:30 PM *The Old Dark House* (1963)
05/07/80 2:19 AM *The Creeping Flesh* (1973)
05/08/80 2:19 AM *Homicidal* (1961)
05/10/80 3:00 PM *Mysterious Island* (1961)
05/17/80 1:30 AM *Isle of the Dead* (1945)
06/01/80 12:00 AM *A Study in Terror* (1965)
07/18/80 1:11 AM *Tower of London* (1962)
07/26/80 1:50 AM *The Body Snatcher* (1945)
08/01/80 1:11 AM *The Two Faces of Dr. Jekyll* (1960)
08/08/80 4:35 AM *Doctor Faustus* (1967)
10/10/80 1:10 AM *Scream of Fear* (1961)
10/31/80 1:11 AM *Strait-Jacket* (1964)
11/09/80 2:00 PM *The Nutty Professor* (1963)
11/14/80 1:10 AM *The Terror of the Tongs* (1961)
01/31/81 2:40 AM *Corruption* (1968)
03/07/81 2:35 AM *Lisa and the Devil* (1973)
04/04/81 12:30 PM *The Old Dark House* (1963)
05/15/81 2:00 AM *The Creeping Flesh* (1973)
05/30/81 12:30 AM *A Study in Terror* (1965)
07/10/81 1:40 AM *Homicidal* (1961)
07/11/81 1:00 PM *Mysterious Island* (1961)
07/12/81 9:00 AM *Abbott and Costello Meet Frankenstein* (1948)
09/25/81 2:00 AM *Scream of Fear* (1961)
10/04/81 9:00 AM *Abbott and Costello Meet the Invisible Man* (1951)
10/23/81 2:15 AM *Bedlam* (1946)
10/30/81 2:00 AM *Strait-Jacket* (1964)
11/08/81 9:00 AM *Abbott and Costello Meet Dr. Jekyll and Mr. Hyde* (1953)
11/20/81 2:00 AM *The Terror of the Tongs* (1961)
11/22/81 9:00 AM *The Incredible Shrinking Man* (1957)
11/26/81 8:00 PM *King Kong* (1933)
02/12/82 3:30 AM *The Leopard Man* (1943)
03/13/82 4:30 AM *Cat People* (1942)
03/19/82 4:35 AM *The Ghost Ship* (1943)
04/03/82 2:45 AM *Mr. Sardonicus* (1961)
04/20/82 2:10 AM *Corruption* (1968)
04/20/82 3:55 AM *The Hunchback of Notre Dame* (1939)
05/02/82 9:00 AM *Mighty Joe Young* (1949)
05/12/82 2:10 AM *The Creeping Flesh* (1973)
05/14/82 1:30 AM *A Study in Terror* (1965)
05/16/82 9:00 AM *Son of Kong* (1933)
05/28/82 1:30 AM *The Seventh Victim* (1943)

06/03/82 3:55 AM *Genius at Work* (1946)
07/03/82 4:25 AM *The Whip Hand* (1951)
07/09/82 1:30 AM *Homicidal* (1961)
07/18/82 9:00 AM *Mysterious Island* (1961)
07/25/82 9:00 AM *Abbott and Costello Meet the Mummy* (1955)
07/28/82 2:10 AM *You'll Find Out* (1940)
07/30/82 1:30 AM *The Old Dark House* (1963)
08/01/82 9:00 AM *The Thing from Another World* (1951)
08/06/82 12:30 AM *The Curse of the Cat People* (1944)
08/27/82 12:30 AM *Isle of the Dead* (1945)
09/25/82 12:30 AM *Shadow of the Hawk* (1976)
10/01/82 3:20 AM *The Terror of the Tongs* (1961)
10/03/82 3:05 AM *Bedlam* (1946)
10/16/82 3:30 PM *Strait-Jacket* (1964)
10/19/82 2:00 AM *The Body Snatcher* (1945)
10/23/82 2:55 AM *Ghosts That Still Walk* (1977)
11/07/82 9:00 AM *Abbott and Costello Meet Frankenstein* (1948)
11/21/82 9:00 AM *The Incredible Shrinking Man* (1957)
12/28/82 2:00 AM *Mummy's Boys* (1936)
01/26/83 2:00 AM *Zombies on Broadway* (1945)
02/06/83 8:30 AM *King Kong* (1933)
02/10/83 2:00 AM *The Leopard Man* (1943)
02/13/83 9:00 AM *Abbott and Costello Meet Dr. Jekyll and Mr. Hyde* (1953)
03/04/83 2:00 AM *Mr. Sardonicus* (1961)
03/08/83 2:00 AM *Corruption* (1968)
03/19/83 4:15 AM *Cat People* (1942)
03/24/83 2:55 AM *Thirteen Women* (1932)
03/30/83 12:00 AM *Dr. Jekyll and Mr. Hyde* (1941)
04/28/83 1:30 AM *The Hunchback of Notre Dame* (1939)
05/01/83 9:00 AM *Son of Kong* (1933)
05/03/83 2:00 AM *The Hunchback of Notre Dame* (1939)
05/04/83 2:00 AM *A Study in Terror* (1965)
05/14/83 4:20 AM *The Whip Hand* (1951)
05/27/83 1:30 AM *The Creeping Flesh* (1973)
05/29/83 4:10 AM *Sasquatch: The Legend of Bigfoot* (1976)
06/10/83 1:30 AM *The Old Dark House* (1963)
07/01/83 3:30 AM *Isle of the Dead* (1945)
07/24/83 2:00 PM *Mysterious Island* (1961)
07/28/83 3:05 AM *Genius at Work* (1946)
08/11/83 1:30 AM *Scream of Fear* (1961)
08/18/83 1:30 AM *Shadow of the Hawk* (1976)
09/03/83 3:15 AM *The Terror of the Tongs* (1961)
09/13/83 1:30 AM *Mr. Sardonicus* (1961)
09/30/83 2:10 AM *Strait-Jacket* (1964)
10/01/83 11:30 PM *The Day the Earth Stood Still* (1951)
10/02/83 9:00 AM *Abbott and Costello Meet the Mummy* (1955)
10/09/83 9:00 AM *Mighty Joe Young* (1949)
10/15/83 11:30 PM *Eyes of Laura Mars* (1978)
10/16/83 4:15 AM *Mummy's Boys* (1936)
10/25/83 3:50 AM *Ghosts That Still Walk* (1977)
10/29/83 1:55 AM *Bedlam* (1946)
10/30/83 3:15 AM *The Body Snatcher* (1945)
11/13/83 9:00 AM *The Incredible Shrinking Man* (1957)
11/23/83 1:00 AM *The Curse of the Cat People* (1944)
11/27/83 9:00 AM *Abbott and Costello Meet the Invisible Man* (1951)
01/07/84 3:25 AM *The Leopard Man* (1943)
01/08/84 9:00 AM *Abbott and Costello Meet Frankenstein* (1948)
01/28/84 11:30 PM *Time After Time* (1979)
02/18/84 4:00 AM *Zombies on Broadway* (1945)
02/25/84 11:30 PM *The Howling* (1981)
02/26/84 9:00 AM *Abbott and Costello Meet Dr. Jekyll and Mr. Hyde* (1953)
03/02/84 12:30 AM *The Howling* (1981)
03/28/84 12:30 AM *Corruption* (1968)
04/23/84 12:30 AM *Cat People* (1942)
05/04/84 4:10 AM *The Whip Hand* (1951)
05/10/84 3:05 AM *Ghosts That Still Walk* (1977)
05/22/84 2:30 AM *The Hunchback of Notre Dame* (1939)
05/29/84 12:30 AM *A Study in Terror* (1965)
06/10/84 3:15 AM *Thirteen Women* (1932)
07/06/84 4:25 AM *Genius at Work* (1946)
07/13/84 1:00 AM *One Million Years, B.C.* (1967)
07/15/84 1:30 AM *The Nanny* (1965)
07/21/84 1:35 AM *King Kong* (1933)
08/17/84 1:30 AM *Quatermass and the Pit* (1967)
08/18/84 2:30 AM *The Shuttered Room* (1967)
08/24/84 2:55 AM *Isle of the Dead* (1945)
09/02/84 8:00 AM *Son of Kong* (1933)
10/03/84 1:00 AM *One Million Years B.C.* (1966)
10/06/84 2:10 AM *The Swarm* (1978)
10/13/84 1:30 PM *The Lost World* (1960)
10/13/84 11:30 PM *Eyes of Laura Mars* (1978)
10/20/84 11:30 PM *The Exorcist* (1973)
10/20/84 1:55 AM *The Body Snatcher* (1945)
10/24/84 12:30 AM *Two on a Guillotine* (1965)
10/26/84 2:30 AM *I Walked with A Zombie* (1943)
10/27/84 11:30 PM *Exorcist II: The Heretic* (1977)
10/27/84 1:35 AM *House of Wax* (1953)
10/27/84 2:30 AM *Mummy's Boys* (1936)
10/30/84 12:30 AM *The Old Dark House* (1963)
10/31/84 12:30 AM *The Curse of the Cat People* (1944)
11/04/84 9:00 AM *Abbott and Costello Meet the Invisible Man* (1951)
11/08/84 3:00 AM *Ghosts That Still Walk* (1977)
11/11/84 9:00 AM *The Incredible Shrinking Man* (1957)
11/30/84 2:35 AM *Shadow of the Hawk* (1976)
12/31/84 3:00 AM *King Kong* (1933)
12/31/84 4:45 AM *Son of Kong* (1933)
02/10/85 9:00 AM *Mighty Joe Young* (1949)
02/13/85 12:30 AM *The Legacy* (1978)
02/24/85 9:00 AM *Abbott and Costello Meet the Mummy* (1955)
04/06/85 3:30 AM *Zombies on Broadway* (1945)
04/13/85 3:35 AM *The Leopard Man* (1943)
04/14/85 9:00 AM *Abbott and Costello Meet Frankenstein* (1948)
04/27/85 3:10 AM *Bedlam* (1946)
05/10/85 12:30 AM *Time After Time* (1979)
05/17/85 3:10 AM *The Whip Hand* (1951)
05/26/85 9:00 AM *Abbott and Costello Meet Dr. Jekyll and Mr. Hyde* (1953)
05/31/85 2:35 AM *Cat People* (1942)
06/23/85 1:30 AM *The Hunchback of Notre Dame* (1939)
06/28/85 12:30 AM *Dracula* (1979)
07/08/85 12:30 AM *The Nanny* (1965)
07/19/85 3:55 AM *Thirteen Women* (1932)

07/20/85 1:30 AM *Quatermass and the Pit* (1967)
08/03/85 12:30 AM *The Haunting of Julia* (1977)
08/06/85 12:30 AM *The Nanny* (1965)
08/09/86 1:00 PM *The Swarm* (1978)
08/07/85 12:30 AM *The Haunting of Julia* (1977)
08/10/85 11:30 PM *Things to Come* (1936)
08/31/85 1:00 AM *One Million Years B.C.* (1966)
09/02/85 12:30 AM *The Shuttered Room* (1967)
09/05/85 1:30 AM *Shadow of the Hawk* (1976)
09/07/85 1:25 AM *The Swarm* (1978)
09/14/85 3:30 AM *The Body Snatcher* (1945)
09/21/85 2:05 AM *Two on a Guillotine* (1965)
09/24/85 3:20 AM *Isle of the Dead* (1945)
10/05/85 11:30 PM *The Exorcist* (1973)
10/12/85 11:30 PM *Exorcist II: The Heretic* (1977)
10/13/85 9:00 AM *Abbott and Costello Meet the Invisible Man* (1951)
10/19/85 12:00 AM *Dracula* (1979)
10/20/85 9:00 AM *The Incredible Shrinking Man* (1957)
10/25/85 2:00 AM *House of Wax* (1953)
10/26/85 11:30 PM *Love at First Bite* (1979)
10/26/85 1:20 AM *The Thing from Another World* (1951)
10/26/85 2:20 AM *I Walked with A Zombie* (1943)
10/26/85 3:40 AM *Mummy's Boys* (1936)
10/29/85 2:00 AM *Cat People* (1942)
12/15/85 1:00 AM *The Legacy* (1978)
12/28/85 11:30 PM *King Kong* (1976)
12/31/85 2:35 AM *King Kong* (1933)
12/31/85 4:20 AM *Son of Kong* (1933)
01/17/86 1:00 AM *Quatermass and the Pit* (1967)
01/31/86 1:30 AM *One Million Years B.C.* (1966)
02/09/86 9:00 PM *Abbott and Costello Meet the Mummy* (1955)
03/15/86 1:30 AM *Time After Time* (1979)
03/20/86 12:30 AM *The Nanny* (1965)
03/27/86 1:00 AM *Dr. Jekyll and Mr. Hyde* (1941)
04/11/86 1:30 AM *Exorcist II: The Heretic* (1977)
04/13/86 9:00 AM *Abbott and Costello Meet Frankenstein* (1948)
04/26/86 1:00 PM *The Shuttered Room* (1967)
05/06/86 12:30 AM *Quatermass and the Pit* (1967)
05/12/86 12:30 AM *The Stepford Wives* (1975)
05/30/86 1:30 AM *The Swarm* (1978)
06/01/86 7:00 PM *Time After Time* (1979)
06/08/86 9:00 AM *Abbott and Costello Meet Dr. Jekyll and Mr. Hyde* (1953)
06/17/86 12:30 AM *The Hunchback of Notre Dame* (1939)
06/20/86 12:30 AM *King Kong* (1976)
06/24/86 1:30 AM *Mighty Joe Young* (1949)
07/02/86 12:30 AM *One Million Years B.C.* (1966)
07/18/86 3:50 AM *The Curse of the Cat People* (1944)
07/27/86 2:00 PM *King Kong* (1933)
08/29/86 2:00 AM *Two on a Guillotine* (1965)
09/07/86 3:35 AM *Thirteen Women* (1932)
09/12/86 2:00 AM *Shadow of the Hawk* (1976)
09/16/86 4:25 AM *Genius at Work* (1946)
09/30/86 1:30 AM *The Legacy* (1978)
10/03/86 1:00 AM *Quatermass and the Pit* (1967)
10/19/86 9:00 AM *Abbott and Costello Meet the Invisible Man* (1951)

10/24/86 1:00 AM *Dracula* (1979)
10/25/86 1:00 PM *Theater of Blood* (1973)
10/25/86 12:30 AM *Love at First Bite* (1979)
10/25/86 1:30 AM *The Thing from Another World* (1951)
10/25/86 3:30 AM *I Walked with A Zombie* (1943)
10/25/86 4:40 AM *Mummy's Boys* (1936)
10/26/86 9:00 AM *The Incredible Shrinking Man* (1957)
10/26/86 1:00 AM *House of Wax* (1953)
10/30/86 3:45 AM *Cat People* (1942)
10/31/86 1:00 AM *The Exorcist* (1973)
10/31/86 3:55 AM *Isle of the Dead* (1945)
11/14/86 1:00 AM *Time After Time* (1979)
12/06/86 4:00 AM *Bedlam* (1946)
12/25/86 3:45 AM *Son of Kong* (1933)
02/04/87 1:30 AM *The Shuttered Room* (1967)
02/07/87 1:55 AM *The Exorcist* (1973)
02/14/87 1:00 PM *Eyes of Laura Mars* (1978)
02/14/87 1:55 AM *Exorcist II: The Heretic* (1977)
03/28/87 1:00 PM *The Swarm* (1978)
04/23/87 2:00 AM *The Legacy* (1978)
06/20/87 1:30 AM *King Kong* (1976)
07/22/87 2:00 AM *Mighty Joe Young* (1949)
07/31/87 2:30 AM *House of Wax* (1953)
08/07/87 3:00 AM *The Hunchback of Notre Dame* (1939)
08/18/87 2:00 AM *Shadow of the Hawk* (1976)
08/21/87 2:30 AM *Two on a Guillotine* (1965)
08/22/87 1:30 AM *The Swarm* (1978)

Channel 20

Date   Time   Title   Year
02/14/67 12:00 PM *Flesh and Fantasy* (1943)
02/23/67 11:00 PM *Bluebeard* (1944)
03/09/67 11:00 PM *Jack the Ripper* (1959)
03/23/67 11:00 PM *What A Carve Up!* (1961)
04/02/67 7:30 PM *Invaders from Mars* (1953)
04/07/67 9:00 PM *The Whip and the Body* (1963)
04/13/67 11:00 PM *Violent Midnight* (1963)
04/14/67 11:00 PM *Uncle Was a Vampire* (1959)
05/20/67 11:00 PM *The White Spider* (1963)
06/13/67 2:00 PM *Flesh and Fantasy* (1943)
07/08/67 6:30 PM *The Whip and the Body* (1963)
07/22/67 6:30 PM *Violent Midnight* (1963)
08/09/67 11:00 PM *Mystery of Edwin Drood* (1935)
09/12/67 9:00 PM *Jack the Ripper* (1959)
10/18/67 12:00 PM *Flesh and Fantasy* (1943)
11/10/67 9:00 PM *Ghidorah, the Three-Headed Monster* (1964)
11/10/67 11:00 PM *Bluebeard* (1963)
11/17/67 11:00 PM *Uncle Was a Vampire* (1959)
01/10/68 11:00 PM *Dead of Night* (1945)
01/23/68 11:00 PM *Tower of Terror* (1941)
01/26/68 9:00 PM *Mothra* (1961)
01/28/68 2:30 PM *Mothra* (1961)
02/13/68 9:00 PM *Five* (1951)
03/08/68 9:00 PM *Ghidorah, the Three-Headed Monster* (1964)
03/09/68 8:00 PM *Ghidorah, the Three-Headed Monster* (1964)
03/10/68 2:30 PM *Ghidorah, the Three-Headed Monster* (1964)
05/05/68 9:00 PM *The Phantom of the Opera* (1943)
05/19/68 7:00 PM *It Came from Beneath the Sea* (1955)

09/25/68 8:30 PM *Godzilla vs. The Thing* (1964)
09/27/68 8:30 PM *Godzilla vs. The Thing* (1964)
09/28/68 7:00 PM *Godzilla vs. The Thing* (1964)
09/29/68 2:30 PM *Godzilla vs. The Thing* (1964)
09/29/68 7:00 PM *Godzilla vs. The Thing* (1964)
11/14/68 12:00 PM *The Phantom of the Opera* (1943)
01/29/69 8:30 PM *Godzilla vs. The Thing* (1964)
01/31/69 8:30 PM *Godzilla vs. The Thing* (1964)
02/01/69 10:00 AM *Godzilla vs. The Thing* (1964)
02/01/69 8:30 PM *Godzilla vs. The Thing* (1964)
02/02/69 11:00 PM *Godzilla vs. The Thing* (1964)
02/03/69 1:00 PM *Godzilla vs. The Thing* (1964)
02/12/69 8:30 PM *Jack the Ripper* (1959)
02/14/69 8:30 PM *Jack the Ripper* (1959)
02/16/69 11:00 PM *Jack the Ripper* (1959)
02/17/69 1:00 PM *Jack the Ripper* (1959)
02/26/69 11:30 PM *The Phantom of the Opera* (1943)
02/27/69 1:00 PM *The Phantom of the Opera* (1943)
03/27/69 11:30 PM *Dead of Night* (1945)
03/28/69 1:00 PM *Dead of Night* (1945)
05/25/69 3:00 PM *The Phantom of the Opera* (1943)
06/16/69 9:00 PM *Bluebeard* (1963)
06/23/69 6:00 PM *Die, Monster, Die!* (1965)
06/30/69 6:00 PM *The Spider Woman Strikes Back* (1946)
07/07/69 6:00 PM *The Giant Claw* (1957)
07/14/69 6:00 PM *It Came from Beneath the Sea* (1955)
07/21/69 6:00 PM *Curse of the Demon* (1957)
07/28/69 6:00 PM *Mothra* (1961)
08/01/69 11:30 PM *A Game of Death* (1945)
08/04/69 1:00 PM *A Game of Death* (1945)
08/04/69 6:00 PM *The Tingler* (1959)
08/11/69 6:00 PM *Bela Lugosi Meets a Brooklyn Gorilla* (1952)
08/18/69 6:00 PM *Serpent Island* (1954)
09/08/69 10:00 PM *Jack the Ripper* (1959)
09/26/69 1:00 PM *The Amazing Mr. X* (1948)
10/05/69 10:00 PM *The Phantom of the Opera* (1943)
10/08/69 1:00 PM *Flesh and Fantasy* (1943)
02/28/70 9:00 PM *Diabolique* (1955)
05/17/70 6:30 PM *Jack the Ripper* (1959)
07/10/70 9:00 PM *Ghidorah, the Three-Headed Monster* (1964)
07/19/70 6:30 PM *The Phantom of the Opera* (1962)
07/31/70 9:00 PM *Hangover Square* (1945)
09/12/70 9:00 PM *Diabolique* (1955)
10/31/70 12:00 AM *The Tingler* (1959)
11/03/70 12:00 AM *The Phantom of the Opera* (1962)
11/08/70 6:30 PM *Journey to the Center of the Earth* (1959)
11/09/70 1:00 PM *Tomb of Torture* (1963)
11/20/70 1:00 PM *Hangover Square* (1945)
11/20/70 9:00 PM *Voyage to the Bottom of the Sea* (1961)
12/19/70 9:00 PM *Bluebeard* (1963)
12/26/70 11:00 PM *The Human Monster* (1939)
01/13/71 1:00 PM *Back from the Dead* (1957)
01/19/71 1:00 PM *Bluebeard* (1944)
01/24/71 8:30 PM *Diabolique* (1955)
02/17/71 8:30 PM *What Ever Happened to Baby Jane?* (1962)
02/21/71 6:30 PM *What Ever Happened to Baby Jane?* (1962)
03/02/71 8:30 PM *Picture Mommy Dead* (1966)
03/03/71 8:30 PM *Hush…Hush, Sweet Charlotte* (1964)

03/07/71 6:30 PM *Hush…Hush, Sweet Charlotte* (1964)
03/30/71 11:00 PM *Tomb of Torture* (1963)
05/01/71 6:30 PM *Voyage to the Bottom of the Sea* (1961)
05/07/71 8:30 PM *Journey to the Center of the Earth* (1959)
05/08/71 6:30 PM *Journey to the Center of the Earth* (1959)
06/11/71 1:00 PM *Hangover Square* (1945)
07/09/71 8:30 PM *Village of the Giants* (1965)
07/10/71 6:30 PM *Village of the Giants* (1965)
08/10/71 11:00 PM *Tomb of Torture* (1963)
08/15/71 10:30 AM *The Bowery Boys Meet the Monsters* (1954)
08/26/71 1:00 PM *Back from the Dead* (1957)
09/13/71 8:30 PM *Back from the Dead* (1957)
09/28/71 11:00 PM *The Lodger* (1944)
10/03/71 8:30 PM *Diabolique* (1955)
10/25/71 11:00 PM *Bluebeard* (1944)
12/06/71 9:00 PM *The 10th Victim* (1965)
12/25/71 10:30 AM *Abbott and Costello Meet the Invisible Man* (1951)
12/31/71 8:30 PM *Mad Monster Party?* (1967)
01/02/72 4:30 PM *Mad Monster Party?* (1967)
02/13/72 4:30 PM *Journey to the Center of the Earth* (1959)
02/20/72 10:30 AM *Master Minds* (1949)
02/25/72 8:00 PM *Voyage to the Bottom of the Sea* (1961)
02/26/72 6:30 PM *Voyage to the Bottom of the Sea* (1961)
02/27/72 4:30 PM *Voyage to the Bottom of the Sea* (1961)
05/30/72 11:00 PM *The Lodger* (1944)
09/16/72 9:30 AM *Abbott and Costello Meet Dr. Jekyll and Mr. Hyde* (1953)
09/23/72 9:30 AM *Abbott and Costello Meet the Invisible Man* (1951)
09/24/72 10:30 AM *The Bowery Boys Meet the Monsters* (1954)
10/19/72 1:00 PM *Hangover Square* (1945)
10/26/72 8:00 PM *Journey to the Center of the Earth* (1959)
10/31/72 1:00 PM *The Mad Magician* (1954)
11/02/72 8:00 PM *Voyage to the Bottom of the Sea* (1961)
11/04/72 6:30 PM *Voyage to the Bottom of the Sea* (1961)
11/05/72 4:30 PM *Voyage to the Bottom of the Sea* (1961)
11/15/72 8:00 PM *Fantastic Voyage* (1966)
11/18/72 2:30 PM *Fantastic Voyage* (1966)
11/19/72 6:30 PM *Fantastic Voyage* (1966)
11/20/72 1:00 PM *The Lodger* (1944)
12/01/72 8:00 PM *Mad Monster Party?* (1967)
12/03/72 4:30 PM *Mad Monster Party?* (1967)
12/14/72 8:00 PM *Diabolique* (1955)
01/04/73 8:00 PM *What Ever Happened to Baby Jane?* (1962)
01/06/73 6:30 PM *What Ever Happened to Baby Jane?* (1962)
01/07/73 4:00 PM *What Ever Happened to Baby Jane?* (1962)
01/25/73 8:00 PM *Hush…Hush, Sweet Charlotte* (1964)
01/28/73 5:00 PM *Hush…Hush, Sweet Charlotte* (1964)
03/03/73 11:00 AM *Abbott and Costello Meet Dr. Jekyll and Mr. Hyde* (1953)
03/10/73 11:00 AM *Abbott and Costello Meet the Invisible Man* (1951)
03/17/73 11:00 AM *Abbott and Costello Meet Frankenstein* (1948)
03/18/73 10:30 AM *Master Minds* (1949)
03/20/73 1:00 PM *The Maze* (1953)
04/19/73 1:00 PM *Hangover Square* (1945)
05/04/73 9:00 PM *Master of the World* (1961)

05/05/73 3:30 PM *Master of the World* (1961)
05/06/73 3:00 PM *Master of the World* (1961)
05/11/73 9:00 PM *The Shuttered Room* (1967)
05/12/73 3:30 PM *The Shuttered Room* (1967)
05/13/73 3:00 PM *The Shuttered Room* (1967)
05/18/73 9:00 PM *The Sorcerers* (1967)
05/19/73 3:30 PM *The Sorcerers* (1967)
05/20/73 3:00 PM *The Sorcerers* (1967)
05/25/73 9:00 PM *Black Sabbath* (1963)
06/02/73 11:00 AM *Abbott and Costello Meet the Mummy* (1955)
07/06/73 9:00 PM *Fantastic Voyage* (1966)
07/07/73 3:30 PM *Fantastic Voyage* (1966)
07/08/73 3:00 PM *Fantastic Voyage* (1966)
07/13/73 9:00 PM *Voyage to the Bottom of the Sea* (1961)
07/14/73 3:30 PM *Voyage to the Bottom of the Sea* (1961)
07/15/73 3:00 PM *Voyage to the Bottom of the Sea* (1961)
07/20/73 9:00 PM *The Lost World* (1960)
07/21/73 3:30 PM *The Lost World* (1960)
07/22/73 3:00 PM *The Lost World* (1960)
07/27/73 9:00 PM *Bluebeards Ten Honeymoons* (1960)
07/28/73 3:30 PM *Bluebeards Ten Honeymoons* (1960)
07/29/73 3:00 PM *Bluebeards Ten Honeymoons* (1960)
09/07/73 9:00 PM *Pyro* (1964)
09/08/73 3:30 PM *Pyro* (1964)
09/09/73 3:00 PM *Pyro* (1964)
09/14/73 9:00 PM *Burn, Witch, Burn* (1962)
09/15/73 11:00 AM *Abbott and Costello Meet Frankenstein* (1948)
09/15/73 3:30 PM *Burn, Witch, Burn* (1962)
09/16/73 3:00 PM *Burn, Witch, Burn* (1962)
09/21/73 9:00 PM *The Castle of the Living Dead* (1964)
09/22/73 3:30 PM *The Castle of the Living Dead* (1964)
09/23/73 3:00 PM *The Castle of the Living Dead* (1964)
09/28/73 9:00 PM *Terror in the Crypt* (1964)
09/29/73 11:00 AM *Abbott and Costello Meet Dr. Jekyll and Mr. Hyde* (1953)
09/29/73 3:30 PM *Terror in the Crypt* (1964)
09/30/73 3:00 PM *Terror in the Crypt* (1964)
10/05/73 9:00 PM *The Day the Earth Stood Still* (1951)
10/06/73 11:00 AM *Abbott and Costello Meet the Invisible Man* (1951)
10/06/73 3:30 PM *The Day the Earth Stood Still* (1951)
10/07/73 3:00 PM *The Day the Earth Stood Still* (1951)
10/12/73 9:00 PM *Goliath and the Vampires* (1961)
10/13/73 3:30 PM *Goliath and the Vampires* (1961)
10/14/73 3:00 PM *Goliath and the Vampires* (1961)
10/15/73 9:00 PM *The Ghost Breakers* (1940)
10/26/73 9:00 PM *Circus of Fear* (1966)
10/27/73 3:30 PM *Circus of Fear* (1966)
10/28/73 10:00 AM *Mad Monster Party?* (1967)
10/28/73 3:00 PM *Circus of Fear* (1966)
10/30/73 12:30 PM *Bluebeard* (1944)
11/02/73 9:00 PM *4D Man* (1959)
11/03/73 3:30 PM *4D Man* (1959)
11/04/73 3:00 PM *4D Man* (1959)
11/09/73 10:30 PM *Torture Garden* (1967)
11/10/73 3:30 PM *Torture Garden* (1967)
11/11/73 3:00 PM *Torture Garden* (1967)
11/16/73 9:00 PM *The Mad Room* (1969)
11/17/73 3:30 PM *The Mad Room* (1969)
11/18/73 3:00 PM *The Mad Room* (1969)
11/23/73 9:00 PM *The Mad Doctor* (1940)
11/24/73 3:30 PM *The Mad Doctor* (1940)
11/25/73 3:00 PM *The Mad Doctor* (1940)
11/28/73 12:30 PM *The Mad Magician* (1954)
11/30/73 10:00 PM *The Evil Eye* (1963)
12/01/73 3:30 PM *The Evil Eye* (1963)
12/02/73 3:00 PM *The Evil Eye* (1963)
12/07/73 9:00 PM *Picture Mommy Dead* (1966)
12/08/73 3:30 PM *Picture Mommy Dead* (1966)
12/09/73 3:00 PM *Picture Mommy Dead* (1966)
12/14/73 9:00 PM *Circus of Horrors* (1960)
12/15/73 11:00 AM *Abbott and Costello Meet the Mummy* (1955)
12/15/73 3:30 PM *Circus of Horrors* (1960)
12/16/73 3:00 PM *Circus of Horrors* (1960)
12/21/73 9:00 PM *The Innocents* (1961)
12/22/73 3:30 PM *The Innocents* (1961)
12/23/73 3:00 PM *The Innocents* (1961)
01/04/74 10:00 PM *Curse of the Voodoo* (1965)
01/05/74 3:30 PM *Curse of the Voodoo* (1965)
01/06/74 3:00 PM *Curse of the Voodoo* (1965)
01/11/74 11:00 PM *Blood and Black Lace* (1964)
01/12/74 3:30 PM *Blood and Black Lace* (1964)
01/13/74 3:00 PM *Blood and Black Lace* (1964)
01/18/74 10:00 PM *The Shuttered Room* (1967)
01/19/74 3:30 PM *The Shuttered Room* (1967)
01/20/74 3:00 PM *The Shuttered Room* (1967)
02/01/74 10:00 PM *House on Haunted Hill* (1959)
02/02/74 3:30 PM *House on Haunted Hill* (1959)
02/03/74 3:00 PM *House on Haunted Hill* (1959)
02/09/74 3:30 PM *Frankenstein 1970* (1958)
02/10/74 3:00 PM *Snake People* (1971)
02/15/74 9:00 PM *Snake People* (1971)
02/16/74 3:00 PM *Theatre of Death* (1967)
02/22/74 9:00 PM *Theatre of Death* (1967)
02/23/74 3:00 PM *The Human Duplicators* (1965)
03/01/74 9:00 PM *The Human Duplicators* (1965)
03/02/74 3:00 PM *Castle of Terror* (1964)
03/08/74 8:00 PM *Castle of Terror* (1964)
03/16/74 3:00 PM *War of the Monsters* (1966)
03/22/74 9:00 PM *War of the Monsters* (1966)
03/23/74 3:00 PM *Mission Stardust* (1967)
03/29/74 9:00 PM *Mission Stardust* (1967)
03/30/74 3:00 PM *Gamera vs. Monster X* (1970)
04/05/74 9:00 PM *Gamera vs. Monster X* (1970)
04/06/74 3:30 PM *Destroy All Monsters* (1968)
04/12/74 9:00 PM *Destroy All Monsters* (1968)
04/13/74 3:30 PM *Frankenstein Conquers the World* (1965)
04/20/74 10:30 AM *Abbott and Costello Meet Dr. Jekyll and Mr. Hyde* (1953)
04/20/74 3:30 PM *From the Earth to the Moon* (1958)
04/26/74 9:00 PM *From the Earth to the Moon* (1958)
04/27/74 3:00 PM *Curse of the Demon* (1957)
05/03/74 9:00 PM *Curse of the Fly* (1965)
05/04/74 3:00 PM *Curse of the Fly* (1965)
05/04/74 10:30 AM *Abbott and Costello Meet the Invisible Man* (1951)
05/10/74 9:00 PM *Hush... Hush, Sweet Charlotte* (1964)
05/11/74 3:00 PM *Hush... Hush, Sweet Charlotte* (1964)

05/17/74 9:00 PM *What Ever Happened to Baby Jane?* (1962)
05/18/74 3:00 PM *What Ever Happened to Baby Jane?* (1962)
05/24/74 9:00 PM *Journey to the Center of the Earth* (1959)
05/25/74 3:00 PM *Journey to the Center of the Earth* (1959)
05/27/74 9:00 PM *A Reflection of Fear* (1972)
05/31/74 9:00 PM *The Uninvited* (1944)
06/01/74 3:00 PM *The Uninvited* (1944)
07/17/74 12:00 PM *Village of the Giants* (1965)
07/19/74 9:00 PM *The Day of the Triffids* (1963)
07/20/74 3:00 PM *The Day of the Triffids* (1963)
07/22/74 12:00 PM *The 10th Victim* (1965)
07/25/74 12:00 AM *The 10th Victim* (1965)
07/26/74 9:00 PM *The Day the Earth Stood Still* (1951)
07/27/74 3:00 PM *The Day the Earth Stood Still* (1951)
08/29/74 12:00 AM *The Lodger* (1944)
08/31/74 5:00 PM *Abbott and Costello Meet the Mummy* (1955)
09/13/74 9:00 PM *The Mysterians* (1957)
09/14/74 1:30 PM *The Mysterians* (1957)
09/20/74 9:00 PM *Snake People* (1971)
09/21/74 1:00 PM *Snake People* (1971)
09/27/74 9:00 PM *Snake People* (1971)
09/28/74 1:00 PM *Snake People* (1971)
10/04/74 9:00 PM *Psychomania* (1973)
10/05/74 1:00 PM *Psychomania* (1973)
10/11/74 9:00 PM *Crucible of Terror* (1971)
10/12/74 1:00 PM *Crucible of Terror* (1971)
10/18/74 9:00 PM *In the Devil's Garden* (1971)
10/19/74 1:00 PM *In the Devil's Garden* (1971)
10/25/74 9:00 PM *Torture Chamber of Dr. Sadism* (1967)
10/26/74 1:00 PM *Corridors of Blood* (1958)
11/01/74 9:00 PM *The Castle of Fu Manchu* (1969)
11/02/74 1:00 PM *The Castle of Fu Manchu* (1969)
11/08/74 9:00 PM *Mad Doctor of Blood Island* (1969)
11/10/74 1:00 PM *Fantastic Voyage* (1966)
11/15/74 9:00 PM *The Vampire People* (1964)
11/16/74 1:00 PM *The Vampire People* (1964)
11/22/74 9:00 PM *The Fury of the Wolfman* (1972)
11/23/74 1:00 PM *Daughter of Dr. Jekyll* (1957)
11/30/74 1:00 PM *The Fury of the Wolfman* (1972)
12/13/74 9:00 PM *Queen of Blood* (1966)
12/14/74 1:00 PM *Queen of Blood* (1966)
12/20/74 9:00 PM *Voyage to the Prehistoric Planet* (1965)
12/21/74 1:00 PM *Voyage to the Prehistoric Planet* (1965)
12/27/74 9:00 PM *The Eye Creatures* (1965)
12/28/74 1:00 PM *The Eye Creatures* (1965)
01/11/75 9:00 PM *Torture Garden* (1967)
01/18/75 9:00 PM *Horror Express* (1972)
01/21/75 12:00 PM *The Bamboo Saucer* (1968)
01/25/75 9:00 PM *Theatre of Death* (1967)
02/01/75 9:00 PM *The Sorcerers* (1967)
02/04/75 12:00 PM *The Ghost Breakers* (1940)
02/09/75 3:00 PM *Hush...Hush, Sweet Charlotte* (1964)
02/09/75 6:00 PM *What Ever Happened to Baby Jane?* (1962)
04/17/75 12:00 PM *The Lodger* (1944)
04/26/75 10:30 AM *Abbott and Costello Meet the Mummy* (1955)
04/27/75 6:00 PM *Voyage to the Bottom of the Sea* (1961)
05/10/75 10:30 AM *Abbott and Costello Meet Dr. Jekyll and Mr. Hyde* (1953)
05/17/75 10:30 AM *Abbott and Costello Meet the Invisible Man* (1951)
07/21/75 9:00 PM *Voyage to the Bottom of the Sea* (1961)
07/22/75 9:00 PM *Fantastic Voyage* (1966)
07/26/75 3:00 PM *Fantastic Voyage* (1966)
08/22/75 9:00 PM *The 10th Victim* (1965)
08/25/75 9:00 PM *The Hound of the Baskervilles* (1959)
09/19/75 8:00 PM *Torture Garden* (1967)
10/10/75 8:00 PM *Master of the World* (1961)
10/17/75 8:00 PM *Curse of the Fly* (1965)
10/26/75 5:00 PM *Mad Monster Party?* (1967)
10/31/75 8:00 PM *Theatre of Death* (1967)
11/04/75 1:00 AM *The Hound of the Baskervilles* (1959)
11/07/75 8:00 PM *Doctor Faustus* (1967)
11/12/75 8:00 PM *The Collector* (1965)
11/14/75 8:00 PM *The Mad Room* (1969)
11/20/75 1:00 AM *The Hound of the Baskervilles* (1959)
11/21/75 8:00 PM *Snake People* (1971)
11/22/75 1:30 PM *The Ghost Breakers* (1940)
11/28/75 8:00 PM *Assignment Terror* (1970)
12/05/75 8:00 PM *Dracula vs. Frankenstein* (1971)
12/06/75 1:30 PM *Abbott and Costello Meet the Mummy* (1955)
12/08/75 1:00 AM *The Hound of the Baskervilles* (1959)
12/09/75 8:00 PM *U.F.O.* (1956)
12/12/75 8:00 PM *Frankenstein 1970* (1958)
12/24/75 1:00 AM *The Hound of the Baskervilles* (1959)
12/26/75 8:00 PM *The Mysterians* (1957)
01/02/76 8:00 PM *The Day the Earth Stood Still* (1951)
01/10/76 4:00 PM *The Mummy's Curse* (1944)
01/17/76 11:30 AM *Abbott and Costello Meet Dr. Jekyll and Mr. Hyde* (1953)
01/17/76 3:00 PM *The Invisible Man's Revenge* (1944)
01/24/76 11:30 AM *Abbott and Costello Meet the Invisible Man* (1951)
01/24/76 3:00 PM *Creature from the Black Lagoon* (1954)
01/30/76 8:30 PM *Hush...Hush, Sweet Charlotte* (1964)
01/31/76 3:00 PM *The Wolf Man* (1941)
02/01/76 5:00 PM *The Two Faces of Dr. Jekyll* (1960)
02/06/76 8:30 PM *Fantastic Voyage* (1966)
02/07/76 3:00 PM *Gorgo* (1961)
02/13/76 8:30 PM *What Ever Happened to Baby Jane?* (1962)
02/14/76 3:00 PM *One Million B.C.* (1940)
02/21/76 3:00 PM *Godzilla vs. the Smog Monster* (1972)
02/28/76 3:00 PM *Son of Godzilla* (1967)
03/06/76 3:00 PM *The Amazing Transparent Man* (1960)
03/13/76 3:00 PM *Dagora, the Space Monster* (1964)
03/20/76 3:00 PM *Creature with the Blue Hand* (1967)
03/27/76 3:00 PM *The Angry Red Planet* (1959)
04/03/76 3:00 PM *The Invisible Man Returns* (1940)
04/10/76 3:00 PM *Return of the Giant Monsters* (1967)
04/12/76 12:00 PM *Hangover Square* (1945)
04/17/76 11:30 AM *Abbott and Costello Meet Frankenstein* (1948)
04/17/76 3:00 PM *Frankenstein Meets the Wolf Man* (1943)
04/19/76 12:00 PM *Alias John Preston* (1955)
04/24/76 3:00 PM *X* (1963)
04/25/76 1:00 PM *The Omega Man* (1971)
05/08/76 3:00 PM *Yog, Monster from Space* (1970)
05/18/76 12:00 PM *The Lodger* (1944)
05/22/76 3:00 PM *Gog* (1954)
05/29/76 3:00 PM *Voyage to the Prehistoric Planet* (1965)

06/19/76 3:00 PM *Konga* (1961)
06/26/76 3:00 PM *The Brain that Wouldn't Die* (1962)
07/07/76 12:00 PM *The Ghost Breakers* (1940)
07/24/76 1:00 PM *Voyage to the Bottom of the Sea* (1961)
08/29/76 1:00 PM *Voyage into Space* (1970)
09/09/76 9:00 PM *Berserk* (1967)
09/19/76 5:00 PM *Fantastic Voyage* (1966)
09/24/76 4:30 AM *The Bamboo Saucer* (1968)
10/04/76 12:30 PM *Doctor Faustus* (1967)
10/10/76 1:00 PM *Mad Monster Party?* (1967)
10/17/76 1:00 PM *One Million B.C.* (1940)
10/17/76 5:00 PM *Silent Running* (1972)
10/18/76 9:00 PM *A Reflection of Fear* (1972)
11/06/76 1:30 PM *Abbott and Costello Meet the Mummy* (1955)
11/07/76 4:30 PM *Planet of the Apes* (1968)
11/13/76 1:30 PM *Abbott and Costello Meet Dr. Jekyll and Mr. Hyde* (1953)
11/17/76 12:30 PM *The Collector* (1965)
11/21/76 1:00 PM *Master of the World* (1961)
11/21/76 5:00 PM *Beneath the Planet of the Apes* (1970)
11/28/76 1:00 PM *The Hound of the Baskervilles* (1959)
12/25/76 2:00 PM *Journey to the Center of the Earth* (1959)
12/26/76 3:00 PM *From the Earth to the Moon* (1958)
02/05/77 1:30 PM *Abbott and Costello Meet Dr. Jekyll and Mr. Hyde* (1953)
02/12/77 1:30 PM *Abbott and Costello Meet the Mummy* (1955)
02/19/77 1:30 PM *Abbott and Costello Meet Frankenstein* (1948)
02/25/77 4:00 AM *The College Girl Murders* (1967)
02/26/77 1:30 PM *Abbott and Costello Meet the Invisible Man* (1951)
02/27/77 5:30 PM *Conquest of the Planet of the Apes* (1972)
03/20/77 1:00 PM *The Lost World* (1960)
04/02/77 3:00 PM *Picture Mommy Dead* (1966)
04/09/77 3:00 PM *The Innocents* (1961)
04/16/77 3:00 PM *The Shuttered Room* (1967)
04/22/77 12:00 AM *The Little Shop of Horrors* (1960)
04/23/77 3:00 PM *The Mad Room* (1969)
04/29/77 12:00 AM *The Blancheville Monster* (1963)
04/29/77 2:00 AM *Last Woman on Earth* (1960)
04/30/77 3:00 PM *You'll Like My Mother* (1972)
05/06/77 12:00 AM *Terror in the Crypt* (1964)
05/06/77 2:00 AM *The Hypnotic Eye* (1960)
05/07/77 3:00 PM *Dear Dead Delilah* (1972)
05/13/77 12:00 AM *Circus of Horrors* (1960)
05/13/77 2:00 AM *Hands of a Stranger* (1962)
05/19/77 9:00 PM *The Omega Man* (1971)
05/20/77 12:00 AM *Graveyard of Horror* (1971)
05/27/77 12:00 AM *Frankenstein 1970* (1958)
05/27/77 2:00 AM *Indestructible Man* (1956)
06/03/77 12:00 AM *Bluebeards Ten Honeymoons* (1960)
06/04/77 3:00 PM *Night Tide* (1961)
06/04/77 8:00 PM *Village of the Giants* (1965)
06/10/77 12:00 AM *Daughter of Dr. Jekyll* (1957)
06/11/77 3:00 PM *Blood and Lace* (1971)
06/14/77 12:00 PM *The Ghost Breakers* (1940)
06/17/77 12:00 AM *Invisible Creature* (1960)
06/18/77 3:00 PM *The Evil Eye* (1963)
06/24/77 12:00 AM *Not of This Earth* (1957)

06/28/77 9:00 PM *The 10th Victim* (1965)
07/01/77 12:00 AM *The Sorcerers* (1967)
07/02/77 3:00 PM *Violent Midnight* (1963)
07/08/77 12:00 AM *House on Haunted Hill* (1959)
07/15/77 12:00 AM *Frankenstein's Bloody Terror* (1968)
07/15/77 4:00 AM *The Disembodied* (1957)
07/22/77 12:00 AM *The Bloody Judge* (1970)
07/22/77 4:00 AM *From Hell It Came* (1957)
07/23/77 2:30 PM *Hush...Hush, Sweet Charlotte* (1964)
07/23/77 8:00 PM *Voyage to the Bottom of the Sea* (1961)
07/29/77 12:00 AM *Track of the Vampire* (1966)
08/05/77 4:00 AM *Beast from Haunted Cave* (1959)
08/06/77 3:00 PM *Burn, Witch, Burn* (1962)
08/12/77 12:00 AM *Terror in the Haunted House* (1958)
08/12/77 4:00 AM *The Bride and the Beast* (1958)
08/13/77 3:00 PM *Face of Terror* (1962)
08/19/77 12:00 AM *Mesa of Lost Women* (1953)
08/19/77 4:00 AM *The Mermaids of Tiburon* (1962)
08/26/77 12:00 AM *The Brain from Planet Arous* (1957)
08/26/77 4:00 AM *War of the Satellites* (1958)
08/27/77 3:00 PM *Portrait in Terror* (1965)
09/02/77 12:00 AM *Goliath and the Vampires* (1961)
09/06/77 12:00 AM *Blood and Black Lace* (1964)
09/08/77 12:00 AM *Murder in the Blue Room* (1944)
09/22/77 12:00 AM *Secret of the Blue Room* (1933)
09/24/77 8:00 PM *Blood of Ghastly Horror* (1971)
10/01/77 12:00 PM *Abbott and Costello Meet Dr. Jekyll and Mr. Hyde* (1953)
10/01/77 8:00 PM *Gog* (1954)
10/05/77 7:30 PM *Silent Running* (1972)
10/08/77 12:00 PM *Abbott and Costello Meet the Invisible Man* (1951)
10/08/77 8:00 PM *The Snow Devils* (1967)
10/09/77 1:00 PM *Fantastic Voyage* (1966)
10/15/77 12:00 PM *Abbott and Costello Meet the Mummy* (1955)
10/16/77 5:00 PM *The Andromeda Strain* (1971)
10/23/77 1:00 PM *Master of the World* (1961)
10/26/77 9:00 PM *Run Stranger Run* (1973)
11/01/77 12:00 PM *The Uninvited* (1944)
11/05/77 12:00 PM *Abbott and Costello Meet Frankenstein* (1948)
11/06/77 1:00 PM *Beneath the Planet of the Apes* (1970)
11/07/77 12:00 AM *The Hound of the Baskervilles* (1959)
11/12/77 8:00 PM *War of the Planets* (1966)
11/13/77 1:00 PM *Escape from the Planet of the Apes* (1971)
11/20/77 1:00 PM *Conquest of the Planet of the Apes* (1972)
11/26/77 8:00 PM *The Day the Earth Caught Fire* (1961)
11/27/77 1:00 PM *Battle for the Planet of the Apes* (1973)
12/15/77 11:30 PM *The Evil Eye* (1963)
12/29/77 11:30 PM *Calling Dr. Death* (1943)
12/31/77 8:00 PM *Voyage to the Prehistoric Planet* (1965)
01/05/78 11:30 PM *Dementia 13* (1963)
01/07/78 8:00 PM *Dracula vs. Frankenstein* (1971)
01/09/78 8:00 PM *The Collector* (1965)
01/12/78 9:00 PM *Frankenstein 1970* (1958)
01/15/78 5:00 PM *Planet of the Apes* (1968)
01/16/78 7:00 PM *The Day the Earth Stood Still* (1951)
01/29/78 1:00 PM *The Nutty Professor* (1963)
05/06/78 12:00 PM *Abbott and Costello Meet the Mummy* (1955)

05/13/78 12:00 PM *Abbott and Costello Meet Dr. Jekyll and Mr. Hyde* (1953)
05/15/78 7:00 PM *The Legend of Boggy Creek* (1972)
05/20/78 12:00 PM *Abbott and Costello Meet the Invisible Man* (1951)
06/12/78 9:00 PM *A Reflection of Fear* (1972)
06/25/78 1:00 PM *Fantastic Voyage* (1966)
07/22/78 12:00 PM *Abbott and Costello Meet Frankenstein* (1948)
08/23/78 12:00 PM *The Uninvited* (1944)
09/01/78 1:00 AM *The Hound of the Baskervilles* (1939)
10/01/78 5:30 PM *Battle for the Planet of the Apes* (1973)
10/07/78 8:00 PM *The Lost World* (1960)
10/08/78 1:00 PM *The Nutty Professor* (1963)
10/14/78 8:00 PM *The Omega Man* (1971)
10/22/78 5:00 PM *Planet of the Apes* (1968)
11/05/78 5:00 PM *Escape from the Planet of the Apes* (1971)
11/06/78 9:00 PM *The Andromeda Strain* (1971)
11/19/78 5:00 PM *Beneath the Planet of the Apes* (1970)
11/25/78 12:30 PM *Abbott and Costello Meet the Invisible Man* (1951)
12/02/78 12:30 PM *Abbott and Costello Meet Dr. Jekyll and Mr. Hyde* (1953)
12/09/78 8:00 PM *Master of the World* (1961)
12/16/78 8:00 PM *Zontar, the Thing from Venus* (1966)
12/30/78 8:00 PM *Queen of Outer Space* (1958)
01/04/79 9:00 PM *The Illustrated Man* (1969)
01/19/79 1:00 AM *The Hound of the Baskervilles* (1939)
01/20/79 8:00 PM *U.F.O.* (1956)
01/21/79 5:00 PM *Fantastic Voyage* (1966)
02/04/79 10:00 AM *Abbott and Costello Meet Frankenstein* (1948)
02/10/79 8:00 PM *Silent Running* (1972)
02/11/79 10:00 AM *Abbott and Costello Meet the Invisible Man* (1951)
02/13/79 12:00 PM *The Ghost Breakers* (1940)
03/03/79 12:30 PM *Abbott and Costello Meet the Mummy* (1955)
03/03/79 8:00 PM *Terror Beneath the Sea* (1966)
03/06/79 12:00 PM *The Uninvited* (1944)
03/10/79 8:00 PM *The Diabolical Dr. Z* (1966)
03/24/79 8:00 PM *The Human Duplicators* (1965)
03/31/79 8:00 PM *4D Man* (1959)
04/01/79 1:00 PM *The Ghost Breakers* (1940)
04/09/79 12:00 PM *Godzilla vs. The Thing* (1964)
04/10/79 12:00 PM *Space Monster* (1965)
04/11/79 12:00 PM *In the Year 2889* (1967)
04/12/79 12:00 PM *It Came from Outer Space* (1953)
04/13/79 12:00 PM *X* (1963)
04/19/79 12:00 PM *The Mermaids of Tiburon* (1962)
04/22/79 10:00 AM *Abbott and Costello Meet Dr. Jekyll and Mr. Hyde* (1953)
05/05/79 12:30 PM *Abbott and Costello Meet the Invisible Man* (1951)
05/21/79 9:00 PM *The Nightcomers* (1972)
06/09/79 8:00 PM *The Sorcerers* (1967)
06/16/79 8:00 PM *War Gods of the Deep* (1965)
06/30/79 8:00 PM *War Between the Planets* (1966)
07/01/79 10:00 AM *Abbott and Costello Meet Frankenstein* (1948)
07/07/79 8:00 PM *Quatermass and the Pit* (1967)
07/08/79 1:00 PM *The Nutty Professor* (1963)
07/14/79 8:00 PM *One Million Years B.C.* (1966)
07/28/79 12:30 PM *Abbott and Costello Meet Dr. Jekyll and Mr. Hyde* (1953)
08/11/79 12:30 PM *Abbott and Costello Meet the Mummy* (1955)
08/11/79 8:00 PM *Journey to the Center of the Earth* (1959)
08/18/79 8:00 PM *Riders to the Stars* (1954)
08/25/79 12:30 PM *Abbott and Costello Meet the Invisible Man* (1951)
09/01/79 8:00 PM *From the Earth to the Moon* (1958)
09/09/79 10:00 AM *Abbott and Costello Meet the Invisible Man* (1951)
09/15/79 8:00 PM *Terror in the Haunted House* (1958)
09/22/79 8:00 PM *Nightmare Castle* (1965)
10/12/79 9:00 PM *The Hound of the Baskervilles* (1959)
10/28/79 3:00 PM *The Collector* (1965)
10/31/79 8:00 PM *Dracula* (1931)
10/31/79 10:00 PM *Frankenstein* (1931)
11/03/79 12:00 PM *Abbott and Costello Meet Frankenstein* (1948)
12/16/79 1:00 PM *Billy the Kid vs. Dracula* (1966)
12/30/79 1:00 PM *Jesse James Meets Frankenstein's Daughter* (1966)
01/04/80 1:00 AM *The Creation of the Humanoids* (1962)
01/06/80 10:00 AM *Abbott and Costello Meet Frankenstein* (1948)
01/11/80 1:00 AM *War Between the Planets* (1966)
01/19/80 12:00 PM *Abbott and Costello Meet the Mummy* (1955)
01/20/80 1:00 PM *The Nutty Professor* (1963)
01/20/80 3:00 PM *The Spiral Staircase* (1946)
01/22/80 8:00 PM *What Ever Happened to Baby Jane?* (1962)
02/01/80 1:00 AM *The House of Seven Corpses* (1974)
02/03/80 10:00 AM *Abbott and Costello Meet the Invisible Man* (1951)
02/08/80 8:00 PM *Things to Come* (1936)
02/08/80 1:00 AM *The Human Duplicators* (1965)
02/09/80 12:00 PM *Abbott and Costello Meet Dr. Jekyll and Mr. Hyde* (1953)
02/10/80 1:00 PM *Beneath the Planet of the Apes* (1970)
02/15/80 8:00 PM *Fantastic Voyage* (1966)
02/15/80 1:00 AM *Snake People* (1971)
02/22/80 1:00 AM *The Stranglers of Bombay* (1959)
05/11/80 10:00 AM *Abbott and Costello Meet Dr. Jekyll and Mr. Hyde* (1953)
05/18/80 10:00 AM *Abbott and Costello Meet the Invisible Man* (1951)
05/18/80 1:00 PM *Voyage to the Bottom of the Sea* (1961)
06/18/80 1:00 PM *Sisters* (1973)
08/02/80 2:00 PM *Beneath the Planet of the Apes* (1970)
08/03/80 1:00 PM *Battle for the Planet of the Apes* (1973)
08/10/80 7:00 PM *The Uninvited* (1944)
09/06/80 2:00 PM *Panic in Year Zero* (1962)
09/13/80 8:00 PM *The Collector* (1965)
09/14/80 7:00 PM *The Collector* (1965)
09/20/80 12:00 PM *Quatermass and the Pit* (1967)
09/27/80 1:00 PM *Mothra* (1961)
09/27/80 3:00 PM *The Incredible 2-Headed Transplant* (1971)
10/04/80 1:00 PM *Them!* (1954)
10/04/80 2:30 PM *The Tingler* (1959)
10/11/80 2:30 PM *Godzilla vs. the Smog Monster* (1971)
10/18/80 2:30 PM *X* (1963)
10/25/80 2:30 PM *Bride of Frankenstein* (1935)

11/01/80 1:00 PM *Frankenstein* (1931)
11/01/80 2:30 PM *Dracula* (1931)
11/08/80 1:00 PM *Reptilicus* (1961)
11/09/80 12:00 PM *Planet of the Apes* (1968)
11/09/80 2:00 PM *Escape from the Planet of the Apes* (1971)
11/09/80 4:00 PM *Fantastic Voyage* (1966)
11/15/80 1:00 PM *Conquest of the Planet of the Apes* (1972)
11/15/80 2:30 PM *Return of the Fly* (1959)
11/22/80 1:00 PM *The Invisible Man* (1933)
11/22/80 2:30 PM *Godzilla vs. The Thing* (1964)
11/23/80 12:00 PM *The Nutty Professor* (1963)
11/29/80 1:00 PM *The Giant Behemoth* (1959)
11/29/80 2:30 PM *Frankenstein Meets the Wolf Man* (1943)
12/06/80 1:00 PM *It Conquered the World* (1956)
12/13/80 1:00 PM *Zontar, the Thing from Venus* (1966)
12/13/80 2:30 PM *House on Haunted Hill* (1959)
12/27/80 1:00 PM *Invasion of the Saucer Men* (1957)
12/27/80 2:30 PM *Indestructible Man* (1956)
01/23/81 8:00 PM *Things to Come* (1936)
01/30/81 8:00 PM *The Nanny* (1965)
02/15/81 12:00 PM *Battle for the Planet of the Apes* (1973)
02/15/81 2:00 PM *The Day the Earth Stood Still* (1951)
02/15/81 4:00 PM *Journey to the Center of the Earth* (1959)
03/08/81 10:30 AM *The Bowery Boys Meet the Monsters* (1954)
04/03/81 8:00 PM *Berserk* (1967)
05/01/81 8:00 PM *Terror of Mechagodzilla* (1975)
06/06/81 8:00 PM *Murders in the Rue Morgue* (1932)
06/07/81 10:30 AM *The Bowery Boys Meet the Monsters* (1954)
07/19/81 12:00 PM *The Legend of Boggy Creek* (1972)
07/19/81 4:00 PM *The Andromeda Strain* (1971)
07/20/81 8:00 PM *What Ever Happened to Baby Jane?* (1962)
07/26/81 10:30 AM *Abbott and Costello Meet the Mummy* (1955)
10/18/81 12:00 PM *Planet of the Apes* (1968)
10/18/81 2:00 PM *Escape from the Planet of the Apes* (1971)
10/18/81 4:00 PM *Quatermass and the Pit* (1967)
10/25/81 12:00 PM *One Million Years B.C.* (1966)
10/30/81 1:00 PM *Phantom of the Rue Morgue* (1954)
10/31/81 8:20 PM *Dracula* (1931)
11/01/81 12:00 PM *King Kong* (1933)
11/01/81 2:00 PM *Mighty Joe Young* (1949)
11/01/81 4:00 PM *Them!* (1954)
11/08/81 2:00 PM *Fantastic Voyage* (1966)
11/22/81 2:00 PM *The Nutty Professor* (1963)
01/24/82 12:00 PM *Journey to the Center of the Earth* (1959)
02/05/82 8:00 PM *Carrie* (1976)
02/11/82 8:00 PM *The Birds* (1963)
02/21/82 10:30 PM *Abbott and Costello Meet Frankenstein* (1948)
05/02/82 10:30 AM *Abbott and Costello Meet the Invisible Man* (1951)
05/06/82 8:00 PM *Audrey Rose* (1977)
05/07/82 8:00 PM *Burnt Offerings* (1976)
05/16/82 10:30 AM *Abbott and Costello Meet Dr. Jekyll and Mr. Hyde* (1953)
05/21/82 8:00 PM *Revenge of the Creature* (1955)
05/25/82 8:00 PM *Audrey Rose* (1977)
07/19/82 8:00 PM *What Ever Happened to Baby Jane?* (1962)
10/03/82 12:00 PM *Munster, Go Home!* (1966)
10/16/82 12:00 PM *Abbott and Costello Meet the Mummy* (1955)
10/24/82 2:00 PM *Escape from the Planet of the Apes* (1971)

10/24/82 4:00 PM *Them!* (1954)
10/30/82 8:00 PM *Dracula* (1931)
11/12/82 8:00 PM *Gorilla at Large* (1954)
11/13/82 12:00 PM *Abbott and Costello Meet Frankenstein* (1948)
11/14/82 12:00 PM *The Nutty Professor* (1963)
11/28/82 12:00 PM *King Kong* (1933)
11/28/82 2:00 PM *Mighty Joe Young* (1949)
11/28/82 4:00 PM *Planet of the Apes* (1968)
02/28/83 8:00 PM *Burnt Offerings* (1976)
03/01/83 8:00 PM *Carrie* (1976)
03/02/83 8:00 PM *Audrey Rose* (1977)
03/04/83 8:00 PM *Murder by Decree* (1979)
04/07/83 12:00 PM *The Hunchback of Notre Dame* (1939)
05/08/83 2:00 PM *The Time Machine* (1960)
07/05/83 8:00 PM *What Ever Happened to Baby Jane?* (1962)
07/06/83 8:00 PM *The Nanny* (1965)
10/09/83 2:00 PM *The Day the Earth Stood Still* (1951)
10/31/83 8:00 PM *Phantasm* (1979)
11/06/83 4:00 PM *The Nutty Professor* (1963)
11/18/83 8:00 PM *Carrie* (1976)
01/01/84 4:00 PM *Munster, Go Home!* (1966)
01/06/84 8:00 PM *Audrey Rose* (1977)
02/19/84 4:00 PM *King Kong* (1933)
02/26/84 12:00 PM *Voyage to the Bottom of the Sea* (1961)
03/04/84 12:00 PM *Return to Boggy Creek* (1977)
05/26/84 8:00 PM *He Knows You're Alone* (1980)
07/21/84 8:00 PM *The Nanny* (1965)
08/23/84 9:00 PM *The Birds* (1963)
08/24/84 9:00 PM *Squirm* (1978)
09/16/84 12:00 PM *Fantastic Voyage* (1966)
10/28/84 12:00 PM *Return to Boggy Creek* (1977)
11/01/84 8:00 PM *Carrie* (1976)
11/06/84 8:00 PM *The Amityville Horror* (1979)
11/10/84 12:00 PM *King Kong* (1933)
11/10/84 2:00 PM *Mighty Joe Young* (1949)
12/08/84 12:00 PM *One Million Years B.C.* (1966)
01/21/85 8:00 PM *The Legend of Hell House* (1973)
01/22/85 8:00 PM *The Other* (1972)
01/23/85 8:00 PM *He Knows You're Alone* (1980)
01/24/85 8:00 PM *The Mephisto Waltz* (1971)
01/25/85 8:00 PM *Audrey Rose* (1977)
02/10/85 12:00 PM *Voyage to the Bottom of the Sea* (1961)
02/17/85 2:00 PM *The Nutty Professor* (1963)
02/24/85 12:00 PM *The Thing from Another World* (1951)
02/24/85 2:00 PM *The Day the Earth Stood Still* (1951)
03/01/85 8:00 PM *A Stranger is Watching* (1982)
03/03/85 4:00 PM *A Stranger is Watching* (1982)
03/17/85 12:00 PM *Munster, Go Home!* (1966)
04/27/85 12:00 PM *Race with the Devil* (1975)
05/16/85 8:00 PM *Prom Night* (1980)
05/17/85 8:00 PM *Invasion of the Body Snatchers* (1978)
06/09/85 12:00 PM *Mystery on Monster Island* (1981)
06/23/85 12:00 PM *Planet of the Apes* (1968)
07/06/85 12:00 PM *Beneath the Planet of the Apes* (1970)
07/06/85 2:00 PM *Escape from the Planet of the Apes* (1971)
07/20/85 8:00 PM *The Mask* (1961)
08/01/85 8:00 PM *Phantasm* (1979)
08/02/85 8:00 PM *Squirm* (1976)
08/10/85 12:00 PM *My Blood Runs Cold* (1965)

08/10/85 2:10 PM *The Frozen Dead* (1966)
09/01/85 12:00 PM *Fantastic Voyage* (1966)
10/20/85 12:00 PM *Return to Boggy Creek* (1977)
10/26/85 12:00 PM *Conquest of the Planet of the Apes* (1972)
10/26/85 2:00 PM *Battle for the Planet of the Apes* (1973)
10/31/85 8:00 PM *Damien: Omen II* (1978)
11/01/85 8:00 PM *The Amityville Horror* (1979)
11/04/85 8:00 PM *The Birds* (1963)
11/08/85 8:00 PM *Carrie* (1976)
11/10/85 2:00 PM *The Nutty Professor* (1963)
12/02/85 8:00 PM *Audrey Rose* (1977)
12/03/85 8:00 PM *Burnt Offerings* (1976)
01/05/86 12:00 PM *The Thing from Another World* (1951)
01/05/86 2:00 PM *Mighty Joe Young* (1949)
01/05/86 4:00 PM *King Kong* (1933)
01/07/86 8:00 PM *The Other* (1972)
01/30/86 8:00 PM *Invasion of the Body Snatchers* (1978)
01/31/86 8:00 PM *Prom Night* (1980)
02/06/86 8:00 PM *The Legend of Hell House* (1973)
02/09/86 12:00 PM *Voyage to the Bottom of the Sea* (1961)
02/09/86 2:00 PM *The Day the Earth Stood Still* (1951)
03/16/86 12:00 PM *Munster, Go Home!* (1966)
03/29/86 12:00 PM *Race with the Devil* (1975)
04/04/86 8:00 PM *The Mephisto Waltz* (1971)
04/05/86 12:00 PM *Planet of the Apes* (1968)
05/15/86 12:30 PM *The Hound of the Baskervilles* (1959)
05/19/86 8:00 PM *Massacre at Central High* (1976)
05/26/86 8:00 PM *The Fury* (1978)
06/07/86 2:00 PM *Quatermass and the Pit* (1967)
06/11/86 8:00 PM *Phantasm* (1979)
06/14/86 12:00 PM *Godzilla: King of the Monsters* (1956)
06/14/86 2:00 PM *Godzilla vs. The Thing* (1964)
06/16/86 8:00 PM *The Birds* (1963)
06/26/86 8:00 PM *Murder by Decree* (1979)
07/07/86 12:30 PM *Mothra* (1961)
07/08/86 12:30 PM *Master of the World* (1961)
07/09/86 12:30 PM *Dracula vs. Frankenstein* (1971)
07/10/86 12:30 PM *The Phantom of the Opera* (1962)
07/11/86 12:30 PM *Godzilla vs. the Smog Monster* (1971)
07/19/86 12:00 PM *Fantastic Voyage* (1966)
07/19/86 2:00 PM *Escape from the Planet of the Apes* (1971)
08/30/86 12:00 PM *The Beast from 20,000 Fathoms* (1953)
09/06/86 8:00 PM *Race with the Devil* (1975)
09/13/86 12:00 PM *Destroy All Planets* (1968)
09/13/86 2:00 PM *Destroy All Monsters* (1968)
09/25/86 12:00 AM *Tower of London* (1962)
09/29/86 12:00 AM *Two on a Guillotine* (1965)
10/03/86 8:00 PM *A Stranger is Watching* (1982)
10/12/86 10:30 AM *Abbott and Costello Meet the Mummy* (1955)
10/31/86 12:00 AM *Holocaust 2000* (1977)
11/01/86 12:00 PM *Battle for the Planet of the Apes* (1973)
11/01/86 8:00 PM *Burnt Offerings* (1976)
11/02/86 10:30 AM *Abbott and Costello Meet Frankenstein* (1948)
11/06/86 12:00 AM *The Illustrated Man* (1969)
11/08/86 12:00 PM *The Day the Earth Stood Still* (1951)
11/09/86 10:30 AM *Abbott and Costello Meet the Invisible Man* (1951)
11/10/86 8:00 PM *Prom Night* (1980)
11/11/86 8:00 PM *The Shining* (1980)
11/13/86 8:00 PM *Carrie* (1976)
11/14/86 8:00 PM *The Legend of Hell House* (1973)
11/16/86 10:30 AM *Abbott and Costello Meet Dr. Jekyll and Mr. Hyde* (1953)
11/26/86 12:00 AM *The Frozen Dead* (1966)
12/17/86 12:00 AM *The Shuttered Room* (1967)
12/19/86 8:00 PM *Damien: Omen II* (1978)
12/19/86 12:00 AM *Homebodies* (1974)
12/26/86 8:00 PM *Audrey Rose* (1977)
01/02/87 12:30 AM *Munster, Go Home!* (1966)
01/02/87 2:30 AM *Munster, Go Home!* (1966)
01/03/87 12:00 PM *The Manitou* (1977)
01/04/87 12:00 PM *Hush…Hush, Sweet Charlotte* (1964)
01/06/87 12:00 AM *Curse of the Demon* (1957)
01/08/87 8:00 PM *The Amityville Horror* (1979)
01/13/87 12:00 AM *The Nightcomers* (1972)
01/14/87 7:00 PM *Squirm* (1976)
01/16/87 12:00 AM *Psychic Killer* (1975)
01/17/87 2:00 PM *The Bubble* (1966)
01/19/87 8:00 PM *Planet of the Apes* (1968)
01/20/87 8:00 PM *Beneath the Planet of the Apes* (1970)
01/22/87 12:30 PM *Things to Come* (1936)
01/22/87 8:00 PM *Escape from the Planet of the Apes* (1971)
01/22/87 2:30 AM *Things to Come* (1936)
02/07/87 12:00 PM *Voyage to the Bottom of the Sea* (1961)
02/07/87 2:00 PM *The Nutty Professor* (1963)
02/13/87 8:00 PM *The Omen* (1976)
02/15/87 2:00 PM *He Knows You're Alone* (1980)
02/15/87 4:00 PM *The Other* (1972)
02/20/87 8:00 PM *Invasion of the Body Snatchers* (1978)
02/21/87 2:00 PM *Master of the World* (1961)
02/25/87 8:00 PM *The Fog* (1980)
03/08/87 10:30 AM *The Astro-Zombies* (1968)
03/08/87 12:00 PM *The Eye Creatures* (1965)
03/08/87 1:30 PM *Return of the Fly* (1959)
03/08/87 3:00 PM *Curse of the Fly* (1965)
03/08/87 4:30 PM *The Mysterians* (1957)
03/14/87 12:00 PM *No Survivors Please.* (1964)
03/14/87 2:00 PM *Panic in Year Zero* (1962)
03/17/87 12:00 AM *The Beast with Five Fingers* (1946)
03/20/87 12:00 AM *You'll Like My Mother* (1972)
03/27/87 12:00 AM *Silent Running* (1972)
03/31/87 9:00 PM *Dorian Gray* (1970)
04/30/87 8:00 PM *Phantasm* (1979)
05/16/87 2:00 PM *Massacre at Central High* (1976)
05/24/87 10:30 AM *Abbott & Costello Meet Frankenstein* (1948)
05/28/87 8:00 PM *The Birds* (1963)
06/13/87 2:00 PM *Return to Boggy Creek* (1977)
06/27/87 12:00 PM *Mighty Joe Young* (1949)
07/03/87 11:30 PM *Ghoulies* (1984)
07/05/87 6:00 PM *Ghoulies* (1984)
07/12/87 10:30 AM *Abbott & Costello Meet the Mummy* (1955)
07/24/87 8:00 PM *The Fury* (1978)
07/26/87 10:30 AM *Abbott & Costello Meet Dr. Jekyll and Mr. Hyde* (1953)
08/19/87 11:30 PM *Mighty Joe Young* (1949)
09/03/87 8:00 PM *Massacre at Central High* (1976)

Channel 26

Date   Time   Title   Year
08/22/74 9:00 PM *The Hunchback of Notre Dame* (1923)
08/24/74 6:00 PM *The Hunchback of Notre Dame* (1923)
01/18/75 10:00 PM *Ugetsu* (1953)
06/28/75 10:00 PM *The Hunchback of Notre Dame* (1923)
07/05/75 10:00 PM *Dr. Jekyll and Mr. Hyde* (1920)
04/24/76 9:00 PM *The Most Dangerous Game* (1932)
06/03/76 1:00 PM *Nosferatu* (1922)
06/05/76 1:00 PM *Nosferatu* (1922)
06/27/76 1:00 PM *The Most Dangerous Game* (1932)
06/28/76 1:00 PM *The Most Dangerous Game* (1932)
12/21/76 1:00 PM *Metropolis* (1927)
12/24/76 1:00 PM *Metropolis* (1927)
12/28/76 1:00 PM *Nosferatu* (1922)
12/31/76 1:00 PM *Nosferatu* (1922)
02/17/77 1:00 PM *The Most Dangerous Game* (1932)
04/08/77 1:00 PM *The Cabinet of Dr. Caligari* (1920)
04/25/77 12:45 PM *Metropolis* (1927)
04/29/77 12:45 PM *Nosferatu* (1922)
05/14/77 10:00 PM *The Cabinet of Dr. Caligari* (1920)
05/15/77 1:00 PM *The Most Dangerous Game* (1932)
05/21/77 10:00 PM *Metropolis* (1927)
05/28/77 10:30 PM *Nosferatu* (1922)
06/28/77 1:00 PM *Metropolis* (1927)
07/04/77 2:00 PM *The Cabinet of Dr. Caligari* (1920)
08/08/77 2:00 PM *Nosferatu* (1922)
09/09/77 2:00 PM *The Most Dangerous Game* (1932)
09/19/77 2:00 PM *Metropolis* (1927)
11/09/77 2:00 PM *The Cabinet of Dr. Caligari* (1920)
01/17/78 2:00 PM *Metropolis* (1927)
01/24/78 2:00 PM *The Most Dangerous Game* (1932)
02/13/78 2:00 PM *Nosferatu* (1922)
06/16/78 2:00 PM *The Cabinet of Dr. Caligari* (1920)
09/06/78 2:00 PM *The Most Dangerous Game* (1932)
09/30/78 10:30 AM *The Cabinet of Dr. Caligari* (1920)
10/06/78 2:00 PM *The Cabinet of Dr. Caligari* (1920)
10/31/78 2:00 PM *Nosferatu* (1922)
12/12/78 2:00 PM *The Most Dangerous Game* (1932)
05/23/79 2:00 PM *The Cabinet of Dr. Caligari* (1920)
06/21/79 2:00 PM *The Most Dangerous Game* (1932)
07/04/79 2:00 PM *Nosferatu* (1922)
10/25/80 9:00 PM *Dracula* (1979)
11/01/80 9:00 PM *The Plumber* (1979)
10/31/83 10:30 PM *In Search of Dracula* (1975)
02/04/84 9:00 PM *Invasion* (1965)

Channel 45

Date   Time   Title   Year
04/11/71 11:00 PM *The Hound of the Baskervilles* (1959)
04/16/71 11:30 PM *It! The Terror from Beyond Space* (1958)
04/23/71 11:30 PM *The Day the Earth Stood Still* (1951)
04/30/71 11:30 PM *Destination Moon* (1950)
05/05/71 7:00 PM *Flight to Mars* (1951)
05/07/71 11:30 PM *Gog* (1954)
05/14/71 11:30 PM *The Man from Planet X* (1951)
05/28/71 11:30 PM *U.F.O.* (1956)
06/04/71 11:30 PM *Curse of the Faceless Man* (1958)
06/18/71 11:30 PM *The 27th Day* (1957)
06/19/71 12:00 PM *The Mad Executioners* (1963)
06/25/71 11:30 PM *Mothra* (1961)
07/02/71 11:30 PM *Battle in Outer Space* (1959)
07/09/71 11:30 PM *Ghidorah, the Three-Headed Monster* (1964)
07/16/71 11:30 PM *12 to the Moon* (1960)
07/23/71 11:30 PM *It! The Terror from Beyond Space* (1958)
07/30/71 11:30 PM *Destination Moon* (1950)
08/06/71 11:30 PM *Riders to the Stars* (1954)
08/13/71 11:30 PM *Planets Against Us* (1962)
08/15/71 11:00 PM *The Creeper* (1948)
08/20/71 11:30 PM *The Final War* (1960)
08/27/71 11:30 PM *The Creation of the Humanoids* (1962)
09/03/71 11:30 PM *Red Planet Mars* (1952)
09/10/71 11:30 PM *The Diabolical Dr. Z* (1966)
09/17/71 11:30 PM *The Dungeon of Harrow* (1962)
09/24/71 11:30 PM *The Flame Barrier* (1958)
10/01/71 11:30 PM *Panic in Year Zero* (1962)
10/03/71 7:00 PM *Beyond the Time Barrier* (1960)
10/08/71 11:30 PM *Planet of the Vampires* (1965)
10/10/71 7:00 PM *Journey to the Seventh Planet* (1962)
10/15/71 11:30 PM *The Neanderthal Man* (1953)
10/17/71 7:00 PM *Die, Monster, Die* (1965)
10/22/71 11:30 PM *Atragon* (1963)
10/24/71 7:00 PM *The Angry Red Planet* (1959)
10/29/71 11:30 PM *The Phantom Planet* (1961)
10/31/71 7:00 PM *Invasion of the Body Snatchers* (1956)
11/07/71 7:00 PM *The Day the Earth Froze* (1959)
11/19/71 11:00 PM *The Bamboo Saucer* (1968)
11/20/71 11:00 PM *The Day the Earth Caught Fire* (1961)
11/21/71 7:00 PM *The Eye Creatures* (1965)
11/28/71 11:00 PM *The Hound of the Baskervilles* (1959)
12/10/71 1:00 PM *Svengali* (1931)
02/01/72 11:30 PM *Dead Eyes of London* (1961)
02/07/72 1:00 PM *The Horrible Dr. Hichcock* (1962)
02/11/72 12:45 AM *U.F.O.* (1956)
02/22/72 8:30 PM *Forbidden Planet* (1956)
02/22/72 11:30 PM *The Maze* (1953)
02/29/72 11:30 PM *Diabolique* (1955)
03/03/72 12:55 AM *Mars Needs Women* (1967)
03/04/72 12:00 PM *Day the World Ended* (1955)
03/10/72 1:20 AM *The 27th Day* (1957)
03/11/72 12:00 PM *Voyage to the End of the Universe* (1963)
03/12/72 11:05 PM *The Creeper* (1948)
03/17/72 1:20 AM *Space Monster* (1965)
03/18/72 2:00 PM *The Monster that Challenged the World* (1957)
03/24/72 1:25 AM *Invasion* (1965)
03/25/72 2:00 PM *Planets Against Us* (1962)
03/31/72 1:20 AM *Voyage to the Planet of Prehistoric Women* (1968)
04/01/72 2:00 PM *Gog* (1954)
04/02/72 11:05 PM *The Mad Magician* (1954)
04/07/72 7:00 PM *Invasion of the Saucer Men* (1957)
04/08/72 2:00 PM *Creature with the Atom Brain* (1955)
04/09/72 11:05 PM *Pharaoh's Curse* (1957)
04/14/72 7:00 PM *Maneater of Hydra* (1967)
04/16/72 11:05 PM *The Hound of the Baskervilles* (1959)
04/21/72 7:00 PM *Rome Against Rome* (1964)

04/22/72 12:00 PM *Destination Moon* (1950)
04/26/72 11:30 PM *Repulsion* (1965)
04/28/72 7:00 PM *Attack of the Puppet People* (1958)
04/30/72 11:05 PM *The Black Sleep* (1956)
05/01/72 7:00 PM *Teenage Caveman* (1958)
05/02/72 7:00 PM *The Beast with a Million Eyes* (1955)
05/03/72 7:00 PM *It's Alive!* (1969)
05/04/72 7:00 PM *Invisible Creature* (1960)
05/04/72 11:30 PM *Curse of the Demon* (1957)
05/05/72 7:00 PM *Queen of Blood* (1966)
05/06/72 12:00 PM *The Gamma People* (1956)
05/07/72 11:05 PM *The Amazing Transparent Man* (1960)
05/08/72 7:00 PM *Blood of Dracula* (1957)
05/09/72 7:00 PM *Curse of the Swamp Creature* (1966)
05/10/72 7:00 PM *It Conquered the World* (1956)
05/11/72 7:00 PM *Terror from the Year 5000* (1958)
05/12/72 7:00 PM *Zontar, the Thing from Venus* (1966)
05/13/72 12:00 PM *12 to the Moon* (1960)
05/14/72 11:05 PM *Circus of Horrors* (1960)
05/15/72 7:00 PM *I Was a Teenage Werewolf* (1957)
05/16/72 7:00 PM *Cat Girl* (1957)
05/17/72 7:00 PM *Night of the Blood Beast* (1958)
05/18/72 7:00 PM *The She-Creature* (1956)
05/19/72 7:00 PM *One Million B.C.* (1940)
05/21/72 11:05 PM *The Hand* (1960)
05/22/72 7:00 PM *War of the Colossal Beast* (1958)
05/23/72 7:00 PM *Track of the Vampire* (1966)
05/24/72 7:00 PM *Die, Monster, Die* (1965)
05/25/72 7:00 PM *The Screaming Skull* (1958)
05/25/72 11:30 PM *Dead of Night* (1945)
05/26/72 7:00 PM *Creature of Destruction* (1967)
05/26/72 11:00 PM *The Day the Earth Stood Still* (1951)
05/28/72 11:05 PM *Alias John Preston* (1955)
05/29/72 7:00 PM *Planet of the Vampires* (1965)
06/02/72 7:00 PM *The Amazing Colossal Man* (1957)
06/04/72 11:05 PM *The Awful Dr. Orlof* (1962)
06/06/72 7:00 PM *The Beast of Hollow Mountain* (1956)
06/07/72 7:00 PM *It! The Terror from Beyond Space* (1958)
06/08/72 7:00 PM *Yongary, Monster from the Deep* (1967)
06/09/72 7:00 PM *The Neanderthal Man* (1953)
06/11/72 11:05 PM *Bride of the Monster* (1955)
06/12/72 7:00 PM *Majin, Monster of Terror* (1966)
06/13/72 7:00 PM *The Lost Missile* (1958)
06/14/72 7:00 PM *The Killer Shrews* (1959)
06/15/72 7:00 PM *The Manster* (1959)
06/16/72 7:00 PM *Terror is a Man* (1959)
06/18/72 11:05 PM *Chamber of Horrors* (1940)
06/19/72 7:00 PM *Attack of the Mushroom People* (1963)
06/20/72 7:00 PM *The Giant Gila Monster* (1959)
06/21/72 7:00 PM *The Flame Barrier* (1958)
06/22/72 7:00 PM *Red Planet Mars* (1952)
06/23/72 7:00 PM *The Angry Red Planet* (1959)
06/25/72 11:05 PM *The Incredibly Strange Creatures Who Stopped Living and Became Mixed-Up Zombies!!?* (1964)
07/09/72 11:00 PM *Invasion of the Body Snatchers* (1956)
07/14/72 1:40 AM *The Mask of Diijon* (1946)
07/23/72 11:00 PM *Gammera the Invincible* (1966)
08/20/72 11:00 PM *Bluebeard* (1944)

09/03/72 11:00 PM *U.F.O.* (1956)
09/04/72 1:00 PM *The Body Disappears* (1941)
09/05/72 12:05 AM *Diabolique* (1955)
09/10/72 11:00 PM *The Son of Dr. Jekyll* (1951)
09/29/72 8:00 PM *Forbidden Planet* (1956)
10/13/72 8:00 PM *The Day the Earth Caught Fire* (1961)
10/18/72 12:00 AM *The Bamboo Saucer* (1968)
12/13/72 1:00 PM *Diabolique* (1955)
12/21/72 12:00 AM *The Hound of the Baskervilles* (1959)
12/27/72 12:00 AM *Dead Eyes of London* (1961)
12/31/72 3:30 AM *The Black Cat* (1941)
03/02/73 12:00 AM *Gorilla at Large* (1954)
03/09/73 8:00 PM *The 27th Day* (1957)
03/15/73 12:00 AM *Hunter of the Unknown* (1966)
03/26/73 12:00 AM *The College Girl Murders* (1967)
03/29/73 12:00 AM *Dead of Night* (1945)
05/01/73 11:30 PM *Portrait in Terror* (1965)
06/19/73 11:30 PM *The Mad Executioners* (1963)
07/18/73 11:30 PM *Tower of Terror* (1941)
07/31/73 1:00 PM *The Night Has Eyes* (1942)
09/25/73 11:30 PM *The Mad Magician* (1954)
10/12/73 12:00 AM *Forbidden Planet* (1956)
11/10/73 8:00 PM *The Lost World* (1960)
11/26/83 9:00 AM *Battle for the Planet of the Apes* (1973)
12/20/73 1:00 PM *The Woman in White* (1948)
02/02/74 1:00 PM *The Night the World Exploded* (1957)
03/08/74 10:00 AM *The Horror of Party Beach* (1964)
03/25/74 10:00 AM *The Curse of the Living Corpse* (1964)
05/03/74 12:00 AM *Day the World Ended* (1955)
05/31/74 8:00 PM *Gorilla at Large* (1954)
06/01/74 11:00 PM *Dead Eyes of London* (1961)
06/07/74 12:00 AM *The Day the Earth Stood Still* (1951)
07/03/74 8:00 PM *Dorian Gray* (1970)
07/05/74 10:00 AM *Flight to Mars* (1951)
08/26/74 10:00 AM *A Game of Death* (1945)
09/27/74 12:30 AM *Forbidden Planet* (1956)
10/18/74 10:00 AM *12 to the Moon* (1960)
10/28/74 10:00 AM *The Stranglers of Bombay* (1959)
10/29/74 10:00 AM *The 27th Day* (1957)
10/30/74 10:00 AM *The Tingler* (1959)
10/30/74 12:30 AM *Gorilla at Large* (1954)
12/17/74 12:30 AM *U.F.O.* (1956)
01/28/75 12:00 AM *Repulsion* (1965)
02/14/75 9:00 PM *The Lost World* (1960)
02/20/75 9:00 PM *House of Wax* (1953)
03/03/75 10:00 AM *The New Invisible Man* (1958)
03/05/75 10:00 AM *Frozen Alive* (1964)
03/14/75 10:00 AM *Red Planet Mars* (1952)
03/18/75 10:00 AM *She Demons* (1958)
03/21/75 10:00 AM *The Black Sleep* (1956)
04/04/75 8:30 PM *The Day the Earth Caught Fire* (1961)
04/04/75 12:30 AM *The College Girl Murders* (1967)
05/10/75 11:00 PM *The Hound of the Baskervilles* (1959)
05/15/75 10:00 AM *Castle of Evil* (1966)
05/20/75 10:00 AM *The Gamma People* (1956)
05/24/75 11:00 PM *Dead Eyes of London* (1961)
05/30/75 8:30 PM *Forbidden Planet* (1956)
06/06/75 10:00 AM *Gorilla at Large* (1954)

07/10/75 10:00 AM *The Day the Earth Stood Still* (1951)
08/12/75 1:00 PM *Dorian Gray* (1970)
09/18/75 10:00 AM *Forbidden Planet* (1956)
10/04/75 1:00 PM *The Night the World Exploded* (1957)
10/10/75 9:30 PM *The Day the Earth Stood Still* (1951)
10/28/75 1:00 PM *20 Million Miles to Earth* (1957)
11/30/75 2:00 PM *Circus of Horrors* (1960)
03/12/76 1:00 PM *Gorilla At Large* (1954)
04/17/76 1:00 PM *Strangler of the Swamp* (1946)
05/19/76 10:00 AM *House of Wax* (1953)
05/31/76 10:00 AM *U.F.O.* (1956)
05/31/76 9:00 PM *Creature with the Atom Brain* (1955)
06/04/76 9:00 PM *Assignment: Outer Space* (1960)
06/07/76 9:00 PM *Beyond the Time Barrier* (1960)
06/08/76 9:00 PM *Circus of Horrors* (1960)
06/09/76 9:00 PM *Journey to the Seventh Planet* (1962)
06/10/76 9:00 PM *Konga* (1961)
06/11/76 9:00 PM *The Phantom Planet* (1961)
06/15/76 9:00 PM *Mothra* (1961)
06/16/76 10:00 AM *Burn, Witch, Burn* (1962)
06/16/76 9:00 PM *12 to the Moon* (1960)
06/17/76 9:00 PM *The Giant Claw* (1957)
06/18/76 9:00 PM *Battle in Outer Space* (1959)
06/21/76 9:00 PM *The Angry Red Planet* (1959)
06/22/76 9:00 PM *Attack of the Mushroom People* (1963)
06/23/76 9:00 PM *Battle Beyond the Sun* (1963)
06/24/76 9:00 PM *Invasion of the Saucer Men* (1957)
06/25/76 9:00 PM *Dr. Orloff's Monster* (1964)
06/26/76 1:00 PM *The Undying Monster* (1942)
06/28/76 9:00 PM *The Brain That Wouldn't Die* (1962)
06/29/76 9:00 PM *The Blancheville Monster* (1963)
06/30/76 9:00 PM *I Was a Teenage Werewolf* (1957)
07/01/76 9:00 PM *Space Monster* (1965)
07/02/76 9:00 PM *Curse of the Demon* (1957)
07/03/76 1:00 PM *Valley of the Zombies* (1946)
07/05/76 9:00 PM *It's Alive!* (1969)
07/06/76 9:00 PM *Attack of the Puppet People* (1958)
07/07/76 9:00 PM *The Beast with a Million Eyes* (1955)
07/09/76 9:00 PM *The Day the Earth Stood Still* (1951)
07/19/76 9:00 PM *The Quatermass Xperiment* (1955)
07/20/76 9:00 PM *The Magnetic Monster* (1953)
07/21/76 9:00 PM *Gog* (1954)
07/22/76 9:00 PM *Unearthly Stranger* (1963)
07/26/76 9:00 PM *Queen of Blood* (1966)
07/27/76 9:00 PM *Voyage to the Prehistoric Planet* (1965)
07/28/76 9:00 PM *Planet of the Vampires* (1965)
07/29/76 10:00 AM *Black Sabbath* (1963)
07/29/76 9:00 PM *Die, Monster, Die* (1965)
07/30/76 9:00 PM *Attack of the Robots* (1966)
08/02/76 9:00 PM *Beast of Morocco* (1966)
08/04/76 9:00 PM *The Time Travelers* (1964)
08/05/76 9:00 PM *The Lost World* (1960)
08/06/76 9:00 PM *Monster from a Prehistoric Planet* (1967)
08/09/76 9:00 PM *Godzilla vs. The Thing* (1964)
08/10/76 9:00 PM *War of the Monsters* (1966)
08/11/76 9:00 PM *Ghidorah, the Three-Headed Monster* (1964)
08/12/76 9:00 PM *Riders to the Stars* (1954)
08/13/76 9:00 PM *In the Year 2889* (1967)

09/28/76 1:00 PM *The Maze* (1953)
11/05/76 9:00 PM *Planet of the Apes* (1968)
11/12/76 9:00 PM *Beneath the Planet of the Apes* (1970)
12/31/76 9:00 PM *The Hound of the Baskervilles* (1959)
04/02/77 1:30 PM *Two Lost Worlds* (1951)
08/06/77 12:00 PM *Ghidorah, the Three-Headed Monster* (1964)
08/13/77 12:00 PM *The Lost World* (1960)
11/05/77 9:00 PM *Hush…Hush, Sweet Charlotte* (1964)
11/14/77 9:00 PM *Planet of the Apes* (1968)
11/15/77 9:00 PM *Beneath the Planet of the Apes* (1970)
11/16/77 9:00 PM *Escape from the Planet of the Apes* (1971)
11/17/77 9:00 PM *Conquest of the Planet of the Apes* (1972)
11/18/77 9:00 PM *Battle for the Planet of the Apes* (1973)
11/19/77 12:00 PM *Journey to the Center of the Earth* (1959)
11/23/77 9:00 PM *Voyage to the Bottom of the Sea* (1961)
12/14/77 11:30 PM *X the Unknown* (1956)
12/16/77 9:00 PM *The Fly* (1958)
12/19/77 1:00 PM *Dorian Gray* (1970)
12/21/77 1:00 PM *Tam Lin* (1970)
12/24/77 1:15 PM *The Time Travelers* (1964)
12/25/77 11:30 PM *The Hound of the Baskervilles* (1959)
01/13/78 1:00 PM *The Day the Earth Stood Still* (1951)
01/18/78 11:30 PM *Phantom of the Rue Morgue* (1954)
01/24/78 11:30 PM *The Beast from 20,000 Fathoms* (1953)
03/03/78 9:00 PM *Them!* (1954)
05/13/78 9:00 AM *The Bowery Boys Meet the Monsters* (1954)
06/13/79 9:00 PM *The Fly* (1958)
06/14/78 11:30 PM *The Woman in White* (1948)
06/27/78 9:00 PM *House of Wax* (1953)
07/03/78 9:00 PM *The Creeping Terror* (1964)
07/04/78 9:00 PM *The Castle of Fu Manchu* (1969)
07/05/78 9:00 PM *Attack of the Mushroom People* (1963)
07/06/78 9:00 PM *The Vampire* (1957)
07/07/78 9:00 PM *Horrors of the Black Museum* (1959)
07/10/78 9:00 PM *Dracula vs. Frankenstein* (1971)
07/11/78 9:00 PM *The Crimson Cult* (1968)
07/12/78 9:00 PM *Blood and Lace* (1971)
07/13/78 9:00 PM *Assignment Terror* (1970)
07/14/78 9:00 PM *The Navy vs. the Night Monsters* (1966)
07/17/78 9:00 PM *Graveyard of Horror* (1971)
07/18/78 9:00 PM *The Clones* (1973)
07/19/78 9:00 PM *Blood Mania* (1970)
07/20/78 9:00 PM *First Spaceship on Venus* (1960)
07/21/78 9:00 PM *Dracula's Castle* (1969)
07/25/78 9:00 PM *Vampire Circus* (1972)
07/26/78 9:00 PM *Countess Dracula* (1971)
07/27/78 9:00 PM *Crucible of Terror* (1971)
07/28/78 9:00 PM *Horror Express* (1972)
09/20/78 11:30 PM *The Lost World* (1960)
10/27/78 11:30 PM *The Hound of the Baskervilles* (1959)
11/02/78 9:00 PM *The Other* (1972)
11/13/78 9:00 PM *The Legend of Hell House* (1973)
12/02/78 9:00 AM *Master Minds* (1949)
01/12/79 9:00 PM *The Brotherhood of Satan* (1971)
01/19/79 1:00 PM *X the Unknown* (1956)
02/08/79 9:00 PM *Planet of the Apes* (1968)
02/08/79 11:30 PM *What Ever Happened to Baby Jane?* (1962)
02/09/79 9:00 PM *Beneath the Planet of the Apes* (1970)

02/15/79 11:30 PM *Hush...Hush, Sweet Charlotte* (1964)
02/16/79 9:00 PM *Battle for the Planet of the Apes* (1973)
02/17/79 9:00 PM *Rosemary's Baby* (1968)
02/23/79 1:00 PM *Voyage to the Bottom of the Sea* (1961)
02/23/79 9:00 PM *Escape from the Planet of the Apes* (1971)
03/02/79 9:00 PM *Conquest of the Planet of the Apes* (1972)
04/03/79 11:30 PM *The Bamboo Saucer* (1968)
04/14/79 9:00 AM *The Bowery Boys Meet the Monsters* (1954)
04/30/79 11:30 PM *Them!* (1954)
05/18/79 11:30 PM *Let's Scare Jessica to Death* (1971)
06/04/79 11:30 PM *The Astro-Zombies* (1968)
06/05/79 1:00 PM *The Maze* (1953)
06/05/79 11:30 PM *Creature with the Blue Hand* (1967)
06/06/79 11:30 PM *The Crimson Cult* (1968)
06/07/79 11:30 PM *Deathmaster* (1972)
06/08/79 1:00 PM *The Bamboo Saucer* (1968)
06/08/79 11:30 PM *Countess Dracula* (1971)
06/11/79 11:30 PM *Horror House* (1969)
06/12/79 11:30 PM *The Incredible 2-Headed Transplant* (1971)
06/13/79 11:30 PM *Blood Mania* (1970)
06/14/79 11:30 PM *Nightmare in Wax* (1969)
06/15/79 11:30 PM *Dracula vs. Frankenstein* (1971)
06/18/79 9:00 PM *Tam Lin* (1970)
06/18/79 11:30 PM *Point of Terror* (1971)
06/19/79 11:30 PM *Stanley* (1972)
06/20/79 11:30 PM *Terrified* (1963)
06/21/79 11:30 PM *Theatre of Death* (1967)
06/22/79 11:30 PM *Frankenstein's Bloody Terror* (1968)
06/23/79 12:30 PM *The Night the World Exploded* (1957)
06/25/79 11:30 PM *Twisted Brain* (1973)
06/26/79 11:30 PM *The Terror* (1963)
06/27/79 11:30 PM *Blood and Lace* (1971)
06/28/79 11:30 PM *The Bloody Judge* (1970)
06/29/79 1:00 PM *Unknown Island* (1948)
07/05/79 11:30 PM *Dorian Gray* (1970)
08/02/79 1:00 PM *House of Wax* (1953)
09/03/79 11:30 PM *Invisible Agent* (1942)
09/04/79 11:30 PM *The Invisible Man* (1933)
09/06/79 11:30 PM *The H-Man* (1959)
09/07/79 11:30 PM *12 to the Moon* (1960)
09/10/79 11:30 PM *The Ghost of Frankenstein* (1942)
09/11/79 11:30 PM *House of Horrors* (1946)
09/13/79 11:30 PM *The Day of the Triffids* (1963)
09/14/79 11:30 PM *20 Million Miles to Earth* (1957)
09/17/79 11:30 PM *My Son, The Vampire* (1952)
09/19/79 11:30 PM *First Spaceship on Venus* (1960)
09/20/79 11:30 PM *Night of Terror* (1933)
09/21/79 11:30 PM *The Invisible Ray* (1936)
09/24/79 11:30 PM *Earth vs. the Flying Saucers* (1956)
09/25/79 11:30 PM *Crucible of Terror* (1971)
09/26/79 11:30 PM *X the Unknown* (1956)
09/27/79 11:30 PM *The Invisible Woman* (1940)
09/28/79 11:30 PM *The Day the Earth Stood Still* (1951)
11/12/79 9:00 PM *What Ever Happened to Aunt Alice?* (1969)
11/29/79 1:00 PM *The Legend of Hell House* (1974)
01/17/80 1:00 PM *The Brotherhood of Satan* (1971)
01/18/80 11:30 PM *Voyage to the Bottom of the Sea* (1961)
02/05/80 1:00 PM *Phase IV* (1974)

02/07/80 1:00 PM *Let's Scare Jessica to Death* (1971)
02/21/80 11:30 PM *Rosemary's Baby* (1968)
03/21/80 11:30 PM *Them!* (1954)
05/07/80 11:30 PM *The Other* (1972)
05/13/80 11:30 PM *The Legend of Hell House* (1974)
05/29/80 11:30 PM *Journey to the Center of the Earth* (1959)
08/08/80 9:00 PM *Planet of the Apes* (1968)
08/15/80 9:00 PM *Escape from the Planet of the Apes* (1971)
08/22/80 1:00 PM *The Gamma People* (1956)
08/22/80 9:00 PM *Beneath the Planet of the Apes* (1970)
08/28/80 9:00 PM *Battle for the Planet of the Apes* (1973)
08/29/80 9:00 PM *Conquest of the Planet of the Apes* (1972)
09/04/80 11:30 PM *Dr. Jekyll and Mr. Hyde* (1941)
09/16/80 11:30 PM *Night Must Fall* (1964)
09/21/80 11:30 PM *The Hound of the Baskervilles* (1939)
10/17/80 9:00 PM *The Picture of Dorian Gray* (1945)
11/30/80 11:30 PM *The Hound of the Baskervilles* (1939)
12/02/80 11:30 PM *What Ever Happened to Baby Jane?* (1962)
01/01/81 1:00 PM *Journey to the Center of the Earth* (1959)
02/07/81 9:00 PM *Rosemary's Baby* (1968)
04/17/81 1:00 PM *X the Unknown* (1956)
06/14/81 11:30 PM *The Hound of the Baskervilles* (1939)
08/07/81 1:00 PM *The Baby* (1973)
08/15/81 12:30 PM *Return of the Fly* (1959)
09/25/81 1:00 PM *Night Must Fall* (1964)
10/12/81 1:00 PM *What Ever Happened to Aunt Alice?* (1969)
12/10/81 1:00 PM *The Picture of Dorian Gray* (1945)
01/09/82 9:00 AM *Planet of the Apes* (1968)
01/27/82 11:30 PM *The Other* (1972)
02/06/82 12:00 PM *Battle for the Planet of the Apes* (1973)
02/13/82 12:00 PM *Beneath the Planet of the Apes* (1970)
02/24/82 1:00 PM *Phase IV* (1974)
02/27/82 9:00 AM *Conquest of the Planet of the Apes* (1972)
03/13/82 12:00 PM *The Beast from 20,000 Fathoms* (1953)
03/23/82 1:00 PM *Let's Scare Jessica to Death* (1971)
05/01/82 12:00 PM *Escape from the Planet of the Apes* (1971)
07/05/82 9:00 PM *Blood Mania* (1970)
07/07/82 9:00 PM *The Spectre of Edgar Allan Poe* (1974)
07/08/82 9:00 PM *Demons of the Mind* (1972)
07/09/82 9:00 PM *Dracula's Castle* (1969)
07/12/82 9:00 PM *Nightmare in Wax* (1969)
07/13/82 9:00 PM *Point of Terror* (1971)
07/14/82 9:00 PM *Terrified* (1963)
07/15/82 9:00 PM *Theatre of Death* (1967)
07/16/82 9:00 PM *Stanley* (1972)
07/19/82 9:00 PM *The Curse of the Werewolf* (1961)
07/20/82 9:00 PM *Night Creatures* (1962)
07/21/82 9:00 PM *Island of Terror* (1966)
07/22/82 9:00 PM *The Evil of Frankenstein* (1964)
07/23/82 9:00 PM *Dracula vs. Frankenstein* (1971)
07/26/82 9:00 PM *They Saved Hitler's Brain* (1963)
07/27/82 9:00 PM *Agent for H.A.R.M.* (1966)
07/28/82 9:00 PM *The Bloody Judge* (1970)
07/29/82 9:00 PM *Assignment Terror* (1970)
07/30/82 9:00 PM *The Phantom of the Opera* (1962)
09/05/82 12:30 PM *What Ever Happened to Aunt Alice?* (1969)
09/10/82 1:00 PM *Dr. Jekyll and Mr. Hyde* (1941)
09/15/82 11:30 PM *Rosemary's Baby* (1968)

09/21/82 1:00 PM *Let's Scare Jessica to Death* (1971)
09/27/82 12:00 AM *Phase IV* (1974)
10/08/82 12:00 AM *Conquest of the Planet of the Apes* (1972)
10/19/82 9:00 PM *The Other* (1972)
10/30/82 9:00 PM *Friday the 13th* (1980)
11/01/82 12:00 AM *Friday the 13th* (1980)
11/05/82 12:00 AM *Battle for the Planet of the Apes* (1973)
12/10/82 9:00 PM *Escape from the Planet of the Apes* (1971)
02/22/83 1:00 PM *Let's Scare Jessica to Death* (1971)
05/06/83 9:00 PM *Beneath the Planet of the Apes* (1970)
05/09/83 9:00 PM *Planet of the Apes* (1968)
06/03/83 9:00 PM *The Fan* (1981)
06/06/83 9:00 PM *The Legend of Hell House* (1973)
06/06/83 11:30 PM *The Fan* (1981)
06/16/83 1:00 PM *Return of the Fly* (1959)
07/09/83 9:00 AM *Them!* (1954)
08/04/83 12:30 AM *Blood Mania* (1970)
08/08/83 12:30 AM *The Phantom of the Opera* (1962)
08/09/83 12:30 AM *Theatre of Death* (1967)
08/12/83 12:30 AM *The Devil's Hand* (1961)
08/15/83 12:30 AM *The Projected Man* (1966)
08/16/83 12:30 AM *Twisted Brain* (1973)
08/17/83 12:30 AM *Terrified* (1963)
08/18/83 1:00 PM *Agent for H.A.R.M.* (1966)
08/18/83 12:30 AM *First Spaceship on Venus* (1960)
08/19/83 12:30 AM *The Creeping Terror* (1964)
08/22/83 1:00 PM *Let's Scare Jessica to Death* (1971)
08/23/83 12:30 AM *Varan the Unbelievable* (1962)
08/24/83 12:30 AM *Point of Terror* (1971)
08/25/83 12:30 AM *Plan 9 From Outer Space* (1959)
08/26/83 12:30 AM *Nightmare in Wax* (1969)
08/30/83 12:30 AM *The Night Walker* (1964)
09/01/83 12:30 AM *They Saved Hitler's Brain* (1963)
09/02/83 12:30 AM *Stanley* (1972)
10/01/83 12:00 PM *Beneath the Planet of the Apes* (1970)
10/29/83 9:00 PM *Friday the 13th Part 2* (1981)
10/31/83 12:30 AM *Friday the 13th Part 2* (1981)
11/12/83 9:00 AM *Curse of the Fly* (1965)
12/17/83 9:00 AM *The Legend of Hell House* (1973)
01/11/84 9:00 PM *The Nutty Professor* (1963)
02/02/84 9:00 PM *Crack in the World* (1965)
02/09/84 12:30 AM *Carrie* (1976)
02/19/84 1:00 AM *The Swarm* (1978)
02/21/84 9:00 PM *The War of the Worlds* (1953)
03/17/84 9:00 AM *Planet of the Apes* (1968)
03/20/84 9:00 PM *The Picture of Dorian Gray* (1945)
03/24/84 9:00 AM *Escape from the Planet of the Apes* (1971)
03/31/84 9:00 AM *Battle for the Planet of the Apes* (1973)
04/07/84 12:00 PM *Dr. Jekyll and Mr. Hyde* (1941)
05/21/84 1:00 PM *Night Must Fall* (1964)
06/17/84 1:00 AM *The Omen* (1976)
06/24/84 1:00 AM *Dressed to Kill* (1980)
07/05/84 12:45 AM *Tower of London* (1962)
07/22/84 1:00 AM *Dracula* (1979)
07/24/84 1:00 PM *The Legend of Hell House* (1973)
08/03/84 1:00 PM *The Devil's Hand* (1961)
08/04/84 12:00 PM *Graveyard of Horror* (1971)
08/05/84 1:00 AM *The Changeling* (1980)

08/06/84 12:30 AM *Killer Fish* (1979)
08/09/84 1:00 PM *The Creeping Terror* (1964)
08/10/84 9:00 PM *Mystery of the Wax Museum* (1933)
08/13/84 9:00 PM *Equinox* (1970)
08/13/84 12:30 AM *Horror House* (1969)
08/14/84 9:00 PM *Assignment Terror* (1970)
08/15/84 9:00 PM *The Astro-Zombies* (1968)
08/17/84 1:00 PM *Conquest of the Planet of the Apes* (1972)
08/17/84 9:00 PM *The Hound of the Baskervilles* (1959)
08/17/84 12:30 AM *Theatre of Death* (1967)
08/23/84 12:30 AM *Blood Mania* (1970)
08/24/84 12:30 AM *Dracula's Castle* (1969)
08/27/84 1:00 PM *Terrified* (1963)
08/27/84 9:00 PM *The Crimson Cult* (1968)
08/27/84 12:30 AM *The Bloody Judge* (1970)
08/28/84 1:00 PM *Plan 9 From Outer Space* (1959)
08/28/84 9:00 PM *Deathmaster* (1972)
08/29/84 9:00 PM *Dracula vs. Frankenstein* (1971)
08/30/84 9:00 PM *Creature with the Blue Hand* (1967)
08/30/84 12:30 AM *Nightmare in Wax* (1969)
08/31/84 9:00 PM *Frankenstein's Bloody Terror* (1968)
09/05/84 1:00 PM *The Medusa Touch* (1978)
09/09/84 1:00 AM *Point of Terror* (1971)
10/27/84 9:00 PM *The Legend of Hell House* (1973)
11/05/84 1:00 AM *What Ever Happened to Aunt Alice?* (1969)
11/14/84 1:00 AM *Blood Mania* (1970)
11/24/84 10:00 AM *Curse of the Fly* (1965)
01/17/85 9:00 PM *The Medusa Touch* (1978)
01/30/85 9:00 PM *Killer Fish* (1979)
03/06/85 1:00 AM *The Nutty Professor* (1963)
03/07/85 9:00 PM *A Stranger is Watching* (1982)
03/09/85 12:00 PM *A Stranger is Watching* (1982)
04/06/85 10:00 AM *Conquest of Space* (1955)
04/19/85 1:00 AM *The War of the Worlds* (1953)
05/07/85 1:00 AM *Beneath the Planet of the Apes* (1970)
05/27/85 1:00 AM *Escape from the Planet of the Apes* (1971)
06/22/85 10:00 AM *When Worlds Collide* (1951)
07/06/85 10:00 AM *Tower of London* (1962)
07/31/85 1:00 PM *The Legend of Hell House* (1973)
08/02/85 8:00 PM *Planet of the Apes* (1968)
08/13/85 1:00 PM *Psycho* (1960)
08/30/85 1:00 PM *Fahrenheit 451* (1966)
09/15/85 12:30 AM *The Nutty Professor* (1963)
09/25/85 8:00 PM *The Picture of Dorian Gray* (1945)
10/02/85 8:00 PM *Psycho* (1960)
10/25/85 1:00 AM *Halloween II* (1981)
10/29/85 8:00 PM *Mystery on Monster Island* (1981)
10/31/85 8:00 PM *Halloween II* (1981)
11/01/85 8:00 PM *Damien: Omen II* (1978)
11/12/85 1:00 AM *The Medusa Touch* (1978)
11/25/85 8:00 PM *Saturn 3* (1980)
11/27/85 8:00 PM *The Day the Earth Stood Still* (1951)
11/29/85 8:00 PM *The War of the Worlds* (1953)
12/03/85 1:00 AM *The Picture of Dorian Gray* (1945)
12/23/85 1:00 PM *Killer Fish* (1979)
12/26/85 1:00 PM *Saturn 3* (1980)
12/26/85 3:00 AM *Saturn 3* (1980)
01/12/86 3:00 PM *The War of the Worlds* (1953)

01/12/86 1:55 AM *The War of the Worlds* (1953)
01/25/86 12:00 PM *Crack in the World* (1965)
02/07/86 8:00 PM *Strange Invaders* (1983)
03/03/86 1:00 PM *What Ever Happened to Aunt Alice?* (1969)
03/18/86 8:00 PM *Colossus: The Forbin Project* (1970)
04/02/86 8:00 PM *Ghost Story* (1981)
04/06/86 3:00 PM *Ghost Story* (1981)
04/20/86 11:30 PM *Psycho* (1960)
06/12/86 8:00 PM *Bluebeard* (1972)
06/14/86 12:00 PM *Bluebeard* (1972)
06/20/86 9:00 PM *Frankenstein Conquers the World* (1965)
06/28/86 12:00 PM *The Power* (1968)
07/01/86 8:00 PM *Piranha II: The Spawning* (1981)
07/02/86 8:00 PM *Cat People* (1982)
07/03/86 1:00 PM *Mystery on Monster Island* (1981)
07/03/86 1:15 AM *Piranha II: The Spawning* (1981)
07/05/86 10:00 AM *Cat People* (1982)
07/27/86 3:00 PM *The Day the Earth Stood Still* (1951)
07/27/86 2:45 AM *The Day the Earth Stood Still* (1951)
08/02/86 12:00 PM *The Omen* (1976)
09/02/86 1:00 AM *Dr. Jekyll and Mr. Hyde* (1941)
09/06/86 9:00 PM *Monster Zero* (1965)
09/08/86 8:00 PM *Games* (1967)
09/18/86 8:00 PM *The War of the Worlds* (1953)
10/15/86 8:00 PM *The Legend of Hell House* (1973)
10/21/86 12:00 AM *A Reflection of Fear* (1972)
10/29/86 8:00 PM *Amityville: The Demon* (1983)
10/30/86 8:00 PM *The Omen* (1976)
10/31/86 8:00 PM *Damien: Omen II* (1978)
11/01/86 9:00 PM *Psycho* (1960)
11/12/86 12:00 AM *Don't Look Now* (1973)
11/29/86 9:00 PM *Godzilla vs. The Thing* (1964)
12/01/86 8:00 PM *The Mephisto Waltz* (1971)
12/26/86 1:00 PM *Scared Stiff* (1953)
12/26/86 3:00 AM *Scared Stiff* (1953)
01/20/87 8:00 PM *Strange Invaders* (1983)
02/01/87 1:00 AM *Scared Stiff* (1953)
02/10/87 12:00 AM *Ruby* (1977)
02/11/87 8:00 PM *Soylent Green* (1973)
02/15/87 12:00 PM *The Nutty Professor* (1963)
02/16/87 12:00 AM *The Two Faces of Dr. Jekyll* (1961)
03/09/87 8:00 PM *Planet of the Apes* (1968)
03/10/87 8:00 PM *Beneath the Planet of the Apes* (1970)
03/11/87 8:00 PM *Escape from the Planet of the Apes* (1971)
03/12/87 8:00 PM *Conquest of the Planet of the Apes* (1972)
03/13/87 8:00 PM *Battle for the Planet of the Apes* (1973)
03/27/87 8:00 PM *The Deadly Bees* (1967)
03/27/87 1:00 AM *Don't Look Now* (1973)
03/29/87 1:00 AM *Die! Die! My Darling* (1965)
04/06/87 8:00 PM *Death Ship* (1980)
04/07/87 8:00 PM *Kingdom of the Spiders* (1977)
04/08/87 8:00 PM *The Changeling* (1980)
04/09/87 8:00 PM *Son of Frankenstein* (1939)
04/10/87 8:00 PM *Nightmare in Wax* (1969)
04/20/87 1:00 PM *The Nutty Professor* (1963)
04/29/87 8:00 PM *Psycho* (1960)
05/13/87 12:00 AM *Westworld* (1973)
05/15/87 1:00 AM *Saturn 3* (1980)

06/03/87 12:00 AM *Beneath the Planet of the Apes* (1970)
07/08/87 8:00 PM *Firestarter* (1984)
07/12/87 2:00 PM *Firestarter* (1984)
07/14/87 8:00 PM *Westworld* (1973)
07/22/87 1:00 PM *A Reflection of Fear* (1972)
08/07/87 1:30 AM *The Other* (1972)
08/17/87 12:30 AM *Crack in the World* (1965)
09/01/87 1:00 PM *The Collector* (1965)
09/01/87 12:30 AM *The Old Dark House* (1963)
09/05/87 1:30 AM *The Colossus of New York* (1958)

Channel 50
Date   Time   Title   Year
12/17/86 9:00 PM *What Ever Happened to Aunt Alice?* (1969)
12/31/86 7:00 PM *The Lost World* (1960)
12/31/86 9:00 PM *Humanoids from the Deep* (1980)
02/13/87 1:00 AM *They Came from Within* (1975)
03/15/87 8:00 PM *The Changeling* (1980)
05/05/87 1:00 PM *Three Cases of Murder* (1953)
05/26/87 1:30 AM *The Vampire Lovers* (1970)
05/28/87 1:30 AM *Jennifer* (1978)
06/11/87 7:00 PM *The Hound of the Baskervilles* (1978)
06/18/87 4:00 PM *Phantom of the Paradise* (1974)
06/22/87 9:00 PM *Things to Come* (1936)
06/25/87 12:30 PM *The Psychic* (1977)
07/10/87 4:00 PM *The Lost World* (1960)
07/24/87 4:00 PM *Willard* (1971)
07/24/87 7:00 PM *Uncle Was a Vampire* (1959)
08/10/87 12:30 AM *Mako: Jaws of Death* (1976)
08/17/87 9:00 PM *A Boy and His Dog* (1975)
08/19/87 9:00 PM *Night of the Living Dead* (1968)
08/20/87 9:00 PM *Invasion of the Body Snatchers* (1956)
08/21/87 9:00 PM *The Conqueror Worm* (1968)
08/26/87 7:00 PM *Whoever Slew Auntie Roo?* (1972)

Channel 54
Date   Time   Title   Year
10/08/82 8:00 AM *Doctor X* (1932)
10/13/82 8:00 AM *The Mad Genius* (1931)
11/08/82 5:00 PM *Hush…Hush Sweet Charlotte* (1964)
11/09/82 8:00 AM *The Walking Dead* (1936)
11/22/82 5:00 PM *Dark Star* (1974)
11/23/82 5:00 PM *Voyage to the Bottom of the Sea* (1961)
11/24/82 5:00 PM *Invaders from Mars* (1953)
12/15/82 8:00 AM *Doctor X* (1932)
01/03/83 5:00 PM *Gorgo* (1961)
01/05/83 5:00 PM *The Fabulous World of Jules Verne* (1958)
01/06/83 5:00 PM *The Mysterians* (1957)
01/07/83 5:00 PM *From the Earth to the Moon* (1958)
02/10/83 8:00 AM *Svengali* (1931)
02/26/83 12:00 PM *Things to Come* (1936)
02/27/83 12:30 PM *Black Dragons* (1942)
03/31/83 8:00 AM *The Mad Genius* (1931)
04/12/83 8:00 AM *The Walking Dead* (1936)
05/30/83 5:00 PM *Invaders from Mars* (1953)
05/31/83 8:00 AM *The Devil Doll* (1936)
05/31/83 5:00 PM *Gorgo* (1961)
06/01/83 5:00 PM *Voyage to the Bottom of the Sea* (1961)

06/02/83 5:00 PM *The Mysterians* (1957)
06/07/83 8:00 AM *Svengali* (1931)
06/20/83 8:00 AM *The Unholy Three* (1930)
06/21/83 8:00 AM *The Mask of Fu Manchu* (1932)
06/22/83 8:00 AM *Mad Love* (1935)
06/23/83 8:00 AM *Mark of the Vampire* (1935)
07/21/83 5:00 PM *Hush…Hush Sweet Charlotte* (1964)
09/11/83 1:30 PM *The Mask of Fu Manchu* (1932)
09/18/83 1:30 PM *Dr. Cyclops* (1940)
10/31/83 5:00 PM *Night of the Living Dead* (1968)
11/01/83 5:00 PM *The Bubble* (1966)
11/03/83 5:00 PM *Things to Come* (1936)
11/04/83 5:00 PM *The Devil Doll* (1936)
12/09/83 5:00 PM *The Uninvited* (1944)
02/27/84 5:30 PM *The Unholy Three* (1930)
02/28/84 5:30 PM *The Mask of Fu Manchu* (1932)
02/29/84 5:30 PM *Mad Love* (1935)
03/01/84 5:30 PM *Mark of the Vampire* (1935)
03/02/84 5:30 PM *Dr. Cyclops* (1940)
03/16/84 5:30 PM *Island of Lost Souls* (1933)
03/19/84 9:00 AM *The Woman in White* (1948)
04/10/84 9:00 AM *The Uninvited* (1944)
06/12/84 5:00 PM *Kongo* (1932)
06/25/84 5:00 PM *The Alien Factor* (1978)
06/28/84 5:00 PM *No Survivors Please.* (1964)
07/06/84 5:00 PM *The Innocents* (1961)
07/07/84 1:00 PM *The Alien Factor* (1978)
07/11/84 9:00 AM *The Innocents* (1961)
07/14/84 1:00 PM *The Lucifer Complex* (1978)
07/21/84 1:00 PM *The Fabulous World of Jules Verne* (1958)
07/22/84 1:30 PM *The Devil Doll* (1936)
07/28/84 1:30 PM *Gorgo* (1961)
08/04/84 1:00 PM *The Bubble* (1966)
08/11/84 1:00 PM *From the Earth to the Moon* (1958)
08/13/84 9:00 AM *The Woman in White* (1948)
08/18/84 1:00 PM *Kong Island* (1968)
08/25/84 1:00 PM *Star Pilot* (1966)
08/27/84 5:00 PM *The Fabulous World of Jules Verne* (1958)
08/28/84 5:00 PM *Invaders from Mars* (1953)
08/29/84 5:00 PM *The Fly* (1958)
08/30/84 5:00 PM *Dark Star* (1974)
09/01/84 1:00 PM *From the Earth to the Moon* (1958)
09/15/84 1:00 PM *Voyage to the Bottom of the Sea* (1961)
09/22/84 1:00 PM *Gorgo* (1961)
12/03/84 12:00 PM *Hush…Hush Sweet Charlotte* (1964)
12/30/84 1:00 PM *Dr. Cyclops* (1940)
12/30/84 2:30 PM *The Mask of Fu Manchu* (1932)
01/01/85 12:00 PM *Night of the Living Dead* (1968)
01/27/85 1:00 PM *Fantastic Voyage* (1966)
02/12/85 9:00 AM *Kongo* (1932)
03/18/85 12:00 PM *The Mysterians* (1957)
03/20/85 12:00 PM *The Uninvited* (1944)
03/25/85 9:00 AM *The Innocents* (1961)
06/13/85 12:00 PM *Kong Island* (1968)
06/16/85 1:00 PM *Mad Love* (1935)
08/13/85 12:00 PM *Gorgo* (1961)
08/14/85 9:00 AM *Dr. Cyclops* (1940)
08/14/85 12:00 PM *No Survivors Please.* (1964)
08/15/85 12:00 PM *The Eyes Behind the Stars* (1978)
08/16/85 9:00 AM *Island of Lost Souls* (1933)
08/16/85 12:00 PM *The Lucifer Complex* (1978)
08/22/85 12:00 PM *The Devil Doll* (1936)
09/01/85 1:00 PM *Voyage to the Bottom of the Sea* (1961)
09/15/85 1:00 PM *Invaders from Mars* (1953)
09/29/85 1:00 PM *Fantastic Voyage* (1966)
10/02/85 12:00 PM *Hush…Hush, Sweet Charlotte* (1964)
10/13/85 1:00 PM *Sisters* (1973)
10/27/85 1:00 PM *Futureworld* (1976)
10/31/85 9:00 AM *Old Dracula* (1974)
11/10/85 1:00 PM *Ben* (1972)
11/24/85 1:00 PM *The Abominable Dr. Phibes* (1971)
12/22/85 1:00 PM *The Food of the Gods* (1976)
01/05/86 1:00 PM *Frogs* (1972)
01/12/86 1:00 PM *The Island of Dr. Moreau* (1977)
01/19/86 1:00 PM *Dr. Phibes Rises Again* (1972)
01/21/86 9:00 AM *The Fly* (1958)
02/23/86 1:00 PM *Tentacles* (1977)
03/02/86 1:00 PM *The Little Girl Who Lives Down the Lane* (1976)
03/09/86 1:00 PM *The Premature Burial* (1962)
03/24/86 8:00 PM *Squirm* (1976)
04/12/86 1:00 PM *The Attic* (1980)
04/19/86 1:00 PM *Futureworld* (1976)
04/26/86 1:00 PM *Fantastic Voyage* (1966)
04/28/86 8:00 PM *Journey to the Center of the Earth* (1959)
04/29/86 8:00 PM *The Lost World* (1960)
04/30/86 8:00 PM *The Land that Time Forgot* (1974)
05/01/86 8:00 PM *The Island of Dr. Moreau* (1977)
05/01/86 11:30 PM *Old Dracula* (1974)
05/05/86 8:00 PM *The Amityville Horror* (1979)
05/06/86 8:00 PM *Dressed to Kill* (1980)
05/08/86 8:00 PM *Sisters* (1973)
05/10/86 1:00 PM *Empire of the Ants* (1977)
05/12/86 8:00 PM *Phantasm* (1979)
05/13/86 8:00 PM *Hell Night* (1981)
05/14/86 8:00 PM *Terror Train* (1980)
05/15/86 8:00 PM *Prom Night* (1980)
05/16/86 8:00 PM *Godzilla 1985* (1984)
06/03/86 12:00 PM *Old Dracula* (1974)
06/07/86 1:00 PM *Gorgo* (1961)
06/09/86 8:00 PM *Asylum* (1972)
06/18/86 11:30 AM *The Woman in White* (1948)

06/20/86 11:30 AM *Hangover Square* (1945)
06/25/86 8:00 PM *At the Earth's Core* (1976)
06/28/86 1:00 PM *The Vengeance of Fu Manchu* (1967)
07/10/86 8:00 PM *Hush…Hush, Sweet Charlotte* (1964)
07/19/86 1:00 PM *Prisoners of the Lost Universe* (1983)
07/22/86 12:00 PM *The Woman in White* (1948)
07/23/86 12:00 PM *Hangover Square* (1945)
08/02/86 1:00 PM *Warriors of the Wasteland* (1983)
08/09/86 1:30 PM *The Mask of Fu Manchu* (1932)
08/23/86 1:30 PM *The Alien Factor* (1978)
08/30/86 1:00 PM *Dracula A.D. 1972* (1972)
09/06/86 1:00 PM *Kong Island* (1968)
09/12/86 11:30 PM *The Uninvited* (1944)
09/13/86 1:00 PM *The Eyes Behind the Stars* (1978)
10/13/86 12:00 PM *The Uninvited* (1944)
10/19/86 1:00 PM *THX 1138* (1971)
10/20/86 8:00 PM *Friday the 13th* (1980)
10/21/86 8:00 PM *The Entity* (1982)
10/22/86 8:00 PM *The Haunting* (1963)
10/23/86 8:00 PM *The Beast Must Die!* (1974)
10/24/86 8:00 PM *Ben* (1972)
10/28/86 8:00 PM *Night of the Living Dead* (1968)
10/29/86 8:00 PM *Friday the 13th: Part 2* (1981)
10/30/86 8:00 PM *The Howling* (1981)
10/31/86 8:00 PM *Halloween II* (1981)
11/14/86 8:00 PM *Young Frankenstein* (1974)
11/18/86 8:00 PM *Invasion of the Body Snatchers* (1978)
11/19/86 8:00 PM *Forbidden Planet* (1956)
01/02/87 8:00 PM *Phantom of the Paradise* (1974)
03/30/87 9:00 AM *Doctor X* (1932)
03/31/87 9:00 AM *The Mask of Fu Manchu* (1932)
04/01/87 9:00 AM *Mad Love* (1935)
04/02/87 9:00 AM *Mark of the Vampire* (1935)
04/03/87 9:00 AM *Svengali* (1931)
04/23/87 8:00 PM *The Reincarnation of Peter Proud* (1975)
04/24/87 8:00 PM *At the Earth's Core* (1976)
04/26/87 1:00 PM *Holocaust 2000* (1977)
05/01/87 8:00 PM *Bug* (1975)
05/18/87 8:00 PM *Terror Train* (1980)
05/19/87 8:00 PM *The Boogeyman* (1980)
05/20/87 8:00 PM *My Bloody Valentine* (1981)
05/21/87 8:00 PM *Phantasm* (1979)
05/22/87 8:00 PM *The Texas Chain Saw Massacre* (1974)
05/27/87 8:00 PM *Dressed to Kill* (1980)
05/30/87 8:00 PM *Fortress* (1985)
05/31/87 3:00 PM *Voyage to the Bottom of the Sea* (1961)
06/06/87 1:00 PM *The Alien Factor* (1978)
06/12/87 8:00 PM *Fortress* (1985)
06/13/87 1:00 PM *Fortress* (1985)
06/27/87 1:00 PM *Invaders from Mars* (1953)
07/13/87 8:00 PM *Ghoulies* (1984)
07/14/87 8:00 PM *The Fog* (1980)
07/15/87 8:00 PM *Demon Seed* (1977)
07/16/87 8:00 PM *Creature* (1985)
07/17/87 8:00 PM *Prom Night* (1980)

Channel 67

<u>Date   Time   Title   Year</u>
08/04/73 8:00 PM *The Monster* (1925)
09/08/73 8:00 PM *The Unholy Three* (1925)
09/22/73 8:00 PM *West of Zanzibar* (1929)
05/04/74 8:00 PM *The Monster* (1925)
06/08/74 8:00 PM *The Unholy Three* (1925)
06/22/74 8:00 PM *West of Zanzibar* (1929)
01/16/75 9:00 PM *Ugetsu* (1953)

Chapter 9

Life After September 5, 1987
Final Memories, Thoughts and Reflections

One more horror host should be mentioned, although he was *not* a home-grown entity, so to speak. *Morgus Presents*, featuring Morgus the Magnificent, aired *very* briefly on WBFF Channel 45 at 6:00 p.m. on Saturday evenings. Unlike the previous hosts, however, Morgus' material was not filmed locally but was instead a syndication pickup. Approximately half an hour of host material was provided to subscribing stations, who could then present it with a program of their own choosing. Channel 45 went with several Universal classics.

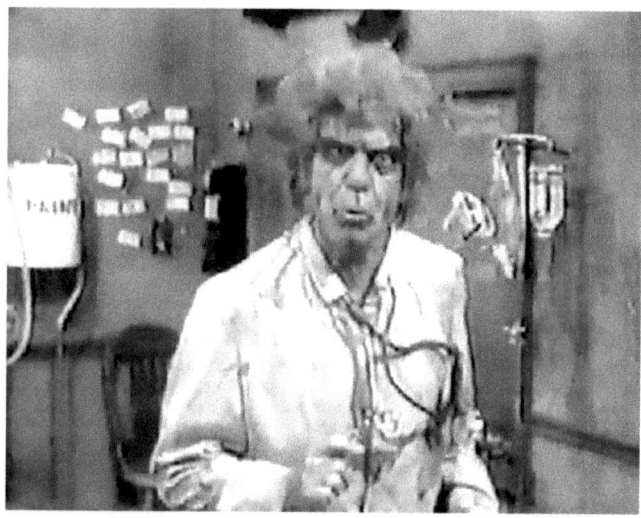

Morgus made a brief appearance on Baltimore air waves.

Louisiana disc jockey Sidney Noel Rideau (1929-2020) created Morgus in 1959 for the *House of Shock* program, which debuted January 3 on WWL-TV Channel 4 in New Orleans. Each week, along with six-foot-seven masked assistant Chopsley, Morgus attempted some doomed experiment ("Get your notebooks ready."), such as trying to cure baldness, convert criminals to model citizens, or preserve life through near-instant organ replacements. Always popular in his hometown, Morgus branched out in the late 1980s into other markets, including Maryland.

Unfortunately, the disheveled, stained-lab-coat-wearing Morgus never caught on in Charm City. Part of the problem may have been publicity, or complete lack thereof. There were no adverts for the show in *TV Guide* or *The Baltimore Sun*. TV listings did not point out Morgus was even hosting. In fact, when Channel 45 general manager Bruce Lumpkin discussed fall programing with *The Evening Sun* columnist Steve McKerrow for an August 31, 1988, article, Lumpkin did not even mention that the upcoming Saturday "rubber monster movies" were going to be hosted! So much for promotion. It was quite by accident that this viewer even discovered Morgus, which was a result of seeing a listing for *Son of Dracula* and wanting to tape it. And there was Morgus. A few weeks later, however, he had vanished, which makes his final show rather appropriate: it was *The Invisible Man*. Below is a believed-to-be complete filmography of *Morgus Presents* showings in the Baltimore-Washington era.

10/01/88 *Creature from the Black Lagoon* (1954)
10/08/88 *The Creature Walks Among Us* (1956)
10/15/88 *Cult of the Cobra* (1955)
10/22/88 *It Came from Outer Space* (1953)
10/29/88 *Frankenstein* (1931)
11/05/88 *Bride of Frankenstein* (1935)
11/12/88 *Dracula* (1931)
11/19/88 *The Wolf Man* (1941)
11/26/88 *Frankenstein Meets the Wolf Man* (1943)
12/03/88 *Son of Dracula* (1943)
12/10/88 *House of Frankenstein* (1944)
12/17/88 *The Mummy* (1932)
12/24/88 *The Invisible Man* (1933)

Looking back, the Horror Host era can be summed up by stealing from one of the most famous novel openings in history: "It was the best of times; it was the worst of times…" To address the second assertion first: the viewer did not have the kind of power or control he or she has today. There were no VCRS, no cable television, no DVRS, no streaming; the viewer was at the mercy of the programmers. If you wanted to watch something, you had to be there in front of your set or wait until the next showing. Even if you did manage to sneak downstairs for the 1:00 a.m. weeknight showing of a favorite, you could still be disappointed thanks to a last-minute program change. In short: the stations had you where they wanted you. Thankfully, we didn't know any better at the time. It was the way it was. And while no one would want to go back to the time of edited features, un-skippable commercials, battered prints, and inconvenient airtimes, some of us are thankful for the era when the edited, interrupted, late-night airings were presided over by local talent dressed up for Halloween each week.

However, the pressure of having to be in front of your TV set at a specific time made the viewing something special. One looked forward to the show. There was anticipation as you went through your ritual: gather your snacks, adjust the antenna, darken the room if you were brave enough, and find that comfortable spot. The weekly ritual made it memorable. Today, we have too much flexibility and this negates the "specialness" of it.

It *was*, in many ways however, the best of times. The amount of horror and sci-fi movies shown regularly is staggering when one compares it to the wasteland of genre fare airing today. It's practically nonexistent. Look at the TV listings for a typical Friday or Saturday night and you will be shocked and horrified for all the wrong reasons. Where did our horror movies go? If you are lucky enough to get digital substation MeTV, you can at least watch Svengoolie (Richard Koz) every Saturday night. Otherwise, odds are, you are out of luck, unless you have built a personal library of favorites from which to choose. That's not a bad thing though, right? Well…

In the earlier days of the medium, with only a handful of channels at one's disposal, you might be forced to take a chance on something you wouldn't otherwise have watched. Imagine, you are in the mood to sit in front of your television set, but all the dramas and sitcoms either are repeats or not up your alley. The independent stations however have several movie choices to offer. You read the descriptions in the TV listings and decide to take a chance. Before the film is over, you have discovered a new actor you admire, a new genre you are curious about, or a new favorite movie. These "accidental discoveries" are how most of us pre-cable, etc. viewers became fans. We took chances. (It was either that or read a book.)

This approach to home viewing no longer exists. There are *too many* choices, too many options. There is no incentive to give some old film a chance because classic films have been relegated to the likes of Turner Classic Movies, and TCM cannot possibly show *everything*. If you are a young person curious about *Frankenstein*, you had better hope an older person will buy or rent it for you, or at least tape it *if* it does air during October. In short: there is no active mechanism in place to create young horror fans; they are at the mercy of not only the programmers, but the grownups too. And when *these* grownups were kids, it was around the time horror hosts were leaving the airwaves as stations made changes to compete with the ever evolving and growing cable and home video markets. How can we aging classic horror fans be replaced by new ones, and keep the love of these films alive, if there is so little exposure?

> **㊺ Ghost Host Double Feature.**
> "Curse of the Demon." (1957).
> **⑤ Metromedia Movie.**
> "Send Me No Flowers." (1964).
> **⑦ Saturday Movie 7.**
> "Ocean's 11." (1960). Frank Sinatra, Dean Martin,
> **⑨ Saturday Night Late Show.**
> "El Condor." (1970). Jim Brown,
> **⑯ WBOC-TV Late, Movie.**
> "The Catered Affair." (1956).
> **⑳ Creature Feature.**
> "The Incredible Two-Headed Transplant." (1971). Bruce Dern,

And that's why this period *was* the best of times. On February 25, 1978, for example, you could watch a *Ghost Host* double feature of *Curse of the Demon* and *Terror in the Crypt* starting at 11:30 p.m., and then catch *The Curse of the Cat People* at 3:20 a.m. on Channel 13's *Late Late Show*. On the other hand, you could alternatively view *Creature Feature*'s 11:30 p.m. presentation of *The Incredible 2-Headed Transplant*. (Hey, it has its charms.) Good luck finding such an eclectic collection of options today.

Thankfully, though, in this age of nostalgia and everything-old-is-new-again, the horror host phenomena of the *Shock!* era has been, and continues to be, documented both nationally and locally in the form of books, blogs, websites, and documentaries. Count Gore De Vol continues to host *Creature Feature: The Weekly Web Program*. Svengoolie can be seen every Saturday night. What footage that does exist of our favorite horror hosts can be found and sometimes purchased online. YouTube is a goldmine of horror host segments, even if the gold tends to be blurry and distorted. And of course, a lion's share of the films we watched all those years ago can be rented, streamed, or purchased in near-perfect audio and visual presentations. But viewing these films in all their glory on our home theater systems isn't quite the same as stretching out (or curling up) on the floor in front of our parents' television set, awaiting with joy and dread the arrival of our favorite host and what they had to offer. Even better, you could then chat about your experience with like-minded friends the next school day. Sharing such experiences on modern day message boards is not quite the same thing as a face-to-face exchange.

Even more impressive is that the hosts *inspired* their young viewers, some of whom grew up to become actors, directors, writers, or horror hosts themselves. Count Gore watched Chicago's Marvin in the 1950s. Author Gregory William Mank, whose body of work includes such important works as *It's Alive! The Classic Cinema Saga of Frankenstein* and *Bela Lugosi and Boris Karloff: The Story of a Haunting Collaboration*, viewed Dr. Lucifer. The youthful experiences of these viewers followed them into adulthood, compelling them to share their memories by continuing to celebrate the genre in creative ways. Not a bad accomplishment for local performers who most likely never imagined their efforts would go noticed beyond their broadcast area.

Yes, these horror host years were the best of times. It's no wonder we want to remember the hosts and to thank the people who helped create them…*whatever* they were.

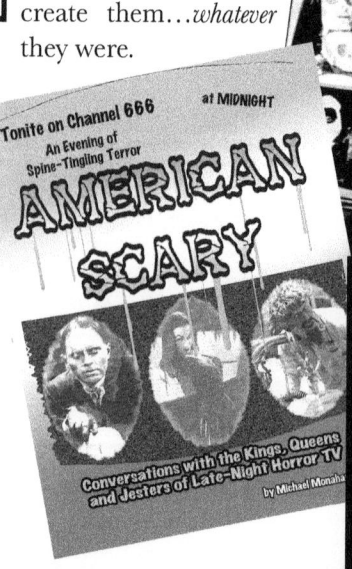
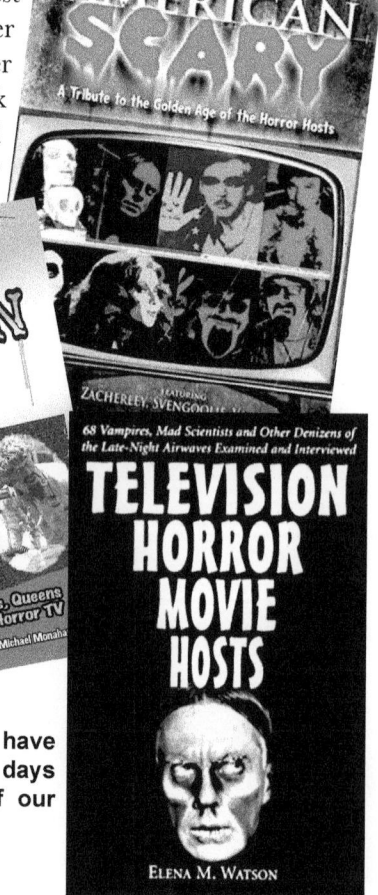

Many mags and books have not forgotten the glory days of the horror hosts of our youth.

Chapter 10

Baltimore Horror Film Fandom

Luckily for horror fiends, Baltimore is under a cloud of weirdness that rivals any city in the world. Movies, books, magazines and conventions help feed the monster kids' quest to find horror films on TV. Here is a list of Baltimore's finest things that go bump in the night.

Film Conventions

FANEX Film Festival (1984-2003)

FANEX became a meeting ground for classic horror/sci-fi/fantasy film fans to spend a weekend with like-minded people and indulge in movies, panels, guests from classic genre films and often ice cream sundaes. The guest list was amazing and many of the stars and filmmakers from the previous horror hosts lists were guests—and they actually enjoyed meeting their fans. The following is a list of guests who appeared in Baltimore (or Crystal City for two shows) and their genre credits. If you would like to know all the credits of FANEX guests, you'll have to look them up on IMDB. They were all working actors and filmmakers with many, many credits—Westerns, dramas, musicals, film noir, mysteries and lots of television—including *Thriller*, *Star Trek*, *One Step Beyond* and *Twilight Zone*. To see many of the guest talks visit FANEX YouTube Channel at https://www.youtube.com/channel/UCOqz6MA2kIVNs-xW1S_aa8Q

FANEX 1
September 1987
Really small, about 80 people showed up—which made the staff of volunteers thrilled.
Greg Mank: local film historian
Bill Littman: local film historian did the Emergo show from William Castle's House on Haunted Hill
Rick Shanklin: local comic shop owner/author
Gary J. Svehla: publisher/editor of Midnight Marquee

FANEX 2
November 1988
John Agar (FANEX's first movie star!) John and his wife Loretta were so lovely and really enjoyed meeting their fans. FANEX 2 was the beginning of a "beautiful friendship" between FANEX and Fred Olen Ray (who only missed one show) & Ted Bohus. Fred helped FANEX get many guests and Fred and Ted gamely hosted our charity auctions, awards shows, the Ed Wood Awards at Monster Rally and other kindnesses too many to mention.

John Agar signs autographs at FANEX 2

Guests
John Agar (1921-2002)
The Vampire Hunters Club (2001)
The Naked Monster (2005)
Body Bags (1993)
Nightbreed (1990)
Fear (1990)
Miracle Mile (1988)
Attack of the B Movie Monsters (1985)
King Kong (1976)
Curse of the Swamp Creature (1968)
Night Fright (1967)
Zontar: The Thing from Venus (1967)
Women of the Prehistoric Planet (1966)
Journey to the Seventh Planet (1962)
Hand of Death (1962)
Invisible Invaders (1959)
Destination Space (1959)
Attack of the Puppet People (1958)
Daughter of Dr. Jekyll (1957)
The Brain from Planet Arous (1957)
The Mole People (1956)

Revenge of the Creature (1955)
Tarantula (1955)
The Rocket Man (1954)
Adventure in Baltimore (1949, not a genre film, but hey it's Baltimore)

Ted Bohus (b. 1952-)
Destination Fame (2012 Video) (co-director)
Vampire Vixens from Venus (1995)
Regenerated Man (1994)
Fantastic Film Show (1991 Video)

Ted Bohus and Ernie Farino show off one of Ernie's models.

Ernie Farino (b. 1954-)
Emmy Award-winning SPFX artist who got his start on Baltimore's *The Alien Factor*

The Adventures of Sharkboy and Lavagirl 3-D (2005)
Children of Dune (2003, TV mini-series, won Emmy)
Dune (2000, TV mini-series, won Emmy)
From the Earth to the Moon (1998, TV mini-series, nominated for Emmy)
Snow White: A Tale of Terror (1997)
Screamers (1995)
Tales from the Darkside (1990)
Cyborg (1989)
The Abyss (1989)
Lady in White (1988)
Dead Heat (1988)
The Lost Empire (1984)
Dreamscape (1984)
The Dungeonmaster (1984)
The Terminator (1984)
Spacehunter: Adventures in the Forbidden Zone (1983)
The Thing (1982)
Nightbeast (1982)
Slapstick of Another King (1982)
Saturday the 14th (1981)
Galaxy of Terror (1981)
The Alien Factor (1978)

Fred Olen Ray (b. 1954-) Director/Writer
Stage Fright (TV Movie) (2017)
Abner, the Invisible Dog (2013)
Dirty Blondes from Beyond 2012, (TV Movie) (as Nicholas Medina)
Super Shark (2011)
Sexual Witchcraft (2011, TV Movie) (as Nicholas Juan Medina)
Bikini Time Machine (2011, TV Movie) (as Nicholas Juan Medina)
Housewives from Another World (2010, Video) (as Nicholas Medina)
Bikini Jones and the Temple of Eros (2010, TV Movie) (as Nicholas Medina)
Twilight Vamps (2010, Video)
Bikini Frankenstein (2010, Video) (as Nicholas Medina)
Dire Wolf (2009)
Voodoo Dollz (2008, TV Movie) (as Nicholas Medina)
Solar Flare (2008)
The Girl from B.I.K.I.N.I. (2007, Video) (as Nicholas Medina)
Girl with the Sex-Ray Eyes (2007, TV Movie) (as Nicholas Medina)
Super Ninja Doll (2007, TV Movie) (as Nicholas Medina)
Bewitched Housewives (2007, TV Movie) (as Nicholas Medina)
Bikini Girls from the Lost Planet (2006, Video) (as Nicholas Medina)
Ghost in a Teeny Bikini (2006, Video) (as Nicholas Medina)
Teenage Cavegirl (2004, Video) (as Nicholas Medina)
Tomb of the Werewolf (2004, Video)
Haunting Desires (2004, TV Movie) (as Nicholas Medina)
Thirteen Erotic Ghosts (2002) (as Nicholas Medina)
Venomous (2001, Video) (as Ed Raymond)
Invisible Mom II (1999, Video)
The Kid with X-ray Eyes (1999, Video) (as Sherman Scott)
Prophet (1999, Video) (as Ed Raymond)
Billy Frankenstein (1998)
Mom's Outta Sight (1998) (as Peter Stewart)
Mom, Can I Keep Her? (1998, Video)
Little Miss Magic (1998)
Invisible Dad (1998, Video)
Hybrid (1997, Video)
Invisible Mom (1996, Video)
Star Hunter (1996, Video) (as Sherman Scott)
Witch Academy (1995)
Droid Gunner (1995)
Attack of the 60 Foot Centerfolds (1995)
Bikini Drive-in (1995)
Inner Sanctum II (1994)
Possessed by the Night (1994, Video)
Dinosaur Island (1994)
Mind Twister (1993)
Evil Toons (1992)
Scream Queen Hot Tub Party (1991, Video) (as Bill Carson)
Inner Sanctum (1991)
Wizards of the Demon Sword (1991)
Bad Girls from Mars (1990)
Spirits (1990)
Haunting Fear (1990, Video)
Alienator (1990)
Beverly Hills Vamp (1989)
Warlords Vamp (1988)

The Phantom Empire (1988, Video)
Deep Space (1988)
Hollywood Chainsaw Hookers (1988)
Evil Spawn (1987, uncredited)
Cyclone (1987)
Star Slammer (1986)
The Tomb (1986)
Grave's End (1985, co-director)
Biohazard (1985)
Scalps (1983)
The Alien Dead (1980)
The Brain Leeches (1978)

Jay Schlossberg-Cohen
Producer/Director/Maryland Film Commissioner
Night Train to Terror (1985)

Sam Sherman (b. 1940-) Producer
Beyond This Earth (2020, executive producer)
Bloody Slumber Party (2014, consulting producer)
Drive-in Madness! (1987, Documentary) (producer)
Cinderella 2000 (1977, executive producer)
Terror of Frankenstein (1977, executive producer)
Dracula vs. Frankenstein (1971, producer—uncredited)
Brain of Blood (1971, producer)
Satan's Sadists (1969, producer)
Blood of Ghastly Horror (1967, associate producer)

Dawn Wildsmith (b. 1963-)
Lake of Shadows (1995)
Jack-O (1995)
Wizards of the Demon Sword (1991)
Empire of the Dark (1990)
Alienator (1990)
Future Force (1989)
Beverly Hills Vamp (1989)
Warlords (1988)
The Phantom Empire (1988, Video)
Deep Space (1988)
Hollywood Chainsaw Hookers (1988)
Evil Spawn (1987)
Surf Nazis Must Die (1987)
Cyclone (1987)
It's Alive III: Island of the Alive (1987)
Star Slammer (1986)
The Tomb (1986)
Evils of the Night (1985)

FANEX 3
September, 1989

Jeff Morrow! He didn't have the most genre credits—but what he had were top drawer!

Guests
Forrest J Ackerman (1916-2008)
Editor *Famous Monsters* magazine
Ted Bohus (see FANEX 2)

Conrad Brooks (1931-2017)
Conrad, who lived in Western Maryland attended most shows.
Night of the Ghouls (1959)
Plan 9 from Outer Space (1957)
Bride of the Monster (1955)

Dave DeCoteau (b. 1962-) Director
Asian Ghost Story (2016)
Sorority Slaughterhouse (2016)
The Pit and the Pendulum (2009)
Alien Presence (2009)
House of Usher (2008)
Frankenstein & the Werewolf Reborn (2005)
Possessed (2005)
Prison of the Dead (2000)
Voodoo Academy (2000)
Ancient Evil: Scream of the Mummy (1999)
Teenage Alien Avengers (1999)
Frankenstein Reborn (1998)
Prehysteria! 3 (1995)
Beach Babes from Beyond (1995) (as Ellen Cabot)
Test Tube Teens from the Year 2000 (1994, Video) (as Ellen Cabot)
Beach Babes from Beyond (1993) (as Ellen Cabot)
Puppet Master III: Toulon's Revenge (1991, Video)
Dr. Alien (1989)
Sorority Babes in the Slimeball Bowl-O-Rama (1988)
Nightmare Sisters (1988)
Creepozoids (1987)

Anna Karen (1914-2009)
Did mostly TV work. Married to Jeff Morrow
Lights Out (1950-1951).
One Step Beyond (1960)
Star Trek (1969)
Project UFO (1978)

Jeff Morrow (1907-1993)
As far as we know, FANEX was the only convention Jeff Morrow ever attended—he didn't make many genre films, but

Left to Right: Ted Bohus, Brinke Stevens, Jeff Morrow, Fred Olen Ray and HFFS member Ellie Green.

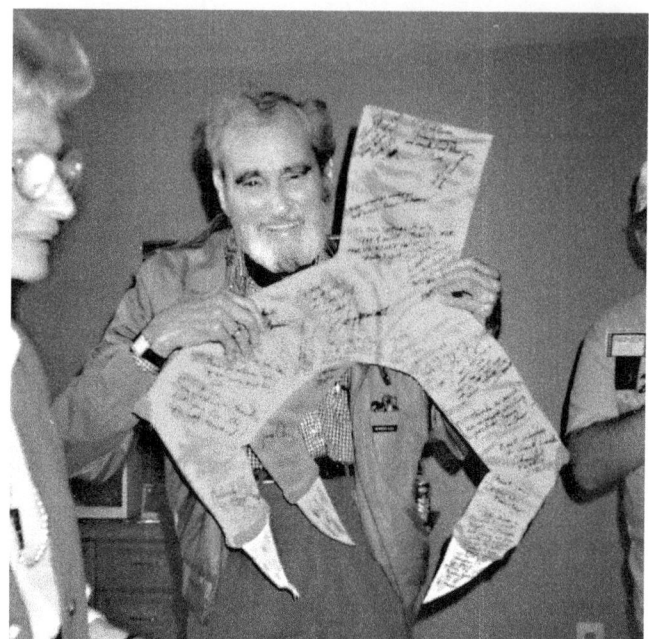
Jeff Morrow laughs at the Giant Claw autographed by members of the FANEX 3 staff.

boy he picked the best (*The Giant Claw* the exception, but still lots of fun).
Octaman (1971)
The Giant Claw (1957)
Kronos (1957)
The Creature Walks Among Us (1956)
This Island Earth (1955)

Linnea Quigley (b. 1958-)
Triassic Hunt (2021)
The Good Things Devils Do (2020)
Clownado (2019)
Hooker with a Hacksaw (2017)
Cabaret Diabolique (2015)
Girls Gone Dead (2012)
Beach Babes from Beyond (1993)
Innocent Blood (1992)
Nightmare Sisters (1988)
Night of the Demons (1988)
Hollywood Chainsaw Hookers (1988)
Sorority Babes in the Slimeball Bowl-O-Rama (1988)
Creepozoids (1987)
The Return of the Living Dead (1985)
Silent Night, Deadly Night (1984)

Fred Olen Ray (see FANEX 2)

Brinke Stevens (b. 1954-)
It Wants Blood (2019)
RoboWoman (2019)
Meathook Massacre 4 (2018)
Psychosomatika (2010)
The Naked Monster (2005)
Sideshow (2000)
Mom, Can I Keep Her? (1998)
Mommy (1995)
Scream Queen Hot Tub Party (1991)
Teenage Exorcist (1991)
Sorority Babes in the Slimeball Bowl-O-Rama (1988)
Slave Girls from Beyond Infinity (1987)

FANEX 4
August 1990

We couldn't believe the king of SPFX was coming to FANEX!

Guests
Ted Bohus and **Fred Olen Ray** (see FANEX 2)

Veronica Carlson (1944-2022)
Veronica Carlson became a well-loved guest at FANEX and returned many times. She was as beautiful inside as outside.
House of the Gorgon (2019)
Stellar Quasar and the Scrolls of Dadelia (2016)
Freakshow (1995)
Black Easter (1994)
The Ghoul (1975)
Old Dracula (1974)
The Horror of Frankenstein (1970)
The Ghost Who Saved the Bank at Monte Carlo (1969)
Frankenstein Must Be Destroyed (1969)
The Double Death of Charlie Crippen (1969)
Dracula Has Risen from the Grave (1968)

Ray Harryhausen (1920-2013)
Clash of the Titans (1981)
Sinbad and the Eye of the Tiger (1977)
The Golden Voyage of Sinbad (1973)
The Valley of Gwangi (1969)
One Million Years B.C. (1966)
First Men in the Moon (1964)
Jason and the Argonauts (1963)
Mysterious Island (1961)

Ray Harryhausen displays his work at FANEX 4.

The 3 Worlds of Gulliver (1960)
The 7th Voyage of Sinbad (1958)
20 Million Miles to Earth (1957)
Earth vs. the Flying Saucers (1956, special photographic effects—uncredited) (technical effects created by)
It Came from Beneath the Sea (1955, visual effects—uncredited)
The Beast from 20,000 Fathoms (1953)
Mighty Joe Young (1949, technician—uncredited)

Mike Jittlov (b. 1948-)
Special effects wizard who became a legend at sci-fi conventions. His animation in commercials would make Harryhausen proud.
The Wizard of Speed and Time (1988)

Elizabeth Russell (1916-2002)
What a time we had tracking down this Val Lewton actress, we think FANEX was her only convention appearance.
Bedlam (1946)
The Curse of the Cat People (1944)
Weird Woman (1944)
The Uninvited (1944)
A Scream in the Dark (1943)
The Seventh Victim (1943)
Hitler's Madman (1943)
Cat People (1942)
The Corpse Vanishes (1942)

FANEX 5
August 1991

Guests
Forrest J Ackerman (see FANEX 3)

John Agar (see FANEX 2)

Ted Bohus and **Fred Olen Ray** (see FANEX 2)

William K. Everson (1929-1996) Author and Film Historian

Lisa Gaye (b. 1960-)
Local Baltimore Girl and Troma Star
Shakespeare's Sh*tstorm (2020)
Return to Nuke 'Em High Volume 1 (2013)
Citizen Toxie: The Toxic Avenger IV (2000)
Terror Firmer (1999)
Class of Nuke 'Em High Part 3: The Good, the Bad and the Subhumanoid (1994)
State of Mind (1994)
Class of Nuke 'Em High Part II: Subhumanoid Meltdown (1991)
Sgt. Kabukiman N.Y.P.D. (1990)
The Toxic Avenger Part III: The Last Temptation of Toxie (1989)
The Toxic Avenger Part II (1989)

Richard Gordon (1925-2011) Producer
Horrorplanet (1981)
The Cat and the Canary (1978)
Horror Hospital (1973)
Tower of Evil (1972)
Bizarre (1970)
Island of Terror (1966, executive producer—uncredited)
The Projected Man (1966, producer—uncredited)
Naked Evil (1966, executive producer—uncredited)
Voodoo Blood Death (1965, producer)
Devil Doll (1964, executive producer—uncredited)
The Playgirls and the Vampire (1960, executive producer)
First Man Into Space (1959, executive producer—uncredited)
Corridors of Blood (1958, executive producer—uncredited)
Fiend Without a Face (1958 executive producer—uncredited)
The Haunted Strangler (1958, executive producer—uncredited)
The Electronic Monster (1958 executive producer—uncredited)

Count Gore De Vol (b. 1947-) *Creature Feature* Host (Dick Dyszel), see Chapter 6, page 78)
Revenge of the Devil Bat (2020)
Monster Movie Night: Yule Scaremas Special (2016, TV Movie)
The Dead Matter (2010)
Raising the Stakes (2005)
Crawler (2004, Video)
Chainsaw Sally (2004
Countess Dracula's Orgy of Blood (2004, Video)
Stakes (2002, Video)
The Galaxy Invader (1985, Video)

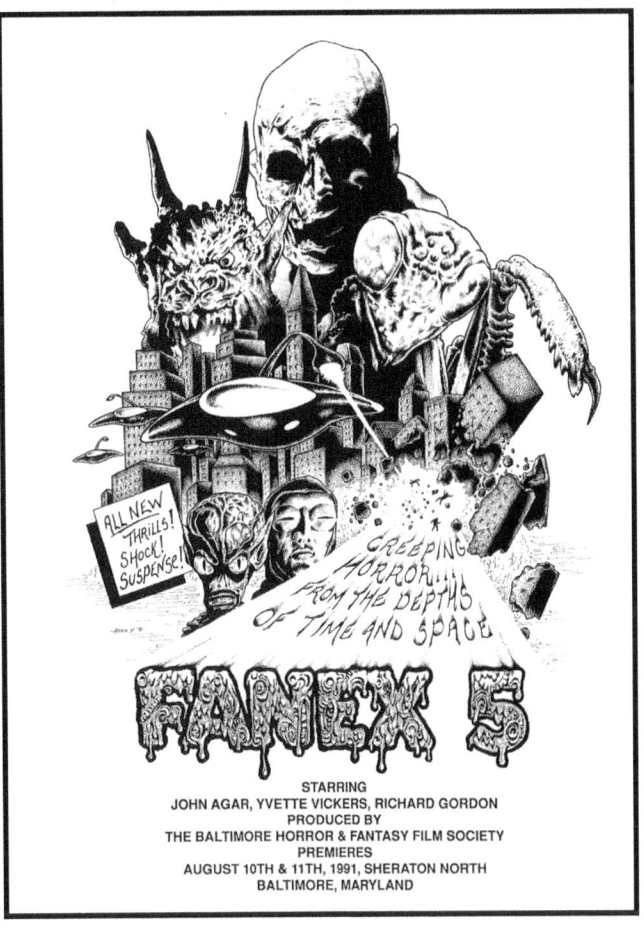

Nightbeast (1982)
The Alien Factor (1978)

Janie Howard Hanky (b. 1948-)
Daughter of Curly Howard

Gus Russo (b. 1950-) Composer: Another Baltimore Boy
Brain Damage (1988)
Basket Case (1982)

Yvette Vickers gave us "Fever!"; Richard Svehla on sax

Yvette Vickers (1928-2010)
Yvette was a sweet soul and truly enjoyed meeting the fans. She did a smoking version of "Fever" at the FANEX Awards.
Evil Spirits (1991)
What's the Matter with Helen? (1971)
Attack of the Giant Leeches (1959)
Attack of the 50 Foot Woman (1958)

FANEX 6
August 1992
FANEX 5 and 6 were so much fun and something attendees will never forget.

Acquanetta (1921-2004)
Lost Continent (1951)
Tarzan and the Leopard Woman (1946)
Dead Man's Eyes (1944)
Jungle Woman (1944)
Captive Wild Woman (1943)

Ted Bohus and **Fred Olen Ray** (see FANEX 2)

Veronica Carlson (See FANEX 4)

Jim Danforth (b. 1940-) SPFX Artist
The Prophecy (1995, matte artist: angel effects and Mesa mattes, Effects Associates, Inc.) (matte photographer: angel effects and Mesa mattes, Effects Associates, Inc.)
Dark Universe (1993, Video) (matte painter)
Body Snatchers (1993, matte artist—uncredited)
Robot Wars (1993, additional stop-motion)
Memoirs of an Invisible Man (1992, matte artist—uncredited) (matte photographer—uncredited) (matte supervisor)
The NeverEnding Story II: The Next Chapter (1990, additional matte paintings: from The NeverEnding Story)
Flatliners (1990, matte artist—uncredited)
Friday the 13th Part VIII: Jason Takes Manhattan (1989, special photographic effects: Effects Associates, Inc.)
DeepStar Six (1989, matte artist) (miniature effects
Prince of Darkness (1987, matte artist—uncredited) (matte painter)
Day of the Dead (1985, matte artist—uncredited) (matte photographer—uncredited)
The Stuff (1985, matte artist)/(miniature photography) (optical effects)
The Ewok Adventure (1984, TV Movie) (matte artist) (matte photographer)
The NeverEnding Story (1984, matte painter: ILM)
Twilight Zone: The Movie (1983, effects photography—uncredited)/(matte artist—uncredited)/(visual effects—segment "4")
Megaforce (1982, matte artist—uncredited)/(matte photographer—uncredited)
The Thing (1982, matte artist—uncredited)
Creepshow (1082, matte artist—uncredited)
Conan the Barbarian (1982, matte artist—uncredited)
Clash of the Titans (1981, animator—uncredited) (assistant to Ray Harryhausen)
Caveman (1981, dinosaur and effects designer—uncredited)
The Day Time Ended (1979, The "City of Light" by) (matte artist—uncredited)/(matte photographer—uncredited)
The Crater Lake Monster (1977, assistant model animator—uncredited)

Russ Tamblyn, Veronica Carlson, Acquanetta, Jim Danforth at FANEX 6

The Reincarnation of Peter Proud 1975, (matte artist—uncredited)
Flesh Gordon (1974, creator: special visual effects—as Mij Htrofnad) (matte artist—uncredited) (stop-motion animator—uncredited)
Dark Star (1974, matte painter—uncredited)
Willy Wonka & the Chocolate Factory (1971, model animator: Wonkavator—uncredited) (optical effects—uncredited)
When Dinosaurs Ruled the Earth (1970, effects cameraman—uncredited)/special visual effects/visual effects designer/director—uncredited)
Equinox (1970, cel animator—uncredited) (matte artist—uncredited)/(special equipment—uncredited) (special photographic effects)
7 Faces of Dr. Lao (1964, special visual effects) (stop-motion animator—uncredited)
The Wonderful World of the Brothers Grimm (1962, stop-motion animator—uncredited) (visual effects technician—uncredited)
Jack the Giant Killer (1962, stop-motion animator—uncredited)
Journey to the Seventh Planet (1962, stop-motion animator: cyclops—uncredited)
Master of the World (1961, miniature maker—uncredited)
Atlantis: The Lost Continent (1961, stop-motion animator—uncredited)
The Time Machine (1960, assistant animator—uncredited) (visual effects assistant—uncredited)

Dan Golden
Director/Producer/Actor

Dances with Werewolves (2017)
Satanic (2006)
The Haunted Sea (1997)

Russ Tamblyn (b. 1934-)
One of the favorite FANEX guests, he was then appearing in Twin Peaks..
Little Miss Magic (1998)
My Ghost Dog (1997)
Attack of the 60 Foot Centerfold (1995)
Wizards of the Demon Sword (1991)
The Bloody Monks (1988)
Necromancer (1988)
The Phantom Empire (1988)
Dracula vs. Frankenstein (1971)
Satan's Sadists (1969)
The War of the Gargantuas (1966)
The Haunting (1963)
The Wonderful World of the Brothers Grimm (1962)
Tom Thumb ((1958)

Nostalgia Vision
February, 1993
Classic TV Convention but let's face it, Beverly Garland and Russell John were 1950s and '60s horror royalty. HFFS members gamely did a version of *Family Feud* with *Star Trek* crew vs. *Gilligan's Island* crew. Russell Johnson roared each time the Mary Ann character said, "coconut cream pies."

**February 26-28, 1993
Baltimore, Maryland**

**Guests of Honor
*Beverly Garland
Russell Johnson***

Richard Dix (d. 1998)
Baltimore Horror Host, Dr. Lucifer

Dick Dyszel Washington D.C. Horror Host
Count Gore De Vol (see FANEX 5)

Beverly Garland (1928-2008)
Twice-Told Tales (1963)
The Alligator People (1959)
Not of This Earth (1957)
Curucu, Beast of the Amazon (1956)
It Conquered the World (1956)
The Rocket Man (1954)
The Neanderthal Man (1953)

Russell Johnson (1924-2014)
Attack of the Crab Monsters (1957)
This Island Earth (1955)
It Came from Outer Space (1953)

George Lewis (1926-2000)
Baltimore Horror Host, The Ghost Host

FANEX 7
July-August 1993
FANEX Goes to the (Bengie's) Drive-In

Ted Bohus and **Fred Olen Ray** (see FANEX 2)

Robert Clarke (1920-2005)
The Naked Monster (2005)
Haunting Fear (1990)

Midnight Movie Massacre (1989)
Frankenstein Island (1981)
Terror of the Bloodhunters (19620
Beyond the Time Barrier (1960)
The Incredible Petrified World (1959)
From the Earth to the Moon (1958, uncredited narrator)
The Hideous Sun Demon (1958)
The Astounding She-Monster (1957)
Captive Women (1952)
The Man from Planet X (1951)
Genius at Work (1946, uncredited radio announcer)
Bedlam (1946, uncredited)
Zombies on Broadway (1945, uncredited)
The Body Snatcher (1945, uncredited)

Sam Sherman (See FANEX 2)

FANEX 8
July 1994

FANEX's first all Hammer Show! All the Hammer guests over the years were the loveliest people.

Guests

James Bernard (1925-2001) Composer
The Legend of the 7 Golden Vampires (1974)
Frankenstein and the Monster from Hell (1974)
Scars of Dracula (1970)
Taste the Blood of Dracula (1970)
Frankenstein Must Be Destroyed (1969)
Dracula Has Risen from the Grave (1968)
The Devil Rides Out (1968)
Torture Garden (1967)
Frankenstein Created Woman (1967)
Dracula: Prince of Darkness (1966)
The Plague of the Zombies (1966)
The Secret of Blood Island (1965)
She (1965)
The Gorgon (1964)
The Kiss of the Vampire (1963)
The Damned (1962)
The Terror of the Tongs (1961)
The Stranglers of Bombay (1959)
The Hound of the Baskervilles (1959)
Horror of Dracula (1958)
Quatermass 2 (1957)
The Curse of Frankenstein (1957)
X the Unknown (1956)
The Quatermass Xperiment (1955)
Nosferatu (1922) (1997, New Original Music)

Martine Beswick (b. 1941-)
Saturnalia (2022)
Cowgirls vs. Pterodactyls (2021)
House of the Gorgon (2019)
Magic Island (1995, Video)
Night of the Scarecrow (1995)
Critters 4 (1992)
Evil Spirits (1991)
Trancers II (1991)
Strange New World (1975)
Dr. Jekyll and Sister Hyde (1971)
Prehistoric Women (1957)
One Million Years B.C. (1966)
Thunderball (1965)

Ted Bohus (see FANEX 2)

Veronica Carlson (see FANEX 4)

Yolande Donlan (1920-2014)
Mr. Drake's Duck (1951)
The Devil Bat (1940)

Val Guest (1911-2006) Writer/Director
When Dinosaurs Ruled the Earth (1970)

The Day the Earth Caught Fire (1961)
The Abominable Snowman (1957)
Quatermass 2 (1957)
The Quatermass Xperiment (1955)
Mr. Drake's Duck (1951

Ingrid Pitt (1937-2010)
Ingrid kept the FANEX staff on their toes!
Minotaur (2006)
The Wicker Man (1973)
The House that Dripped Blood (1971)
Countess Dracula (1971)
The Vampire Lovers (1970)

FANEX 9
July 1995

Such a fun show and what a pleasure to meet William Marshall, and boy was he tall! But still so handsome.

Guests
Jane Adams (1918-2014)
Master Minds (1949)
Batman and Robin (1949)
The Brute Man (1946)
House of Dracula (1945)

Ted Bohus and **Fred Olen Ray** (see FANEX 2)

Richard Gordon (see FANEX 5)

Lucille Lund (1912-2002)
The Black Cat (1934)

William Marshall (1924-2003)
Dinosaur Valley Girls (1996)
Sorceress (1995)
Amazon Women on the Moon (1987)
Abby (1974)
Scream Blacula Scream (1973)
Blacula (1972)
Sabu and the Magic Ring (1957)

Robert Quarry (1925-2009)
Invisible Mom II (1999)
Little Miss Magic (1998)
Inner Sanctum II (1994)
Mind Twister (1993)
Evil Toons (1992)
Teenage Exorcist (1991)
Evil Spirits (1991)
Spirits (1990)
Haunting Fear (1990)
Alienator (1990)
Beverly Hills Vamp (1989)
The Phantom Empire (1988)
Sugar Hill (1974)
Deathmaster (1972)
Dr. Phibes Rises Again (1972)

The Return of Count Yorga (1971)
Count Yorga, Vampire (1970)
Colossus: The Forbin Project (1970, uncredited)

Greta Thyssen (1927-2018)
Journey to the Seventh Planet (1962)
Terror is a Man (1959)

Elena Verdugo (1925-2017)
Day of the Nightmare (1965)
The Frozen Ghost (1945)
House of Frankenstein (1944)

FANEX 10
July 1996

Guests
Forrest J Ackerman (see FANEX 3)

John Agar (see FANEX 2)

Ted Bohus and **Fred Olen Ray** (see FANEX 2)

Robert Clarke (see FANEX 7)

Kathleen Crowley (1929-2017)
Curse of the Undead (1959)
The Flame Barrier (1958)
Target Earth (1954)

Dolores Fuller (1923-2011)
Bride of the Monster (1955)

FANEX 10 GUESTS

John Agar • Robert Clarke • Kathleen Crowley
Dolores Fuller • Linda Harrison • Ann Robinson
William Schallert • Robert Wise • Forrest J Ackerman

Mesa of Lost Women (1953)
Glen or Glenda (1953)

Linda Harrison (1945-)
A local girl born in Berlin, Maryland
Midnight Massacre (2021)
Planet of the Apes (2001)
Cocoon: The Return (1988)
Cocoon (1985)
Beneath the Planet of the Apes (1970)
Planet of the Apes (1968)

Val Lewton, Jr. (1937-2015)
Son of Val Lewton, the RKO legend whose 1940s horror films became the stuff of legend: Cat People, Bedlam, I Walked with a Zombie, The Seventh Victim, and The Body Snatcher insured him an honored place in Horrorwood!

Anne Robinson (1929-)
Began her career as a stuntwoman.
Tales of Frankenstein (2018)
War of the Worlds (2005)
The Naked Monster (2005)
My Lovely Monster (1991)
Midnight Movie Massacre (1989)
Rocky Jones, Space Ranger (1954)
The War of the Worlds (1953)

William Schallert (1922-2016)
William Schallert and Robert Clarke ended up being a horror film star comedy duo! They were so funny together and the audience did not want their talk to end! I didn't note it but Schallert was in the Star Trek fave "The Trouble with Tribbles."
Innerspace (1987)
Gremlins (1984, uncredited)
Twilight Zone: The Movie (1983)
Colossus: The Forbin Project (1970)
The Computer Wore Tennis Shoes (1969)
The Monolith Monsters (1957, uncredited)
The Incredible Shrinking Man (1957)
Them! (1954, uncredited)
Gog (1954)
Captive Women (1952)
Mighty Joe Young (1949, uncredited)

Robert Tinnell (b. 1961-)
Requiem for the Damned (2012)
Surf Nazis Must Die (1987, producer)
Frankenstein and Me (1996)

Robert Wise (1914-2005)
Star Trek: The Motion Picture (1979)
Audrey Rose (1977)
The Andromeda Strain (1971)
The Haunting (1963)
The Day the Earth Stood Still (1951)
The Body Snatcher (1945)
The Curse of the Cat People (1944)

FANEX 11
July 1997
Hammer Has Risen from the Grave, again!

Guests
Ted Bohus and **Fred Olen Ray** (see FANEX 2)

Veronica Carlson (see FANEX 4)

Freddie Francis (1917-2007)
Director/Academy Award-winning Cinematographer
What an amazing guest he was! He filmed the convention with a camera he had just been given by David Lynch.
Dark Tower (1987, as Ken Barnett)
The Doctor and the Devils (1985)
Dune (1984, Photographed by)
The Ghoul (1975)
Legend of the Werewolf (1975)
Tales That Witness Madness (1973)
Son of Dracula (1973)
The Creeping Flesh (1973)
Tales from the Crypt (1972)
The Vampire Happening (1971)
Trog (1970))
Dracula Has Risen from the Grave (1968)
Torture Garden (1967)

PETER CUSHING

Like old Dracula himself, it would seem that Hammer Films are 'un-knockoutable'! - and it is thanks to the likes of you dear people that keeps 'em alive and kicking.

How grateful all old Hammeronians must be, and may the recent revival of that Company give you even more pleasure in the years to come.

From my 'rocking-chair-by-the-fire' I salute you, regretting that the toll taken by eighty-one summers prevents me from being at the Baltimore Convention.

With my kindest wishes, and may God's be with you all always.

In all sincerity,

Peter Cushing, O.B.E.

Veronica Carlson — Yolande Donlan — Freddie Francis
Richard Gordon — Val Guest — Caroline Munro
Mary Peach — Jimmy Sangster — Virginia Wetherell

They Came from Beyond Space (1967)
The Deadly Bees (1966)
The Psychopath (1966)
The Skull (1965)
Hysteria (1965)
Dr. Terror's House of Horrors (1965, as Freddy Francis)
The Evil of Frankenstein (1964, directed by)
Nightmare (1964)
Paranoiac (1963)
Invasion of the Triffids (1963, uncredited)
The Brain (1962)

Richard Gordon ()see FANEX 5)

Val Guest (see FANEX 8)

Caroline Munro (b 1949-)
House of the Gorgon (2019)
Stellar Quasar and the Scrolls of Dadelia (2016)
Vampyres (2015)
Flesh for the Beast (2003)
The Black Cat (1989)
Howl of the Devil (1988)
Slaughter High (1986)
Grave's End (1985)
Don't Open Till Christmas (1984)
The Last Horror Film (1982)
Maniac (1980)

Starcrash (1978)
At the Earth's Core (1976)
Captain Kronos: Vampire Hunter (1974)
The Golden Voyage of Sinbad (1973)
Dr. Phibes Rises Again (1972)
Dracula A.D. 1972 (1972)
The Abominable Dr. Phibes (1971)

Mary Peach (b. 1934-)
Wife of Jimmy Sangster
The Projected Man (1966)
Scrooge (1970)
Cutthroat Island (1995)

Jimmy Sangster (1927-2011) Writer/Director
Fear in the Night (1972, screenplay)
Whoever Slew Auntie Roo? (1972, screenplay)
A Taste of Evil (1971, written by)
The Horror of Frankenstein (1970, screenplay)
Dracula; Prince of Darkness (1966, screenplay as John Sansom)
Hysteria (1965, written by)
Maniac (1963)
Paranoiac (1963, screenplay)
Scream of Fear (1961, written by)
The Terror of the Tongs (1961, written by)
The Brides of Dracula (1960, screenplay)
The Mummy (1959, screenplay)
The Man Who Could Cheat Death (1959, screenplay)
Jack the Ripper (1959, screenplay)
The Crawling Eye (1958, screenplay)
Blood of the Vampire (1958, screenplay)
The Revenge of Frankenstein (1958, written by)
Horror of Dracula (1958, screenplay by)
The Curse of Frankenstein (1957, screenplay)
X the Unknown (1956, screenplay)

Virginia Wetherell (b. 1943-)
Married to Ralph Bates until his death.
Disciple of Death (1972)
Demons of the Mind (1972)
A Clockwork Orange (1971)
Dr Jekyll & Sister Hyde (1971)
The Crimson Cult (1968)

FANEX 12
July 1998

Guests
Ted Bohus and **Fred Olen Ray** (see FANEX 2)

Karolyn Grimes (b. 1940-)
The Bishop's Wife (1947)
It's a Wonderful Life (1946)

Peggy Moran (1918-2002)
Horror Island (1941)
The Mummy's Hand (1940)

Betsy Jones-Moreland (1930-2006)
Creature from the Haunted Sea (1961)
Last Woman on Earth (1960)
The Saga of the Viking Women and Their Voyage to the Waters of the Sea Serpent (1957)

Kevin McCarthy (1914-2010)
Matinee (1993, uncredited)
The 'Burbs (1989, uncredited)
Dark Tower (1987)
Innerspace (1987)
Twilight Zone: The Movie (1983)
The Howling (1981)
Invasion of the Body Snatchers (1978)
Piranha (1978)
Invasion of the Body Snatchers (1956)

Lori Nelson (1933-2020)
The Naked Monster (2005)
Mom, Can I Keep Her? (1998)
Day the World Ended (1955)
Revenge of the Creature (1955)

Mala Powers (1931-2007)
Doomsday Machine (1972)
The Colossus of New York (1958)
The Unknown Terror (1957)

Dee Wallace (b. 1948-)
Ouija House (2018)
Death House (2017)
All Hallow's Eve (2016)
The House of the Devil (2019)

Little Red Devil (2018)
Curse of the Creeps (2006)
The Frighteners (1996)
Invisible Mom (1996)
Alligator II (1991)
Critters (1986)
E.T. (1982)
The Howling (1981)
The Stepford Wives (1975)

For the first 12 years all the FANEX guests signed free autographs. (Although Guest Liaison Barry Murphy had to get down on his hands and knees to beg several of the FANEX 12 guests to sign for free.)

FANEX: Monster Rally
August 1999

Guests
Forrest J Ackerman (see FANEX 3)

Jane Adams (see FANEX 9)

Ted Bohus and **Fred Olen Ray** (see FANEX 2)

Joyce Broughton
Long-time secretary for Peter Cushing

Veronica Carlson (see FANEX 4)

Ron Chaney (b. 1955-)
Son of Lon Chaney, Jr. and Grandson of Lon Chaney

Anne Francis (1930-2011)
The Satan Bug (1965)
Forbidden Planet (1956)
The Rocket Man (1954)
Portrait of Jennie (1948)

Basil Gogos (1939-2017)
Famous Monsters cover artist

Count Gore De Vol (see FANEX 5)

Coleen Gray (1922-2015)
The Phantom Planet (1961)
The Leech Woman (1958)
The Vampire (1957)

Linda Harrison (see FANEX 10)

Ray Harryhausen (see FANEX 4)

Sara Karloff (b. 1938-)
Daughter of Boris Karloff

Ed Kemmer (1920-2004)
The Spider (1958)
Giant from the Unknown (1958)
Space Patrol (1950-1955, Television series with Kemmer staring as Commander Buzz Corry)

Carla Laemmle (1909-2014)
Niece of Universal founder Carl Laemmle
Dracula (1931)
The Phantom of the Opera (1925, uncredited)

Christopher Lee (1922-2015)
Getting Lee's autograph in his autobiography was something the lucky attendees will never forget. Mr. Lee requested that he only sign copies of his book. He was wonderful with his fans and signed his autobio for hours. He would only hint about the upcoming film of his favorite book, *Lord of the Rings*! Lee has 248 credits, so we will just list his best remembered films.
The Hobbit (2012)
Dark Shadows (2012)
Star Wars: The Clone Wars (2008)

FANEX Monster Rally opening ceremony: (left to right) Carla Laemmle, Jane Adams, Elena Verdugo, Christopher Lee, Bela Lugosi, Jr., Victoria Price, Ann Francis, Collen Gray, Ed Kemmer, Rex Reason, Yvette Vickers, Ingrid Pitt, Yutte Stensgaard, Linda Harrison, Ray Harryhausen, Terry Moore, Suzanna Leigh (several guests are behind Christopher Lee). What a night for horror film fans!

Charlie and the Chocolate Factory (2005)
Star Wars III: Revenge of the Sith (2005)
Lord of the Rings (Three films, 2001, 2002, 2003)
Star Wars II: Attack of the Clones (2002)
Gremlins 2: The New Batch (1990)
Howling II (1985)
House of Long Shadows (1983)
Dracula and Son (1976)
To the Devil a Daughter (1976)
The Wicker Man (1973)
The Satanic Rites of Dracula (1973)
The Creeping Flesh (1973)
Horror Express (1972)
Dracula A.D. 1972 (1972)
Scars of Dracula (1970)
Taste the Blood of Dracula (1970)
The Crimson Cult (1968)
Dracula Has Risen from the Grave (1968)
Dracula (1968)
The Devil Rides Out (1968)
The Torture Chamber of Dr. Sadism (1967)
Theatre of Death (1967)
Dracula: Prince of Darkness (1966)
She (1965)
Dr. Terror's House of Horrors (1965)
The Gorgon (1964)
The Castle of the Living Dead (1964)
Crypt of the Vampire (1964)
The Mummy (1959)
Horror of Dracula (1958)
The Curse of Frankenstein (1957)

Susanna Leigh (1945-2017)
Son of Dracula (1973)
Lust for a Vampire (1971)
The Lost Continent (1968)
The Deadly Bees (1966)

Val Lewton, Jr. (see FANEX 10)

Bela Lugosi, Jr. (b. 1938-) Son of Bela Lugosi

Terry Moore (b. 1929-)
Mighty Joe Young (1998)
The Great Rupert (1950)
Mighty Joe Young (1949)

Victoria Price (b. 1962-) Daughter of Vincent Price

Ingrid Pitt (see FANEX 8)

Rex Reason (1928-2015)
The Creature Walks Among Us (1956)
This Island Earth (1955)

Michael Ripper (1913-2000)
British character actor with 244 credits
Dracula Has Risen from the Grave (1968)

The Lost Continent (1968)
Torture Garden (1967)
The Mummy's Shroud (1967)
The Deadly Bees (1966)
Rasputin: The Mad Monk (1966)
The Reptile (1966)
The Plague of the Zombies (1966)
The Curse of the Mummy's Tomb (1964)
Night Creatures (1962)
The Phantom of the Opera (1962)
The Curse of the Werewolf (1961)
The Brides of Dracula (1960)
The Mummy (1959)
The Revenge of Frankenstein (1958)
Quatermass II (1957)
X the Unknown (1956)

Yutte Stensgaard (b. 1946-)
Lust for a Vampire (1971)
Scream and Scream Again (1970)

Bob Tinnell (see FANEX 10)

Elena Verdugo (see FANEX 9)

Yvette Vickers (see FANEX 5)

FANEX Classic Filmfest
July 2000

Guests
Samuel Z. Arkoff (1918-2001)
Producer/Executive Producer
Has 203 credits, we have picked the genre highlights.
The Haunting (1999, executive producer–uncredited)
Q: The Winged Serpent (1982, executive producer— uncredited)
Dressed to Kill 1980 (executive producer—uncredited)
The Amityville Horror (1978, executive producer)
Love at First Bite (1979, executive producer)
The Incredible Melting Man (1977, executive producer— uncredited)
Empire of the Ants (1977, executive producer)
The Island of Dr. Moreau (1977, executive producer)
The People That Time Forgot (1977, executive producer)
Sugar Hill (1974, executive producer)
Scream Blacula Scream (1973, executive producer)
Blacula (1972, executive producer)
Dr. Phibes Rises Again (1972, executive producer)
The Abominable Dr. Phibes (1971, executive producer)
The Dunwich Horror (1970, producer)
Witchfinder General (1968, executive producer–uncredited)
Dr. Goldfoot and the Girl Bombs (1966, executive producer)
Queen of Blood (1966, producer–uncredited)
Planet of the Vampires (1965. executive producer)
The Tomb of Ligeia (1964, producer–uncredited)
The Comedy of Terrors (1963, producer)
The Haunted Palace (1963, executive producer–uncredited)

FANEX Classic Filmfest opening ceremony: (left to right) Pat Hitchcock, Robert Skotak, Linda Harrison, Sam Arkoff, Candace Hilligoss, Ib Melchior, Kevin McCarthy, Betsy Jones-Moreland, Yvonne Monlar, Janet Leigh, Veronica Carlson, Elena Verdugo, Robert Dwan, Jessica Rains, Margaret O'Brien, Randall Malone. Roger Corman was stuck in Chicago because of severe thunderstorms.

Black Sabbath (1963, executive producer–uncredited)
X: The Man with the X-Ray Eyes (1963, executive producer)
The Raven (1963, executive producer)
Invasion of the Star Creatures (1962, producer–uncredited)
Journey to the Seventh Planet (1962, producer–uncredited)
The Premature Burial (1962, producer–uncredited)
The Pit and the Pendulum (1961, executive producer)
Master of the World (1961, executive producer)
Reptilicus (1961, producer)
Black Sunday (1960, executive producer–US version, uncredited)
Circus of Horrors (1960, producer)
A Bucket of Blood (1959, executive producer–uncredited)
The Spider (1958, executive producer)
Teenage Cave Man (1958, executive producer)
War of the Colossal Beast (1958, executive producer)
Terror from the Year 5000 (1958, executive producer)
The Saga of the Viking Women and Their Voyage to the Waters of the Great Sea Serpent (1957, executive producer)
Invasion of the Saucer Men (1957, executive producer)
I Was a Teenage Werewolf (1957, executive producer–uncredited)
Voodoo Woman (1957, executive producer)
The She-Creature (1956, executive producer)
It Conquered the World (1956, executive producer–uncredited)
Day the World Ended (1955, executive producer–uncredited)
Phantom from 10,000 Leagues (1955, executive producer–uncredited)
The Beast with a Million Eyes (1955, executive producer–uncredited)

Ted Bohus and **Fred Olen Ray** (see FANEX 2)

Veronica Carlson (see FANEX 4)

Roger Corman (b. 1925-)
A FANEX Hero! Roger has 515 credits, we have listed what we consider highlights.
Frankenstein Unbound (1990)
The Tomb of Ligeia (1964)
The Masque of the Red Death (1964)
The Haunted Palace (1963)
X: The Man with the X-Ray Eyes (1963)
The Raven (1963)
Tales of Terror (1962)
The Premature Burial (1962)
The Pit and the Pendulum (1961)
Creature from the Haunted Sea (1961)
Last Woman on Earth (1960)
The Little Shop of Horrors (1960)
House of Usher (1960)
A Bucket of Blood (1959)
The Wasp Woman (1959)
War of the Satellites (1958)
The Saga of the Viking Women and Their Voyage to the Waters of the Great Sea Serpent (1957)
Attack of the Crab Monsters (1957)

After the Laemmle Awards at Classic Filmfest: (left to right) Susan Svehla, Margaret O'Brien, Pat Hitchcock, Janet Leigh and Paul Naschy. They are holding their Laemmle Awards.

Not of This Earth (1957)
It Conquered the World (1955)
Day the World Ended (1955)
The Beast with a Million Eyes (1955, some scenes, uncredited)

Robert Dwan (1915-2005) Director of *You Bet Your Life*

Linda Harrison (see FANEX 10)

Dorothy Herrmann
Daughter of famed composer Bernard Herrmann

Candace Hilligoss (b. 1935-)
The Curse of the Living Corpse (1964)
Carnival of Souls (1962)

Pat Hitchcock (1928-2021)
Daughter of Alfred Hitchcock and Alma Hitchcock
Psycho (1950)
Strangers on a Train (1951)

Betsy Jones-Moreland (see FANEX 12)

Janet Leigh (1927-2004)
Halloween H20: 20 Years Later (1998)
Night of the Lepus (1972)
Psycho (1960)

Randall Malone (1959)
Dr. Jekyll and Mr. Hyde (2017)
Don't Look in the Cellar (2008)
Hollywood Mortuary (2002)
The Crawling Brain (2002)
Vampyre Femmes (1999)
Creaturerealm: From the Dead (1998)
The Mark of Dracula (1997)

Kevin McCarthy (see FANEX 12)

IB Melchior (1917-2015) Writer/Director
Death Race (1975 story Death Race 2000)
Death Race 2000 (1975, story The Racer)
Planet of the Vampires (1965, screen story)/(screenplay–English version)
The Time Travelers (1964, Director/screenplay))
Robinson Crusoe on Mars (1964, screenplay)
Journey to the Seventh Planet (1962, screenplay)
Reptilicus (1961, screenplay)
The Angry Red Planet (1969, Director, screenplay by)
Gigantis, the Fire Monster (1959, original story: American version—"The Volcano Monsters")
Godzilla Raids Again (1955, original story—American version, "The Volcano Monsters")

Yvonne Monlaur (1935-2017)
The Terror of the Tongs (1961)
The Brides of Dracula (1960)
Circus of Horrors (1960)

Paul Naschy (1934-2009)
King of Spanish horror movies! Writer/Director/Actor! He and his family were so lovely.
Valdemar Legacy II: The Forbidden Shadow (2010)
The Valdemar Legacy (2010)
A Werewolf in the Amazon (2005)
Countess Dracula's Orgy of Blood (2004, Video)
Tomb of the Werewolf (2004, Video)
El lado oscuro (2002)
Lycantropus: The Moonlight Murders (1997)
Horror en el museo de cera (1990)
The Beast and the Magic Sword (1983)
Buenas noches, señor monstruo (1982)
Night of the Werewolf (1981)
Mystery on Monster Island (1981)
The Beasts' Carnival (1980)
The People Who Own the Dark (1976)
The Man with the Severed Head (1976)
Exorcismo (1975)
The Mummy's Revenge (1975)
Night of the Howling Beast (1975)
Devil's Possessed (1974)
Curse of the Devil (1973)
Vengeance of the Zombies (1973)
Horror Rises from the Tomb (1973)
Count Dracula's Great Love (1973)
Dr. Jekyll vs. The Werewolf (1972)
Fury of the Wolfman (1972)
The Werewolf Versus the Vampire Woman (1971)
Assignment Terror (1970)
Las noches del Hombre Lobo (1968)
Frankenstein's Bloody Terror (1968)

Margaret O'Brien (b. 1937-)
Dr. Jekyll and Mr. Hyde (2017)
Frankenstein Rising (2010)
The Canterville Ghost (1944)

Jessica Rains (b. 1938-)
Daughter of Claude Rains

Robert Skotak (b. 1945-)
Academy Award-winning SPFX artist.
Starship Troopers 3: Marauder (2008, Video) (visual effects supervisor)
Anamorph (2997, matte artist: Whodoo EFX) (special animator: Whodoo EFX)
The Stepford Wives (2004, visual effects art director: Whodoo EFX)
Tremors 4: The Legend Begins (2004, Video) (visual effects supervisor)
X2: X-Men United (2003, visual effects supervisor: 4 Ward productions)
The Tuxedo (2002, visual effects design)
House on Haunted Hill (1999, visual effects supervisor: 4 Ward Productions)
Mousehunt (1997, visual effects supervisor: 4-ward productions)
Mars Attacks! (1996, visual effects designer: 4-Ward Productions–uncredited)
The Arrival (1996, visual effects supervisor: 4-Ward Productions)
Tank Girl (1995, visual effects supervisor: 4-Ward Productions)
Honey, I Blew Up the Kid (1992, visual effects: 4-Ward Productions)
Batman Returns (1992, visual effects supervisor: 4-Ward Productions)
Terminator 2: Judgment Day (1991, special visual effects sequences: 4-Ward Productions) (visual effects supervisor: 4-Ward Productions)
Darkman (1990, visual effects supervisor: 4-ward productions)
Tremors (1990, visual effects supervisor: 4-ward productions)
The Abyss (1989, visual effects supervisor: Los Angeles surface unit)
Aliens (1986, visual effects supervisor)
Strange Invaders (1983, visual effects consultant)
Slapstick of Another Kind (1982, special visual consultant: Private Stock Effects)
Forbidden World (1982, production designer: special visual effects)
Galaxy of Terror (1981, special visual effects–uncredited)
Escape from New York (1981, matte artwork–as Bob Skotak) (visual effects supervisor)
Battle Beyond the Stars (1980, miniature design and construction)/(special designs/effects creations)

Elena Verdugo (see FANEX 9)

FANEX 15
July 2001

Guests
Forrest J Ackerman (see FANEX 3)

Ted Bohus and **Fred Olen Ray** (see FANEX 2)

Veronica Carlson (see FANEX 4)

Curtis Harrington (1926-2007) Director/Writer
Queen of Blood (1966)
Voyage to the Prehistoric Planet (1965, as John Sebastian)
Night Tide (1961)

Jonathan Haze (b. 1929-)
The talk with Jonathan Haze and Jackie Joseph was one of the funniest events FANEX has ever seen!
Blood Bath (1966)
X: The Man with the X-Ray Eyes (1963)
The Terror (1963)
The Little Shop of Horrors (1960)
Cave Man (1958)
The Saga of the Viking Women and Their Voyage to the Waters of the Great Sea Serpent (1957)
Not of This Earth (1957)
It Conquered the World (1956)
Swamp Women (1956)
Day the World Ended (1955)
Dementia (1955)
Monster from the Ocean Floor (1954)

Jackie Joseph (b. 1933-)
Small Soldiers (1998)
Gremlins 2 (1990)
Gremlins (1984)
The Little Shop of Horrors (1960)

Yvonne Monlaur (see FANEX Monster Rally)

Paul Picerni (1922-2011)
Has 207 credits, mostly TV including:
Men Into Space (1960)
Batman (1967)
Capricorn One (1967, Film)
Project UFO (1978)
)

Michael J. Pollard (1939-2019)
House of 1000 Corpses (2003)
Sleepaway Camp III (1989)
Scrooged (1988)
American Gothic (1988)

Barbara Shelley poses with staffer Polly Lynn at FANEX 15.

Barbara Shelley (1932-2021)
Ghost Story (1974)
Quatermass and the Pit (1967)
Dracula: Prince of Darkness (1966)
The Gorgon (1964)
The Shadow of the Cat (1961)
Village of the Damned (1960)
Blood of the Vampire (1958)
Cat Girl (1957)

FANEX 16
August 2002

Guests
Ted Bohus and Fred Olen Ray (see FANEX 2)

Robert Z'Dar (1950-2015)
Voices from the Graves (2006)
Vampire Blvd. (2004)
Zombiegeddon (2003, Video)
Future War (1997, Video)
Night Realm (1994)
The Devil's Pet (1994)
Maniac Cop 3: Badge of Silence (1992)
The Legend of Wolf Mountain (1992)
Through the Portal of Time (1991)
Soultaker (1990)
A Gnome Named Gnorm (1990)
Evil Altar (1988)
Maniac Cop (1988)
Cherry 2000 (1987)
The Night Stalker (1986)

Susanna Leigh (see FANEX Monster Rally)

Carol Lynley (1942-2019)
Howling VI (1991)
Spirits (1999)
The Shape of Things to Come (1979)
The Cat and the Canary (1978)
Beware the Blob (1972)
The Night Stalker (1972)

Gary J. Svehla poses with John Saxon at FANEX 16.

John Saxon (1936-2020)
From Dusk Till Dawn (1996)
The Arrival (1991)
My Mom's a Werewolf (1989)
A Nightmare on Elm Street 3 (1987)
A Nightmare on Elm Street (1984)
Battle Beyond the Stars (1980)
Beyond Evil (1980)
Queen of Blood (1966)
Blood Beast from Outer Space (1965)
The Evil Eye (1963)

FANEX 16 staffers pose with Ted Bohus and Fred Olen Ray (in front).

SON OF FANEX
April 2003

Guests
Ted Bohus and Fred Olen Ray (see FANEX 2)

Edward de Sousa (b. 1932-)
The Golden Compass (2007)
Rocket to the Moon (1967)
Kiss of the Vampire (1963)
The Phantom of the Opera (1962)

Susan Gordon (1949-2011)
Tormented (1960)
Attack of the Puppet People (1958)

FANEX 17
August 2003

Guests
Ted Bohus and Fred Olen Ray (see FANEX 2)

Carol Cleveland (b. 1942-)
Alice, Through the Looking Glass (2021)
The Meaning of Life (1983)
Life of Brian (1979)
Monty Python and the Holy Grain (1975)
Old Dracula (1974)
Moon Zero Two (1969)

Francis Matthews at FANEX 17

Hank Garrett (b. 1931-)
The Amityville Horror (1979)
Exorcist II (1977)
The Sentinel (1977)

Francis Matthews (1927-2014)
Captain Scarlet and the Mysterons (1967-1968, TV Series)
Dracula: Prince of Darkness (1966)
The Hellfire Club (1961)
Corridors of Blood (1958)
The Revenge of Frankenstein (1958)

Beverly Washburn (b. 1943-)
Tales of Frankenstein (2013)
Spider Baby (1967)
Superman and the Mole-Men (1951)

Sean Yseult (b. 1966-)
(former White Zombie bassist)

Other Baltimore Conventions

Balticon

Now in its 56th year, all things sci-fi and, when they ran Worldcon in Baltimore in September 1983, fans were able to meet Jim Henson and cast members promoting *The Right Stuff*.

Baltimore Comic-Con

Farpoint
In its 19th year features all things *Star Trek* and sci-fi.

Shore Leave
Now in its 42nd year began with all things Trek, but has been bringing stars from across the sci-fi universe.

Mid-Atlantic Nostalgia Convention

Baltimore-Washington Area Horror Hosts and More! (1957-1987)

Magazines/Fanzines

Thanks to *Famous Monsters* and *Castle of Frankenstein*, kids in Bmore were inspired to start their own fanzines.

Bits and Pieces
Published by The Horror and Fantasy Film Society

Black Oracle
Publishers/Editors Charlie Ellis and Bill George
Publisher George Stover

Cinemacabre
Publisher George Stover

Cinemagic
Publisher Don Dohler

Gore Creatures (see Midnight Marquee)

The Late Show
Publisher Bill George

Mad About Movies
Publisher Gary J. Svehla

Midnight Marquee
2023 will be *MidMar*'s 60th Anniversary!
Publisher/Editor Gary J. Svehla

Monsters from the Vault
Publisher/Editor Jim Clatterbaugh

Movie Club
Editor/Publisher Don Dohler

Movie Mystique
Editor Susan Svehla

Prodigy
Editor: Marty Kirscher

Independent Filmmakers

Of course Baltimore's claim to Hollyweird immorality is director John Waters. But there are many filmmakers making low-budget horror/sci-fi movies. Baltimore is filled with dedicated filmmakers—who make movies with their blood, sweat and tears, and usually their own money. And while we probably have missed some, here are local directors of genre mayhem.

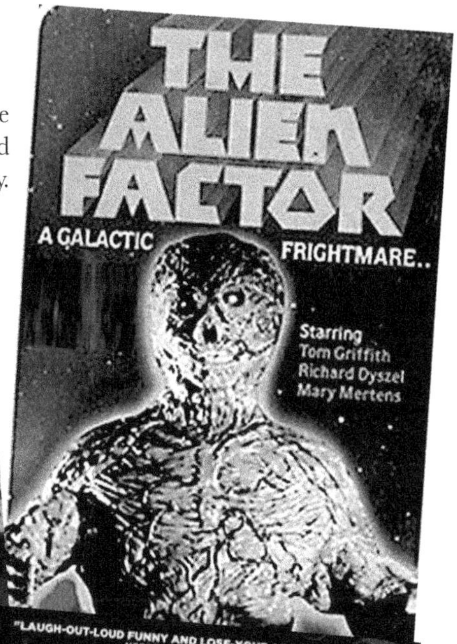

Jimmyo Burril
Known for Chainsaw Sally
Johnny Daggers
Known for Noctambulist
Joel Denning
Known for Canvas of Blood and Sward of the Snakehead
Don Dohler
Known for Alien Factor and Nightbeast
Alvin Gary
Known for Sweet Dreams
Mike Gutridge
Known for The Bone Garden
Kevin Kangus
Known for Fear of Clowns and Hunting Humans
Frank Lama
Known for Swarm of the Snakehead
Chris Lamartina
Known for Call Girl of Cthulhu and Graves Mistakes
Eric Christopher Myers
Known for 8 Ball Clown II
Kevin Perkins
Known for My Boring Zombie Apocalypse
Mark Redfield
Known for The Death of Poe
Joe Ripple
Known for Harvesters and Vampire Sisters
Susan Svehla
Known for Terror in the Pharaoh's Tomb and Stellar Quasar and the Scrolls of Dadelia
Justin Timpane
Known for Ninjas vs. Monsters
Tom Towsend
Known for Zombie Doomsday and Ghosts that Hunt Back

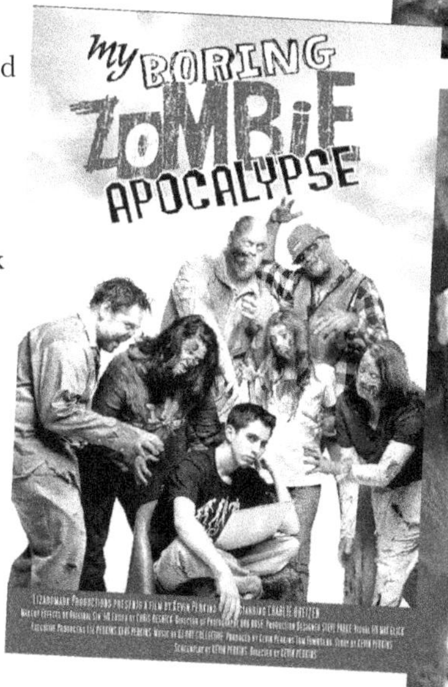

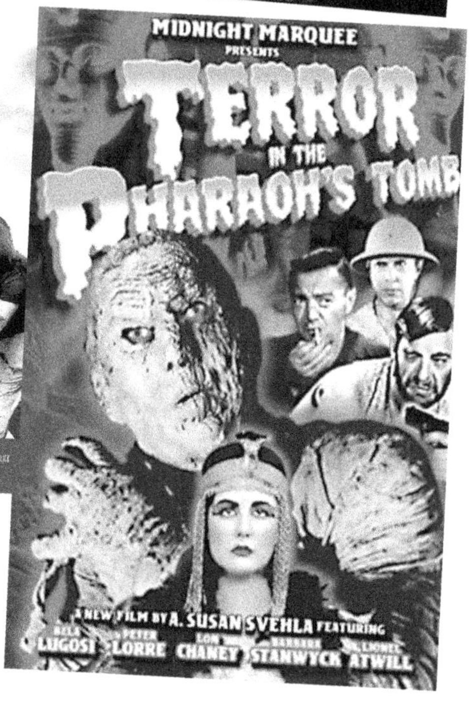

Fanex Panel Participants

Joe Alexander
Mark Altman
Trish Antonucci
Joe Auslander
Pam Banner
Ed Bansak
Mark Bialek
Stephen Bissette
The Blob
Ted Bohus
Greg Boggia
Jack Brent
Michael Brunas
Dorothy Burke
Tom Burke
Amy Byrne
Michael Caputo
Robin Chaney
Ralph Chapman
Jim Clatterbaugh
John Clayton
Jim Cochran
Cindy Ruth Collins
Linda Conrad
Danny Contreras
Amy Crowell
Angie Crowell
Gene Crowell
Tim Davis
Thomas DeJa
Deborah Del Vecchio
Joe Demers
Melinda DiLeonardi
Vince DiLeonardi

Some of the staff from FANEX 1. Front: John Freyer, Harry Eisel, Back: Jeff Feaster, Sharon Landrum, Ellie Green and Debbie Feaster.

Glen DiMatto
Michael Dobbs
Dick Dyszel
Harry Eisel
Charlie Ellis
John Ellis
Donald Farmer
Tod Feiertag
Tim Ferrante
John Flynn
Carl Friedel
John Freyer
Ann Frith
Bill George
Michael Gingold
Joe Guilfoyle
Bruce Hallenbeck
Steve Ham
Gary Harner
Bill Harrison
Dave Henderson
Phil Holthaus
James Janis
Barbara Jarvis
Michael Jeffers
Paul Jensen
J.J. Johnson
Tom Johnson
Jenny Keith
Charles Kilgore
Mitch Klein
Dick Klemensen
David Karmer
Michael Kronenberg

FANEX 10 staff members and writers accompany the guests to the Baltimore Inner Harbor.

Steve Kronenberg
Jonathan Lampley
Don Leifert
Jessie Lilley
Bill Littman
Lelia Loban
Donna Lucas
Tim Lucas
Lawrence Luers
Lillian Luers
Arthur Lundquist
Jeff Lynn
Polly Lynn
Bob Madison
Barbara Mank
Greg Mank
Lorne Marshall
Kevin Michael
Mark A. MIller
Ben Miner
Nathan Miner
Randy Palmer
Tony Oliveri
Marian Owens
Tom Parker
John Parnum
Rob Parr
Phil Perry
Jerry Pleines
Keith Poston
Fred Olen Ray
Chuck Reinitz
Gary Don Rhodes
Steve Rifkin
Terry Roark
Mark Rollie
Bob Sargent
Michael Schilling
Jay Schlossberg-Cohen
Bryan Senn
Wes Shank
Jay Sher

Midnight Marquee's Gary Svehla (center) with writers (Left to Right) Bryan Senn, Dick Klemensen, Mark A. Miller, Harvey Clarke and Paul Jensen

Don Smith
Jeff Smith
Stephen Smith
Larry Springer
John Stell
George Stover
Michael Brett-Surman
Gary Svehla
Susan Svehla
Joe Szczepaniak
Dan Taylor
Jeff Thompson
Steve Thornton
Richard Valley
Joe Vannicola
Steve Vertlieb
Mark Walker
Robert Walters
Tom Weaver
David Willard
Delbert Winans
Chuck Winton
Charlie Wittig
Nathalie Yafet

Thanks to Jim Clatterbaugh and Susan Svehla for contribution to this listing.

The bar always did big business at FANEX! Fred Olen Ray, Ted Bohus and George Stover relax.

Author John Stell with fellow FANEX staffer Leo Dymowski.

Appendix 1
Filmography

This is an alphabetical list of all films (with brief comments) covered in Chapters 2 through 8, for the period November 9, 1957 (Dr. Lucifer's debut) through September 5, 1987 (Ghost Host's presumed sign-off). United States home video availability (announced through January 2022) is also noted in the at-present believed-best format available (e.g. VHS, Laserdisc, DVD, BR for Blu Ray, or NA for not available on US format), although titles go out-of-print and formats are discontinued. Lastly, the two films unavailable for review are noted with NR. The mini-review ratings are out of 4.0.

The 10th Victim (1965) 2.5
Before *The Hunger Games* and *The Purge*, there was The Big Hunt, a competition where participants sign up for 10 rounds, five as the hunter (who knows all about her target) and five as the hunted (who must figure out the identity of his pursuer), and it's kill, or be killed. The grand prize is fame and fortune. Ursula Andress pursues Marcello Mastroianni in her final contest, and wants his execution filmed for a TV commercial. Then things get complicated. Strange blend of sci-fi, satire, and humor is unique enough to keep one's full attention. Ultimately, the film isn't as satisfying as one would like. (BR-Blue Underground)

12 to the Moon (1960) 2.0
An international dozen board Lunar Eagle No. 1 to travel to the moon and claim it as international territory. Cultural tensions surface during the trip but the more pressing problem is that, once they arrive, something doesn't want them there. Performances are uneven and the budget low, preventing the film from being anything special, despite the admirable intentions. (DVD-Mill Creek as part of *Vintage Sci-Fi: 6 Movie Collection*)

13 Ghosts (1960) 2.5
An impoverished American family gets sort-of lucky when Uncle Plato dies and leaves them his haunted house. There are, at present, 12 ghostly inhabitants with the promise another will join them before film's end. Director William Castle's gimmick this time is Illusion-O, a process whereby a viewer can choose to see the ghosts or not via special glasses. (In fact, the first DVD release had the option to watch in Illusion-O, complete with glasses.) The film has the look of a TV show, and the direction is lackluster. But it's also kind of fun and highly watchable. (BR —Mill Creek with *13 Frightened Girls*)

2020 Texas Gladiators (1982) 1.5
In the stereotypical-looking post-apocalyptic world of 2020, a former Texas Ranger joins forces with Nazi-inspired bad guys to take on his former comrades. Lots of uninspired (and silly) action scenes in this Italian-made knockoff of the *Mad Max* films, with amusing attempts to make it appear the setting is America, such as a container marked, "Danger: Exsplosive [sic]." Nonstop action keeps things moving but the sleaze quotient (frequent female exploitation) leaves a sour taste. There is an English-friendly German DVD available if you must. (NA)

20 Million Miles to Earth (1957) 2.5
Upon its return to Earth, the first US rocket ship to Venus crashes in the Mediterranean near Sicily. Contained within is an alien specimen that soon breaks free of its gelatin capsule and starts growing too fast for comfort. Ray Harryhausen's marvelous stop-motion effects are the reason to see this very familiar giant-monster-on-the-loose effort which is somewhat marred by stereotypes and tepid romantic subplot. Highlights include an exciting battle with an elephant and the finale inside the Roman Colosseum. (BR-Sony)

The 27th Day (1957) 3.0
An alien from a dying planet selects five earthlings from various nations to receive deadly weapons, which they can use to destroy their enemies at the risk of wiping out all human life. When a TV broadcast announces the names of the individuals, the nation's rulers must decide between war and peace. Intelligent science fiction thriller certainly has a message to deliver but never becomes too preachy. Ending has a nice twist too. (DVD-Mill Creek as part of *Vintage Sci-Fi: 6 Movie Collection*)

4D Man (1959) 3.0
Researcher thinks he's come up with impregnable metal called Cargonite, until his also-scientist brother reveals how he *willed* a pencil to pass through steel with aid of amplifier. Their experiments result in the ability to enter the fourth dimension and pass through objects at will. But there are severe consequences. Colorful sci-fi features jazzy music score and intriguing plot, along with good effects. Robert Lansing is well cast as stoic doctor who loses it when his gal dumps him. (BR-Kino)

Abbott and Costello Meet Dr. Jekyll and Mr. Hyde (1953) 2.5
A&C are American Bobbies in London who cross paths with Boris Karloff's Jekyll/Hyde. Some fine moments (Lou turning into a mouse, for example) and well-executed slapstick. But it's not as funny as the previous monster encounters. (BR-Shout! Factory as part of *Abbott and Costello: The Complete Universal Pictures Collection*)

Abbott and Costello Meet Frankenstein (1948) 4.0
Best of the Universal monster mashes—the writers finally came up with a story that involves all the classic figures (Dracula, the Wolf Man, the Monster) in the same continuous story, as opposed to the *House of...* pictures that featured the Count as Act I, the tortured Talbot as Act II, and then a brief Act III for the Monster. Dracula (Bela Lugosi) wants Wilbur's (Lou Costello) brain for the Frankenstein Monster (Glenn Strange). Lawrence Talbot (Lon Chaney, Jr.) tries to prevent this while battling his own demons. It's very well plotted and funny, one of the greatest horror comedies. The finale is a beautifully choreographed piece of creepy craziness. (BR-Universal)

Abbott and Costello Meet the Invisible Man (1951) 3.0
The first client for new PIs Bud and Lou is boxer framed for murder. His doctor friend was willed the invisibility formu-

la from Jack Griffith, so you can guess what happens. This entry lacks the Gothic ambiance and occasional hair-raising moments of the previous A&C monster film but has genuine laughs and a lively boxing match. The effects are great too. (BR— Universal)

Abbott and Costello Meet the Killer (1949) 2.5
Abbott and Costello work at hotel as house detective and bellhop, respectively. When famous criminal attorney is murdered after having Lou fired, guess who the prime suspect is. Boris Karloff wears a turban and acts suspiciously but seems bored. Pleasant enough outing works rather well as whodunit. (BR-Shout! Factory as part of *Abbott and Costello: The Complete Universal Pictures Collection*)

Abbott and Costello Meet the Mummy (1955) 2.0
Lou comes into possession of valuable amulet that various parties need either to find a buried treasure or to revive treasure's bandaged protector. Tired A&C vehicle should have been better. The problem is there's very little interaction with the Mummy. Most of the time the team is dealing with human thieves and connivers. The finale should have been a lot livelier too what with three mummies running around. (BR-Universal)

The Abominable Dr. Phibes (1971) 3.0
Vincent Price is the title character who takes revenge on the nine doctors who couldn't save his wife on the operating table. Ultra-stylish, visually breathtaking film is scary, funny, clever, and most enjoyable. See Phibes commit murder via boils, bats, frogs, blood draining, hail, rats, locusts, and a unicorn! (BR-Shout! Factory as part of *The Vincent Price Collection*)

The Abominable Snowman (1957) 3.0
One of the last of Hammer Film Productions' black-and-white science fiction thrillers, which pretty much ended after the success of the same year's *The Curse of Frankenstein*. As the title suggests, a team travels through the Himalayas in search of the elusive Yeti. Peter Cushing is the botanist who is sympathetic to the Yeti's plight; Forrest Tucker is the obnoxious showman whose intentions are less than honorable. Director Val Guest had a real gift for bringing realism to the most fantastic of tales, as he does here. The ending is not what is expected. (BR-Shout! Factory)

Agent for H.A.R.M. (1966) 1.5
Originally filmed as a TV pilot, this was released to theaters instead. The United States Human Aetiological Relations Machine sends casually dressed secret agent to stop spread of deadly bacteria that eats the human body from within. When the contagion first touches skin, one looks as though covered in green oatmeal. The TV origins are all too apparent in this bland, unexciting spy effort. Barbara Bouchet *is* lovely as the "innocent" niece of scientist attempting to find antidote. (NA)

Alias John Preston (1955) 2.5
Christopher Lee is excellent in the title role of this mild thriller about successful businessperson who may not be all he seems. Talky but intelligent and involving. But at 66 minutes, it feels as though it ends just as it should be kicking into high gear. (DVD-R-Sinister Cinema)

Alibi for Murder (1936) 2.0
Radio reporter ear-witnesses "suicide" of renowned chemist but thinks that it's murder and sets out to prove it. Dwight Frye is a suspect. Passable standard programmer clocks in just under an hour and features the usual fast-talking reporter, clueless cops, blooming romance, ineffectual thugs, and irritating comedy relief. (DVD-R-Sony)

The Alien Factor (1978) 1.0
Space creatures that have crashed on Earth are mutilating anyone they come across. This micro-budget effort was filmed in Baltimore and features Count Gore himself, Richard Dyszel, as the unhelpful mayor more interested in his potential amusement complex. Director Don Dohler's first film plays more like a bloodless slasher film given the high body count and numerous point-of-view shots. Whatever you call it, the effects are chintzy, the acting below average, and the pacing erratic. The synthesizer score has dated horribly. (BR-Retromedia)

Alien Zone (1978) 2.0
On a rainy night, an adulterous plumber has problems finding his hotel, so friendly mortician Ivor Francis invites him in to get warm. Then the host shows his guest four corpses and tells their stories: a schoolteacher who hates kids is terrorized in her own home; a photographer likes filming the murders he commits; an American detective and British inspector compete for world's greatest sleuth; and an obnoxious businessman gets put through various tortures when he steps into the wrong store. Those familiar with how anthologies work will guess where this is going. Uneven like most films with multiple tales, this low-budget effort has good atmosphere and a nice performance by Francis. But too many of the stories fall flat for this to really score. (BR-Vinegar Syndrome as *The House of the Dead*)

Aliens from Spaceship Earth (1978) 1.5
Despite the title, this has nothing to do with UFOs or aliens. Instead, it's a sleep-inducing look at man's search for a higher consciousness, a result of the hippy movement of the 1960s and 1970s. The primary focus of the film is Eastern religions and interviews with several leaders, along with several actors. There's also plenty of acoustic peace songs throughout. Perhaps interesting as a cultural artifact, but the approach is so laid back the film ultimately becomes monotonous and rather dreary. (DVD-UFO TV)

Alligator (1980) 3.0
Late entry in the "animals on the loose" subgenre that flourished in the 1970s. A cute little alligator flushed down the toilet survives the sewers by dining on discarded laboratory test subjects. Now 36 feet long, he decides to come topside. If you're going to make a giant-alligator-attacks-the-city film, this is the way to do it: good cast, well-staged attack scenes, and a sense of humor ("Harry Lime lives!" is written on the

sewer walls). Henry Silva is a hoot as big-game hunter brought in to stop the carnage. (BR-Shout! Factory)

The Alpha Incident (1978) 1.5
A nosy train engineer inadvertently releases an alien microorganism, resulting in the quarantine of several station employees and government biochemist. They bide their time while scientists try to discover an antidote. Eerie but talky thriller has a mixed bag cast and very little happens until the last 15 or so minutes. (BR-Arrow as part of *Weird Wisconsin: The Bill Rebane Collection*)

The Amazing Colossal Man (1957) 2.0
Army colonel blunders into plutonium bomb test. He survives but then starts growing and growing. Director Bert I. Gordon specialized in '50s giant monster movies starting with *King Dinosaur* in 1955. Most of them are overly talky with poor special effects. This is one of his better efforts thanks to Glen Langan's sympathetic performance as the afflicted male. There was even a sequel, *War of the Colossal Beast*, in 1958. (VHS-Columbia/Tristar)

The Amazing Mr. X (1948) 2.5
Engaged widow is still mourning the death of her husband, so when a medium comes into her life she tries reaching out to the deceased. To reveal any more of the plot would be unfair, as the story twists like a snake even if these twists have been seen plenty of times before. Cinematography by John Alton is the chief asset here; cast is mostly good too. Nothing original but still entertaining. (BR-The Film Detective)

The Amazing Transparent Man (1960) 1.5
Smooth-talking crackpot arranges the prison escape of notorious safecracker as part of plan to create invisible army. Absurdly plotted thriller drags at only 58 minutes and offers nothing you haven't seen before. (BR-Kino as part of *Edgar G. Ulmer Sci-Fi Collection*)

The Amityville Horror (1979) 2.5
The Lutz family moves into a home where a family was murdered a year earlier, and then find themselves plagued by flies, bleeding walls, and a hidden room in the basement. Putting to one side the veracity of this being based on fact, the film is a mishmash of haunted house clichés that reduces the proceedings to a string of incidents and contrivances. (One relative is a nun; the wife of the husband's partner is a medium; etc.) In a subplot that doesn't really lead anywhere, Rod Steiger hams it up shamelessly as a priest whose peers don't believe him. Despite all the above however, the film is still watchable thanks to leads James Brolin and Margot Kidder who have great chemistry and make a sympathetic couple. (BR-Shout! Factory)

Amityville: The Demon (1983) 2.0
Reporter for sleazy *Reveal* magazine moves into infamous house to write serious novel. Instead, he must put his skepticism aside and deal with the demon that apparently lives there. Loud, nonsensical horror (how did that force cause a building's elevator to plummet or make a person's car brakes fail?) is just another haunted house story. Some effective moments but mostly overly familiar. (BR-Shout! Factory as *Amityville 3-D* as part of *The Amityville Horror Trilogy*)

Amphibian Man (1962) 3.0
Beautiful Russian fairy tale. Title creature falls in love with young woman when he saves her from a shark attack. But treacherous ship owner claims to be the hero and makes plans to marry her, so the "sea devil" makes his own arrangements to win her love. Stunning photography, memorable music score, and impressive production design complement touching script. (DVD-Image)

Anatomy of Terror (TV-1973) 2.5
American couple in England for their second honeymoon run into problems when hubby starts acting strangely, including calling his wife Susie "Theresa." Intriguing episode of *Thriller* has a good central idea but even at 67 minutes, the story is stretched out a bit. Original British title: *An Echo of Theresa*. (DVD-VEI as part of *Thriller: The Complete Collection*)

And Now the Screaming Starts (1973) 2.5
On her wedding night, virgin bride discovers her new home has a terrible secret. While family curses have served as the plot for countless films, this entry has some pretty effective moments, including the ending. Peter Cushing shows up about 45 minutes into the story. Stylish direction by Roy Ward Baker also helps. (BR-Severin)

The Andromeda Strain (1971) 3.0
In a high-security laboratory in Nevada, scientists study a lethal alien life form brought back by a crashed satellite. When the organism starts mutating, it threatens to destroy the group along with the whole facility. Gripping, tense thriller directed by Robert Wise. The cast is perfect, giving believable performances. (BR-Arrow)

The Angry Red Planet (1959) 2.0
Traumatized scientist recounts the events of doomed Mars exploration. The film's gimmick is showing the Mars scenes with red tint, a process called Cinemagic; it adds little to the story. Highlights include the many creatures that show up, one of which is a 40-ft tall bat. A jelly-like monster absorbs one crewmember. (BR-Shout! Factory)

The Ape (1940) 2.0
When murderous ape escapes from the circus, crazed doctor Boris Karloff decides he can commit murder to continue his spinal fluid experiments, putting blame on the beast. Nonsensical, low-budget Monogram offering is routine and nothing special although Karloff delivers an earnest performance, which keeps this watchable. (BR-Kino)

The Ape Man (1943) 2.0
Bela Lugosi plays doctor who transformed himself into apeman and now can't master the antidote. Lugosi does what he can, but this is weak tea. A razor and a visit to a chiropractor may have solved his problems and made for a better movie. (BR-Retromedia with *Doomed to Die*)

Ape Man of the Jungle (1964) 1.5
The peaceful chief of the Leopard Men (they don leopard heads and skins) has died, and his replacement wants a return to the bloodthirsty days of terrorizing the land. They start by abducting several American vacationers, including a blonde-haired beauty they intend to sacrifice. Luckily, Zoltak of the forest is nearby to save the day. Italian *Tarzan* knockoff is cliché-ridden effort; peaceful tribe members plot against violent ones, while Zoltak tosses Leopard Men about like ragdolls, laughs in the face of danger, pulls large vehicles from the mud, and wrestles alligators. Funniest scene has Zoltak impersonating witch doctor, as if the tribe wouldn't notice a white guy beneath the headpiece. For Tarzan and bad movie completists only. (NA)

Appointment with A Killer (TV-1975) 2.0
Wife of private detective attempts to solve the five-year-old murder of 17-year-old Annabella. Like several *Thriller* episodes, the basic idea is okay but can't sustain the running time, causing the viewer to lose interest. Original British title: *A Midsummer Nightmare*. (DVD-VEI as part of *Thriller: The Complete Collection*)

Assignment: Outer Space (1960) 1.0
Reporter is given permission to cover activities of space station, much to the chagrin of those running the place. He causes problems but ultimately must help prevent the destruction of Earth! The most bored-sounding actors ever dubbed this Italian space opera. Instead of building tension, film creeps along daring viewer to stay interested. (DVD-Mill Creek as part of *Sci-Fi Classics: 50 Movie Pack*)

Assignment Terror (1970) 2.0
Aliens from a dying planet reanimate the corpses of two dead scientists, who in turn revive a vampire, werewolf, Frankenstein monster, and mummy. The hope is superstitious Earth people will be scared to death! Attempt by Paul Naschy to do a Universal monster rally (the vampire is revived in the exact same manner as in *House of Frankenstein*) is only moderately successful as too much time is spent on the buildup. Some of the duels during the finale are pretty good. Just one of many outings for Naschy's tragic werewolf character Waldemar Daninsky. (BR-Scorpion Releasing)

The Astounding She-Monster (1957) 0.0
Low-rent thugs kidnap heiress and wind up at lonely geologist Robert Clarke's cabin in the woods. Soon title alien creature who can kill with her touch is hunting them all. Incredibly bad sci-fi seems much longer than its 62 minutes. Poorly acted for the most part with molasses pacing and terrible script. (DVD-Image)

The Astro-Zombies (1968) 1.0
Scientist John Carradine is developing synthetic-human hybrid beings. The CIA is on to him, and enemy agents want his secret. Noisy, excruciatingly paced film jumbles science fiction and crime drama elements unsuccessfully. The zombie gets almost no screen time. Carradine deserves award for delivering his non-stop pseudo-scientific lines with a straight face. (BR-Kino)

Asylum (1972) 3.0
Another solid anthology from Amicus. New doctor must determine which patient was the former head of the asylum by listening to the stories of the most violent inmates. Tales include a dismembered corpse that won't stay still; a tailor who must make a special suit; a mysterious friend who commits murder; and a doctor whose little robots may have strange powers. (BR-Severin)

At the Earth's Core (1976) 2.5
Peter Cushing and Doug McClure test their revolutionary burrowing machine and end up in fantastical world of rubbery monsters, enslaved tribes, and Caroline Munro. Amicus sci-fi adventure seems to be for kids with its campy tone and Cushing's hammy performance. Still, it's never dull, and is often rousing, achieving a certain giddiness if one is in the right mood. (BR-Kino)

Atom Age Vampire (1960) 1.0
Scientist who's trying to perfect cell regeneration falls in love with his latest subject—a stripper who was disfigured in a car accident. Eventually he must kill to preserve her beauty, transforming into title creature to do so. Our heroine spends most of her screen time crying, while villain is nothing we haven't seen before. Worst of all is that the story grows more nonsensical as it progresses, with character motivation becoming inconsistent and confused. (DVD-Alpha)

The Atomic Brain (1963) 1.0
Rich, elderly woman is financing mad doctor with the hopes he can put her 80-year-old brain inside a beautiful 20-year-old body. One of his experiments acts like a cat, while another prowls the estate grounds acting like a guard dog. Sloppily assembled horror opus has irritating music score, uneven performances, too much voice-over narration, and too few scares. (BR-R-Moth, Inc. as *Monstrosity*)

The Atomic Man (1955) 2.5
Magazine reporter is naturally puzzled when a gunshot victim looks exactly like a nuclear physicist who's working on top secret experiments involving radioactive materials. Convinced some nefarious plot is afoot, he and his photographer girlfriend investigate. Intriguing sci-fi ideas (the patient seems to be 7.5 seconds ahead of the rest of us) are somewhat overshadowed by standard 1930s-style wise-guy-reporter approach to the mystery. The original British version *Timeslip* runs about 15 minutes longer. (DVD-R-Sinister Cinema)

Atomic Rulers of the World (1965) 1.0
Starman (the creature made of the strongest steel) is sent to earth to disrupt plot to blow up Japan with nuclear bomb. Bland actioner features mostly fistfights and rudimentary action scenes. In a desperate move to create suspense, children are endangered. It's all a big yawn. On-screen title is *Atomic Rulers*. This is the first of four movies derived from nine Japanese short films made between 1957 and 1959 featuring Super Giant (aka Starman). They were released to US television in 1965. The remaining three are *Invaders from Space, Attack from*

Space, and *Evil Brain from Outer Space*. (DVD-Image with *Invaders from Space*)

The Atomic Submarine (1959) 2.0
Submarine *Tiger Shark* journeys to investigate why various vessels are meeting with disasters; discovers underwater flying saucer "Cyclops" is the cause. Ultra-cheap, standard thriller boasts great sci-fi cast including Dick Foran, Arthur Franz, and Tom Conway. Some of the dialogue between Franz and the alien is hilarious. (DVD-Criterion as part of *Monsters and Madmen*)

Atragon (1963) 2.0
The Mu empire thought destroyed some 10,000 years ago has thrived underwater and now wants to take over the world. But the rulers are worried about a state-of-the-art submarine and want its inventor turned over to them. Routine and slow going for the most part. Giant fire-spurting serpent shows up with about 20 minutes left to battle the sub and wake viewers up. (DVD-Media Blasters)

Attack from Space (1964) 1.0
Third Americanized Starman film. This time our hero is trying to find scientist kidnapped by vicious alien race who dress like Nazis and plan to attack Earth. Poor effects and uninspired fisticuffs. If Republic at its worst had ripped off *Superman*, the result might resemble this sluggish actioner that offers zero novelty. (DVD-Image with *Evil Brain from Outer Space*)

Attack of the 50 Foot Woman (1958) 2.0
Neglected wife Allison Hayes runs afoul an alien and starts growing. Silly film that's very enjoyable in a bad sort of way. Terrible effects. But at only 66 minutes, it moves quickly, and the climax is hilarious. HARRYYYYYYYYYY! (DVD-Warner Bros.)

Attack of the Crab Monsters (1957) 2.5
Island-stranded scientists learn one of the effects of H-bomb testing was the creation of smart, extra jumbo-sized crabs. Low-budget Roger Corman effort is a little talky but mostly works thanks to Charles B. Griffith's audacious script, which gives the crustaceans the power to speak in the voices of those whose brains they have consumed! The cast is solid and the effects convincing enough. (BR-Shout! Factory)

Attack of the Giant Leeches (1959) 2.0
Huge bloodsuckers are hiding in local swamp, their exploits blamed on alligators and jealous husbands. Dreary low-budget AIP outing lacks a compelling lead character. On the other hand, leech-bait Yvette Vickers smolders as unfaithful wife who pays for her infidelity in the worst way. (BR-Retromedia with *Teenagers from Outer Space*)

Attack of the Monsters (1969) 2.0
Alien pair kidnaps two young pals and brings them to planet Tera, where monster Guiron, with its razor-sharp schnoz, watches over things. Luckily, superhero monster Gamera, the giant flying turtle, is watching over the boys, because the aliens want to eat the children's brains. Obviously produced for the under-14 set, the fifth *Gamera* film is imaginative, goofy fun, with some lively monster battles. Just don't expect high art. (BR-Arrow as *Gamera vs. Guiron* as part of *Gamera: The Complete Collection*)

Attack of the Mushroom People (1963) 3.0
Storm strands friends out for some boating fun on mysterious island. They find a wrecked ship that contains mushrooms possibly subject to radiation poisoning. When one unwise castaway decides to try the fungus, the real nightmare begins. Starts out as study of the psychological effects of being isolated and hungry, with exposure of resentments and jealousies and some wanting to die. The attack finally comes with less than 10 minutes left. Highly effective slow-burn thriller is creepy and haunting and boasts excellent use of sound and makeup. (DVD-Media Blasters as *Matango*)

Attack of the Puppet People (1958) 2.0
Owner of Dolls Incorporated shrinks those he likes so they won't leave him; houses them in display cases when he's not forcing them to have "fun." Hit or miss Bert I. Gordon effort features less-than-special effects and predictable story. A nice performance by John Hoyt as the deranged villain makes things bearable. (BR-Shout! Factory)

Attack of the Robots (1966) 2.5
A retired spy is forced back to work to learn why assassin's skin color changed when he died. It seems a criminal organization has perfected a method of transforming humans of a certain blood type into obedient robots, and our hero shares that very type! Tongue-in-cheek spy spoof is rather entertaining, with Eddie Constantine quite good in the lead. Too bad Fernando Rey doesn't seem to be having as much fun the chief villain. One of the few films from director Jess Franco that could be described as charming. (BR-Kino)

The Attic (1980) 2.5
Carrie Snodgrass gives sympathetic performance as spinster who was jilted at the altar 19 years ago and now lives with her cruel father (Ray Milland). When she loses her librarian job and her pet chimpanzee Dickie (a gift from the only friend she has) vanishes, she begins her journey to madness. Plays out as expected but Snodgrass keeps you watching and interested. (DVD-MGM with *Crawlspace*)

Audrey Rose (1977) 3.0
Well-mannered English gentleman informs New York couple that their daughter Ivy is his reincarnated daughter Audrey Rose, who died in a car fire minutes before Ivy was born. The parents are ready to dismiss such a claim as nonsense, until they realize the nightmares Ivy is having involve her being trapped in a fire. Engrossing thriller is very well acted and directed and builds to gut-wrenching climax. (BR-Twilight Time)

The Avenger (1960) 2.0
Criminal who calls himself "The Executioner" has just decapitated his 12th victim and so Scotland Yard assigns new inves-

tigator, who goes undercover at movie shoot to question latest victim's niece. Potentially exciting thriller gets bogged down in movie-making clichés and setting up obvious red herrings. Things do get interesting in the last 15 minutes or so, however. (DVD-R-Sinister Cinema)

The Awful Dr. Orlof (1962) 2.5
Dr. Orlof murders beautiful young women to restore beauty to his disfigured daughter. Jess Franco's first "big movie" has some creepy atmosphere and a menacing blind henchman to make this an above-average surgical-horror flick. (BR-Kino)

The Baby (1973) 3.0
Social worker takes case of adult male who is still being treated like a baby by his mother and sisters: he wears diapers, sleeps in a crib, crawls, and can't speak. And it seems anyone who tries to help Baby is stopped. Fascinating, uncomfortable, bizarre, and frightening. There is a twist to the story that is beautifully set up, culminating in a GREAT ending that makes this a winner. (BR-Arrow)

Back from the Dead (1957) 1.5
When Dick Anthony's second wife has an epileptic seizure and suffers a miscarriage, his dead first wife possesses her and wreaks havoc. Apparently, the ex-mother-in-law is an expert in the black arts. Uninvolving thriller with lackluster cast and predictable plot. Really bland direction doesn't help either. (NA)

Back to the Planet of the Apes (TV-1974) 2.5
After five theatrical features, *Planet of the Apes* became a short-lived TV series that debuted Friday, September 13, 1974 (the same night as *Kolchak: The Night Stalker*'s premiere) but was gone by the end of the year. Ten of the 14 episodes were re-edited into five syndicated movies consisting of two episodes each. This is the first one, pairing the premiere and third episodes, "Escape from Tomorrow" and "The Trap," respectively. Three astronauts take off in 1980 and land on ape-dominated Earth in 3085. The two that survive eventually team up with Galen (Roddy McDowall), a chimpanzee sympathetic to the humans, who gets in trouble when he tries to help them. The trio are pursued by Urko and his Gorilla army to a dilapidated city that may provide a means of returning to a present-day Earth. While neither a great nor revolutionary series, it was enjoyable enough for *Apes* aficionados. This "movie" rates as above-average entertainment. (DVD-Fox as part of *Planet of the Apes: The Complete TV Series*)

The Bamboo Saucer (1968) 2.5
No one believes test pilot who claims he saw a flying saucer during routine exercises. After a Chinese peasant provides a sketch of a UFO that's residing in a deserted church, the flyer is recruited to join the exploratory team heading to China. Thing is, there's a Russian team headed there too. Enjoyable if unspectacular sci-fi does have unusual plot element of US/Russian cooperation. Likeable cast includes Dan Duryea in his final film role. (BR-Olive)

Baron Blood (1972) 3.0
Curious about his heritage, young scholar visits uncle in Austria and learns about villainous ancestor, whom he unintentionally raises from the dead when he recites spell from parchment. Director Mario Bava's uber-stylish Gothic is ultra-creepy, with Joseph Cotten seemingly having a blast playing sadistic Baron. (BR-Kino)

The Bat (1959) 2.5
Re-telling of the exploits of super criminal The Bat, who terrorizes mystery writer and her guests at rented home as he searches for hidden loot. Vincent Price is a suspect. Agreeable mystery horror. (BR-R-The Film Detective)

The Bat People (1974) 2.0
Recently married doctor is bitten by bat while cave exploring, and then begins to transform into blood-thirsty monster. Modest thriller features good performance by Michael Pataki as determined lawman and fine makeup by Stan Winston, which is kept in the shadows until finale. Stewart Moss is okay in the lead, but his frequent seizures get repetitive and ultimately silly. (BR-Shout! Factory)

Battle Beneath the Earth (1967) 1.5
The Chinese have been building tunnels beneath the US with the goal of detonating atomic bombs. But several unnatural disasters alert scientists to their nefarious plan. Campy, unconvincing sci-fi actioner with terrible makeup and laughable script. Good for some unintentional chuckles. (DVD-Warner Bros. with *The Ultimate Warrior*)

Battle Beyond the Sun (1963) 1.5
Francis Ford Coppola is the pseudonym-credited director of this Americanized version of 1959 Soviet Union film *Nebo Zovyot*. It's 1997 and a nuclear war has resulted in the new nations of North Hemis and South Hemis. They're in a race to be the first to land on Mars. Interestingly shaped monsters are waiting for them. Some of the effects are impressive but overall, this is slow-moving, dialogue-heavy stuff. (DVD-Retromedia with *Star Pilot*)

Battle for the Planet of the Apes (1973) 2.5
Following the events of *Conquest of the Planet of the Apes* and a nuclear war, apes and humans must learn to coexist. But a gorilla named Aldo thinks the only good human is a dead human, setting the stage for the ultimate battle. Mostly entertaining final installment in the original ape series ties things together nicely. Human attack caravan may have inspired the *Mad Max* series. (BR-Fox)

Battle in Outer Space (1959) 2.0
Alien race has set up shop on the moon with the intention of taking over Earth. Abundant special effects include mother ships, attack saucers, space torpedoes and laser battles. Ending of course sees the proverbial destruction of Tokyo. Diverting but nothing special; there's not much here in the way of character. (BR-Mill Creek with *The H-Man*)

Battle of the Worlds (1961) 1.0
Claude Rains plays a disagreeable genius who realizes the strange planet that has started orbiting Earth means us harm. Rains gives a vigorous performance as an unlikeable character. But it's in the service of a poorly edited film with drawn-out story that fails to hold viewer's interest. The finale is excruciating. OK effects. (BR-The Film Detective)

The Beach Girls and the Monster (1965) 0.5
Former Invisible Agent Jon Hall shot, directed and stars in this low-budget offense about sea monster killing young people who just want to live the beach life. Bad on nearly every level, but at least the "surprise" ending explains why the monster is so goofy looking. Aired under the title *Monster from the Surf*. (DVD-Image)

Beast from Haunted Cave (1959) 2.5
Thieves plan their escape route via the snowy mountains of Deadwood, South Dakota, not realizing title fiend lies in wait. Some great, witty dialogue here along with solid performances. Needed more monster attacks to really score though. (BR-Retromedia with *The Wasp Woman*)

The Beast from 20,000 Fathoms (1953) 2.5
Atomic testing frees previously frozen dinosaur, which goes on rampage. A Ray Bradbury story receives the Ray Harryhausen effects treatment in this monster-on-the-loose thriller. Great effects of course. The film sags when the beast is off screen. (BR-Warner Bros.)

The Beast in the Cellar (1971) 2.0
Title tells most in this British chiller about two sisters who keep their savage brother in the basement. He figures out a way to escape and starts murdering local soldiers. The attack/murder sequences are little varied, and the film is mostly exposition. Beryl Reid and Flora Robson are very good as the siblings and give the film a certain gravitas it may not have had without them. (BR-Severin)

The Beast Must Die! (1974) 2.0
It's another variation on Agatha Christie's *And Then There Were None*, except the murderer this time is a werewolf. Hunter gathers suspects on an island hoping to discover werewolf's identity. Can you figure out the guilty party by the end of the Werewolf Break? Silly thriller with Peter Cushing on hand to give it a much-needed boost. (BR-Severin)

Beast of Blood (1970) 1.0
Third, last, and least of the Blood Island Trilogy. Dr. Lorca did *not* perish in the fire that supposedly consumed him in *Mad Doctor of Blood Island*. He's back to creating "green men" while trying to revive his decapitated monster, with whose living head he has one-way conversations. It takes too long to get to the good stuff this time around, making the lousy acting and technical ineptness even more obvious. Our beloved monster hardly has any screen time. (BR-Severin as part of *The Blood Island Collection*)

The Beast of Hollow Mountain (1956) 2.5
On a Mexican ranch cattle are being killed seemingly by local wildlife. The true culprit however is a dinosaur that soon sets its sights on the nearby village. About 75% of the film is a standard western with greedy villain that resents American newcomer, and the woman who loves them both. Then the monster finally shows its face, and the last quarter of the movie is a rousing monster-on-the-loose thriller. Result is entertaining if imperfect hybrid. (BR-Shout! Factory with *The Neanderthal Man*)

Beast of Morocco (1966) 2.0
Grieving architect, plagued by horrific nightmares involving his dead family, travels to Morocco and becomes enchanted by local woman who happens to be a life-draining vampire. Having lost the will to live, he considers joining her. Starts out as intriguing, living nightmare narrative but then gets bogged down in romantic subplot and metaphoric discussions about light versus darkness and such. Opening nightmare sequence is effectively creepy. (VHS-Video Yesteryear)

The Beast with a Million Eyes (1955) 1.0
Alien being with power to control the minds of animals and weak humans arrives on Earth to begin its reign of terror, menacing troubled ranch family and the local wildlife. No-budget, talky bore with inappropriate music, poor post-synching, and villain who talks like a disc jockey. (BR-Scorpion Releasing)

The Beast with Five Fingers (1946) 3.0
Good, creepy flick about a deceased musician's hand that seems to have a life of its own. Peter Lorre's confrontations with the hand are the highlights. Great direction by Robert Florey. (DVD-R-Warner Archive)

Beasts (1983) 1.0
A savage grizzly and the two quarreling ex-cons who are hunting it for the reward ruin a couple's reunion retreat to a mountain cabin. Poor entry in Killer Grizzly subgenre has likeable leads but leaden pace and unconvincing bear attacks. The "beast" looks like he's hugging his "victims." The true beasts are the hunters, who are little more than stereotypes. Corny Cub Scout subplot and lousy ending don't help matters either. (VHS-Star Classics)

Bedlam (1946) 3.0
Final Val Lewton horror production features Boris Karloff as head of St. Mary's of Bethlehem Asylum. He runs afoul reformer Anna Lee who is not pleased with the poor conditions, so he has her committed. Good production values and fine, menacing Karloff performance. (BR-Warner Archive with *The Ghost Ship*)

The Bees (1978) 1.5
Scientists are trying to take the fatal sting out of South American killer bees when a series of unfortunate events send the buzzing villains to the US A good B-movie cast (John Saxon, Angel Tompkins, and John Carradine, attempting a German

accent) isn't enough to save this laughable nature attacks entry. The music score is inappropriate, the effects not effective, and the overall tone off-putting. Carradine is a hoot as buzzing scientist affectionately called Ziggy. (BR-Vinegar Syndrome)

Before I Hang (1940) 2.5
Awaiting his execution for a mercy killing, an elderly scientist (Boris Karloff) continues his experiments on an anti-aging serum while on death row. He appears to succeed, and the twists and turns start coming. Pretty good thriller starts to get repetitive as the climax approaches, though Karloff is as watchable as always. Edward Van Sloane is a kindly prison doctor. (DVD-Sony as part of *Icons of Horror Collection: Boris Karloff*)

Before Midnight (1933) 1.5
On a dark and stormy night, Inspector Trent (Ralph Bellamy) tries to prevent a murder supposedly tied to a family curse. He can't, so he must solve it instead. Archaic Columbia whodunit is mostly painful, with stodgy, lackluster performances; awkward and slow line delivery; and an unconvincing plot that ultimately makes little sense. First of the studio's four Inspector Trent films. (DVD-R-Sinister Cinema)

Beginning of the End (1957) 2.0
Giant grasshoppers threaten Chicago in director Bert I. Gordon's second directing effort. Peter Graves is the scientist who deals with bad effects and flat dialogue. Competent performances are what keep the film afloat. (DVD-Image)

Behind the Mask (1932) 2.5
US Secret Service agent goes undercover to find head of drug ring. Boris Karloff plays a none-too-bright henchman; Edward Van Sloan a bearded, sinister doctor, who is introduced fooling around with electronic gadgets. Sloan and Karloff have some great scenes together and the film, though a crime picture, features numerous elements more at home in a Gothic thriller: a thunderstorm, a creepy mansion, a late-night cemetery visit, a clock striking midnight, a scenery-chewing mad scientist, etc. (DVD-Sony as part of *Karloff: Criminal Kind*)

Bela Lugosi Meets a Brooklyn Gorilla (1952) 0.0
Poor Bela. After having fun with the Ritz Brothers (*The Gorilla*), the East Side Kids (*Spooks Run Wild, Ghosts on the Loose*), Brown and Carney (*Zombies on Broadway*), Abbott and Costello (*Meet Frankenstein*), and Old Mother Riley (*My Son, the Vampire*), he got stuck with the imitation Martin and Lewis team of Duke Mitchell and Sammy Petrillo. Result is awful comedy where Lugosi is jungle mad scientist testing his theories of evolution on love rival Mitchell, hoping to make a gorilla out of him. Lewis' goofy-voiced schtick may be a product of its time. But if you're going to watch that sort of thing you may as well watch the original in something like *Scared Stiff*. Lugosi's next stop was Ed Wood, Jr. Make that poor, poor Bela. Also aired as *The Boys from Brooklyn*. (DVD-Image)

Ben (1972) 1.5
Sequel to *Willard* picks up after rats have torn Willard to ribbons. While the police are scouring the neighborhood looking for rodents, a young introvert befriends Ben, the rat leader. Uninvolving thriller that consists of tame rat attack scenes and overly cute boy-and-his-rat moments. Theme song performed by Michael Jackson was nominated for an Oscar. (BR-Shout! Factory)

Beneath the Planet of the Apes (1970) 2.0
First sequel to classic *Planet of the Apes*. In 3955, astronaut James Franciscus lands on ape planet in search of Taylor (Charlton Heston) from the previous entry. He finds city of apes and community of telepathic humans living underground. Disappointing follow-up repeats many beats from the first film to no avail and then loses its audience with overlong sequences involving manipulative mutants. Bleak finale is bold but too little too late. (BR-Fox)

Berserk (1967) 2.5
Someone is murdering circus owner Joan Crawford's performers. Not that she minds—it's great for business! Michael Gough is her ex-lover; Judy Geeson her grumpy daughter. Horror-whodunit is entertaining enough while it lasts. (BR-Mill Creek with *Strait-Jacket*)

Beware! The Blob (1972) 1.5
Fools bring Blob specimen back from the Artic; it thaws and starts consuming all manner of life forms. Uneasy mix of supposedly funny character bits (which pad the running time) and thrills that scream 1970s. The bowling alley attack is cool. Otherwise, beware indeed. (BR-Kino)

Beyond the Time Barrier (1960) 2.5
Air Force test pilot zooms into 2024; learns of bleak future where sterile mutants and deaf mutes populate Earth due to plague and radiation. Visually captivating low-budget sci-fi with good lead performance by Robert Clarke and fast-paced direction by Edgar G. Ulmer. (BR-Kino as part of *Edgar G. Ulmer Sci-Fi Collection*)

Billy the Kid vs. Dracula (1966) 2.0
John Carradine's hammy turn as Dracula makes this horror-western entertaining for all the wrong reasons. Dracula assumes the identity of ranch owner and sets his teeth on his "niece." But her boyfriend is none other than Billy the Kid! Most hilarious scene happens at the end, when, after firing all his bullets at Dracula with no effect, Billy then tosses his gun at the villain—which hits Drac square in the face, knocking him out cold!! Who knew? (BR-Kino)

The Birds (1963) 3.5
Chilling Alfred Hitchcock thriller about the sudden attack on humankind by our feathered friends. Lack of a music score adds to the eeriness, and the bird attacks remain harrowing. The final shot is a kicker. (BR-Universal)

The Black Abbot (1963) 2.5
Cloaked figure stabs man at the abbey near Chelford Manor. Scotland Yard sets up shop at the estate to find the killer, his motivation a rumored hidden treasure—two and half tons of

gold! Klaus Kinski is a butler with a criminal past. The nighttime scenes with various characters prowling fog-enshrouded ruins are sufficiently creepy, as is the music. Eddi Arent's bumbling policeman on the other hand threatens to derail the whole thing. (DVD-R-Sinister Cinema)

The Black Castle (1952) 2.0
English nobleman goes undercover to find out what happened to his two friends, victims of a sinister Count (he wears an eyepatch after all) who likes hunting leopards and such. Boris Karloff is the villain's on-hand doctor. Has good atmosphere but lacks a strong bad guy. (BR-Shout! Factory as part of *Universal Horror Collection: Volume 6*)

The Black Cat (1934) 4.0
Critics have praised Boris Karloff for making his monsters sympathetic in both *Frankenstein* (1931) and *The Mummy* (1932). But there is no sympathy to be had for his Hjalmar Poelzig, a Satanist and murderer who plans to sacrifice a newlywed during what was supposed to be her honeymoon. Luckily, doctor Bela Lugosi has plans of his own. This makes the short-list of best horrors of the 1930s due to its intense performances, marvelous production design, and unrelentingly grim atmosphere. It's unique in that it deals with outright evil. Many people can dismiss vampires and mummies as the stuff of make-believe. The devil on the other hand… (BR-Shout! Factory as part of *Universal Horror Collection: Volume 1*)

The Black Cat (1941) 2.5
Familiar story of greedy relatives, a will, and murder given a boost thanks to a cast that includes Basil Rathbone and a young Alan Ladd. Bela Lugosi chases cats ("Here kitty, kitty!"). The villain of the piece is nicely concealed but the obtrusive comedy relief by Hugh Herbert always ruins the mood. (BR-Shout! Factory as part of *Universal Horror Collection: Volume 3*)

The Black Cobra (1963) 2.0
An innocent truck driver is caught up with drug smugglers and the police, who think he's a killer. Austria-produced thriller has the look and feel of a German *krimi*, including a routine plot and secret master villain. But Adrian Hoven is likable as the man out to prove his innocence. Klaus Kinski is a junkie who plays the piano, while the gangsters are played rather broadly for the most part. The encounter with the cobra is admittedly intense though. (DVD-VCI with *No Survivors Please.*)

Black Dragons (1942) 1.5
Dull and illogical Bela Lugosi Poverty Row outing has Lugosi avenge himself on the Japanese agents who double-crossed him. There are some real howlers of dialogue here, but it's not as much fun as some of Lugosi's other low budget thrillers. Favorite Lugosi line, responding to someone wondering if they'll meet again: "Who knows, in this crazy world?" (DVD-Roan Group as part of *The Black & Blue Collection*)

Black Friday (1940) 2.5
Boris Karloff saves his friend's (Stanley Ridges) life by giving him part of a dying gangster's (Ridges again) brain, and then realizes he might be able to get his hands on the $50K the thug has hidden. Fast-paced horror/sci-fi thriller boasts excellent dual performance by Ridges. Bela Lugosi is fun, if wasted, in the role of hoodlum's rival. (BR-Shout! Factory as part of *Universal Horror Collection: Volume 1*)

The Black Panther of Ratana (1963) 2.5
A murderous black panther is apparently loose in Thai mining village, attacking respected local businessman as well as visiting ex-cons. Does it have something to do with the blue sapphire stolen during the pre-credits sequence? Shades of *The Leopard Man* with respect to the mystery plot, this German adventure is lightweight, escapist entertainment with a sense of humor. The bar fight sequence is especially amusing as the owner keeps track of his destroyed furniture. There's also a surprise or two at the end. All that is missing is a sense of focus. Having so many characters gives the film an erratic quality that hinders the narrative. (NA)

The Black Pit of Dr. M (1958) 3.0
One of the best Mexican horrors, and a unique film still today. Two doctors make a deal. The first one who dies will come back and show the other what awaits after death. The other will then return his friend to the living. When one does indeed die, the agreement comes to fruition, although not exactly as imagined. The Rube Goldberg-like machinations of the plot are fascinating, and patience is rewarded with a dizzying final act. A minor gem. (DVD-Casa Negra)

The Black Raven (1943) 2.5
Criminals, seedy types, and people who cannot leave town thanks to a washed-out bridge gather at the Black Raven Inn. Murder and mayhem ensue. Pretty entertaining Poverty Row thriller includes George Zucco and Glenn Strange in the cast. The motivations of Zucco's character, a criminal known as the Raven, are perplexing as he emerges something of a hero by film's end. But this is a must for fans of old dark house cinema. (BR-Retromedia with *The Ape*)

The Black Room (1935) 3.5
Karloff plays twin brothers whose family is cursed. When the ruling older brother is about to be ousted due to his less than civil behavior, he calls back his younger brother to assume the leadership role. But of course, there's a double cross in store. Neglected thriller features some of Karloff's finest, most subtle work. The film looks beautiful too. (DVD-Sony as part of *Icons of Horror Collection: Boris Karloff*)

Black Sabbath (1963) 3.0
Italian anthology film directed by Mario Bava and narrated by Boris Karloff, who stars in the last segment as a vampire-like creature. The first story, "The Drop of Water," is the best and one of the most effective ghost stories this viewer has ever seen. Middle segment, "The Telephone," is largely forgettable but may have been special back in '63. (The sequence of the stories is different in the original Italian version. Both are available on home video.) (BR-Kino)

The Black Scorpion (1957) 2.5
Willis O'Brien's effects work is the reason to see this familiar "giant fill-in-the-blank on the loose" picture. A volcanic eruption unleashes the title beast on Mexican village. The attack scenes are staged with verve and the stadium finale is a wow. (BR-Warner Archive)

The Black Sleep (1956) 2.5
Basil Rathbone conducts brain experiments in hope of reviving his wife, who's been in a coma for many months. Bela Lugosi, Lon Chaney, John Carradine, and Tor Johnson are also in the cast. A decidedly watchable, old-fashioned mad scientist yarn released one year before the Gothic horror revival. (BR-Kino)

Black Sunday (1960) 3.5
One of the great Italian horrors, oozing atmosphere and dread thanks largely to cinematographer-turned-director Mario Bava. A witch plans to return as a vampire to avenge her death. Barbara Steele plays the two female leads. Complete with graveyard visits, spooky castles, secret passageways, frightened animals, looming thunderstorms, angry torch-bearing peasants, family curses, raging fires—it's all here. (BR-Kino)

Black Tide (1958) 2.0
Standard murder tale about married man drowning his lover, under the cover of fog, as she swims the English Channel. Unfortunately for him, her swim partner suspects foul play, making the meddler the killer's next target. Not too many surprises here and the ending is disappointing, although the setting is atmospheric, and the cast is fine. There is a Region 2 DVD release under the title *Stormy Crossing*. (NA)

Blacula (1972) 3.0
Great vampire film with William Marshall impressive as cursed African prince unleashed in Los Angeles. Director William Crain stages some fabulous terror sequences. But it's Marshall that makes the film as memorable as it is. Love the main title music! (BR-Shout! Factory with *Scream, Blacula, Scream*)

The Blancheville Monster (1963) 2.0
Northern France 1884: A week before her 21st birthday, young woman returns to her castle home and learns that her bellowing, disfigured father is being kept chained in the castle tower and wants to kill her! Atmospheric Italian Gothic has the requisite trappings (e.g. a family curse, late-night strolls, castle graveyard, thunderstorms, cries in the night) but suffers from languid pacing and too-familiar plot. (DVD-Retromedia as *Horror*)

The Blob (1958) 2.5
One of the best-known titles of the '50s; it even has its own theme song! Meteor crashes on earth and curious onlooker unwittingly releases what it contains: a glob of purple jelly that consumes living beings. The more it eats, the bigger it grows. Steve McQueen plays a determined teenager whom the police don't believe. OK effects in this colorful, mostly fun effort. A sequel, *Beware! The Blob*, followed some 14 years later. Effectively remade in 1988. (BR-Criterion)

Blood and Black Lace (1964) 2.5
Director Mario Bava's atmospheric mystery set at a fashion house, where figure in black is viciously murdering models. The first true *giallo* (assuming color is a prerequisite) is beautiful and stylish, if emotionally cold. The plot is sufficiently complicated to keep the viewer guessing. (BR-Arrow)

Blood and Lace (1971) 2.0
After her mother is murdered, a young woman is sent to orphanage where mistress stores troublemakers in the freezer. Mostly ineffective jumbling of familiar horror tropes further harmed by atrocious use of music. Notable for Gloria Grahame's appearance as chief baddie. The opening sequence features point-of-view shot of killer using hammer. The final twist, however, is delightfully nasty. (BR-Shout! Factory)

Blood from the Mummy's Tomb (1971) 2.5
As her birthday approaches, daughter of archaeology professor starts having nightmares about centuries-old Queen of Darkness, whose crypt Dad and company violated the night she was born. Is she the reincarnation of the vengeful queen? Not a traditional mummy film, there are no bandages, tana leaves, or high priests to be found; this handsome, atmospheric Hammer Film production features a striking lead in Valerie Leon and solid veteran cast. The problem is a script that doesn't know where to go when the plot has been fully established. Highlight is asylum scene where a cobra statue seems to have come to life. Based on Bram Stoker's *Jewel of the Seven Stars*; one of the characters is named Tod Browning! (BR-Shout! Factory)

Blood Mania (1970) 1.5
The sordid tale of two "young and evil" souls: he's a doctor in need of $50,000 to pay off a blackmailer, and she's a nutcase whose rich, sick father is confined to his bed. There's murder and lots of skin in this sleazy flick. The best sequences are at the very beginning (a dazzlingly hallucinatory credit sequence) and the very end. Too bad what happens in between isn't as interesting. (BR-Vinegar Syndrome with *Point of Terror*)

Blood of Dracula (1957) 1.5
Dad and his new bride ship troubled teen Sandra Harrison off to boarding school. Her violent outbursts make her a candidate for mad professor's experiments involving hypnosis and an ancient amulet. Pretty much a reworking of *I Was a Teenage Werewolf* that could just as easily been titled *I Was a Teenage Vampire*. But the result is nowhere near as enjoyable. Part of the problem is that Louise Lewis' playing of the villain is too staid, lacking the verve that Whit Bissell brought to the earlier feature. The finale is a bust, and the slack pacing and repetitious nature of the plot don't help either. (DVD-Lionsgate with *How to Make a Monster*)

Blood of Ghastly Horror (1971) 1.0
Years ago, neurologist John Carradine created electronic gizmo that helped revive injured parts of the brain. Unfortunately, his test case turned into homicidal madman. Now, seeking vengeance on those he holds responsible for the maniac's death, the father of that test case has created a zombie of sorts to do

his dirty work. Notorious for starting out as a crime drama, and then having footage added to turn it into a horror film. The resulting confused mess *is* ghastly but not in a good way. (BR-Severin as part of *Al Adamson: The Masterpiece Collection*)

The Blood of Nostradamus (1962) 1.5
Final of four films culled from 12-part Mexican serial given the K. Gordan Murray treatment for AIP Television. Vampire Nostradamus taunts police chief by sending death announcement while the man is still alive. Luckily, expert scientist is on hand to offer his advice and invent headache-inducing machine that gives the vampire migraines. Nostradamus plays his violin for amusement of his hunchback assistant and hypnotizes plenty of people, never following through with his various schemes. A couple of decent scenes in this otherwise talky bore filled with ludicrous dialogue and lethargic pacing. (DVD-R-Sinister Cinema)

Blood of the Vampire (1958) 2.5
Really a mad scientist yarn about "vampire" doctor who was staked through the heart for his unorthodox experiments. Now he's governor of a prison for the criminally insane where he carries on with his work. Donald Wolfit is very good as the villain and makes the film worth seeing. Written by Jimmy Sangster. Barbara Shelley plays the heroine. (BR-Shout! Factory)

Blood Song (1982) 2.0
High schooler Donna Wilkes is having visions of flute-playing psychopath Frankie Avalon who, 27 years earlier, witnessed his father kill himself after murdering his wife and her lover. The two are linked because she received Avalon's blood during a transfusion. Now he's escaped the state mental hospital and is heading her way. Pure 1980s horror with synthesizer score, gory kills, and teen in peril. But Avalon is good as the psycho and Wilkes makes a sympathetic heroine. (DVD-BCI with *Mausoleum*)

The Blood Spattered Bride (1972) 3.0
Newlywed Susan moves into her husband's palatial home and starts having violent nightmares involving mysterious woman who encourages the young bride to murder her spouse. When hubby brings home a look-a-like stranger he found on the beach, Susan is convinced the woman is the ghost of Mircalla Karenstein, an ancestor of her husband who murdered her own spouse centuries ago on her wedding night. This Spanish version of Sheridan Le Fanu's *Carmilla* is violent and sexy and features a few scenes of shocking violence. It's also well-acted and compelling viewing. This review is for the uncut 102-minute version, which no doubt was heavily censored for its TV incarnation. Aired on Channel 2's *Chiller Theater* as *Till Death Do Us Part*. (BR-Mondo Macabro)

Bloodlust! (1961) 1.5
Reworking of short story "The Most Dangerous Game" shot in 1959 for the teenage set. Youths make mistake of investigating seemingly deserted island; find madman who wants to hunt them like animals instead. Dreary and uninspired; of note perhaps for appearance by future *The Brady Bunch* dad Robert Reed. (DVD-Film Chest)

The Bloody Judge (1970) 2.0
Christopher Lee plays true-life Lord Chancellor George Jeffreys who presides over cases of witchcraft and traitors against King James II in 17th-century England. Not historically accurate of course, and since it's Jess Franco behind the camera there is a misogynistic streak running throughout. Lee's commanding performance keeps this watchable. But the film suffers when he's not on screen. Aired as *Night of the Blood Monster*. (DVD-Blue Underground)

The Bloody Vampire (1962) 2.5
Vampire Count Frankenhausen keeps his beautiful female victims tucked away in coffins in his castle cellar, biding his time until he can take over the world! Meanwhile Count Cagliostro continues the family tradition of trying to rid the world of the undead bloodsuckers. This has one of the best openings of any Mexican horror, as a horse-drawn carriage glides in slow motion along fog-enshrouded roads. Its driver is a cloak-wearing skeleton! There's also a big-ass bat flapping about and a phenomenal use of music and eerie sound effects. Unfortunately, the film is also frequently talky, spoiling the well-mounted atmosphere. Still, a good choice for a Saturday night spook show. Followed by *The Invasion of the Vampires*. (DVD-Beverly Wilshire)

Blue Sunshine (1977) 3.0
Headaches, hair loss, nightmares, and homicidal rampages—these are the delayed side effects of a drug called Blue Sunshine several people took 10 years ago in college. A friend (Zalman King) of one of the killers is blamed for the crimes and takes it upon himself to investigate. Clever, inventive thriller by writer/director Jeff Lieberman is highly entertaining but somewhat hampered by King's lackluster lead performance. Brion James does an amusing Rodan imitation early in the film. (BR-Filmcentrix)

Bluebeard (1944) 3.0
John Carradine gives a strong performance as the title character, a puppeteer and artist who, motivated by revenge, strangles women. Some nice visual flourishes by director Edgar G. Ulmer complement the Parisian setting. Only gripe is a music score that doesn't stop. (DVD-Image)

Bluebeard (1963) 2.5
Directed by the acclaimed Claude Chabrol (France's answer to Alfred Hitchcock), this semi-comedic version of the familiar story has a seemingly respectable family man using newspaper ads to lure unwary widowed ladies to their doom. Unevenly paced film is still fascinating due to the story itself. One running gag includes couple complaining to each other about the smell every time Bluebeard burns a corpse in his villa's stove. Aired sometimes under its original title *Landru*. (BR-Kino)

Bluebeard (1972) 2.0
Bizarre version of the wife-killer legend played for laughs at times. Richard Burton stars as Austrian World War I hero who murders his brides in various ways. When his latest missus discovers the freezer where he keeps the corpses, he explains to

her why each one had to die. Burton seems to be having fun but the audience, not so much. The ladies are stunning and the production attractive, with good Ennio Morricone score. Unfortunately, the film is more curio than entertainment. (BR-Shout! Factory)

Bluebeards Ten Honeymoons (1960) 2.5
George Sanders plays lonely man who becomes infatuated with money-hungry club singer. He tries at first to raise funds honestly. When an accidental death gets him what he wants without consequence, he goes on a killing spree to secure further income. The script is heavily contrived, but Sanders is very good in the lead and makes this recommended viewing. The climax features thunder, lightning, and a damsel in distress (and another one burning in the oven). (NA)

The Body Disappears (1941) 2.5
Passed out from too much libation at his bachelor party, rich golf champion is mistaken for a corpse and "resurrected" by scientist Edward Everett Horton. Unfortunately, the doctor's formula turns the subject invisible. Comedic sci-fi is amiable enough, with most of the laughs provided by Willie Best and his non-stop one-liners. Courtroom framing device doesn't really add anything to the story though. (NA)

The Body Snatcher (1945) 4.0
Perhaps the best horror film of the 1940s. Boris Karloff has never been better as the charming but ruthless cabman John Gray who steals bodies for Dr. MacFarlane (Henry Daniell) in 19th-century Edinburgh. Bela Lugosi plays MacFarlane's doomed employee. The scenes between Karloff and Daniell crackle with tension, and director Robert Wise beautifully handles the murder sequences. And what an ending! (BR-Shout! Factory)

The Boogeyman (1980) 2.5
A mirror "witnesses" a young boy stabbing his mother's abusive boyfriend. Many years later, the mirror is shattered, and the boyfriend's evil spirit is set free. Derivative but stylish slasher film offers some nicely choreographed death sequences and good lead performance by charming Suzanna Love. But other parts are silly, and the ending is a real letdown. (DVD-Anchor Bay)

The Boogie Man Will Get You (1942) 2.5
Amusing Boris Karloff effort where he plays daffy scientist conducting experiments on traveling salesmen. Peter Lorre is his partner in crime. The two horror stars make a great comedy team. (DVD-Sony as part of *Icons of Horror Collection: Boris Karloff*)

Bowery at Midnight (1942) 2.0
By day, Bela Lugosi is a respected college professor. By night, he leads a daring crime syndicate. And there's a drug-addicted mad doctor in his employ who performs weird experiments on Lugosi's victims. Another humdrum Monogram outing made watchable by Lugosi and his joyously evil performance. (BR-Retromedia with *The Corpse Vanishes*)

The Bowery Boys Meet the Monsters (1954) 2.5
By this point, the Boys were just Leo Gorcey and Huntz Hall, but they work well enough together. The duo visits an eccentric family hoping to secure location where underprivileged children can play baseball. But the family is comprised of a vampire, a woman who feeds people to her plant, and a couple of mad scientists. And there's another gorilla! Silly but a lot of fun, with Gorcey still mangling the English language and Hall playing the lovable idiot. (DVD-Warner Archive as part of *The Bowery Boys: Volume Two*)

A Boy and His Dog (1975) 3.0
2024 A.D. after World War IV: sex-starved young Vic and his telepathic, wiseacre dog Blood wander the wasteland in search of food and amusement. Vic doesn't realize he's been selected by leader of underground society for a very special purpose. Frequently hilarious black comedy is also cold and rather bleak. But it's never less than entertaining. Based on Harlan Ellison's Nebula Award-winning novella. (BR-Shout! Factory)

The Boy Who Cried Werewolf (1973) 2.0
While on a nature outing, werewolf bites young lad's father, who then goes on killing spree. A decidedly odd take on the werewolf myth, with any savagery toned down due to the PG rating. This wolf man will dig pits to hide severed heads, open and close doors, and leisurely pull back bed covers. Religious hippy subplot also adds to the weird vibe. The biggest problem though is a total lack of atmosphere, partly due to the inept handling of day-for-night scenes. (BR-Shout! Factory)

The Brain (1962) 2.5
This remake of *Donovan's Brain* stars Peter van Eyck as scientist working to keep animal brains alive once the bodies have stopped working. When he's called upon to provide medical assistance to a nearly dead plane crash survivor, he realizes he can keep the victim's brain alive. But the strong-willed brain overtakes his personality and forces him to do its bidding. More of a murder mystery with supernatural elements than an outright horror tale, the film has an eerie, noirish style and taut pace courtesy of director Freddie Francis, making his horror film directing debut. Enjoyable if not particularly memorable. (DVD-R-Sinister Cinema)

The Brain Eaters (1958) 2.0
Strange creatures from within the earth take over residents of small town. The beings attach themselves to the necks of their victims and then exact control. The film's cheapness shows every step of the way and prevents this *Invasion of the Body Snatchers* variant from succeeding. The best moment is a point-of-view shot where creature attacks a victim while asleep in her bed. Leonard Nimoy appears near the end, made up with a bushy beard and dressed like Obi-Wan Kenobi. (BR-Shout! Factory)

The Brain from Planet Arous (1957) 2.0
Giant, evil brain (complete with eyes) overtakes Earth scientist John Agar to carry out his dastardly plans. Luckily, a kindly brain hides out in a dog while figuring out how to save the

planet. Downright goofy story earnestly told, and is fascinating to watch, even if for the wrong reasons. The finale is a hoot. (BR-The Film Detective)

Brain of Blood (1971) 0.0
Ruler of presumably Middle Eastern country dies but mad medico transfers his brain to body of disfigured brute. Doctor's assistant Angelo Rossitto keeps women chained in a dungeon. Grant "Shrinking Man" Williams plays a good guy and wears a funny hat in his last film role. Viewer will have a hard time giving a damn about anything in another one of director Al Adamson's god-awful genre offerings. Aired as *The Creature's Revenge*. (BR-Severin as part of *Al Adamson: The Masterpiece Collection*)

The Brain That Wouldn't Die (1962) 1.5
Arrogant young scientist keeps his fiancée's head alive after a car crash. She isn't too happy about this but at least makes friends with the thing held captive in the closet. Talky, flat, and tedious; good for a few laughs though. (BR-Shout! Factory)

The Brainiac (1962) 2.0
In 1661, a warlock is put to death, only to return 300 years later to murder the descendants of his persecutors. Film wastes great movie monster in what becomes a repetitive revenge picture. Worth seeing at least once, but once you've seen the first murder, you've seen them all. (DVD-Casa Negra)

Breaking Point (1976) 2.5
Family man witnesses fatal beating and agrees to testify against the killers. The problem is the attack was a mob hit and wise guys don't like witnesses. Largely predictable story is still fun for those who enjoy watching tough guys get their asses handed to them by the common man. (DVD-Fox)

The Bribe (1949) 2.5
Robert Taylor is agent tracking down thieves in South America, where he falls in love with Ava Gardner who is married to the prime suspect. Charles Laughton and Vincent Price are also somehow involved. Sluggishly paced film noir still has the great cast and an exciting climax to recommend it. (DVD-R-Warner Archive)

The Bride and the Beast (1958) 1.0
Newlywed thinks she was a gorilla in past life; flirts with her husband's pet gorilla Spanky (no, I'm not making this up); and then goes on hunting trip to hook up. They should have called this film *Stock Footage Meets the Reincarnated Gorilla Slut*. (DVD-VCI)

Bride of Frankenstein (1935) 4.0
Universal's crowning horror achievement: the monster talks and demands a mate! Although the monster rallies didn't officially begin until the 1940s, this classic film boasts two mad scientists, two man-made monsters, and Una O'Connor. Ernest Thesiger practically steals the show as the flamboyant Dr. Pretorious. Karloff brings such marvelous humanity to his role that his performance here must rank as one of the all-time greats. (BR-Universal)

Bride of the Gorilla (1951) 2.0
Six years before *Perry Mason* made him a superstar Raymond Burr starred in this Lewtonesque jungle thriller as a murderer who, cursed by his victim's servant, may turn into a gorilla and wreak havoc when night falls. The local police chief (Lon Chaney) thinks a legendary creature called the succarath is on the prowl. Curt Siodmak (*The Wolf Man*) wrote and directed this unremarkable feature, originally intended to be an "is it all in his mind?" tale. The producers nixed that idea. For gorilla film aficionados only. (DVD-Image)

Bride of the Monster (1955) 2.0
Bela Lugosi plays Dr. Vornoff, a disgraced German scientist who now resides in the US, conducting experiments that will lead to a race of super beings! He also keeps a giant rubber octopus in his backyard. Lugosi gives his last major role his all, and that makes this Ed Wood effort entertaining if far, far from good. (DVD-Image)

Bride of Vengeance (1949) 2.0
Because the Duke of Ferrara would not agree to join him in a military alliance against Venice, Cesare Borgia frames the Duke for the murder of Borgia's brother-in-law. The new widow Lucretia (Paulette Goddard) agrees to marry the man she believes murdered her husband as part of intricate revenge plot, but things don't go quite as planned. Goddard, who was so innocent and adorable in *The Cat and the Canary* and *The Ghost Breakers*, does well enough as the title character. But the script lacks suspense, and the finale is a bust. (NA)

Brides of Blood (1968) 2.0
Scientist, his sex-starved wife, and a Peace Corps volunteer visit small island to aid in its modernization. Unfortunately, atomic testing from years earlier has created mutations in plant life as well as a monster that attacks on a nightly basis. Indefensible on any artistic level, this creepy, sleazy, and disturbing thriller is nevertheless compulsively watchable. It really does have to be seen to be believed. The first of the infamous Blood Island Trilogy; followed by *Mad Doctor of Blood Island*. Aired as *The Island of Living Horror*. (BR-Severin)

The Brides of Dracula (1960) 3.5
One of Hammer Film Productions' best with Peter Cushing tracking down vampire who has his sights set on lovely teaching assistant. Beautiful, haunting film, with many great supporting performances. David Peel as the fanged one lacks Christopher Lee's intimidating presence. But he still does well in the role of the vampiric Baron. (BR-Shout! Factory)

The Brides of Fu Manchu (1966) 2.5
Fu Manchu (Christopher Lee) has kidnapped the wives and daughters of leading industrialists and scientists to blackmail them into constructing death ray. Commissioner Nayland Smith vows to stop him. Lee is good as is German *krimi* star Heinz Drache, who plays a scientist. Not quite as strong as the first film. Still quite lively and entertaining. (DVD-Warner Bros. with *Chamber of Horrors* [1966])

The Brighton Strangler (1945) 2.5
American stage actor in London is looking forward to his final performance as the Brighton Strangler. Unfortunately, the theater district is bombed, and he suffers a head injury, which causes him to believe he really is the villain he's been playing! Set during the Christmas holidays, this is nicely atmospheric but strangely lacking in the expected tension. John Loder is okay in the lead but oh what Laird Cregar could have done with this. (VHS-RKO Home Video)

The Brotherhood of Satan (1971) 3.0
Over the last three days, the small town of Hillsboro has been plagued by multiple murders and disappearing children. No one can get in or out, except for birthday girl K.T., her father, and father's girlfriend. Meanwhile elderly Satanists have gathered for some horrific event. Eerie, intense, atmospheric chiller is well-directed and features disturbing ending. (BR-Arrow)

The Brute Man (1946) 1.5
Final Universal Horror (before the International merger) is one of the studio's worst. It's an origin story for The Creeper and how he became embittered and homicidal. Rondo Hatton still can't deliver a line and the attempts at humor don't work at all. Trivia note: Universal sold the film to Poverty Row studio PRC instead of distributing it themselves. (DVD-Image)

The Bubble (1966) 1.0
The first film shot in Space Vision, this 3D effort concerns airborne pregnant couple and their pilot who land during a thunderstorm in mysterious small town when wife goes into labor. The citizens speak in either clichés or bizarre codes and walk around like the living dead. The marrieds must discover what's going on and escape with their newborn. Writer-director Arch Obler gained fame as the creator of radio's *Lights Out*, so he knows how to tell a good scary tale. Here his at-times preachy, overwrought script is little more than a too-long *Twilight Zone* episode that relies on 3D for its impact. The ending stinks too. Aired as *Fantastic Invasion of Planet Earth*. (BR-Kino)

Buck Rogers (1939) 2.0
Film version of the Universal 12-chapter serial of the same name. Buck and his sidekick Buddy are discovered in state of suspended animation 500 years after crashing. They agree to help their rescuers do battle with gangster Killer Kane, who wants to control the universe. As with all serials butchered and forced into a feature film, this is episodic and unevenly paced. The likability of our heroes makes this better than most. Features music cues from *Bride of Frankenstein*, *WereWolf of London*, and *Dracula's Daughter*. Also known as *Destination Saturn*. (DVD-Mill Creek in edited version as *Planet Outlaws* as part of *Sci-Fi Classics: 50 Movie Pack*)

A Bucket of Blood (1959) 3.0
Dick Miller first played the character Walter Paisley in this Roger Corman black comedy. Walter accidentally kills a cat, covers it in plaster and calls it a sculpture. The next thing he knows he's a hit with the beatniks at the cafe where he works. When poor Walter unknowingly accepts heroin from an admirer, an undercover agent moves in to bust Walter, with fatal consequences. This is unquestionably Miller's best film role as *he's* the show here, as a lovable loser who just wants to be accepted. (BR-Olive)

Bug (1975) 2.5
After an earthquake, hybrid beetles with the power to set fires plague small rural town. Scientist Bradford Dillman tries to find a way to stop them, or at least understand them, possibly losing his mind in the process. Starts out like many revenge-of-nature films but eventually develops its own identity, with several harrowing scenes before the bravura finale. Last film produced by William Castle, who also co-scripted. (BR-Shout! Factory)

Burn, Witch, Burn (1962) 3.5
Second film version of Fritz Leiber's *Conjure Wife* (the first was *Weird Woman*), this superior story of witchery takes place on a college campus where a professor attempts to rid his wife of her belief in protective spells. Bad move. Suspenseful, intense thriller with perfect performances and several hair-raising sequences, including an unforgettable ending. Scripted by Richard Matheson, Charles Beaumont, and George Baxt (who also wrote *City of the Dead* aka *Horror Hotel*). (BR-Kino)

Burnt Offerings (1976) 3.0
Happy family rents disheveled, isolated mansion for the summer, only to find their relationships deteriorating while the house seems to rebuild itself. The great cast includes Oliver Reed, Karen Black, and Bette Davis, and they create a believable family dynamic that pays dividends as the horror unfolds in slow-burn fashion. Director Dan Curtis creates the proper mood and stages several impressive set-pieces. A different take on the haunted house story that holds up well today. (BR-Kino)

Bury Me Dead (1947) 2.5
June Lockhart plays woman believed to have burned to death in stable fire. Now, she must figure out who tried to kill her before he or she gets a second chance. For a film that is typically classified as film noir, this is awfully light-hearted—Lockhart playing the whole thing with a smile on her face, making it hard to worry about her too much. Other characters, such as the soon-to-be ex-husband and amorous boxer, are played as buffoons. Still, flashback approach to solving the crime holds one's interest as does John Alton's cinematography. (DVD-VCI with *The Chase*)

The Cabinet of Dr. Caligari (1920) 3.5
Justifiably classic piece of German Expressionism features somnambulist Cesare (Conrad Veidt) who may be committing murders under the instruction of demented doctor. One-of-a-kind picture with startling visuals, haunting visages, and a twist ending. After 100 years, this film can still give one the creeps if approached with an open mind. (BR-Kino)

Calling Dr. Death (1943) 2.5
First of the six *Inner Sanctum* series is pretty good. Lon Chaney plays therapist whose cheating wife is murdered, so of course

he's a suspect. It's rather absurd that the man eventually arrested for the crime, as well as his invalid wife, would ask Chaney to clear him when Chaney's not even a detective! But these Inner Sanctums are a lot of fun despite their shortcomings. (BR-Mill Creek as part of *Inner Sanctum Mysteries: The Complete Film Series*)

Caltiki, the Immortal Monster (1959) 2.5
Italian sci-fi production set in Mexico borrows from America's *The Blob* and Great Britain's *X the Unknown* and *The Quatermass Xperiment*. Expedition is attacked by glob creature that is supposedly an incarnation of Mexican god, then mistakenly brings back a sample for further study. Photographed by Mario Bava, who gives the film a Gothic look and feel. Story is rather clumsily developed, however. (BR-Arrow)

A Candle for the Devil (1973) 2.0
Judy Geeson arrives at Spanish inn to meet her sister, unaware the proprietors have just murdered her for the crime of sunbathing on the roof. Not terribly convincing story of religious zealotry and sexual repression is mostly predictable even though well-acted. Aired as *Nightmare Hotel*. (BR-Scorpion Releasing)

The Cape Canaveral Monsters (1960) 0.5
The director of *Robot Monster* strikes again but for the last time. Aliens who are planning an Earth invasion send two bickering emissaries to thwart missile launches. They kill two beachgoers and then inhabit their deceased bodies. Lots of talk, hammy acting, and unintentional comedy, including a villain who keeps losing his arm. (NA)

Captain Blackjack (1950) 2.5
George Sanders stars in this European thriller as lawyer-turned-smuggler who falls in love and decides his next job will be his last. Everyone's a liar or double-crosser in this entertaining, if hardly credible, crime drama. Agnes Moorehead is great as wealthy ditz who is really a ruthless competitor. (NA)

Captive (1980) 1.5
After their ship crashes on Earth, a pair of hostile aliens take a grandfather and his grandkids hostage at their farmhouse. One of the invaders is shot and starts bonding with the young woman forced to take care of him. Story wise this is obvious and predictable. The effects are weak due to the budget. The mostly adequate performances help somewhat but this is below average entertainment. On Region 2 DVD as part of *The Renown Pictures Vintage Sci-Fi Collection Volume One*. (NA)

Captive Wild Woman (1943) 2.5
John Carradine is good as villainous doctor conducting horrific experiments at his clinic, following in the footsteps of Dr. Moreau. Lively hour of circus footage features the debut of ape woman Paula Dupree, played by Acquanetta. (We learn in the next film why they didn't let her speak in this one.) (BR-Shout! Factory as part of *Universal Horror Collection: Volume 5*)

The Car (1977) 2.5
Demonic auto terrorizes small desert town, blowing its horn and running over various citizens. A *Jaws*-on-land wannabe succeeds some of the time, fails miserably at others. The cast is generally good, and there are some terrific stunts. On the other hand, some of the dialogue is poor and several situations just plain goofy, the confrontation at the cemetery for instance. (BR-Shout! Factory)

The Carnation Killer (TV-1973) 3.0
After he's found guilty but insane for nine murders, a psycho killer escapes custody and, through a case of mistaken identity, finds himself on a train with potential victim number 10. There are some clever nods to *Psycho* as well as the requisite twists. The final shot is shudder-inducing. Original title: *The Colour of Blood*. (DVD-VEI as part of *Thriller: The Complete Collection*)

Carnival of Crime (1962) 1.0
Architect returns from work trip to find his wife has left him; discovers she has lots of boyfriends and starts interrogating them to find her. Shot in Brazil, this is an unforgivably dull and uninvolving mystery. Music score at times recalls that of *The Third Man*, which any viewer would be much better off watching. (DVD-Mill Creek as part of *Cult Terror Cinema: 12 Movie Collection*)

Carnival of Souls (1962) 3.0
Car accident survivor tries to get on with her life, but ghoulish, mysterious figure pursues her. Gripping, moody thriller with a great ending and many memorable sequences. One of the few films that successfully captures the idea of living in a nightmare. (BR-Criterion)

The Carpet of Horror (1962) 2.0
Exotic poison gas is the means used to murder those who threaten international crime organization. There's lots of running, fighting, and chasing in this disjointed thriller, which adds ludicrous romantic subplot to no avail. One might find amusement in guessing the identity of the mystery boss, who communicates to his underlings via type-written messages on video monitor. (DVD-R-Sinister Cinema)

Carrie (1976) 3.5
Stephen King's first novel makes for classic Brian De Palma-directed tale. Social outcast comes into womanhood and is invited to the prom. You know the rest. Suspenseful, shocking, funny, heartbreaking, and horrifying. (BR-Shout! Factory)

Castle of Evil (1966) 1.5
Supposedly dead scientist arranges for his enemies to be brought to island for reading of his will. Instead, robot zombie starts murdering the guests. Despite a cast including Scott Brady and Virginia Mayo, this is a familiar story cheaply told that fails to build the atmosphere and suspense necessary to make its ancient premise succeed. (VHS-Republic)

The Castle of Fu Manchu (1969) 0.0
Probably Christopher Lee's worst film, his final turn as the evil genius Fu Manchu who this time is planning to freeze the ocean unless world meets his demands. God-awful pacing, obnoxious camera zooms, and lack of action are only some

of the problems in this sleep-inducing mess. (BR-Blue Underground with *The Blood of Fu Manchu*)

Castle of Terror (1964) 2.5
Writer accepts wager to spend the night in a haunted castle. He encounters ghosts who reenact horrible events and he's now one of their targets. Barbara Steele is one of the specters in this typically atmospheric Italian offering. The ending is especially well done—and harsh. Highly recommended for fans of Gothic spookers. Remade as *Web of the Spider*. (BR-Severin with *Nightmare Castle*)

The Castle of the Living Dead (1964) 2.5
Set in 19th-century Europe, just after the Napoleonic Wars have ended, a traveling circus is hired by Count Drago (Christopher Lee) and discover he has sinister plans in store for them. Lee is good but looks in desperate need of sleep. Donald Sutherland makes his film debut playing elderly witch ("Beware the castle of the living dead!") and goofy soldier. Also look for a killer wielding a scythe. Atmospheric Italian horror with some interesting characters caught in standard horror plot. (BR-Severin as part of *The Eurocrypt of Christopher Lee Collection*)

The Cat Creature (TV-1973) 3.0
The former gardener of deceased collector of Egyptian artifacts steals amulet from mummified disciple of cat goddess. Soon after, the title monster is clawing her way through the city in search of the stolen item. Made by (Curtis Harrington directs, Robert Bloch writes), and featuring (Gale Sondergaard, John Carradine, Milton Parsons) several horror pros this is a highly entertaining throwback to classic thrillers of yesteryear. The opening sequence recalls *The Mummy* (1932) and there's a stalk scene reminiscent of *Cat People* (1942), whose star Kent Smith is this film's first victim. (NA)

The Cat Creeps (1946) 1.5
As does this film: it limps along with tired clichés after a decent opening. Killer is trying to find money hidden somewhere in creepy old house. There's a black cat wandering around too. No surprises here in this sub-par Universal chiller. (NA)

Cat Girl (1957) 2.5
Uncle summons woman to family castle where he passes the family curse onto her, allowing her spirit to enter that of a cheetah, which can murder her enemies. Barbara Shelley stars as the title creature in this atmospheric but familiar tale; she gives the film a sensual quality that makes it worth checking out. (VHS-Columbia/Tristar Home Video)

Cat People (1942) 3.5
First and one of the best of producer Val Lewton's chillers made for RKO. A young woman refuses intimacy with her new husband for fear her inner beast will be unleashed, the result of an ancient curse. But when hubby turns his attentions to a pretty coworker…The horror here is mostly suggested by clever use of sound and camera placement; the scenes of a walk to the bus stop and a late-night dip in the pool are especially memorable. (BR-Criterion)

Cat People (1982) 3.0
Young Irena is distressed to learn she is of a race that transforms into panthers after sex and can't return to human form until they kill. Remake of the great Val Lewton chiller lacks all subtlety; star Nastassja Kinski literally transforms, as does her loony brother Malcolm McDowell, into bloodthirsty feline. Bloody, sexy, intense, and well-acted. Good music score too. (BR-Shout! Factory)

Cat-Women of the Moon (1953) 2.0
The first and relative best of the lost-women-civilization-on-planet-whatever films of the 1950s. Here astronauts exploring the moon find race of shapely females (and some giant spiders too) who plot to steal their spaceship. Takes itself seriously, which helps a bit, as does good cast. Sometimes aired as *Rocket to the Moon*. (DVD-Image)

The Catman of Paris (1946) 2.0
In 1896 Paris a legendary creature is murdering the enemies of controversial author, making him prime suspect. Not bad Jekyll/Hyde type thriller has some good moments but is otherwise standard stuff. (NA)

Cauldron of Blood (1970) 1.5
Blind sculptor Boris Karloff doesn't realize his latest commissioned work features the skeletons of those his wife and her lover have murdered. It's not just about the money either. Filmed over three years (the copyright is 1967) and released after Karloff's death, this is an erratically edited, over-scored jumble whose central idea is poorly served. It's saving graces are Karloff and Viveca Lindfors, who plays the villainous spouse with relish. (BR-Olive)

Chamber of Horrors (1940) 2.0
Young woman comes into possession of one of seven keys needed to open treasure-filled tomb. When the man who sent her the key is murdered, she finds herself wrapped up in a mystery of missing keys and conniving thieves. Good cast (including Leslie Banks doing his Court Zaroff) does its best with clunky, overlong old dark house tale based on Edgar Wallace story. (BR-Kino)

Chamber of Horrors (1966) 2.0
Kooky Jason Cravatte strangles his lover and then forces a minister to marry them. He escapes the hangman's knot by severing his hand! It's up to Anthony Draco and Harold Blount, who run the "House of Wax" and assist the police in their spare time, to find the demented Cravatte before he kills again. Set in 19th-century Baltimore, this was initially a pilot for a TV series called *House of Wax* but was deemed too horrifying for television. Features the gimmicks the Fear Flasher and Horror Horn to warn audiences of potentially frightening scenes. Great period flavor and Patrick O'Neal, as the villain, seems to be having fun. But its overall tone is rather light-weight, and it runs too long. Still, it may have made a fun TV series since Cesare Danova and Wilfrid Hyde-White make a fine detective team. (BR-Shout! Factory)

Chandu the Magician (1932) 2.0
Edmund Lowe is heroic title character battling Bela Lugosi's evil scientist Roxor who wants to rule the world, with the help of his death ray. Hokey artifact has its moments. The lead performances are very flowery, but the production design and effects make this worth seeing at least once. (BR-Kino)

The Changeling (1980) 3.0
Four months after his wife and daughter are killed, composer moves into historical home for some seclusion only to find that it's haunted. Straightforward ghost story/mystery has several memorable scenes, including a hair-raising séance. George C. Scott is commanding as the haunted father determined to solve the puzzle. (BR-Severin)

Charlie Chan at the Circus (1936) 3.0
The Chan family is invited to circus where co-owner is getting threatening letters. Soon a killer strikes and Charlie goes to work. Very enjoyable entry in the Chan series, with humor nicely balanced with good mystery. J. Carrol Naish is a suspect. Since the prime suspect is an ape one can kind of see why this film aired on *Ghost Host*. But the other Chans…? (DVD-Fox as part of *Charlie Chan: Volume 2*)

Charlie Chan at the Olympics (1937) 2.5
Charlie's fishing jaunt with Number 2 son is interrupted when they discover missing plane and a dead pilot. Also missing is technology for remote-controlled aircraft, the search for which takes the sleuth to Olympic Games in Berlin. Lesser Chan entry is unevenly paced but still entertaining. (DVD-Fox as part of *Charlie Chan: Volume 2*)

Charlie Chan at the Opera (1936) 3.0
It's Warner Oland vs. Boris Karloff in what is probably the best of the Charlie Chan series. Karloff plays mad amnesiac who escapes from asylum and becomes prime suspect when bodies start piling up at the opera. Echoes of *The Phantom of the Opera* pervade this atmospheric mystery set mostly during intense night at the theater. Villain isn't too surprising but there's no denying this entry has palpable suspense not typically present in the studio-era B-mystery series. (DVD-Fox as part of *Charlie Chan: Volume 2*)

Charlie Chan at the Race Track (1936) 3.0
Charlie takes a sea voyage to uncover killer of friend whose horse Avalanche lost in fixed race. Strong entry in the series, with well-planted clues and satisfying denouement. (DVD-Fox as part of *Charlie Chan: Volume 2*)

Charlie Chan at the Wax Museum (1940) 2.5
An escaped gangster who's tucked away in wax museum run by thug has marked Charlie Chan for death. There's plenty of atmosphere in this nicely structured mystery, although the low budget is rather obvious. (DVD-Fox as part of *Charlie Chan: Volume 5*)

Charlie Chan in the Secret Service (1944) 2.0
The first Charlie Chan for Monogram Pictures is a rather drab affair. Sidney Toler returns as the famed sleuth trying to figure out which houseguest murdered inventor. This is missing the zing and fine pacing of the Fox features, even though the mystery itself is okay. Mantan Moreland is more interesting than Chan's two offspring. (DVD-MGM as part of *The Charlie Chan Chanthology*)

Charlie Chan on Broadway (1937) 3.0
Charlie is to be honored by New York's Finest at fancy dinner; gets involved in former gangster gal's murder instead. One of the series best episodes is well-plotted and fast-paced. Lon Chaney, Jr. is in it for about three seconds as newspaper desk jockey. (DVD-Fox as part of *Charlie Chan: Volume 3*)

Children of the Damned (1964) 2.5
Six super-intelligent but deadly kids from various parts of the world take refuge in a London church while international authorities wonder what to do with them. Less involving than its predecessor *Village of the Damned* (we already know what these tykes are capable of) but still has several intense moments. (BR-Warner Archive)

Children Shouldn't Play with Dead Things (1972) 2.5
Film troop gathers at cabin near island cemetery, the leader deciding to play games with the dead. Talky but very atmospheric and creepy. The makeup by star Alan Ormsby is suitably grotesque. (BR-VCI)

Chinatown Squad (1935) 2.0
After an embezzler is murdered in Chinatown restaurant, a former police officer steps in to solve the mystery. Pretty flat whodunit from Universal was part of the original *Shock!* package. The ending is especially weak, as is most of the humor. (NA)

The Chinese Cat (1944) 2.0
Stepdaughter of murdered businessman asks Charlie Chan to solve the months-old case. There's more comedy relief than usual thanks to Mantan Morland. The real problem is the film's lack of a compelling mystery. It's hardly even a whodunit! (DVD-MGM as part of *The Charlie Chan Chanthology*)

Christina (1974) 2.0
A woman offers an unemployed aircraft designer $25,000 to marry her so she can stay in the United States. He agrees, they get hitched, and then she vanishes. But he's fallen in love with her, so he tries to learn what happened to his bride. Intriguing premise gives way to a routine procedural that gets less interesting and more ridiculous as story progresses. The good cast keeps it watchable. (VHS-MPI)

Circus of Fear (1966) 2.5
As the title suggests, a circus is the setting for a series of murders, the motive for which involves a cop killer who is hiding out amongst the performers. Could it be lion tamer Christopher Lee, who wears a mask due to his scarred face? British-made Edgar Wallace mystery is colorful and stylish, thanks to director John Llewellyn Moxey. The villain is obvious though, and the script holds few surprises. (BR-Blue Underground with *Five Golden Dragons*)

Circus of Horrors (1960) 2.5
Disgraced plastic surgeon utilizes a circus as cover, so he can continue his experiments. If the people he helps want to leave, they meet with mysterious accidents. Enjoyable enough but becomes repetitive. Anton Diffring is appropriately sinister in the lead. (BR-Shout! Factory)

The Claw Monsters (1966) 1.5
One of the many serials re-edited to movie length in 1966 and syndicated, this is from *Panther Girl of the Kongo* (1955). A chemical researcher has discovered a diamond mine in fictional Utanga and doesn't want to share, so he creates giant crawfish to frighten away the natives and anyone else who gets nosy. Thankfully, there's photographer-come-Panther Girl, so named because she shot dead "evil" black panther, to save the day. Plenty of fistfights that don't leave bruises; shoot outs where no one can shoot; and barely seen bad special effects in this tired jungle opus. (NA)

The Climax (1944) 2.5
Boris Karloff is rather sullen in this *Phantom* follow up. He plays a murderous opera doctor determined to stop new ingénue from performing his dead beloved's final role. It looks great and sounds pretty good. But Boris is too low key in his first color film. (BR-Shout! Factory as part of *Universal Horror Collection: Volume 4*)

The Clones (1973) 2.5
Dr. Gerald Appleby discovers he's the subject of a cloning experiment and those responsible apparently want him dead. He tries to learn the reason why while evading capture. Low budget sci-fi is essentially one long chase chock full of gunfights, car chases, foot pursuits, and a duel involving a rollercoaster! Entertaining with a memorable ending. (DVD-Peter Rodgers Organization)

Coast of Skeletons (1965) 2.0
Given the title, it's not too surprising this turned up on a few horror theaters. In truth this is a lukewarm crime drama, based on a story by Edgar Wallace, about an African diamond operation, a missing ship, and a search for gold. Standard action scenes and some double-crosses; the ending fizzles with an explosion. Nothing here to keep one up at night. (DVD-R-Warner Archive)

The Cobra Strikes (1948) 2.0
After a scientist is shot and his invention stolen, people start inexplicably dying from cobra venom. Obvious low-budget mystery in terms of whodunit. But the method used is unique. The police chief delivers some good zingers too. (NA)

Cobra Woman (1944) 2.0
Maria Montez plays twins, one good, one bad, the latter ruling over Cobra Island in the South Seas. She's set her sights on her sister's fiancé, Jon Hall, and will stop at nothing to possess him. There's also a cobra jewel, Lon Chaney as a deaf-mute priest, a cute chimpanzee, and Sabu. Beautiful looking Technicolor nonsense will pass as camp entertainment for some. Others will not be so forgiving of Montez's inadequate performances and the over-ripe dialogue. (BR-Kino)

The Collector (1965) 3.0
Hoping she'll fall in love with him, lonely bank clerk and butterfly collector Terence Stamp kidnaps Samantha Eggar and takes her to his isolated home, where he's prepared a special place for her. Director William Wyler's study of obsession and madness is essentially a two-character piece, beautifully acted by the leads, with a potent ending. (BR-Image)

The College Girl Murders (1967) 2.0
Criminal organization is poisoning college gals while crimson-clad monk roams the school grounds, whip in hand, strangling on occasion. Not-at-all convincing German *krimi* just goes through the familiar motions and has ludicrous denouement. (DVD-MPI)

Color Him Dead (TV-1974) 1.5
Husband and wife detective team try to find out who is trying to kill business bigwig. Everyone is rather flip and pleased with themselves, and this approach quickly grates on a viewer's nerves. Tedious and at times unbearable. One of the least of the *Thriller* episodes. Original British title: *K is for Killing*. (DVD-VEI as part of *Thriller: The Complete Collection*)

The Colossus of New York (1958) 2.5
When his beloved son dies in a freak accident, a grieving but brilliant scientist keeps the brain alive, ultimately transplanting it into giant robot. As time moves on, the once-gentle robot begins to realize how powerful he is and threatens to harm those around him. Rather effective sci-fi tale works because the motivations of the "mad" scientists revolve around family and humanitarian efforts for a change. There are also elements of *The Golem* present. No real surprises, but quite affecting in its own way. (BR-Olive)

Colossus: The Forbin Project (1970) 3.0
Dr. Charles Forbin has invented a computer called Colossus that has just been given control of the entire defense of the United States. At almost the same time, the Russians come online with their own system called Guardian, and the two systems become pals. Then the US makes the mistake of trying to end the relationship, and Colossus retaliates. Top-notch sci-fi is a gripping look at the dangers of relying too much on technology, stylishly directed and well-acted. The ending is devastating. (BR-Shout! Factory)

Come Die with Me (TV-1974) 2.5
In a moment of anger, man in debt to gamblers kills his older brother. The housekeeper that loves him agrees to be his alibi. In return, she wants to remain at his brother's home. An installment of ABC's Wide World Mystery elevated by Eileen Brennan's performance as lonely servant. A twist towards the end is not particularly believable, however. (DVD-MPI with *The Invasion of Carol Enders*)

Come Out, Come Out, Wherever You Are (TV-1974) 2.0
Lynda Day George wakes up at country hotel to find her cousin has vanished. Even worse, the landlord denies the relative even checked in! Potentially intriguing story drags things out

until the requisite twist, subsequently ruined by character actions that make little sense. Peter Jeffrey is over the top as abusive policeman. (DVD-VEI as part of *Thriller: The Complete Collection*)

The Comedy of Terrors (1963) 3.5
There should be a lot more love for this movie; it's hilarious, with numerous quotable lines. ("I regard your actions as inimical to good fellowship.") Even the cat is lovable. Vincent Price plays a thoroughly reprehensible funeral parlor owner who creates his own clients when business is bad. Peter Lorre is the unwilling assistant; Boris Karloff the father-in-law he's trying to poison; Joyce Jameson the wife who wants to sing opera; and Basil Rathbone the would-be latest victim. They're all wonderful, having a grand ole time hamming it up. Lots of slapstick and verbal comedy, with a rousing final chase/duel (those stunt doubles are rather obvious though). One can sense the fun they're all clearly having. One of the best horror comedies. (BR-Kino)

The Conqueror Worm (1968) 3.5
Vincent Price is Matthew Hopkins, Witchfinder General, who arranges to have "witches" executed for the right price. But he errs when he executes a priest out of jealousy and finds himself the hunted instead of the hunter. Intense, serious thriller features one of Price's best performances and has convincing period atmosphere. The supporting cast is excellent. Original title: *The Witchfinder General*. (BR-Shout! Factory as part of *The Vincent Price Collection*)

Conquest of Space (1955) 2.5
In the future, group leaves the comfort of their space station to journey to Mars. They encounter difficulties along the way, including a captain who seems to be cracking under the stress. George Pal production is moderately successful; good effects work and lively characters make up for bizarre subplot involving religious fanaticism. (DVD-Paramount)

Conquest of the Planet of the Apes (1972) 3.0
In 1991, Cornelius and Zira's son leads the first ape revolt against their enslavement. Fascinating chronicle of how humanity started to lose its foothold at the top of the food chain. Viewer will be rooting for the simians. Fourth in the series. (BR-Fox)

Convicted Woman (1940) 2.5
A down-on-her-luck jobseeker is mistaken for notorious thief and gets sent to corrupt prison. Now she must try to survive her year-long sentence without becoming hard and cynical. Entertaining if hardly credible story of reform, romance, and sisterhood. (NA)

The Corpse Vanishes (1942) 2.0
Bela Lugosi poisons and kidnaps would-be brides on their wedding days so he can use them to keep his own wife young. Not as enjoyably zany as *The Devil Bat* but has enough unintentional laughs to keep it watchable. Favorite line: "My poor son, why did he have to be born?" (BR-Retromedia with *Bowery at Midnight*)

Corridors of Blood (1958) 2.5
Boris Karloff plays gifted surgeon in the days before anesthesia who wants to remove pain from surgery. His experiments turn him into addict who is now involved with murderers. Another good 1950s role for Karloff but the film, which does have its gruesome moments, is only fitfully successful. Francis Matthews plays Karloff's son, while Christopher Lee plays the villainous Resurrection Joe. (DVD-Criterion as part of *Monsters & Madmen*)

Corruption (1968) 2.5
Fiancée of brilliant surgeon Peter Cushing is burned by a toppling flood light, which is career-ending since she's a model. He vows to restore her beauty even though it means murder. There were several films with this basic plot made in the wake of France's *The Horror Chamber of Dr. Faustus*. This one boasts the always-watchable Cushing, and Sue Lloyd is good as the victim who has no problem with what her lover is doing. The ending involving a laser is off the wall. But the film is harmed by final twist and awful, dated music. (BR-Grindhouse Releasing)

The Cosmic Man (1959) 2.0
John Carradine arrives in an oversized ping-pong ball causing women to scream and the military to fear the worst, even though his initial behavior is that of an intergalactic Peeping Tom. All he seems to really want is to let us earthlings know we're not alone in the universe. Basically, this is *The Day the Earth Stood Still* told from the scientist's point of view; Carradine has very little screen time. Not bad, but nothing special either. (DVD-Image)

Cosmic Monsters (1958) 2.0
Sluggish jumble of sci-fi staples. Experiments that have punctured the ionosphere result in friendly tramps committing murder and harmless insects ballooning to deadly proportions. Most of the action takes place in the last 20 minutes; the first 55 is chock full of talk that grows tiresome. (VHS-Rhino)

Count Dracula (1970) 2.5
Christopher Lee gets to play the most famous vampire as Bram Stoker wrote him, as an aged fiend who grows younger in appearance with each victim whose blood he drains. Herbert Lom is Van Helsing and Klaus Kinski is Renfield in director Jess Franco's attempt to make the most faithful version of the classic novel to date. The main cast is good, especially Lee. Franco, however, can neither control his zoom lens nor build enough momentum as the story progresses. More respectable than good. (BR-Severin)

Count Dracula's Great Love (1972) 2.0
Count Dracula must get a virgin to fall in love with him, so he can live again...or something like that. Repetitive, one-location Paul Naschy outing that seemingly features blood and boobs as its main selling points. But the film drags even at 83 minutes. (BR-Vinegar Syndrome)

Count Yorga, Vampire (1970) 3.5
Robert Quarry plays the title role: a suave, deadly bloodsucker who's taken up residence in modern day Los Angeles. This is

one of the first vampire films to take the classic monster out of Gothic environs and put him in present society, and it works beautifully. Yorga, as played by Quarry, is one of this viewer's favorite vampires and this film did what Hammer couldn't do when they brought Dracula into the 1970s. Quarry had a brief but memorable horror resume (*Dr. Phibes Rises Again, Deathmaster, Madhouse, Sugar Hill*) in the 1970s thanks to this film's success. Director/writer Bob Kelljan knows how to stage jump scares as well as anybody. He went on to direct the *Blacula* sequel. (BR-Twilight Time)

Countess Dracula (1971) 2.0
Recently widowed countess discovers (in a clumsily handled scene) that young blood restores her beauty. Unfortunately, it's not permanent so she becomes mass murderer. In the meantime, she masquerades as her own daughter and romances stable owner. Based on the exploits of Elizabeth Bathory, this plays more like *As the Vampire Turns* as it focuses on various jealousies and double crosses. Ingrid Pitt is good in the lead, however. (BR-Synapse)

Crack in the World (1965) 2.5
Scientist Dana Andrews wants to blast his way to the center of earth via atomic missile to harness limitless power source. Then the earthquakes start. Well-acted, convincing sci-fi disaster picture is somewhat hobbled by subplot involving Andrews' wife. (BR-Olive)

The Crater Lake Monster (1977) 0.0
The heat from a crashed meteor leads to the hatching of an aquatic dinosaur egg. Soon mysterious accidents and deaths (and terrible comedy relief) plague the peaceful town of Crater Lake. Mostly poor throwback to 1950s giant monster movies has okay stop motion effects by David Allen for those interested. But they can't save this awful film. (BR-Mill Creek with *Galaxina*)

The Crawling Eye (1958) 2.5
Giant, tentacled eye creatures that can also possess the dead have trapped mountain resort patrons, one of whom is a psychic who may hold the secret to stopping the fiends. Good performances in tense creature feature with decent effects. (DVD-Image)

The Crawling Hand (1963) 1.5
The second man sent to the moon comes back with the compulsion to kill, so he insists mission control blow up his spacecraft, which they do. But his severed arm is discovered by Swedish exchange student and her boyfriend, who brings it home so it can start strangling people. Although this effort has a creepy feel to it, the script suffers from wordiness and ill-conceived comedy relief that seriously interfere with the pacing. At almost 90 minutes, it's way too long. (DVD-VCI with *The Slime People*)

The Crazies (1973) 2.5
A plane carrying a bioweapon crashes, and the military quarantines the nearby town. As the incurable, insanity-causing virus spreads creating violent outbursts, armed forces invoke martial law but meet with resistance from the locals. George A. Romero directs at a breakneck pace and creates convincing atmosphere of chaos. Overall weak performances prevent this from being completely satisfying. (BR-Arrow)

The Creation of the Humanoids (1962) 2.5
A nuclear war practically wiped out humanity and led to the creation of robots as a labor force. Now, advanced technology has resulted in humanoids that can pass for the real thing. This doesn't sit well with the prejudiced The Order of the Flesh and Blood, which wants "clickers" to remain distinguishable from man. Low budget yields a feeling of intimacy with the characters, with lots of good ideas and dialogue as the film ponders the true meaning of what makes a man. But it's also exposition-heavy, unsubtle, and too preachy at times. Beautifully shot by Hal Mohr, who won an Oscar for lensing 1943's *The Phantom of the Opera*. Also notable as Jack Pierce's final film. (DVD-MPI with War *Between the Planets*)

Creature (1985) 2.0
On the Saturn moon Titan, a corporate-funded investigatory team discovers ancient life form that has the power to reanimate and control the victims it has killed. Low budget *Alien* variation has great atmosphere and production design. Unfortunately, it loses momentum as it progresses, and the derivative nature is all too obvious. Klaus Kinski is fun as German who was the lone survivor of a previous attack. (BR-Vinegar Syndrome)

Creature from Black Lake (1976) 2.5
This is one of the best of several Bigfoot films of the 1970s, which isn't that much of a compliment. University of Chicago anthropology students head to Louisiana in search of legendary creature. They find it soon enough. Low budget effort features engaging cast and some very tense moments, including scary finale. Lensed by Dean Cundey. (DVD-UAV)

Creature from the Black Lagoon (1954) 3.0
Scientists go in search of title monster, unprepared for just how fierce, persistent, and vengeful this thing can be. Highly regarded Universal horror/sci-fi introduces the Gill-man, the only truly classic creation of the 1950s (it got two sequels). The Creature costume is great as is the suspense. But without the ability to speak or even emote, Gill-man isn't as powerful as the 1930s/'40s monsters on an emotional level. (BR-Universal)

Creature from the Haunted Sea (1961) 2.0
Roger Corman and writer Charles Griffith couldn't recreate the magic of *The Little Shop of Horrors* with this comedy/horror about thieves who stumble upon ridiculous-looking monster. (DVD-Legend)

Creature of Destruction (TV-1967) 1.5
This film starts out with an almost-effective chase sequence, "almost" because when the monster shows up one is most likely to bust a gut. Oh well. This is a color remake of *The She-Creature*, with Les Tremayne playing the Chester Morris part as "investigative hypnotist" who can connect subjects with their past lives. Specifically, that means bringing forth

murderous sea monsters. Tremayne is fine; most everyone else isn't in yet another Larry Buchanan schlock fest. (DVD-Retromedia as part of *Sci-Fi Trash O-Rama*)

The Creature Walks Among Us (1956) 2.5
Another expedition goes after the Gill-man. This time they succeed where others have failed and make him more man than fish. Domestic problems lay the groundwork for a violent finale. There's a bit too much marital bickering eating up the running time. But there are also some interesting ideas and a much more sympathetic Creature. (BR-Universal as part of *Creature from the Black Lagoon: Complete Legacy Collection*)

Creature with the Atom Brain (1955) 2.0
Intriguing idea given mundane treatment in this tale of a gangster's revenge via atomically reanimated corpses. Cast is OK, and the walking dead sequences recall old school zombie flicks. But the script is merely adequate, and some scenes are unintentionally hilarious. (Check out the scene where the investigating police medical officer and his wife lie to their daughter.) (BR-Arrow as part of *Cold War Creatures: Four Films from Sam Katzman*)

Creature with the Blue Hand (1967) 2.0
Klaus Kinski plays twin brothers, one of whom escapes the asylum to which he was sent for committing murder. Soon after, more murders begin, the killer using a blue-tinted iron hand with knives for fingers as his weapon. German *krimi* in color has one of those impossibly complicated plots you'll never figure out, so just try to enjoy it for the atmosphere and occasional terror sequences. (DVD-Image with alternate version *The Bloody Dead*)

The Creeper (1948) 2.0
Low-budget nonsense about killer who has a cat's paw as a hand and is not afraid to use it. No atmosphere, no chills, and a grating heroine. Only the adequate performances by reliable stars such as Eduardo Ciannelli, Onslow Stevens, and Ralph Morgan keep this thing afloat—barely. Bears no relation to Rondo Hatton's Universal character. (VHS-VCI)

The Creeping Flesh (1973) 3.0
1893: Scientist Peter Cushing returns home with skeletal remains of what he thinks is proof of intelligent life predating Neanderthal man. Meanwhile envious half-brother Christopher Lee runs an asylum where he conducts his own "electrical wave" experiments while dealing with escaped lunatic. Subplots concerning Cushing's insane wife and sheltered daughter meld well with main story and lead to nail-biting finale. Unique and compelling thriller. (BR-Mill Creek as part of *Psycho Circus: 3 Rings of Terror*)

The Creeping Terror (1964) 0.0
A monster resembling a carpet with feet and elephant trunk lands on Earth and attacks the citizenry with the speed of molasses. Notoriously awful film is yet another candidate for all time worst, with most of the action narrated due to either lost soundtrack or shortness of funds, whichever one wants to believe. There is absolutely nothing to recommend this; so bad, it's just effing bad. (BR-Synapse with *The Creep Behind the Camera*)

The Cremators (1972) 0.5
300 years ago, an alien life form resembling a giant ball of flame plunged to Earth and settled in the ocean. But the discovery of some pretty pebbles somehow releases it, and it rolls around a small town unnoticed, setting people on fire. An overwrought music score, indifferent performances, and flat direction make this an endurance test. The ball effect is cool though. (BR-Retromedia with *Octaman*)

The Crime of Doctor Hallet (1938) 2.5
Doctor impersonates deceased research assistant to continue their work on finding cure for Red Fever, as well as to assuage his own guilt over the death. Interesting plot is ultimately rather predictable and a bit too pat. (NA)

The Crime of Helen Stanley (1934) 2.5
An arrogant, controlling movie star with a secret is shot and killed while filming her latest feature. Inspector Trent takes the case, searching for the victim's diary that could hold the key to the mystery. Much better than the other Trent whodunit (*Before Midnight*) shown on Baltimore's *Shock!*, this entry is fast-paced and entertaining. Remade as *Who Killed Gail Preston?* (NA)

Crimes at the Dark House (1940) 2.5
Based on the novel *The Woman in White*, Tod Slaughter stars as murderer who impersonates heir only to discover his victim inherited debt, not a fortune. Now, to become solvent, he plans to marry lovely woman who was promised to him years ago, while getting rid of those who know the truth about him. If you're a fan of Slaughter (imagine a more intense Vincent Price), then you'll find much to enjoy here, as the actor oozes villainy in every scene. (DVD-VCI as part of the *British Cinema Classic 'B' Film Collection: Volume 1*)

The Crimes of Stephen Hawke (1936) 2.5
Britain's favorite villain Tod Slaughter stars as title character—respected moneylender by day, murderous thief known as the Spine Breaker by night. Things get complicated for the fiend when his daughter becomes target of blackmailer. Twisty, fast-paced thriller with Slaughter at his hammy best, although not everyone may appreciate his flamboyant style. (DVD-Mill Creek as part of *Horror Classics: 100 Movie Pack*)

The Crimson Canary (1945) 3.0
The no-good songstress for a jazz band is snuffed after breaking her engagement with drummer. So, which one of the five bumped her off? Good whodunit, with clever vital clue. John Litel is terrific as the investigating officer, who happens to be a hard-core jazz fan. (NA)

The Crimson Cult (1968) 2.5
Antique dealer goes in search of his missing brother and discovers witchery. Boris Karloff and Christopher Lee play the possible villains, while Barbara Steele wears green makeup and a goofy hat, and Michael Gough plays an idiot servant.

Colorful Tigon production made very watchable by its roster of stars. (BR-Kino)

The Crosby Case (1934) 2.5
A disgraced doctor is shot and then hit by a cab. His girlfriend and her former lover are among the suspects in this Universal whodunit. The opening credits introduce various actors as numbered suspects, one of whom is Edward Van Sloan, who speaks with a German accent this time around. Pretty good, with an interesting denouement that reveals tragic fates of several "innocent" characters. (NA)

Crowhaven Farm (TV-1970) 3.0
No sooner has she moved into her recently inherited farm when Maggie starts feeling a sense of déjà vu and having visions of being crushed to death. It turns out her new hometown has a history of witchcraft. One of the first great made-for-TV horror films. There's a clever script, fine direction, and game cast. The ending is unsettling. John Carradine plays a creepy handyman. (DVD-R-Sinister Cinema)

Crucible of Terror (1971) 2.5
Several people gather at home of reclusive artist, including his drunkard son and a would-be business partner. They've also brought their attractive female companions. The weekend is anything but relaxing, however, especially when the murders begin. Appears to be a standard whodunit at first but features an unpredictable twist to explain it all. Opening and closing scenes are the best parts. Flawed but interesting. (DVD-Severin)

Cry of the Banshee (1970) 2.0
Disappointing witchcraft outing with Vincent Price playing crooked magistrate. After a witch curses him, a mysterious beast starts attacking his family members. Unforgivably dull most of the time, with predictable plot and nary an original idea. Only the cast's professionalism keeps it watchable. (BR-Shout! Factory as part of *The Vincent Price Collection III*)

Cry of the Bewitched (1957) 1.0
In 1850 Cuba, woman almost murdered 15 years earlier for being a witch uses her beautiful granddaughter Yambaó (Ninón Sevilla) as means of revenge. Yambaó becomes infatuated with married plantation owner whose wife is pregnant and puts a love spell on him. Film seems more interested in showing off renowned Rumba dancer Sevilla's abilities than telling anything resembling a compelling story. Viewer will lose interest *long* before film's end. (DVD-VCI with *The Mermaids of Tiburon*)

Cry of the Werewolf (1944) 2.0
Columbia copied Universal for *The Return of the Vampire* and seems to be copying Val Lewton's formula here. Nina Foch is fetching as Marie Letour, the daughter of a legendary werewolf. When a museum professor starts digging around her family tree, she plots to stop it. One of the rare horrors where a female is the main monster, making it even more disappointing that so little is done with it. The werewolf, which is rarely shown, is hardly the savage beast it's made out to be and boredom sets in quickly. (VHS-Goodtimes)

Cry Terror (TV-1975) 2.0
Gang pursues recently released thief to secure his ill-gotten gains. Two American tourists, a drunken former doctor, and the owners of a café become involved. Nothing special here, although the cast is good. Original British title: *Kill Two Birds*. (DVD-VEI as part of *Thriller: The Complete Collection*)

Cult of the Cobra (1955) 2.5
GIs about to return to US stop and disrupt sacred ceremony; a curse is put on them in the form of Faith Domergue. She has a problem when she falls in love with one of her targets. Above average characterizations help make this one of the better '50s Universals. (BR-Shout! Factory as part of *Universal Horror Collection: Volume 6*)

Curse of Bigfoot (TV-1975) 0.0
Director Dave Flocker took his barely released early 1960s film *Teenagers Battle the Thing* and added almost a half hour of new footage to give the world this dross, which started hitting our small screens in September 1975. To take advantage of the Sasquatch craze, he threw Bigfoot in the title even though the monster is a mummy. A science teacher recounts for a modern-day class an archaeological field trip he and five students took 15 years ago that resulted in tragedy. A jaw-droppingly inept mix of pompous narration, bored performances, meaningless scenes with loggers, and the expected laughable makeup effects. A "perfect" bad movie. (DVD-Mill Creek as part of *Pure Terror: 50 Movie Pack*)

The Curse of Frankenstein (1957) 3.0
The pivotal horror film of the decade, which kick-started the return to classic monsters and Gothic stylings. Peter Cushing is a ruthless Baron Victor Frankenstein, who will even commit murder to realize his life's ambition: the creation of life! Christopher Lee plays the creature well enough, but he's never given the opportunity to bring the pathos that Karloff brought to the character. The pacing could have used some tightening too, as the story gets repetitive (Paul Krempe's repeated warnings to Elizabeth grow tiresome). But this is still a fine thriller with Cushing an excellent Frankenstein. (BR-Warner Archive)

The Curse of Nostradamus (1961) 1.5
A 12-part Mexican serial was divided into four separate films for the US market. This is the first. German Robles from *El Vampiro* is the title character, a vampire who insists his ancestor gets some respect from a noted debunker of superstitions. Otherwise, Nostradamus will murder 13 people. Character actions are contradictory and ridiculous at the same time, and the movie repeats itself too much. The remaining films include *The Monsters Demolisher*, *The Genie of Darkness* and *The Blood of Nostradamus*. (DVD-R-Sinister Cinema)

The Curse of the Aztec Mummy (1957) 2.0
Sequel to *La Momia Azteca* is better simply because it's shorter (a little over an hour) and keeps moving. The Bat, captured by the police, nevertheless escapes, and plans to go after the Aztec treasure. This time a mysterious masked man called the Angel (think Mexican wrestler Santo) shows up to help, although he keeps getting captured too. Silly, serial-like film saves the mum-

my for the last act, but it's a fast-paced ride that doesn't wear out its welcome. (DVD-BCI/Eclipse as part of *The Aztec Mummy Collection*)

The Curse of the Cat People (1944) 3.5
The ghost of Irena (Simone Simon) befriends lonely seven-year-old Amy, the daughter of the now-married lovers from *Cat People*. Meanwhile a kindly but senile elderly woman incurs the wrath of her own daughter when the woman befriends Amy. A film that has the technical strengths of the other Lewton horrors (acting, script, photography) but has more emotional punch than his previous films. Ann Carter is excellent as the little lass. (BR-Shout! Factory)

Curse of the Crying Woman (1963) 3.0
Woman comes to stay with her aunt little realizing that auntie intends to use her in bizarre resurrection ritual. Good Mexican film is nicely paced, is atmospheric, and features one of the longest knockdown, drag-out fistfights you're likely to see. (DVD-Casa Negra)

Curse of the Demon (1957) 4.0
Noted American paranormal investigator Dana Andrews arrives in England to help discredit Dr. Karswell (Niall MacGinnis), the leader of a satanic cult. Karswell marks the skeptic for death by passing him a parchment that will summon an ancient fire demon at an appointed time. Will Andrews find a way to lift the curse before it is too late? Directed by Jacques Tourneur (*Cat People, I Walked with A Zombie*), this movie starts with a bravura demonic attack and never lets up. The audience knows what Andrews doesn't and watches him slowly come to realize the danger he's in. There are several memorable sequences, including a sudden windstorm, a walk through a forest at night, an unauthorized visit to Karswell's house, etc. The finale aboard the train is sweat inducing, as the moment of death approaches. And MacGinnis is marvelous as the charming but evil Karswell, whose cat-and-mouse game with an equally fine Andrews dominates the picture. Pretty much a perfect chiller. (DVD-Columbia/Tristar)

The Curse of the Doll People (1961) 1.5
Voodooist uses well-dressed, creepy-looking dolls to punish the four men (and their families) who stole sacred idol. Luckily, a friend of the group is a doctor who understands what's going on every step of the way and she tries to help them, unfazed by their mockery. The killer toys are nothing but people of short stature wearing masks, and there's too much telling instead of showing. Not as atmospheric as other Mexican horrors either. (DVD-BCI/Eclipse with *Night of the Bloody Apes*)

Curse of the Faceless Man (1958) 2.0
The body of a mummified warrior is discovered at Pompeii and transported to a museum. He awakens and wreaks the usual havoc while seeking his reincarnated lover. Some effective moments along the way but the story feels awfully familiar. (BR-Kino)

Curse of the Fly (1965) 1.5
Second *The Fly* sequel is pretty lousy despite a *great* opening scene. Shattered glass hurls towards the audience in slow motion as mental-house patient escapes; she's soon picked up by grandson of *The Fly* and they get married nine days later. Maybe if she had known about his family's experiments with teleportation and the resulting mutants that live in the family stables, she would have had second thoughts. The Delambre family is a reprehensible group here, and the film is little more than a parade of grotesques when it's not boring us with family arguments. (BR-Shout! Factory as part of *The Fly Collection*)

The Curse of the Hidden Vault (1964) 2.0
Edgar Wallace *krimi* about gangsters plotting to gain access to booby-trapped vault that contains accumulated loot, shares of which several believe they are entitled. Scotland Yard is of course on their trail in this average crime drama, with Eddi Arent getting too much screen time as the comedy relief. Klaus Kinski lurks in the shadows. (DVD-R-Sinister Cinema)

The Curse of the Living Corpse (1964) 1.5
New England, 1892: wealthy curmudgeon who feared being buried alive has just passed. His will forces his family to take certain precautions if they are to inherit. If they don't obey, they will each die in a manner that exploits their worst phobias. Faces are beaten and burned, throats stabbed, and heads lopped off in this gruesome, shrill thriller that might have really been something with atmospheric direction and calmer performances. (DVD-MPI with *The Horror of Party Beach*)

The Curse of the Mummy's Tomb (1964) 2.5
Same standard mummy story: a tomb is violated so a mummy is sent out to avenge said violation. The variation here is the nature of who is controlling the mummy's actions; it's actually a nice surprise. Typically handsome Hammer production takes a while for things to get really going. But it's well-done enough to make it recommendable. (BR-Mill Creek as part of *Hammer Films: The Ultimate Collection: 20 Film Set*)

Curse of the Stone Hand (1965) 0.5
There are few directors in the annals of filmdom whose credits are as 100% awful as Jerry Warren's are. For this effort, he took two unrelated Chilean films and reconfigured them into an anthology about a house cursed by a stone hand. The first story, based on Robert Louis Stevenson's *The Suicide Club*, concerns a bankrupt newlywed who engages in a deadly game for some fast cash. The second part, for which John Carradine was cast to ham things up as a groundskeeper, deals with three siblings, the oldest a domineering type who sets his sights on his brother's fiancée. Poor dubbing and narration were used in failed effort to cover the story gaps. The first tale seems worth tracking down in its original form due to several stunning images. But in this form, it's a disjointed mess, as is the whole enterprise. (DVD-VCI as part of *Jerry Warren Collection: Volume 1*)

Curse of the Swamp Creature (TV-1966) 0.0
Group looking for oil in swamplands meet mad scientist who is attempting to create "beautiful, indestructible fishman." Despite the presence of John Agar and Francine York, this is a wretched affair where very little happens and what does happen is wholly uninteresting. We don't even get the enjoyment of watching a poorly designed creature mope about during

the picture; it shows its pathetic face only during the finale. Perhaps the worst of the seven horror/sci-fi pictures director Larry Buchanan made for AIP Television. But it's too close to call. (DVD-Elite Entertainment)

Curse of the Undead (1959) 2.5
In the Old West, a vampire puts the moves on ranch owner who wants her brother's assassin dead. Her preacher boyfriend objects. Michael Pate is great as the vampire, and there's a terrific scene between him and the holy man as they each make their case against the other. The main cast is overall very strong. (BR-Kino)

Curse of the Vampires (1966) 1.5
As he nears death, father reveals to his son and daughter that their missing mother is a vampire who is hiding in the basement. Soon Mom passes the family curse onto her boy, who starts putting the bite on the locals. Poorly paced horror from the Philippines lays the romance and religion on thick. Director Gerardo de Leon stages a few effective and atmospheric sequences. (BR-Severin)

Curse of the Voodoo (1965) 1.5
Africa, "where the penalty for killing a lion is death." Well, hunter Bryant Haliday does just that and soon after returning to London, his wife leaves him and he's hearing lion growls. The cast does their best, but the pacing is just too lethargic for this film to gain any traction. Catchy title theme though. (DVD-Elite)

The Curse of the Werewolf (1961) 3.5
This Hammer outing is structured as a fairy tale, with the background laid out setting up the tragic future of Leon, played by Oliver Reed with his typical intensity, who was born on Christmas day, the result of a rape. One of Hammer's most emotionally powerful films, with a slow build that really pays off at the end. (BR-Shout! Factory)

The Curse of the Yellow Snake (1963) 2.0
Half-brothers battle for Chinese artifact that promises victory in war for the one who possesses it. Eventually they're also fighting over young woman since marrying her will result in a large inheritance. Atmospheric *krimi* that gets bogged down in talky, repetitive back-and-forth between adversaries. (DVD-Retromedia with *The Phantom of Soho*)

Curucu, Beast of the Amazon (1956) 1.0
Dreadful "thriller" about legendary monster that has committed five murders, causing the hired help to flee back into the jungle. Stud McMuffin investigates along with lady scientist who's looking for special headhunter formula, thinking it will help with her cancer research. The sexist hero is unbearable as is the near-constant droning music. Random close-ups of piranha, snakes, etc. do little to add thrills. And the *Scooby-Doo*-esque script (before there even was *Scooby-Doo*) is unconvincing. (NA)

Cyborg 2087 (1966) 2.0
Michael Rennie plays title role. He/it is sent back to 1966 to prevent scientist from perfecting his radio telepathy technology that will allow one to control another's thoughts. Our future government apparently uses it to control the minds of the populace and sends its own cyborgs to stop Rennie. *The Terminator* (1984) wasn't the first film to borrow Harlan Ellison's basic story for his "Soldier" episode of *The Outer Limits*. What could have been an intense, fascinating story is neutered by misplaced comedy relief; silly attempts to appeal to the far-out young folk (e.g. grooving to would-be hip instrumentals); and lackluster production values. Rennie's no-nonsense performance is probably the film's sole saving grace. (BR-Kino)

The Cyclops (1957) 2.0
Woman who commissioned an expedition to find her long-missing fiancé crash-lands and finds giant monsters instead. OK Bert I. Gordon effort features Lon Chaney as uranium-seeking pain in the butt. (BR-Warner Archive)

Cyclotrode "X" (1966) 2.0
Feature version of the 1946 serial *The Crimson Ghost*. A skull-donning, skeletal gloves-wearing criminal kingpin is after the title device that can interfere with electric currents and cause all kinds of panic. Visually impressive villain is the only distinction between this and any other Republic serial of one's choosing, although we get a couple of airplane crashes in addition to the usual gun battles and fisticuffs, and the slave collar is cool. Ghost may be the first baddie to keep a key to his secret lair hanging from a nearby rock. (NA)

Dagora, the Space Monster (1964) 2.5
A squishy energy glob (at one point it looks like a jellyfish) in need of carbon starts pilfering coal and diamonds from planet Earth, interfering especially with a syndicate's diamond heist operation. One of director Ishirô Honda's most unusual efforts, spoofing police procedurals while providing some wild visual effects (various trucks and structures are sucked up into the blob; its tentacles rip a bridge off its girders) and an interesting monster. (DVD —Media Blasters as *Dogora*)

Daleks' Invasion Earth 2150 A.D. (1966) 2.5
Dr. Who (Peter Cushing), his niece, his granddaughter, and unfortunate law officer travel to year 2150, where Earth is in ruins and the robot-like Daleks have taken control. It's up to this unlikely team to help the survivors reclaim the planet! Sequel to *Dr. Who and the Daleks* offers more campy fun, a mostly enjoyable mix of action and humor. But those Dalek speech patterns can still be grating. (BR-Kino)

Damien: Omen II (1978) 2.5
Damien, the devil's spawn, is attending military school when he learns the truth about himself. More concerned with creative deaths than storytelling, but one rarely loses interest in the proceedings. Best moment is Damien humiliating his history teacher. (BR-Shout! Factory as part of *The Omen Collection*)

Danger Woman (1946) 2.0
After a three-year absence, the title female returns to her scientist husband—one of the people who helped with the atomic bomb—who now has ideas for practical uses of nuclear

energy that he won't share. He soon finds his reputation in tatters while gang plots against him. Patricia Morison is fun as duplicitous wife. Milburn Stone is a sneaky houseguest. OK drama that wraps things up too neatly. (NA)

A Dangerous Game (1941) 1.0
Residents of a sanitarium become involved in murder when criminals show up looking for the $250,000 one patient just inherited. Incredibly poor mix of comedy and mystery consists mostly of yelling and screaming. Enthusiastic cast can do only so much. Opens to music cues from *Black Friday* and then it's all downhill from there. (NA)

Dark Intruder (1965) 3.0
Originally meant as a TV pilot, this enjoyable supernatural mystery stars Leslie Nielsen as occult detective investigating gruesome murders in late 19th-century San Francisco. Despite some miscasting (especially Nielsen's girlfriend), this atmospheric thriller is highly recommended due to tight pacing, clever plotting, and several genuinely frightening sequences. (BR-Kino)

Dark Star (1974) 3.0
Scout ship Dark Star travels the cosmos to destroy unstable planets using intelligent bombs; faces various perils. It has also picked up an alien "mascot" resembling a beach ball with Gill-man feet that gives the crew trouble. Clever, funny sci-fi comedy from writers John Carpenter and Dan O'Bannon that makes the most of its low budget. Plenty of great moments, including extended sequence of the alien escaping its room, and arguments between the ship's computer and bomb number 20. Carpenter's theatrical directing debut. O'Bannon plays one of the crew. (BR-VCI)

Daughter of Dr. Jekyll (1957) 2.0
After terrified townspeople kill Dr. Jekyll by driving a stake through his heart (because we all know that's how you kill a mad scientist) legend has it he returns as a werewolf. On the eve of her 21st birthday Jekyll's daughter (Gloria Talbott) returns to her father's estate to claim her inheritance, although she is unaware of this until her guardian reveals all. She then has nightmares whereby she murders several locals, who do in fact turn up dead. Is she really the killer? This obviously low-budget picture (no matter how much fog machine mist they use they cannot disguise the fact the castle is clearly a miniature) was directed by Edgar G. Ulmer, whose 1934 Universal horror *The Black Cat* is one of the all-time greats. Here he does what he can (the atmosphere is strong) with an obvious, overly familiar script. John Agar, playing the fiancé, doesn't engage our sympathies when he calls his bride-to-be a "little idiot." (DVD-Image)

Daughter of the Mind (TV-1969) 2.5
"Oh Daddy, I hate being dead," says the recently deceased daughter of cybernetics genius Ray Milland. To determine if he's going mad, Pop consults a parapsychologist to get to the truth of the matter. Intriguing "What's really going on here?" thriller may not hold up under scrutiny, but it's entertaining enough while it lasts. (NA)

Daughter of the Sun God (1962) 1.0
Awkward, low-budget bore about search for lost Incan city and the gold located therein. Heroes discover Incan princess, overgrown snakes, and underfed crocodiles. Lethargic pacing and unimaginative direction make for a grueling 70 minutes. (NA)

Dawn of the Mummy (1981) 1.0
"He will rise and kill!" warns the stereotypical prophet of doom during the pre-credits sequence-a sequence so clichéd and humorous one can be forgiven thinking this film might be a parody. Nope. New York City fashion models travel to Cairo, run afoul desecrators of a mummy's tomb, and help unleash the dreaded curse. Rather routine and dull for the most part, until the gory finale. No atmosphere whatsoever and the performances are lackluster. (DVD-Madacy)

Day of the Animals (1977) 2.0
The ozone layer's deterioration has somehow affected animals in high altitude areas. That's bad news for Christopher George's camping party that's just been dumped in such a location for two weeks. There are assaults by vicious birds, a grizzly, cougars, rattlesnakes, etc. Back home flying rats attack the sheriff. The cast is good and the locations attractive in this "when nature attacks" offering. But the pacing is a bit too leisurely to sustain tension and Leslie Nielsen's advertising executive going psycho feels contrived. (BR-Severin)

The Day of the Triffids (1963) 2.5
A fireworks-like meteor shower has the unfortunate effects of blinding most of the earth's population and creating giant, mobile man-eating plants. The clicking sounds the florae make are creepy, and there are some effective terror sequences. Hampered by iffy special effects and too many scenes of the blind populace behaving stupidly. (DVD-Allied Artists)

The Day the Earth Caught Fire (1961) 3.5
The combined nuclear testing by the US and Russia has jolted the Earth off its axis, sending the planet on a collision course with the sun. In the meantime, natural disasters wreak havoc with the citizenry. Set primarily in the environs of Howard Hawks-type newspaper office where cynical men talk fast and drink hard, this is a gripping end-of-the-world drama shot in documentary style by director Val Guest. Terrific, witty dialogue too. (BR-Kino)

The Day the Earth Froze (1959) 2.5
Finnish fairy tale about young maiden Annikki whose falling in love will trigger the forging of a sampo: a magical mill that will give its owner anything asked for, from flour to gold. But an impatient witch kidnaps Annikki to force her blacksmith brother to build a sampo. Poorly dubbed Americanized version of Finnish production cuts a third of the original film, the combined result being a heavily compromised film. As it stands, this is still a colorful, visually interesting fantasy even if the characters come off as one-note. (DVD-Retromedia with *Magic Voyage of Sinbad*)

The Day the Earth Stood Still (1951) 3.5
Emissary Klaatu comes to Earth to warn us that the other planets will no longer tolerate our violent ways. The recent world war and our interest in space exploration apparently threaten the galaxy! Intelligent, involving sci-fi with memorable robot Gort and great performance by Michael Rennie as friendly alien. (BR-Fox)

The Day the Sky Exploded (1958) 2.0
Italian sci-fi moodily photographed by Mario Bava. American astronaut is all set to orbit the moon when he needs to eject from his ship. The abandoned rocket effectively becomes nuclear missile that causes asteroids to hurl towards Earth. Intense but familiar world-in-peril story. Takes its time to get going but the finale is well done. (DVD-Alpha)

Day the World Ended (1955) 2.0
Director Roger Corman's first credited genre film behind the camera concerns seven survivors of atomic war all trying to get along in survivalist's rural home while a mutant lurks outside. Good cast makes do with talky script; most of the action consists of fistfights and verbal tussles. Monster finally shows its face during the last 12 minutes. (BR-Shout! Factory)

The Day Time Ended (1979) 2.0
Extended family moves into their new desert house just in time to witness UFO landing. Soon dancing aliens visit and various creatures attack. Decent performances and enchanting special effects somewhat compensate for lousy script. (BR-Full Moon)

D-Day on Mars (1966) 1.0
Yet another film culled from a 1940s serial; in this case, it's *The Purple Monster Strikes* from 1945. Martian has invented "distance eliminator" which allows him to travel to Earth to construct interplanetary jet plane. His goal is the eventual invasion of Earth. The fact he can assume various identities makes catching him a bit of a problem. Fistfights and car chases are of course ever-present since this a Republic serial. It's also hard to get too worked up over cries of, "The Purple Monster!" when it's just a guy in a stocking and beady headpiece. A repetitive bore. (NA)

Dead Eyes of London (1961) 2.5
Scotland Yard investigates baffling accidents where rich men are falling into the Thames, and the same company has insured each one of them. Pretty solid Edgar Wallace tale, previously filmed as *The Human Monster* with Bela Lugosi, has memorable villains and nice atmosphere. Over-length dilutes some of its impact, however. (DVD-Retromedia with *The Ghost*)

Dead Man's Eyes (1944) 2.5
Inner Sanctum entry #3, with artist Lon Chaney accidentally blinded. His wealthy future father-in-law can pay for a restorative operation. Of course, there's a murder, and a rather obvious solution. Acquanetta, as Chaney's subject, is awful. But the film is still compulsively watchable. (BR-Mill Creek as part of *Inner Sanctum Mysteries: The Complete Film Series*)

Dead Men Walk (1943) 2.0
George Zucco plays twin brothers-one's a respected doctor, the other a vampire. OK PRC production has a welcome appearance by Dwight Frye as hunchbacked assistant to the bloodsucker. Low budget helps with the atmosphere. (DVD-Roan Group with *The Monster Maker*)

Dead of Night (1945) 3.5
Classic anthology film, one of the very best, features architect arriving for weekend stay at home he recognizes from his dreams, or rather, his nightmares. When he tells the other guests of his situation, they in turn recount their own brushes with the supernatural. Except for a comedy interlude that destroys the mood, the stories are atmospheric and effective. The final tale, with Michael Redgrave as a deranged (?) ventriloquist, is the most popular and rightfully so. But the story about a mirror which reflects an image from the past is also top notch. (BR-Kino)

Dead of Night (TV-1977) 3.0
A follow-up of sorts to *Trilogy of Terror* containing three tales of the fantastic. "Second Chance" concerns a restored automobile that takes its new owner back in time. In "No Such Thing as a Vampire," a woman's illness may be due to a vampire. And in "Bobby" a woman gets a visit from her dead son one stormy night. The third tale is the best, with a final reveal that's a shocker. (DVD-MPI)

The Deadly Bees (1967) 2.0
Singer has breakdown and goes for some rest and quiet. What she gets instead is involved with bizarre rivalry between bee owners. Boring Amicus horror-mystery involving repetitive bee attacks. Written by Robert Bloch, who was a *long* way from *Psycho* with this. (BR-Olive)

The Deadly Mantis (1957) 2.5
A giant praying mantis causes problems in the tradition of *Them!* The romantic subplot bogs down the script in the early stages but once the film gets going, it means business, with plenty of action and destruction. The effects and music are great, and the heroes well-played. (BR-Shout! Factory)

Dear Dead Delilah (1972) 2.5
In 1943 Luddy ax-murdered her mother. Now she's been released and is staying at South Hall Plantation where owner Agnes Moorehead lords over her family. Believing she's near death, Agnes tells her siblings that $600,000 is hidden somewhere on the estate. Naturally, someone starts bumping off the competition. Slow-burn Gothic thriller is ripe with atmosphere and idiosyncratic characterizations. There are several brutal kills too. Cast and sense of humor make this an above average horror whodunit. One of 13 titles included in Avco Embassy's Nightmare Theater package syndicated in 1975. The other 12 are *Bell from Hell, Death Smiles on a Murderer, Doomwatch, Fury of the Wolfman, Hatchet for the Honeymoon, Horror Rises from the Tomb, The Murder Mansion, Marta, The Mummy's Revenge, The Night of the Sorcerers, The Witch*, and *The Witches Mountain*. (BR-Vinegar Syndrome)

Death at Broadcasting House (1934) 2.5
An actor is strangled during live performance of radio play; Scotland Yard investigates. Enjoyable whodunit has some great lines as cast and crew insult each other during the investigation. But there's nothing special about the crime itself and the villain is easy to guess. Available on Region 2 DVD. (NA)

Death Curse of Tartu (1966) 1.0
When dancing young people disturb his Florida burial site, the spirit of the mummified Indian medicine man Tartu takes the form of various deadly creatures (e.g. snakes, sharks, alligators) and kills the defilers. Colorful Everglades scenery and a gruesome looking mummy are not nearly enough to offset the film's unbearable tedium and poor acting. (BR-Arrow Video as part of *He Came from the Swamp: The William Grefé Collection*)

Death in Deep Water (TV-1975) 3.0
Man hiding from the mob starts relationship with beautiful free spirit while hiding in small fishing village. Nicely plotted tale with the expected twists. The final episode of the British television series *Thriller*. (DVD-VEI as part of *Thriller: The Complete Collection*)

Death is a Woman (1966) 2.0
An undercover agent is suspected in the murder of a casino owner, whose partner was fatally shot the night before. But just how did the killer manage to chain the door from the inside of the victim's high-rise apartment after stabbing the poor man, and where is the murder weapon? Unsatisfying blend of spy and mystery genres: the who is obvious and the how isn't hard to figure out, so what we're left with is so-so caper tale. The ladies are lovely as is the scenery. Available on Region 2 DVD. (NA)

Death Policy (TV-1973) 2.5
Robert Powell plays schemer who woos and marries lonely American Barbara Feldon. But why? And to whom is he making all those ominous phone calls? Debut outing of British TV series *Thriller*, whose episodes were syndicated as movies in the US Pretty good suspenser with a couple of nifty twists. The original title of this was *Lady Killer*. (DVD-VEI as part of *Thriller: The Complete Collection*)

The Death Ray Mirror of Doctor Mabuse (1964) 2.0
As the title suggests, "the embodiment of evil" Mabuse is attempting to procure a death ray to wreak havoc and must be stopped! Talky and routine, this is a weak entry in the series, with little cleverness and less Mabuse. (DVD-Retromedia as part of *The Terrible Dr. Mabuse*)

Death Ship (1980) 1.5
A haunted freighter demolishes a pleasure cruise ship, and the survivors eventually find the same vessel anchored at sea, although they don't seem to realize it. After boarding, a force systematically attacks and terrorizes them. Tedious shocker with bland characters, ham-fisted direction, and poor pacing. (BR-Scorpion Releasing)

Death: The Ultimate Mystery (1979) 2.0
Cameron Mitchell, in the guise of a journalist who almost died, narrates this exploration of Mexican mummies, near-death experiences, Egyptian pharaoh death rites, India's belief in reincarnation, after-death experiences, and hypnotherapy. Mitchell is a good orator, and the background music is appropriately moody. But the fact is this film is dull and doesn't really offer the great insights one might hope. The regression sequence goes on far too long. (DVD-VCI as part of *Worlds Bizarre*)

Deathdream (1974) 3.0
Andy returns home from Vietnam, much to his parents' delight. The problem is he's developed a taste for blood. Between *Children Shouldn't Play with Dead Things* and *Black Christmas*, Bob Clark directed this frightening, atmospheric zombie tale that fits perfectly with the 1970s zeitgeist: the corruption of the American Dream and destruction of the family. The ending is particularly powerful. (BR-Blue Underground)

Deathmaster (1972) 2.5
Robert "Count Yorga" Quarry plays vampire who assumes leadership of a bunch of hippies; he puts the bite on them in between his philosophizing about day versus night and eternal life. Quarry is great, and first-time director Ray Danton delivers some harrowing moments. Leisurely pacing is the film's main liability. (DVD-Retromedia)

Dementia 13 (1963) 3.0
Before he made history with *The Godfather* films, Francis Ford Coppola (here billed sans Ford) directed this effective low-budget thriller produced by Roger Corman. A family gathers at an Irish estate to hear the matriarch read her will as well as remember the tragic death of young Kathleen, who drowned in a pond. Then the axe murders start. The plot is nothing spectacular, but the film is undeniably eerie and intense with several effective murder set-pieces. (BR-Lionsgate)

The Demon Murder Case (TV-1983) 2.0
Based on the infamous Brookfield, Connecticut murder trial where the defense claimed the defendant was possessed when he committed murder, this plays very much like *The Exorcist* by way of *Perry Mason*. Kevin Bacon's girlfriend's young brother is exhibiting signs of possession, so Bacon challenges the demons and gets possessed himself. The film would have played more effectively if there had been any doubt about the devil being at work. Instead, we get clichés, several silly scenes of the supernatural, and a perfunctory trial. Features characters based on the Warrens, married paranormal investigators who became popular in the 21st century thanks to *The Conjuring* films. (VHS-Media Entertainment)

Demon Seed (1977) 3.0
Super-intelligent computer decides it would like to reproduce with human female to understand humanity. It traps its target (Julie Christie) in her home and begins to terrorize her, while eliminating anyone who tries to help her. A tour de force for Christie and Robert Vaughn as the voice of Proteus, the com-

puter. Sometimes bogged down by director Donald Cammell's visuals, but overall unnerving stuff. (BR-Warner Archive)

Demonoid (1980) 1.5
Devil's hand possesses American miner while he's in Mexico. He brings the villainous appendage back to the US where it causes much mayhem. His wife tries to convince people evil is at work. Unconvincing performances is just one problem in this poorly edited tale where characters reach conclusions with no reason as to why. At least the film isn't dull: there are several gory murders, a car chase, and plenty of scenes of the persistent disembodied hand. (BR-Vinegar Syndrome)

Demons of the Mind (1972) 2.5
Unique Hammer horror that just misses the mark. Father imprisons his two adult children (who are a little *too* close) at home estate out of fear they carry his tainted bloodline. Meanwhile a murderer who leaves rose pedals by his victims roams the countryside. Patrick Magee is a psychiatrist trying to help. Some good ideas in Christopher Wicking's script, which is alas muddled at times. (BR-Shout! Factory)

Destination Inner Space (1966) 2.5
At the bottom of the sea, scientists from the Institute for Marine Science are picking up signals from unknown object. Soon alien relative of the Gill-man stalks the group. The budget is low, but the sense of fun is high in this 1950's–style monster movie. The cast is good and the fishman is one mean SOB. (DVD-Cheezy Flicks)

Destination Moon (1950) 2.0
Key science fiction film of the 1950s deals with the United States' desire to be the first country to the moon, and the challenge faced when the rocket is too heavy to bring everyone back to Earth with the fuel they have left. Woody Woodpecker shows up to give a basic lesson on space travel. Respectable but cold and aloof; the filmmakers relied too much on the film's novelty and didn't put enough heart into the story. (DVD-Image)

Destination Unknown (1942) 2.0
Missing jewels that are supposed to help fund the Chinese war effort against Japan are of interest to various parties in this espionage tale from Universal. William Gargan's affable spy is a bit *too* affable, and the tension that should be building throughout the story is consistently undone by his "What, me worry?" performance. The rushed climax doesn't help things either. Edward Van Sloan and Turhan Bey have small roles. (NA)

Destroy All Monsters (1968) 2.5
In 1999, the island called Monster Land serves as home to Godzilla, Rodan, Mothra, Anguirus, Gorosaurus, and others. Unfortunately, outer space forces free the beasts to destroy major cities in order to take over Earth. Somewhat disappointing monster bash promises more than it delivers. There is too much time spent on the tracking down of the aliens' hideaway and not enough monster goodness. The climactic battle involving King Ghidorah and a destructive fireball is a long time coming. (BR-Criterion as part of *Godzilla: The Showa-Era Films, 1954–1975*)

Destroy All Planets (1968) 1.0
Aliens planning to attack Earth kidnap two boy scouts to force super turtle Gamera to do their evil will. In the last 10 minutes, Gamera faces squid monster Viras. Poor entry in the series with too much talk; too much footage from earlier *Gamera* films; and leads that need a good spanking. A shame because the final duel is kind of fun. (BR-Arrow as *Gamera vs. Viras* as part of *Gamera: The Complete Collection*)

The Devil Bat (1940) 2.5
Feeling unappreciated by the cosmetics company he works for, a ticked off scientist (Bela Lugosi) plots revenge using a specially scented shaving lotion and an over-sized bat. Corny, campy fun, with Bela delivering his patented mad doctor antics. (BR-Kino)

Devil Bat's Daughter (1946) 1.0
Ludicrous "thriller" has the daughter of Bela Lugosi's *The Devil Bat* character accused of murder. Obvious and predictable. To come up with the needed happy end the writers had to negate Lugosi's villainy in the first film! Such a contrived plot point is indicative of the film's overall lazy nature. (DVD-Image)

The Devil Commands (1941) 2.5
One of Boris Karloff's mad scientist films made for Columbia. Here he plays scientist trying to contact his late wife via use of brainwaves, eventually putting his own daughter in danger. Many Gothic touches are present, such as setting most of the action in gloomy mansion, and Karloff is good as usual. Predictable story arch is film's main problem. (DVD-Sony)

Devil Dog: The Hound of Hell (TV-1978) 2.0
Martine Beswick buys a hound for five grand and immediately performs ceremony so that demon impregnates the poor pooch. Then her cult murders a family's pet so that one of the dog's pups can take its place. In a year Lucky's made mom and the kids his evil minions. Well, if you're trying to introduce evil into the common person's everyday existence, man's best friend is a perfect vehicle. Plays like a variation on *The Omen*, with canine causing trouble such as setting the maid on fire or trying to force Dad to lose his hand to a spinning lawnmower blade. Hard to take seriously as a terror tale. But the novelty of the whole thing makes it entertaining, to a certain degree. Originally aired Halloween 1978. (BR-Shriekshow)

The Devil Doll (1936) 3.0
Lionel Barrymore plays wrongly-convicted man who escapes and goes undercover-as a female doll maker! But *his* dolls have a life of their own, and he uses them to exact revenge. Director Tod Browning mixes elements of his *The Unholy Three* (1925) with terrific special effects. Barrymore is great. (DVD-Warner Bros. as part of *Hollywood Legends of Horror Collection*)

Devil Doll (1964) 2.0
The Great Vorelli is an evil ventriloquist-hypnotist with a large dummy named Hugo. Vorelli plans using his abilities to force wealthy Yvonne Romain to marry him, which starts a chain of events leading to the shocking truth about Hugo. The story is nifty and the twist at the end a good one. But Lindsay Shon-

teff's direction is, as usual, uninspired, and the film plays out in mundane fashion. A real missed opportunity. (DVD-Image)

Devil Girl from Mars (1954) 2.0
A Scottish country inn is the setting for this straight-faced tale of female Martian, clad in black cape and shower cap, who wants to bring virile men back with her for breeding. She's also seen *The Day the Earth Stood Still*, so she brings a robot along to help. A good British cast, including Hazel Court, almost pulls off this campy effort. (DVD-Image)

The Devil Rides Out (1968) 3.5
Excellent Hammer horror featuring Christopher Lee as occult expert Duc de Richleau, who is trying to save the son of deceased friend from satanic cult. Terrific script and direction, with a harrowing attack by the Angel of Death and neat twist ending. Released in the US as *The Devil's Bride*. (BR-Shout! Factory)

The Devil Within Her (1975) 1.0
When Joan Collins rejected the affections of a little person, he cursed her so that her offspring would be a demon baby. Now a new mum, she thinks her kid is responsible for all sorts of terrible happenings. Absurd melding of *Rosemary's Baby* and *The Exorcist* is too darn funny most of the time to build any aura of terror. Having a mildly annoyed-looking tyke dubbed with ear-piercing screams is just one of the film's many problems trying to make us afraid of this cutie. Biggest guffaw: seeing a little hand push a nurse into the lake. (BR-Scorpion Releasing)

The Devil's Hand (1961) 2.0
Robert Alda finds himself haunted by visions of a mystery woman who turns out to be a witch. And she's set her sights on him. Standard, predictable voodoo tale with OK performances. Final shot is more humorous than chilling. (DVD-BCI/Eclipse as part of *Drive-In Cult Classics: Vol. 2*)

Devil's Island (1939) 2.5
Boris Karloff plays a surgeon sent to the crooked Parisian penal colony on Devil's Island for giving aid to an escaped condemned patient. While serving his term he stands up to corruption, and then the daughter of the man in charge is in a serious accident. Entertaining if standard prison film is given gravitas thanks to Karloff's committed performance. (DVD-R-Warner Archive as part of *Boris Karloff Triple Feature*)

The Devil's Messenger (1961) 1.5
Three installments of a Swedish television program called *13 Demon Street* were cut together to make this anthology film. Playing the Devil, Lon Chaney, Jr. was brought in to connect the segments. The stories concern a photographer who's haunted by a murder victim, a woman frozen in ice, and a fortune teller who predicts murder. The stories have neither the style nor wit of an average *Twilight Zone* or *Alfred Hitchcock Presents* episode, and the cast is merely OK. Chaney is fun as Beelzebub but is not around that much. (DVD-Alpha)

Devils of Darkness (1965) 2.0
After his friends die under mysterious circumstances, a British author investigates and encounters 16th-century French vampire and the satanic cult he oversees. When our hero gets hold of an ancient talisman, he becomes marked for death. A jumbled, sluggish script made watchable by attractive production and some effective moments. (DVD-Fox with *Witchcraft*)

The Devil's Rain (1975) 3.0
In barren, rural town, a centuries-old hunt for satanic volume holding condemned souls plays out in gruesome fashion. It's literally a battle between good and evil. Ernest Borgnine is terrific as the demonic priest, and Robert Fuest directs with intensity. Creepy in the extreme, with incredibly gloppy finale. Check out William Shatner in his eye-less makeup; he looks like the Michael Myers Halloween mask come to life, which is appropriate since a mask of the actor was the starting point for Michael. (BR-Severin)

The Devil's Web (TV-1975) 3.0
A throw from a horse leaves active young woman paralyzed. Luckily, Nurse Bessy has a way to make things better. Good episode of *Thriller* features infectious performance by Diana Dors as the nasty nurse with a diabolical secret. Original title: *Nurse Will Make It Better*. (DVD-VEI as part of *Thriller: The Complete Collection*)

The Diabolical Dr. Z (1966) 3.0
Dr. Zimmer claims he can pinpoint the areas of the body that control good and bad. When his fellow scientists mock him and he dies, his daughter swears vengeance. Stylish shocker from director Jess Franco features many atmospheric touches, a rousing fight scene near the end, and the beautiful Estella Blain as Miss Muerte, a performance artist whose lengthy fingernails are put to sinister use. (BR-Kino)

Diabolique (1955) 4.0
French classic concerning schoolmaster's wife and his mistress who together plot his murder. Things seem to have gone according to plan, until his body disappears. Peerless suspenser, with nonstop tension once the murder plot kicks in and a socko, influential ending. Lack of music at key moments adds to the overall impact. (BR-Criterion)

Dial A Deadly Number (TV-1975) 2.0
No-good hard-up actor takes advantage of frightened woman who has dialed the wrong number, thinking she's called a psychiatrist. She's plagued by nightmares in which she has murdered a man and is afraid she's losing her mind. Thoroughly predictable, right down to the "surprise" ending. (DVD-VEI as part of *Thriller: The Complete Collection*)

Diary of a Madman (1963) 2.5
Vincent Price plays a French magistrate under control of evil force called the Horla. Colorful, gruesome tale benefits from always-reliable Price and Nancy Kovack as scheming lover. Dialogue is sometimes downright awful ("Ah, this stupid murder...") and the film has its fair share of corny moments. Still quite enjoyable. (BR-Shout! Factory as part of *The Vincent Price Collection III*)

Die! Die! My Darling (1965) 2.5
Tallulah Bankhead plays a woman whose grief over her son's death has driven her mad. When his former fiancée arrives to say she's engaged to another man, Mom doesn't react very well. Bankhead is fun to watch in this colorful Hammer Films production. There are no real surprises in the script though. (BR-Mill Creek as part of *Hammer Films: The Ultimate Collection: 20 Film Set*)

Die, Monster, Die (1965) 2.0
American student visits English estate to see his girlfriend, and finds nasty goings on involving her father, played by Boris Karloff. Although based on an H.P. Lovecraft story, this plays more as a variation on the Poe Gothic tales filmed by Roger Corman: the arrival at an estate surrounded by arid landscapes; the portraits of ancestors that adorn the walls; the fact that most of the action takes place in one location; the repeated orders to "leave this place;" etc. But if Karloff is playing the Vincent Price part he is never nearly as sympathetic as Price always was. And the film grows tiresome despite the fine sets and atmospheric lighting. (BR-Shout! Factory)

Die Screaming Marianne (1971) 2.0
Susan George plays woman on the run from her father and stepsister, both of whom want her returned home for less-than-familial reasons. Title promises tense thriller; actual film is leisurely-paced drama that nevertheless builds to affecting climax thanks to George's ingratiating performance. (BR-Kino)

Die Sister, Die! (1978) 2.0
Title gives main plot away. Brother hires disgraced nurse to tend to his suicidal sister, with the goal being his sister dies. But there are family secrets about to be uncovered so things don't go as planned. Sufficiently involving if unspectacular Gothic suspense effort. Although this has the look and feel of a made for television film, it played theatrically starting November 22, 1978, as the co-feature to the US release of *The Satanic Rites of Dracula*. Aired on television as *The Companion*. (DVD-Scorpion Releasing with *Lurkers*)

Dinosaurus! (1960) 2.5
Construction-related blasting in the Caribbean leads to discovery of two frozen dinosaurs. Lightning revives them shortly thereafter. A thawed, friendly caveman joins the fun too, providing plenty of intentional laughs. The script suffers from a split personality: parts of it are extremely juvenile while at the same time it presents vicious Tyrannosaurus Rex attacks. Still, the effects are charming and there's entertainment to be had. (BR-Kino)

Disciple of Death (1972) 1.5
Once upon a time, there was a disciple of death! British period piece concerns devil's lackey (Michael Raven) who's resurrected when virgin plasma is spilled on his grave during a couple's blood oath. The local parson suspects the truth as soon as the virgin sacrifices begin. Incredibly cheap and dreary, with too many close-ups and nary a thrill in sight. Raven's kind of fun as the baddie. The music score consists mostly of cues from Bach's "Toccata and Fugue in D minor." I pray thee, make it stop. (DVD-Retromedia)

The Disembodied (1957) 1.5
Voodoo priestess Allison Hayes, bored with her husband and African life in general, puts the moves on a safari member. There's heart sacrifice, ritualistic dances, attempted murder, voodoo dolls, and other spooky stuff—all played out in an unconvincing Africa—that add up to a real yawner. (DVD-R-Warner Archive)

Doctor Blood's Coffin (1961) 2.5
Peter Blood returns home after studying in Vienna, hellbent on proving that he can revive the dead with a proper heart replacement. He also woos his father's widowed nurse Hazel Court, who grows suspicious after discovering him with Curare poison. Standard mad scientist stuff benefits from good performances, nice color, and lovely location work. (BR-Shout! Factory)

Doctor Faustus (1967) 2.0
Co-director/co-producer Richard Burton stars in this opulent retelling of the legend. Scholar sells his soul for knowledge, then regrets his decision and begs both heaven and hell to release him from his bargain. Not a film in the conventional sense; more like a series of Shakespearean soliloquies punctuated by visual flourishes. The result is an interesting curio but little more. Elizabeth Taylor plays a mute Helen of Troy. (DVD-Mill Creek)

Dr. Goldfoot and the Girl Bombs (1966) 1.0
Vincent Price returns as title villain (he wears golden booties) in sequel to *Dr. Goldfoot and the Bikini Machine*. In this outing, the bad doctor builds female robots who blow up when kissed. He teams with the Chinese to start war between the US and Russia. Directed by the great Mario Bava, this ill-conceived parody of James Bond films is intentionally silly, focusing too much attention on bumbling doormen-turned-spies and their unfunny slapstick. Even Price camping it up can't save things. (BR-Kino)

Doctor of Doom (1963) 1.5
K. Gordon Murray strikes again by Americanizing a Mexican combination of mad scientist themes and, of all things, wrestling. A mysterious doctor is attempting brain transplants, but the women subjects keep dying. He decides that a woman athlete, such as a wrestler, would be the perfect candidate because of her physical strength. Unintentional (?) hilarity ensues. If you like lovely, full-figured gals wrestling you still must sit through the other 7/8's of the film which features bad dialogue, nonexistent logic, and stupid characters. It is, in its own way, rather fun. (BR-VCI with *Night of the Bloody Apes*)

Doctor X (1932) 2.5
The police have traced the moon-killer murderer to the home of Dr. Xavier (Lionel Atwill), whose house guests are a strange assortment of scientists. There is a four-star movie trapped in *Doctor X*. The problem-and it's a big one-is the constant unfunny comedy relief from our "hero," an obnoxious newspaper

man. Whenever the film focuses on Xavier, his experiments, etc., the film is terrific. And the "synthetic flesh" sequence is one of the creepiest things ever put on film. Sadly, these moments are buffered by the buffoonery of Lee Tracy's Lee Taylor. His romance with Fay Wray is unbelievable and ridiculous. Like she would fall in love with the guy after he betrayed her father. Absolutely maddening. (BR-Warner Archive)

Dominique (1979) 2.0
Dominique misplaces things and hears voices. But she thinks her husband is behind it, trying to drive her mad. Then she hangs herself, leaving a request that her Etruscan bracelet be buried with her. Now, it's the husband's turn to deal with strange noises in the night. Old-fashioned ghost story is *too* old-fashioned: it offers no original variations on the theme and builds to an unsurprising climax. Good cast though. (BR-Vinegar Syndrome)

Donovan's Brain (1953) 3.0
Solid adaptation of Curt Siodmak's novel. Lew Ayers plays dedicated researcher who comes under the control of millionaire Walter Donovan—or rather, his brain—when plane crash supposedly kills the tyrannical tycoon. Ayers then starts acting like Donovan as he carries out the mogul's last wishes. Successful mix of sci-fi, film noir, and crime drama largely due to Ayers' performance in what is essentially a dual role. (BR-Kino)

Don't Look in the Basement (1973) 2.5
Young nurse arrives at sanitarium and learns patient has killed the doctor who hired her. She stays on to assist the new director, unaware at least one of the patients has it in for her. Low-budget grindhouse effort has a decent story and generally acceptable if one-note performances. Script is initially talky, but director S.F. Brownrigg keeps the mood suitably creepy and delivers intense, bravura finale. (BR-VCI with *Don't Open the Door*)

Don't Look Now (1973) 3.5
After the accidental drowning death of their daughter, grieving architect and his wife travel to Venice so the husband can restore a church. While there, wifey meets psychic who says hubby is in danger. Meanwhile, a series of murders plagues the city. Haunting, evocative thriller with arresting visuals, outstanding performances, and a tragic ending. (BR-Criterion)

Doomsday Machine (1972) 0.0
In 1975, the men and women of rocket *Astra* sent on two-year journey to Venus watch helplessly as China's doomsday device destroys Earth. Now, they must look to restart humanity if they can stop their bickering. Started in 1967 but shelved, the film was completed in 1972 using conflicting effects footage from other films and poorly concealed new cast members. The result is something awful: dull, grating, and deeply offensive in its treatment of the female characters. It doesn't appear to have ever played in theaters, showing up on television as early as 1978. (DVD-Mill Creek as part of *Nightmare Worlds: 50 Movie Pack*)

The Door with Seven Locks (1962) 3.0
Two murder victims who died with similar keys on their person are somehow tied to creepy English estate, a young lord about to turn 21, and a doctor studying "constructive biology." One of the best of the many *krimis* based on Edgar Wallace stories. The fast-paced plot is nicely complicated with its share of bizarre turns, and the humor is well integrated. The film also has some nice visuals, including a neat shot through a glass wall map. (DVD-R-Sinister Cinema)

Dorian Gray (1970) 1.5
Handsome, wealthy, and vain Dorian Gray (Helmut Berger) has his portrait painted and wishes it would age instead of him. He gets his wish and lives a life of debauchery. Berger is well-cast in this over-sexed version of Oscar Wilde's classic novel. The various sex scenes, however, are clumsily tossed into the story and slow down the first hour. And the build up to Dorian's confrontation with the portrait is poorly handled. Marie Liljedahl is a beautiful Sybil Vane. (BR-Raro Video as *The Secret of Dorian Gray*)

The Double Kill (TV-1975) 3.0
A man who's married to wealthy woman blackmails a burglar to kill his wife. The thief however has his own ideas. Nicely twisted "perfect murder" episode of *Thriller*. (DVD-VEI as part of *Thriller: The Complete Collection*)

Dr. Cyclops (1940) 2.5
Demented scientist who has discovered shrinking properties of radium-bearing ore miniaturizes visiting fellow scientists who get a bit too curious about his experiments. Albert Dekker is very good in the lead, and the Oscar-nominated effects are top notch. The film gets a case of the cutes too often, which diminishes (pun intended) the impact. (BR— Kino)

Dr. Jekyll and Mr. Hyde (1920) 3.0
Fine silent rendering of the oft-told story of scientist trying to split the good and bad sides of man's dual nature. John Barrymore does well with both roles, and the transformation sequences are well handled. (BR-Kino)

Dr. Jekyll and Mr. Hyde (1931) 4.0
Frederic March deservedly won an Oscar for his intoxicating performance(s) of the title roles. The film shows that, contrary to what some people seem to believe, the early films were not innocent and naive. Dr. Jekyll desperately wants to marry his fiancée because he's horny as hell. He starts to live the life of Hyde after she informs him that she will be away for a month. So, Hyde shacks up with a lovely prostitute. Easily the best filmed version of the story. (DVD-Warner Bros. with 1941 version)

Dr. Jekyll and Mr. Hyde (1941) 3.0
Good version of story of a brilliant doctor's desire to separate the good and evil aspects of man's nature. Spencer Tracy in the title roles and Ingrid Bergman as Hyde's whipping girl are very good, and their scenes together are very intense. Tracy isn't as flamboyant as March was back in 1931 but Hyde's evil nature comes through just the same. (BR-Warner Archive)

Dr. Jekyll & Sister Hyde (1971) 3.0
Intriguing variation on the familiar tale. Dr. Jekyll tries to develop elixir of life, so he can live to cure diseases. But his female hormone-based formula transforms him into villainous Martine Beswick. Writer Brian Clemens even throws in a Jack the Ripper subplot to keep things interesting. Bates and Beswick are terrific in what may be Hammer's best film of the 1970s. (BR-Shout! Factory)

Dr. Orloff's Monster (1964) 2.0
In-name-only sequel features another villainous doctor who continues Orloff's work. This one uses a robot-like henchman (his own adulterous brother whom he killed!) to commit murder. Repetitive murder sequences and too many musical numbers. Nothing memorable about this film, despite the well-mounted atmospherics. (BR-Kino)

Dr. Phibes Rises Again (1972) 2.5
Indeed, he (Vincent Price) does, and finds that someone has stolen the ancient papyrus that could bring eternal life to him and his wife. He goes looking for it, dispatching all those who interfere. The murders are gruesome but the contrivances (where did he get that giant fan?) get a little much. Robert Quarry is good as Phibes' nemesis. (BR-Shout! Factory as part of *The Vincent Price Collection II*)

Dr. Renault's Secret (1942) 2.5
New York doctor travels to France to collect his fiancée, whose uncle (George Zucco) is also a scientist with a most curious handyman played by top-billed J. Carrol Naish. Familiar but neat little mad scientist yarn with Naish and Zucco doing typically fine genre work. (DVD-Fox as part of *Fox Horror Classics Vol. 2*)

Dr. Satan's Robot (1966) 2.5
Movie derived from Republic's 1940 serial *Mysterious Doctor Satan*. Eduardo Ciannelli makes a great villain as Doctor Satan, who is after scientist's remote-control technology that he needs for his gigantic robots. Thankfully, there's the heroic Copperhead who manages to thwart Satan at every turn. While the original serial is the preferable viewing experience, this film version is one of the best serial-to-movie efforts by Republic. The perils are varied and there is some impressive stunt work, while the viewer is not distracted by silly costumes. (NA)

Dr. Terror's House of Horrors (1965) 3.5
The first official Amicus horror film is an exceptional anthology with Peter Cushing as Dr. Shrek, a mysterious fortuneteller who uses the Tarot deck to foretell supernatural fates. Five strangers on a train learn their futures involving vampires, a creeping vine, a werewolf curse, a disembodied hand, and voodoo rites. Christopher Lee (as pompous art critic) and Donald Sutherland are in the cast. Colorfully and atmospherically directed by Freddie Francis, with some neat story twists (especially in the final tale) by screenwriter Milton Subotsky. Great, great fun. (BR-Olive)

Dr. Who and the Daleks (1965) 2.5
Dr. Who (Peter Cushing) makes the mistake of showing his granddaughter's clumsy boyfriend (Roy Castle in full pratfall mode) his time and space machine Tardis. The bungler accidently sends the Who family and himself to another planet where they all become involved in battle for control of the strange world. Lightweight, campy film version of the popular BBC television serial looks nice and features cute performance by Cushing. There's an exciting finale as well. Castle's buffoonery is a bit much at times though. And. I. Wish. The. Daleks. Could. Have. Spoken. A. Little. More. Quickly. Too. (BR-Kino)

Dracula (1931) 3.5
This film gets the back-handed compliment of being "important" due to its initiating the Universal horror cycle while not being "good" because of the stage-bound second half. Baloney. Bela Lugosi makes such a powerful impression in his early scenes that even when he's *not* on screen one can *feel* his threatening presence in every cobwebbed nook and cranny. Add to this Dwight Frye's Renfield and Edward Van Sloan's Van Helsing and you have a genuine classic, flaws and all. (BR-Universal)

Dracula (TV-1973) 3.0
Jack Palance makes for a grand Count Dracula in director Dan Curtis' first-class adaptation. When he sees a photograph featuring a woman who looks like his late wife, Dracula decides she will be his and dispatches anyone who gets in his way. Reverent, handsome production features Robert Cobert's best score. This was originally scheduled to premiere on CBS Friday October 12, 1973. However, it was preempted by Richard Nixon's presidential address concerning the October 10 resignation of vice-president Spiro Agnew. It debuted the following February instead. (BR-MPI)

Dracula (1979) 2.5
Frank Langella was such a hit on Broadway as the legendary Count that Universal decided to bring him to the big screen. The writers make first victim Lucy the daughter of Dr. Van Helsing (Laurence Olivier) in hopes of bringing some pathos to the proceedings. Langella is good and there *are* some creepy moments, but the overlong film is slowly paced, and the performers don't seem committed to the material. One never gets the sense the characters appreciate the true horror that has befallen them. Available in both the original colorful theatrical version and director John Badham's preferred version with virtually all the color drained. (BR-Shout! Factory)

Dracula A.D. 1972 (1972) 2.0
Hammer's first attempt to bring Dracula (Christopher Lee) into the 20th century doesn't work. The Count's descendant Johnny Alucard recruits his pals to bring Dracula back. Now the caped one sets his red-eyed sights on the current Van Helsing (Peter Cushing) and his granddaughter. Lee's actions are pretty much restricted to an abandoned church, while the rest of the story plays out in a horribly dated London. The result is an unsuccessful melding of the modern and the Gothic. (BR-Warner Archive)

Dracula Has Risen from the Grave (1968) 2.5
Picking up a year after *Dracula: Prince of Darkness*, Christopher Lee's third Hammer outing as Dracula is pretty good entry. Dracula seeks revenge on the monsignor who defiled his castle, and that means going after the holy man's niece, Veroni-

ca Carlson. Lovely to look at and with likable characters, this doesn't break any new ground but is still entertaining for Lee and/or Hammer fans. (BR-Warner Bros.)

Dracula vs. Frankenstein (1971) 0.5
Dracula hunts down descendant of Dr. Frankenstein (J. Carrol Naish in his last film) to force him to revive swollen-faced monster. Lon Chaney, Jr. (in his penultimate flick) is mute assistant who loves puppies and axing hippies to death. Naish delivers lots of meaningless scientific monologues. Dreadful film but has a memorable climax involving vampire and man-made monster. Thought of very highly by the so-bad-it's-good crowd. (BR-Severin as part of *Al Adamson: The Masterpiece Collection*)

Dracula: Prince of Darkness (1966) 3.0
Tourists: they always cause trouble. Ten years after the events played out in *Horror of Dracula*, a foursome unwittingly help bring Dracula back. Dracula doesn't even appear until the movie's nearly half over, and he doesn't speak a word. But the film does a great job setting up its characters so that there is genuine emotion to be found when the horror begins. Andrew Keir's priest makes a fine Van Helsing-type character and the whole cast is quite good. (BR-Shout! Factory)

Dracula's Castle (1969) 1.0
Photographer brings his girlfriend to the castle he's just inherited, unaware the current tenants are vampires. Their butler John Carradine keeps women in the cellar from whom he draws blood for his employers' nightly cocktails. Tongue is planted firmly in cheek in this rather dull camp fest. The vampires do little but gab, and director Al Adamson can't stage an action scene for spit. For the television version, an extra seven minutes of footage was shot, which changed the houseguest character from a psycho killer to a werewolf. (BR-Severin as *Blood of Dracula's Castle* as part of *Al Adamson: The Masterpiece Collection*)

Dracula's Daughter (1936) 3.0
Good sequel doesn't just repeat plot of its predecessor. Drac's kid hopes Dad's death means she's free of the vampire curse. Fat chance. Gloria Holden is marvelous in the title role, and Irving Pichel is perfect as her assistant Sandor. He's the creepiest thing about the movie. And the finale is well-staged. The only real problem is too much comedy relief, or rather, failed attempts at comedy. (BR-Universal as part of *Dracula: Complete Legacy Collection*)

Dressed to Kill (1980) 3.0
Once again, director Brian De Palma borrows from Alfred Hitchcock in telling this tale of a woman whose frustration with her husband has her seeking other companionship elsewhere. Her son, her psychiatrist, and a prostitute who witnesses a crime get caught up in story's mechanics. Stylish, fast-moving, and darkly humorous, this film might be trash but it's entertaining-as-hell trash. (BR-Criterion)

The Dungeon of Harrow (1962) 1.0
Two shipwreck survivors wash ashore an island presided over by a demented count. Really strange blend of fantasy, horror, and the plot of *The Most Dangerous Game* has its creepy moments. Unfortunately, the performances are a mixed bag and there is no emotional involvement whatsoever. Aired as *Dungeons of Horror*. (BR-Vinegar Syndrome as part of *5 Films, 5 Years-Vol. 2: Horror and Exploitation*)

The Dunwich Horror (1970) 2.0
Dean Stockwell plays young warlock Wilbur Whateley who seeks ancient book the Necronomicon to bring back ancient evil race. Sandra Dee is his planned sacrifice. Based on H.P. Lovecraft's short story, this a mixed bag. The interiors of the Whateley house are gorgeous, Les Baxter's score is one of his best, and art-director-turned-director Daniel Haller manages some striking scenes. But the main performances by Stockwell and Dee leave something to be desired and the psychedelic touches are hopelessly dated. (BR-Shout! Factory with *Murders in the Rue Morgue* [1971])

Earth II (TV-1971) 3.0
After the establishment in outer space of peaceful, independent station dubbed *Earth II*, China launches a thermonuclear bomb that regularly passes the base. Now, the people of Earth must decide whether to risk starting World War III by deactivating the threat, which the Chinese have expressly forbidden. Good effects and fine cast in tense sci-fi drama dealing with familiar challenge of keeping the peace in the face of violence. (DVD-R-Warner Archive)

Earth vs. the Flying Saucers (1956) 3.0
Scientist Russ Marvin (Hugh Marlowe) learns that alien beings are responsible for shooting down the 11 rockets sent into orbit. Now, the ETs plan to take over Earth and have given Marvin 56 days to arrange a meeting in Washington, D.C. or else. One of the very best of Ray Harryhausen's efforts for Columbia. The effects are top notch and the script involving, with thrilling attack sequences. (BR-Sony)

The Electronic Monster (1958) 2.0
When a film star dies in an apparent car accident and his insured studio wants its money, an insurance investigator stars looking into the death. He discovers a clinic that has a unique approach to psychotherapy. Science fiction drama plays more like a straightforward mystery, and the results are mixed. The basic story is good, some nightmare sequences effective, and the performances adequate. But there's more talk than action, which makes the film drag in spots instead of building the needed tension. (DVD-R-VCI)

Elevator to the Gallows (1958) 3.0
Slow-burn thriller about businessman who's just murdered his lover's husband, only to be trapped in an elevator when attempting to retrieve incriminating evidence. Things get even more complicated when a young punk and his girlfriend steal the killer's car! Fascinating tale of a perfect murder gone wrong, and the ensuing unpredictable events that follow. Miles Davis composed the jazzy score. Aired as *Frantic*. (BR-Criterion)

Empire of the Ants (1977) 1.5
Pesky favorite radioactive waste is responsible for the giant ants overrunning real estate hustler Joan Collins' latest scam.

Potential buyers visit beach property Dreamland Shores and are attacked by director Bert I. Gordon's bad special effects. Corny dialogue delivered by hokey characters doesn't help matters either. H.G. Wells deserved better. (BR-Shout! Factory with *Jaws of Satan*)

Enemy Agent (1940) 2.0
Spy ring frames young engineer for the theft of aircraft plans and ruin his life. So, he sets out to prove his innocence. OK programmer gets interesting when the victim starts putting the screws to the villains while an opportunistic waitress hatches a scheme of her own. But it also closes with an unconvincing finale. Music from *Son of Frankenstein* and *Black Friday* figures prominently. (NA)

Enter the Devil (1972) 2.5
Low budget, Texas-lensed shocker about mysterious cult gathering at night and murdering tourists and locals in ritualistic ways. No real surprises here. But an appropriately uneasy mood is maintained throughout and most of the performances are engaging enough to keep viewers interested. (BR-Massacre Video)

The Entity (1982) 2.5
Invisible force repeatedly rapes single mother of three. It even causes a car accident. Her psychiatrist is of little help. Based on a true story, the film is truly horrific, and Barbara Hershey deserves props for her committed performance. But the distasteful nature of the story itself and the continued denial by her doctor(s) that something supernatural is at work ultimately make this a rather unpleasant experience. (BR-Shout! Factory)

Equinox (1970) 2.5
Two young couples go for a picnic in the woods while planning a visit to a professor friend. There they encounter devilish creatures somehow tied to mysterious ancient book. Unique blend of Lovecraftian themes and stop motion animation on a low budget. Acting wise, the cast is hit or miss but the youths are likeable enough. Some great effects work by future big shots Dennis Muren and Jim Danforth. (DVD-Criterion)

Escape from Hell Island (1963) 1.0
Captain who used to run liquor agrees to pick up Cuban refugees and bring them back to Florida. When he falls in love with one of his married passengers, her husband plots murder. "Escape" of the title is accomplished within the first half hour, and then the film becomes tedious chronicle of a budding love triangle. (DVD-Mill Creek as part of *Cult Terror Cinema: 12 Movie Collection*)

Escape from the Planet of the Apes (1971) 3.0
Terrific second sequel to *Planet of the Apes*. Three chimpanzees in astronaut garb land on 1973 Earth and find themselves subject to scrutiny and interrogation. Deft blend of sci-fi and comedy, with stellar performances by Roddy McDowall and Kim Hunter who reprise their roles from the original. Builds to emotionally powerful climax that cleverly sets up the next installment. (BR-Fox)

Evil Brain from Outer Space (1965) 1.0
Final Starman film derived from Japan's Super Giant short films. The brain of a malevolent alien being plots the takeover of Earth, unleashing fanged, cobalt-clawed mutants with goofy headdresses to do his malicious bidding. Oh, sometimes they can appear in human form to rob banks. More Starman silliness, with mutants providing some chuckles amidst the sleep-inducing plot mechanics and fight scenes. (DVD-Image with *Attack from Space*)

The Evil Eye (1963) 2.5
Mystery thriller concerns a series of murders by the Alphabet Killer. The lovely Leticia Roman finds herself a possible target when she thinks she witnesses the latest crime. The film is sometimes a bit too jokey, and the actions of our heroine aren't always credible (especially that which sets up the climax). But this is still a highly watchable effort from director Mario Bava. The original Italian version *The Girl Who Knew Too Much* has a different edit. (BR-Kino)

Evil of Dracula (1974) 2.0
The third and final Toho vampire film with Shin Kishida again playing the bloodsucker as he did in *Lake of Dracula*. This time he is a girl's school principal who ultimately sets his sights on the students. Again, there are loud echoes of Hammer Films here in both look and style, with the occasional powerful sequence. The attempt to blend the modern and the Gothic isn't quite successful though. (BR-Arrow as part of *The Bloodthirsty Trilogy*)

The Evil of Frankenstein (1964) 2.5
Peter Cushing plays the title mad scientist for the third time. He shows up at his old digs, finds his monster frozen in ice, and then has problems with a mesmerist and the locals. Cushing makes this film watchable, and it looks beautiful. Good music score too. (BR-Shout! Factory)

The Exorcist (1973) 4.0
This film has lost none of its power despite the imitations and sequels, probably because it features an A+ cast and Oscar-winning director who all take this stuff seriously. Young girl begins to exhibit strange behaviors, prompting her mother to seek medical help. But it's not a doctor she needs. (BR-Warner Bros.)

Exorcist II: The Heretic (1977) 1.0
Richard Burton plays a priest who's sent to investigate Father Merrin's death. Meanwhile Regan is "synching up" with psychiatrist whereby they can share thoughts and memories. And it turns out it wasn't the devil that possessed Regan, but a demon named Pazuzu-and it's still inside her wanting to be evil again! Scenes of a one-note Burton roaming around Africa are mixed with scenes of Linda Blair looking dazed and confused, speaking such awful lines as, "Come—fly the teeth of the wind; share my wings." Rife with mind melds, locusts, total boredom, and pretentiousness. (BR-Shout! Factory)

The Eye Creatures (TV-1965) 1.0
Remake of *Invasion of the Saucer Men* isn't nearly as much fun. Alien beings frame innocent teen for death by auto, so they

can continue plotting their attack on humankind undeterred. Weak performances and failed attempts at humor are only two of the problems in this cheap, feeble programmer. The first of several dreadful color remakes director Larry Buchanan filmed for AIP television's syndication package. The others include *Zontar, the Thing from Venus*, *In the Year 2889* and *Creature of Destruction*. Buchanan is also to blame for *Curse of the Swamp Creature*, *Mars Needs Women*, and *It's Alive!* (1969), all of which received regular airplay on many a horror theater. (DVD-Retromedia with *Zontar, the Thing from Venus*)

Eye of the Cat (1969) 3.0
Scheming beautician reunites nephew with his estranged dying, wealthy aunt. In return, she wants half the inheritance after they bump auntie off. The only challenge is the numerous cats who seem determined to protect their owner. Nicely mounted thriller with great sense of humor and some nice story turns. (BR-Shout! Factory)

Eye of the Devil (1966) 2.5
Marquis is summoned to his vineyard because of failing crops. His wife is horrified to learn how he plans to fix things. The film is worth seeing for the cast alone, which includes David Niven, Deborah Kerr, Donald Pleasence, Sharon Tate, and David Hemmings. The script is muddled, and director J. Lee Thompson's arty approach can be off-putting sometimes, but he stages some impressive scenes, including Kerr being pursued in broad daylight by figures clad in black. (BR-Warner Archive)

The Eyes Behind the Stars (1978) 1.0
Reporter believes aliens have abducted his missing photographer friend. He investigates and for his trouble is abused by mysterious "group of silencers" while other citizens are murdered. Tedious, uninvolving dross plays more like '70s paranoia thriller with monotonous point-of-view shots announcing alien's presence. The last 15 minutes or so are ridiculous. A real chore to sit through. (DVD-Mill Creek as part of *Sci-Fi Invasion: 50 Movie Pack*)

The Eyes Have It (TV-1973) 3.0
Thinking they can go undetected, a trio of assassins set up shop at school for the blind, which is the best vantage point from which to carry out their plans. Student Sally senses something is wrong. It's always fun to watch the seemingly helpless turn the tables on their oppressors. (DVD-VEI as part of *Thriller: The Complete Collection*)

Eyes of Laura Mars (1978) 2.5
Photographer Faye Dunaway, whose art revolves around violence, finds herself psychically linked to killer in that she sees through his eyes when he starts murdering her friends. Cop Tommy Lee Jones tries to find out who and why. Co-scripted by John Carpenter (based on his story) and filmed by the director of *The Empire Strikes Back*, this initially engrossing thriller ultimately doesn't make a lot of sense but remains watchable mainly because of its great cast. (BR-Mill Creek)

The Fabulous World of Jules Verne (1958) 3.0
Based on various works by Jules Verne and presented in the new format Mysti-Mation, a combination of live action, animation, and sundry visual effects that make the film look like a storybook come to life. Pirates kidnap scientist and his assistant; they trick the professor into building invention they intend to use as a weapon. Meanwhile the imprisoned assistant tries to communicate the villains' plans to both the scientist and the outside world. Dazzling visuals keep the viewer's attention even if the basic story is standard stuff. (BR-Criterion as *Invention for Destruction* as part of *Three Fantastic Journeys by Karel Zeman*)

The Face at the Window (1939) 2.5
Who is the "Wolf," a killer responsible for sundry stabbings? What is his connection to the horrific face at the window that figures into the crimes? British ham Tod Slaughter's enthusiastic performance makes this fun. The finale involves bringing a victim back to life to identify his killer! (BR-Kino)

The Face Behind the Mask (1941) 3.5
After hotel fire disfigures Hungarian emigre (Peter Lorre), he turns to a life of crime to survive. The love of a blind woman (Evelyn Keyes) may just be his salvation. Terrific horror/crime thriller moves like a bullet and Lorre is excellent. Finale is especially memorable. Directed by Robert Florey, who almost directed *Frankenstein*. Only reservation is that Keyes' character is just too good to be true at times. Available on region-free Blu Ray from Australia's Imprint label. (NA)

The Face of Fu Manchu (1965) 3.0
First in the series of thrillers starring Christopher Lee as archfiend Fu Manchu. In this outing, Fu has gotten hold of Tibetan poison so toxic that "a pint could kill every human and animal in London." Lively, colorful thriller well-directed by Don Sharp. Lee makes a great villain, and Nigel Green is intense as police commissioner Nayland Smith. Also, great to see the charismatic Joachim Fuchsberger in something other than a German *krimi*. (DVD-R-Warner Archive)

The Face of Marble (1946) 2.0
John Carradine plays well-meaning scientist who can revive the dead, which take on physical feature of the title. Believe it or not, the main villain is a ghost dog! The doctors here are the sympathetic characters while the soap opera going on behind their backs leads to the real treachery of the film. Minor fun. (DVD-Timeless Media Group as part of *Movies 4 You: Timeless Horror*)

Face of Terror (1962) 2.0
Doctor who has made a breakthrough in plastic surgery doesn't realize his disfigured test subject is a mentally unstable woman who walked away from an asylum. When he learns the truth, she flees, incorrectly believing the operation's results are permanent. Predictable thriller at least has good lead performances and some sassy dialogue to hold one's attention. (DVD-R-Sinister Cinema)

Fahrenheit 451 (1966) 3.0
In the future, firemen don't put out fires because nearly all homes are fireproof. Instead, they burn books because reading is forbidden and makes people unhappy. So, society is kept busy with wall screens (televisions), sports, and lots of pills. But one fireman decides to risk everything and start reading anyway. Engrossing film version of Ray Bradbury's novel; some of his visions of future life have certainly come true. (BR-Universal)

Fame and the Devil (1949) 2.0
Mongolian trinket gives smitten professor opportunity to make a deal with the devil. He takes over the bodies of various recently deceased men (famous tenor, a middleweight boxer, politician) in the hopes of winning the heart of the woman he loves. Comedic complications ensue with each incarnation. Amusing trifle from Italy is pleasant if familiar. (DVD-R-Sinister Cinema)

The Fan (1981) 2.0
Lauren Bacall plays legendary stage and screen performer who's become target of obsessed fan and letter-writer Michael Biehn. When she doesn't answer his missives, he lashes-or rather slashes-out at those close to her. Largely predictable thriller still has its strong points. There's an impressive title sequence, a great cast, and fine music score too. (BR-Shout! Factory)

Fangs of the Living Dead (1969) 1.5
Engaged model is informed two weeks before her wedding that she's inherited her late mother's estate. Upon meeting her creepy uncle, she learns the truth about her ancestors. Disappointing Spanish horror looks great but suffers from poor pacing and all too familiar plot beats; certain scenes seem directly lifted from other vampire films. And the film's sense of humor is misplaced. (BR-Shout! Factory)

Fanny by Gaslight (1944) 2.5
After horse tramples her brothel-running father during a street fight, 19-year-old Fanny goes to work for wealthy man who turns out to be her real pop! Soon she discovers her dad's wife is having an affair with her foster father's killer! Engrossing look at hypocritical Victorian society features hissable villains and likeable heroes. A bit sluggish here and there, and the final duel seems anticlimactic, but still worthwhile. (DVD-VCI)

Fantastic Voyage (1966) 3.0
Neat sci-fi about miniaturized submarine and its crew injected into dying scientist to remove blood clot. They have only 60 minutes to do so because they'll start growing to normal size and be attacked by the body's viral defenses. Visually impressive with good cast and plenty of nail-biting moments. (BR-Fox)

Farewell to the Planet of the Apes (TV-1974) 2.5
Two episodes from the *Planet of the Apes* TV series were combined for this movie. In "Tomorrow's Tide," the two astronaut heroes are captured and must become fishermen to save their hides. In the series' final episode "Up Above the World So High," an ape scientist wishes to learn how humans constructed and flew a hang glider. Roddy McDowall is fun as the helpful chimpanzee Galen and the makeup is excellent. Stories themselves are only OK. (DVD-Fox as part of *Planet of the Apes: The Complete TV Series*)

Fear in the Night (1972) 2.5
Late addition to the Hammer "twist" films that aimed to emulate *Psycho*, this effort concerns a newly married woman who's recovering from a nervous breakdown. She takes up residence at the boys' school that employs her teacher husband. But the one-armed man who attacked her in her apartment before the move soon terrorizes her. There are several twists until the big reveal, which isn't that surprising. The cast is good (Peter Cushing, Joan Collings, Judy Geeson, Ralph Bates) and co-writer/producer/director Jimmy Sangster does a nice job keeping us interested. (BR-Shout! Factory)

Fearless Frank (1967) 1.0
The mob murders innocent bumpkin when he unknowingly tries to help their hostage. However, wacky scientist restores him to life and decides to turn him into a force for good. With opening credits looking like comic book pages and characters having Dick Tracy-like names (e.g. Screwnose), this comedy is meant as a parody and/or satire of superhero stories. The problem is this would-be cult film just isn't funny. At all. (DVD-R-Fox)

The Fellowship of the Frog (1959) 2.5
The first in the popular Edgar Wallace-based German *krimis* concerns notorious criminal known as the Frog. His 300-some underlings bear frog tattoos while he wears a gas mask during burglaries and murders. Scotland Yard can't seem to catch him. Now, the Frog is in love and has a scheme to win the woman's affections. Ultimately silly but still entertaining mystery has some good action sequences and likeable leads. (DVD-Retromedia with *The Mad Executioners*)

Fiend Without a Face (1958) 3.0
Near a remote US army base, invisible creatures are sucking the brains and spinal cords from the citizenry, who blame the deaths on nuclear fallout. Major Cummings vows to solve the mystery. Intense and atmospheric with a gangbuster's finale involving materialized flying brains, this nifty sci-fi thriller has aged well. Those brains are some of the coolest of the 1950s monsters. (DVD-Criterion)

File It Under Fear (TV-1973) 2.5
Someone is strangling young women and the victims all have ties to the Penbrury Library. Could the killer be Steve, who rents a room in the house where librarian Liz lives with her mother? Or maybe it's Liz's irritating assistant George? Then there's Mr. Stubbs, a lonely older gentleman who practically lives at the library by day. And there's that skulking serviceman who was romancing one of the victims. Maybe it's not a man at all. Few people act rationally, and obvious red herrings abound. (DVD-VEI as part of *Thriller: The Complete Collection*)

The Final War (1960) 2.5
The accidental detonation of nuclear bomb starts a chain reaction that leads to World War III. Shot in stark black-and-white and told in documentary style from the perspectives of both young and old, the film's low-key presentation is punctuated by tracking shots of panicking crowds, and scenes of drivers carelessly running down pedestrians as they exit an in-danger Tokyo. Downbeat to be sure, it's superior to *The Last War*, released the following year, that told pretty much the same story in a much more ham-fisted fashion. (DVD-R-Sinister Cinema)

Fire Maidens of Outer Space (1956) 0.0
Earth males land on Jupiter moon and find tribe of beautiful women; a monster lurking in the surrounding forest threatens to attack at any moment. Sleep-inducing, cheapjack effort has lots of pretty girls but little else. The creature is a joke. Be warned: you may never be able to enjoy *Stranger in Paradise* again after seeing this turkey. (BR-Olive)

Firestarter (1984) 3.0
A film where this viewer parts company with the consensus. Drew Barrymore plays young girl (whose parents were given experimental drugs) with the ability to start fires by just thinking about them. Her father doesn't like the idea of turning his daughter over to the government so the two go on the run. George C. Scott plays a true sicko who looks forward to killing the child after she's been thoroughly studied. Lots of flames and things blowing up, as well as the fine cast, make this a guilty pleasure. You'll really be cheering for the little lass. (BR-Shout! Factory)

First Man into Space (1959) 2.0
Cocky, obnoxious test pilot disobeys orders, is contaminated by meteorite dust, and returns to Earth a bloodthirsty monster. Not particularly involving despite some effective suspense scenes. (DVD-Criterion as part of *Monsters and Madmen*)

First Men in the Moon (1964) 3.0
Crew landing on the moon is shocked to find a British flag and correspondence, both left there in 1899. United Nations representatives track down one of the voyagers to the nursing home where he now lives, and he recounts for them how his team came to land on the moon—and the dangers it holds! Visually impressive adaptation of H.G. Wells' novel boasts Ray Harryhausen's effects and imaginative production design. Great fun. (BR-Twilight Time)

First Spaceship on Venus (1960) 2.5
In 1985, a spaceship fragment is found in the Gobi Desert and scientists theorize it originated from Venus. Soon after, an international expedition is assembled to journey to the second planet from the sun. Visually arresting sci-fi from Germany was cut for its US release so some sequences seemingly end before they should. But the creativity and imagination that went into the production still survive. Listen for music cues from *Son of Frankenstein* and *Creature from the Black Lagoon*. (DVD-Image)

Five (1951) 3.0
The five survivors of a nuclear bomb explosion must learn to get along so they can restart society. Engrossing if talky study of the strengths and weaknesses of humankind when faced with the struggle to survive. Eerie and haunting, with a good cast. (DVD-Sony)

The Flame Barrier (1958) 1.5
Woman hires mercenary and his brother to find her wealthy husband, who disappeared while searching for fallen satellite in Mexican jungle. Cheap, talky would-be adventure film for the first hour; the sci-fi part concerns an immobile but supposedly growing blob-type being protected by force field. Meh. (NA)

Flesh and Fantasy (1943) 3.0
Trio of stories built around the supernatural. "Ugly" woman gets a new face during Mardi Gras courtesy of a mysterious mask seller. In story two, Edward G. Robinson is told by psychic he will murder someone. The last story has Charles Boyer as a high-wire artist having nightmares about falling to his doom. The middle story is the best, with Eddy G. having conversations with himself about getting the murder "out of the way." (DVD-R-Universal)

The Flesh Eaters (1964) 3.0
Grandly entertaining low-budget feature serves as a showcase for Martin Kosleck. Pilot and his passengers must make an emergency landing on island that's home to a Nazi-inspired mad scientist (Kosleck) and his flesh eaters. Kosleck pulls out all the stops as the seemingly concerned and helpful biologist who is secretly plotting the unwanted visitors' doom. Gory deaths and intentional humor make this a lot of fun. (DVD-MPI)

Flight of the Lost Balloon (1961) 1.5
In 1878, explorer from the London Geographical Society boards a hot-air balloon and heads to Africa in search of missing fellow traveler. One of his companions is the man responsible for the disappearance, motivated by his search for the lost treasure of Cleopatra. The low budget (check out the attack on the balloon by screeching condors) really prevents the film from maintaining any sense of genuine wonder; the racist stereotypes don't help either. Too low-key for its own good. It is worth mentioning, however, that James Lanphier makes a smooth, cunning villain. (DVD-R Synergy)

Flight to Mars (1951) 2.0
Monogram Pictures' contribution to the wave of space exploration films, in Cinecolor no less. Reporter accompanies scientific team to Mars. They discover civilization of seemingly friendly Martians. But some are planning to use the Earth rocket for invasion. Good cast does what they can with script that focuses more on intrigue and double crosses than the excitement of discovering life on Mars. The result is a middling suspense picture. (BR-The Film Detective)

The Fly (1958) 3.0
Ingeniously structured thriller has respected scientist allegedly murdered by his wife. But the victim's brother (Vincent Price) thinks there's more to the story—and he's right! Very well-done sci-fi horror, with memorable climax. (BR-Shout! Factory as part of *The Fly Collection*)

The Flying Serpent (1946) 1.0
Re-working of *The Devil Bat* plot just never really comes together. This time George Zucco sends out prehistoric bird to kill those who may discover hidden treasure. Instead of shaving lotion it's a feather that spells doom. (DVD-Image)

Foes (1977) 2.0
Married lighthouse keepers take notice of UFO that's settled near their Southern California island while research scientist and military work to assess the danger. Eerie low-budget sci-fi is intermittently effective but suffers from uneven performances and some iffy effects. (BR-Garagehouse Pictures)

The Fog (1980) 3.5
The town of Antonio Bay is on the verge of celebrating its 100th Birthday when a ghostly fog slithers across the township, leading to discovery of circumstances surrounding the village's founding. Considered a disappointment when it premiered in February 1980, director John Carpenter's horror follow-up to *Halloween* has aged very well and is one of his best films: efficiently told, moody, genuinely creepy, well-acted, and wonderfully scored. As in *Halloween*, Carpenter is more interested in creating atmosphere and suspense than showing gory killings, and the film is the better for it. (BR-Shout! Factory)

Fog for A Killer (1962) 2.5
When a young woman's strangled body is found, Scotland Yard suspect recently paroled robber is responsible. Entertaining quickie with good cast and suspenseful moments. Hammer Films regular Michael Ripper plays one of the alternate suspects. On Region 2 DVD as *Out of the Fog*. (NA)

Fog Island (1945) 1.5
Seeking revenge against the people who double crossed him and sent him to prison for five years, George Zucco invites them to his booby-trapped island. One of them may have killed Zucco's wife too. It's hard to care in this talky, routine old dark house-style chiller that has atmosphere and good finale, but little else. Lionel Atwill is one of Zucco's intended victims. (DVD-Alpha)

The Food of the Gods (1976) 1.5
Religious farming folk have discovered a food that causes wasps, chickens, worms, and rats to grow to enormous size, and they all go on the attack. Based on H.G. Wells' novel, director Bert I. Gordon-the man whose sized-obsessed oeuvre is beloved by 1950s sci-fi fans-also scripted and provided the visual effects for this hilarious remake of his own *Village of the Giants* (1965). It wasn't a good idea to have a giant poultry attack so early in the film because it's just not possible to take this thing seriously after that—and the tone seems to be serious.

By the way, rats *can* swim; Google says so. (BR-Shout! Factory with *Frogs*)

Footsteps on the Moon (1969) 2.5
Interesting but sometimes ponderous documentary about Apollo 11 moon landing. Footage from both ground control and Apollo 11 are edited together with occasional narration to take the viewer through the events leading up to and including the historic event. A bit too detail-oriented for the casual viewer but still fascinating. *Ghost Host Theatre* ran this several times since it was one of the 13 films in Gold Key Entertainment's 1978 "Scream Theater" package. The other 12 titles were: *Blood Mania*, *The Curse of Bigfoot*, *The Devil's Hand*, *Escape from Hell Island*, *First Spaceship on Venus*, *The Hostage*, *Plan 9 from Outer Space*, *Point of Terror*, *Stanley*, *Theatre of Death*, *Twisted Brain*, and *Varan, the Unbelievable*. (DVD-VCI as *Footprints on the Moon: Apollo 11*)

Forbidden Planet (1956) 3.5
Relief crew from Earth lands on Altair 4 and discovers scientist and his daughter are the only survivors from the previous party, most of whom were killed by mysterious force that tore them limb from limb! It's somehow related to an extinct people called the Krell whose advances in science were not all positive. Dazzling sci-fi mystery is a visual treat, with intelligent script, fine cast, and Robby the Robot. Unpretentious, with a great sense of humor too. (BR-Warner Bros.)

The Force on Thunder Mountain (1978) 0.0
Father takes his son and the family dog on camping trip to notorious Thunder Mountain. We already know something sinister exists there because we saw a UFO cause a rockslide in the pre-credits sequence. Ninety minutes of dull, amateur filmmaking is for people who like looking at nature footage without wanting anything interesting to happen. (VHS-United Home Video)

The Forger of London (1961) 2.0
Newlywed suspects her husband may be the notorious title villain. Fueling her suspicions are his memory lapses and several characters that make unpleasant insinuations. Too much talk and inconsistent characterizations (even after all is revealed) make this one of the weakest German *krimis*. (DVD-R-Sinister Cinema)

Forgotten City of the Planet of the Apes (TV-1974) 2.5
One of five telefilms derived from the short-lived *Planet of the Apes* series. This entry melds the episodes "The Gladiators" and "The Legacy." In the former, which was the series' second installment, our two human heroes must face dueling to the death with other members of their race. In the latter, the fugitive trio find ancient recording that could lead to learning about man's effective destruction. Enjoyable thanks largely to its game cast. (DVD-Fox as part of *Planet of the Apes: The Complete TV Series*)

Fortress (TV-1985) 2.5
Hoping for a big payday, four gun-toting, mask-wearing hoods kidnap a teacher and her nine students and force them into a

cave. The villains, however, underestimate the survival instinct of their captives. Suspenseful people-in-peril outing is somewhat hampered by bizarre tonal shifts, dated music score, and uneven lead performance by Rachel Ward. The film's final shot is a kicker though. (DVD-HBO)

Fortress of the Dead (1965) 2.0
World War II veteran goes on vacation in the Philippines to reunite with an old army buddy. But he's still haunted by the 20-year-old battle that only he survived, so he visits the location of the attack in hopes of purging his demons. Plays like an overlong *Twilight Zone* episode with a predictable ending. Decent acting keeps it bearable. (DVD-R-Sinister Cinema)

Four Sided Triangle (1953) 2.5
A love triangle develops among three former childhood friends. Luckily, the males have invented a "reproducer" machine that replicates anything, so they can both have the same girl! Not surprisingly, the experiment doesn't go as planned. Interesting early Hammer Films effort offers good premise but so-so delivery; Barbara Payton is inadequate in key role. (DVD-Anchor Bay)

The Four Skulls of Jonathan Drake (1959) 2.5
Henry Daniell makes a good villain in this tale of ancient curses and shrunken heads. Enjoyable enough, especially for those who have a skull fetish when it comes to horror films. It would have been better if director Edward L. Cahn had poured on the atmosphere to compensate for the low budget. (BR-Shout! Factory)

Frankenstein (1931) 4.0
Classic tale of mad doctor trying to play God by creating a man. Sometimes a viewer may get antsy waiting for a film's Monster to show up, but this has never been the case with *Frankenstein*. Colin Clive's turn as the mad doctor just about matches Boris Karloff's as his creation; this film contains two of horror's best all-time performances. When you're not listening to the rapturous ravings of Clive, you're marveling at the subtle sympathetic touches Karloff brings to *his* role. *Frankenstein* was the first film shown on both Baltimore and Washington, D.C.'s *Shock Theater*. (BR-Universal)

Frankenstein (TV-1973) 2.5
Not realizing his own strength, The Giant (Bo Svenson), as he's called here, accidentally kills Dr. Frankenstein's lab assistant while learning the game of catch, and then escapes from the laboratory. When he fails to find a friend in the outside world, he vows to make his creator's life miserable. A miscast Robert Foxworth is the title doctor, but Svenson is excellent as his creation. Produced and co-scripted by Dan Curtis, this two-part version of the classic novel originally aired as part of ABC's late-night *Wide World Mystery* in January 1973. (DVD-MPI)

Frankenstein 1970 (1958) 2.0
Needing money Baron Frankenstein rents his castle out to TV crew. Meanwhile he's constructing new monster for not very noble reasons. Karloff is hammy and humorless, but he's still Karloff. Story itself ultimately plays like a warmed-over *Son of Frankenstein* (what happened to the butler?) but nowhere near as tasty. (BR-Warner Archive)

Frankenstein and the Monster from Hell (1974) 2.5
In the final Hammer Films *Frankenstein* entry, Dr. F is pretty much running the asylum to which he's been confined, building yet another monster. There's no new ground broken here but Peter Cushing is as watchable as always. (BR-Shout! Factory)

Frankenstein Conquers the World (1965) 2.0
Radiation from the Hiroshima bombing has created an atomic age Frankenstein monster, which means he's huge. He does battle with Baragon (making its debut) when it emerges from the soil. The writers of this thing forgot Frankenstein is the name of the scientist, *not* the monster. But whatever. This is typical *kaiju eiga* formula: mostly talk until the extended battle scene finale. Not bad but hardly a good example of the genre. (DVD-Media Blasters)

Frankenstein Created Woman (1967) 3.0
Dr. F is now exploring the transference of souls! And he has his chance to test his theories when an innocent man is hanged, and the wronged fellow's girlfriend then commits suicide. Peter Cushing is excellent as always, especially in the scene where he must take the stand at trial. The revenge angle recalls *Son of Frankenstein*. Again, Hammer delivers sympathetic performances from a fine cast that sell the story. (BR-Shout! Factory)

Frankenstein Meets the Spacemonster (1965) 1.0
Martian princess and her mini Nosferatu-looking sidekick Dr. Nadir head to Earth looking for Earth women to repopulate their decimated planet. When they destroy an android-manned spaceship, the brain-damaged android survives but goes on a rampage in Puerto Rico where he crashes. Low-budget silliness might have been more fun if the space monster had more screen time. As it stands there are too many stretches of dullness. Bad but entertainingly so. (DVD-MPI)

Frankenstein Meets the Wolf Man (1943) 2.5
Lon Chaney, Jr. returns as the tortured Larry Talbot, seeking out the notes of Dr. Frankenstein but finding the Monster (Bela Lugosi) instead. This film gets off to a good start (the opening scene where graverobbers pick the wrong tomb is terrific) but then falters in the midsection. Patric Knowles is miscast as the friendly doctor who must have a "mad scientist" moment and revive the Monster, and it's not convincing at all. Still, a pretty good film that does have its great moments. (BR-Universal as part of *Frankenstein: Complete Legacy Collection*)

Frankenstein Must Be Destroyed (1969) 3.0
Cushing's mad doc is nastier than ever: murdering, blackmailing, raping, kidnapping, and on and on. This time he's focusing on brain transplants. Nice performance by Freddie Jones as the subject of Frankenstein's experiments. And Veronica

Carlson gets soaked by a broken water pipe. (BR-Warner Bros.)

Frankenstein: The True Story (TV-1973) 3.0
Handsome, engrossing version of Mary Shelley's novel with some nice variations on the familiar story. Michael Sarrazin plays the creature (aka the second Adam) who starts out well-mannered and beautiful, but then starts deteriorating as time passes, horrifying his creator. James Mason plays an entertaining variation of Dr. Pretorius, who blackmails Frankenstein into creating an Eve for his Adam. Originally shown in two parts that aired as NBC's *World Premiere Movie* on November 30 and December 1, 1973. (BR-Shout! Factory)

Frankenstein's Bloody Terror (1968) 2.5
An important film for Euro-horror aficionados: the debut of Paul Naschy's tragic werewolf Waldemar Daninsky. After the silver crucifix is removed from Daninsky's werewolf ancestor, Waldemar helps track down the revived fiend but is bitten in the process. Vampires join the fun as Waldemar seeks a cure. Full of atmospheric touches, savage werewolf attacks, and a sympathetic monster, the film meanders here and there and doesn't always make sense. (Why do the vampires tease the werewolves like they do?) (DVD-Media Blasters)

Frankenstein's Daughter (1958) 1.5
Grandson of the original doctor Frankenstein tries to carry on the family tradition. Creates silly monster, laughable film. Funniest moment has the monster politely knocking on the doctor's front door to regain entry, even though it broke the door down when leaving the house. (BR-The Film Detective)

Freedom to Die (1961) 3.0
Prison escapee wants to collect his share of post office robbery that inadvertently landed him behind bars. Meanwhile the mastermind behind the theft arranges to have the convict bumped off. Twisty, compact British quickie moves like a bullet to its nasty conclusion. Available on Region 2 DVD. (NA)

Friday the 13th (1980) 2.5
Counselors arrive to set up for summer camp, not realizing a brutal, psychotic killer plans murdering them all. Watershed horror film has atmosphere, suspense, and some ground-breaking special effects. But it also lacks characterization and originality. (BR-Shout! Factory as part of *Friday the 13th Collection: Deluxe Edition*)

Friday the 13th Part 2 (1981) 2.0
Five years after the events in the first film, a counselor training camp is opened near Camp Crystal Lake, where Jason Vorhees is rumored to prowl. Amy Steel is one of the best "final girls" to ever grace a slasher film, and the last 20 minutes or so is a great, extended piece of peek-a-boo. Unfortunately, the first hour is by-the-numbers and thus pretty blah. (BR-Shout! Factory as part of *Friday the 13th Collection: Deluxe Edition*)

Fright (1956) 1.5
Psychiatrist hypnotizes/regresses new patient and discovers part of her past is as a 19th-century Austrian baroness who committed suicide. His attempt to cure her eventually involves a multiple murderer. The story itself isn't bad; the execution, however, is sorely lacking. The main culprits are lackluster performances and W. Lee Wilder's leaden direction. (DVD-Alpha with *Stark Fear*)

Fright (1971) 2.0
Susan George takes a babysitter's job unaware the mother's ex-husband has escaped from a mental facility and is heading home. Ian Bannen is over the top as the psycho, and the film relies too much on putting a three-year-old in danger to build suspense. (BR-Shout! Factory)

Frogs (1972) 2.5
A more apt title would have been *Noise*. A well-to-do family gathers for its annual July birthdays celebration on island plantation, where the surrounding non-human life has plans of its own. Misleading title since more than just frogs attack: lizards, spiders, snakes, and alligators do most of the dirty work. It takes a while to get going. But when it finally does, most people will be squirming left and right. (BR-Shout! Factory with *The Food of the Gods*)

From Beyond the Grave (1973) 3.0
Peter Cushing is the proprietor of Temptations Ltd., a most unusual antique store where, if you lie, cheat, or steal to get what you want, you will pay the ultimate price. Stories concern a haunted mirror, an avenging angel, an invisible demon, and a possessed door. Suitably intense when it wants to be but also has some well-handled humor. Horror familiars David Warner, Diana Dors, Donald Pleasence, and Ian Ogilvy are in the cast. Based on stories by R. Chetwynd-Hayes. (BR-Warner Archive)

From Hell It Came (1957) 2.0
When his wife and members of his clan betray him, a tribesman vows to come back from the dead to seek revenge. He makes good on his promise by taking form of scowling tree monster called Tabonga. Acting is a mixed bag, and the monster is a laugh riot resulting in a somewhat entertaining debacle. Aired sometimes as *The Strange Creature*. You think? (BR— Warner Archive)

From the Earth to the Moon (1958) 2.0
Jules Verne story about two rivals who team for the construction of the first rocket to the moon. Good cast does what it can in this low budget affair set shortly after the Civil War's end. Not bad but not particularly involving either. (VHS-VCI)

Frozen Alive (1964) 1.0
Scientist experimenting with freezing chimps and bringing them back to life is ready to play human guinea pig. Unfortunately, his jealous wife inadvertently makes him a murder suspect. Flatly directed with molasses pacing, this low-budget crime drama with sci-fi elements severely tests the viewer's patience. The payoff has no resonance whatsoever. (BR-Retromedia with *Phantom from Space*)

The Frozen Dead (1966) 2.5
Dana Andrews, the hero from the excellent *Curse of the Demon*, here plays Nazi scientist trying unsuccessfully to revive frozen

important members of the Third Reich. He ends up using the decapitated head of his daughter's visiting friend to help him figure out his mistakes. Amusing if ludicrous thriller has several haunting images and a memorable final scene. (DVD-R-Warner Archive)

The Frozen Ghost (1945) 2.0
Inner Sanctum #4: hypnotist Lon Chaney thinks he killed a man during his act, so he retreats to wax museum and finds greater problems. Martin Kosleck is good as villainous figure maker. But the film fails to build up atmosphere and Chaney is not very convincing in his role. (BR-Mill Creek as part of *Inner Sanctum Mysteries: The Complete Film Series*)

The Funhouse (1981) 3.0
Two couples plan to spend the night in a carnival funhouse but get more than they bargained for when they witness a murder. Underrated Tobe Hooper horror has a playful nature in the beginning but becomes increasingly intense as the story progresses. Sound design is exceptional aiding in the jumps and jolts. (BR-Shout! Factory)

The Fury (1978) 3.0
Boss John Cassavetes double crosses government agent Kirk Douglas so he can kidnap Douglas' psychically gifted son and develop his abilities for nefarious purposes. Meanwhile young psychic Amy Irving is just discovering *her* abilities and forms link with Douglas' boy. Entertaining if sometimes corny mix of action and science fiction. Fine cast and stylish direction by Brian De Palma make for bloody good time. Music by John Williams. (BR-Twilight Time)

The Fury of the Wolfman (1972) 1.0
Jacinto Molina Álvarez (Paul Naschy) played his famous werewolf Waldemar Daninsky in a dozen or so films spanning 35 years give or take. This is far from the best. "Walderman" returns from Tibet to find his unfaithful wife plotting his murder. He turns into a werewolf, kills her and her lover, and then is electrocuted after fleeing the scene! He's promptly dug up by crazy scientist who plans to use him for her mind control experiments. Sloppily told, poorly paced and badly dubbed, this does have a couple of energetic wolf man attacks. (BR-Scorpion Releasing)

Future Woman (1969) 1.5
Ruler of the all-women city Femina plans to take over the world but needs financing. She arranges the kidnapping of wealthy stud who's also the target of mobster George Sanders. Can the men put aside their differences long enough to defeat their female adversary? Anemic comic book thriller has beautiful women and attractive photography but little else. For fans of its director, Jess Franco, only. (BR-Blue Underground as *The Girl from Rio* with *The Million Eyes of Sumuru*)

Futureworld (1976) 2.0
Two years after the tragedy at Delos Corporation's ultimate amusement park, things are up and running again, bringing visitors' fantasies to life with the assistance of robots. Shortly after the reopening of the park, however, a former Delos employee is murdered after contacting reporter Peter Fonda about nefarious goings-on. Now, Fonda is determined to learn the truth behind the new and improved guest attraction. Disappointing sequel to *Westworld* lacks the sense of fun and humor of the first film and horribly misuses Yul Brynner in a cameo. It also takes too long to get to the big twist, which isn't that surprising but still makes for a good last half hour. (BR-Shout! Factory)

Gallery of Horrors (1967) 0.0
Incredibly cheap anthology whose art direction budget must have been $7.49 including tax and shipping. John Carradine presents five dreadful tales involving a haunted clock, a vampire loose in London, a vengeful corpse, a disciple of Dr. Frankenstein and some character named Count Alucard. Acting is amateurish and the unoriginal stories quite predictable. Lon Chaney completists may want to suffer through this to see him play a mad science professor. Not even "so bad, it's good." But if you must watch, listen for music from *Queen of Outer Space*. Aired on television with the bland title *Return from the Past*. (DVD-Image)

A Game of Death (1945) 3.0
Good version of the short story "The Most Dangerous Game" follows the 1932 version very closely, even to the point of adding a love interest that is not present in the original material. John Loder makes a good hero, and the basic premise is as strong as ever. Robert Wise directs. (BR-Kino)

Gamera Super Monster (1980) 1.5
Three "space women" are hiding on Earth, pursued by aliens who want to take over the planet. To that end, the invaders arrange various monster attacks, which are no more than footage from the *Gamera* oeuvre of the giant turtle battling various foes. The eighth *Gamera* outing is beyond cheesy, with poor special effects, erratic editing, and no sense of pacing. Briefly comes alive in a duel involving the most incompetent villain ever. But seeing those pixies do their transformation routine once was quite enough. (BR-Arrow as part of *Gamera: The Complete Collection*)

Gamera vs. Monster X (1970) 2.0
An ancient statue is removed from its resting place and transported to the Big Expo '70. Unfortunately, that unleashes ancient monster Jiger. Thankfully, Gamera is around to save the day. Rubber monster fans should enjoy this spirited if standard series entry. Highlight is Jiger impregnating Gamera! (BR-Arrow as *Gamera vs. Jiger* as part of *Gamera: The Complete Collection*)

Games (1967) 2.5
Colorful thriller about wealthy young couple whose harmless games-playing takes a sinister turn when stranger Simone Signoret comes into their lives. Enjoyable to a certain extent, but the whole story set-up is so darn odd that it's hardly believable. Signoret's *Cat People* co-star Kent Smith is also in the cast, but they have no scenes together. One character watches a few seconds from 1931's *Dracula* during a particularly unnerving evening. (BR-Shout! Factory)

The Gamma People (1956) 2.5
Two stranded reporters discover Nazi-like scientist conducting experiments on "immature minds" utilizing gamma rays; turns some subjects into geniuses but most into imbeciles. Odd mix of sci-fi and comedy is engaging but uneven. (VHS-RCA Columbia)

Gammera the Invincible (1966) 2.0
The Cold War between the US and Russia leads to atomic explosion that releases giant, fire-breathing flying turtle from the Artic. Gammera then proceeds to go on the usual rampage, including decimating Tokyo, while familiar cast of character actors argue whether Gammera is real or hoax. For US television, the original 1965 Japanese *Gamera* film was Americanized by removing the "action" footage and blending it with newly shot scenes featuring American cast. Subplot involving turtle-loving boy is also carried over. The result is passable entertainment for the undemanding. The original (shorter) version is available on Blu-Ray from Arrow as part of *Gamera: The Complete Collection*. (BR-Arrow at part of *Gamera: The Complete Collection*)

Gargoyles (TV-1972) 2.5
A well-respected anthropologist/author travels with his daughter to Arizona to see what local shop owner has discovered, which turns out to be a hundreds-year-old horn-headed skeleton. The visitor is skeptical-until claw-bearing creatures attack them. The first 40 or so minutes of this is good stuff, scary and intriguing. Once we get to the gargoyle cave, however, things get cheesy. Won an Emmy for Outstanding Achievement in Makeup. (DVD-VCI)

Genesis II (TV-1973) 2.5
Scientist working for NASA finds himself in the 22nd century, caught in a war between peace loving humans and domination-bent mutants. Lots of action and plot turns in unsubtle story about dangers of war and power. Written and produced by Gene Roddenberry. (BR-Warner Archive with *Planet Earth*)

The Genie of Darkness (1962) 2.0
Third film derived from 12-part Mexican serial follows *The Monsters Demolisher*. Vampire-hunter professor is developing machine that uses soundwaves to mess with bloodsucking Nostradamus. Plus, the heroes learn of parchment that might mean the fiend's destruction. There's a witch and a ghost mixed in too. This is probably the best of the four-film series: it is better paced than the others and less repetitive in terms of plot development. Some good cat-and-mouse in the early going between Nostradamus and his arch enemy Igor too. The "prisoner-rival" scene is a hoot. Followed by *The Blood of Nostradamus*. (DVD-R-Sinister Cinema)

Genius at Work (1946) 2.0
Lionel Atwill is the notorious Cobra and Bela Lugosi is his henchman in this horror comedy from RKO. Plot involves radio writer who starts to get close to the truth. Atwill and Lugosi are fine and keep this watchable. (DVD-R-Warner Archive as part of *The RKO Brown & Carney Comedy Collection*)

Ghidorah, the Three-Headed Monster (1964) 2.5
Godzilla, Rodan, and Mothra join forces to battle outer space monster Ghidorah. It takes quite a while for the main encounter to take place. In the meantime, we get some mini-tussles between Godzilla and Rodan, as well as subplot of Martian-possessed princess foretelling Ghidorah's presence. Last half hour makes this worth catching. (BR-Criterion as part of *Godzilla: The Showa-Era Films, 1954–1975*)

The Ghost Breakers (1940) 3.0
Bob Hope and Paulette Goddard, who co-starred together in the 1939 version of *The Cat and the Canary*, reunite for this funny horror/comedy/mystery. Goddard inherits a castle in Cuba with Hope, as gossip radio personality, tagging along to help solve the riddle as to why someone or something doesn't want her there. Hope is great as he delivers zinger after zinger, most of which work well. Goddard is adorable. The art direction of the castle gives the film a spooky atmosphere once they get there. (BR— Kino)

Ghost Catchers (1944) 2.5
Wacky comedy starring Ole and Johnson as nightclub owners who help their neighbors with a ghost problem. Lively and frantic and sometimes funny. Lon Chaney, Jr. is in the cast and wears a bear suit. (NA)

Ghost Diver (1957) 2.0
Diver kills his partner when they find idol with one eye of gold, the other of silver, which indicates a buried treasure is close by. TV adventure host purchases the idol, sans eyes, and brings his son and secretary to search for the goodies. Unfortunately, they unknowingly hire the killer (along with his girlfriend, daughter of the murder victim who thinks Dad was attacked by a shark) to help them. There's lots of diving footage as tensions mount in this OK drama. Title refers to corpse of victim that pops up at inopportune time. (NA)

Ghost of Dragstrip Hollow (1959) 1.0
Flat, tedious horror-comedy about group of drag-racing teens who run afoul a monster in their new digs. Very much of its time, this film has not aged well at all. (DVD-MGM with *The Ghost in the Invisible Bikini*)

The Ghost of Frankenstein (1942) 3.0
Ygor (Bela Lugosi) goes in search of the second son (Cecil Hardwicke) of Dr. Frankenstein to restore the monster's (Lon Chaney) power. A better film than it has any right to be, the fourth Frankenstein entry is all warm and fuzzy thanks to a top notch, familiar cast (Lugosi, Chaney, Hardwicke, Lionel Atwill, Evelyn Ankers, Dwight Frye and those other familiar townspeople performers) doing well with the by-now expected material. The finale is especially grand, unintentionally setting the stage for Lugosi playing the Monster in the next film in the series, *Frankenstein Meets the Wolf Man*. (BR-Universal as part of *Frankenstein: Complete Legacy Collection*)

The Ghost Ship (1943) 3.0
New third mate on ship discovers his Captain is cuckoo. And the psycho might be trying to kill him. Richard Dix is perfect in the

role of the unstable captain who is convincing whether playing charming or crazy. This is Skelton Knaggs' (as mute shipmate) first Val Lewton appearance. (BR-Warner Archive with *Bedlam*)

Ghost Ship (1952) 2.0
A couple buy a haunted yacht and then try to solve the mystery behind the ghost(s). Talky, low-budget thriller seems longer than it is, and director Vernon Sewell can't manage to generate the necessary atmosphere to sustain the film. Hazel Court is in the cast. (DVD —Televista)

Ghost Story (1981) 3.0
Four elderly gentlemen share a 50-year-old secret that has literally come back to haunt them. Beautifully shot and acted slow-burn thriller that overcomes its more predictable elements by creating a strong atmosphere that keeps the viewer's attention throughout. Alice Krige is mesmerizing as the vengeful spirit. (BR-Shout! Factory)

Ghosts on the Loose (1943) 1.0
Bela Lugosi is Nazi spy leader trying to scare the East Side Kids out of the house they're fixing up. A follow-up to *Spooks Run Wild*, this isn't nearly as amusing, and *Spooks* wasn't terribly amusing anyway. Notable only for Lugosi's utterance of the 's' word during a sneeze. Slow, unfunny, and clichéd, this is for Kids completists only. (DVD-VCI with *Spooks Run Wild*)

Ghosts That Still Walk (1977) 0.0
A teenager is suffering from unexplained aches and pains. So, the hospital refers him to a psychiatrist who hypnotizes his grandmother because *her* husband recently died from a heart attack. It turns out the elderly couple was attacked by flying boulders while driving in their RV in the desert, while Ronald Stein's theme from *Spider Baby* played in the background. Then, the doctor reads from the diaries of the lad's mother, who went insane. See, *she* tried to connect with an Indian mummy via astral projection. Then…oh, the hell with this. This is a film of badly dramatized, disconnected ideas that build to nothing. Another problem is that potentially horrific scenes go on far too long, making the events ridiculous instead of terrifying. Just awful. (VHS-VCI)

Ghoulies (1984) 1.5
The son of a satanic cult leader with lovely green eyes inherits dad's mansion and starts practicing occult rituals. Soon the title creatures are popping out of his backyard and attacking his friends. This low-budget oddity isn't the *Gremlins* rip-off it might appear to be, nor does it seem that most of the laughs are intentional. It's mostly juvenile tedium for the first hour. But the final 20 or so minutes are lively-or deadly rather. The puppet ghoulies aren't as much fun as they should be. (BR-Shout! Factory with *Ghoulies 2*)

The Giant Behemoth (1959) 2.0
Radioactive dinosaur is on the loose in Cornwall and plans making London a future stop. Standard monster-on-the-loose fare: too talky during the first hour, with most of the monster attacks saved for the last 20 minutes. (BR-Warner Archive)

The Giant Claw (1957) 1.5
Bad movie staple about goofy monster from outer space threatening Earth. Stars Jeff Morrow and Mara Corday are earnest. Even before the monster shows up the story is a pale imitation of other giant monster films. But boy are the effects ineffective—you can see the strings! The monster looks like Beaky Buzzard from the Looney Tunes shorts. (BR-Arrow as part of *Cold War Creatures: Four Films from Sam Katzman*)

Giant from the Unknown (1958) 1.5
Freed from his suspended animation state centuries-old Spanish Conquistador Vargas (dubbed the Diablo Giant) goes on rampage in mountains. Likeable leads, but the lame monster (he throws rocks!), dumb sheriff, and weak ending make this below average sci-fi. Features a character named Charlie Brown. (BR-The Film Detective)

The Giant Gila Monster (1959) 2.0
Title creature is causing traffic accidents in small Texas town. The special effects are poor, but the approach is unpretentious and sincere enough to make this somewhat enjoyable. Don Sullivan is agreeable as the lead. (DVD-Retromedia with *The Killer Shrews*)

The Giant Spider Invasion (1975) 1.5
A meteor crashes in a small Wisconsin town, bringing spiders that grow to above-average sizes. Barbara Hale plays a scientist, Alan Hale, Jr. the sheriff, in this special effects-challenged laugh riot. The film admittedly has some effective moments, usually those involving normal-sized spiders creeping about, and the first giant spider attack is sufficiently gruesome. But the poor editing and poorer effects derail the film's potential effectiveness. I do give it props for having the balls to reference *Jaws* by saying the spider makes the shark look like a goldfish in comparison. Uh-huh. (BR-Dark Force)

Gigantis, the Fire Monster (1959) 2.5
Gigantis (Godzilla) does battle with an Ankylosaurus, and their melee threatens Osaka. Enjoyable *kaiju eiga* is on par with the American version of the first film, but not as good as the Japanese original *Godzilla*. Still rather serious in tone, with a great monster battle. Released in Japan in 1955 as the first sequel to *Godzilla*, this US version was released in 1959. (BR-Criterion as *Godzilla Raids Again* as part of *Godzilla: The Showa-Era Films, 1954–1975*)

The Glass Tomb (1955) 2.0
Carnival man John Ireland does a favor for an old pal and winds up getting involved in murder. Potentially interesting story done in by poor script. One murder takes place off screen and a would-be harrowing kidnapping with escape from moving car is merely talked about! Aren't movies supposed to *show* us this stuff? Title refers to location where man will starve for 70 days as part of carnival act. (DVD-VCI with *Paid to Kill*)

Godzilla: King of the Monsters (1956) 2.5
Near Tokyo a gigantic beast, brought forth from its slumber due to the atomic bomb, starts terrorizing the citizenry. Soon

it's on its way to stomping across Tokyo. Between 1954 and 1984 Toho released 16 Godzilla films, all of which aired between 1957 and 1987 locally. Unfortunately, the version of the first film shown was the Americanized one created in 1956, with Raymond Burr as reporter covering Godzilla's attacks. Some of the original's power remains. But it's best to view the 1954 version, which rates 3.5. (BR-Criterion as part of *Godzilla: The Showa-Era Films, 1954–1975*)

Godzilla 1985 (1984) 2.5
America, Russia, and Japan must come to an agreement on how to deal with a returning Godzilla. A direct sequel to the 1954 classic, this was re-edited for US release, with Raymond Burr returning as his reporter character in newly filmed inserts. Both versions are imperfect. But there's enough giant monster action to make this enjoyable enough. (BR-Kraken Releasing as *Godzilla 1984: The Return of Godzilla*)

Godzilla on Monster Island (1972) 2.0
Godzilla and Anguirus leave Monster Island to do battle with King Ghidorah and new foe Gigan, summoned by alien cockroaches wanting to make Earth their own. Standard plotting and stock footage from previous entries are major detriments to this Godzilla outing. The final battle involving all four monsters is a lengthy one and almost makes up everything leading up to it-that and hearing Godzilla speak in the American version. (BR-Criterion as *Godzilla vs. Gigan* as part of *Godzilla: The Showa-Era Films, 1954–1975*)

Godzilla vs. Megalon (1973) 1.5
Nuclear testing has destroyed nearly a third of the underwater country Seatopia. Its irked ruler releases Megalon, who is later joined by Gigan, to wipe out humanity. That's okay because super robot Jet Jaguar has recruited Godzilla to help fight the good fight. Weak, tedious entry filmed on the cheap, with more Jet than Godzilla, who doesn't even show up until well into the proceedings. Interestingly, this is the only Godzilla film to air on network prime time, premiering at 9:00 p.m., March 15, 1977, on NBC affiliates Channels 11 and 4 hosted by Saturday Night Lives' John Belushi. He was dressed in a Godzilla costume and the film re-edited (with a new dub) into a comedy. (BR-Criterion as part of *Godzilla: The Showa-Era Films, 1954–1975*)

Godzilla vs. the Cosmic Monster (1974) 2.5
Ape-like aliens (apparently, someone at Toho noticed how well the *Planet of the Apes* movies were doing) have created cyborg Godzilla to do battle with the real one, fearing he may hinder their plans to conquer Earth. A somewhat return to form, as this a great improvement over the last two entries. Good monster battles and a more serious approach to the material, but the jazzy score seems out of place. (BR-Criterion as *Godzilla vs. Mechagodzilla* as part of *Godzilla: The Showa-Era Films, 1954–1975*)

Godzilla vs. the Sea Monster (1966) 2.0
When a young man, along with three unwitting accomplices, steal a boat to search for his missing brother they all get stranded on island thanks to hellacious storm and giant lobster-type monster named Ebirah. Evil organization controls the isle and tries to capture them. Thankfully, Godzilla is entombed on said island and ready for a fight. Mothra gets in on the action too. OK Godzilla entry doesn't really offer anything new until near the end when the monsters duel in the sea. (BR-Criterion as *Ebirah, Horror of the Deep* as part of *Godzilla: The Showa-Era Films, 1954–1975*)

Godzilla vs. the Smog Monster (1971) 2.5
In this pollution-themed entry, the mighty Godzilla battles alien creature that feeds on waste, then spews sulfuric acid mist as one of its means of attack. Along with the usual battles, this features hallucinogenic dance scene with people wearing fish masks, bizarre animated sequences, and James Bond-like title sequence. (BR-Criterion as *Godzilla vs. Hedorah* as part of *Godzilla: The Showa-Era Films, 1954–1975*)

Godzilla vs. The Thing (1964) 3.0
American International Pictures released this Japanese Godzilla entry stateside. Monster egg comes ashore, later purchased by shady entrepreneur. Soon the twin fairies from Mothra Island show up asking for its return. Initially refused, things change when Godzilla is unearthed, and Japan realizes their only hope is an aging Mothra (annoyingly called The Thing in the US version). Great fun; there's never a dull moment in this fast-paced sequel. Terrific music score too. (BR-Criterion as *Mothra vs. Godzilla* as part of *Godzilla: The Showa-Era Films, 1954–1975*)

Godzilla's Revenge (1971) 2.0
Americanized version of 1969's *All Monsters Attack*. Bullied youth dreams that he travels to Monster Island where he meets Godzilla's son (who speaks); has ringside seat to sundry monster battles taken from previous entries. Then Godzilla battles new monster that's picking on his boy. Obviously meant as a kiddie pic, this does nothing to advance the franchise. Somewhere between cute and cloying; at least it's mercifully short at 69 minutes. (BR-Criterion as *All Monsters Attack* as part of *Godzilla: The Showa-Era Films, 1954–1975*)

Gog (1954) 2.5
Investigators arrive at site where two scientists working on space station project have died under mysterious circumstances; discover supercomputer NOVAC and the "frightening" robots under its control. Intriguing mystery with great effects and ideas. Talky first hour lessens overall impact. (BR-Kino)

Goliath and the Vampires (1961) 2.0
Goliath returns to his village to find it destroyed and the women kidnapped. The main villain is a vampire. Weird, unsatisfying blend of horror and sword & sandal has lots of action and some atmosphere. But the film feels more like a string of incidents than a well thought out story. Aired as *The Vampires* and *Samson vs. the Vampires*. (DVD-Wild East with *Goliath and the Barbarians*)

Gorath (1962) 2.0
A star called Gorath that is 6,000 times that of Earth's mass is on a collision course to wipe out the blue planet. So, it's time to

force Earth out of its orbit. Handsome Toho production with great music score saddled with a preposterous script as far as actual science goes. (VHS-Prism)

Gorgo (1961) 2.5
British salvagers capture 65-foot-high prehistoric creature off the coast of Ireland and sell it to London circus. Eventually its mother shows up and together they tear up London. Colorful English answer to Godzilla has convincing effects and well-staged action. While the plot is mostly standard stuff, one's sympathies will be with the monsters this time out. (BR-VCI)

The Gorgon (1964) 3.0
Effective updating of the gorgon story, with Christopher Lee playing a brash investigator. He's a hoot in a rare hero role for Hammer. Peter Cushing is the doctor who knows what's really going on. (BR-Mill Creek as part of Hammer Films: The Ultimate Collection: 20 Film Set)

Gorilla at Large (1954) 2.5
Who-or what-is responsible for the murders plaguing the Cyrus Miller circus? Is it Goliath the gorilla? Another 3D scare fest, with a terrific cast including Cameron Mitchell, Anne Bancroft, Raymond Burr, Lee J. Cobb, and Lee Marvin. This is no less than the third '50s film to feature a gorilla as its central monster. (DVD-Fox with Mystery on Monster Island)

The Gorilla Man (1943) 2.0
In wartime England, a wounded captain, nicknamed the Gorilla Man for his climbing abilities, is being treated at hospital run by Nazi doctors. They're able to learn what the captain knows and act on it while trying to frame their patient for murder. Okay but hardly credible thriller; it's difficult to believe the powers-that-be would dismiss the hero's claims so readily. Because of the title Channel 5's Chiller Theater ran this positively non-horror entry several times. (DVD-R-Warner Archive)

Graduation Day (1981) 0.5
Poorly acted slasher about killer loose at high school campus, apparently avenging the death of female athlete. Killer's identity is obvious, and Patch MacKenzie tries but fails as the athlete's sister, determined to find out why her sister died unexpectedly. Guilty pleasure material for some, endurance test for others. (BR-Vinegar Syndrome)

Grave of the Vampire (1972) 3.0
An excellent example of low-budget 1970s horror. Michael Pataki plays centuries-old vampire that rapes young woman after killing her fiancé. She conceives a son who drinks blood instead of milk and grows up wanting to track down his father. This nasty little gem is fierce and intense, with plenty of shocks and twists. David Chase wrote the screenplay, two years before he worked on Kolchak: The Night Stalker. (BR-Shout! Factory)

Graveyard of Horror (1971) 1.5
A film that defies description! A man determined to find out why his wife died during childbirth discovers horrific secret about local cemetery. There are sudden zooms, over-zealous music cues, wild plot turns, inconsistent character behaviors, mad scientists, globs of atmosphere, consistent harmonica playing, bad dubbing, tiresome cries of "Michael!," and a cool monster that likes consuming human flesh. Nonsensical and fascinating at the same time. (DVD-Image)

The Great Alligator (1979) 1.5
American developer has destroyed African land to build awesome Paradise House resort. This has angered a local god that takes the form of giant alligator to wreak havoc. Italian Jaws rip-off is largely uneventful and plodding for much of its running time. But the action-packed finale is appropriately frenzied and offers a few late-in-the-game thrills. (BR-Code Red)

The Great Flamarion (1945) 2.5
Stage trick-shot artist has just strangled the woman who shot him. Now dying, he recounts the events leading to the crime. Moderately entertaining film noir has a good cast, but its script lacks any surprises. (DVD-Mill Creek as part of Mystery Classics: 100 Movie Pack)

The Great Impersonation (1935) 2.5
Set in pre-WWI England, this melding of spy melodrama with ghost story concerns an impostor taking the place of nobleman. Meanwhile jarring howls are heard periodically coming from the woods. Some good twists and atmosphere help make this an above average thriller. (NA)

The Green Archer (1961) 2.0
Not-particularly-involving Edgar Wallace krimi stars Goldfinger himself, Gert Frobe, as a crooked American businessman who returns to his London home after a murder has been committed there. The culprit is supposedly a ghostly Green Archer. Meanwhile his new neighbor pesters him about her mother's disappearance. An obnoxious reporter keeps showing up trying to get a story. Too much gangster-type stuff and not enough archer. (DVD-R-Sinister Cinema)

The Green Slime (1968) 2.5
A team sent to destroy an asteroid inadvertently brings back title substance to its space station. The slime produces one-eyed, tentacled monsters, which thrive on energy and go on the attack. The low-budget special effects will either charm you or make you laugh. But the monsters are wicked, especially when brandishing their electrified extensions. (BR-Warner Archive)

Grizzly (1976) 2.0
Gruesome Jaws clone features title creature, who stands at least 15 feet tall and weighs 2,000 pounds, slashing its way through popular forest. Plenty of POV shots and severed body parts. Spirited attack sequences help somewhat overcome poorly scripted dialogue and several unconvincing characterizations. (BR-Severin)

The H-Man (1959) 3.0
Atomic testing has created gelatinous green substance that hides in the sewers, sometimes venturing out to dissolve anyone with whom it comes in contact. Even in its shortened,

Americanized form, this is a nifty effort from Toho and legendary director Ishirô Honda, featuring great special effects and genuine suspense. Originally released in Japan in June 1958 a few months before *The Blob* started hitting US screens. (BR-Mill Creek with *Battle in Outer Space*)

Halloween (1978) 4.0
Halloween night six-year-old Michael Myers murders his sister, and then escapes the psychiatric hospital fifteen years later to kill again. Watershed film is nonstop exercise in suspense, with Jamie Lee Curtis making a marvelous person to cheer for. Director John Carpenter has style to spare and makes extraordinary use of the widescreen frame. (BR-Shout! Factory as part of *Halloween: The Complete Collection*)

Halloween II (1981) 2.5
This picks right up after Loomis looks over the balcony and is shocked by what he *doesn't* see. Michael continues his killing spree while Loomis continues his hunt. The problem with the film is that it lacks a strong lead. Laurie Strode is in a hospital bed for most of the film. But the atmosphere is still strong, and the movie works for the most part in maintaining suspense. (BR-Shout! Factory)

The Hand (1960) 2.0
In World War II, captured British soldiers each lose a hand when failing to answer a Japanese interrogator's questions. Years later, police find derelict with missing hand. What is the connection? Intense opening scenes eventually give way to a standard police procedural. Some good atmosphere helps. (DVD-Elite Entertainment as part of *Drive-In Discs: Volume Three*)

The Hand of Power (1968) 2.0
At Sir Oliver's burial, mourners hear his corpse laughing from its coffin. Shortly thereafter, a skeletal figure bearing Sir Oliver's poison ring starts murdering many people. Talk of zombies abounds. This color-lensed Edgar Wallace *krimi* may have worked better in black-and-white, as there are potentially atmospheric trips to Sir Oliver's tomb beneath the church and multiple appearances of the skeleton. As it is, the film grows tiresome as it offers little variety in the murder scenes and the big reveal doesn't hold up. (DVD-R-Sinister Cinema)

Hands of a Stranger (1962) 2.0
Unofficial remake of *The Hands of Orlac* concerns concert pianist losing his hands in auto accident, only to have them replaced by over-zealous doctor; madness ensues. Characters don't so much engage in dialogue as deliver speeches time and time again. But the bigger problem is none of the main characters are that sympathetic. The film sits on its hands instead of grabbing the viewer. The silent version with Conrad Veidt and the earlier sound version with Peter Lorre are much better. (DVD-R—Warner Archive)

The Hands of Orlac (1960) 2.0
A plane crash leaves pianist Stephen Orlac's hands "burned to the bone." So, he receives the hands of an executed strangler as replacements. Fearing he'll kill his fiancée he tries hiding in a hotel. But all that does is make him a target of blackmailer Christopher Lee. Mostly dull and uneventful version of the classic tale, with Lee's villainous turn being the sole point of interest. (DVD-R-Sinister Cinema)

Hands of the Ripper (1971) 2.5
Psychiatrist unknowingly takes on Jack the Ripper's daughter as a patient. She witnessed her father kill her mother, and now she too murders when certain events take place. Sympathetic characters are the main selling point of this Hammer thriller, which plays out with few surprises. There are some gory murders, and a lovely main theme by Christopher Gunning. (BR-Synapse)

Hangover Square (1945) 3.0
Laird Cregar is back, this time as disturbed composer George Harvey Bone, who goes into murderous blackouts when distressed and hearing a discordant noise. Contrived film (the noises and moments of anger are all too conveniently timed) nevertheless works thanks again to Cregar's committed performance and John Brahm's stylish direction. Bernard Herrmann's score is a big plus too. (BR-Kino)

Happy Birthday to Me (1981) 2.0
As her 18th birthday approaches, Virginia is still dealing with her mother's death and her own grip on reality. When her friends start dying in gruesome ways, she wonders if she is responsible. Much more plot heavy than your typical '80s slasher film, this effort suffers from over-length and leisurely pacing. Still, the cast is good and the end a surprise. (BR-Mill Creek with *When a Stranger Calls*)

Hatchet for the Honeymoon (1970) 2.5
Wedding dress designer starts slaying brides-to-be because, with each murder, he comes closer to remembering whom he witnessed murder his own mother. Given *that* set-up, it's no surprise who that villain turns out to be. Upping the ante, director Mario Bava throws in a ghost subplot by having the antihero murder his nagging wife who ends up sticking around. It's nonsense but it's stylish, watchable nonsense. (BR-Kino)

The Hatchet Man (1932) 2.5
Edward G. Robinson stars as Tong hitman Wong sent to kill his best friend, who has willed everything-including his own six-year-old daughter-to Wong! Years later, Wong is a successful businessman hoping to marry the now-grown child, as his Tong prepares for war. Interesting curio from a time when Caucasians played ethnic roles, which today hinders totally embracing such efforts. Robinson is good as always, and the ending is terrific. Aired once on *Ghost Host Theatre* probably by mistake. Perhaps someone saw the title and made an incorrect assumption about the subject matter. (DVD-Warner Archive as part of *Forbidden Hollywood Collection: Volume 7*)

The Haunted Palace (1963) 3.0
Primarily based on H.P. Lovecraft's *The Case of Charles Dexter Ward*, Price's great-great-grandfather was a warlock who now wants to possess his descendant. Lon Chaney, Jr. is a fellow

practitioner of the black arts. Tremendously spooky and vicious, as Price sets people on fire and forces himself on his wife, who knows something is wrong. Plus, the ending's implication is not something typical of horror films of the period. (BR-Shout! Factory as part of *The Vincent Price Collection*)

The Haunted Strangler (1957) 2.5
Boris Karloff is good as novelist whose research into the possible innocence of an executed killer yields surprising results. Clever plot is dragged out a bit, but the film is still enjoyable. (DVD-Criterion as part of *Monsters and Madmen*)

The Haunting (1963) 4.0
Taking a page from the "what you don't see is scarier than what you do" school of horror, this magnificently mounted tale concerns a group of people investigating a reportedly haunted house. And it certainly seems to be, as various and sundry screams, cries, moans, bangs, and other assorted noises can be heard, especially at night. But what exactly does Hill House want? Maybe Eleanor (Julie Harris), the mousy psychic who feels she's come "home." Truly classic thriller is a treat for the eyes and ears, and the tension never lets up. (BR-Warner Bros.)

The Haunting of Julia (1977) 3.0
Mia Farrow plays woman whose daughter chokes to death, driving the distraught mom to leave her husband and rent a creepy old house that turns out to be haunted. Julia decides to investigate the reason for the haunting, leading to tragic results. A neglected gem of a ghost story done 1970s–style; a slow-burn thriller with a great lead performance and a *really* downbeat conclusion. Decidedly not for those who want their horror capped with a happy end. (VHS-Media Home Entertainment)

He Knows You're Alone (1980) 1.5
Psycho killer targets brides-to-be while being hunted by the detective whose fiancée was one of the previous victims. Tedious early slasher just drags and features one of the least interesting villains in the subgenre. Mostly notable for Tom Hanks first credited role as a psych student who explains why people like to be scared. (BR-Shout! Factory)

The Head (1959) 2.5
Dr. Ood removes the head of his brilliant, but dying, boss so they can continue their transplant experiments. Very moody film, with tremendously eerie music score, is somewhat sabotaged by sleazier aspects concerning strip club. Overlong too, but it's still worth checking out. (DVD-Alpha)

The Headless Ghost (1959) 2.0
Three exchange students camp out at haunted British museum. They get involved in scheme to reunite title character with his head. At barely an hour, it moves quickly but is neither very funny nor scary. (DVD-VCI with *Horrors of the Black Museum*)

Hell Night (1981) 2.5
Linda Blair plays one of four pledges who must spend the night in estate where, 12 years ago, deranged father killed his family. Not surprisingly, the group is being set up for a night of screams and terror. What the tormentors don't realize, however, is that someone or something else is also lurking in the shadows. Rather tame for a "slasher" film: there's little blood and no T&A. What it does have is atmosphere and several effective jump scares. The finale is especially well handled. (BR-Shout! Factory)

The Henderson Monster (TV-1980) 2.5
Noble Prize-winning scientist is genetically engineering bacteria at university lab when he gets into hot water for refusing to follow required safety protocols. One long debate about the risks of playing Dr. Frankenstein is interesting but the same arguments are repeated one too many times. Be forewarned that, contrary to title, there is no literal monster. (DVD-Platinum with *The Infinite Worlds of H.G. Wells*)

Hercules in the Haunted World (1961) 2.0
Hercules returns home to marry Princess Deianira only to find her in a trance-like state. To release her, he must travel to Hades and retrieve the Stone of Forgetfulness. Christopher Lee is the villain responsible for Deianira's predicament. Directed by Mario Bava, the film looks gorgeous and has the occasional effective moment, such as when corpses rise and leap from their fog-enshrouded tombs to attack. Attempts at comedy fail, and the story drags too frequently. (BR-Kino)

The Hideous Sun Demon (1958) 2.0
The sun causes scientist to transform into title creature thanks to his exposure to radiation. Low-budget outing features great monster and sincere performance from director-star Robert Clarke. It also has the typical low-budget faults: talky script, clunky editing, and mixed-bag performances. (DVD-Image)

Holocaust 2000 (1977) 2.0
Is industrialist Kirk Douglas' proposed nuclear power plant the "dragon of the apocalypse"? Is his unborn child the antichrist? This Italian *The Omen* clone shamelessly steals plot points from its inspiration. But it does have an interesting premise, tapping into fears of the time, and features great cast. Watchable but hardly memorable. (BR-Shout! Factory as *The Chosen*)

Homebodies (1974) 3.0
When the elderly residents of a condemned building notice construction "accidents" stop work, they come up with a plan to save their living quarters. Entertaining blend of horror, humor, and commentary doesn't completely succeed. But it's performed to the hilt by a gifted cast and is a lot of fun. (BR-Kino)

Homicidal (1961) 2.5
One of the more blatant *Psycho* rip-offs still works well enough. Cold blonde Emily starts stabbing people left and right. Why? The film probably won't fool anyone today and that fright break is just plain ludicrous. The mystery elements keep the story interesting. (BR-Mill Creek with *Mr. Sardonicus*)

The Hooded Terror (1938) 2.0
Tod Slaughter stars as the Snake, the head of sinister organization taking on our heroes Sexton Blake and his assistant

Mr. Tinker, who are Sherlock Holmes and Dr. Watson clones; they even reside on Baker Street! Slaughter plays this one low-key, probably because this was the third of three Sexton Blake films instead of being strictly a Slaughter vehicle. The result is a mostly tedious affair as Blake tracks down criminals' hideout, leading to rushed finale. (DVD-VCI as part of the *British Cinema Classic 'B' Film Collection: Volume 1*)

The Horrible Dr. Hichcock (1962) 3.0
Esteemed surgeon likes to drug his wife during hanky-panky. She overdoses and dies. He remarries and brings to his old mansion his new spouse (Barbara Steele), who is eventually tormented by *something*. Loaded with various horror accoutrements including thunderstorms, a black cat, various skulls, a cackling hag, squeaky footsteps, and a fiery climax. There's not a whole lot of dialogue and what little there is purely plot stuff. The film works because of the atmospheric visuals: they're mesmerizing. (BR-Olive)

Horror Castle (1963) 2.5
Italian shocker in glorious color! Murders connected to a lavishly furnished German castle may be the work of The Punisher, a 300-year-old villain whose statue is part of the manor's torture chamber. Or could the real killer be Christopher Lee, the scarred servant? Fans of 1960s Italian Gothics should eat this up; others may find it rather dull. The music score, however, can be quite grating. (DVD-Media Blasters as *The Virgin of Nuremberg*)

The Horror Chamber of Dr. Faustus (1959) 3.5
After automobile accident disfigures his daughter, ingenious surgeon kidnaps young women to perform skin graft operations. Haunting French chiller is loaded with striking images, a detailed look at one of those skin graft operations, and other gruesomeness. (BR-Criterion as *Eyes Without a Face*)

Horror Express (1972) 3.0
Christopher Lee plays an archaeologist who is transporting a fossil aboard the Trans-Siberian Express. But this relic houses a force that can take over bodies and wreak havoc, which it does. Peter Cushing plays Lee's curious colleague. Nifty blending of horror, mystery, and sci-fi elements with great atmosphere and music. Several plot points would be used to great advantage in *The Thing* (1982) and various *The X-Files* episodes. (BR-Arrow)

Horror Hospital (1973) 2.5
Wheelchair-bound Michael Gough runs a health clinic that is a cover for mind control experiments. His wife's niece shows up and realizes something is amiss. Tongue-in-cheek mad scientist yarn is gruesome and funny too, when it wants to be, even if it runs out of steam before wrapping things up. Check out Gough's auto, which, in the best James Bond tradition, has a retracting blade that can lop the heads off pesky pedestrians. (DVD-MPI)

Horror Hotel (1960) 3.5
Excellent, moody story of witchcraft at work in a small town where witch Elizabeth Selwyn was burned in 1692. A college student visits the town to do her term paper only to find...Well, no need to spoil it for those who haven't seen it. Christopher Lee is in the cast. Better known today by its original British title, *The City of the Dead*. (BR-VCI)

Horror House (1969) 1.5
Some bored, hip party types dressed in dated '60s clothing head to a deserted, allegedly haunted, mansion for some thrills. There's a bloody murder, a cover-up, and a killer who may kill again. Structured as a 'who-done-it?', but don't bother trying to figure out the killer's identity as it features one of those no-way-you-can-guess motives. The film has some power in its final moments, but it's too little too late. Frankie Avalon is in the cast to give this British production from Tigon some American appeal. Available on UK Blu-Ray as *The Haunted House of Horror*. (NA)

Horror Island (1941) 2.5
Dick Foran offers interested parties a trip to a "haunted" island; terror ensues. Horror-whodunit blend is diverting if not particularly memorable. (BR-Shout! Factory as part of *Universal Horror Collection: Volume 3*)

Horror of Dracula (1958) 3.5
Christopher Lee makes an impressive vampire and Peter Cushing a compelling Van Helsing in Hammer Film Productions' version of the classic novel. Beautifully shot and designed with a terrific climax that's been reworked in other vampire films such as *The Night Stalker* (1971) and *Fright Night* (1985). Was it really a good idea for Dracula to hide his coffin where he did? (BR —Warner Archive)

The Horror of Frankenstein (1970) 3.0
Hammer's reboot of its own *Frankenstein* series. Young Victor Frankenstein (Ralph Bates) decides he wants to attend University and arranges an accident for his disagreeable father. Then he decides he wants to build a man and lets no one stand in his way to accomplish this goal either. This much-maligned film seems to depend on one's acceptance of Bates as the charming but villainous doctor. This viewer thoroughly enjoyed Bates' take on the infamous scientist, as well as the vein of black humor running throughout, such as when a body part number appears on the head of Frankenstein's dinner guest. A film that deserves a reappraisal. (BR-Shout! Factory)

The Horror of Party Beach (1964) 0.5
The first monster musical! Big deal. Radioactive chemicals are dumped in the ocean and create blood thirsty, laughable monsters. Awful film with lame attempts at humor, flat direction, and no sense of pacing whatsoever. The monster theme music is effectively creepy though. (BR-Severin)

Horror Planet (1981) 0.5
An alien life form impregnates one of the scientists exploring its planet. Mom-to-be then goes on slasher-type rampage killing the other members of her team. Awful *Alien* rip-off is gory and tasteless as well as being dull, even during the various attack scenes. Judy Geeson does a good job as the murderous

mother. But that's not nearly enough to make this thing bearable. (BR-Shout! Factory as *Inseminoid*)

Horror Rises from the Tomb (1973) 1.5
Head of decapitated warlock (Paul Naschy), discovered by treasure seekers, starts controlling those around him and once rejoined to his body, begins a reign of terror. A gorgeous looking film with absolutely no sense of pacing or logic. The women are beautiful, but the attack scenes are repetitive and sometimes downright funny, such as when Naschy is tormented by a talisman in a scene that goes on forever. (BR-Shout! Factory as part of *The Paul Naschy Collection*)

Horrors of the Black Museum (1959) 2.5
Michael Gough's first lead role as a horror villain is his typically hammy turn. Here he plays crime writer who institutes series of gruesome murders, so he can write about them, using male youth as his unwitting accomplice. Colorful and violent. (DVD-VCI with *The Headless Ghost*)

The Hostage (1967) 2.0
Young troublemaker gets trapped in moving van driven by two killers. When they move the body to bury it, he's discovered and must make a run for it. Middling suspense picture has some amateurish performances and incredibly corny theme song. John Carradine is a panhandler whom the parents think may have swiped their son. (DVD-Mill Creek as part of *B-Move Blast: 50 Movie Pack*)

The Hound of the Baskervilles (1939) 4.0
Is a ghostly hound responsible for the death of Sir Charles Baskerville? Does the same fate await heir, Sir Henry? Terrific first outing for Basil Rathbone and Nigel Bruce as Holmes and Watson. Lionel Atwill and John Carradine are suspects. Atmospheric and chilling in spots. (BR-MPI as part of *The Complete Sherlock Holmes Collection*)

The Hound of the Baskervilles (1959) 3.0
Fine Hammer version of the Sherlock Holmes classic, with Peter Cushing and Andre Morell excellent as Holmes and Watson. Christopher Lee is their client, Sir Henry Baskerville. Beautiful and moody, with only negative the changes to the original story. (BR-Twilight Time)

The Hound of the Baskervilles (1978) 0.5
Peter Cook and Dudley Moore, who worked their magic in *The Wrong Box* and *Bedazzled*, reteam as Sherlock Holmes and Dr. Watson, respectively, in this comic retelling of the classic thriller. Very few laughs; everyone is over the top; the piano-driven music score seems to parody silent films for no reason. Eventually becomes unbearable, especially the scene with Moore playing Holmes' phony-psychic mother. (BR-Code Red)

House of Dracula (1945) 2.5
Dracula, the Wolf Man, and the Frankenstein monster end up at castle clinic of kindly doctor Onslow Stevens, who goes mad when Dracula messes with a blood transfusion. Fun but familiar stuff. (BR-Universal as part of *Dracula: Complete Legacy Collection*)

The House of Fear (1939) 2.5
Remake of the silent 1929 film *The Last Warning*. One year after the corpse of a murdered stage actor vanishes, morbid producer plans to reopen the supposedly haunted theater where the crime took place. He wants to put on the same play the actor was in when he died, along with the same cast, who are all murder suspects. Fast paced with a good mystery and less obnoxious comic relief than usual. (NA)

House of Frankenstein (1944) 3.0
Boris Karloff is the mad scientist who escapes from prison and attempts to revive Frankenstein's monster (Glenn Strange), finding Lon Chaney's Wolf Man and John Carradine's Dracula too. Acting honors go to J. Carrol Naish who plays Karloff's hunchbacked assistant and makes him incredibly sympathetic. (BR-Universal as part of *Frankenstein: Complete Legacy Collection*)

House of Horrors (1946) 2.5
Martin Kosleck plays artist who gets no respect. He teams up with murderous Creeper (Rondo Hatton) to silence his critics while sculpting the perfect Neanderthal Man. Kosleck is great and makes this an above average outing. (BR-Shout! Factory as part of *Universal Horror Collection: Volume 4*)

House of Mystery (1961) 2.5
Pretty good if talky ghost story about house-hunting couple that learns the history of a house they are considering. Low budget but the story is interesting enough to keep one's interest. On Region 2 DVD as special feature on *The Edgar Wallace Mysteries: Volume Four*. (NA)

The House of Seven Corpses (1974) 2.5
As a film crew shoots at house where multiple murders have been committed, tensions build, a cat is slain, John Carradine beds down in a grave, and people start dying. Low budget, moody shocker builds slowly but surely to horrific climax with a neat twist to top things off. (BR-Severin)

House of Usher (1960) 3.0
First of the Roger Corman/Vincent Price Poe films sets the standard: beautiful atmosphere, sumptuous production design, gorgeous cinematography, and themes of death, life after death, and being buried alive. Suitor shows up looking for his fiancée, only to find she's been confined to her bed on her brother's orders. Price sports white hair but he's his usual wonderful self. A fine premiere entry in the series. (BR-Shout! Factory as part of *The Vincent Price Collection*)

House of Wax (1953) 3.5
One of the most successful 3D films of the 1950s; the first great horror film of the decade; and the flick that launched Vincent Price on a new career path in terms of the genre with which he would become most identified. In this remake of 1933's *Mystery of the Wax Museum*, Price plays the gifted sculptor who burns his hands trying to extinguish a deliberately set fire. He starts his own wax museum with a unique way of getting his wax figures to look the way he wants them to. The film seems to improve with age, with Price in excellent form as the sympa-

thetic but mad villain. And the script is very good too, making the unusual choice, for example, to have the police ultimately solve the crimes instead of some amateur. (BR-Warner Bros.)

House on Haunted Hill (1959) 3.5
Vincent Price invites five strangers to a party at a haunted house. He says it was his wife's idea. She thinks he wants to kill her. This is director William Castle's best movie: an extremely fun visit to a haunted attraction with well-timed screams and interesting twists. Every home should have an acid vat in their cellar just in case. (BR-Shout! Factory as part of *The Vincent Price Collection II*)

The House That Dripped Blood (1971) 3.0
Very enjoyable Amicus anthology concerning a cursed house. An author's latest villain has seemingly come to life; a businessman is haunted by the Salome figure at the local waxworks; a parent has serious child issues; a horror actor gets more than he bargained for after acquiring authentic vampire cape; and the wrap-around tale about a Scotland Yard inspector investigating the disappearance of the aforementioned actor. Great fun, with Peter Cushing and Christopher Lee in the cast. (BR-Shout! Factory)

The House That Screamed (1970) 2.5
Headmistress of boarding school for "poisoned" girls keeps her asthma-afflicted teenaged son tucked away, although he has a habit of spying on the students and meeting with a female now and again. Then there's the matter of the missing young women who are believed to be runaways but are instead murder victims. There is no surprise in the killer's identity. The motivation behind the killings chillingly caps this atmospheric, if overlong, Gothic thriller. (BR-Shout! Factory)

How to Make a Monster (1958) 2.0
After new management purchases American International Studios, they fire the makeup man who's worked there for 25 years. He plots revenge by hypnotizing the youths playing the werewolf and Frankenstein's Monster in his latest, and final, effort and has them attack. As the motivating scenario sounds like the way Universal dumped Jack Pierce after his accomplishments, it's easy to have a soft spot for this admittedly bland AIP effort. There's not much depth to Robert H. Harris' portrayal of the artist. But there are some good sequences, the final act is in color, and it's cool to see all those AIP monsters at the end. The finale is a shameless steal from *House of Wax* though. (BR-Shout! Factory)

The Howling (1981) 3.5
After being attacked while covering a story, newswoman Dee Wallace Stone goes to retreat for some much-needed rest, unaware that it's home to werewolves. Superior horror outing with well-placed humor and dazzling special effects. Many characters are named after directors of werewolf films. (BR-Shout! Factory)

The Human Duplicators (1965) 1.5
Reputable scientists are suddenly committing thefts of equipment and then dying in mysterious ways. It all has to do with visiting alien Richard Kiel, who is attempting to build race of androids. Uneven performances and lack of tension doom this one. (VHS-Thriller Video)

The "Human" Factor (1975) 2.5
NATO computer engineer working in Naples comes home to learn terrorists have murdered his wife and three children. He decides to track down the killers using the technology of his employer. Sort of a high-tech, international *Death Wish* meets *Dirty Harry*, with some good action sequences and a bravura finale. A guilty pleasure. Final directing effort for Edward Dmytryk (*The Devil Commands, Captive Wild Woman*). (DVD-MPI)

The Human Monster (1939) 2.0
Bela Lugosi is a crooked insurance man who commits murder to collect on his policies. He is also linked to home for the blind that has something horrific in its basement. Low budget prevents this crime melodrama with horror trappings from rising above the ordinary. (BR-VCI)

The Human Vapor (1960) 2.5
Innocent librarian becomes guinea pig of unscrupulous scientist, who transforms him into being that can become invisible at will. After murdering the scientist, the title being starts robbing banks to finance the dancing career of the woman he loves. Unusual Toho production first has much narration as villain tell his story to press, and then becomes hybrid of *The Invisible Man* and *The Phantom of the Opera*. Strange but quite watchable. (VHS-Prism)

Humanoids from the Deep (1980) 2.5
Mutated salmon creatures who want to mate are attacking fishing village residents! The performances are a mixed bag and the film's plot is right out of the 1950s. Rob Botin's creatures are impressive, and the attack scenes filled with verve. (BR-Shout! Factory)

The Hunchback of Notre Dame (1923) 3.0
One of Lon Chaney's most famous makeups has resulted in his Quasimodo joining the ranks of Universal monsters. It's a rather cruel classification given the character is quite human, and ultimately heroic, protecting the unjustly persecuted gypsy Esmeralda, subject of a cleric's lust. Still an impressive film both visually and in how Chaney lets Quasimodo's humanity shine through. (BR-Flicker Alley)

The Hunchback of Notre Dame (1939) 3.5
Charles Laughton is memorable as the title character who gets involved in murder and false accusations surrounding the Notre Dame Cathedral. Beautifully realized version of the Victor Hugo novel. (BR-Warner Bros.)

The Hunchback of Notre Dame (1956) 3.0
Gina Lollobrigida is Esmeralda and Anthony Quinn is Quasimodo in this gorgeous retelling of the Victor Hugo classic. Gypsy Esmeralda is framed for the attempted murder of her lover by cleric who cannot have her himself. To the rescue comes the misshapen bellringer of Notre Dame who offers

her sanctuary in the church. Both the stars are fine, but it's the relative faithfulness to the novel (in comparison to other versions) which makes this one worth seeing. (DVD-Miramax)

Hunter of the Unknown (1966) 2.0
AIP edit of Italian/French/Spanish co-production. American agent is sent to Republic of San Felipe to find Russian scientist and discover what he's up to. Meanwhile the Russians send in their own spy to kill the American and then bring the scientist back home. And there's a lovely blonde British agent too. Not very inspired James Bond clone has a couple of good action set pieces, including a truck that descends and then climbs street stairs. But the budget prevents this film from having the panache of its inspiration. Showdowns with the main villains are over all too soon. One character looks like Robert Shaw of *From Russian With Love*. Bondsian theme song *Get Ready for Trouble* is pretty good too. (NA)

Hush…Hush, Sweet Charlotte (1964) 3.0
In 1927, someone hatchet-murders Charlotte's (Bette Davis) lover, severing his hand and head. Everyone thinks she did it but, officially, the crime is unsolved. In present day, she's a lonely spinster whose Louisiana mansion is about to be razed by the county. Charlotte sends for her cousin Miriam (Olivia de Havilland) hoping she can help. But the relative's arrival has unexpected consequences, including digging up ghosts from the past. Outstanding cast enlivens this twisty, sometimes gruesome Gothic. Overlong perhaps but still compelling. (BR-Twilight Time)

The Hypnotic Eye (1960) 2.5
Hypnotist "The Great Desmond," with the aid of his beautiful assistant Justine (Allison Hayes), is responsible for several beautiful women disfiguring themselves. Detective's girlfriend decides to find out how he does it, while the audience wonders why he does it. Fun if farfetched thriller relies on ineffectual cops to keep the plot going. (DVD-R-Warner Archive)

I Bury the Living (1958) 3.0
Gripping thriller about cemetery employee who thinks he can cause plot owners' deaths. All he must do is change the pin designation (white for living, black for dead). Intriguing and involving, with Richard Boone giving appropriately anguished lead performance. The only misstep is the resolution, which doesn't pass muster. (BR-Shout! Factory)

I Married a Monster from Outer Space (1958) 2.5
Just before he's married, groom-to-be is abducted by alien and replaced with duplicate. His new wife wonders why she can't get pregnant and eventually discovers the truth. Low-key sci-fi thriller piles on the paranoia as aliens take over more and more people. Obviously, a variation on the superior *Invasion of the Body Snatchers* (1956) but still enjoyable. (DVD-Paramount)

I, Monster (1971) 2.0
Disappointing update of the Jekyll/Hyde story given Christopher Lee plays monster of the title. His Dr. Marlowe becomes Mr. Blake, who grows more evil and uglier with each trans- formation. Peter Cushing is also in this Amicus production, which suffers from stolid direction and ponderous story development despite capturing period flavor. (DVD-Retromedia)

I Saw What You Did (1965) 3.0
Two teenage girls prank call random people saying, "I saw what you did, and I know who you are." The problem is they call someone who has just murdered his wife. Gimmick-free William Castle outing has some good suspense scenes and a few effective jump scares. Of course, this scenario would never work today thanks to caller ID, star 69, and all that. Joan Crawford is woman in love with killer John Ireland. (BR-Shout! Factory)

I Walked with A Zombie (1943) 4.0
One of the very best of the Val Lewton productions has nurse tend to a zombie-like patient while she finds herself falling in love with her charge's husband. Beautifully atmospheric with excellent performances, a complex script, and some truly haunting imagery. The best zombie movie before George Romero redefined the monster in 1968. (DVD-Warner Bros. as part of *The Val Lewton Horror Collection*)

I Was a Teenage Frankenstein (1957) 2.0
Dr. Frankenstein, visiting America for a lecture tour, decides to build his own man, starting with the body of teen killed outside Frankenstein's lab. Whit Bissell is a fun mad scientist, and the monster makeup is suitably cheesy. Gary Conway's performance as the creature, on the other hand, is poor and the plot overly familiar and repetitive. The title shows the filmmakers confusing the name of the monster with the doctor. (VHS-Columbia/Tristar Home Video)

I Was a Teenage Werewolf (1957) 2.5
Michael Landon plays a teenager who has anger issues. The doctor (Whit Bissell) who is supposed to help instead injects him with a serum that turns the poor boy into a werewolf. Entertaining first, and probably best, entry in the AIP teenage monster cycle (dig those crazy kids with their Halloween pranks and musical interludes). The first murder sequence is suspenseful, as a lone teen makes his way home through a forest and hears footsteps behind him. Future angel Landon is quite fine as the misunderstood (?) teen. (VHS-Columbia/Tristar Home Video)

If It's a Man, Hang Up (TV-1975) 3.0
Successful model Carol Lynley starts receiving menacing phone calls. Then the men in her life start dying. Twisty story will keep you guessing; one of the best *Thriller* episodes. (DVD-VEI as part of *Thriller: The Complete Collection*)

The Illustrated Man (1969) 2.0
Young hitchhiker encounters man (Rod Steiger) covered in skin illustrations that "come alive" if one stares at them for too long, leading to anthology of three separate visions of the future, none of them particularly hopeful. Steiger gives it his all (maybe too much) but the stories just are not very involving. (BR-Warner Archive)

In Search of Dracula (1975) 2.0
Well-intentioned docudrama exploring historical and fictional vampires and their influences, with Christopher Lee providing narration as well as playing various nefarious characters in dramatization sequences. Lots of great information, but it's all delivered in a flat, lecture-like style that grows tiresome. (BR-Kino)

In the Devil's Garden (1971) 2.0
A rapist-killer is targeting students of all-girls high school. Art teacher Suzy Kendall sort of saw the villain, whom she describes as looking like Satan, and now she wants to help the police trap the murderer. OK thriller has too few suspects for the reveal to be that surprising. Major complaint though is the overbearing music score. Aired as *Tower of Terror*. (DVD-VCI)

In the Steps of a Dead Man (TV-1974) 2.5
While the parents and girlfriend of slain soldier are still grieving, his best friend shows up and captivates the mourners. But this charmer isn't who he pretends to be. The final story turns help elevate this standard *Thriller* episode (DVD-VEI as part of *Thriller: The Complete Collection*)

In the Year 2889 (TV-1967) 0.0
Remake of *Day the World Ended*. Survivors of nuclear holocaust must get along while waiting for world to become inhabitable again. There's also a poorly costumed mutant lurking about. Just a bunch of amateur thespians endlessly yacking for most of the 80 minutes. One of the absolute worst of the Larry Buchanan features made for American International Television. (DVD-Retromedia with *It's Alive!*)

The Incredible Melting Man (1978) 1.5
Contaminated astronaut becomes title monster after returning from latest mission and terrorizes the citizenry. Despite Rick Baker's terrific special effects, this is a poorly acted, repetitious affair. It does however have guilty pleasure-like charms. (BR-Shout! Factory)

The Incredible Petrified World (1959) 0.5
After their diving bell cable breaks, the four occupants are trapped in underwater maze of tunnels. Meanwhile the bell's inventor (John Carradine) tries to find out what has happened. Another cure for insomnia from producer/director Jerry Warren. Nothing really happens until the film's final moments. By then you won't care. (DVD-Image with *The Atomic Brain*)

The Incredible Shrinking Man (1957) 3.0
Title explains the predicament of our hero, who eventually must do battle with his cat and a house spider, as well as his unwelcome celebrity status. Intelligent script and approach to the material work well with the special effects, yielding a fine sci-fi entry. (BR-Criterion)

The Incredible 2-Headed Transplant (1971) 1.0
Scientist transplants head of psychotic killer onto muscular body of man with intellect of an eight-year-old. Of course, the two-headed monstrosity escapes and starts killing because the evil noggin is in control. For a PG-rated film, this is an awfully sleazy affair as the killer goes after scantily clad young women. Bruce Dern's mad doctor doesn't quite come off and the extra head effect is laughable. Good for some unintended chuckles. (BR-Kino)

The Incredibly Strange Creatures Who Stopped Living and Became Mixed-Up Zombies!!? (1964) 2.0
Jerry visits a carnival where he gets mixed up with dancer Carmelita and her fortune teller sister. Soon he's being hypnotized and turned into a knife-wielding killer. There are musical numbers, stand-up comedy, black cats, bad dancing, a creepy henchman, goofy nightmares, disfigured victims, an absurd final chase, and lots of gorgeous color photography. A glorious mess of a film, but one that is compulsively watchable. (DVD-Media Blasters)

Indestructible Man (1956) 1.5
Scientist restores executed baddie Lon Chaney, Jr. to life, but with the side effect that he's now impervious to bullets and scissors. Filmmakers take advantage of Chaney's physique but not his voice; he's silent nearly the entire picture. More a mundane police procedural, complete with pointless voice-over narration, than a full-blooded thriller. Chaney bulges his eyes a lot in this drab affair. (DVD-Image as part of *The Lon Chaney Collection*)

The Indian Scarf (1963) 2.0
And Then There Were None German *krimi* style. The potential beneficiaries of wealthy man's will must spend six days together in isolated peace and harmony if they are to inherit. Now cut off from civilization, a killer starts strangling them with the title instrument. This may be the first film where a peephole is concealed in a nude woman's portrait at her nipple. Other than that, there really isn't much to distinguish this from all the other films with similar set ups. Klaus Kinski plays a bastard drug addict. (DVD-R-Sinister Cinema)

The Inheritance (1947) 2.5
Based on the novel by Sheridan Le Fanu. Uncle Silas becomes guardian of his niece after her father dies. Unfortunately, Silas is a rotten egg who plots her demise so he can inherit her fortune. Handsomely filmed and well-plotted suspenser lacks subtlety and features over-the-top villains. There's also a terrible rendition of *God Rest Ye Merry Gentlemen*. (DVD-R-Sinister Cinema)

Inn of Frightened People (1971) 2.5
When the man suspected of a series of rapes and murders is released by the police, several of the victims' family members plot their revenge, some eventually having second thoughts after kidnapping him. Intense telling of familiar story doesn't completely succeed but is still worth seeing. (DVD-Scorpion Releasing as *Revenge!*)

The Inn on Dartmoor (1964) 2.0
Scotland Yard and a private detective are trying to figure out why escapees from Dartmoor prison are never heard from

again. Opening with a jazzy version of *Green Sleeves* and the latest prison escape, the film gets off to an atmospheric and beautifully shot start (a secret bridge emerges from the nearby swamp, a cop on bicycle gets a knife in the back) before settling down to a typically talky German *krimi* which comes alive only in fits and starts. The villain makes so many dumb moves during the finale it almost undermines the whole film. (NA)

The Inn on the River (1962) 3.0
Scotland Yard is hunting The Shark: a bank robber, whiskey smuggler, and killer who uses a spear gun instead of a more conventional weapon. One of the best in the series of German *krimis*: the plot is nicely convoluted, the villain's identity is well-hidden, and the humor is nicely played. (DVD-Retromedia with *The Terrible People*)

The Innocents (1961) 3.5
Chilling adaptation of Henry James' *The Turn of the Screw*, with Deborah Kerr doing outstanding work as governess who thinks her new charges are possessed by deceased former employees/lovers. Beautifully filmed by DoP Freddie Francis in widescreen black-and-white, the film can be read as a straight up ghost story or the tale of mentally unbalanced woman finally losing it. Either way the ending is hard to forget. (BR-Criterion)

Invaders from Mars (1953) 3.0
Boy witnesses a spaceship land, and then watches in horror as alien technology takes over his friend Cathy and various adults, including his own parents. Now he must get unaffected grownups to help him. Told primarily from a child's perspective, this is compelling, colorful sci-fi that has some great ideas (the aliens hide beneath the sand) and terrific visuals to match. (BR-Ignite)

Invaders from Space (1965) 1.5
Starman returns to Earth to stop alien salamander men from spreading deadly virus and lethal soundwaves so they can take over. Children are dangled above gloomy sea. The fish fellows perform a weird dance that makes Starman laugh. Effectively creepy at times, with interesting makeups but also extremely cheesy. Probably the best of the four Starman films. (DVD-Image with *Atomic Rulers of the World*)

Invasion (1965) 3.0
Motorist takes the pedestrian he's just hit to nearby hospital, not realizing the victim is a just-arrived alien. Soon afterwards, a force field traps the clinic's employees. Intelligent, moody, and atmospheric low-budget effort that recalls Hammer's excellent 1950s efforts. Available on Region B Blu Ray. (NA)

The Invasion of Carol Enders (TV-1974) 3.0
Carol Enders is attacked and near death when she is apparently taken over by the spirit of doctor's wife who has just been murdered. Now Carol is determined to find the killer. Good performances and cleverly handled script make this one of the best *Wide World Mystery* entries. (DVD-MPI with *Come Die with Me*)

Invasion of the Animal People (1962) 0.0
Producer Jerry Warren took a 1959 Swedish film, re-edited it adding US-shot footage and narration by John Carradine, and then released it to television in a much-altered form. The result is a talky bore perfect for insomniacs. Geologists investigate meteorite crash that turns out to be alien landing; encounter creature that likes to kill reindeer. Romance subplot further drags things out. Absolutely dreadful. (DVD-Image with *Terror in the Midnight Sun*)

Invasion of the Bee Girls (1973) 2.0
A series of heart attacks due to sexual exhaustion have claimed the lives of several men, some of whom worked in government-sponsored research facility. State Department Security agent investigates and discovers experiments involving bees are taking place at the facility, presided over by quirky female scientist. Initially amusing throwback to 1950s sci-fi efforts stretches its simple premise too thin and runs out of steam way too soon. The women are of course lovely to look at. (BR-Shout! Factory)

Invasion of the Body Snatchers (1956) 4.0
Classic thriller stars Kevin McCarthy as small-town doctor whose patients start exhibiting the strangest form of paranoia he's ever seen. They claim their loved ones aren't really their loved ones. He slowly comes to realize there may be something going on after all. Intense direction of well-plotted story leads to pulse-pounding suspense. Studio tampering forced addition of happy ending which thankfully doesn't really hurt the picture. (If you want to be even more freaked out just turn off the film when the camera pulls away from the freeway around the 79-minute mark.) (BR-Olive)

Invasion of the Body Snatchers (1978) 3.5
Top-notch second film version of Jack Finney novel. Several San Franciscans come to realize space flowers are responsible for replacement of humans with emotionless duplicates. As more of the populace become victims their situation grows even more desperate. Director Philip Kaufman fills the screen with creepy throwaway shots that build sense of dread. Great cast makes it all believable. Worth seeing just to learn the fate of the street singer and his dog. (BR-Shout! Factory)

Invasion of the Neptune Men (1964) 0.0
American version of 1961 Japanese film. Title creatures wear cone-shaped helmets and attack little kids. They also make trains move backwards, mess with the weather, and threaten Earth. Thankfully, Space Chief (Sonny Chiba!) arrives to save the day. Awful kiddie fare features laughable villains, boring hero, and hopeless script. Lots of things blow up in the last 10 minutes or so but no…just no. (DVD-MPI with *Prince of Space*)

Invasion of the Saucer Men (1957) 2.0
Unearthly visitors kill drifter who has discovered their presence and then frame two teenagers for the crime. Granted, the characters are exaggerated and some of the humor is lame (a bull drinks a discarded beer, complete with sound effects). But this jokey sci-fi effort has atmosphere and a certain low-budget

charm, and the aliens are cute. Poorly remade for television in 1965 as *The Eye Creatures*. (VHS-Columbia/Tristar)

Invasion of the Star Creatures (1962) 0.0
Two beautiful alien scientists planning world domination capture a pair of moronic army privates. The film is supposed to be a comedy, and everyone in front of the camera tries. They overact, mug, and deliver writer Jonathan Haze's dialogue thinking it's funny. The musicians try to help with cartoonish music. Director Bruno Vesota tries by speeding up the camera and staging silly chase scenes. It's all for naught in this dreadful, painfully unfunny film. To quote one of the aliens, "It's completely illogical and infantile." (DVD-MGM with *Invasion of the Bee Girls*)

The Invasion of the Vampires (1963) 2.0
Sequel to *The Bloody Vampire* finds doctor visiting the Haunted Hacienda to research mysterious murders. It seems Count Frankenhausen is up to his old tricks near Dead Man's Lake. Not as inventively atmospheric as its predecessor, this follow-up nevertheless has its moments, especially during the finale. Otherwise, it's a familiar talk fest, although the village priest's rant about the stupid townspeople is hilarious. (DVD-R-Sinister Cinema)

Invasion of the Zombies (1962) 2.0
Professor writing a book on his experiences in Haiti vanishes, and his daughter turns to the authorities for help. Soon after, three slow-moving, oddly dressed gents break into a jewelry store and are shot during their escape but are unharmed. It's up to the Saint (Santo) to find out what the hell is going on. Given the villain wears a black hood and works in a secret lab, this recalls many a Republic serial versus the Gothic horrors future Santo adventures emulated. Unfortunately, between all the talk and wrestling matches, Santo doesn't get busy until the film is half over, and then it's all standard stuff. Available on Mexican DVD as *Santo Contra Los Zombies* with an English subtitles option. (NA)

Invisible Agent (1942) 2.0
Man goes invisible for the war effort and infiltrates Germany; he spies on meetings between Sir Cedric Hardwicke and Peter Lorre. The least of the *Invisible Man* series is more about making Nazi's look ridiculous than anything else. It might have worked in 1942 but today it's mostly eye-rolling. (BR-Universal as part of *The Invisible Man: Complete Legacy Collection*)

The Invisible Boy (1957) 2.0
Scientist's son becomes pawn in smart computer's plot to take over the world. Luckily, Robby the Robot is around to help save the day. Despite good concept, this is an uneven mix of thrills, childish comedy, and sci-fi peril. (BR-Warner Bros. with *Forbidden Planet*)

Invisible Creature (1960) 2.0
Woman with no-good husband inherits her aunt's house, complete with ghost dubbed Patrick. When Patrick finds out hubby is up to no good, he steps in to protect the new owner. Okay variation on the standard haunted house tale plays more like lesser *Alfred Hitchcock Presents* episode. (DVD-R-Sinister Cinema)

The Invisible Dr. Mabuse (1962) 2.5
When an FBI agent is murdered while on assignment in Germany, his cohort is summoned to help continue investigating Operation X, which involves a missing professor, the actress he loves, invisibility, and the thought-dead Dr. Mabuse. Not as good as the Fritz Lang-directed entries, this is still entertaining, with fast pace and good atmosphere. (DVD-Retromedia as part of *The Terrible Dr. Mabuse*)

Invisible Ghost (1941) 2.0
Bela Lugosi plays a sympathetic villain in this poorly conceived story of man haunted by the wife he thinks is dead. But she's alive and living on the estate, hidden away by the gardener. Character motivation is nonsensical, but the film is so earnest that it works well enough. (BR-Kino)

Invisible Invaders (1959) 2.0
When the people of Earth fail to surrender to alien beings, the title creatures occupy corpses to carry out their attack. Good idea hampered by flat direction and needless narration. The zombie makeup works well in black-and-white. (BR-Kino)

The Invisible Man (1933) 4.0
Perfect blend of horror and comedy, with Claude Rains giving a bravura vocal performance as invisible doctor going insane and terrorizing nearby village. Entertaining as heck and the special effects are still mostly a wow. (BR-Universal)

The Invisible Man Returns (1940) 3.0
Falsely condemned for murder, Vincent Price is fortunate that he has in his employ the brother of the Invisible Man, who helps Price literally vanish, so she can prove his innocence. Since the title character is the hero, he doesn't wreak havoc like Claude Rains did. The effects are top notch and Price deliciously hammy. (BR-Universal as part of *The Invisible Man: Complete Legacy Collection*)

The Invisible Man's Revenge (1944) 2.5
Insane killer hooks up with kindly scientist and becomes invisible; plots revenge against former business partners who left him for dead. Jon Hall is good as villain. John Carradine is fun as the scientist. Moral of the story: a dog is *not* an invisible man's best friend. (BR-Universal as part of *The Invisible Man: Complete Legacy Collection*)

The Invisible Ray (1936) 2.5
Karloff is scientist exposed to Radium X, which gives him the touch of death, complete with glowing hands and face. The antidote given to him by fellow scientist Lugosi drives him mad, so he starts killing those who accompanied him on an African expedition. Starts out as Gothic thriller and then evolves into a standard revenge story. The stars and some nifty effects make it watchable though. (BR-Shout! Factory as part of *Universal Horror Collection: Volume 1*)

The Invisible Terror (1963) 2.0
An invisible man thriller by way of German *krimi*; it's a whodunit where you must guess who the title character is! A brilliant scientist perfects his invisibility formula the same night a burglary takes place where he works. He's suspected of the theft and the murder of the night watchman, but no one can find him. His brother and future sister-in-law step in to help. Too much time spent on the routine crime elements and not enough on the more fantastic aspects until late in the story. There is a neat early transformation scene where skeletal arms check a wristwatch, along with an unexpected finale. (DVD-R-Sinister Cinema)

The Invisible Woman (1940) 2.5
Comedy that just misses the mark. Virginia Bruce agrees to be John Barrymore's subject for invisibility experiment. Meanwhile an ostracized gangster plots to steal the invention. Funny at times with great effects naturally. Likable cast makes this watchable. (BR-Universal as part of *The Invisible Man: Complete Legacy Collection*)

Island Claws (1980) 1.0
Leakage from a nuclear power plant creates giant killer crab. You won't see much of it in this uninspired, tedious offering that throws in various subplots concerning various characters—some romantic, some tragic—to no avail. The attacks by regular-sized, ill-tempered crabs are mostly comical. They are the Pepe Le Pew of the sea world. (BR-Scorpion Releasing)

Island of Doomed Men (1940) 2.5
Peter Lorre is the reason to catch this quickie suspense drama. He plays owner of Dead Man's Island where he recruits parolees to mine his diamonds, turning them into slave labor and having them beaten on his whims. Enter undercover agent who plans to expose Lorre's illegal operations. Illogical plotting is somewhat overcome by watching Lorre at his most villainous. (DVD-R-Sony)

The Island of Dr. Moreau (1977) 2.5
On his own private island, Dr. Moreau (Burt Lancaster) conducts genetic experiments transforming animals into humans. Enter shipwreck survivor Michael York who is both fascinated and repulsed by what he discovers. Lancaster does well in title role, playing Moreau as more determined scientist than madman. Richard Basehart is good too as Sayer of the Law. Director Don Taylor, however, approaches this more as an action film, with bombastic music and too many chase scenes, robbing it of the intensity that made the 1933 version of H.G. Wells' novel so memorable. The doctor's fate is not nearly as powerful either. (BR-Kino)

Island of Lost Souls (1933) 4.0
Charles Laughton plays the mad doctor who makes "things-part man, part beast!" in his secret island lab. The plot thickens when he gets an unwelcome visitor. Those screams from the House of Pain continue to chill, as do Laughton's cries during the finale. One of the few early horrors that has retained its power to truly frighten and disturb. (BR-Criterion)

Island of Terror (1966) 2.5
On a small island near Ireland, tentacled monstrosities turn humans to jelly, removing their bones in the process. The local doctor consults pathologist Peter Cushing and bone expert Edward Judd thinking the cause is an infectious disease. Standard creatures-on-the-loose thriller aided by good cast. Director Terence Fisher stages at least one memorable scare sequence around the 40-minute mark when our heroes first encounter the creepy-crawlies. (BR-Shout! Factory)

Island of the Burning Doomed (1967) 2.0
While the areas surrounding it are experiencing typical near-freezing temperatures, the island of Fara is dealing with temps in the 90s. Christopher Lee is the no nonsense scientist who knows that an other-worldly force is responsible. Peter Cushing is the friendly doctor. Too leisurely paced by director Terence Fisher to really score; the aliens are lame; and the ending is disappointing. (DVD-Cheezy Flicks as *Island of the Burning Damned*)

Island of the Lost (1967) 1.5
Anthropologist takes his family on expedition to isolated South Seas island. There they encounter savage ostriches, Sabre-Toothed wolves, and young native left behind to prove himself worthy of being future tribal king. When a typhoon destroys their ship, they must figure out how to leave the island. Anemic adventure fantasy where much happens (native attacks, shark battles, earthquake) but little of it is exciting. Kids might like Drip the sea lion that tags along. (DVD-Trinity)

Isle of the Dead (1945) 3.0
King Karloff is a Greek military officer who becomes unhinged while being quarantined. Could the victims of a plague really be victims of a legendary vampire-like creature? Val Lewton-produced chiller is even more slow burn than his other horrors. But Karloff is so good, and the tension nicely built up, that the final act works wonderfully. (BR-Warner Archive)

It! (1967) 2.0
Roddy McDowall stars as nutty assistant curator at a museum where the latest attraction is a genuine golem. He figures out how to control it and gets even nuttier. McDowall is the whole show in this rather flat, clichéd thriller that rips off a main plot point from *Psycho* just for the hell of it. If you're a McDowall fan you're bound to enjoy his hammy turn here. All others are advised to visit another museum. (DVD-Warner Bros. with *The Shuttered Room*)

It Came from Beneath the Sea (1955) 2.5
Giant radioactive octopus attacks sea vessels as it makes its way to San Francisco's Golden Gate Bridge. Exciting attack sequences courtesy of Ray Harryhausen's effects work make this required viewing. The silly battle-of-the-sexes subplot between submarine captain Kenneth Tobey and scientist Faith Domergue takes up too much time, however. (BR-Sony)

It Came from Outer Space (1953) 2.5
Scientist Richard Carlson realizes a spaceship, not a meteor, has crash-landed nearby. Then some of his pals start acting

strangely. Universal's first pure sci-fi of the 1950s (in 3D, no less) is intelligent and moody but suffers from languid pacing and repetition of the fact no one believes Carlson. (BR-Universal)

It Conquered the World (1956) 2.5
Being from Venus has convinced scientist Lee Van Cleef that superior Venetians should control bad Earth people. Luckily, scientist Peter Graves is around to lecture and set things right. This Roger Corman-directed effort is sure sincere and thus almost works. Beverly Garland is terrific as Van Cleef's wife, who eventually confronts the invader. (VHS-Columbia/Tristar)

It! The Terror from Beyond Space (1958) 3.0
In 1974, a rescue team travels to Mars to bring back the lone survivor from a previous expedition and charge him with the murder of his nine fellow explorers! He insists a creature killed his crew, and soon the new group realizes they have a murderous stowaway on board their own ship. The basic plot of this nifty thriller is said to have inspired *Alien*. While this film doesn't have that classic's production values, it still is a nicely done bit of claustrophobic sci-fi with solid performances and an ugly monster. Watch out for a great "discovering the body" scene that predates all those slasher films by 20-some years. (BR-Olive)

It's Alive! (TV-1969) 0.5
Traveling married couple make a wrong turn, find themselves in need of gas, and stop at the wrong farm in search of petrol. The wacko farmer imprisons them in his cave with pet monster. Film features two of the most disagreeable husbands ever, little screen-time for the monster, and perhaps the most excruciatingly lengthy flashback scene you're likely to see. Final Larry Buchanan film for American International Television reuses the costume from *Creature of Destruction*. (DVD-Retromedia with *In the Year 2889*)

J.D.'s Revenge (1976) 2.0
In 1942, hustler J.D. Walker is gunned down by his sister's murderer immediately after he discovers her body. In present day New Orleans, he possesses overworked law school student (Glynn Turman) and hunts down his sibling's killer, who was successful in framing J.D. for the crime. Sluggish pacing lessens the impact of several intense moments; film is longer than it should be for such a simple story. Turman is a lot of fun in his J.D. Walker persona. (BR-Arrow)

Jack the Ripper (1959) 2.5
British thriller chronicling the exploits of the infamous slasher, apparently looking for Mary Clark. Atmospheric direction and some good performances. A brief shot of blood during the finale is shown in color. (BR-Severin)

The Jade Mask (1945) 2.0
Charlie Chan (Sidney Toler) visits a stereotypical creepy mansion to solve murder of hated scientist. Pacing seems off in average Monogram mystery that features what is certainly a most unusual solution. Mantan Morland keeps the laughs coming; final gag is a hoot. (DVD-MGM as part of *The Charlie Chan Chanthology*)

Jaws (1975) 4.0
Gigantic shark makes tourist season a nightmare for small town of Amity Island. Classic thriller from director Steven Spielberg boasts great characters, memorable score, harrowing attack sequences, and dark sense of humor. The first summer blockbuster has aged beautifully. (BR-Universal)

Jennifer (1978) 1.5
Jennifer is a bright teenager who's received a full scholarship to prestigious (e.g. expensive) high school where she's tormented by psychotic rich girl. Jennifer also has a psychic link to snakes, which allows her ultimately to take her revenge. This blatant *Carrie* clone (with a helping of *Stanley*) lacks its source's style, and it takes too long for Jennifer to start kicking butt. The first hour just piles on the tortures to the point of annoyance and frustration. One-note characterizations don't help matters either. (BR-Scorpion Releasing)

Jesse James Meets Frankenstein's Daughter (1966) 1.5
Notorious outlaw Jesse James and his able-bodied but injured partner Hank wind up guests of Frankenstein's *grand*daughter (Narda Onyx), who plans to use the later in her experiments. As silly as it sounds, with a hammy performance by Onyx and plenty of hilarious dialogue. Nevertheless, it's entertaining enough in its own way if one's in the proper mood. (DVD-Elite Entertainment)

Journey into Fear (1975) 2.0
American engineer/geologist working in Turkey has discovered oil and that makes him a target of certain business interests. (There are two attempts on his life before the opening credits!) Now, he's traveling on a boat with an all-star cast (including Vincent Price and Donald Pleasence), at least one of whom may be a hired killer. Disappointing thriller has great cast but muted, muddled direction that plods when it should be maintaining tension. (BR-Dark Force)

Journey to the Center of the Earth (1959) 3.0
Edinburgh professor and his student travel to Iceland in hopes of finding entrance to the center of the earth. Rousing adventure film features kidnapping, murder, a tumbling boulder, prehistoric monsters, over-sized mushrooms, perilous waters, a lovable pet duck, Pat Boone crooning, and more. A little long perhaps but a lot of fun. (BR-Twilight Time)

Journey to the Center of Time (1967) 1.0
Lab researchers are caught in time warp, tossed first into the future and then back to one million years B.C. There's a lot of arguing, button pushing, and spouting of scientific nonsense in this labored effort. (DVD-Brentwood as part of *Time Travelers: 4 Movies*)

Journey to the Far Side of the Sun (1969) 3.0
American astronaut and British astrophysicist journey to Earth's just-discovered mirror planet on the opposite side of the sun. But there are complications, leading to a startling dis-

covery. Intriguing premise and great special effects combine to make this a solid sci-fi outing. (BR-Universal)

Journey to the Seventh Planet (1962) 2.0
In 2001, five (mostly) horny men travel to Uranus where they find beautiful women, memories that come to life, and an evil force that plans to use them to take over Earth. OK low-budget effort builds creepy atmosphere, but its story is derivative of prior films. Alien spends much of the film talking to itself. (BR-Kino)

Journey to the Unknown (TV-1969) 2.0
Joan Crawford hosts two episodes of the British television series of the same name. In "Matakitas Is Coming," author of magazine mystery stories is trapped in library while researching 1927 multiple murderer who claimed the devil made him do it. In "The Last Visitor," woman recovering from a breakdown at seasonal hotel wakes up to find a strange man in her room. First story is pretty good, with some fine atmosphere and a bleak ending. The second tale, however, is as unsurprising as they come, despite several red herrings, and leaves a sour taste in the mouth. (NA)

The Jungle (1952) 1.5
American hunter in India claims woolly mammoths are the reason behind elephants attacking villagers. He's right, but the believed-extinct beasts don't show up until the film is nearly over. In the meantime, we're treated to attacking bears, slithering snakes, assassination attempts, and blooming romance. Unfortunately, the film's episodic nature and slow pace ultimately work against it. (DVD-VCI with *King Dinosaur*)

The Jungle Captive (1945) 2.0
Final Paula Dupree film is helped by Otto Kruger's performance as vicious scientist who of course wants to revive the ape woman. Rondo Hatton plays his murderous henchman. Vicky Lane takes over the Paula role and does little with it. Good riddance, Paula. (BR-Shout! Factory as part of *Universal Horror Collection: Volume 5*)

Jungle Woman (1944) 1.5
The nadir of the Universal horror series, a sequel to *Captive Wild Woman* that features J. Carrol Naish on trial for killing Paula the ape woman. He tries to explain what happened. The lovely Acquanetta is terrible, seemingly reading her lines from cue cards (and having trouble with *that*), and pretty much ruins the movie. Rest of characters fail to register and engage the viewer. Lewton-esque touches abound (the opening shot taking place on windy evening, view of the monster withheld until the end, a murder shown via shadows on a wall, final walk of frightened potential victim) but are all for naught. As one character says, "It's a gyp!" (BR-Shout! Factory as part of *Universal Horror Collection: Volume 5*)

Killer Fish (1979) 2.0
As a precaution, the mastermind behind a diamond theft fills the lake where he's hidden the booty with piranha. His plan backfires, however, when a storm causes the damn to break, dumping the hungry fish into the sea while he's trying to make his aquatic getaway. A good cast does what it can in rather blah horror-crime hybrid that had the misfortune of being released after Joe Dante's terrific *Piranha*. Not bad, just formulaic and predictable. (BR-Kino)

A Killer in Every Corner (TV-1975) 3.0
Renowned psychiatrist invites three students to his home allegedly for an intimate seminar. His real motive, however, is horrifying. He plans to use them as guinea pigs in his latest research project involving murder. Intriguing story is well-served by its cast, especially Patrick Magee as the unethical scientist. (DVD-VEI as part of *Thriller: The Complete Collection*)

The Killer Shrews (1959) 2.0
Shrews the size of medium-sized doggies attack group of bickering adults trapped in island cabin. Shadowy photography and wind effects add to the creepy atmosphere. On the other hand, the shrew "makeup" is ineffective, and the characters are largely unpleasant. Maybe if teens had been the protagonists this would have been more fun instead of just dreary. (DVD-Retromedia with *The Giant Gila Monster*)

Killer with Two Faces (TV-1974) 2.0
Ian Hendry stars as escaped psychotic strangler who meets beautiful Donna Mills on a train...sort of. Hendry is good, but this episode grows tedious as we wait for Mills to realize the danger that she is in. (DVD-VEI as part of *Thriller: The Complete Collection*)

Killers from Space (1954) 1.0
Nuclear scientist Peter Graves miraculously survives a plane crash, claiming aliens swiped him and that they are now planning an invasion. The aliens look hilarious. Clad in black body stockings, their eyes look like eggshells with holes carved out for irises. When they're not on screen, we're subjected to stock footage and drab dialogue scenes. Graves is OK though as the lead. (DVD-R-Reel Vault)

The Killings at Outpost Zeta (1980) 1.5
The Pathfinder Group is the latest expedition being sent to planet Zeta "our steppingstone to a new sector of the galaxy." Previous groups have disappeared. What happened to them? Will this new team be more successful? Inert *Alien* clone, with POV shots to hide the killer; characters that wander about alone when they should know better; and a low budget that prevents anything remotely convincing from happening. Sincere approach to the material helps a little. (DVD-R-VCI)

The Killing Game (TV-1975) 3.0
Wealthy, psychotic gambler arranges for kidnappings of deemed worthy opponents. He then forces them to engage in games with the highest stakes imaginable. Nicely mounted suspense tale, with ultra-sexy Ingrid Pitt looking for a new squeeze. Original British title: *Where the Action Is*. (DVD-VEI as part of *Thriller: The Complete Collection*)

King Dinosaur (1955) 0.5
Four scientists visit planet Nova, which has just joined the solar system. There they discover stock footage and giant creatures,

including title beast, which is an over-sized lizard. The directing debut of Bert I. Gordon is probably his worst film. At just over an hour, it's a cut-and-paste show with lethargic pacing and poor effects. The actors are fine but their characters uninteresting. (DVD-VCI with *The Jungle*)

King Kong (1933) 4.0
Simply the greatest giant monster movie ever made. Film crew goes in search of legendary god known as Kong. Once they discover him, there's absolutely no letup in this thrilling picture. Not only do we get Kong, but also sundry prehistoric creatures thrown in just to keep things interesting. A must! (BR-Warner Bros.)

King Kong (1976) 2.5
An oil company executive charters a vessel to a hidden island he believes holds an abundance of oil. What he, the crew, a rescued actress, and a stowaway paleontologist find instead is Kong. Reviled by some, this is an entertaining remake with some good performances and a great music score. The special effects lack the charm of the original film, and the darn thing is overlong at two-and-a-quarter hours. Still, it is *fun* in many ways, and Rick Baker does well in the ape suit. (BR-Shout! Factory)

King Kong Escapes (1968) 1.5
Mad scientist Dr. Who (!) builds Robot Kong to dig for Element X, which he will use to build nuclear weapons. When things go wrong, he arranges for the kidnapping of the real King Kong. Kong battles several creatures (and throws a mean boulder) before the final showdown with his metallic counterpart. At 96 minutes the film is painfully overlong with a mid-section that drags badly. Unfortunately, with over 10 years of giant monster movies at this point, the film offers nothing new. Original version was released in Japan in 1967. (BR-Universal)

King Kong vs. Godzilla (1962) 2.5
Now freed from the glacier that held him, Godzilla goes on his usual rampage. Compelled to get his own monster, TV station owner has King Kong kidnapped from his island home. After Kong escapes, he and Godzilla eventually butt heads en route to Tokyo. Deliberately silly in places (the original version was meant as satire), but fun for giant monster fans. Since Universal released this American version, cues from *Creature from the Black Lagoon* can be heard. (BR-Criterion as part of *Godzilla: The Showa-Era Films, 1954–1975*)

King of the Zombies (1941) 2.0
Rather dull zombie tale about stranded airplane passengers and their fate at the hands of zombie master Henry Victor. Mantan Moreland steals the film-and seems to have the most screen time-doing his standard scared-servant routine. Most of the time he's quite funny. (BR-Retromedia with *The Monster Maker*)

Kingdom of the Spiders (1977) 2.5
William Shatner plays small-town veterinarian caught up in invasion of lethal tarantulas. Spends a lot of time on the build-up. But once the spiders get serious in the last half-hour, this is an intense creepy-crawly fest. (BR-Code Red)

KISS Meets the Phantom of the Park (TV-1978) 1.5
Fired genius (Anthony Zerbe) behind many amusement park attractions decides to use the rock band Kiss as a means of revenge by creating destructive, lookalike robots. Zerbe is good as the villain and has the most screen time. But giving Kiss magic powers was a bad idea and renders this thing more silly than scary. The band members aren't particularly charismatic actors either. (Laserdisc-Image)

Kiss, Kiss, Kill, Kill (TV-1974) 3.0
Killer who marries and then murders wealthy women takes a break to woo beautiful Helen Mirren just for pleasure. When a perfect target shows up, he must juggle both relationships. One of the very best *Thriller* episodes (it kicked off Series 3) with top-notch performances and an extremely satisfying ending. Original British title: *A Coffin for the Bride* (DVD-VEI as part of *Thriller: The Complete Collection*)

Kiss of the Tarantula (1976) 2.0
Lonely teenager has a thing for tarantulas. In fact, when she was younger, she used one to frighten her cruel mother to death. Now, her sleazy cop-uncle is making advances and her schoolmates are giving her a hard time. Time to get out those spiders again. Okay low-budget *Willard* clone relies on audience's fear of eight-legged creatures to generate terror, as the camera lingers on the slow-moving creatures as they crawl all over the victims. (BR-VCI)

Kiss of the Vampire (1963) 3.0
Vampires interfere with young newlyweds' honeymoon. Colorful, engaging Hammer thriller with a nice variation on the vampire theme. The ending is a highlight. Apparently, the finale was too much for television so Universal recut the film for TV and redubbed it *Kiss of Evil*. (BR-Shout! Factory)

Konga (1961) 1.5
Botanist who crashed in Africa returns after a year with new theories regarding plant and animal life. He experiments on chimpanzee that grows to huge proportions. We're not even 15 minutes in when Michael Gough starts serving the ham, shooting his pet cat because it wandered into the lab. Uninvolving story hampered by poor special effects. (BR-Kino)

Kong Island (1968) 0.0
Mad scientist puts the brains of humans into the heads of gorillas, while female Tarzan frolics about in the surrounding jungle. Some movies exist on their own plane of awfulness. This is one of them. (DVD-Retromedia)

Kongo (1932) 3.0
Remake of *West of Zanzibar* with Walter Huston in the Lon Chaney role. Huston plays crippled former stage magician who now rules African colony while plotting diabolical revenge against the man who caused his injury and stole his wife. Huston is great in sadistic tale that remains potent even today. (DVD-R-Warner Archive)

Kronos (1957) 3.0
Soon after landing in ocean near Mexico, an alien machine emerges and begins path of destruction in order to harness Earth's energy. Well-mounted sci-fi story is unique among its peers and gripping all the way. (DVD-Image)

Laboratory (1980) 1.0
Six earthlings are "secured for study" by aliens whose outfits make them look like human-shaped disco balls. The subjects are forced to take part in various experiments including mild shocks and vanishing doorways while the shimmery scientists comment in electronic voices. This might have made an interesting *Twilight Zone* episode but at 90 minutes, the damn thing is just too long to endure. (VHS-United Home Video)

The Lady and the Monster (1944) 2.5
Probably low-budget studio Republic's best thriller, the first filmed version of Curt Siodmak's novel *Donovan's Brain*. After an accident kills millionaire W.H. Donovan, scientist Erich von Stroheim keeps his brain alive for let's-see-what-happens reasons. But the will of Donovan survives his death, and he possesses medical assistant Richard Arlen to take care of unfinished business. This is a moodily shot film with several intriguing ideas. Longer than it needs to be, the main debit is top-billed Vera Hruba Ralston whose character is incidental to the story and whose performance is severely lacking. Available as a bonus feature on region-free Blu Ray set from Australia's Imprint label called *Silver Screams Cinema*. (NA)

Lady Frankenstein (1971) 2.0
In this Italian Gothic, Joseph Cotten plays Dr. Frankenstein who again is using damaged brains when he should know better. His lovely daughter (Rosalba Neri) wants to be just like dad, so she plans to create her own monster with the help of her father's associate. Trashy but sort-of fun thanks to Neri's ruthless, sexy performance. She alone makes the film worth seeing. (DVD-Shout! Factory as part of *Vampires, Mummies & Monsters*)

Lady in a Cage (1964) 3.0
When the power fails on a hot summer day woman finds herself trapped in her home elevator. Things get even worse when several home invaders show up and terrorize her. Unflinching, intense thriller about society's coldness is unfortunately as relevant and believable as ever. (BR-Shout! Factory)

Lady of Vengeance (1957) 2.5
The ward of newspaper tycoon William Marshall throws herself in the path of an oncoming commuter train. In response, Marshall coerces master criminal (Anton Diffring) into helping him murder the man he holds responsible. Even at just over 70 minutes, the story drags. On the plus side, Diffring is great as the hesitant accomplice and there's a neat twist to the story. (NA)

The Lady Vanishes (1979) 2.0
Comedy remake of Alfred Hitchcock's classic set in 1939 aboard train leaving Bavaria for London as world prepares for war. Cybil Shepherd stars as wealthy American who likes her whiskey and strikes up friendship with English nanny Angela Lansbury. When the latter vanishes, everyone denies the woman exists. A throwback of sorts to the screwball comedies of the 1930s, Shepherd is rather shrill in what is supposed to be a sympathetic role and Elliott Gould as the man who ultimately helps her doesn't fare much better. Lucky for them (and us) there's still a compelling mystery going on too. (DVD-VCI)

Lake of Dracula (1971) 2.0
After a coffin is mysteriously delivered to the caretaker of a lakeside resort, a vampire with strange yellow eyes is murdering the locals. His main target seems to be Akiko, a woman who at age five encountered the vampire but managed to escape. Not really a Dracula picture, this Toho production takes its basic story from *The Brides of Dracula* but isn't nearly as memorable. Effective moments are few and far between, despite good demise for the villain. (BR-Arrow as part of *The Bloodthirsty Trilogy*)

Land of the Minotaur (1976) 1.0
Donald Pleasence plays a priest out to stop Satanist Peter Cushing from sacrificing young people to nostrils-flaming statue. Alternately dull and silly, with the worst decision probably being letting the Minotaur speak. Good atmosphere is wasted. (BR-Indicator as *The Devil's Men*)

The Land That Time Forgot (1974) 2.5
During World War I, a German submarine crew and the survivors of a ship it attacked find themselves on an uncharted island whose inhabitants are of a prehistoric nature. They must work together to survive not only ancient creatures but also tribe of Neanderthals. Charming adventure-fantasy doesn't have the most convincing dinosaur effects we've seen. The film, however, is too rife with incident for a viewer to lose interest. Followed by *The People That Time Forgot*. (BR-Kino)

The Land Unknown (1957) 2.0
Four people crash land in lost world rife with dinosaurs and sea creatures. They also find a missing scientist who has a seashell from hell. The effects are hit-and-miss, and the sexual tensions tediously handled. Film still has its moments. (BR-Kino)

Laserblast (1978) 1.5
Alienated youth, whose girlfriend wishes he'd act "more ordinary," discovers blast gun left behind by battling aliens. The weapon takes him over, compelling him to attack his enemies. There's some neat stop-motion animation work, a bossy bureaucrat in a suit, Roddy McDowall as a confused doctor, comic relief police officers, stuff blowing up, and abrupt ending. OK for a while but doesn't have a strong enough story to sustain an entire feature, so it eventually just starts repeating itself. (BR-Full Moon)

The Last Days of Planet Earth (1974) 1.5
Droughts, trees that consume living things, smog, mutated birds, nuclear fallout, rice riots, destruction of the ozone layer: had we listened to Nostradamus' prophecies, maybe we could

have avoided the apocalypse. Toho production purports to show cumulative effects of man's mistreatment of the earth in this message picture that's a fascinating disaster itself. Jarring transitions between scenes of human interaction and the latest "event" make for a frequently off-putting experience. Favorite scene: a car decides to plow through a traffic jam, flips over, and then ignites, causing the entire line of autos to explode! (Laserdisc-Paramount)

The Last Man on Earth (1964) 2.5
Based on Richard Matheson's novel *I Am Legend*, Vincent Price plays the lone survivor of a plague that has turned people into vampires. The first half or so is fascinating as we watch Price go about his daily routine of survival, mostly relayed by voice-over and simple visuals. Then the film loses steam and becomes routine. Still worth catching. (BR-Shout! Factory as part of *The Vincent Price Collection II*)

The Last War (1961) 2.0
Message movie from Toho. Average Japanese family watches with horror as world moves towards nuclear war. Lots of things blow up in the last five minutes or so. Kids sing *It's A Small World After All* in complete oblivion. The filmmakers' intentions may have been noble, but the result is hokey. (VHS-Video Gems)

The Last Warning (1938) 2.5
Entry in Universal's "Crime Club" series. Detective duo goes undercover at California estate looking for writer of threatening letters with pen name The Eye. There's kidnapping and murder too. More comedy than mystery here, although what mystery there is *is* good and most of the comedy is at least amusing. (NA)

Last Woman on Earth (1960) 1.5
Crook, his wife, and his lawyer go scuba diving in Puerto Rico and survive fatalistic event, which seems to have killed everyone else. Soon the men are fighting over the final living female. Producer/director Roger Corman can do only so much with Robert Towne's talky script; one loses interest well before film has concluded. (DVD-Image as part of *The Roger Corman Puerto Rico Trilogy*)

Latitude Zero (1969) 2.0
Joseph Cotten plays 204-year-old submarine commander who lives in beautiful underwater title city, doing battle with madman Cesar Romero, who creates fake-looking but cuddly human-animal hybrids. Some good effects work but lots of silliness too. Romero hams it up. Features the Bath of Immunity, which makes bathers impervious to all harm for 24 hours! (DVD-Media Blasters)

The Leech Woman (1960) 1.5
Older woman who is about to divorce her scientist husband gains the secret of youth (albeit temporarily) and becomes selfish monster. There isn't a single likable character in this thing: the husband is a pig, his wife a killer, her lawyer a simpleton, and the lawyer's fiancée pulls a gun on a rival. It's depressing and not very fun although Coleen Gray does give a good lead performance. Too bad that's not enough. (BR-Shout! Factory)

The Legacy (1978) 2.5
American architect brings her boyfriend to England for job opportunity and is then lured to estate where sinister forces are at work. Enjoyable if muddled shocker, based on a story by Hammer Film vet Jimmy Sangster, features several gruesome deaths and the ubiquitous kitty, which is never a good sign. (BR-Shout! Factory)

Legacy of Blood (1971) 0.5
John Carradine has died leaving a $136 million inheritance to be divided among his four "screwball" offspring. The catch is they must spend a week together in the family home. Then the murders start. Great to see Jeff Morrow and Faith Domergue again; not so great to see them is this sluggish, talky, and bland thriller. Gets worse and worse as it fumbles along. (DVD-Mill Creek as part of *Horror Classics: 100 Movie Pack*)

Legacy of Horror (1978) 1.0
Director Andy Milligan's remake of his own *The Ghastly Ones*. Three sisters and their respective husbands must spend three days and two nights at late father's island home if they want to inherit fortune. Of course, a mystery killer shows up and starts eliminating heirs. Technically the film is a disaster: the editing is frequently jarring and the dialogue difficult to make out. The acting is a mixed bag too. Still, the flick has a certain creaky charm despite the awfulness. (BR-Severin as part of *The Andy Milligan Dungeon*)

The Legend of Boggy Creek (1972) 2.0
Docudrama about Bigfoot-type monster scaring the residents of Fouke, Arkansas and nearby Texarkana. One of the earliest in the numerous Sasquatch films that emerged during the 1970s. This one isn't bad; it's hokey in spots because non-actors were used in various roles, and some of those songs are corny. On the other hand, several of the attack sequences manage to raise a neck hair or two. (BR-Boggy Creek LLC)

The Legend of Hell House (1973) 3.0
In the days leading up to Christmas, a team of paranormal investigators make themselves uncomfortable at reportedly haunted house. Director John Hough employs many odd camera angles and close-ups to generate tension, of which this film has a lot. Creepy music score too. Based on the novel by Richard Matheson. (BR-Fox)

Legend of the 7 Golden Vampires (1974) 2.0
In 1904 Dr. Van Helsing (Peter Cushing) is lecturing in China when he is asked by student to assist in eliminating six vampires who terrorize his village. His grandfather had killed the seventh many years ago. Unsuccessful marriage of horror and martial arts results in busy but tedious enterprise. Van Helsing's final face off with Dracula is a joke. (BR-Shout! Factory)

Lemora, the Lady Dracula (1973) 2.5
Devout 13-year-old choir singer Lila Lee goes to visit her ailing father who is on the run for murdering his wife. Lila doesn't realize however she is being set up by title creature to join her strange world. Often fascinating attempt to film horrific fairytale about loss of innocence is rife with atmosphere, hideous

creatures, and sense of dread. It's also slow and meandering, with Lesley Gilb's performance as Lemora ranging from hypnotic to awful. Good music score too. (DVD-Synapse Films as *Lemora: A Child's Tale of the Supernatural*)

The Leopard Man (1943) 3.0
Another winner from the Lewton company, this one concerning an escaped panther and some vicious murders. The early sequence involving a frightened girl's late-night walk home from the store is one of the very best terror passages from '30s/'40s horror. (BR-Shout! Factory)

Let's Scare Jessica to Death (1971) 3.5
Woman who's just getting over a breakdown moves to farmhouse with husband and his pal. There they discover a squatter named Emily who bears a chilling resemblance to a legendary vampire said to haunt the countryside. Unjustly neglected horror film is creepy, intense, unnerving, and ultimately terrifying, with Zohra Lampert giving utterly believable performance as tortured Jessica. (BR-Shout! Factory)

Life, Liberty, and Pursuit on the Planet of the Apes (TV-1974) 2.5
Two episodes from the TV series. In "The Surgeon," one of the human fugitives takes a bullet and must be moved to medical facility, risking exposure. In "The Interrogation," the apes plan to try brainwashing techniques on one of the captured heroes. Entertaining enough for apes' fans. (DVD-Fox as part of *Planet of the Apes: The Complete TV Series*)

Lifepod (1981) 1.5
The maiden voyage of White Star Lines' luxury space cruiser *Arcturus* is on its way to Jupiter when the main computer orders everyone to abandon ship. Those left trapped on the vessel try to find a way out while debating, arguing, and assigning blame about the situation. Low-budget variation on *2001: A Space Odyssey* consists mostly of talk and lackluster performances. Eerie mood helps a bit. (DVD-R-VCI)

Lisa and the Devil (1973) 2.5
While shopping during her jaunt to Spain, Elke Sommer sees fellow customer Telly Savalas and thinks he's the devil come to life because he resembles Satan's likeness in a fresco. Things get worse when she takes shelter in a home where Savalas is the butler. The matriarch of the house is blind and creepy, while her son berates someone or something that occupies an upstairs room. There's also infidelity, a dummy which may or may not be alive, and murder. Director Mario Bava's nightmare come to life is a beguiling piece of work-beautiful, haunting, confusing, and original. Not for all tastes. Avoid the bastardized version *House of Exorcism*, which added exorcism scenes with Robert Alda to cash in on *The Exorcist*. (BR-Kino)

The Little Girl Who Lives Down the Lane (1976) 3.0
Thirteen-year-old girl (Jodie Foster) has a secret. It has something to do with her father never seeming to be around. A pervert (Martin Sheen) lurking about intends to find out what is really going on. Very well-done thriller with great performances and several twists. Great ending. (BR-Kino)

The Little Shop of Horrors (1960) 3.0
Very funny Roger Corman quickie about skid row flower store employee who learns his new plant loves blood. Jack Nicholson has funny cameo as dental patient who loves pain. Charles B. Griffith's dialogue is terrific, especially as delivered by Mel Welles who plays the store's owner. (BR-Legend Films)

The Living Ghost (1942) 2.0
A wealthy financier is missing, and retired PI agrees to find out what happened. When the "victim" shows up zombie-like, however, the real mystery begins. Average blend of humor and thrills. (BR-Retromedia with *The Mysterious Mr. Wong*)

The Living Head (1963) 2.5
After violating an Aztec tomb, three friends/archaeologists are marked for death. Wild but repetitive Mexican horror film re-teams German Robles and Abel Salazar. Has good, albeit unintentional, laughs along the way. (DVD-Beverly Wilshire)

The Lodger (1944) 3.0
Well-done Jack the Ripper thriller with Laird Cregar as the title character, Mr. Slade. He sets his sights on the lovely actress who shares his boarding address. Cregar is very good, as is George Sanders as the detective on the case and Merle Oberon as the woman in peril. Nice period flavor too. Slade's numerous soliloquies do get a little tired as the film progresses. (BR-Kino)

Look Back in Darkness (TV-1975) 2.0
A pianist returns to England where, 10 years ago, his wife was murdered, and he was blinded during a bank robbery. While playing at a swanky engagement party, he hears a voice that he believes belongs to the killer. Starts out fine but ultimately the story grows tedious, as we're repeatedly shown the villain's shoes to the point of annoyance. Original British title: *The Next Voice You See* (DVD-VEI as part of *Thriller: The Complete Collection*)

Lost Battalion (1960) 1.5
Tepid World War II outing about romance that develops between Filipino guerrilla fighter and American girl (Diane Jergens) as they flee the Japanese, trying to reach submarine that will rescue her. Nicely filmed but almost entirely uninvolving, partly due to Jergens' stiff performance. (DVD-Timeless Media Group as part of *Movies 4 U: Timeless Military Film Collection*)

Lost Continent (1951) 2.0
Team sent to recover missing rocket discovers dinosaurs and other prehistoric creatures as well. Low-budget effort has likeable cast, but the story drags in places. Stop-motion animated creatures pale in comparison to previous efforts such as *King Kong*. (DVD-Image)

The Lost Continent (1968) 2.0
Hammer Film Productions fantasy about cargo ship headed to Caracas caught in hurricane. The survivors wind up stranded in sea village of wrecked ships, vicious vines, giant crabs, and descendants of the Spanish Inquisition. Amusing but silly

adventure stretches things out with character melodramatics that amount to very little. Kudos to the cast for playing this straight. (BR-Shout! Factory)

The Lost Missile (1958) 2.5
Scientists need to figure how to stop low-flying alien missile-like object traveling at 4,000 miles an hour that destroys everything in its path. Scary and intense story, with brutal climax. Lots of stock footage due to low budget lessens impact somewhat. (DVD-Cheezy Flicks)

Lost Planet Airmen (1951) 2.0
Revered scientists are dying in mysterious accidents. The culprit is the mysterious Dr. Vulcan, who is trying to steal the Decimator, so he can hold New York City for ransom. It's up to the Rocket Man (a scientist with a pointy helmet and jet pack strapped to his back) to foil Vulcan's plans. This feature version of the Republic serial *King of the Rocket Men* (1949) is rife with fist- fights, car chases, and views of the button-controlled rocket suit. The result is a routine 65 minutes. (NA)

The Lost World of Sinbad (1963) 2.5
Japanese legend Toshirô Mifune plays Sinbad in American International Pictures version of Toho's *Samurai Pirate*. A shipwrecked Sinbad is rescued by demoted wizard who has an eye for the ladies and the ability to transform into a fly. Our hero decides to save a king's daughter from a corrupt premier; he faces the Black Pirate, a fanged, white-haired witch, trap doors, and other perils. Handsome, ornate, and well-cast actioner needed more consistent adventure to fully succeed. (NA)

The Lost World (1960) 2.0
Claude Rains plays irascible professor (with injurious umbrella) leading search for dinosaurs in the Amazon. Irwin Allen's colorful remake of 1925 film, based on Sir Arthur Conan Doyle's novel, has good cast but disappointing effects, which aren't much better than what we saw in 1950s low-budgeters. It also suffers from padding by adding the ubiquitous love triangle and out-for-revenge subplots. (DVD-Fox)

Love at First Bite (1979) 3.0
Dracula (George Hamilton) is kicked out of his Transylvania home and heads to New York, where he tracks down the model with whom he's fallen in love. Funny, heartfelt vampire comedy with great turns by Artie Johnson as Renfield and Richard Benjamin as psychiatrist who can't keep his vampire mythos straight. Very cute ending with great final line. (BR-Shout! Factory with *Once Bitten*)

The Lucifer Complex (1978) 0.0
Robert Vaughn plays a disgraced agent who's discovered a Nazi cloning plot on remote island. The whole film is being watched on computer by bored-looking loner via memory crystals, which is absurd since Vaughn's character has a few flashbacks that could hardly be viewed on stored data. So, someone must have run out of money or saw what a disaster this thing was, took what footage they had shot, and created the wrap-around, which first bores us with 20 minutes of war footage before introducing our hero. Lots of stuff blows up at the end but you won't care. The pits. (DVD-East West DVD with *Beyond the Bermuda Triangle*)

Lust for a Vampire (1971) 2.0
Middle and least entry in Hammer Film Productions' Karnstein trilogy. This time Carmilla/Mircalla lands at girl's Finishing School and puts bite on students and teachers alike. Yutte Stensgaard is stunning as the bloodthirsty object of desire. The story itself is unspectacular and uninvolving. (BR-Shout! Factory)

Macabre (1958) 2.0
William Castle's first excursion into the horror field focuses on disgraced town doctor and his kidnapped daughter. It seems almost everyone has a reason to hate him. There are so many scenes of explaining all the relationships and their history that the film drags when it should be charging ahead, considering the poor little girl may be buried alive. There's a good twist at the end, but it doesn't have the punch it should. (DVD-R-Warner Archive)

Macumba Love (1960) 1.0
Cynical writer who exposes myths has targeted voodoo rites in cliché island paradise, but he still has time to romance wealthy divorcee. Then his busty daughter and her new dim bulb husband show up and upset the locals. Overall, the acting is poor, the pacing haphazard, and the interest level nonexistent. An early scene where a corpse upsets an ocean swim is effective though. (VHS-Sinister Cinema)

The Mad Doctor (1940) 2.5
Basil Rathbone plays psychiatrist who has murdered his wealthy wife with aid from partner in crime Martin Kosleck. Now he has wedding bells planned for wealthy but suicidal debutante. Plenty of horror trappings in the early going, including the opening sequence where rain pours from the credits. Unfortunately, things settle down to standard melodrama. Rathbone and Kosleck make a great team. (BR-Kino)

Mad Doctor of Blood Island (1969) 2.0
Dr. Lorca's experiments with chlorophyll have created green-blooded, savage monster. Second entry in the Blood Island Trilogy is much like the first: sleazy, technically challenged, fascinating, and compelling. Ronald Remy is good as title medico. Watch out for the pulsating camera! Aired as *Tomb of the Living Dead*. (BR-Severin)

The Mad Doctor of Market Street (1942) 2.0
Lionel Atwill's turn as mad scientist is what makes this clunky thriller watchable. He escapes justice for killing a test subject only to end up on the proverbial hostile island, where he continues his experiments. His comeuppance is terrific. (BR-Shout! Factory as part of *Universal Horror Collection: Volume 2*)

The Mad Executioners (1963) 2.5
The Executioners of London are a group of hood-wearing hangmen who hold court against criminals, and then carry out the death penalty for those found guilty. They leave the bodies in public places to be found, complete with the evi-

dence gathered against them. Meanwhile, a madman is decapitating young women, including the sister of Scotland Yard inspector. German *krimi* based on Bryan Edgar Wallace story is atmospheric and well paced, if hard to swallow. (DVD-Retromedia with *The Fellowship of the Frog*)

The Mad Genius (1931) 2.5
Puppeteer (John Barrymore), who always dreamed of being a great dancer, decides to teach abused but graceful young Fedor, and has no problem taking all the credit for his protégé's eventual success in the ballet. When Fedor falls in love with fellow performer, however, the obsessed Barrymore decides to interfere, with tragic results. Barrymore makes a good human monster as he did in 1931's *Svengali*. The ending though, while appropriately gruesome, is unconvincing. (DVD-R-Warner Archive)

The Mad Ghoul (1943) 3.0
George Zucco is once again up to no good, this time poisoning a medical student whom he then uses to do his murderous bidding. An early variation on the zombie theme, this has plenty of creepy moments, especially the death of Carl Denham himself, Robert Armstrong, who plays a pushy journalist. Evelyn Ankers is the woman everybody loves. (BR-Shout! Factory as part of *Universal Horror Collection: Volume 2*)

Mad Love (1935) 3.5
Peter Lorre made his American film debut with this superlative version of *The Hands of Orlac*. Colin Clive is the pianist whose hands are destroyed in a train wreck, and Lorre is the doctor (Gogol) who grafts the hands of an executed knife-thrower onto Clive. Frances Drake is Orlac's wife, whom Gogol loves. Madness ensues. Delirious horror film with great cast firing on all cylinders. (BR-Warner Archive)

The Mad Magician (1954) 3.0
Vincent Price plays creator of brilliant illusions who meets with dirty tricks when he tries performing them himself. He goes mad and murders those who cross him, even disguising himself as his victims. Columbia's 3D answer to *House of Wax* (albeit in black-and-white) is a lot of fun with Price in fine form. Director John Brahm borrows elements from his own 1940s' efforts *The Lodger* and *Hangover Square*. The "Paddle Ball Man" from *Wax* shows up here briefly tossing yo-yos at the audience. (BR-Twilight Time)

The Mad Monster (1942) 1.5
George Zucco is disgraced scientist who transforms handyman Glenn Strange into a wolf man of sorts. He wants the US army to transform its soldiers into wolf men to help the war effort. First, however, Zucco plots revenge against the doctors who humiliated him. Strange's simpleton shtick gets old fast and the whole film has a dreary look and feel. Even the beautiful Anne Nagel, playing Zucco's daughter, looks drab here. (DVD-Retromedia)

Mad Monster Party? (1967) 2.5
Baron Von Frankenstein (voiced by Boris Karloff) intends to retire as head of monster community and leave his secrets with his nephew. This doesn't sit well with Dracula, etc. Mostly entertaining stop-motion outing from the Rankin Bass team. The voice artists seem to be having fun and all the nods to classic monsters will make this more appealing to lovers of the 1930s classics. (BR-Lionsgate)

The Mad Room (1969) 2.0
Stella Stevens plays housekeeper to Shelley Winters, whose stepson she plans to marry. But Stevens has two younger siblings who are being released from an asylum into her care, committed when they were six and four for murdering their parents. Of course, it's not long before there's another body. No real surprises here, but Stevens' off-kilter performance offers some amusement, as does Beverly Garland's drunken tirade at charity lunch. Good score by Dave Grusin. (DVD-R-Sony)

Madhouse (1974) 3.0
Underrated Vincent Price thriller features the master of menace as Paul Toombes, a retired horror legend brought to London to star in a TV series. Soon however his return to his Doctor Death character results in murder and mayhem. Is Toombes responsible? Along for the ride in this horror whodunit are Robert "Count Yorga" Quarry as Price's producer and, as his writer and best friend, Peter "Van Helsing" Cushing. Footage from at least six of Price's Edgar Allan Poe films with Roger Corman show up as Toombes' previous work. (BR-Kino)

The Mafu Cage (1978) 2.5
Mentally unstable woman has a bad habit of beating her pet monkeys to death. When the older sister she lives with refuses to supply her with any more victims, she decides to secure a different kind of pet. Unique, well-acted slow-burn chiller is sluggish at times but builds to haunting climax. (BR-Scorpion Releasing)

Magic (1978) 2.5
Future Dr. Hannibal Lecter Anthony Hopkins plays deranged ventriloquist who finally crosses the line when reunited with his married former girlfriend. Hopkins is very good, as is Burgess Meredith as his concerned agent, in overlong film that offers few surprises. (BR-MPI)

Magic Serpent (1966) 2.5
Son of murdered Japanese lord plots revenge against the killers of both his parents and the wizard that saved his life. Although the characterizations are one-note, this is a mostly entertaining fantasy that blends enchanting effects, giant monsters, wizardry, and other fairy tale elements. That sea dragon is a scary sight. (DVD-Retromedia with *Gamera: Return of the Giant Monsters*)

The Magnetic Monster (1953) 3.0
Richard Carlson is doctor working for Office of Scientific Investigation whose "A-Men" need to stop newfangled, hungry radioactive element from growing strong enough to fly Earth out of its orbit. Intriguing, original story is well told and tense, with some nifty effects work. (BR-Kino)

Majin, Monster of Terror (1966) 3.0
When disbelieving warlord attempts to have its image destroyed, the god of oppressed village comes to life in the form of giant statue to take vengeance. Entertaining blend of samurai action and *kaiju eiga* genres boasts great effects (starting an hour in), intense situations, and sympathetic characters. First of a trilogy, the final installment of which doesn't appear to have ever aired in the Maryland area. (BR-Arrow as *Daimajin* as part of *The Daimajin Trilogy*)

Mako: Jaws of Death (1976) 1.0
Touching (snicker) tale of man who protects Mako sharks from those that would do them harm. The sharks like him because he wears a sacred amulet. He kills fishermen, and then uses the sharks to take out his enemies. Another *Willard* variation, this time combined with elements of *Jaws*. Watch either of those instead. (BR-Arrow Video as part of *He Came from the Swamp: The William Grefé Collection*)

The Man and the Monster (1959) 2.5
Second-rate pianist sells his soul to the devil to become world's greatest artist-except now every time he plays, he turns into hideous monster. His mom sticks around to protect him. A rather original take on the Faust legend, this Mexican horror would have worked better if the monster makeup hadn't made the beast look like a puppy with a huge schnoz. (DVD-Casa Negra)

Maneater of Hydra (1967) 1.5
A dubbed Cameron Mitchell welcomes tourists to his botanical garden where he experiments with various plants. He's made cucumbers that taste like meat, and a bloodsucking, mobile tree that stalks the guests trapped on Mitchell's island. A sort-of horror variation on *And Then There Were None*, except the human entrees are a mostly obnoxious lot, making the non-horror moments tough going. (DVD-Shout! Factory with *The House That Screamed*)

The Man from Planet X (1951) 3.0
On the Scottish island Burray, scientist has set up a castle observatory to monitor Planet X, which is on course to possibly collide with Earth. He summons a reporter to cover the phenomenon. When an alien crashes on the nearby fog-enshrouded moors, everyone wonders whether it is friend or foe. Directed by Edgar G. Ulmer, who always made the most of his low budgets, this is best-described as science fiction-noir, with its voice-over narration, shadowy photography, twisty plot, and constant sense of dread. William Schallert does well in a rare villainous role. (BR-Kino as part of *Edgar G. Ulmer Sci-Fi Collection*)

Man in Black (1949) 2.5
When her wealthy father dies, young heiress gets the *Gaslight* treatment from her greedy stepmother and stepsister. Twisty thriller from Hammer Film Productions offers snappy dialogue, plenty of mood, and some great villains. Unfortunately, the damsel in distress is a bit too whiney to be as sympathetic as she should be. (DVD-R-Sinister Cinema)

The Man in Half Moon Street (1944) 2.5
Scientist has found the secret to eternal youth but needs some replacement glands. He's also tired of being alone so he gets engaged, which doesn't sit well with the doctor who's helping with the experiments. Leisurely-paced mood piece looks nice and features a smooth turn by Nils Asther as the youthful codger. Remade by Hammer as *The Man Who Could Cheat Death*. (NA)

Man in Outer Space (1962) 2.5
Sci-fi comedy about nebbish who clumsily causes the launch of rocket he's repairing, lands on the Blue Star, and is then sent back to earth centuries later with bald alien to observe humanity. Known as the Man from the First century, he takes advantage of his celebrity (food, money) and tries to woo the woman he desires, to no avail. Cute effort with plenty of sight gags and interesting visuals. Milos Kopecký gives a spirited performance as the lead, although he plays things rather broadly. (DVD-R-Sinister Cinema)

Man Made Monster (1941) 3.0
Lon Chaney, Jr. is Dynamo Dan, whose performance as the Electric Man saves him when his bus crashes and gets a hot foot. He is now a subject of interest for a good scientist (Samuel S. Hinds) and a bad scientist (Lionel Atwill). Fast pace, great cast, and dazzling effects add up to a most enjoyable quickie. (BR-Shout! Factory as part of *Universal Horror Collection: Volume 3*)

The Man Who Changed His Mind (1936) 2.5
Boris Karloff plays brilliant scientist who can swap personalities between animals. When his research is threatened, he decides to experiment on humans. There is much humor to be found here, especially after Karloff starts exchanging personas and people don't act like themselves. Amusing performances and droll script make for an entertaining if laid back thriller. (DVD-Shanachie)

The Man They Could Not Hang (1939) 3.0
Faithful assistant brings his hanged employer back from the dead, who promptly plots his revenge against the justice system that proclaimed him guilty of homicide! Tight and entertaining little thriller has Boris Karloff in top form, who cleverly contrives to bring death to those trapped in his home. (DVD-Sony as part of *Icons of Horror Collection: Boris Karloff*)

The Man Who Could Cheat Death (1959) 2.5
To retain his youth, a 104-year-old scientist must have surgery every so often to replace his pituitary gland. Things get tricky when he reunites with old love. Anton Diffring, Hazel Court, and Christopher Lee head fine cast, even if the story offers few surprises. Pretty good Hammer chiller is a remake of Paramount's *The Man in Half Moon Street*. (BR-Kino)

The Man Who Could Work Miracles (1936) 3.0
Deities that don't think much of humanity grant one member of the race the power to make any command come true just to see what happens. The lucky subject is meek clerk who doesn't

quite know what to do with his newfound power, making him vulnerable to other people's desires. Delightful sci-fi comedy from H.G. Wells is genuinely funny but has serious undertones. Roland Young is terrific in the lead. (Laserdisc-Image)

The Man Who Cried Wolf (1937) 2.5
The police think stage actor is confessing to murders he didn't commit to drum up publicity for his play "The Death Cry." But he's really setting up his alibi for a murder he's been planning for 20 years: the execution of his ex-wife's killer. Good plot starts well but sputters during the midsection and never quite recovers. (NA)

The Man Who Haunted Himself (1970) 2.5
Screen version of Anthony Armstrong's *The Strange Case of Mr. Pelham*. Sir Roger Moore plays businessman who survives car accident only to learn he seemingly has a double taking over his life. Moore is very good in the lead and the film holds one interest for the first hour or so. Then things start dragging as the story is a bit too thin to sustain full-length feature. Ending isn't particularly satisfying either. Handled better as an episode of *Alfred Hitchcock Presents*. (BR-Kino)

The Man Who Lived Twice (1936) 2.5
Columbia programmer about wanted criminal who gets a new face and undergoes brain surgery; wakes up with no memory of his past and becomes solid citizen. But the past eventually catches up with him. Ralph Bellamy is good in the lead and the basic story proposes an interesting dilemma. Unfortunately, the last reel contains too many newspaper headlines and story contrivances. (NA)

The Man Who Reclaimed His Head (1934) 3.0
Set when France was on the brink of entering WWI, Claude Rains plays a pacifist newspaper writer whose boss Lionel Atwill decides he'd make more money if the publication went pro-war. Joan Bennett is Rains' beautiful wife on whom Atwill sets his sights because he's a scoundrel. The three key players are great, and the final showdown appropriately horrific. Reworked as Inner Sanctum entry *Strange Confession*. (NA)

The Man Who Turned to Stone (1957) 2.0
At woman's house of detention, centuries-old scientists who've discovered the secret to eternal life use prisoners' "energy" to keep alive. The basic idea isn't bad, and lead baddie Victor Jory has one of the great movie voices. But the story is told in a much too straight-forward, bland manner to be memorable. (DVD-Mill Creek as part of *Classic Horror: 4 Movie Collection*)

The Man Who Wouldn't Die (1942) 2.5
Detective Michael Shayne goes undercover posing as client's new husband; she claims a ghost took a shot at her while visiting her father's home. The first 10 minutes will make any fan of old dark house thrillers smile. The remaining 55 minutes are an agreeable, breezy mix of mystery and humor. There *is* a working laboratory that would make Dr. Frankenstein proud. (DVD-Fox as part of *Michael Shayne Mysteries: Volume 1*)

The Man with Nine Lives (1940) 2.5
Boris Karloff plays research scientist whose frozen therapy may lead to cure of disease. Discovered 10 years after he'd frozen himself and several others, he vows to continue his work, even if it costs other people their lives. Columbia B-picture is fast-paced and fun due to Karloff's performance and the eventful script. By this point Karloff's various mad doctor portrayals could be distinguished largely by his hairdo. (DVD-Sony)

The Man Without a Body (1957) 1.5
Gruff businessman learns he has inoperable brain tumor and seeks out doctor experimenting with brain transplantation. Naturally he wishes to have the head of Nostradamus swapped with his own. Poor script and dialogue do ridiculous premise no favors. (NA)

Mania (1960) 3.0
To get bodies to conduct research, university professor Dr. Knox (Peter Cushing) utilizes the corpse-snatching services of Burke and Hare, two immigrants who eventually turn to murder as their primary source of income. Excellent retelling of the Burke and Hare story, with director John Gilling creating a vivid 19th-century Edinburgh. Cushing is compelling as the arrogant medico as is Donald Pleasence as the treacherous William Hare. (BR-Kino as *The Flesh and the Fiends*)

Maniac (1963) 2.5
When he learns his daughter was sexually assaulted, an angry father takes a blowtorch to the attacker and is then committed to an asylum. Years later, the dad's wife wants to remarry. Her husband will agree to a divorce only if the lovers free him. This was one of Hammer Film Productions' thrillers meant to cash in on *Psycho*. So, there are twists and turns, some of them surprising. Cold and clever, but not altogether satisfying. (BR-Mill Creek as part of *Hammer Films: The Ultimate Collection: 20 Film Set*)

The Manitou (1977) 1.5
Woman has a fetus growing on her neck, so she consults her former boyfriend Tony Curtis because he reads tarot cards. It turns out an ancient medicine man is about to be reborn and threaten the world. Curtis is miscast in the lead, and the film takes a kitchen sink approach to spectacle. It all adds up to a silly venture into Native American legend that has a few effective shocks but many more moments of unintentional comedy. (BR-Shout! Factory)

The Manster (1959) 3.0
This film means business. It starts out with a brutal attack on nubile Japanese bathers; quickly moves to the basement of scientist's laboratory where deformed creatures reside; and then has a reporter poisoned since he is to be the next experiment. In many ways, this American/Japanese co-production is the definitive late-night horror movie, complete with atmospheric black-and-white photography, unscrupulous mad doctor, agonized hero, and incredible monster. It's also creepy as hell. (BR-Shout! Factory)

Mark of the Devil (1970) 2.5
Herbert Lom is very good as an Austrian witchfinder par excellence (with a grand entrance a half hour in) in this nasty clone of *The Conqueror Worm*. There are gruesome torture scenes and some over-the-top villains to be sure. But the darn thing becomes more involving as it progresses and leads to an emotionally brutal climax. (BR-Arrow)

Mark of the Vampire (1935) 3.0
Atmospheric chiller about the investigation into a murder that may have been committed by a vampire! Lots to savor here in terms of atmosphere and visuals, as well as Bela Lugosi as Count Mora, but the ending is disappointing. (DVD-Warner Bros. as part of *Hollywood Legends of Horror Collection*)

Marooned (1969) 2.0
Three astronauts are seemingly unable to return to Earth when their equipment malfunctions. Meanwhile mission control must decide if they can initiate a rescue attempt. All-star cast and Oscar-winning effects can do only so much to help humorless, draggy script. Some of the drama is laughable. (DVD-Columbia/Tristar)

Mars Needs Women (TV-1967) 1.0
Five Martians land on Earth, get some nice suits, and go looking for women who will help replenish their dwindling race. Of course, they snatch an exotic dancer, a flight attendant, and the homecoming queen. One of the aliens, however, falls in love with scientist Yvonne Craig, an authority on space genetics. Little happens in this hopelessly padded, sluggishly paced Larry Buchanan film. The result is sleep-inducing. Viewers need caffeine! (DVD-MGM)

The Mask (1961) 1.5
A case of the tail wagging the dog: nightmare sequences shot in 3D are what give this film its notoriety. But they're surrounded by a bland. cold story of ancient mask that drives people to murder. Dialogue is bad at times, and the police investigation scenes are repetitive and mood-killing. The Kino 3D Blu Ray looks very nice and features the complete 83-minute print. Too bad the overall film isn't better. (BR-Kino)

The Mask of Diijon (1946) 2.0
Erich von Stroheim is retired magician who discovers the secret of mesmerism. He uses it for evil instead of niceness. Stroheim is OK, but the ending is so ridiculous (why does he even run away to begin with?) that it hurts the entire film. (DVD-Image)

The Mask of Fu Manchu (1932) 3.0
Boris Karloff plays the notorious Dr. Fu Manchu is this campy, fun outing. He kidnaps various folks to acquire the mask and sword of Genghis Khan, which will give him incredible powers. Karloff really seems to be enjoying himself. (DVD-Warner Bros. as part of *Hollywood Legends of Horror Collection*)

The Masque of the Red Death (1964) 3.5
Satan-worshiping Prince Prospero (Vincent Price) holds a lavish ball at his castle while the nearby villagers suffer from deadly plague. Death has other party plans. The penultimate Roger Corman Poe entry boasts sumptuous production design and costumes, as well as literate script by Charles Beaumont and R. Wright Campbell. Great dialogue includes Price discussing the positive aspects of evil. Hazel Court is one of Satan's disciples who gets more than she bargained for. (BR-Shout! Factory)

Massacre at Central High (1976) 3.0
A high school transfer student runs afoul the school bullies, so he proceeds to eliminate them, with unexpected consequences. A fine young cast impresses in this entertaining psycho killer movie that hasn't dated a bit; unofficially remade as *Heathers* in 1989. (BR-Severin)

Master Minds (1949) 2.5
When a toothache gives Sach (Huntz Hall) the ability to foretell the future, he gets a job at carnival as psychic Ali Ben Sachmo. His gift attracts the attention of mad scientist who wants to transplant his mental powers into monstrous Glenn Strange (made up by Jack Pierce). Fitfully amusing Bowery Boys shenanigans, with Strange's sporadic Hall imitation the highlight. Universal veterans Alan Napier, Jane Adams, and Skelton Knaggs are also in the cast. (DVD-Warner Archive as part of *The Bowery Boys: Volume 1*)

Master of the World (1961) 2.5
Vincent Price stars as slightly mad 19th-century genius who roams the skies in his futuristic airship, destroying military targets. His pacifist extremism doesn't sit well with his prisoners, so they set out to interfere with his plans. Enjoyable fantasy is a little too cute at times and features an unnecessary love triangle to create additional tension. Charles Bronson seems ill at ease as the hero. (BR-Shout! Factory as part of *The Vincent Price Collection III*)

The Maze (1953) 2.0
Woman shows up at her ex-fiancé's castle home in Scotland looking for answers; realizes he's hiding some terrible secret. Moody, well-mounted tale might be termed Gothic sci-fi. The ending though is disappointing, almost laughable, souring the whole film. (BR-Kino)

The Medusa Touch (1978) 3.0
Author Richard Burton has been viciously beaten and hovers near death. Psychiatrist Lee Remick tells investigating detective that Burton believes he has the power to create catastrophe, whether it's causing a school fire or forcing a plane to crash. Should the patient be saved so he can bring more destruction? Engrossing hybrid of mystery and terror with strong performances; fine music score too. (BR-Hen's Tooth Video)

Melody of Hate (TV-1975) 2.0
Man, who faked his death, returns 11 years later to blackmail his "widow," a famed opera singer who is about to marry a very wealthy man. Susan Flannery's strong lead performance makes this obvious suspense tale bearable. Original British title: *Nightmare for a Nightingale*. (DVD-VEI as part of *Thriller: The Complete Collection*)

The Mephisto Waltz (1971) 2.0
Dying pianist Curt Jurgens, a Satanist, transfers his soul to Alan Alda, whose wife must now figure out why her husband has changed so much. The story is not bad, and director Paul Wendkos likes his odd camera angles. But at almost two hours the film is too long for the material, and Jerry Goldsmith's score is frequently obtrusive. (BR-Kino)

The Mermaids of Tiburon (1962) 1.5
Marine biologist goes in search of pearls near isolated island but instead finds mermaids. Unfortunately, there's also a killer hunting for the treasure too. Beautifully shot film with terrific underwater photography is flatly narrated with several stretches of tedium. It feels much longer than its 76 minutes. (DVD-with *Cry of the Bewitched*)

Mesa of Lost Women (1953) 0.0
A mad scientist is attempting to create race of super spider women who would be under his control. Unfortunately, they're seen only in the opening moments and during the rushed finale. Take your pick as to what is the worst aspect of the film: the bad performances, the grating music, the laughable effects, the clunky script, or all the above. (DVD-Image)

Metropolis (1927) 4.0
Director Fritz Lang's visionary tale of class struggle in futuristic society still dazzles after all these years. The son of "the master of Metropolis" is shocked to discover an impoverished working class that lives beneath the surface. He joins the cause to unite the classes. In response, his father consults an inventor/mad scientist pal to help thwart such efforts. Striking visuals and grand production design complement story still relevant today. (BR-Kino)

Mighty Joe Young (1949) 3.0
Carl Denham has changed his name to Max O'Hara apparently and goes to Africa looking for a way to promote his new nightclub. There he finds Mr. Joseph Young. Likable characters and top-notch effects work make for an entertaining if familiar tale. (BR-Warner Bros.)

Mill of the Stone Women (1960) 2.5
Grieving father joins mad scientist to conduct sinister experiments; puts victims on display as part of bizarre carousel. Colorful Euro-horror film has a great look and feel but drags in spots; still quite watchable. (BR-Arrow)

The Million Eyes of Sumuru (1967) 1.5
Jokey adventure about man hating Sumuru and her followers who hook-up with wealthy men to acquire their fortunes in pursuit of world takeover. American agent on vacation gets involved and is soon wanted for murder. Literally starts with a bang and a pair of assassinations; then becomes only intermittently interesting. Klaus Kinski shows up halfway through and seems to be having a good time. Many viewers will not. (BR-Blue Underground with *The Girl from Rio*)

The Mind Benders (1963) 3.0
Physiologist studying effects of isolation exits a moving train, committing suicide. The military suspects he was guilty of treason. His Oxford University associate doesn't agree and is willing to undergo bizarre experiment to prove his friend's innocence. For his trouble, he becomes victim of brainwashing experiment. Fascinating if occasionally sluggish sci-fi drama benefits from fine, sympathetic performances and intense final act. (BR-Kino)

Mirror of Deception (TV-1975) 3.0
When both of her roommates take the same job and seem to disappear, American newlywed decides to investigate. Neat plot effectively sustained throughout its running time. Original British title: *Good Salary, Prospects, Free Coffin*. (DVD-VEI as part of *Thriller: The Complete Collection*)

Missile Monsters (1958) 1.5
Edited version of Republic's 1950 serial *Flying Disc Man from Mars*. Earth scientist joins forces with visitor from Mars he had inadvertently shot down to take over the world. It seems Earth's experiments with nuclear energy threaten the entire universe! Sounds exciting, except all the action takes place on Earth and it's all the same old Republic blend of well-dressed men in fistfights and car chases. Some airplanes explode too. A bore. (NA)

Missile to the Moon (1958) 1.5
Ticked-off scientist recruits two escaped convicts to join him in trip to the moon. Before the rocket takes off, they're joined by scientist's partner and partner's fiancée. Once on the moon they discover willful female inhabitants, slow-moving rock people, giant arthritic spider, and obese diamonds. Remake of *Cat-Women of the Moon* isn't as entertaining; poor effects and lackluster performances don't help matters. (BD-R-Snappy Video)

Missiles from Hell (1958) 2.5
Michael Rennie stars as Polish resistance member who allows himself to be captured so he can spy on Germans. Soon he and his partner are working in research facility where the Nazis are constructing V-1 bomb; they become involved in plot to destroy the plant and war effort overall. Solid cast and interesting story, with some intense moments, including the diffusion of a bomb. Unfortunately, Vernon Sewell's direction is occasionally flat. Christopher Lee has brief part as Nazi. (DVD-R-Sinister Cinema)

The Missing Corpse (1945) 2.0
While on vacation at his hunting lodge, newspaper publisher J. Edward Bromberg discovers the body of crooked rival in his trunk. Now he must hide the body before the police find it and draw the wrong conclusion. Meanwhile the real killer realizes he needs to locate the corpse to retrieve incriminating evidence. Sporadically amusing comedy from PRC is fun when the focus is on Bromberg's predicament. Isabel Randolph's shtick as the ditzy wife gets old quick. (DVD-Alpha)

The Missing Guest (1938) 2.0
Here's the first redo of *Secret of the Blue Room*, with some modifications as to motive. A reporter sneaks into a party celebrating the reopening of an allegedly haunted house. (A piano plays by itself without apparent explanation.) There's a disappearance and another murder. Unfunny PI's are called in.

The house is sufficiently creepy and there's a nifty early POV entrance sequence. But Universal never could work comedy into mysteries like this and the villain's explanation at the end just goes on and on. (NA)

Mission Stardust (1967) 2.0
Moon expedition sent to investigate possible new element instead finds marooned human-looking aliens, one of whom has leukemia. In hopes of saving the being's life, they all return to Earth but run afoul African Federation Army and mob boss. So-so combo of sci-fi and spy thrillers fitfully amuses but ultimately disappoints. (DVD-Mill Creek as part of *Sci-Fi Invasion: 50 Movie Pack*)

The Mole People (1956) 2.0
After too much stock footage, a trio of archaeologists finally find lost city beneath a mountain but tick off the high priest of the people who live there. This civilization also has "dark beasts" which are used as slave labor. Alan Napier is fun as the scheming cleric and the beasts are awesome. On the negative side, the film is hopelessly padded and repetitive, with an unnecessarily downer ending. One of the least of the Universal '50s horrors. (BR-Shout! Factory)

The Monolith Monsters (1957) 2.5
Meteor crashes and generates rock "stalks" which threaten small town. Original premise keeps this interesting despite numerous talking heads segments. Main issue is that rocks have no personality. (BR-Shout! Factory)

The Monster (1925) 2.5
At a supposedly closed sanitarium, a mad scientist (Lon Chaney) arranges automobile accidents to provide subjects for his experiments. Amateur sleuth investigates. Rather standard mix of laughs and chills boasts at least one memorable sequence: the hero trying to balance himself on telephone pole wires during a thunderstorm. (DVD-R-Warner Archive)

The Monster and the Girl (1941) 2.0
Man framed by mobsters for murder is executed. Mad doctor then puts his brain into a gorilla, and the gorilla escapes to avenge his death. Thinly disguised remake of the superior *The Walking Dead* with only change being a gorilla instead of a zombie. Story handles transplant angle in quick, perfunctory manner. Uneven performances don't help matters either. (BR-Shout! Factory as part of *Universal Horror Collection: Volume 5*)

Monster from a Prehistoric Planet (1967) 2.0
Expedition swipes just-born creature from its island home and brings it back to Japan. Its concerned parents come looking, causing the usual destruction. Jokey *kaiju eiga* has plenty of Tokyo carnage and some amusing-looking monsters. Probably just for fans of the sub-genre though. (BR-Tokyo Shock as *Gappa: The Triphibian Monsters*)

Monster from the Ocean Floor (1954) 1.0
Roger Corman's first solo producer effort is an abysmal debut. A one-eyed octopus-like creature is terrorizing Mexican seaside village. Visiting American is determined to destroy the menace. The monster's first moonlight appearance is eerie, and the underwater photography looks nice. Too bad most of the picture is a dull talkfest, making the film feel much longer than its 64 minutes. (DVD-VCI with *Serpent Island*)

The Monster Maker (1944) 2.5
J. Carrol Naish and Frank Morgan's performances make this seedy horror tale quite watchable. Naish injects Morgan with formula causing the latter to develop acromegaly. It's all due to Naish's lust for Morgan's daughter, a lookalike of the doctor's late wife. Subject matter might turn some viewers off. But this *is* a horror film after all. (BR-Retromedia with *King of the Zombies*)

The Monster of Piedras Blancas (1959) 2.0
Entertaining for some of the right but mostly wrong reasons. Title beast likes meat and decapitating people. Low budget but rather nasty outing has at least one genuine jump scare and a cool monster. When the monster is not on screen, the film suffers. (BR-Olive)

Monster on the Campus (1958) 2.5
Blood of prehistoric fish causes nice college scientist to revert to prehistoric savage. Largely familiar and predictable tale is well paced with good performance by Arthur Franz. The Blu-Ray really brings out the strings holding the giant dragonfly. (BR-Shout! Factory)

The Monster that Challenged the World (1957) 3.0
One of the better giant monster movies of the fifties. Giant mollusks plague the Salton Sea and devour military personnel and nubile swimmers. Standard plotting (hiding the appearance of the monster initially: check; scientist showing others film about sea life: check) enlivened by terrific monster scenes and a creature that is quite scary. (BR-Kino)

Monster Zero (1965) 2.5
A joint American Japanese space mission to Planet X leads to the discovery that Ghidorah has relocated and forced X's inhabitants to live underground. They request the services of Godzilla and Rodan to rid themselves of this "demon of the galaxy," striking a deal with the astronauts. But the true nature of the appeal is much more sinister. Enjoyable Godzilla entry with above average characterizations and interesting subplots confines most of the monster action until the last 20 minutes. Nick Adams, however, is out of place as one of the leads. His tough-guy act doesn't mesh with every other element of the production. (BR-Criterion as *Invasion of Astro-Monster* as part of *Godzilla: The Showa-Era Films, 1954–1975*)

The Monsters Demolisher (1962) 1.5
Second film derived from 12-part Mexican serial follows *The Curse of Nostradamus*. This installment opens with the vampire Nostradamus' body found and unearthed by hunchbacked henchman Leo. Now freed he resumes his threats against professor who refuses to acknowledge the vampire's powerful ancestors. The heroes and villains of these films are equally inept, so you watch in absolute disbelief as each side constant-

ly screws up. But even the least of the Mexican horrors offer atmospheric passages now and again. Followed by *The Genie of Darkness*. (DVD-R-Sinister Cinema)

The Most Dangerous Game (1932) 3.0
Exciting film version of the classic short story. Shipwrecked hunter discovers a horrifying secret about his host's little island hideaway. Made by the team that later produced *King Kong*, this is less elaborate but still quite enjoyable. Leslie Banks makes a great Count Zaroff. Other characters are likeable and sympathetic. (BR-Flicker Alley)

Most Dangerous Man Alive (1961) 2.0
Double-crossed by his own people and convicted of murder, an escaped mob boss becomes a literal man of steel when exposed to cobalt element X. Of course, he takes his revenge against those who plotted against him. Standard sci-fi stuff given a slight boost by the lovely leading ladies whose sex appeal is exploited by the filmmakers. Made in 1958. (NA)

Mothra (1961) 3.0
Shameless promotor swipes two diminutive, telepathic "secret fairies" from their island home to use in his show, little realizing the island god Mothra will come to rescue them. There is much destruction as Mothra starts out as giant caterpillar before becoming enormous full-fledged moth. One of the best of Japan's *kaiju eiga* films. (The American version released in 1962 wisely dispenses with any narration.) It's colorful and well paced, and you will be cheering for the monster. Only negative is some distracting goofiness from comic-relief reporter. (BR-Mill Creek)

Mr. Sardonicus (1961) 2.5
One of the most original thrillers ever produced. Evil Baron, his face frozen in a hideous grin, blackmails renowned doctor to cure him. Guy Rolfe, who acts mostly with his voice, is very good as is Oscar Homolka as evil assistant to Sardonicus. But William Castle's direction is lackluster. (BR-Mill Creek with *Homicidal*)

The Mummy (1932) 3.5
First and still unique mummy film, with Karloff in bandages only during the opening segment. For the rest of the film, he is trying to woo his reincarnated love. Karloff is great as usual; the opening segment ("He went for a little walk.") is one of the best in Universal's oeuvre. (BR-Universal)

The Mummy (1959) 3.0
Hammer takes various plot points from the Universal Mummy movies and delivers a solid thriller. Christopher Lee as the Mummy is both physically intimidating (this fellow *moves*) and sympathetic (note his reaction to seeing whom he believes is his reincarnated love). Perhaps the best Mummy film next to the Karloff classic. (BR-Warner Bros.)

Mummy's Boys (1936) 2.0
Wheeler & Woolsey comedy has the boys hired to help return stolen treasures to a desecrated tomb because the original treasure hunters are dying off. Sporadically amusing piffle isn't one of the duo's best films. Even the chased-by-a-mummy finale seems tired. (DVD-R-Warner Archive as part of *Wheeler & Woolsey: RKO Comedy Classics Collection*)

The Mummy's Curse (1944) 2.0
Final Kharis film is tired retread, despite New Orleans setting and Virginia Christine's good performance as reincarnated Ananka. It's too hard to care anymore about a Mummy that just takes orders most of the time. (BR-Universal as part of *The Mummy: Complete Legacy Collection*)

The Mummy's Ghost (1944) 2.5
Pretty good rehash of Mummy lore, with beloved Ananka reincarnated as fetching Ramsay Ames. No wonder John Carradine's high priest is ready to betray his oath. (BR-Universal as part of *The Mummy: Complete Legacy Collection*)

The Mummy's Hand (1940) 2.5
The first of the four Kharis films is probably the best, setting up the formula of tana leaves; the high priest who's supposed to protect Ananka but ultimately lusts after the damsel in distress; and the slow-moving Mummy who nevertheless has no problem trapping his prey. Wallace Ford overdoes the comedy relief something awful. The Mummy scenes are great (as is the bandaged Tom Tyler), George Zucco is menacing, Peggy Moran is adorable, and the atmosphere strong. (BR-Universal as part of *The Mummy: Complete Legacy Collection*)

The Mummy's Revenge (1975) 1.5
Having already played a werewolf, Dracula, and a hunchback, among others, Spanish horror star Paul Naschy finally plays a mummy. Unfortunately, the only variation he can offer is gore. In London, a descendant of a ruthless, mummified pharaoh revives his ancestor and helps him look for mostly female victims. There are head bashings and throat slashings, though the mummy gets to kiss a sleeping beauty. The editing is at times haphazard and the whole affair eventually becomes dull, topped off with an uninspired finale. On the other hand, the sets are attractive, as are the ladies, and the Mummy may be the most ruthless in cinema history. (BR-Scorpion Releasing)

The Mummy's Shroud (1967) 2.0
Routine outing offers yet another mummy legend with yet another mummy (this time a king's slave) avenging the tomb desecration of his master. Virtually a remake of *The Curse of the Mummy's Tomb*, but it has Andre Morell and, especially, Michael Ripper to keep it watchable. Good death sequences are particularly brutal this time out. (BR-Shout! Factory)

The Mummy's Tomb (1942) 2.0
A rather troublesome sequel to *The Mummy's Hand* for three main reasons. 1) This film *must* be set in 1970 since there's no doubt the previous film is set in 1940. That's rather lazy on the part of the writers, unless they really thought WWII was going to last 30 years. 2) It's not really a proper film: 10 minutes is repeated from *The Mummy's Hand* meaning this film is barely 50 minutes of new stuff. 3) The victims are all elderly persons.

That's right: the Mummy goes after defenseless old people; not much of a challenge for the all-powerful Kharis. On the other hand, the brief running time means the film moves at high speed with the death toll of a slasher film. The kill scenes are handled well-enough with atmospheric night-for-night shooting. (BR-Universal as part of *The Mummy: Complete Legacy Collection*)

Munster, Go Home! (1966) 2.5
Herman Munster's English uncle dies leaving his entire estate to his American nephew. But not many people are happy to have the Munsters in town, including mysterious criminal known as the Griffin. Fans of the TV series should enjoy what is essentially an extended episode in color without the familiar laugh track. Good-natured silliness, with game cast. John Carradine is almost unrecognizable as a sinister butler. (BR-Shout! Factory)

Murder! (1930) 2.5
Early Alfred Hitchcock effort about juror who investigates a murder after he's already helped convict someone for the crime. Memorable climax and some inventively staged scenes give needed boost to talky thriller. (BR-Kino)

Murder by Decree (1979) 3.0
Handsome production of Sherlock Holmes (Christopher Plummer) and Dr. Watson's (James Mason) pursuit of Jack the Ripper. Plummer and Mason are terrific, as is a great supporting cast, in this complex mystery-thriller. (BR-Kino)

Murder by the Clock (1931) 3.0
Wealthy widow who fears being buried alive has horn installed in the family crypt. Soon after changing her will, she's strangled, presumably by her idiot son. You can guess what happens not long after she's entombed, although there's much more to the story. A fine example of old dark house thrillers, with Lilyan Tashman's portrayal of a conniving, money-grubbing wife something to behold. Irving Pichel does well as the slow-witted prime suspect, although he did better as Sandor in *Dracula's Daughter*. (DVD-R-Sinister Cinema)

Murder by Two (1960) 3.0
Unhappily married Mel Ferrer is having an affair with his wife's half-sister, who looks very much like her. Meanwhile his engaged niece is cavorting with a man who turns out to be a blackmailer. Then comes the murder. Nicely plotted whodunit courtesy of France keeps things moving and twisting, even if the end isn't terribly surprising. Good cast keeps one interested throughout. (DVD-R-Sinister Cinema)

The Murder Clinic (1966) 1.5
Hooded killer dressed in black and bearing a straight razor stalks the halls of private clinic. Despite attractive photography and a good opening, this quickly becomes tedious affair of people walking through corridors while red herrings are tossed about with abandon. The villain's identity consequently is rather obvious. (DVD-Code Red as part of *Six Pack Volume 2*)

Murder, Inc. (1960) 3.0
Gripping drama about the rise of organized crime during the 1930s and the people who tried to secure convictions against those in charge. Peter Falk as hitman Abe Reles is "introduced" and is a standout in an Oscar-nominated performance. (He also refers to Bela Lugosi while discussing places where drugs can be hidden in swanky apartment.) Loses steam before arriving at the climax but remains engrossing. (DVD-Fox)

Murder in Mind (TV-1973) 2.5
Woman who can't remember who she is or whom she's killed shows up at police station saying she's committed murder. While the film does have its suspenseful moments, the overall plot trajectory is obvious. (DVD-VEI as part of *Thriller: The Complete Collection*)

Murder in the Blue Room (1944) 2.0
Another trip to the murder room with the color of the sky. It starts out as a scene for scene redo of *The Missing Guest* but eventually does its own thing with a trio of lady singers determined to solve the murder mystery. A ghost does, ahem, appear but he's just comedy relief. Not as entertaining as it thinks it is. (DVD-R-Sinister Cinema)

Murder in the Red Barn (1935) 2.5
The first of stage villain Tod Slaughter's melodramatic thrillers. He plays murderous country squire who kills the woman he's impregnated. Slaughter is a lot of fun hamming it up, such as when he challenges the thunder to wake up his victim or makes use of his marvelously expressive face. He brings so-so script to life. (DVD-Kotch with *The Face at the Window*)

The Murder Mansion (1972) 2.0
Impenetrable fog forces several strangers to take refuge in gloomy manor. The owner speaks of her witch ancestor and a history of vampires. Chills and thrills soon follow. Atmospheric outing takes a while to get going, and ultimately the story is hardly credible. Good for a few shudders but that's it. (BR-Vinegar Syndrome as part of *Forgotten Gialli: Volume 3*)

Murder Motel (TV-1975) 1.5
No, not a *Psycho* clone. Instead, this is a disappointing tale of embezzlement, murder, and blackmail connected to sinister inn. Lovely Robyn Millan is dreadful as concerned fiancée of victim Ralph Bates. Other characters behave like idiots when they should know better. One of the least of the *Thriller* series. (DVD-VEI as part of *Thriller: The Complete Collection*)

Murder on the Midnight Express (TV-1975) 2.5
Judy Geeson stars as distraught young woman whose train ride is disturbed by a disappearing corpse. Although the suspense is intermittent, the characters are well drawn, and Charles Gray is a hoot as Geeson's pompous neighbor. Original British title: *Night is the Time for Killing*. (DVD-VEI as part of *Thriller: The Complete Collection*)

Murder Over New York (1940) 3.0
Charlie Chan agrees to help police find killer of old Scotland Yard friend, a victim of poison gas. Good entry in the series moves like a bullet to its harrowing finale on plane. (DVD-Fox as part of *Charlie Chan: Volume 5*)

Murder Will Out (1952) 2.5
Valerie Hobson (*Bride of Frankenstein*, etc.) stars in this who-

dunit involving murder of convicted blackmailer who was at it again. Complications ensue when Hobson begins affair with one of the suspects. Good cast sustains interest in this above average mystery drama that drags now and again. James Robertson Justice is a hoot as Hobson's spouse, insulting everyone around him, even himself! (DVD-R-Sinister Cinema as *The Voice of Merrill*)

Murders in the Rue Morgue (1932) 2.5
Middling Universal horror, with Bela Lugosi playing sideshow scientist mixing ape and human blood. It has a great look to it and Lugosi is hammy fun. But the plot is so threadbare that it can't even sustain an hour; a painful, lengthy comedy routine where three people argue about what language the killer spoke stops the film dead in its tracks. (BR-Shout! Factory)

Murders in the Rue Morgue (1971) 2.0
Present and former theater group members are being viscously murdered via acid, and the prime suspect has supposedly been dead for 12 years. Meanwhile the leading lady is having bizarre nightmares somehow tied to the death of her mother. Director Gordon Hessler manages some stylish scenes, and Herbert Lom is good as the killer. Unfortunately, a miscast Jason Robards is the lead and Christine Kaufmann is lifeless as the distressed damsel. (BR-Shout! Factory with *The Dunwich Horror*)

Murders in the Zoo (1933) 3.0
Lionel Atwill plays a deranged hunter who provides animals to the zoo, but also utilizes it as a backdrop for his various murder plots. Gruesome outing with Atwill in top form. Kathleen "Panther Woman" Burke plays Atwill's doomed wife. (BR-Shout! Factory as part of *Universal Horror Collection: Volume 2*)

Mutiny in Outer Space (1965) 2.0
Space crew inadvertently picks up fungus from moon's ice caves, and then must deal with sick Colonel who denies there's a growing problem in the lab. Now, there's a risk all of Space Station X-7 may be infected. Mediocre special effects and uneven performances made bearable by tense, claustrophobic setting, and palatable sense of dread. Features music cues from *The Ghost of Frankenstein*! (DVD-R-Vidway)

My Blood Runs Cold (1965) 2.5
A traffic mishap introduces handsome but unstable Ben to lovely Julie, whom he believes is the reincarnation of his lost love. But there's more to this story than we at first realize. Entertaining enough chiller may be unbelievable trash, but it's still fun most of the way. (DVD-R-Warner Archive)

My Bloody Valentine (1981) 2.0
The town of Valentine Bluffs is holding its first Valentine's Day party in nearly 20 years. On this day, a deranged coal miner named Harry Warden murdered the two supervisors he held responsible for a fatal mining accident and warned he'd be back if the town ever again celebrated the holiday. When the police discover a heart-shaped box bearing a real human heart, they go looking for Harry. Director George Mihalka nicely captures the blue-collar mining town atmosphere and forgoes stereotypes. It's the formulaic nature of the script that ultimately renders the film routine. (BR-Shout! Factory)

My Son is Guilty (1939) 2.5
Ex-con son of good beat cop hooks up with thugs; uses his job as police radio operator to help commit piano factory hold up that goes wrong. Lays it on thick emotionally but still entertaining. (NA)

My Son, The Vampire (1952) 2.0
Starting in 1936 with *Stars on Parade*, British comedian Arthur Lucan starred as Old Mother Riley in no less than 17 features, of which this is the last. Bela Lugosi co-stars as the "vampire," a mad scientist whose robot mistakenly is shipped to Mother Riley. Would-be hilarity ensues. There are laughs and songs to be sure. But the film wouldn't make it onto a list of good horror comedies. (DVD-Image)

The Mysterians (1957) 2.5
Ginormous pointy-nosed robot starts destroying small Japanese town, paving the way for title creatures that want to reside on section of Earth and breed with human women to maintain their dying, alien race. Colorful, action-heavy invasion thriller from Toho may be familiar stuff but it's still enjoyable. Rousing music score too. (DVD-Media Blasters)

The Mysterious Doctor (1943) 2.5
A headless specter roams a tin mine thus thwarting the English war effort. Fast-paced thriller from Warner Brothers is fun and atmospheric. The plot could function just as easily as an episode of *Scooby-Doo, Where are You?* (DVD-R-Sinister Cinema)

Mysterious Island (1961) 3.0
In 1865, Union soldiers escape from Confederate prison using a hot air balloon. Soon after they crash on island inhabited by various obese animals (birds, bees, crabs, etc.) that threaten their survival. Ray Harryhausen's effects work highlights this vivid and charming Jules Verne tale with good cast and Bernard Herrmann score. (BR-Twilight Time)

The Mysterious Magician (1964) 2.5
When his sister is murdered, infamous criminal known as The Ringer (or The Hexer, or The Magician depending on which language/dub you're viewing) returns to London to seek revenge on those responsible. Tricky, enjoyable German *krimi* has you cheering for the villain since the people he's hunting are even worse. Great ending too. (DVD-R-Sinister Cinema)

Mystery of Edwin Drood (1935) 3.0
Charles Dickens' unfinished novel makes for a solid if unspectacular mystery. Claude Rains is jealous of his nephew for being engaged to the beautiful Rosa. Then a foreigner shows up to compete for Rosa's affections and all heck breaks loose. Rains is his fine self, and so is the rest of the cast. David Manners is the title character and does a good job too. (BR-Kino)

Mystery of Marie Roget (1942) 2.5
Edgar Allan Poe story based on real-life case makes for mildly entertaining mystery. Patric Knowles is sleuth trying to solve

grisly murders where faces are smashed, rendering the victims unrecognizable. Just as in *Murders in the Rue Morgue* (1932), there's a roof-top chase finale. (DVD-R-Universal)

Mystery of the Wax Museum (1933) 3.0
After his wax museum has burned to the ground, disfigured sculptor Lionel Atwill finds unique way to rebuild his wax figures. Nicely done chiller also stars Fay Wray. The comedy relief does the film no favors but at least it isn't as consistently obnoxious as it was in *Doctor X*. (BR-Warner Archive)

Mystery of the White Room (1939) 2.0
Universal "Crime Club" entry concerns stabbing that takes place during surgery. Potentially interesting whodunit stunted by largely flat performances and obnoxious comedy relief courtesy of squeaky-voiced nurse and her moronic suitor. (NA)

Mystery on Monster Island (1981) 1.0
Peter Cushing buys Spencer Island for $5 million, much to the chagrin of Terence Stamp who wanted it for the riches contained therein. Then the two big stars get wise and pretty much vanish, and instead it's Cushing's nephew who is sent to the island, along with his music teacher (David Hatton), where the pair face various rubbery monsters and other dangers. Even giving this thing some leeway for being a children's film, there's still no excuse for Hatton's grating, over-the-top performance; the overbearing music; and film's ungodly length. It's too fever pitch to be fun; dreadful is a better description, or, as Hatton's character puts it, "Blasted turkey!" Based on Jules Verne's novel *L'École des Robinsons*. (DVD-Fox with *Gorilla at Large*)

Naked Space (1983) 1.0
Would-be *Airplane!*-like spoof of *Alien* and related films is pretty much a bust. Cindy Williams, Leslie Nielsen, and Patrick Macnee are among exploratory crew that brings small blob aboard its ship. Sure enough, the blob grows into one-eyed creature that starts consuming the humans. There is one inspired moment in the entire film: a musical number with the alien singing, "I Want to Eat Your Face." Other than that, this is a painful experience. Broadcast as *The Creature Wasn't Nice*. (DVD-Palm Beach Entertainment)

The Nanny (1965) 3.0
Hammer Film Productions scored Bette Davis for the lead in this gripping chiller. An obnoxious 10-year-old boy insists it wasn't he who drowned his little sister in the bath; Nanny did it! Is he in denial or is he possibly telling the truth? Davis is of course great here, playing an *awfully* patient caregiver. The climax is a real nail-biter. (DVD-Fox)

The Navy vs. the Night Monsters (1966) 0.5
Title creatures are discovered in Antarctica and come to omnivorous life during transport to naval base; the tree monsters then raise hell. Mamie Van Doren gets top billing as a Navy nurse. Dull shocker isn't even good for laughs. Where's Tabonga when you need him? (VHS-Paragon)

The Neanderthal Man (1953) 1.5
Scientist believes prehistoric man was just as smart as his modern counterpart and sets out to prove it via regression serum. He only half succeeds. Robert Shayne is one of the least likable mad doctors ever to grace the screen, constantly insisting on everyone else's stupidity. But he does deliver a hilariously brutal dressing down of fellow scientists who are skeptical of his theories. (BR-Shout! Factory with *The Beast from Hollow Mountain*)

Necromancy (1972) 1.0
Poor Pamela Franklin: her baby is stillborn, and hubby just got a new job working for Orson Welles, who is a Satanist in need of Franklin's untapped powers to bring his own dead son back to life. Pamela does her best but is constantly thwarted by poor dialogue, poor direction, and even worse editing. A disjointed, barely watchable mess. (BR-Code Red)

The New Invisible Man (1958) 2.0
Mexican remake of *The Invisible Man Returns*, with scientist turning his brother invisible to beat false murder conviction. The drug eventually turns the escapee mad, and he threatens to poison the populace! The effects are decent, but the film is overlong and lacks energy. After seeing this, one will really appreciate what Vincent Price brought to the title role in the original. (DVD-VCI)

The Next Victim (TV-1975) 2.5
Woman confined to wheelchair due to auto accident is a potential victim of psychotic strangler. Occasionally effective *Thriller* entry hampered by obvious red herring, obnoxious lead detective and a bad case of padding. (DVD-VEI as part of *Thriller: The Complete Collection*)

Night Caller from Outer Space (1965) 3.0
Landing of small, spherical object near London intrigues both scientists and the military. Soon afterwards, *something* escapes from it to carry out dastardly plan involving earthly females. Much of the credit for this film's success goes to director John Gilling, who takes a plot we've seen before and turns it into eerie, noirish thriller with Lewton-esque touches (the first appearance of the alien hand, keeping the villain in shadow). A little talky in the early going, but, overall, a compelling film. (DVD-Image)

Night Creatures (1962) 2.5
The Marsh Phantoms haunt an 18th-century village that may hide smugglers. More an adventure picture even though it typically makes the list of Hammer Horrors, the visuals involving skeletal figures riding horses are very cool. Peter Cushing and a subdued Oliver Reed are in the cast. Original title: *Captain Clegg*. (BR-Shout! Factory)

The Night Digger (1971) 3.0
Maura (Patricia Neal) lives a life of servitude taking care of her blind, adoptive mother and the crumbling Victorian house in which they live. Then Mom hires handsome stranger to take care of the home, and Maura starts developing feelings

for him. The only wrinkle is that he's a serial killer. Moody, well-acted thriller delivers a serious case of the creeps. Ending is unexpectedly poignant. (DVD-R-Warner Archive)

The Night Evelyn Came Out of the Grave (1971) 2.0
Wealthy lord grieving the loss of his unfaithful wife Evelyn picks up redheads and murders them at his creepy castle. When he remarries thinking it may stop his psychotic tendencies, the gruesome killings continue. Middling blend of Gothic horror and *giallo* offers lots of skin, creative deaths, a doozy of a rise-from-the-dead scene, and several wacky twists. Sadly, there's no one to care about here in this ultimately mechanical exercise and director Emilio Miraglia overdoes it with the flashbacks. (BR-Arrow)

Night Gallery (TV-1969) 3.0
Pilot for the Rod Serling series is solid entertainment, as morbid paintings serve as impetus for tales of terror. The stories include: a man murdered by his nephew who may be seeking vengeance from beyond the grave; a blind woman (Joan Crawford) who pays to get a new set of eyes; and a Nazi war criminal who thinks he's found the perfect escape in a museum. The middle installment was Steven Spielberg's directing debut. (BR-Kino as part of *Night Gallery: Season One*)

The Night Has Eyes (1942) 2.5
Two teachers on holiday visit the Yorkshire moors where their friend presumably died a year earlier. During a storm, they meet a recluse (James Mason) who offers them shelter and who may know something about the missing pal. Mostly effective mix of thrills and romance, with memorable climax, still feels longer than it needs to be. (DVD-R-Sinister Cinema as *Terror House*)

Night Key (1937) 2.5
Boris Karloff is kindly scientist who's been double-crossed one too many times. So, he deliberately causes problems for the alarm company owner that screwed him. Things get complicated when gangsters get involved. Enjoyable kind-of sci-fi thriller. (BR-Shout! Factory as part of *Universal Horror Collection: Volume 4*)

Night Monster (1942) 3.0
Good horror-mystery hybrid about brutal murders by hideous creature at The Oaks estate. The frogs stop croaking any time the fiend is near. The cast is good too although Lugosi has another one of his thankless roles playing a seemingly sinister butler. (BR-Shout! Factory as part of *Universal Horror Collection: Volume 4*)

Night Must Fall (1964) 2.5
Charming psycho killer Albert Finney worms his way into the good graces of his girlfriend's employer, as well as those of other household members. Soon he takes up residence as decorator, cook, and games-player, while we wait for him to kill again. The 1937 film version of the stage play was an effectively subtle, slow-burn thriller. Here, Finney is first seen shirtless, brandishing an axe as he chops up a body. It's all rather blunt and obvious, with an intrusive music score. Still, Finney is good enough to keep us watching. Beautifully lensed by Freddie Francis. (DVD-R-Warner Archive)

Night of Terror (1933) 2.0
There's a mad scientist working in the lab, a knife-wielding maniac roaming the grounds, and Bela Lugosi stalking the halls in this amusing old dark house–type chiller. Unintentionally funny much of the time but still worth seeing if only for the terrific coda involving the maniac. (DVD-R-Sinister Cinema)

Night of the Blood Beast (1958) 1.5
Astronaut who's killed when returning to earth has brought alien passenger with him. The alien resurrects the deceased, so he can carry unearthly embryos to term, and kills any earthling that interferes. There are some good ideas story wise, but the execution is sorely lacking. Some of the dialogue is laughable, as is the monster. Fans of low-budget efforts, however, will probably find some enjoyment here. (DVD-Retromedia)

Night of the Cobra Woman (1972) 1.0
During World War II, firebrand cobra bite gives nurse the power of healing and eternal youth. 25 years later, an anti-venom researcher for UNICEF tracks down the nurse with shocking results. Strange, poorly acted exploitation effort is good for chuckles instead of chills. (BR-Scorpion Releasing)

Night of the Living Dead (1968) 4.0
The film that literally redefined zombies for cinema: they were now flesh eaters instead of cheap labor (See pre-1968 efforts such *White Zombie* or *The Plague of the Zombies*, for examples). Shot in documentary style black-and-white, the film is believable from the first scene, with natural sounding dialogue and performances. A group of mostly strangers hole up in a Pennsylvania farmhouse while reanimated corpses of the recent dead surround them. Duane Jones is excellent as the self-appointed leader, and the ending is one of the most emotionally brutal you're likely to see. A truly great film and the best entry in director George A. Romero's *Dead* series. (BR-Criterion)

The Night of the Sorcerers (1974) 1.5
Group arrives in African jungle to conduct "photographic survey of animals near extinction." Instead, they find a tribe of zombies that rise from the dead to continue voodoo rites, including the decapitation of meddlers, who then become vampires. The very definition of Euro-sleaze: gruesome scenes of horror mixed with moments of soft-core and nudity. Occasionally eerie and effective. But just as often silly and tedious. (BR-Shout! Factory with *The Loreley's Grasp*)

Night of the Witches (1970) 1.5
A coven that offers horoscopes has set up shop somewhere in Mexico. A conman posing as a preacher thinks he's going to take advantage of these ladies. Big mistake. Obvious and tiresome low-budget horror mixes humor, pop song interludes, dancing witches, and bible quotes to little avail. Kathryn Loder is fun as head witch Cassandra, however. (NA)

The Night Stalker (TV-1972) 4.0
Proof that a classic movie monster could be effective in a modern setting, this record-setting TV thriller casts a flawless Darren McGavin as Las Vegas reporter Carl Kolchak, a former New York hot shot looking for that one story that will send him back East. He gets it when he realizes a genuine vampire is on the loose. Funny and thrilling, sometimes simultaneously, this perfectly realized shocker led to a sequel (*The Night Strangler*) and a single-season TV series. (BR-Kino)

The Night the World Exploded (1957) 2.0
A series of earthquakes leads to discovery of explosive new Element 112 that threatens to blow the Earth to pieces! Competent handling of decent story idea hobbled by obvious low budget. (DVD-Mill Creek as part of *Vintage Sci-Fi: 6 Movie Collection*)

Night Tide (1961) 2.5
The woman that sailor Dennis Hopper loves may just be a real mermaid, whose lovers have a habit of dying. Creepy, atmospheric low-budget horror-mystery hampered only by its sometimes-sluggish pacing. (BR-Kino)

The Night Walker (1964) 3.0
Barbara Stanwyck's blind, wealthy husband is killed in an explosion. Afterwards, she begins suffering strange nightmares that threaten to drive her mad. Directed by William Castle with a script by Robert Bloch, this is a twisty tale with several nice surprises. Catchy theme by Vic Mizzy too. (BR-Shout! Factory)

Night Watch (1973) 3.0
On a lovely dark and stormy night, Elizabeth Taylor looks out her flat's window and sees a dead body in the abandoned, dilapidated house across the street. When the police investigate, they find nothing. Well-directed thriller may appear obvious at first but there are some great twists, as well as a literal blood and thunder climax. An underappreciated, minor gem. (DVD-R-Warner Archive)

The Nightcomers (1972) 1.5
Would-be prequel to *The Turn of the Screw* documents what transpired between Quint (Marlon Brando) and Ms. Jessel that corrupted youths Miles and Flora. Brando is engaging but the film lacks atmosphere and never really comes to life. Poor direction is the true villain here. (BR-Kino)

Nightmare (1942) 2.5
Down-on-his-luck-gambler sneaks a meal in a home he thinks is abandoned. Turns out a murder has just taken place there and the lady of the house needs his help getting rid of the body. London-set thriller starts out as intriguing, noirish mystery before becoming routine spy story. Great cast though. (NA)

Nightmare (1964) 2.5
More Hammer Film Productions plot-twisting, with adolescent girl haunted by memories of her mother murdering her father. This is a very busy film, with two distinct parts that dare not be spoiled here. Hardly credible but very enjoyable. (BR-Shout! Factory)

Nightmare Alley (1947) 3.5
Tyrone Power is exceptional as carnival barker who has big plans for himself as he tries to secure mind-reading code from fellow performer. But that's just the beginning in this twisty, fascinating film noir with hints of the supernatural. (BR-Criterion)

Nightmare Castle (1965) 2.5
Barbara Steele plays woman who gets busted by her husband while cheating; ticked-off spouse tortures and murders the adulterous pair and then must deal with late wife's half-sister, also played by Steele, who inherits the spooky castle home. Sexy, violent, but overlong Italian chiller filmed in luscious black-and-white, so it has atmosphere to spare. It also has bad dubbing and odd dialogue, probably the result of translation difficulties. Pretty good but not great Steele vehicle. (BR-Severin)

Nightmare at 43 Hillcrest (TV-1974) 2.5
During a drug bust, cops break into the wrong house but decide to frame the innocent family to cover their crooked butts. While the basic story is compelling, the villains are two-dimensional, and the film suffers because of it. Based on a true story. (DVD-MPI with *Shadow of Fear*)

Nightmare in Wax (1969) 1.5
Stars of Paragon Studios are disappearing, soon after which, they're appearing as wax figures at Vincent Renard's (Cameron Mitchell) wax museum. He wears an eyepatch and is disfigured, as well as being the studio's former makeup artist. Coincidence? Uninspired *House of Wax* clone lacks that film's style, fun, and Vincent Price. Mitchell is okay in the lead though, and there is one harrowing scene of someone catching fire. The ending will anger some viewers; most won't care. (DVD-Rhino as part of *Horrible Horrors Collection: Volume 2*)

Nightmares (1983) 2.5
Refreshing change-of-pace 1980s horror film, which returns to the long-absent anthology format. The four stories include: 1) A woman encounters a killer when making a late-night run for cigarettes; 2) A video-game whiz is taken to new levels of terror while facing The Bishop of Battle; 3) A tortured priest encounters a demonic vehicle in the desert; and 4) The Houston family find they have a *major* rat problem. Good cast helps put over mostly familiar material. (BR-Shout! Factory)

No Survivors Please. (1964) 2.5
An expeditionary alien force sent to Earth to annihilate humankind murders important humans and temporarily occupies the corpses. A reporter suspects something is up and romances secretary of possessed ambassador. German thriller is poorly dubbed but undeniably intense and creepy. Plenty of cold-blooded killings and moments of sudden violence. (DVD-VCI with *The Black Cobra*)

Nosferatu (1922) 4.0
Before the vampire became the go-to monster for unrequited and/or tragic love stories, it was an unsympathetic fiend who brought death and disease wherever it went. Maybe that's why this remains the all-time great vampire movie, an unauthorized version of *Dracula* that features one of the ugliest bloodsuckers the other side of *Salem's Lot*. Drenched in atmosphere and stunning visuals, director F.W. Murnau creates a nightmare on screen that has yet to be equaled in other vampire films. (BR-Kino)

Not Guilty! (TV-1974) 3.0
American businessman working in England finds himself framed for wife's murder. Luckily, he knows a terrific private detective who promises to get to the truth. Enjoyable whodunit has a nice twist or two. Original British title: *The Next Scream You Hear*. (DVD-VEI as part of *Thriller: The Complete Collection*)

Not of This Earth (1957) 3.0
Representative of dying alien race visits Earth to collect samples of human blood and in certain cases more than that. Nifty Roger Corman low-budget outing with Beverly Garland effective as the hero and Paul Birch suitably menacing as vampire alien. Dick Miller is a doomed vacuum cleaner salesman. Has a nice sense of humor too. (DVD-Shout! Factory as part of *Sci-Fi Classics: Roger Corman's Cult Classics Triple Feature*)

The Nutty Professor (1963) 3.0
Nerdy high school science teacher wants to build up his body to deal with bullies. Instead, he invents formula that turns him into sociopathic ladies' man. Very funny comedy variation on *Dr. Jekyll and Mr. Hyde* is colorful with plenty of gags but also an unexpectedly touching finale. (BR-Warner Bros.)

The Oblong Box (1969) 2.5
Vincent Price keeps his brother in a locked room because of a voodoo curse. Bro escapes and wreaks havoc, blackmailing doc Christopher Lee along the way. Director Gordon Hessler creates colorful atmosphere in otherwise routine tale. Price and Lee are fine of course. (BR-Kino)

Octaman (1971) 1.5
Title creature gets mad when explorers steal his offspring, so he attacks. The film wastes no time showing us the monster. It's a good-looking monster except his mouth never moves. The film runs out of creative ways to stage the monster attacks quickly and the acting is a mixed bag. (BR-Retromedia with *The Cremators*)

The Old Dark House (1963) 2.5
American is invited to his English flat mate's ancestral home only to discover upon his arrival that his friend has died. He also learns the occupants are crazy and one of them is a murderer. Often maligned William Castle film is his only for Hammer and not that bad. The cast is good as is the production design. Not laugh-out-loud funny but pleasant. (BR-Mill Creek as part of *Hammer Films: The Ultimate Collection: 20 Film Set*)

Old Dracula (1974) 2.0
David Niven plays the classic character who wishes to bring his late wife Vampira (the film's original title) back to life. But the blood he uses has unexpected consequences. Although released before *Young Frankenstein* in its native England, this unsuccessful horror comedy was retitled in the US to cash in on Mel Brook's megahit. Niven is very good and delivers his one-liners and zingers with aplomb. But everything else is rather forced and just not very funny. (BR-Vinegar Syndrome)

The Omega Man (1971) 3.0
It's 1977 and germ warfare has wiped out nearly all of humanity, except for a pack of mutants and machine gun-toting scientist Charlton Heston, who managed to test the right vaccine on himself. Thinking he's the last of his kind, he's shocked to discover this isn't so, and now he must balance his own survival against that of those who need his help. Solid version of Richard Matheson's novel *I Am Legend* has breakneck pace, a good lead performance, some interesting story turns, and haunting music score. (BR-Warner Bros.)

The Omen (1976) 3.5
Big budget thriller about the birth of the antichrist. Getting Gregory Peck and Lee Remick to play the unwitting parents of devil child Damien was a major coup. David Warner and Billie Whitelaw add excellent support, and director Richard Donner keeps things moving briskly. Filled with great moments (that decapitation is a classic) and an Oscar-winning music score. (BR-Shout! Factory as part of *The Omen Collection*)

Once the Killing Starts (TV-1974) 3.0
A married college professor is having an affair, so he plots the "perfect" murder of his wife. But after the deed, he starts getting ominous notes. Seems like a homage to *Columbo* at first-the inspector even wears a raincoat! But this tale has its own version of justice to tell. The final twist is a good one. (DVD-VEI as part of *Thriller: The Complete Collection*)

One Deadly Owner (TV-1974) 2.5
Donna Mills plays a super model who spends her life savings on fancy automobile. Then it starts driving her to places she had no intention of visiting. And it screams too. The main character's actions aren't remotely believable, which hurts this otherwise interesting tale of haunted car aiding in solving a murder. (DVD-VEI as part of *Thriller: The Complete Collection*)

One Million B.C. (1940) 2.5
Largely dialogue-free caveman saga about Rock People tribe member who runs afoul the leader (Lon Chaney, Jr.) and gets kicked out, but finds love and friendship from other tribe, the Shell People. Simple story given boost by well-done action sequences and great special effects, so good they showed up in many future films. (BR-VCI)

One Million Years B.C. (1966) 2.5
Hammer Film Production's remake of 1940 fantasy about evicted tribesman Tumak who discovers a kinder, gentler people during his exile. Boasts Ray Harryhausen's exciting visual

effects and bikini-clad Raquel Welch as Tumak's savior. Like the original, there is some narration at the beginning, but the rest of the film is free of understandable dialogue. Also like the original, interest comes and goes. (BR-Kino)

Only A Scream Away (TV-1974) 2.0
Someone seems to have it in for newlywed Samantha (Haley Mills). They ruin her wedding dress with red paint; cut up a picture of her; and break her wedding cake figurines. And she has this new American neighbor (Gary Collins) who keeps a China doll on his bed. It isn't hard to figure out what is going on and where the story will go. (DVD-VEI as part of *Thriller: The Complete Collection*)

Operation Atlantis (1965) 1.5
American spy travels to North Africa to investigate uranium deposits held hostage by arch villain. Discovers lost city of Atlantis too-maybe. Italian James Bond clone is dull affair, with occasional, pedestrianly staged action sequences to keep the viewer awake. The plot just gets wackier as it goes. (NA)

Orca (1977) 2.0
Hunter Richard Harris decides to capture killer whale for big bucks. When he botches the job, he becomes target of whale's mate. Beautifully shot and scored, the film's cast is a mixed bag, but the main problem is the script, which gets more ludicrous as this tale of revenge plays out. The whale baits Harris to come after him! Director Michael Anderson is more interested in jump-scares than building suspense. (BR-Shout! Factory)

The Other (1972) 3.0
Twins Niles and Holland enjoy playing games on the family farm. When mysterious accidents start plaguing the family, their grandmother suspects they may be up to something sinister. Moody, atmospheric chiller builds to shattering climax that packs a wallop. (BR-Twilight Time)

Panic in Year Zero (1962) 3.0
After a nuclear attack destroys Los Angeles, Ray Milland (who also directs) does what he must to protect his family and survive in a lawless land. Brutal, no-nonsense thriller is utterly convincing and holds up well. (BR-Kino)

Paranoiac (1963) 2.5
Is the man claiming to be a long-thought-dead brother really who he says he is? Why is there a figure wearing a creepy mask moving about the grounds? One of Hammer's Hitchcockian twist films is entertaining but not very surprising. Oliver Reed gets to let loose during the finale. (BR-Shout! Factory)

The Pearl of Death (1944) 3.0
Solid Sherlock Holmes entry that introduces Rondo Hatton's Creeper. Holmes blunders and a valuable pearl is stolen. Then a series of murders begins, whose victims are surrounded by broken China and bric-a-brac. What's the connection? Holmes of course solves it, but the fact remains that Holmes' showing off led to three murders. (BR-MPI as part of *The Complete Sherlock Holmes Collection*)

Peeping Tom (1960) 3.0
Abused son of scientist now likes to photograph women while murdering them. Effective psycho-thriller boasts strong work from the leads and direction by Michael Powell. Sometimes aired as *Face of Fear*. (DVD-Criterion)

The People That Time Forgot (1977) 2.0
Sequel to *The Land That Time Forgot*. Expedition goes in search of missing American Bowen Tyler from the first film. They of course find that island inhabited by dinosaurs and cavemen. But this time there's also a green-skinned warrior tribe to reckon with. Although this effort wastes no time getting to the monsters (there's a pterodactyl attack less than 10 minutes in), this lacks the fun of its predecessor. Patrick Wayne isn't a very likeable lead. (BR-Kino)

Phantasm (1979) 2.0
A pre-adolescent boy discovers mysterious deeds being performed by the "Tall Man" at the Morningside Mortuary. Nightmare logic thriller includes a flying sphere, evil Jawas, a severed finger that transforms into a nasty bug, and other sorts of bizarre happenings. A film easier to admire than like, there is no emotional "in" to becoming involved in the story. Performances needed to be stronger to pull this off. But the film certainly has its moments (and admirers.) (BR-Well Go USA)

The Phantom from 10,000 Leagues (1955) 1.0
Scientist has used radiation to transform sea turtle into murderous monster. Game cast is outwitted by dull script, flat direction, and lack of excitement. Spy subplot adds nothing but padding. (BR-Kino)

Phantom from Space (1953) 1.0
Invisible being from outer space crash lands on Earth; tries to find its way home, killing some people along the way. Nearby scientists employ their dog Venus to save the day. Narration and talk substitute for action most of the time in this drab offering. Comes to life only in the final moments. By that time, it's too late to care. (BR-Retromedia with *Frozen Alive*)

The Phantom of Soho (1964) 2.5
A killer donning golden gloves and skull mask is knifing respectable citizens near seedy nightclub. Scotland Yard teams with crime novelist to stop the killer. Talky at times, as are most German *krimis*, this is one of the better entries. Atmospheric, suspenseful, and well-plotted; the ending is a good one. (DVD-Retromedia with *The Curse of the Yellow Snake*)

The Phantom of the Opera (1925) 3.5
Still one of the great silent films: marvelous sets and Chaney's iconic performance as the title fiend who terrorizes artists and patrons alike. Unfortunately for people today, it's very doubtful they'll see the film for the first time without knowing the visage behind the mask. The sound versions can't hold a candle to the original, which plays up the horror for all it's worth. (BR-Kino)

The Phantom of the Opera (1943) 3.0
Gorgeous-looking remake with Claude Rains doing his typically excellent job. There's more opera than Phantom but this is still an entertaining update. The film won Oscars for its color cinematography and interior art direction. (BR-Universal)

The Phantom of the Opera (1962) 2.0
Herbert Lom plays an overly sympathetic phantom and has a henchman who does the dirty work. Based on what we're shown, the main opera concerning Joan of Arc really stinks. The highlight is Michael Gough's smarmy Ambrose Darcy, who is the true villain of the film. (BR-Shout! Factory)

Phantom of the Paradise (1974) 3.5
Insanely entertaining mix of horror, comedy, and music. Winslow Leach (William Finley) has his compositions stolen by the evil Dorian Swan (Paul Williams), and then gets injured by a record press. He doesn't want his cantata performed by anyone other than Phoenix (Jessica Harper), the singer he's taken a liking to. But that's only the beginning in this twisty tale. Colorful, exciting blend of *The Phantom of the Opera*, *The Picture of Dorian Gray*, and the *Faust* story has style to spare and great music by Williams. The early scene between Swan and one of his thugs plays like a homage to *The Godfather*, with Swan in the Don Corleone part. Another feather in the cap for director/writer Brian De Palma. (BR-Shout! Factory)

Phantom of the Rue Morgue (1954) 2.5
A series of brutal murders plagues 19th-century France. Meanwhile Dr. Marais (Karl Malden) experiments with the conditioning of animal behavior. Malden is fun as the cracked scientist in this colorful, 3D effort from Warner Brothers. Not quite as good as the 1932 version with Bela Lugosi though. (VHS-Warner Bros.)

The Phantom Planet (1961) 1.5
Astronaut finds himself stranded on mysterious planet Rheton that can move from galaxy to galaxy. He shrinks to the size of the other inhabitants and eventually helps battle escaped alien. With meteors that look like caramel popcorn and clichéd love triangle subplot, this barely routine sci-fi feels like something left over from the 1950s. (BR-R-Snappy Video)

Pharaoh's Curse (1957) 2.0
British-American expedition in 1902 Egypt open crypt; spirit of Pharaoh possesses one of the members and then the murders start. Mostly ho-hum outing still has some power once the deaths begin. There is claustrophobia and dread in the sequences inside the mountain tomb. Cast is rather bland though. (DVD-R-Fox)

Phase IV (1974) 2.5
In an Arizona desert research lab, scientists investigate why formally antagonistic ant species now get along while their natural enemies seem to have vanished. Is humankind next? Intense, chilling slow-burn sci-fi is somewhat hampered by aloof cast and repetitive close-ups of ants. (BR-Olive)

Phone Call from a Stranger (1952) 3.0
Man leaving his wife and family becomes involved in the lives of three fellow passengers traveling by air. When tragedy strikes, he becomes involved in the lives of their respective families too. Enjoyable melodrama with nice balance of gravitas and humor; terrific cast too. But why this aired on Channel 20's "Creature Feature" is anyone's guess. (DVD-Fox)

Picture Mommy Dead (1966) 2.0
Teenager is haunted by the memory of her mother, who burned to death three years ago. Now, Mom is haunting the frightened daughter claiming her death was no accident. Director Bert I. Gordon leaves behind the giant monsters for a routine ghost story. Unpleasant characters spouting vitriolic dialogue offers some amusement. (BR-Kino)

The Picture of Dorian Gray (1945) 3.5
Beautifully rendered version of Oscar Wilde's story of man whose portrait grows old while he remains young. George Sanders steals the film as one who lives only for pleasure. Angela Lansbury is lovely as Sybil Vane. Nearly all of Dorian Gray's crimes are left to our imaginations, so just what Gray does against respectability may vary from viewer to viewer. (BR-Warner Bros.)

Pillow of Death (1945) 2.0
In the sixth and final *Inner Sanctum* mystery, Lon Chaney, Jr. plays an adulterous attorney whose wife is murdered. The only notable element of this film is who the villain turns out to be. Otherwise, ho-hum. (BR-Mill Creek as part of *Inner Sanctum Mysteries: The Complete Film Series*)

Piranha (1978) 3.0
A careless skip tracer dumps a school of mutant, genetically altered piranha into the river, threatening the locals, attendees at a nearby summer camp, and guests at a resort's grand opening. Entertaining *Jaws* clone boasts director Joe Dante's typically able blend of humor and horror, good script by John Sayles, and fine music by Pino Donaggio. A *very* bloody good time. (BR-Shout! Factory)

Piranha II: The Spawning (1981) 1.5
Italian-produced sequel is mostly a misfire. Deadly, flying piranha/grunion hybrids call wrecked navy supply ship home, until they decide to move closer inland where a Caribbean vacation paradise brims with potential snacks. Sluggishly paced, uninvolving effort comes to life only in fits and starts, which tend to be horrific. Film served as director James Cameron's first credited theatrical feature, although he reportedly worked on it only a couple of weeks. (BR-Shout! Factory)

Pit and the Pendulum (1961) 3.0
A man shows up at his married sister's home looking for details of her death, but her husband (Vincent Price) is fragile enough as it is. One of the best in the Poe series, with Barbara Steele as Price's wife in flashbacks. Several twists lead to intense finale. (BR-Shout! Factory as part of *The Vincent Price Collection*)

A Place to Die (TV-1973) 3.0
Doctor and his new bride arrive in small town, where the locals think the wife is a *very* special lady. Nicely mounted terror tale is effective if familiar. (DVD-VEI as part of *Thriller: The Complete Collection*)

The Plague of the Zombies (1966) 3.0
The dead seem to be rising from their graves in Cornish village, and the local doctor can't figure out what's going on. He summons learned professor for assistance, and together they discover the terrifying secret. Strong Hammer horror effort, with great performances and terrific zombie makeup. (BR-Shout! Factory)

Plan 9 From Outer Space (1959) 1.0
Notorious "classic" about aliens' plan to invade earth by raising the dead, thereby terrifying the citizenry. Bad acting, bad sets, bad effects, and pretty much bad everything else. But it is entertaining in its own way. Director Ed Wood used footage he'd shot of Bela Lugosi before Lugosi passed away, and clumsily worked it into the story. (BR-Legend Films)

Planet of the Apes (1968) 3.5
In the year 3978, astronaut Charlton Heston and his crew awaken to find they've landed on planet where apes rule and humans are non-verbal slaves. Classic sci-fi with incredible makeups by John Chambers; intelligent ruminations on science, faith, and politics; and a hell of a final shot. Heston is compelling, if occasionally over the top, in the lead. (BR-Fox)

Planet of the Vampires (1965) 2.5
Spaceship lands to investigate planet, and immediately things go wrong as crew members violently turn on each other. Director Mario Bava's low-budget horror/sci-fi hybrid is expectedly stylish with pretty colors and a fog machine on full blast. Some of the ideas the film puts forth are interesting. But the story also gets silly at times and some of dialogue is awkward, and the actors, except for Barry Sullivan, fail to register as characters. Typically aired on television as *The Demon Planet*. (BR-Kino)

Planets Against Us (1962) 1.0
Aliens send cyborgs who look like deceased American scientist to sabotage Earth's various space programs. One of the invaders pursues scientist who has invented coveted gas formula, ends up developing feelings for doctor's daughter. Creepy atmosphere is all for naught in this talky, sleep-inducer. The ending is especially lame. (NA)

The Plumber (1979) 2.5
After her professor-husband leaves for his class, woman is visited by chatty plumber claiming the apartment needs emergency repairs. Already a little spooked, her distress increases when he returns the next day and engages in disturbing conversation. Fairly entertaining battle of wits between the intellectual and working classes. Trivia: although made for Australian television, this had its US premiere during Los Angeles' Filmex on Tuesday, March 11, 1980, at 10 p.m. at Plitt's Century Plaza Theaters and the ABC Entertainment Center, Century City, and then played at the Roxie Cinema in San Francisco from September 19 to October 7, 1980. (DVD-Home Vision Entertainment with *The Cars That Ate Paris*)

Point of Terror (1971) 2.0
Singer has an affair with married woman to advance his career. She doesn't mind because her invalid husband is a real jackass. Familiar story plays out in familiar way, although the sequences where someone ends up dead are interestingly handled. Twist at the end is a groaner. (BR-Vinegar Syndrome with *Blood Mania*)

Port Sinister (1953) 2.0
Bizarre mix of science fiction, gangsters, and adventure. Scientist leading an expedition for legendary pirate city of Port Royal gets assaulted by thugs who then take over ship in hopes of securing fabled treasure; find giant crabs too. Some welcome faces in the cast, such as Paul Cavanagh and William Schallert, help keep this so-so effort afloat. What should have been the film's highlight—Port Royal's rise to the ocean top—is a real disappointment. (NA)

Portrait in Terror (1965) 2.0
Art thief Patrick Magee is alarmed to learn the painting he murdered for is a fake. He proceeds to hunt down the owner's nephew while at the same time deal with a blackmailer. Okay thriller features a good performance by Magee; composer Ronald Stein reuses several of his cues from *Dementia 13* and *The Haunted Palace*. Some of the more atmospheric footage ended up in *Track of the Vampire*. (BR-Arrow as part of *Blood Bath: Limited Edition*)

The Power (1968) 3.0
A scientific committee investigating human endurance finds its numbers dwindling when a killer uses his (or her) telekinetic abilities for murder. The prime suspect is George Hamilton, so he sets out to expose the true villain. One of producer George Pal's most unique movies, a mostly successful blend of science fiction and whodunit. Great cast and a neat theme by Miklós Rózsa. (DVD-R-Warner Archive)

Prehistoric Women (1967) 1.5
Arrogant hunter is thrown back in time where he finds a tribe of brunettes has enslaved a tribe of blondes. He must choose sides or face the jealous wrath of Martine Beswick. Hammer Film Productions adventure has lots of silly dance numbers and unintended chuckles. At least Beswick seems to be having a good time. (DVD-Anchor Bay with *The Witches*)

The Premature Burial (1962) 2.5
Ray Milland plays a man obsessed with being buried alive. Catalepsy also runs in his family. Now his fears threaten his recent marriage to the lovely Emily, played by Hazel Court. Roger Corman once again weaves a Poe-inspired tale that concerns some of the same things that were present in *House of Usher* and *Pit and the Pendulum*. But the film is a bit repetitive despite an amusing scene with Milland showing off his tomb built for escape and the intense finale. (BR-Kino)

Prisoners of the Lost Universe (1983) 1.0
Low-budget glop about people transported to another dimension called Vonya, trying to find a way back home. There's a big caveman, some silly sound effects, green-skinned forest dwellers, squealy water beasts, red-eyed aliens, John Saxon as villain Kleel the Warlord, and *lots* of bad dialogue. Enough cheese to go along with a box of Ritz. (DVD-Mill Creek as part of *Nightmare Worlds: 50 Movie Pack*)

Project Moonbase (1953) 1.5
In 1970, Earth sends scientists to the moon to evaluate suitability for a lunar base, unaware that one of the team is an imposter bent on sabotaging the mission. Routine '50s sci-fi gets docked for the unbelievably sexist treatment of female lead—a colonel—who, for example, is told to shut up and threatened with a spanking. Yeesh. (DVD-Image)

The Projected Man (1966) 2.0
Scientist has developed method of converting matter to pure energy and projecting it. When an all-important demonstration is sabotaged, he foolishly experiments on himself, with horrific results. Derivative to say the least, with large chunks of plot from *The Fly* and *The Invisible Ray*, and it gets bogged down in politics. But there are effective moments, such as the harrowing experiment-goes-wrong scene and the first appearance of the mutated doctor. (BR-Shout! Factory)

Prom Night (1980) 2.5
Above average slasher entry takes the *Halloween* route by focusing on suspense and mystery rather than gore. Vengeful ax-wielding maniac visits several high schoolers at their senior prom. Jamie Lee Curtis is in the cast. (BR-Synapse)

Psyche 59 (1964) 2.5
Patricia Neal plays woman suffering from hysterical blindness, the result of a fall down the stairs while pregnant with her second child. When her trouble-making younger sister shows up after getting divorced, secrets threaten to be revealed. Moody, well-acted drama promises more than it delivers. It builds big to an obvious conclusion. (DVD-R Sony)

PSI Factor (1980) 2.5
Research scientist working for the military inadvertently contacts an alien intelligence, which then visits him in the form of large fireball the very same night. He meets with resistance when he tries to report the incident, and then goes on the run with his computer programmer girlfriend when she swipes a top-secret file for him. This modest blend of man-on-the-run, science fiction and conspiracy thrillers might be low budget, but it features a game cast and decent pace. The script also has moments of cleverness, wit, and dark humor. (VHS-Monarch Home Video)

The Psychic (1977) 2.5
Jennifer O'Neill plays young woman who has psychic vision of murder that took place in her husband's house. When a skeleton is found hidden in the walls, he's arrested for the crime, so she sets out to prove his innocence. One of director Lucio Fulci's better films, with a focus on story and plot development instead of gore-for-gore's-sake murder scenes. Not as twisty and surprising as the best *gialli*, but sufficiently entertaining. Major complaint is overuse of zooms. (BR-Scorpion Releasing)

Psychic Killer (1975) 2.5
Before a wrongly convicted man is released, he learns the art of astral projection. Once freed he uses that power to kill those he blames for his incarceration. Good cast in a story that plays like a psychic mad slasher film, with creative deaths aplenty. It also has a sense of humor, sometimes to its detriment. Still entertaining though. (BR-Vinegar Syndrome)

Psycho (1960) 4.0
Marion Crane steals $40,000 and makes an unwise stop at the Bates Motel. Still potent after umpteen viewings, Alfred Hitchcock's classic boasts Bernard Herrmann's rich score and Anthony Perkins' iconic performance. Suspenseful even when you know what's coming next. (BR-Universal)

Psychomania (1973) 3.0
The leader of *The Living Dead* biker gang has a clairvoyant mother who knows the secret of eternal life: kill yourself believing you'll come back, and you will. So, of course he tries it out and it works, and then the other gang members soon join him. Original, entertaining action-horror blend has a great sense of humor and some harrowing set pieces. George Sanders' last movie, which is rather eerie given the actor committed suicide. Sometimes aired on television as *The Death Wheelers*. (BR-Arrow)

Psychopath (1973) 1.0
The host (Tom Basham) of a lame kid's TV show, who also volunteers at children's hospital, avenges his abused young viewers by offing their abusers. Low-budget effort is poorly made (bad acting, inappropriate music, abundant close-ups of killer's eyes, etc.) but Basham's performance offers some mild amusement. The verbal abuse we hear is the most disturbing element of the film. (VHS-Fox Hills Video)

Pyro (1964) 2.0
When a married man breaks off his affair, his lover arranges a fire to kill his family in the hopes she'll get him back. But the plan backfires (pun intended) when *he* is nearly burned to death too. Now, he plots to torch his ex, her daughter, and the rest of her family as revenge. Fitfully interesting chiller has too many lulls and doesn't adequately maintain suspense. (DVD-Roan)

The Quatermass Xperiment (1955) 3.5
Top-notch Hammer horror/sci-fi about spacecraft that returns to Earth with only one of its three passengers surviving. But he's infected with something that threatens all humankind! Brian Donlevy plays Dr. Quatermass as an arrogant jerk and it works beautifully. Director Val Guest shoots the film as if it were a documentary so that the story has an intensity not seen in most sci-fi pictures of the time. Aired on television as *The Creeping Unknown*. (BR-Kino)

Quatermass 2 (1957) 3.0
The irascible Professor Quatermass is back, this time dealing with alien life forms housed in top secret Government-sponsored plant supposedly making synthetic food. He soon learns the Earth is being invaded, with certain authority figures having been taken over. Exciting sci-fi is almost as good as the first film, with harrowing moments aplenty. Television title: *Enemy from Space*. (BR-Shout! Factory)

Quatermass and the Pit (1967) 3.0
Concluding film in Hammer's Quatermass trilogy features Andrew Keir taking over for Brian Donlevy, making for a warmer, but no less determined, professor. A London construction crew find what they think is an undetonated German missile, as well as five-million-year-old skeleton! But an investigating Quatermass thinks the discovery might not be of this planet. Filled with clever ideas and chilling images, building to apocalyptic climax. Television title: *Five Million Years to Earth*. (BR-Shout! Factory)

Queen of Blood (1966) 2.5
In the year 1990, Earth receives distress signals from Mars. So, scientist Basil Rathbone assembles team to respond to the call; find vampiric creature for their trouble. Very atmospheric and creepy space horror tale. Aired on television as *Planet of Blood*. (BR-Kino)

Queen of Outer Space (1958) 2.0
In 1985, a trio of astronauts join professor to investigate problems on space station. They instead crash land on female-inhabited Venus, which is ruled by grumpy queen. Borders on (and crosses over into) parody territory at times, but it has some good laughs, unintended or not, and high camp entertainment ratio. Zsa Zsa Gabor is memorable as Venusian scientist who sides with the guys. (BR-Warner Archive)

Race with the Devil (1975) 3.0
Vacationing couples witness a satanic ceremony where a girl is murdered. They then must flee the Satanists in this entertaining hybrid of horror and action films. Peter Fonda and Warren Oates make great leads, and the smash-ups are staged with aplomb. The ending is typical '70s gloom and doom. A blast! (BR-Shout! Factory with *Dirty Mary Crazy Larry*)

Rasputin: The Mad Monk (1966) 2.5
Fictionalized account of evil monk who used his powers of healing and hypnotism in a bid to control the Russian empire. Hammer Film Productions effort offers nothing ground-breaking in terms of plot. As the title fiend, Christopher Lee is commanding in one of his most villainous roles and makes the film worth seeing. (BR-Shout! Factory)

The Raven (1935) 3.0
Lugosi is mad surgeon with a Poe obsession; he plots torturous revenge against a judge who isn't keen on Lugosi's interest in his daughter. A disfigured Karloff is a henchman. One of a kind horror film that probably wouldn't have worked with anyone other than Lugosi in the lead. Some of the dialogue is unreal. (BR-Shout! Factory as part of *Universal Horror Collection: Volume 1*)

The Raven (1963) 3.0
Vincent Price, Peter Lorre, and Boris Karloff are all wizards who have their own agendas when they meet at Karloff's castle. More comedy than horror but very entertaining. Jack Nicholson plays Lorre's son and gets to make crazy faces. (BR-Shout! Factory as part of *The Vincent Price Collection II*)

The Red Circle (1960) 2.0
Criminal known as The Red Circle blackmails various persons and then murders them if they go to Scotland Yard for help. Rather routine German *krimi* that's mostly talk and red herrings; several suspects have something to hide. There is a surprise at the end, but it's not the identity of the killer. For Edgar Wallace fans only. AKA *The Crimson Circle*. (DVD-R-Sinister Cinema)

The Red Cloak (1955) NR
In this Italian melodrama set in 1500 Pisa, the son of a murdered banker dons a crimson cape as he takes revenge on those responsible. One of the most obscure and elusive "horror" films to air on local television. The film aired twice on WDCA Channel 20: Tuesday, November 29, 1966, at 11:00 p.m., and then as an installment of *House of Horrors* on Sunday, September 22, 1968. (NA)

The Red Hand (1960) NR
Throughout the world, a notorious group known as the Red Hand is blowing up munition factories. To stop them, even countries that are enemies must join forces. Another one of the most obscure and elusive "horror" films to air on local television. The film aired twice in 1966 on WDCA: Saturday, August 13 as an installment on *House of Horrors*, and then on Thursday, December 29 at 7:30 p.m. (NA)

Red Planet Mars (1952) 2.0
Peter Graves plays scientist whose communicating with Martians—or is it God?—results in panic across the world (runs on banks, coalmines closing, rioting, etc.). Anti-communist propaganda piece is amusing nonsense mixing science, religion, and the Cold War. (Laserdisc-MGM as part of *United Artists Sci-Fi Matinee*)

A Reflection of Fear (1972) 2.5
Robert Shaw returns to his estranged wife seeking a divorce, so he can remarry. She'll grant it if he agrees to never again see the teenage daughter he barely knows anyway. But his child's strange behavior leads dad to believe some further investigation is warranted. The story itself is very familiar and mostly predictable. But it's well-told and well-acted, filmed in a dreamlike manner with dialogue spoken rarely above a whisper. (DVD-R-Sony)

The Reincarnation of Peter Proud (1975) 2.5
Dr. Peter Proud becomes convinced his nightmares about being murdered (in Crystal Lake!) are really memories of a past

life. He investigates and eventually meets his "killer." Intriguing for a while but eventually becomes obvious where the story is headed. (BR-Kino)

Rendezvous at Midnight (1935) 2.5
Spoiled socialite (Valerie Hobson) confesses to fictitious killing in hopes of getting some attention from the police commissioner she loves. She doesn't realize her phony victim has really been murdered! Pleasant, breezy mix of comedy and mystery. Hobson made this shortly before *Bride of Frankenstein*. (NA)

Reported Missing (1937) 2.0
The "Browning Drift Indicator" is supposed to help airplanes manage bad weather. Unfortunately, the experimental passenger flight ends up crashing and being robbed afterwards. Universal mystery hampered by weak comedy relief, hackneyed love triangle, and obvious villain. (NA)

The Reptile (1966) 3.0
Good Hammer horror about bizarre deaths taking place in a Cornish village and the strange creature responsible. The performances are especially strong, including great turn by Michael Ripper as a friendly barkeep. (BR-Shout! Factory)

Reptilicus (1961) 1.0
Copper miners drill into reptile fossil, which is brought to a lab where it thaws, regenerates, and returns to life. Soon it escapes and wreaks bargain-basement havoc, covering people in animated green slime. Poorly edited, goofy mix of giant-monster-on-the-loose antics, broad humor, and tepid romance. (BR-Shout! Factory with *Tentacles*)

Repulsion (1965) 4.0
Catherine Deneuve gives a bravura performance in director Roman Polanski's study of sexual repression and madness. Deneuve is left alone in the apartment she shares with her older sister when the latter leaves for a romantic getaway. She suffers hallucinations and nightmares, leading to violent encounters. Grim, intense, and haunting. Those scenes in the hallways with arms coming out of the walls are not easily forgotten. (BR-Criterion)

Retik, the Moon Menace (1966) 2.0
Feature version of serial *Radar Men from the Moon* (1952). Moon beings, armed with atomic weapons, are planning a takeover of Earth, so it's up to our hero Commando Cody with his flying jetpack to stop them. As typical with Republic serials cut down to feature length, there's an abundance of fistfights and gun battles. There's also plenty of moon action and low-budget effects to keep one amused. The complete serial is available from several companies due to its public domain status. (DVD-R-Alpha in 60-minute version as *Commando Cody vs. the Moon Menace*)

The Return (1980) 1.5
As young ones, deputy Jan-Michael Vincent and scientist Cybill Shepherd witnessed strange alien phenomena in small New Mexico town. 25 years later, they are reunited in the same place, which is currently plagued by mysterious cattle mutilations and murders. Potentially interesting sci-fi mystery with good cast is let down by director Greydon Clark's lifeless pacing and nonsensical turn of events in the last 15 or so minutes, making this one big, "Huh?" (BR-Scorpion Releasing)

The Return of Charlie Chan (TV-1971) 2.0
Charlie Chan (Ross Martin) comes out of retirement to solve the attempted murder of Greek tycoon (Leslie Nielsen) as well as few successful killings. Martin is OK as the famed detective, but the story isn't terribly involving; this isn't the warmest group of suspects, and one doesn't really care what's going on. More problematic is the darn thing turns out to be too complex for its own good, with way too many "surprises." The one aspect that *does* work though is Chan's relationship with his son, who insists on calling him "Pop" even though Charlie keeps asking him to stop. ("Pop is for corn!") Filmed in 1971, it finally had its American premiere on ABC at 11:30 p.m. on Tuesday, July 17, 1979, under the title *Charlie Chan: Happiness Is A Warm Clue*. (NA)

The Return of Count Yorga (1971) 3.0
Sequel to 1970 hit has Yorga revived by those evil Santa Ana winds; he goes after persons associated with an orphanage, falling in love along the way. The strengths of the first film (Quarry, well-directed terror sequences) are present here. But there's also some repetition that lessens the impact a bit. Still quite good though. (BR-Shout! Factory)

The Return of Doctor X (1939) 2.5
Reporter finds a dead body which later returns to life. His investigation puts him in pursuit of a deceased scientist. Humphrey Bogart is the horror heavy here and he's just fine. Fast-paced B picture. (DVD-Warner Bros. as part of *Hollywood Legends of Horror Collection*)

The Return of Dracula (1958) 2.5
Frances Lederer does well in role of vampire terrorizing suburbia while impersonating distant uncle of sickly-sweet family. Predictably plotted and rather sunny, but some of Lederer's dialogue is excellent. Aired on television as *Curse of Dracula*. (BR-Olive)

Return of the Ape Man (1944) 2.0
Bela Lugosi and John Carradine discover frozen caveman in the Arctic, and then bring him back to US for thawing. But Lugosi's plans for the thawed icicle conflict with Carradine's. Typical Monogram silliness at least has nonstop action to go along with such scenes as Lugosi going after the escaped caveman with a small blowtorch. (BR-Olive)

Return of the Fly (1959) 2.0
Poor sequel finds son of research scientist carrying on his father's work. Corporate schemes lead to tragic and predictable outcome. Not nearly as involving as the first film, although the black-and-white photography adds creepy atmosphere. (BR-Shout! Factory as part of *The Fly Collection*)

The Return of Giant Majin (1966) 2.5
Sequel to *Majin, Monster of Terror*. Benevolent ruler Juro is betrayed, and his village overtaken. He escapes capture and is now hunted by would-be killer, who subsequently kidnaps a citizen of yet another village thinking Juro is hiding there. So, the persecuted pray to their god for protection. Pretty much a repeat of the previous film: the bad guys destroy the statue image of Majin and Majin gets his revenge. Good effects and hissable villains who get theirs make this entertaining if familiar. (BR-Arrow as *Return of Daimajin* as part of *The Daimajin Trilogy*)

Return of the Giant Monsters (1967) 2.0
Third *Gamera* film has the giant turtle battling Gyaos, a bat-like creature with laser breath that cuts like a Ginsu. Told with a straight face, which helps, this is still tacky stuff. The monster fight sequences are brutal enough though. (BR-Arrow as *Gamera vs. Gyaos* as part of *Gamera: The Complete Collection*)

The Return of the Vampire (1943) 2.5
Bela Lugosi plays Armand Tesla-vampire. He's out for revenge against the family who stuck a spike in him in 1918. To cash in on Universal's *Frankenstein Meets the Wolf Man*, Columbia added a werewolf assistant (Matt Willis) here. But he's mostly useless (at one point he just stands in the bushes and snarls at a couple of vampire hunters instead of, like, attacking them or something) even if Willis does a good job. Lugosi is restrained, at least compared to his Poverty Row performances. Not without its moments. (BR-Shout! Factory)

Return to Boggy Creek (1977) 1.0
A G-rated adventure for the entire family! Prepubescent Evie Jo, who has a gift for fishing thanks to her secret formula, decides to play Nancy Drew when she and her two younger brothers follow a guide and his client in search of legendary monster. Then the hurricane strikes. Despite the title, not really a sequel to *The Legend of Boggy Creek*; scenarist/director Tom Moore just used the setting to come up with his own Bigfoot-type story. Unfortunately, most of the acting is subpar and the film is greatly lacking in incident, hardly an adventure. Creates convincing picture of fishing village though. (VHS-CBS/Fox)

The Revenge of Frankenstein (1958) 3.0
Dr. Frankenstein has escaped the noose and is now looking for a brain to go with his newly made body. Enjoyable sequel to *The Curse of Frankenstein* has Peter Cushing of course but also strong support from Francis Matthews and Michael Gwynn. There's a nice twist at the end too. (BR-Mill Creek as part of *Hammer Films: The Ultimate Collection: 20 Film Set*)

Revenge of the Creature (1955) 2.5
Pretty good sequel brings the Gill-man to Sea-World type establishment. Of course, he escapes and causes trouble. John Agar makes his first Universal horror appearance, as does Clint Eastwood as a lab tech. (BR-Universal as part of *Creature from the Black Lagoon: Complete Legacy Collection*)

Revenge of the Zombies (1943) 2.0
John Carradine is Nazi mad scientist who turns people into zombies. Title gives away the ending. Has an eerie mood and some interesting camera angles, plus Mantan Morland. But it's still low-budget boredom too often. (DVD-Timeless Media Group as part of *Horror Classics*)

Riders to the Stars (1954) 2.0
Scientists developing rocket technology want to study the outer hulls of full meteors to learn how they survive space travel. So, three scientists are sent individually into space to capture a meteor for study. Languidly paced Ivan Tors production with poor effects and one romantic subplot too many. Ending is sufficiently tense though. (NA)

The Ringer (1952) 2.5
Scotland Yard is after criminal mastermind with a gift for disguises who may be targeting his late sister's employer, a crooked lawyer. Well-cast, enjoyable if at times silly Edgar Wallace-based mystery. (DVD-R-Sinister Cinema)

Robot Monster (1953) 0.0
Aliens have practically annihilated Earth's *hu-man* population, save for one struggling family. So, an alien emissary is sent to finish them off, a task he struggles with. Mind-bogglingly awful film, with the budget of a Halloween party. The *Ro-man* of the title has admittedly become a classic '50s image: gorilla suit, diving helmet, and antennae. But the film is turgid (love those Ro-man monologues and ponderings) and arid. (DVD-Image)

The Robot vs. the Aztec Mummy (1959) 1.0
Dr. Krupp builds a robot with a human inside to combat the Aztec Mummy. Barely a movie, as the first 10 minutes or so just recaps the first two Aztec Mummy films leaving about 50 minutes for this story. At least the hero doctor has married his fiancée in this one. Last and least of the Aztec Mummy trilogy. (DVD-BCI/Eclipse as part of *The Aztec Mummy Collection*)

Rocketship X-M (1950) 2.0
Good cast in dramatically stiff story of first manned trip to the moon. When the rocket is thrown off course, the real drama starts. Decent effects but attempts at character development are strained. Lloyd Bridges' character is a bit too smug. Bleak ending however has quite an impact. (DVD-Image)

Rodan (1957) 2.0
Two giant flying reptiles terrorize the skies of Japan. There is also a cache of oversized prehistoric insects causing trouble in a mine. Average *kaiju eiga* with love affair inconvenienced by lots of explosions. Released in Japan in 1956, the American version was released a year later. (DVD-Classic Media with *The War of the Gargantuas*)

Rome Against Rome (1964) 2.0
John Drew Barrymore plays sinister magician who worships jewel-eyed statue goddess, building an army on her behalf (including soldiers he raises from the dead) that will help him take over Rome. His femme fatale partner uses a voodoo doll and frames the hero for murder. Fair hybrid of horror and Italian peplum genres has some fine atmosphere and a hammy Barrymore, but also poorly integrates stock footage during

key battle scene, spoiling things somewhat. Aired as *Night Star: Goddess of Electra*. (DVD-Substance)

Room 13 (1964) 2.5
Respectable Lord hires PI to protect his daughter who has been threatened by gangsters, former associates of dear old dad who need him for latest crime. Meanwhile, a razor-wielding maniac is on the loose. There's an enjoyable game of cat-and-mouse that ensues between detective and mob boss, especially once the daughter is kidnapped. But psycho subplot is superfluous and obvious. (DVD-R-Sinister Cinema)

Rosemary's Baby (1968) 4.0
Guy and Rosemary Woodhouse move into a building that has a history of witchcraft. Rosemary discovers that evil still exists there-and threatens her baby. What makes this film so powerful is its utter believability, as director Roman Polanski tells this as realistically as possible without making one false step. The film features one of the subtlest, most beautifully chilling endings in horror film history. Excellent performances. (BR-Criterion)

Ruby (1977) 2.0
1951: Former gangster-gal Ruby owns a drive-in that manages to screen 1958's *Attack of the 50 Foot Woman* and is staffed by paroled ex-gang members. Now, Ruby's murdered ex-lover wants vengeance against those very same people who double-crossed him 15 years ago. Starts out as a ghost story and then unnecessarily tosses in elements from *The Exorcist*. The result is something of a mess, although the film has its moments. (BR-VCI)

Run Stranger Run (1973) 2.5
Although Darren "Kolchak" McGavin directed some episodic television, this is his only theatrical effort behind the camera. The fishing village Malone Bay has been plagued by several disappearances. Then an adoptee shows up in search of his birth parents, and gruesome murders begin. Unusual mix of drama and horror is a well-acted, slow-burn thriller with a hell of a "discover the bodies" scene and a nail-biting finish. The secret of the birth father is no real surprise though. Simon "Vincenzo" Oakland plays the town sheriff. (VHS-RCA/Columbia)

The Saga of the Viking Women and Their Voyage to the Waters of the Great Sea Serpent (1957) 1.5
Group of Viking women go searching for their men who have been missing for three years. A sea serpent attack and lightning bolt leave them stranded on an island with whip-bearing males. Starts out fine, but once the women are captured by the Grimaults, things go downhill quickly. We are subjected to a whiney prince and dull political machinations. (DVD-Lionsgate with *Teenage Caveman*)

Samson in the Wax Museum (1963) 2.0
In the basement of his wax museum, mad Dr. Karol displays Mr. Hyde, Frankenstein's monster, the Phantom of the Opera, and Quasimodo, among others. He wants to add a panther woman to his gallery, so he arranges the kidnapping of a pretty photographer whom he will transform. To avert suspicion, he foolishly asks Samson to help prove he's being framed for the disappearance! There's a nifty if derivative plot here sandwiched in between wrestling scenes. But the film is more talk than action and lacks the atmosphere of the best Mexican horrors. Good finale though. (DVD-Beverly Wilshire)

Samson vs. the Vampire Women (1962) 2.5
After a 200-year slumber a group of vampires in league with Satan himself plan to kidnap professor's daughter who bears a vampire birthmark. To protect his child the doc summons Samson (or Santo if you prefer), the wrestler in the silver mask. This Mexican blend of horror and action features a marvelous opening 13 or so minutes, laying on the atmosphere with a shadowy appearance by the devil! Then they go and spoil things with a lengthy wrestling match curiously shot from a distance, which severely curtails the drama. These Santo pictures are certainly of a particular time and need to be appreciated as such. In that regard, the horror elements are terrific, even if the story itself is nothing groundbreaking. (DVD-Beverly Wilshire)

Santa Claus Conquers the Martians (1964) 1.0
The title suggests an all-out battle between the man in red and fabled little green men. We should be so lucky. Martians kidnap Santa so he can bring joy to their sad offspring. Not everyone approves of the plan. Virtually joyless kiddie fare is a slog for adults, with Dropo's "comedy" quite the opposite of relief. (BR-Kino)

Sasquatch: The Legend of Bigfoot (1976) 1.5
Alleged docudrama about expedition in search of legendary creature. Beautifully photographed but incredibly stilted effort bores its audience with details of the journey we don't care about. There are some animal attacks, nervous horses, playful varmints, point of view shots, and insistent music cues before we finally encounter Bigfoot. The final attack on camp is appropriately frenzied but it's too little too late. (BR-Code Red with *Encounter with the Unknown*)

The Satanic Rites of Dracula (1973) 1.0
Christopher Lee's final appearance as Dracula for Hammer is a dismal affair. Dracula plans to release a plague upon the world with help of Satanic cult, as British agents and Van Helsing (Peter Cushing) try to stop him. Dracula spends most of the film tucked away in an office; the evil rituals seem more about nudity than anything else. Hammer just couldn't make a Dracula film set in modern times work. (BR-Warner Archive)

Satanik (1968) 1.0
Doctor has perfected cell regeneration serum with the nasty side effect of making subject susceptible to their primordial instincts. His assistant who's disfigured kills the doctor and takes the drug anyway. Although she does indeed become beautiful, she apparently never saw *The Leech Woman* and thus must take the drug again while committing the occasional murder. Poorly done thriller with zero characterization, unexplained

plot points, and lousy ending. Magda Konopka is a stunning anti-hero, however. (DVD-Retromedia)

Satan's Cheerleaders (1977) 0.5
One of the worst films ever: a movie that tries to be campy and so-bad-it's-good, which of course means it's just awful. Satanists kidnap four cheerleaders and their coach who are on their way to a football game. John Ireland as the chief Satanist looks bored; Yvonne DeCarlo as his wife looks embarrassed; and John Carradine (as a bum) looks amused. Unfunny, unsexy, not scary, and torture to sit through. If this is the best Satan can do for his team, God's doesn't have anything to worry about. There *is* a mild twist at the end. (BR-VCI)

Satan's Satellites (1958) 1.5
Rocket Man is back in this feature derived from Republic's 1952 serial *Zombies of the Stratosphere*. This time he's battling sparkly-dressed Martians who are plotting to blow Earth out of its orbit using an H-bomb. It's the usual Republic template of scientists plotting with the villains while the heroes and hired henchmen duke it out with fists and firearms. There are some underwater sequences including a brief knife battle. Leonard Nimoy plays an alien named Narab. (NA)

Satellite in the Sky (1956) 2.5
The first manned flight into outer space has ulterior motive: the testing of a nuclear bomb. Of course, things don't go as planned and the flight crew is placed in danger. Solid cast and effects propel this pretty good sci-fi effort. Takes a while to get going though; spends time on romantic subplots like so many other 1950s sci-fi films. (DVD-Warner Bros. with *World Without End*)

Saturn 3 (1980) 1.5
At the Saturn 3 experimental food station researchers/lovers Kirk Douglas and Farah Fawcett are visited by murderer Harvey Keitel, who arrives bearing mysterious container. In very short order, Keitel falls in lust with Fawcett and constructs intimidating robot Hector, who is going to take over for Douglas. But Hector has been "implanted' with Keitel's unstable mental state and soon runs amuck. With a cast like this and Stanley Donen credited as director, one expects great-or at least very good-things. Instead, one gets a good-looking but unengaging *Alien* variation with mostly aloof performances. (BR-Shout! Factory)

The Savage Curse (TV-1974) 2.0
American detective comes to small English village looking for his brother, who had fallen for a mysterious beauty with a *very* protective uncle. The pre-credits scene pretty much gives the ending away, although this outing does generate some interest in the fact the uncle is obsessed with Edgar Allan Poe. Original British title: *Kiss Me and Die*. (DVD-VEI as part of *Thriller: The Complete Collection*)

Scanners (1981) 3.5
Drug side effects are the cause behind a group of people with incredible psychic abilities. They cannot only read your mind,

they can also blow it up. Now, there is a battle waging between "good" scanners and "bad" ones, the latter group seeking world domination. Terrific David Cronenberg horror/sci-fi blends many interesting ideas with state-of-the-art effects. (BR-Criterion)

Scared Stiff (1953) 2.5
This remake of *The Ghost Breakers* finds Dean Martin in the Bob Hope role and Jerry Lewis as his bumbling friend. Martin, on the lam from gangsters, decides to help a damsel in distress (Lizabeth Scott) when threats are made against her regarding her newly-inherited-and maybe haunted-Cuban estate. Not as funny as the original, but fans of silly comedies will find laughs here. Lewis has some funny moments, such as talking to himself in a mirror during a should-I-or-shouldn't-I-help-my-friend scene. But with the song interludes and some unnecessary subplots (one involving Carmen Miranda) the film is overlong at 108 minutes. (DVD-Paramount as part of *Dean Martin & Jerry Lewis Collection: Volume One*)

Scared to Death (1947) 1.0
Bela Lugosi's only color horror film is a badly directed and edited mystery that takes place at private clinic presided over by George Zucco. A corpse tells us the story of how she was murdered. Scenes featuring Lugosi and Zucco (who play cousins!) offer some fun for classic horror buffs, as does a figure in a green mask. But the nonsensical script is so bad it ruins everything. Lugosi does have some great dialogue such as, "If I allowed myself to be announced, I doubt I would be received anywhere." (DVD-Lumivision with *The Devil Bat*)

Scared to Death (1980) 1.5
"Some sticky substance" is found at various brutal murder scenes, baffling police, who turn to retired detective for help. The villain turns out to be a synthesized genetic organism (or monster). While the attack scenes work well enough in this low-budget affair, our main character mistakes obnoxious for charming, making most of the first hour an endurance test. Below-average performances don't help things either. The later pursuit through the sewers, however, offers some excitement. (DVD-Retromedia)

The Scarlet Claw (1944) 3.5
Sherlock Holmes and Dr. Watson travel to Canada's La Morte Rouge to solve the vicious murder of Lady Penrose, whose killer is believed to be legendary phantom. The "monster" effect is very good and the atmosphere flawless. Great cast too. Only weakness is the contrived script, that has all the killer's targets conveniently settle in the same place. Martin Scorsese may have borrowed the "housekeeper sequence" for a similar murder scene in his *Cape Fear* remake. (BR-MPI as part of *The Complete Sherlock Holmes Collection*)

The Scarlet Clue (1945) 2.5
Various murders set at radio station tied to espionage plot. This Charlie Chan outing features fatal elevator and a very funny running gag involving Mantan Moreland and his friend, who manage to know exactly what the other is going

to say before they say it. (DVD-MGM as part of *The Charlie Chan Chanthology*)

Scars of Dracula (1970) 2.5
Several young people end up staying at Count Dracula's castle and not all of them live to regret it. Christopher Lee's last period Dracula before entering the 20th century is typical Hammer fare: attractive production, buxom beauties, frightened villagers, and Lee in fine form. Dracula is particularly vicious in this one: he beats and burns his servant; stabs a traitorous bride; and sends bats to attack those hiding in a church (the gruesome aftermath is quite memorable). Overly familiar script beats lessen film's impact. (BR-Shout! Factory)

Scream and Scream Again (1969) 2.5
Vincent Price, Christopher Lee, and Peter Cushing get top billing in this mad scientist thriller. But they have no scenes together and Price and Lee share the screen briefly only during the finale. The tale concerns transplant experiments to create super race. Interesting approach by director Gordon Hessler has seemingly unrelated story lines join as film progresses. Not great but above average. (BR-Kino)

Scream of Fear (1961) 3.0
Hammer's first entry in its post-*Psycho* series of black-and-white thrillers is its best. Young woman goes to visit her father, whom she has not seen in nine years, only to find that he may have been murdered. Or is she just going mad? Some nice twists in Jimmy Sangster's script are aided by good performances and crisp photography. (BR-Mill Creek as part of *Hammer Films: The Ultimate Collection: 20 Film Set*)

Scream of the Demon Lover (1970) 1.5
Biochemist Dr. Ivanna Rakowsky shows up as agreed to assist baron with experiments. She soon learns, however, that her employer's brother burned to death in his laboratory while on the verge of discovering something that would "make you live forever." Now, six women who spent time at the baron's castle have been viciously murdered. Will Ivanna be next? For an obviously brilliant person Ivanna makes several stupid decisions just to keep the labored plot moving towards unsurprising climax. There are some nice Gothic touches along the way, but this is for Euro-sleaze fans only. (DVD-Retromedia as *Blood Castle*)

Screamer (TV-1974) 2.5
After a young woman is attacked, she starts seeing her tormentor's face everywhere. Pretty good *Thriller* entry is largely predictable, right down to its "surprise" ending. (DVD-VEI as part of *Thriller: The Complete Collection*)

Screamers (1979) 2.5
The ads promised, "You will actually see a man turned inside out." No, you won't. What you *will* see is a well-cast variation on *The Island of Dr. Moreau*, concerning doctor who turns humans into fishmen. There's also an evil businessman who's using the mutants to retrieve lost treasure of Atlantis. Moody and atmospheric Italian-made thriller was re-edited for American audiences, with an effective 12-minute opening sequence with gore and beheadings added. The original version, *Island of the Fishmen*, is available on Blu-Ray from Full Moon. (BR-Scorpion Releasing)

The Screaming Skull (1958) 2.5
Newlyweds move into the home of the husband's first wife, who died in a tragic accident. Is her ghost responsible for tormenting the new bride? Despite a cast of only five and just one or two sets, this low-budget effort is nevertheless an occasionally successful-spooker because it's so darn creepy. And yes: a skull does scream. (BR-Shout! Factory)

The Secret of the Black Trunk (1962) 2.5
A baffling series of murders plagues London. The victims come back to their rooms to find their bags packed, and when they leave are promptly knifed in the back by an expert thrower. The motive may be tied to the illegal drug Mescadrine. The first in a series of German *krimis* based on the novels of Bryan Edgar Wallace, this sufficiently atmospheric and complex outing features one coincidence too many when all is said and done. Towards the end, there's a nice sequence in the bowels of a castle. (DVD-R-Sinister Cinema)

The Secret of the Black Widow (1963) 2.0
How's this for a murder weapon: an air pistol whose darts are tipped with poisoned rubber black widows?! Series of murders is connected to a South American treasure expedition where one of the participants died from a black widow bite. An obnoxious reporter investigates while romancing the prime suspect. So badly dubbed that it's painful to listen to at times, this German *krimi* features several familiar faces such as Klaus Kinski, Eddi Arent, and Karin Dor. Decent plot handled in routine fashion with lively finale. (DVD-Televista)

Secret of the Blue Room (1933) 2.5
Pretty good mystery of three suitors trying to win the hand of Gloria Stuart by spending the night in a haunted room. Red herrings abound, and Lionel Atwill makes his debut in a Universal horror film. But to this viewer it was obvious how this was going to play out (it wouldn't have made sense any other way). (BR-Kino)

Secret of the Chateau (1934) 2.0
Ho-hum mystery about a ringing bell predicting death. But it's really about the theft of a valuable Gutenberg Bible and the people who might have stolen it. Claire Dodd is fine as a thief trying to go straight but her male suitor is as bland as a rice cake. (NA)

The Secret of the Chinese Carnation (1964) 2.5
Various parties are after a piece of microfilm and a missing professor whose fuel formula threatens the world's energy producers. More spy thriller than mystery flick, the killers in this are just as dumb as those in any James Bond outing: instead of just shooting the heroes, they tie them up and set a bomb, which of course doesn't work. Klaus Kinski plays thug who works for the owner of "The Chinese Carnation" nightclub,

where a brawl is played mostly for laughs (the microfilm is stuck to the bottom of fishnet stockinged waitress). Climaxes with hair-raising rescue from moving car. (NA)

The Secret of the Red Orchid (1962) 2.0
Former Chicago gangsters have set up shop in London, threatening the wealthy if they don't pay for protection. Fortunately, FBI agent Christopher Lee joins Scotland Yard in hunting down the criminals. Getting used to an American-dubbed Lee takes some time in this German *krimi*. But the real problem is the repetitive nature of the film: someone refuses to pay, that someone dies. Secret villain is obvious too. Eddi Arent gets some laughs as the "Death Butler" whose employers keep getting killed. (DVD-Image with *Monster of London City*)

The Secret of the Telegian (1960) 2.5
Soldier who was left for dead 14 years ago gets revenge on those who betrayed him with the aid of a teleportation machine. Science writer plays reporter to get to the truth. Interesting blend of science fiction and detective procedural features a villain who at first might seem sympathetic but is quite ruthless, delighting in hurting anyone who crosses him. Atmospheric music score helps too. (NA)

The Sentinel (1977) 2.5
Model moves into New York apartment with creepy neighbors and a cat that wears party hats only to discover she and a blind priest who stares out the window all day are the sole occupants. The story is good and compelling, and there are several nifty shocks. But Gil Mellé's score is overbearing, and director Michael Winner is better suited to action pictures. (BR-Shout! Factory)

Serpent Island (1954) 0.0
Great-granddaughter of man who discovered a million dollars in gold treasure thinks she knows where to find it. So, she hires a couple of seafaring studs to help her; gets caught up in voodoo and battle of testosterone. Lousy adventure thriller shot on the cheap certainly looks it. Awful performances, especially from female lead Mary Munday, but then her character is poorly written. First film for Bert I. Gordon, who's credited as producer, director of photography, and supervising editor. (DVD-VCI with *Monster from the Ocean Floor*)

The Seventh Victim (1943) 3.0
When her sister disappears, a boarding school student investigates and finds murder and witchcraft. Yet another winner from Val Lewton with interesting plot and sympathetic performances. Features another terrifying lonely walk at night and a shower scene that's almost as scary as the one in that film from 1960. Fun fact: features Tom Conway as Dr. Judd-the character that was presumably killed in *Cat People*. (DVD-Warner Bros. as part of *The Val Lewton Horror Collection*)

The Severed Arm (1973) 1.5
Five years ago, six pals went cave exploring and got trapped for over two weeks. Fearing starvation, they cut off one of their bud's arms but were rescued before having the chance to dine. They lie and say they cut off Ted's arm because it was crushed during the rock collapse. Now, someone is out for revenge. Eerie with some effective death scenes. But, also poorly paced and nonsensical. (BR-Vinegar Syndrome)

Sh! The Octopus (1937) 2.0
Two bumbling detectives are on the trail of notorious criminal known as the Octopus, who's just murdered his latest victim at lighthouse during the proverbial thunderstorm. There are eyes peering through peepholes, a body dangling from above, large tentacles that threaten to attack, and a great reveal of the villain. But since this is a comedy, it should have been funnier. (DVD-R-Warner Archive as part of *Warner Bros. Horror/Mystery Double Features*)

Shadow of Chinatown (1936) 1.0
Feature version of Bela Lugosi serial. He plays scientist hired to cause problems in Chinatown since it's taking business away from the competition. Thoroughly disposable bore with Lugosi giving a less than enthusiastic performance. (DVD-Mill Creek as part of *Nightmare Worlds: 50 Movie Pack*)

Shadow of Evil (1964) 2.0
Second entry in France's OSS 117 series of the 1960s, their answer to James Bond. Agent is gunned down in Thailand while investigating plague outbreak tied to cholera vaccinations. OSS 117 is sent to find out what's going on; encounters sinister Dr. Sinn and the "Elected People." Not particularly exciting spy flick despite boat chase, ticking car bomb, and various fistfights. The tension just isn't there. Original title: *Panic in Bangkok*. (BR-Kino as part of *OSS 117: Five Film Collection*)

Shadow of Fear (TV-1974) 2.5
Woman comes home from fancy dinner to find her house vandalized and her name written in red lipstick on the mirror-and that's just the beginning. Given the limited budget and cast, this story can play out in only one of two ways, so the ending isn't that much of a surprise. Strong cast keeps the viewer interested. (DVD-MPI with *Nightmare at 43 Hillcrest*)

Shadow of Terror (1945) 2.5
Thieves toss research chemist from moving train after stealing his top-secret formula Solanite. He survives but now has amnesia. That presents a problem when the baddies realize they still need to know the catalytic agent. Not-bad little PRC programmer has likeable leads, fast pace, and slimy villain. Emmett Lynn is a bit much though as Gabby Hayes-type obsessed with pajamas. (NA)

The Shadow of the Cat (1961) 2.5
While she reads "The Raven" aloud to her pet kitty Tabitha wealthy woman is beaten to death by her servant on the orders of her husband. Tabitha sees the whole thing and plots revenge. Sure, it sounds silly. But director John Gilling milks the atmosphere for all its worth, and the fine cast is game. (BR-Shout! Factory as part of *Universal Horror Collection: Volume 6*)

Shadow of the Hawk (1976) 2.0
Jan-Michael Vincent is having bizarre hallucinations involving scary tribal mask; learns they're connected to his Native American heritage and that he must help his grandfather fight vengeful witch. Demon cars, possessed snakes, angry bears, and treacherous bridges are just some of the unspectacular perils faced in this clunky and rather tired affair. Some attractive location work helps. (BR-Mill Creek with *Nightwing*)

The Shanghai Cobra (1945) 2.0
Charlie Chan is after escaped criminal who uses cobra venom as means of murder; gets involved in standard bank robbery plot. OK Chan mystery. (DVD-MGM as part of *The Charlie Chan Chanthology*)

Sharad of Atlantis (1966) 1.5
Feature version of the 1936 serial *Undersea Kingdom*. While investigating earthquake activity using mini-sub, explorers discover lost city of Atlantis and become involved in forthcoming war that threatens not only the underwater city but also the land above! Plenty of wrestling and fistfights in this below-average fantasy, largely due to lacking performances. Lon Chaney, Jr. is one of the villains. The entire serial is available from Alpha Video. (NA)

She (1965) 2.5
Hammer Film Productions' "lost city" fantasy about immortal beauty (Ursula Andress) falling in love with British war vet whom she believes is the reincarnation of her deceased beau. Christopher Lee is a jealous high priest; Peter Cushing is an amused professor; and Andress is a lovely antagonist is this overlong but engaging tale. (DVD-R-Warner Archive)

She Beast (1966) 2.0
Barbara Steele is honeymooning in Transylvania when a car accident results in vengeful witch possessing her. The ugly hag then starts murdering the locals. The film has fun with the Dracula legend, making the Van Helsing family exorcists. In fact, most of the characters are comical, resulting in an odd mix of humor and horror. Some effectively staged shock sequences, but one must wait quite a while for them to arrive. (BR-Raro Video as *Revenge of the Blood Beast*)

The She-Creature (1956) 2.0
Chester Morris, ole' Boston Blackie himself, plays a hypnotist/mentalist who regresses subject to her earliest life, where apparently she was a vicious monster. This prehistoric self emerges from the sea and commits murder, which Morris uses to his advantage. Tom Conway, who played the Falcon in several 1940s films, is one of the potential victims, and his scenes with Morris are the film's non-monster highlights. The she-creature is a great looking monster, and the atmosphere is relentlessly gloomy. The story, however, is little more than a variation on Svengali and becomes repetitive, as well as being highly predictable. (DVD-Lionsgate with *Day the World Ended*)

She Demons (1958) 1.0
Four shipwreck survivors find themselves on an island where former Nazi mad scientist is conducting bizarre experiments, the side effect of which is to turn beautiful women into title creatures. Shoddy, poorly acted effort that will raise not a hair on your back but may force your butt to get up and leave the room. (DVD-Image)

She Devil (1957) 1.5
Doctor tests miracle serum on dying patient (Mari Blanchard); it saves her life but turns her cold, violent, and seemingly immortal. She can even will her hair to change color when needed! Interesting premise blandly explored; Blanchard's portrayal of evil is rather blasé, which is in line with the film's overall flatness. (BR-Olive)

She Gods of Shark Reef (1958) 0.0
Two brothers are stranded on island with female shark cult. Since one is being sought for murder, they both don't want to wait the 10 days for a ship to pass by. Trouble ensues when they try to get one of the women to help them. Awful Roger Corman-directed quickie is dreadfully paced talk-fest that is all scenery and little else. It's impossible to care what's going on. (DVD-Mill Creek as part of *Horror Classics: 100 Movie Pack*)

She-Wolf of London (1946) 2.0
Young woman thinks she's the notorious wolf woman murdering people in turn-of-the-century London. A well-maintained atmosphere makes this watchable. But the film cheats by having the killer make wolfish sounds which makes no sense when all is said and done. (BR-Universal as part of *The Wolf Man: Complete Legacy Collection*)

The Shining (1980) 3.5
Jack Nicholson gives a tour-de-force (or delightfully over-the-top, if you prefer) performance as a man who starts to lose his hold on reality when he and his family agree to watch over a deserted resort during the winter. Thoroughly engrossing film is alternately funny and scary and features a trio of strong performances from the leads. Danny Lloyd is especially impressive as the young psychic boy who senses the danger. (BR-Warner Bros.)

Shock Treatment (1964) 2.5
Prosecutor who thinks murderer of wealthy spinster faked insanity hires actor to go undercover at asylum to see if killer may have stashed a fortune at the murder house. Lauren Bacall plays a psychiatrist who is after the money too. Well-acted eerie, creepy thriller has two great plot turns near the end. The final twist is unconvincing and too convenient, however. Great score by Jerry Goldsmith. (NA)

Shriek of the Mutilated (1974) 0.0
A professor takes four college students on a Yeti hunt. Most of them end up dead. And there's a twist to the story that no one will care about in this poorly acted, directed, scripted, edited, and everything else piece of garbage. Stupefyingly awful film has nothing to recommend it. (DVD-Retromedia)

The Shuttered Room (1967) 2.0
Carol Lynley returns to her parents' abandoned home and discovers a terrifying secret in this predictable adaptation of

a novel by August Derleth and H.P. Lovecraft. Nothing really happens until the climax and the local villagers are clichéd redneck types. (DVD-Warner Bros. with *It!*)

Silent Night, Bloody Night (1972) 2.5
Shortly after an asylum inmate escapes, various townspeople start getting mysterious phone calls from person claiming to be Marianne, who asks them to join "her" at unoccupied estate. Extremely moody thriller features a complex plot, axe murders, and John Carradine. Some of the performances are uneven but the film has much to recommend it. (DVD-Code Red with *Invasion of the Blood Farmers*)

Silent Running (1972) 3.5
After spending eight years tending what's left of Earth's forest-life aboard the spacecraft Valley Forge, Freeman Lowell (Bruce Dern), as well as the rest of the crew, is given orders to destroy the flora and return home. Lowell doesn't approve and takes drastic measures to save what he loves. Engrossing story and impressive effects combine to make this a memorable, one-of-a-kind picture. Dern is sympathetic despite his actions. (BR-Arrow)

Sisters (1973) 3.5
Chilling Brian De Palma thriller about separated Siamese twins (Margot Kidder), one of whom is a psychopathic killer. Co-writer/director De Palma combines elements of *Psycho*, *Rear Window*, and other Hitchcock classics but makes this his own. Bravura filmmaking with outstanding Bernard Herrmann score. (BR-Criterion)

The Skull (1965) 3.0
Peter Cushing collects antiquities related to the occult and purchases the skull of the Marquis de Sade; horror ensues. Director Freddie Francis creates a sustained atmosphere of dread and suspense; this is one of the best visualizations of a living nightmare ever caught on screen. Cushing's performance is a tour de force, frequently carrying scenes sans dialogue. He'd have made a great silent film star. Christopher Lee is in the cast too. (BR-Kino)

Sky Above Heaven (1965) 2.5
Military crew aboard aircraft carrier learns a mysterious satellite, perhaps alien in origin, hovers above them. Not all the men think the visitor means harm, creating additional tension as the world's Great Powers (primarily the US and Russia) decide what to do. Beautifully shot French thriller is very talky for the first hour or so before people spring into action while panic rises. Not much in the way of fancy effects as the satellite is little more than a fast-moving orange flare. The film nevertheless becomes quite gripping. Reportedly, the American dub track to this is currently lost. There is a non-English friendly Region 2 French DVD available. (NA)

Slaughter of the Vampires (1964) 2.0
A vampire sets his sights on the mistress of the castle in which he is hiding, much to the chagrin of her husband. Attractive looking film is rather routine in the story department; the main vampire isn't particularly memorable. (DVD-MPI)

Slaves of the Invisible Monster (1966) 1.0
This is a squished version of the 1950 serial *The Invisible Monster*. The Phantom Ruler and his thugs abduct illegal immigrants to help in his plan of world domination, which he hopes to accomplish via an invisible army. He has a special formula that when applied to clothing and then exposed to a spotlight renders him invisible. A dull insurance agent however is hot on their trail. One can stand only so many tired fistfights and gunfights in a film before total boredom sets in. Maybe if the Phantom Ruler had been a compelling villain this might have been fun. He's not, so this isn't. Now if those two dogs had gotten into a brawl…(The entire serial is available on Blu-Ray from Olive Films)

Sleepwalker (TV-1975) 3.0
Daughter of vacationing horror novelist walks in her sleep, and thinks she's had a premonition of murder. Nicely plotted *Thriller* episode benefits from good performances and satisfying conclusion. (DVD-VEI as part of *Thriller: The Complete Collection*)

The Slime People (1963) 0.5
Goo-covered creatures emerge from the sewers of Los Angeles, create "fog dome" to trap inhabitants, and then start attacking. Poorly paced, flat, dreary sci-fi features first-year-in-drama-class acting. The monsters *are* cool-looking; it's a darn shame they weren't in a better movie. (DVD-VCI with *The Crawling Hand*)

The Smiling Ghost (1941) 2.5
Wayne Morris plays a broke engineer who unwittingly agrees to be the bait to capture the title fiend. Enjoyable horror/comedy/mystery has good characters and a genial atmosphere that holds one's interest, even if the overall film is nothing special. (DVD-R-Warner Archive as part of *Warner Bros. Horror/Mystery Double Features*)

Snake People (1971) 0.0
One of the four notorious Mexican films Boris Karloff shot before his death in 1969, although his ill health forced him to shoot his scenes in Hollywood. He plays wealthy island plantation owner asked to assist new police captain in cracking down on voodoo practices. Karloff's screen time is limited, and he's fine, as expected. However, the film is dull, monotonous, and quite awful. (DVD-Retromedia as *Isle of the Snake People*)

The Snow Creature (1954) 1.0
Botanist tells us how he led a Himalayan expedition, captured a Yeti, brought it back to the US, and then watched as it escaped and wreaked havoc. Static, bland chronicle of mythical monster. Cinematographer Floyd Crosby would do much better work with Roger Corman and company in the 1960s. (DVD-Retromedia as part of *Sasquatch Horror Triple Feature*)

The Snow Devils (1967) 1.5
Some "unknown horror" smashes the window of a Himalayan weather station and kills everyone inside. Was it the legendary yeti? An investigatory team investigates. Yet another story about aliens wanting to take over Earth is all over the

map, but ultimately has little to distinguish it. The villains look rather silly and don't inspire fear. (DVD-R-Warner Archive)

Snowbeast (TV-1977) 1.5
As a Colorado ski resort prepares for its 50th annual winter carnival, a bigfoot/yeti creature decides to attack the citizenry. Unforgivably dull *Jaws* clone that features mostly point of view shots as the little-seen monster prepares to strike. Corny subplot of former Olympic champion trying to find purpose in his life just serves to pad the thin story. (BR-Retromedia)

Sombra, the Spider Woman (1966) 2.0
In this feature version of the 1947 serial *The Black Widow*, several poisoned corpses are tied to Asian spy ring trying to secure rocket fuel formula, their goal being world domination. Newspaper owner brings in mystery writer to help solve the puzzle. Not bad melding of crime and sci-fi, with some clever plotting to offset the usual fisticuffs and car chases. (NA)

Someone at the Top of the Stairs (TV-1973) 3.0
Two young women take a room at a boarding house where floorboards creak nightly and people write "Help me" on the doors. The other "marvelous" occupants sure seem friendly. Nicely mounted what-the-heck-is-going-on chiller with nasty final twist. (DVD-VEI as part of *Thriller: The Complete Collection*)

The Son of Dr. Jekyll (1951) 2.0
Dr. Jekyll's kid plans to clear his father's name by conducting his own experiments. Then the murders begin. Handsome, well-cast Columbia production suffers from lack of a compelling story. It's more mystery than horror, and the villain is revealed too soon. (NA)

Son of Dracula (1943) 3.0
Horror noir that redefines the femme fatale. Woman is obsessed with mysterious Count Alucard (Lon Chaney, Jr.) who's come to settle down in Louisiana. It seems she's about to jilt her fiancé, but all is not what it seems. Chaney isn't that good; he seems to be in a daze most of the film. But everything else about this original take on vampires is top notch, including those great bat transformations and the use of mist. (BR-Universal as part of *Dracula: Complete Legacy Collection*)

Son of Frankenstein (1939) 3.5
Terrific second sequel to *Frankenstein* has first son of famed doctor discovering the monster still lives! The best things about the film, character wise, are Bela Lugosi's Ygor and Lionel Atwill's Inspector Krogh. Karloff's Monster is basically Ygor's puppet, but Karloff still has some great moments. The scenes between Basil Rathbone and Lugosi really crackle. Great sets and music too. (BR-Universal as part of *Frankenstein: Complete Legacy Collection*)

Son of Godzilla (1967) 2.5
Thanks to weather experiments gone awry, giant mantises threaten Godzilla's offspring. There's a giant spider to contend with too. Cute entry that doesn't involve the famed monster attacking defenseless villagers; he's just protecting his kid. (BR-Criterion as part of *Godzilla: The Showa-Era Films, 1954–1975*)

Son of Kong (1933) 2.5
Carl Denham is broke, and dodging subpoenas, so he hops aboard a ship and ultimately returns to Kong Island and finds…Well, you can guess. Nowhere near the quality of the original. The effects are good enough to make this at least watchable. (BR-Warner Bros.)

The Sorcerers (1967) 2.5
Boris Karloff plays scientist who, along with his wife, can dominate the will and actions of young swinger. They get to experience his sensations. Things get out of hand when wifey wants dangerous thrills. Decent thriller from director Michael Reeves has much action but it doesn't connect emotionally. Ian Ogilvy is good as the guinea pig. (DVD-R-Warner Archive)

Sorry, Wrong Number (1948) 3.0
Spoiled rich woman (Barbara Stanwyck) confined to her bed overhears a murder plot while trying to make a phone call. She then attempts to warn people in hopes of saving the would-be victim; discovers troubling facts about her husband. Hits the ground running with pauses for character/plot-establishing flashbacks. Stanwyck is excellent as unsympathetic lead in this well-regarded nail-biter. (DVD-Paramount)

SOS Coast Guard (1942) 2.5
This feature version of the 1937 Republic serial of the same name stars Bela Lugosi (in his only role during the 1937-1938 "horror ban") as scientist developing radioactive disintegration gas for nefarious foreign nation. When he guns down a coast guard member during a rescue mission at sea, the victim's brother swears to bring him to justice. Most serials don't lend themselves to being reformatted but this one is pretty good, if expectedly choppy, offering enough varied action scenes so that it never gets redundant. Lugosi is his reliable self as the villain. (DVD-R-Alpha)

The Soul of a Monster (1944) 2.0
When science is unable to save beloved doctor from dying, his desperate wife unknowingly summons evil emissary who seemingly performs a miracle. Recovered hubby starts acting strangely; around him, dogs bark and flowers wilt. The title gives away the reason. Mundane script given some life by director Will Jason, who employs the Val Lewton approach in key terror scenes. (DVD-R-Sony)

Soylent Green (1973) 2.5
Set in New York 2022 when overpopulation has made food scarce, Charlton Heston investigates the murder of food-producing company executive who was most likely assassinated. His dedication to the case puts his life in peril and leads to shocking revelation. Intriguing, well-cast sci-fi mystery holds one's attention. But the film is also aloof, and Heston isn't the warmest actor. Edward G. Robinson on the other hand is quite powerful in his last theatrical feature. (BR-Warner Bros.)

Space Monster (1965) 1.5

While aboard *Hope I* en route to Taurus, quartet must land on unfamiliar planet's ocean floor to avoid meteor shower. As repairs are made, romance blooms and then "horrible-looking" creatures (five-ton crabs) attack. Sluggish, grating effort will offend the politically correct with its treatment of woman scientist. Original title: *Space Probe-Taurus*. (NA)

Spaceways (1953) 2.0
Scientist is suspected of murdering his wife and her lover and then hiding the bodies on just-launched rocket. The accused decides to prove his innocence by sending a second rocket to retrieve the first, with him on it! Competent performances are the saving grace of this tepid Hammer Film Productions drama. Most of the runtime is spent setting up a rushed finale. (DVD-Image)

The Spaniard's Curse (1958) 2.0
A man sentenced to death for a murder he claims he didn't commit places a curse on all those he blames for his conviction. When the foreman of the jury dies in a freak accident, the trial judge's daughter teams with the victim's brother to find the true killer. Intriguing idea for a horror whodunit doesn't come off due to lackluster performances and casual approach. (DVD-R-Sinister Cinema)

The Spectre of Edgar Allan Poe (1974) 2.0
Poe's (Robert Walker, Jr.) love Lenore dies in his arms-or so he thinks. She's buried alive but luckily, he hears her cries and frees her, her hair now completely white. She's put into a private asylum run by Cesar Romero, where a shaggy inmate commits multiple murders. Walker sure looks the part, and there are snakes, an axe-wielding maniac, and much creepiness as various characters wander halls as thunder booms outside. Sluggish pacing, however, blunts effectiveness. (VHS-Unicorn)

Spell of Evil (TV-1973) 2.0
Witch marries wealthy widower, perhaps with the intention of becoming a widow herself. Routine handling of familiar material. (DVD-VEI as part of *Thriller: The Complete Collection*)

The Spider (1945) 2.0
In New Orleans, woman hires private detective to exchange her valuable brooch for mystery envelope. Instead, he becomes murder suspect when his crooked partner is found strangled. Mantan Moreland provides comedy relief and Martin Kosleck skulks about acting guilty in this routine and obvious programmer. The budget is so cheap they don't even show what should have been an exciting sequence: The PI's escape from police custody. Title comes from phony mind reader known as The Spider Woman. (NA)

The Spider (1958) 2.0
Director Bert I. Gordon's teen take on *Tarantula*. On her birthday Carol wakes up to learn her father hasn't come home after going to get her a present. She and her boyfriend go looking for Dad and find giant spider instead. Soon it's wreaking havoc on the school and town. Iffy special effects and overbearing music score balanced by good performances and several suspenseful sequences. (BR-Shout! Factory)

The Spider Woman Strikes Back (1946) 1.5
Silly would-be thriller about woman (Gale Sondergaard) who pretends to be blind, so she can drain her hired companion's blood and feed it to her plant. Rondo Hatton is the mute henchman. Feels longer than its hour length. (BR-Kino)

The Spiral Staircase (1946) 3.5
Mute girl may be the next victim of a psycho who targets "imperfect" women. Terrific thriller with most of the action playing out in creepy mansion during a nighttime thunderstorm. (BR-Kino)

Spirits of the Dead (1968) 3.5
Three well-respected directors bring us a trilogy of Edgar Allan Poe tales. Roger Vadim is up first with "Metzengerstein" which concerns noblewoman who becomes obsessed with mysterious stallion. Louis Malle is up next with a story about hedonistic man who faces his justice-seeking doppelganger in "William Wilson." The final and best story, "Toby Damnit," is the work Frederico Fellini, who fills the screen with eye-popping imagery. Terence Stamp is a revolting film star whose reckless ways finally catch up with him. While the first two installments have their moments, it's the Fellini segment that makes this must-viewing. (DVD-Home Vision Entertainment)

Spooks Run Wild (1941) 2.0
Bela Lugosi's first teaming with the East Side Kids is endurable, but that's about it. Lugosi is suspected of being "the monster," an escaped murderer. Mugsy, Glimpy, Pee-Wee, et. al. try to capture him. It's harmless enough, with a laugh or two. Mainly this is for the Kids' fans. (DVD-VCI with *Ghosts on the Loose*)

Spy in the Sky! (1958) 1.5
In Vienna, United States agent hunts for kidnapped German scientist whom the Russians had work on their Sputnik satellite. Incredibly flat and dull spy drama fails to build any tension whatsoever. Competent performances. Features villain George Coulouris wearing a neck brace. (NA)

The Squeaker (1963) 2.5
Scotland Yard is after mysterious killer known as The Snake, whose poison of choice is snake venom. The trail leads to a zoologist and family of eccentrics. Klaus Kinski is the villain's henchman, who likes sleeping with animals. Killer is a bit too obvious this time out and the comedy relief intrusive. There are several good scenes, including a snake visiting a potential victim in his bed. (DVD-R-Sinister Cinema)

Squirm (1978) 2.5
An electrical cable comes lose during a storm, falls to the ground, and forces blood worms to leave the safety of the earth, attacking the citizenry on occasion. Enjoyable enough with likable leads and some gory moments. (BR-Shout! Factory)

Sssssss (1973) 3.0
Strother Martin plays the quintessential mad scientist who's performing horrific experiment on student volunteer. As the title suggests, it involves snakes, specifically, the king cobra. Anyone who gets in the doctor's way meets a reptilian fate. This was a favorite growing up and remains an entertaining throwback to sci-fi films of the 1950s. Martin is terrific, as is Patrick Williams' music score. The ending is effectively chilling and tragic. (BR-Shout! Factory)

Stanley (1972) 1.5
Vietnam veteran Tim lives with a cabin full of rattlesnakes in the Florida Everglades. Trouble begins when hammy villain Alex Rocco shows up wanting Tim to help trap snakes for their skins. Eventually Tim uses favorite snake Stanley to exact revenge. *Willard*-inspired dreck is overlong and underperformed, with silly plot turn involving Rocco's nubile daughter. Nicely shot though. (DVD-BCI Eclipse)

Star Odyssey (1979) 0.0
Awful Italian sci-fi about peanut butter cookie-faced alien leading an attack on Earth and those trying to stop him, including an odd group of wacky heroes, a telepathic scientist, and two cute robots that bicker and contemplate suicide. The *Star Wars* influences abound but to little avail in this colossal test of one's patience. (DVD-R-VCI)

Star Pilot (1966) 0.5
Aliens stranded on Earth for two years force scientific team to help them repair their space vehicle. They all journey to visitors' home planet; the trip doesn't go as planned. Poor Italian space saga is alternately tedious and ridiculous. It's assemblage of inept characters is second to none. (DVD-Retromedia with *Battle Beyond the Sun*)

The Steel Claw (1961) 2.0
Philippines December 1941: marine who lost his right hand in drunken boating mishap teams with local guerrilla fighters to rescue kidnapped general. Along the way, he attaches iron hook as replacement. Lots of Technicolor jungle footage in the early going gives way to reasonably entertaining action scenes. Good cast helps somewhat, although Charito Luna's Lolita character starts grating on the nerves. (DVD-Alpha)

The Stepford Wives (1975) 3.0
When Joanna Eberhart and her family move to the idyllic suburb of Stepford, she is puzzled to find the wives of the town behaving like those in 1950s sitcoms, oblivious to the ERA movement of the day as well as their own happiness. Just what is their secret? Based on Ira Levin's novel, this slow but effective chiller (with a great sense of humor) has big reveal that is both shocking and sad. So impactful was the story, the term Stepford Wife became part of pop culture. (DVD-Paramount)

The Stolen Face (1952) 2.5
Terence Fisher directed this Hammer thriller about a plastic surgeon who loses the girl he loves, so he makes an about-to-be-released ex-con into her image. Can she now change her felonious ways? Respected actor (and future director) Paul Henreid plays the lead role with much conviction; he makes the film watchable. The cop-out ending knocks the rating down a bit though. (DVD-VCI)

Strait-Jacket (1964) 3.0
Joan Crawford's star power makes this William Castle thriller work. She's been released from an asylum, where she spent 20 years for murdering her philandering husband. Shortly after taking up residence with her daughter, the murders begin. Robert Bloch's script doesn't contain many surprises. You'll find yourself rooting for Joan. (BR-Shout! Factory)

The Strange Case of Dr. Jekyll and Mr. Hyde (TV-1968) 3.0
Jack Palance stars as title characters in producer Dan Curtis' fine, intense version of the classic story. Great cast and atmosphere. Originally aired on ABC on January 7, 1968, as a primetime two-and-a-half-hour "Sunday Night Special," making it the first horror production to air originally on television. (DVD-MPI)

The Strange Case of Dr. Rx (1942) 2.0
Unconvincing mystery where villain murders acquitted killers and the like. How is he doing it? Familiarity with cast helps somewhat. "Climatic" scene where ape threatens our hero is anything but. (BR-Shout! Factory as part of *Universal Horror Collection: Volume 2*)

The Strange Countess (1961) 3.0
Escaped lunatic Klaus Kinski is trying to kill young woman who is about to take new job as Lady Leonora Moron's secretary. What's his reason? Could it be because she's the daughter of a convicted murderess who's about to be released? Well-mounted tale of mystery and paranoia involves dastardly doctor and a trip to an asylum. (DVD-R-Sinister Cinema)

The Strange Door (1951) 2.5
Charles Laughton is a flavorful ham in this Gothic melodrama, playing vengeful squire who wants his niece to marry a scoundrel. He also has her father (his brother) imprisoned in a dungeon. Boris Karloff is devoted servant, trying to protect the niece. Not great, but Laughton is so much fun, and the atmosphere so well rendered that it's quite enjoyable taken on its meager terms. (BR —Kino)

Strange Invaders (1983) 2.0
When his ex-wife fails to return from supposedly attending her mother's funeral, entomologist investigates and discovers alien race that's been living among us for 25 years. Despite fine cast of familiar faces and some effective sequences, there's something decidedly off about Michael Laughlin's direction, resulting in sluggish film that's just as often off-putting as it is engaging. (BR-Twilight Time)

The Strange Mr. Gregory (1945) 2.0
Magician/hypnotist Gregory the Great (Edmund Lowe) falls in lust with wife of admirer. He sets out to make her his using his nefarious talents. Unconvincing plot made bearable by

Lowe's sinister performance and Ira Morgan's strong photography. (NA)

Stranger in Our House (TV-1978) 2.0
Linda Blair stars in this made for TV chiller directed by Wes Craven. After an auto mishap claims the life of her parents, Blair's cousin comes to live with Blair and family. But there's something amiss with the new family member even though she seems shy and harmless. Standard stuff. Blair goes over the top sometimes with her ranting and raving but overall, this isn't bad, just average. (BR-Doppelganger Releasing as *Summer of Fear*)

A Stranger is Watching (1982) 2.0
Rip Torn plays sadistic psycho who rapes and murders woman while her daughter watches, and then a few years later kidnaps the child along with her father's new girlfriend. Standard suspense picture with a mix of effective scenes and tedious ones. Generally good performances help. (BR-Shout! Factory)

The Strangler of Blackmoor Castle (1963) 2.0
A nine-fingered strangler carves an M into his victims' foreheads to terrorize supposedly upstanding citizen who's about to be knighted. The motive is stolen diamonds. Despite gruesome murders, a spooky swamp, a climax involving a drill, and the presence of title castle complete with catacombs, this is a rather flat entry in the German *krimi* series based on Bryan Edgar Wallace novels. This viewer guessed the killer right away. (DVD-Alpha)

Strangler of the Swamp (1946) 2.5
Creepy PRC production about executed innocent man whose ghost returns to punish those responsible. Whether by accident or design the film has a nice, menacing atmosphere. Future director Blake Edwards has key role. (DVD-Image)

The Stranglers of Bombay (1959) 3.0
Solid Hammer offering with Guy Rolfe battling the Thugee cult in 19th-century India. Pretty gruesome, with eye burning, tongue removal, gut slicing, etc. The climax has a character do an unconvincing about-face that slightly mars the film. (BR-Mill Creek as part of *Hammer Films: The Ultimate Collection: 20 Film Set*)

Student Bodies (1981) 1.5
At Lamab High School, the Breather stalks various teens in sexual congress, using such weapons as paper clips, eggplant, erasers, and trash bags. Parody of mad slasher films starts out great; the first 12 minutes are terrific. Then it settles down into tired comedy with repeated gags and one-note characters. The ending is just too bizarre for words. (BR-Olive)

A Study in Terror (1965) 3.0
Sherlock Homes receives case of surgical instruments that ultimately puts him on the trail of Jack the Ripper. Brisk, entertaining thriller is good showcase for John Neville's Holmes, a man who's as good with his fists and walking stick as he is with his brains. Dame Judi Dench has a minor role as soup kitchen worker. (BR-Mill Creek)

Sugar Hill (1974) 2.0
Familiar revenge story about woman who invokes voodoo to avenge the death of her lover. Some creepy zombie attack moments but they can't sustain such a predictable tale. (BR-Kino)

Supernatural (1933) 2.5
Follow-up from the Halperin brothers to *White Zombie*, this contrived bit of minor horror concerns spirit of executed murderess that enters the body of woman who recently lost her twin brother and is now the target of phony spiritualist, the very man who betrayed the feme fatale. The film moves quickly enough and has a knockout opening. The coincidences needed to make all this happen are collectively hard to swallow. Early roles for Carole Lombard and Randolph Scott. (BR-Kino)

Supersonic Man (1979) 1.0
Dreadful *Superman* rip-off from Spain. Extraterrestrial superhero is sent to Earth to hunt down villain who has kidnapped a scientist and stolen radioactive material. Poor effects and ridiculous action sequences; laughable from the word go. (DVD-VCI with *The War of the Robots*)

Svengali (1931) 3.0
Music instructor with the power of mind control falls in love with model and exerts his influence over her. But can one truly force another to love them? John Barrymore gives a mesmerizing lead performance, and Marian Marsh is quite adorable as the object of affection. Archie Mayo's direction, Anton Grot's sets and Barney McGill's camera work create an effectively haunting atmosphere. The ending is especially powerful. (DVD-The Roan Group)

Swamp Thing (1982) 2.5
At a top-secret lab located in the Florida everglades, scientist Ray Wise has a breakthrough combining plant and animal life, his goal being to grow crops that can deal with any weather situation and therefore help feed the world. An attack by a rival scientist leads to tragic, life-altering results. Writer-director Wes Craven's adaptation of the DC Comics character is an offbeat, good scientist vs. evil scientist story, where the former becomes a victim of his own genius. Louis Jourdan plays the bad guy and he's great, and the relationship between Swamp Thing and Adrienne Barbeau (as a government agent overseeing the research) is quite touching. Not a complete success (humor isn't Craven's strong point) but still fun. (BR-Shout! Factory)

The Swarm (1978) 1.0
Mutant species of the African killer bee attacks military base and small Texas town, and of course threatens the world. Producer-director Irwin Allen's film is an artistic disaster in that it's completely uninvolving: too long with too many characters you won't care about in corny situations. Jerry Goldsmith's score tries but fails to convince viewers exciting things are happening on the screen. (BR-Warner Archive)

Sweeney Todd: The Demon Barber of Fleet Street (1936) 2.0
When barber Sweeney Todd (Tod Slaughter) speaks of "polishing off" his customers, he's usually talking about a nice shave

and haircut. But if you're alone in the world with a nice sum on your person, he'll have you sit in his special chair, which will send you to your death, and then have your body turned into a meat pie, sold by his neighbor and partner in crime. Slaughter is the show here, giggling madly as he plots crime after crime. The story mechanics are no great shakes, and the constant repetition of the main music theme gets annoying. Britain's king of ham, however, is delicious. (DVD-Alpha)

Tales of Terror (1962) 3.0
Three Poe-based chillers all starring Vincent Price. In "Morella," daughter returns to visit her father and finds her dead mother wants revenge. Peter Lorre joins Price (and steals the show) in "The Black Cat" as jealous drunkard who plots the demise of his wife and her lover. In "The Case of M. Valdemar," Basil Rathbone is an unscrupulous mesmerist who has designs on dying man's wife. A very enjoyable anthology. (BR-Kino)

Tales of the Haunted: Evil Stalks this House (TV-1981) 1.5
Jack Palance and his two kids have car trouble and are taken to home of two elderly sisters and their mentally challenged male relative. While there, Palance discovers valuables and plans on stealing them. What he doesn't realize is there's a cult that hangs out in the attic. In its original form, this was a five-part horror tale hosted by Christopher Lee and syndicated during the summer of 1981. Locally, it aired on Channel 5 at 11:30 p.m. from July 13-July 17, and on Channel 45 at 11:00 p.m. from July 20-July 24. The entire series was repeated on *Ghost Host Theatre* on August 8, 1981. The episodes were eventually re-edited into a feature-length version. Directed by Gordon Hessler, shot on videotape, and scored with public domain music, the film version plays like a clunky soap opera that is ultimately too talky and too cheap to work. (NA)

Tales That Witness Madness (1973) 2.0
Psychiatrist Donald Pleasence shares four patient stories with fellow doctor. A boy's imaginary tiger friend doesn't like his pal's parents; after finding a framed picture of his Uncle Albert, a young man is transported back in time; artist brings human-shaped tree into his home, much to his wife's chagrin; and daughter of literary agent gets more than she bargained for when she falls for her mother's new Hawaiian client. Freddie Francis directed this lackluster anthology; the story hooks just aren't interesting enough to make this memorable. Good cast does what it can. (BR-Olive)

Tam Lin (1970) 2.0
Wealthy swinger (Ava Gardner) who likes being in control takes her lover and young groupies to Scottish castle for some decadence. While there, her boyfriend falls for a minister's daughter, setting the stage for revenge. Roddy McDowall's only film as director is not uninteresting, but it's slow, self-indulgent, and overly-arty. (BR-Olive)

Tarantula (1955) 3.0
Good giant spider entry with great effects and direction. Title fiend grows and grows due to genius scientist's formula. John Agar woos Mara Corday in between attacks. Clint Eastwood pilots an attack plane. One of Universal's best 1950's sci-fi films. (BR-Shout! Factory)

Tarantulas: The Deadly Cargo (TV-1977) 2.0
Airliner, carrying coffee beans and deadly spiders, crashes near California town, freeing the eight-legged buggers to cause trouble for orange-packaging plant. Despite good cast, this is mostly an exercise in tedium. (BR-Kino)

Target Earth (1954) 2.0
Several disparate people wake up to an abandoned city; later find giant robots lurking about zapping any humans they find. Switches focus between the frightened citizens and military operation dealing with the invaders. Result is more talk than action. (DVD-VCI)

Taste the Blood of Dracula (1969) 2.5
Worshiper of the black arts invites three well-to-do gentlemen to help him raise Dracula from the dead. They instead murder him but not before Dracula returns, now out for revenge. The idea that Dracula would give a hoot about a mortal is silly given how he uses people. Lee is in fine form as is, ahem, Linda Hayden as one of the killer's daughters. James Bernard's love theme is a beautiful piece of music. (BR-Warner Bros.)

Teenage Caveman (1958) 2.0
Robert Vaughn plays title troublemaker who dares question the Law and traditions of his clan. He especially wants to explore areas outside his home, which are fraught with giant lizards and a strange bug-eyed, beaked creature. Low-budget fantasy directed by Roger Corman has a certain charm thanks to Vaughn's sincere performance, and the end has a couple of interesting twists. (DVD-Lionsgate with *The Saga of the Viking Women and Their Voyage to the Waters of the Great Sea Serpent*)

Teenage Monster (1958) 1.0
In 1880, meteor hits Earth and kills miner while turning his young son into a mutant. Years later Mom (Anne Gwynne) must deal with grown son who can barely speak and is now a hairy killer. He also wants a girlfriend. Laughable tripe gives no true motivation for the killings and introduces blackmail and romance subplots to drag things out. Gwynne does what she can, but the script is hopeless. Aired on television as *Meteor Monster*. (DVD—Image)

Teenage Zombies (1958) 0.0
This is one of the worst films ever made: a poorly produced and acted mad scientist yarn about group of teens trapped on an island; they become potential experimental subjects. Recalling the 1940s war-effort horrors, some mysterious foreign country is trying to turn Americans into mindless, easily controlled zombies. Perhaps the only variation is that the mad doctor is female. Otherwise, this is a tedious affair, with no suspense or surprises. Just awful. (DVD-Retromedia)

Teenagers from Outer Space (1959) 1.0
Aliens plan to use Earth as breeding ground for their dan-

gerous livestock called Gargons (lobsters). This doesn't sit well with young Derek who betrays the mission and flees. Sincerely produced low-budget effort plays better as a comedy than anything else. Beware of the "focusing disintegrator ray" which turns living things into instant skeletons. (BR-Retromedia with *Attack of the Giant Leeches*)

The Tell-Tale Heart (1960) 2.0
Shy Edgar Marsh falls in love with his new neighbor. When she shows more interest in Marsh's best friend, Edgar plots his pal's murder. Only the most basic element of Poe's classic short story remains in this routine exercise. Good atmosphere helps. (DVD-Alpha)

Tentacles (1977) 2.0
Jaws imitation features giant octopus terrorizing boaters and an all-star cast (John Huston, Shelley Winters, Henry Fonda). Not to be outdone, this effort also features two killer whales named Summer and Winter. A reviled film because of the less than great special effects and curious directing choices. (What was up with the oddly edited and scored boat race attack sequence?) There are some effective moments, such as an early attack on two divers. The first victim is a 10-month-old! (BR-Shout! Factory with *Reptilicus*)

The Terrible People (1960) 2.5
Facing execution for multiple crimes, Clay Shelton threatens revenge from beyond the grave against those he blames for his forthcoming death. When the murders do indeed begin, several people think they see Shelton's ghost looming about while the police get calls from someone calling himself The Gallows' Hand. Starts out great, but then introduces romantic subplot where everyone claims to be in love with Karin Dor. Rebounds for a twist-laden finish. (DVD-Retromedia with *The Inn on the River*)

Terrified (1963) 1.0
Masked killer likes to terrify his victims before he finally kills them. Disappointing final film from director Lew Landers (*The Raven* [1935]) has some atmospheric scenes in a ghost town and cemetery; ruined by a poor, overly talky script, several amateurish performances, and sluggish pacing. (DVD-BCI Eclipse as part of *Drive-In Cult Classics Vol. 2*)

The Terror (1963) 2.5
A film made by Roger Corman because he had Karloff under contract for a few more days after *The Raven* (1963) was completed. A separated French soldier (Jack Nicholson) finds himself caught up in some ghostly goings on at stock-footage castle. Colorful and atmospheric outing is better than its reputation suggests. Dick Miller plays Karloff's servant. Corman finally found another way to bring a castle down besides fire. (BD-R-The Film Detective)

Terror Beneath the Sea (1966) 1.0
Future martial arts star Sonny Chiba is one of two reporters captured by mad scientist (who dresses like a James Bond villain) and his race of fish-men hiding in underwater city. It goes without saying the doc plans to rule the world. Even at 79 minutes, this drags as it features one of the most drawn-out transformation scenes ever committed to film. A ridiculous, uninspired cross between spy film and sci-fi thriller. (DVD-MPI)

Terror from the Year 5000 (1958) 2.0
Scientists have built time machine that allows them to swap artifacts with seemingly friendly if mysterious benefactor. Trouble ensues when a citizen from the future shows up, who may not be so benign after all. Imaginative sci-fi is hampered by silly subplots involving scientist's daughter that consume too much of the running time. Basic story is interesting and the monster original. (NA)

Terror from Within (TV-1975) 2.5
Woman visits artists' village seeking her fiancé, who was killed during the pre-credits sequence. Unaware of this, she waits for him and hears a voice calling to her and has various visions (or nightmares). Slow pacing hurts otherwise atmospheric *Thriller* episode; still has its moments though. Original British title: *Won't Write Home Mom, I'm Dead*. (DVD-VEI as part of *Thriller: The Complete Collection*)

Terror in the Crypt (1964) 2.0
Uncredited Italian take on Sheridan Le Fanu's *Carmilla*. Christopher Lee's daughter may or may not be the promised reincarnation of vengeful ancestor declared a witch. As she struggles with her nightmares (or are they visions?), a beautiful stranger comes to stay with the family and make things more complicated. Atmospheric but tedious and repetitive; mainly for Italian Gothic fans. (BR-Severin as *Crypt of the Vampire* as part of *The Eurocrypt of Christopher Lee Collection*)

Terror in the Haunted House (1958) 2.0
Newlywed is horrified to discover the house her husband has rented for them is the same abode from her recurring nightmare! Familiar tale of woman who wonders if she's going mad while the audience wonders if they're watching a remake of *Gaslight*. Neither stylish nor atmospheric enough to create the tension and mounting terror needed, the filmmakers relied on the gimmick of "Psycho-Rama," which utilized scary subliminal imagery at key points. This bland outing needs all the help it can get. (DVD-Rhino)

Terror in the Jungle (1968) 0.0
Astonishingly awful "adventure" movie. Young boy survives plane crash; headhunting tribe finds and venerates him. His dad comes looking. The producer/writer hired non-actors and went through three directors, resulting in a film that moves from one appalling scene to the next. Absolute torture, this just might be the worst film shown during the period this book covers. (DVD-Mill Creek as part of *B-Movie Blast: 50 Movie Pack*)

Terror in the Wax Museum (1973) 2.5
Before John Carradine can sell his wax museum, he is murdered, perhaps by the figure of Jack the Ripper come to life! Enjoyable horror whodunit with nice atmosphere and great

cast, including Ray Milland, Elsa Lanchester, and Patric Knowles. (VHS-Lightning Video)

Terror is A Man (1959) 2.0
Reworking of *Island of Lost Souls* has shipwreck survivor saved by mad scientist. As a thank you, the ungrateful jerk starts an affair with the doctor's wife. Meanwhile man-panther hybrid is on the prowl. Not terribly exciting in the whole, although Francis Lederer is fine in the Moreau-like part. (BR-Severin)

Terror of Mechagodzilla (1975) 2.0
The last of the original Godzilla series that started in 1954, our favorite Japanese monster must once again face Mechagodzilla after aliens revive him. A dinosaur named Titanosaurus controlled by traitorous scientist is thrown into the mix. Stereotypical, cackling, ridiculous-looking aliens undercut serious tone. It also takes too much time to get the fight scenes, which are satisfying enough when they commence. (BR-Criterion as part of *Godzilla: The Showa-Era Films, 1954–1975*)

Terror of the Bloodhunters (1962) 0.0
Sleep inducing bore from Jerry Warren. Robert Clarke plays French inmate (because of his writings) who's approached by the boss' unhappy daughter with a plan of escape. They end up having to endure the dangers of the jungle. Viewers though don't have to endure this cheap, bland, and unexciting movie. Made even worse by additional talking-head footage shot for television. (DVD-Alpha)

The Terror of the Tongs (1961) 2.5
The Red Dragon Tong is terrorizing the Hong Kong citizenry. When they murder the daughter of a British seaman, however, he swears revenge and plots the Tong's demise. Christopher Lee is the top-billed baddie in this lively Hammer thriller. (BR-Mill Creek as part of *Hammer Films: The Ultimate Collection: 20 Film Set*)

Terror on the Beach (TV-1973) 2.5
Dennis Weaver stars as average dad who takes his wife and two college-age children for beach camping trip, only to be harassed by band of dune buggy-driving punks. They steal the distributor cap and the family food and make the vacation a living hell. Tension builds since the audience never knows what the clan is going to do next, or what their true goal is. The villains' motivations are never explained which works to the film's advantage. The ending isn't convincing, however. (NA)

Terror Train (1980) 2.5
Someone is murdering the college seniors aboard a party train. Above average slasher pic is atmospheric, stylish, and clever in spots, but the pacing is off. Jamie Lee Curtis is among the passengers and of course our hero. (BR-Scorpion Releasing)

The Testament of Dr. Mabuse (1962) 2.0
Master criminal orchestrates daring back-to-back thefts of gold and diamonds. He hides behind a plastic curtain like the Wizard of Oz, refers to himself as "Lord and master," and is somehow linked to Dr. Mabuse, who's under constant watch in psychiatric clinic. Humdrum entry in the series comes to life only in the final climatic moments. Otherwise, it's mostly talking heads and standard crime stuff. (DVD-Image)

The Texas Chain Saw Massacre (1974) 4.0
Iconic fright film features five young adults who meet a demented family that specializes in barbecue. Harrowing is an understatement in describing the film's overall tone. Leatherface got all the attention, but Jim Siedow's "Old Man" (later named Drayton in the first sequel), is also great. His disciplinary tendencies of physical and verbal abuse create some of the film's darkest comedy. ("Look what your brother did to the door!") (BR-MPI)

Theater of Blood (1973) 4.0
Vincent Price prepared for this role his whole career. He plays a thought-to-be-dead Shakespearian stage actor who murders the critics who trashed him, his crimes inspired by some of the Bard's most gruesome deaths. Price and a flawless cast help pull this off. Michael Lewis' score is beautiful. The witty script manages the seemingly impossible task of making Price's Edward Lionheart a sympathetic character despite his viciousness. Very gruesome and very fun; maybe Price's best horror film. (BR-Twilight Time)

Theatre of Death (1967) 2.5
Christopher Lee is the director of Grand Guignol-type theater, whose latest production coincides with several vampire-like murders plaguing Paris. Excellent production design and atmosphere are the main assets in this horror whodunit that suffers after Lee pulls a vanishing act halfway through. Is he the killer or one of the victims? (DVD-Anchor Bay)

Them! (1954) 4.0
The title is all a little girl can tell the police after they find her alone. What happened to her family? This is the film that solidified the template for all the giant "something" thrillers of the 1950s; it's also the best. Outstanding cast and characters (you really like these people), outstanding effects, terrific script, taut pacing...exemplary filmmaking. Holds up very well today. Warner Bros. always did like their crime pictures and frequently injected these qualities into their horror and science fiction films. Here it works very well, with some snappy dialogue exchanges and no-nonsense approach. (BR-Warner Bros.)

They Came from Beyond Space (1967) 1.5
Scientist Robert Hutton must single-handedly do battle with his colleagues when they are taken over by alien force that has brought a plague to Earth. Hutton's more action hero than intellectual given all the fistfights and gun battles present. Some good ideas unfortunately get lost in story that gets sillier as it goes along. Dig that pink spiral effect! Michael Gough plays Master of the Moon. (BR-Kino)

They Came from Within (1975) 2.5
At the Starliner Island Apartment Complex in Montreal, parasites invade the tenants, turning their hosts into violent, sex-crazed maniacs. Writer-director David Cronenberg's night-

marish mix of medical horror and mad scientist tropes may not be as polished as his later efforts but still offers plenty of shock moments and a strong premise. Barbara Steele is one of the victims. (BR-Lionsgate as *Shivers*)

They Saved Hitler's Brain (1963) 0.0
Survivors of the Nazi party have preserved their Führer's head; plan to release deadly gas as part of their revenge. Originally a 74-minute film entitled *The Madmen of Mandoras*, about 20 minutes of additional footage was shot at some point and added to the beginning of the film. The IMDB gives a date of 1968 for this expanded version, but the earliest TV appearances appear to be 1976. (The original was still playing drive-ins in '68.) In whatever form, this is lousy stuff, dull with leaden pacing and ridiculous plotting. Might have worked as a comedy if it hadn't taken so damn long for the head to finally show up or if the noggin had more screen time. (DVD-BCI Eclipse as part of *Drive-In Cult Classics Vol. 2*)

The Thing from Another World (1951) 4.0
Justifiably revered thriller about isolated scientists and military personnel hunted by recently thawed alien creature. Producer Howard Hawks is said to have directed, and it shows in the overlapping dialogue and character interaction. Plenty of scares and suspense, with classic closing line. (BR-Warner Archive)

The Thing That Couldn't Die (1958) 1.5
Severed head buried in chest four centuries ago is uncovered and hypnotizes several people into doing his Satanic will. Below average performances and nonsensical backstory (why would righteous people punish evil by allowing it to live forever?) are the main culprits here. And talk about an anticlimax. (BR-Shout! Factory as part of *Universal Horror Collection: Volume 6*)

Things to Come (1936) 2.5
Ambitious look at what may happen to humanity over 100-year period, starting on Christmas Day 1936 as war breaks out and ending in 2036 as the first humans are sent to the moon. Visually, the film is constantly striking and holds one's attention. Unfortunately, the film is one long argument, with characters that are just ideologues giving speeches about why they're right while others counter why they're not. It's telling that in a film about technology, war, and the human condition, the most memorable line of dialogue is, "You've got the subtlety of a bullfrog!" (BR-Criterion)

The Third Man (1949) 4.0
Novelist (Joseph Cotten) travels to post-war Vienna to accept a job offer from pal Harry Lime (Orson Welles). After arriving, he's shocked to learn his friend is dead, and may have been involved in the sale of black-market penicillin. He decides to conduct his own investigation. Deserving of its classic status, this is a thoroughly engrossing mystery told with a visual style second to none. The final chase through the sewers is a wow. (BR-Criterion)

Thirst (1979) 3.0
Taking their cue from Elizabeth Bathory, The Brotherhood cult drinks human blood milked from residents at various farms throughout the world. They kidnap descendant of their founder hoping she will join them, forcing her to drink blood while undergoing horrific "conditioning" that could render her insane. Original variation on vampirism from Australia mixes horror, sci-fi, psychology, and human desire for youth and power into acceptable brew. There are some fine story twists too, and lovely main theme from composer Brian May. (BR-Severin)

The Thirsty Dead (1974) 0.0
Great title; crummy movie. In Manila, cultists wearing monk robes kidnap women-who mostly don't seem too worried-for their blood, which is needed for a youth elixir. Most of the action takes place in the first 10 minutes or so. The rest is a laborious slog through bad filmmaking. (DVD-Vinegar Syndrome with *Blood Thirst*)

Thirteen Women (1932) 2.5
Myrna Loy stars as mixed raced woman who plots revenge, using her hypnotic powers, against the sorority sisters who shunned her 15 years earlier. Cut down from 73 to 59 minutes, the surviving shorter print still manages to build tension in several scenes despite the brief running time. Campy fun, but hardly convincing. (DVD-R-Warner Archive)

This Is Not a Test (1962) 1.5
Police officer starts pulling various drivers over in anticipation of nuclear attack. He suggests they all pile into the back of truck for protection, but not everyone agrees. Not uninteresting drama is hampered by low-budget, uneven performances, and script that's mostly gab. (DVD-Mill Creek as part of *Nightmare Worlds: 50 Movie Pack*)

This Island Earth (1955) 3.0
Entertaining sci-fi with scientists from a dying planet enlisting the unwitting help of Earthly geniuses. Good characterizations and effects, with the Metaluna Mutants making a memorable impression during their brief screen time. (BR-Shout! Factory)

Three Cases of Murder (1953) 3.0
British anthology of three murder stories with a twist: a museum employee is sucked into a painting, meeting the current residents; two friends' feud over a woman leads to murder; and a disgraced politician gets revenge against his nemesis by invading his dreams. The middle story is ho-hum but the first and last stories are great and creepy. Orson Welles plays the object of revenge in the last story and gives a bravura performance, especially in the nightmare segments where he sings and dances. Hammer favorite Andre Morell plays Welles' psychiatrist. (Laserdisc-Criterion)

The Three Stooges in Orbit (1962) 2.5
The down-on-their-luck Stooges move into kooky scientist's creepy castle and get involved with Martians Ogg and Zogg, who've come to Earth to pave the way for invasion since Mars needs more living space. Loaded with spooky atmosphere and old-fashioned slapstick, with the invaders wearing Karloffian Frankenstein monster masks and Dracula capes. Genuine laughs here and there, although the comedy trio aren't everyone's cup of herbal. (DVD-Columbia/Tristar)

Three Strangers (1946) 3.0
At the stroke of midnight on the Chinese New Year, three strangers agree to make same wish before statue of goddess Kwan Yin, believing their fortunes will change via a sweepstakes ticket. Each of these people has skeletons in their respective closets, and their circumstances become more desperate as the drawing approaches. Engrossing story tracks each character's predicament with various twists and turns, leading to powerful climax. (DVD-R-Warner Archive)

THX 1138 (1971) 3.5
Robert Duvall stars as title character, a member of Earth's future society that lives underground. Human intimacy has been outlawed and people are forced to take drugs to deal with this loss of interaction or face prison time. THX 1138 has finally had all he can take. Fascinating story brought to vivid life by co-writer/director George Lucas. The effects work is top notch but it's the various details and situations that make this film so compelling. (BR-Warner Bros.)

Till Death (1978) 2.5
A car accident causes a groom to lose his bride on their wedding night. After he gets out of the hospital, he visits the crypt where she lies, only to discover she's alive! Moody, low-budget shocker kick things off with a terrific, prescient nightmare sequence that it cannot top. But it tries by throwing in a thunderstorm, a black cat, and ghostly apparitions. A nice effort but not completely successful. (NA)

Time After Time (1979) 3.0
In 1893, H.G. Wells (Malcolm McDowell) completes his time machine and is now ready to visit the future. His doctor friend (David Warner) who is Jack the Ripper beats him to the punch. Now, Wells must travel to 1979 to track down the vicious killer. Wonderful blend of thrills, romance, ingenuity, and humor. The cast is great, especially McDowell, who has one his few "normal" roles. (BR-Warner Archive)

The Time Machine (1960) 3.0
H.G. Wells' story of 1899 London scientist who invents time machine and travels into the future, not necessarily liking what he finds. George Pal production has nifty special effects and those creepy Morlocks. Rod Taylor is a likeable hero. (BR-Warner Bros.)

The Time Travelers (1964) 2.0
Researchers create time rift that allows them to literally step into 2071. Trapped in the post-apocalyptic future they must figure out how to return to 1964 while dealing with mutants and benign scientists destined for Alpha Centauri. Imaginative and gripping in parts, self-consciously silly in others. A bit overlong too. (BR-Kino)

The Tingler (1959) 3.0
Scientist Vincent Price discovers creature that grows on the spine during moments of extreme fear. Screaming is the only thing that can stop it. When deaf mute dies with her "tingler" intact, Price removes it and—watch out! Ludicrous premise presented with a straight face is a lot of fun. Director William Castle had certain theater seats wired with electric buzzers that gave audience members their own tingles. (BR-Shout! Factory)

Tobor the Great (1954) 2.0
Scientist develops robot Tobor to use for space exploration in lieu of humans. Grandson Gadge, who is also a genius, befriends Tobor. Of course, foreign forces want Tobor for themselves. Harmless sci-fi for the kids also throws ESP into the mix. Who the heck taught Tobor how to drive a jeep? Gee willikers! (BR-Kino)

Tomb of Ligeia (1965) 3.0
Final Corman-Price-Poe collaboration has different look and feel since Corman filmed it on location versus at a studio. Vincent Price plays a widower who believes his late wife has plans to return to him. A new love interest complicates matters. Familiar Poe themes of life after death, physical affliction, and jealously are trotted out once again but the results are mostly engaging. Price gets to play his romantic side a little bit. Elizabeth Shepherd makes for a compelling heroine. (BR-Shout! Factory as part of *The Vincent Price Collection II*)

Tomb of Torture (1963) 1.5
Doctor's daughter is having nightmares concerning murdered countess whom she resembles. So, Dad brings her to her lookalike's village in hopes a visit to the castle will cure her, unaware there's a giggling, facially deformed hunchback tenant who likes to make use of the manor's torture chamber. Italian shocker features a good opening 15 minutes and a great nightmare sequence. Then a half hour in, the attempts at humor begin, romance blooms out of nowhere, and monotony sets in. (DVD-Image)

Tormented (1960) 2.0
Standard tale of ghostly revenge, as murdered vixen haunts the man (Richard Carlson) who let her fall to her death from a lighthouse. He's going to be married in a week...maybe. Directed by Bert I. Gordon, this is one of his less laughable films thanks to Carlson playing it straight. Some of the would-be scares inspire chuckles (My God! There's seaweed on the wedding dress!). Setting the entire film near a beach gives it a nice atmosphere. (DVD-R-Warner Archive)

Torpedo of Doom (1966) 2.0
Feature version of 1938 serial *The Fighting Devil Dogs*. US marines battle a power-hungry baddie known as The Lightning, so named because he can harness electricity and destroy whatever he chooses with his Electrical Thunderbolt. There are some nifty scenes of the weapon in action to go along with the ubiquitous hand combat. There's also a heavy whodunit component. Weak acting is the real culprit though. Villain looks like an early prototype of Darth Vader. The whole serial is available on French DVD. (NA)

Torture Chamber of Dr. Sadism (1967) 2.5
Christopher Lee has about 20 minutes of screen time as executed count who has returned from the dead. He's arranged

to complete his elixir of life with the blood of one last victim: the daughter of the woman who turned him in 35 years earlier. Heavy on atmosphere and Gothic trappings, this is chock full of arresting visuals. The finale is a bit of letdown unfortunately. (BR-Severin as part of *The Eurocrypt of Christopher Lee Collection*)

Torture Garden (1966) 2.5
Amicus anthology set at a carnival. Dr. Diablo (Burgess Meredith) invites customers to stare into Lady Fate's shears and learn their futures. Stories include: 1) A witch-possessed cat compels fortune-seeking man to commit murder; 2) Wannabe actress learns the secret of Hollywood's Top-Ten performers; 3) A haunted piano is jealous its owner has a new girlfriend; and 4) Poe-obsessed collector discovers a shocking fact about his idol. First and fourth stories are best, the latter featuring engaging performances by Jack Palance and Peter Cushing. (BR-Mill Creek as part of *Psycho Circus: 3 Rings of Terror*)

Tourist Trap (1979) 2.5
Four young people find themselves lost and stranded, so they accept the hospitality of friendly hermit (Chuck Connors) who still lives at his old tourist museum full of functioning mannequins. Soon, the figures seem to come to life and terrorize the guests. Creepy, atmospheric low-budget film provides many chills and a nice turn by Connors. However, some of the acting is lackluster and the film is longer than it should be. (BR-Full Moon)

Tower of Evil (1972) 1.5
Three mutilated bodies are found on Snape Island and the lone survivor is blamed for the crimes. The accused's parents, however, hire a PI to clear their daughter, so he joins a team of archaeologists who are planning an island trip to search for ancient treasures. Soon after they all arrive, more murders occur. Potentially intriguing story done-in by idiotic characters and gratuitous titillation. There's something of a twist at the end if you make it that far. (BR-Scorpion Releasing)

Tower of London (1939) 2.5
Richard III (Basil Rathbone) murders or causes the murders of those who stand in his way to the throne. Boris Karloff runs the torture chamber and assists as needed. Good cast with a sufficiently intricate plot. The battles scenes are a real let down though, especially the final dual between Richard III and Henry Tudor. The *practice* sword bouts lasted longer and were more exciting. (BR-Shout! Factory as part of *Universal Horror Collection: Volume 3*)

Tower of London (1962) 2.5
Vincent Price does a Shakespearean picture via Edgar Allan Poe. He plays Richard III who will let nothing stand in his way of becoming king. His victims however haunt him constantly. The low budget meant no big battle scenes (footage from the 1939 version was used). Price is so much fun to watch that he pretty much saves the picture. (BR-Shout! Factory as part of *The Vincent Price Collection III*)

Tower of Terror (1941) 2.5
British thriller about a mad lighthouse keeper (Wilfrid Lawson) who threatens to thwart an English agent's escape from Germany. Plot elements include a hook for a hand, a potentially reincarnated wife, and a hidden body. Lawson gives an excellent performance in this above average effort. (DVD-R-Sinister Cinema)

Track of the Moon Beast (1976) 1.5
In New Mexico during a meteor shower, mineralogist gets meteorite particle lodged in his brain, and later transforms into "demon lizard monster" of Indian legend. (Man's creation was apparently a deal between a lizard and a coyote.) Reminiscent of 1950s monster flicks crossed with elements of *The Wolf Man*, below-average performances and too-few monster attacks hamper this variation. What attacks *are* present though are done with verve. (DVD-Mill Creek as part of *Chilling Classics: 50 Movie Pack*)

Track of the Vampire (1966) 1.5
Artist who paints nudes of women he's murdered is vampiric reincarnation of ancestor. Infamous mashup by producer Roger Corman of various films, bad dubbing, and reshot footage. This 79-minute version is obviously padded which throws off the pacing. The first shown murder sequence is terrifically atmospheric. But it's all downhill from there. (BR-Arrow as part of *Blood Bath: Limited Edition*)

Trauma (1962) 2.0
When she was 15, Emmaline witnessed the murder of her aunt mere hours after identifying her friend's murdered corpse. Having forgotten everything, she returns to her aunt's estate six years later newly married to her aunt's former suitor! In trying to remember her past Emmaline may be putting her life in danger. OK thriller has some good dialogue and a few red herrings to keep the viewer guessing. It's also talky and overlong. (DVD-R-Sinister Cinema)

Treachery and Greed on the Planet of the Apes (TV-1974) 2.5
TV-movie derived from two episodes of the *Planet of the Apes* series. "The Horse Race" concerns a contest whose stakes include the life of boy who saved Galen's life. In "The Tyrant," the fugitive trio become involved with a district chief's plot to overthrow the prefect, who is a friend of Galen's. Lively apes outing is perhaps the best of the episode matchups. (DVD-Fox as part of *Planet of the Apes: The Complete TV Series*)

Treasure of the Petrified Forest (1965) 1.5
Italian adventure about band of Vikings trying to steal sacred treasure and sword hidden in the petrified valley, guarded by warriors of Valhalla. There are numerous battles with swords and bows and arrows, and Gordon Mitchell's bad guy growls and scowls every chance he gets. The hero is obnoxious, at one point assaulting the woman he wants to marry because their tryst kept him from participating in battle, and *he* blames *her*! One potentially exciting sequence where the heroine is to be ripped apart on wheel of death is dealt with too quickly, and it's back to another standard battle. Beautiful looking, but ultimately rather silly. (NA)

Trick or Treats (1982) 2.0
Jokey Halloween-set thriller about a babysitter, her obnoxious charge, and an asylum-escapee plotting revenge. Its thin prem-

ise is stretched out beyond what it can handle, and it's hard to believe the babysitter continually falls for the kid's pranks after the first few. The performances are uneven to boot. Yet it still has some entertainment value, especially when the madman finally arrives at his former home. (BR-Code Red)

Trog (1970) 2.0
Joan Crawford's last theatrical feature. She plays anthropologist trying to study recently discovered troglodyte. Michael Gough is a bitchy developer who wants Trog destroyed because it lowers property values. Crawford is just fine in this unfairly bashed camp classic. No, it's not very good, but it *is* fun in its own way whenever Trog's on the loose, flashing back to the past, or having a sit-down with Joan. Directed by Freddie Francis. (BR-Shout! Factory)

Turkey Shoot (1982) 3.0
In a future where societal deviants are sent to camps where they are abused until ready to return to the populace, the camp master arranges hunts of select individuals. If they can last until sundown, they earn their freedom. A variation on "The Most Dangerous Game," this is guilty pleasure stuff: violent, over-the-top, and oh so entertaining. Yeah, it's trash. But it's always fun to watch the hunted turn the tables on their hunters, and the formula is well-played here. (BR-Severin)

Turn of the Screw (TV-1974) 2.5
Governess hired to care for orphaned children starts seeing ghosts of deceased lovers who may want to claim the youths' souls. Well-acted adaptation of Henry James' novella pales in comparison to 1961 version, *The Innocents*. The use of videotape and obvious staginess really hinder creating necessary atmosphere. It still has several creepy moments. Megs Jenkins reprises her role as housekeeper Mrs. Grose from the earlier rendering. Originally aired as two-part movie on ABC's Wide World of Entertainment on April 15 and 16, 1974. (DVD-MPI)

Twins of Evil (1971) 2.0
Twin beauties come to live with fanatical uncle (Peter Cushing) who hunts and burns witches for a living. One of the nieces becomes fascinated with local villain, Count Karnstein, and is determined to defy her uncle. Ambitious mix of witchcraft and vampire tales rendered inert due to predictable events and mostly one-note characterizations. Third and final chapter to Hammer Film Productions' Karnstein trilogy. (BR-Synapse)

Twisted Brain (1973) 3.0
A teenage variation on *Dr. Jekyll and Mr. Hyde*. Bullied high school student is forced to drink the formula he developed for Mr. Mumps, his guinea pig science project. It temporarily turns him into a violent killer, allowing him to exact revenge on his tormentors. Low-budget terror tale has its detractors (Leonard Maltin rated it a BOMB). However, lead Pat Cardi is easy to identify with and therefore makes for a sympathetic killer. Highly entertaining, even if that is just nostalgia talking. (I remember seeing this the night it had its *Ghost Host* premiere on June 3, 1978, following the inferior *Stanley*.) (BR-Vinegar Syndrome as *Horror High*)

The Two Faces of Dr. Jekyll (1960) 2.0
Rather downbeat version of the classic story. Jekyll is a wimpy doctor whose wife is cheating on him with his best friend (Christopher Lee). When Mr. Hyde learns the secret, he plots revenge against the adulterers. Some effective moments and a nice score, but Paul Massie as the title character adopts a weird voice to differentiate the two personalities and it's off-putting. There really isn't anyone to care about here. (BR-Mill Creek as part of *Hammer Films: The Ultimate Collection: 20 Film Set*)

Two Lost Worlds (1951) 2.0
Seafaring adventure about pirate-attack victims stranded on island inhabited by dinosaurs. The effects are from *One Million B.C.* and only a third of the film takes place on the island. At just over an hour, this is passable but unspectacular entertainment. (DVD-Image)

Two on a Guillotine (1965) 2.5
Deceased magician leaves his entire estate to his estranged daughter on the condition she stay at his house for seven days, so he can communicate with her from beyond the grave. Entertaining if overlong spooky house thriller where the biggest threat up until the rousing finale is a rabbit out of its hat. (BR-Warner Archive)

The Twonky (1953) 2.0
This may happen to you tomorrow! Comedy about television set (it's a robot from a future dimension) that takes over the life of philosophy professor. The appliance walks; makes counterfeit money; vacuums; and zaps coffee cups at will. A unique picture that has some scattershot laughs. Most of the gags are repeated to death and the film ultimately has nowhere to go. (NA)

U.F.O. (1956) 2.0
The motion picture scoop of the century! "This is *not* fiction," our narrator tells us sternly. Docudrama mostly based on reporter Al Chop's dealings with the Pentagon as it explored various claims that we are not alone. Somber and interesting to a point, the film is still overlong and the acting stiff. On-screen title: *Unidentified Flying Objects: The True Story of Flying Saucers*. (NA)

U-238 and the Witch Doctor (1966) 2.0
Edited version of the 1953 serial *Jungle Drums of Africa*. Witch doctor plots with America's enemies to prevent the US from securing uranium mining rights from the leader of his tribe. Fair adventure at least has varied cliffhangers instead of just one fistfight after another. The cast could have been a little more enthusiastic though. (DVD-R-Grapevine Video)

Ugetsu (1953) 3.5
In war-torn 16th-century Japan, two peasant neighbors abandon their wives to pursue their respective dreams of wealth and becoming a samurai. Neither gets exactly what he had hoped for, and one of them catches the fancy of a ghost! Haunting and emotionally brutal tale with stunning photography. (BR-Criterion)

The Uncanny (1977) 2.5
Peter Cushing plays horror novelist Wilbur Gray (same name as Lou Costello's character in *Abbott and Costello Meet Frankenstein*!) whose latest work exposes cats for what they really are: demonic creatures out to control us all! He shares three of his frightening feline tales with publisher Ray Milland. First: Felines exact punishment when their mistress is murdered. Second: A persecuted adolescent uses witchcraft and her cat to get back at her tormentor. Third: The cat of a murdered woman plots revenge against the villainous husband, a Hollywood actor who can't seem to rid himself of the kitty. Not too many seem to care for this one, but this viewer enjoyed it, maybe due to first seeing it at a young age. (BR-Severin)

Uncle Was a Vampire (1959) 2.0
Italian Baron sells his castle to hoteliers to pay back taxes but stays on as a bellhop. When he learns his wealthy uncle is arriving, he thinks his troubles are over-except uncle sleeps in a coffin. Sporadically amusing horror comedy features Christopher Lee as the vampire. Lots of pretty scenery and a committed performance by Renato Rascel as the Baron, especially once he gets vampirized, keep you watching. (DVD-R-Sinister Cinema)

The Undead (1957) 2.5
Rather unique Roger Corman film about hypnotist who regresses woman back to a past life on the day she's to be executed for witchcraft. But when she escapes, she puts her future lives in jeopardy. Allison Hayes is in the cast as another witch, and Richard Devon plays Satan. There's a neat twist at the end. Quite fun if seen in the right frame of mind. (NA)

The Undying Monster (1942) 2.5
The Hammond family is cursed by a werewolf that terrorizesthe citizenry. This is 20th -Century Fox's combination of *The Hound of the Baskervilles* and Universal's *The Wolf Man* right down to a rhyming ditty ("When stars are bright on a frosty night—Beware the bane on the rocky lane.") The investigating inspectors' tone and attitude are a little too light given the crimes involved and spoil the mood at times. But the film is gorgeously shot with atmosphere to spare, and the finale is exciting. (BR-Kino)

The Unearthly (1957) 2.0
John Carradine plays-what else?-a mad doctor trying to discover the secret to eternal youth. Occasionally atmospheric thriller is also silly. Tor Johnson plays another man-child named Lobo, just like he did in *Bride of the Monster*. Fun for hard-core fans of '50s sci-fi, others should probably stay away. (DVD-Image)

Unearthly Stranger (1963) 3.0
Several scientists connected to space exploration research have died suddenly by brain hemorrhage. The authorities suspect foul play and become very interested in new bride of researcher who has just taken charge of the project. Well-done low-budget shocker moves briskly to its chilling climax. Available on Region 2 Blu-Ray. (NA)

The Unholy Three (1925) 3.0
Three crooks set up shop at a pet store where they conduct robberies of wealthy patrons. Problems develop when the leader's (Lon Chaney) girlfriend falls for the gang's would-be patsy. Fascinating macabre drama executed with aplomb by director Tod Browning and his cast. (DVD-R-Warner Archive)

The Unholy Three (1930) 3.0
Sadly, this was Lon Chaney's only sound picture and shows he would have been great during the sound period too. A remake of the 1925 film of the same name Chaney, in drag, leads a trio of criminals under the guise of a kindly, elderly pet shop owner. Instead of multiple makeups, Chaney uses multiple voices! Almost as good as the original. (DVD-R-Warner Archive)

The Uninvited (1944) 4.0
Perfect cinematic ghost story balances character, humor, mystery, and chills. Brother and sister buy house by the sea only to discover it was the scene of a crime many years ago, and the victim may be haunting the place. They set out to solve the mystery and eventually must confront the ghost! (BR-Criterion)

Unknown Island (1948) 2.0
Engaged couple hires obnoxious captain to deliver them to island of prehistoric creatures. Fine cast can do only so much with one-note characters and a derivative script. Effects consist of people in rubber suits, but a couple of effective scenes sneak in. Filmed in Cinecolor. (DVD-Image)

The Unknown Terror (1957) 2.0
Six months after her brother disappears while searching for the notorious Cueva Muerte (Cave of the Dead) in South America, well-off society gal, her husband, and her ex-boyfriend go searching but instead find scientist experimenting with fungus. He's created bubbly mold that turns people into mutants. Imperfect but watchable thanks to decent cast and some creepy moments inside the drippy cave. Available on a region-free Blu Ray set from Australia's Imprint label called *Silver Screams Cinema*. (NA)

Unknown World (1951) 1.5
To escape a world threatened by the A-bomb, professor forms team to find underground haven by boring to the center of the earth. During the journey, tensions mount and tragedy strikes. Sincere but largely humorless low-budget sci-fi falls flat; it's neither terribly interesting nor convincing. (DVD-Alpha)

Untamed Women (1952) 1.0
During World War II, Air Force bomber crashes and the four survivors find themselves stranded on island ruled by druid women. There's also "monster" footage from *One Million B.C.* to contend with. Poor performances and clunky dialogue abound in this stinker. Check out that flesh-eating plant! For bad movie aficionados only. (DVD-VCI with *Cuban Rebel Girls*)

The Valley of Gwangi (1969) 2.5
Ray Harryhausen's effects work is the main reason to see this variation on *King Kong*. In Mexico, struggling wild west show owner puts captured allosaurus on the program. It escapes, and chaos ensues. Some great battle scenes and rousing score are among the film's assets. Lead actress Gila Golan is obviously (and distractingly) dubbed, and the cliché romance subplot is a yawner. (BR-Warner Archive)

Valley of the Zombies (1946) 2.0
Ian Keith's turn as Ormand Murks, a vampire-like murderer who needs blood to survive, makes for a somewhat endurable Poverty Row thriller. Murks breaks into blood banks and makes unauthorized withdrawals. Now he has his eye on a human benefactor. Title is misleading, as this effort really has nothing to do with zombies, or valleys for that matter. Available on a region-free Blu Ray set from Australia's Imprint label called *Silver Screams Cinema*. (NA)

The Vampire (1957) 3.0
A beloved, small-town doctor is accidentally given (by his own daughter!) experimental pills which transform him into a vampire-like creature. Much like 1956's *The Werewolf* this film uses science to create a familiar monster. But it works very well thanks to a terrific lead performance by John Beal, a fine supporting cast (Kenneth Tobey, Dabbs Greer, Coleen Gray), and the overall tragic story arc that results in an ending with real punch. Aired on television as *Mark of the Vampire*. (BR-Shout! Factory)

The Vampire Bat (1933) 2.5
A mad scientist (Lionel Atwill) performs monstrous experiments on a small village's citizenry. Shot on Universal sets this low-budget effort boasts an impressive cast including Melvyn Douglas, Fay Wray, and Dwight Frye. Maude Eburne provides the comedy relief as hypochondriac Aunt Gussie; Frye is the village idiot Herman who loves, "nice, soft bats." For fans of 1930s horror, this outing is a mini treat. A public domain staple since the dawn of home video, *The Vampire Bat* is best viewed via The Film Detective's restored BR-R.

Vampire Circus (1972) 2.5
A traveling circus visits a small village beset by plague, the result of a vampire's curse years ago. Only gradually do the locals realize the vengeful nature of the performers, one of whom is the bloodsucker's cousin. Unique Hammer horror finds enough variations on the usual vampire clichés to keep this interesting. Beautiful looking too. (BR-Synapse)

The Vampire Lovers (1970) 3.0
Based on Sheridan Le Fanu's story "Carmilla," this is Hammer Film Productions' first nudie vampire film. Ingrid Pitt dazzles as bloodsucker who contrives to be a houseguest of her intended female targets. When she's done with one household, she moves to the next. Handsomely produced and photographed, with several gory scenes including two beheadings. Peter Cushing has what's essentially a cameo as concerned general. Two other Karnstein films followed: *Lust for a Vampire* and *Twins of Evil*. (BR-Shout! Factory)

Vampire Men of the Lost Planet (1970) 0.0
Vampirism apparently originated from outer space, not Transylvania. So, cranky scientist John Carradine and company head to solar system Spectrum where they can learn the secret to stopping a bloodsucker outbreak. The planet they land on is chock full of scenes from other movies, some in black-and-white, which is dealt with by tinting the film various colors throughout and blaming it on radiation effects. There are vampire cavemen, dinosaurs, snake people, and bat creatures. It's another disjointed Al Adamson atrocity, a shocking reminder of what people could get away with releasing once upon a time. (BR-Severin as *Horror of the Blood Monsters* as part of *Al Adamson: The Masterpiece Collection*)

The Vampire People (1964) 2.5
Bald headed vampire Dr. Marco, who also wears sunglasses and cracks a mean whip, needs the heart of his dying lover's twin sister to save her. He starts putting the bite on those close to his target, which gives the police and a priest time to plot the villain's demise. Very stylish horror, with director Gerardo de Leon using color photography for day scenes, and blue and red tints for night and key emotional moments. Atmospheric and creepy, this film's vampire is so evil he uses the twins' own mother in his murder plot! (BR— Severin as *The Blood Drinkers*)

The Vampire's Coffin (1958) 2.5
Count Lavud's staked body is stolen from its tomb, and then the stake is removed! He seeks vengeance on the sweethearts who did him in. Sequel to *El Vampiro* lacks the atmosphere of its predecessor but is redeemed by its likable cast and rousing finale inside a wax museum. (DVD-Casa Negra as part of *The Vampire Collection*)

The Vampire's Ghost (1945) 2.5
Character actor John Abbott gives a strong performance as vampire who owns a bar in Africa, lamenting his cursed existence. Like the best vampire tales, the fiend is alternately sympathetic and ruthless. Perhaps Republic Pictures' finest horror film. (BR-Olive)

El Vampiro (1957) 3.0
The first traditional vampire film of the decade is a terrific Gothic mood piece with German Robles fine as title fiend who plans to bring back late relative. Abel Salazar is great as the likable hero who reminds one of Bob Hope from *The Ghost Breakers*. Assets include cleverly executed bat transformations and some great "jumps" when characters suddenly appear. Another winner from Mexico. (DVD-Casa Negra as part of *The Vampire Collection*)

Vampyr (1932) 3.5
Traveler settles down at an inn for the evening and gets more than he bargained for, becoming involved with sinister doctor and the local vampire. The very definition of a visualized nightmare, with little dialogue and a true sense of the surreal. The best sequence involves the hero being laid to rest in his coffin, as we hear the turning of the hand drill as it secures the lid's screws, while the "corpse" stares open-eyed as if witnessing his own burial. (BR-Criterion)

Varan the Unbelievable (1962) 2.0
A prehistoric monster leaves its home, destroys the small village nearby, and then heads for Tokyo. Familiar stuff—for giant monster fans only. This Americanized version of the 1958 Japanese *kaiju eiga* makes matters worse by adding lengthy set up for American character actor Myron Healey, thereby greatly delaying monster's entrance. Neither version is very good, but the original is preferable. (DVD-Media Blasters [Original Japanese version only])

The Vengeance of Fu Manchu (1967) 2.0
Third entry in the series. As a representative of the world's crime bosses journeys to request Fu Manchu (Christopher Lee) to be their leader, Fu Manchu plots his revenge against Nayland Smith by forcing a plastic surgeon to create a lookalike. The idea that all criminals would follow one boss is a silly one in this disappointing outing that recycles elements of previous films (e.g. kidnapping daughters to force cooperation). (DVD-R-Warner Archive)

The Vengeance of She (1968) 2.0
Hammer's follow-up to *She* (1965) has the deceased Ayesha possibly reborn in confused beauty Carol, guided to lost city of Kuma by ancient forces. Unexciting sequel with lovely lead Olinka Berova's performance blunted by obvious dubbing. Competent performances and nice music score help. (BR-Shout! Factory)

Videodrome (1983) 3.0
A perfectly cast James Woods plays president of cable channel that offers its audience softcore pornography and extreme violence. When a pirate satellite dish picks up an extremely brutal video that may be fact instead of fiction, he becomes involved with a group that believes video is the new reality. Writer/director David Cronenberg's mix of sex, violence, and technology features Rick Baker's eye-popping effects and many intriguing ideas. It doesn't completely work and becomes a little silly before all is said and done. But it is never less than compelling. (BR-Criterion)

Village of the Damned (1960) 3.5
Shortly before 11:00 a.m. one morning, the entire populace of Midwich passes out for nearly three hours. Two months later, all women capable of childbirth realize they're pregnant. The offspring turn out to be golden-haired, glow-eyed, mind reading geniuses whose motives are a mystery. Engrossing, chilling sci-fi is utterly believable and leads to a knockout climax. (BR-Warner Archive)

Village of the Giants (1965) 0.5
Boy genius Ronny Howard accidentally invents growth "goo" that's sampled by group of teen troublemakers. They take over small town while Ronny and company try to defeat them. Loosely based on H.G. Wells' *The Food of the Gods* and very much a product of its time. Director Bert I. Gordon focuses on (primarily female) gyrating body parts as much as he does on giant ducks and the like. Today it's alternately tedious, ridiculous, and laughable. In a word: awful. (BR-Kino)

The Visitor (1979) 2.0
The eight-year-old daughter of divorcee is offspring of evil extraterrestrial force. She and mysterious group of men now want mom to bear a son to effect hell on earth. Luckily, there's a group out to stop this, headed by John Huston. Arty hybrid of 1970's possession and alien films with a touch of the divine thrown in for good measure earns points for its audaciousness. But the result is unsatisfying. In its edited US form, it's muddled and confusing. In its full-length version, it's ponderous and pretentious. Not without its moments though. (BR-Cinedigm)

The Violent and the Damned (1963) 1.0
Jerry Warren took footage from the 1955 film *Mãos Sangrentas*, added narration and too much talking head footage with American actors while removing more than half the original feature, and unleashed this version to theaters in January 1963. After laboriously establishing that prisoners face mental challenges when confined, we move to a brutal escape from Brazilian prison and its aftermath. What survives of the original is certainly gritty and violent but whatever character development there was is gone. Instead, the story gets lost in the mundane Warren re-editing. (DVD-VCI with *No Time to Kill*)

Violent Midnight (1963) 2.0
Wealthy war veteran-turned-painter who believes he murdered his father and who "lost it" when his platoon was killed in the Korean war becomes murder suspect in model's brutal stabbing death shortly after welcoming home his half-sister. Horror whodunit is gruesome and sexy for its time. The direction is rather wanting, and the villain is obvious. Acting is a mixed bag too. Aired on television as *Psychomania*. (DVD-MPI)

Voodoo Island (1957) 2.0
Boris Karloff is a debunker of the supernatural out to disprove voodoo is at work at potential island resort. He's wrong, of course, as he encounters carnivorous plants, voodoo dolls, ouanga bags, and zombie-like inhabitants. Decent cast battles dull script; it's a draw. (DVD-MGM with *The Four Skulls of Jonathan Drake*)

Voodoo Man (1944) 2.5
It's all about the hair—Bela Lugosi sports a beard, George Zucco has feathers in his cap, and John Carradine paid way too much to his stylist. Lugosi kidnaps young girls to transfer their life force into his late wife by means of voodoo. Entertaining in the extreme, even if for the wrong reasons. (BR-Olive)

Voodoo Woman (1957) 1.0
Tom Conway is idiot scientist who transforms murderous thief into title creature, thinking he can control her. AIP stinker with a laughable, barely seen monster and a bored-looking Conway. (VHS-Columbia/Tristar)

Voyage into Space (TV-1970) 2.5
AIP Television patched together several of the 26 episodes from late 1960s Japanese series *Jonny Sokko and his Flying Robot*

for an American audience. The set-up: Emperor Guillotine from the planet Gargoyle brings to Earth monsters and his Gargoyle Gang in bid to take over planet. Lucky for us Earthlings, government agency UNICORN along with kid Jonny and the giant robot he controls are around to save the day. Nonstop action and giant monster silliness make for a fun if repetitive adventure. (BR-Ronin Flix)

Voyage to the Bottom of the Sea (1961) 3.0
When Earth's Van Allen belt catches fire, the planet has about three weeks before totally burning up. Admiral Harriman Nelson suggests firing an atomic missile at the belt from his nuclear submarine. Tensions mount among the crew as the sub deals with various obstacles during the 16-day journey, including a troublesome octopus. Great cast in entertaining if less than scientifically accurate adventure with good effects. (BR-Fox)

Voyage to the End of the Universe (1963) 3.0
Eerie sci-fi from Czechoslovakia. Large expedition is sent to investigate hazards of space while traveling to "green planet," where it is hoped life can be sustained. The length of trip, troubles encountered, and the stress over missing their loved ones eventually take a toll on the crew. Stark, deadly serious drama is never less than compelling. (DVD-R-Sinister Cinema with original version *Ikarie XB 1*)

Voyage to the Planet of Prehistoric Women (1968) 1.0
Rescue team sent to Venus promptly kills pterodactyl that is a god to band of blonde beauties, incurring their wrath, sort of. Movie constructed from Russian films with new footage featuring the women added for no particularly good reason. The men and women therefore never even interact, so the flashback structure makes no sense! Nice to look at for a while, but extreme dullness soon sets in. See also its predecessor *Voyage to the Prehistoric Planet*. (DVD-Retromedia as part of *The Roger Corman Russian Sci-Fi Collection*)

Voyage to the Prehistoric Planet (1965) 1.5
Producer Roger Corman took Russian film *Planeta Bur* and had it reconfigured with added footage featuring Basil Rathbone and Faith Domergue. The result is this tepid journey to Venus. Exploratory teams sent to the second planet from the sun encounter monsters and other dangers. None too thrilling. See also the even worse follow-up *Voyage to the Planet of Prehistoric Women*. (DVD-Retromedia as part of *The Roger Corman Russian Sci-Fi Collection*)

The Vulture (1966) 1.5
Below average tale of a part man, part vulture beast terrorizing descendants of family that wronged his ancestors. Except for Akim Tamiroff, the cast, acting as if they're just in it for the paycheck, give one-note performances that become very off-putting. The script is repetitive also, as characters have the same arguments repeatedly-just before they're killed. (VHS-Congress)

The Walking Dead (1936) 3.0
Boris Karloff plays ex-con framed for judge's murder. After he's executed his innocence is established so he's brought back to life-and he can sense who was part of the plot to frame him. Warner Bros. never could escape its fondness for gangster pictures and there are many elements of that genre present. But Karloff is subtle and haunting in the role, and Michael Curtiz directs with a sure hand. (DVD-Warner Bros. as part of *Karloff & Lugosi Horror Classics*)

War Between the Planets (1966) 2.0
In this Italian feature, a team of officers and scientists is dispatched to destroy an asteroid on course to collide with Earth. Visually arresting in parts, especially when the group reaches the "planet." However, it's also rather dull most of the time, failing to draw the audience into the story. This is one of four "Gamma One" space station movies made over a three-month period in 1965 and then released during 1966 and 1967. The others were *Wild, Wild Planet*, *War of the Planets*, and *Snow Devils*. Aired as *Planet on the Prowl*. (DVD-MPI with *The Creation of the Humanoids*)

War Gods of the Deep (1965) 2.0
Woman is kidnapped and whisked away to city beneath the sea whose inhabitants don't age, and where gill-men swim about looking menacing. Very odd Vincent Price vehicle has lovely atmosphere in the opening sequences but then just fizzles once our would-be heroes go in search of the missing young lady. Ultimately rather blah. (BR-Kino)

The War in Space (1977) 1.5
Autumn 1988: After aliens attack Earth, a team of scientists and astronauts travels to Venus in space battleship to confront the villains. Japanese attempt to take advantage of *Star Wars'* popularity lacks its inspiration's energy and state-of-the-art effects. (Check out the bigfoot-like monster with the obviously plastic, yellow horns.) We're left with mostly dull, derivative space opera that is frequently silly, such as having the main baddie named Commander Hell. (DVD-Discotek)

War of the Colossal Beast (1958) 1.5
Sequel to *The Amazing Colossal Man* finds Glenn Manning alive and stealing delivery trucks so he can eat. His sister tries to intervene, so his life can be saved. Without the study of Manning's descent into insanity this time out, what's left is a cheese fest with dodgy effects and uninteresting script. (BR-Shout! Factory)

The War of the Gargantuas (1966) 2.5
Giant human-like creature resembling the Incredible Hulk if he were a caveman wreaks havoc first at sea and then on land. Eventually a brown-tinted one shows up and soon the "brothers" are duking it out. Sequel to *Frankenstein Conquers the World* is one of the most action-packed *kaiju eiga* entries and therefore a pretty good time. Russ Tamblyn seems out-of-sorts though playing scientist who insists the brown one is good. (DVD-Classic Media with *Rodan*)

War of the Monsters (1966) 2.0
In this first *Gamera* sequel, thieves retrieve what they think is a valuable opal but is really egg that eventually hatches Barugon-a spikey, four-legged beast whose tongue extends and shoots freezing mist. Gamera comes to the rescue. The last of the serious *Gamera* films (you'll find no cute kids here) is decent mix of crime thriller and *kaiju eiga*. But by this point in the sub-genre, there's little in the way of monster mass destruction we haven't seen. (BR-Arrow as *Gamera vs. Barugon* as part of *Gamera: The Complete Collection*)

War of the Planets (1966) 1.0
During a New Year's Eve celebration, aliens that resemble pulsating green lights begin attacking and stealing space stations. They also possess certain persons "for the good of the whole," all part of their efforts to take over humanity! Poor effects and dull script doom this clunky Italian space opera. (DVD-R-Warner Archive)

The War of the Robots (1978) 0.5
Hoping to avoid extinction, a dying alien race sends androids to kidnap geneticist and his lovely assistant. A rescue team is sent after them because without the scientist's help, a reactor may explode on Earth. *Star Wars* clone suffers from subpar effects, acting, and storytelling. Shamelessly steals its action set pieces from a superior film with painful results. (DVD-VCI with *Supersonic Man*)

War of the Satellites (1958) 2.0
Aliens take over dead body of scientist to thwart the Earth's various space programs. Dick Miller swaggers through stock footage and newspaper headlines as the hero. The seams show too easily in this Roger Corman quickie, made bearable by good cast. (DVD-Shout! Factory as part of *Sci-Fi Classics: Roger Corman's Cult Classics Triple Feature*)

The War of the Worlds (1953) 3.5
Martians invade Earth in this superior sci-fi tale based on H.G. Wells' novel. Impressive effects and set pieces combine with believable performances for a riveting thriller. (BR-Criterion)

Warlock Moon (1973) 1.5
Young lovers discover abandoned country spa and the eccentric elderly woman who watches over it, and later learn the macabre reason why the place was closed. Another 1970s low-budget slow burn thriller, this features axe murders, a satanic cult, and some expected twists. Unfortunately, too much padding and repetition greatly dilute the finale's impact. (BR-Code Red)

Warning from Space (1956) 2.0
Aliens that look like a cross between starfish and a cyclops warn Japan that Planet R is on collision course with Earth. Luckily, scientist has developed explosive more powerful than the atomic bomb that might save the planet. First half of the film focuses on random flying saucer sightings; second is mostly talk about how to deal with the horrific situation. Japan's first color sci-fi film is moderately interesting but nothing special. (BR-Arrow)

Warriors of the Wasteland (1983) 1.5
It's 2019 A.D. and the nuclear holocaust is over. The Templars roam the barren countryside killing everyone they find. There's also a wandering ex-gang member named Scorpion who helps those in need. Although this clunky Italian *Mad Max* clone is never exactly boring, it nevertheless ranks high on the cheese meter with its goofy dialogue and bizarre character motivations. (DVD-Mill Creek as part of *Nightmare Worlds: 50 Movie Pack*)

The Wasp Woman (1959) 2.0
In hopes of counteracting falling sales, cosmetics company owner hires genius who has developed youth-restoring cream derived from queen wasp jelly. She insists on being the first human guinea pig and soon resembles a different type of living creature. Susan Cabot is good in the lead and the creature is a nifty sight. Nevertheless, the film is slow going, director Roger Corman stretching the thin script as best he can for the first 40 minutes. (BR-Shout! Factory)

Web of Evidence (1959) 2.0
Van Johnson plays Englishman who returns to Liverpool and learns his father was convicted of murder. He starts his own investigation and comes to believe his father is innocent. The true villain is rather obvious in this familiar story and Johnson is too old to play convincingly a man in his mid-to-late 20s. The ending isn't satisfactory either. (NA)

Web of the Spider (1971) 2.0
Remake of *Castle of Blood* by the same director. Journalist is bet he can't survive the night in haunted castle. Once there he becomes involved in bizarre love triangle, murder, and ghosts. Starts out fine, but then exposition and repetition bog things down. Still, there are plenty of striking visuals and atmosphere to keep one's eyes on the screen. Klaus Kinski has amusing turn as Edgar Allan Poe. (BR-Garagehouse Pictures)

Web of Violence (1966) 3.0
When the ex-fiancée who jilted him disappears, unemployed newspaperman decides to investigate and finds himself in the crosshairs of drug dealers and possibly crooked cops. Engrossing Italian crime picture never slows down as it twists and turns its way through the plot. Identity of the one pulling the strings is a mild surprise. (NA)

Weird Woman (1944) 3.0
Inner Sanctum entry #2: Evelyn Ankers plays her first bad gal in a Universal horror film, as she tries to ruin the marriage of the man she loves (Lon Chaney). But just who is the *Weird Woman* of the title: the wife who believes in witchcraft? Ankers' conniving other woman? The widow of a disgraced professor who accuses Chaney and his spouse of murder? All three are a little weird. (BR-Mill Creek as part of *Inner Sanctum Mysteries: The Complete Film Series*)

Welcome to Arrow Beach (1974) 1.5
Seemingly kind bachelor who lives with his sister (who's also her lover) gives shelter to hitchhiker (Meg Foster). She soon

discovers he's also handy with a meat cleaver. Originally a film about cannibalism, such references were edited out of the American release print leaving an atmospheric, occasionally interesting, but mostly dull exercise with a disappointing climax. Last film for director-star Laurence Harvey. (VHS-Magnetic Video)

The Werewolf (1956) 3.0
The first classic monster to make an appearance in the 1950s, although the cause of lycanthropy is rooted is science, not superstition. A car accident victim receives vaccine against radiation from mad scientist. He turns into a werewolf, escapes, forgets who he is, and goes on rampage when provoked. Steven Ritch is quite fine and sympathetic as the title character, and the film boasts many fine moments, including a transformation into a drooling, hungry wolf. Listen for music cues from 1943's *The Return of the Vampire*. (BR-Arrow as part of *Cold War Creatures: Four Films from Sam Katzman*)

Werewolf in a Girl's Dormitory (1961) 2.0
New teacher shows up at girl's school and werewolf attacks ensue. Another atmospheric Italian horror effort with eccentric characters, which unfortunately never really grabs the audience's attention. (BR-Severin)

WereWolf of London (1935) 3.0
Underrated Universal Horror. Henry Hull is a moody botanist bitten by Sidney Toler in Tibet. Once back in London he alienates his wife by his strange behavior. Dr. Glendon may not be as likable as Larry Talbot, but Hull's performance feels honest and true. It makes it that much more powerful when his wife refuses to obey his orders, which are meant to protect her. The Satanic werewolf makeup is terrific. (BR-Universal as part of *The Wolf Man: Complete Legacy Collection*)

West of Zanzibar (1929) 3.0
When his wife leaves him, and he loses the use of his legs in a freak accident, a bitter man (Lon Chaney) plots revenge against his wife's lover and the resultant offspring. Another macabre outing between Chaney and director Tod Browning has Chaney at his most vicious. Twist is expected but still powerful. (DVD-R-Warner Archive)

Westworld (1973) 3.5
For a $1,000 a day, the Delos Corporation's amusement park complex offers guests the chance to vacation in Medieval World, Roman World, or Western World, all authentic recreations brought to life with the aid of robots. Then one day a mechanical rattlesnake malfunctions and hurts a guest, causing the tech team great concern. Writer-director Michael Crichton's best film is a funny, scary, intelligent, and alarming warning on the dangers of technology, or perhaps humanity's inability to handle it. Yul Brynner's relentless Gunslinger is an ancestor of the Terminator. A great entertainment. (BR-Warner Bros.)

What A Carve Up! (1961) 2.0
In this remake of 1933's *The Ghoul*, scaredy-cat book editor's uncle dies, and he must spend the night in creepy mansion to claim inheritance. Not surprisingly, various relatives start dropping dead. Despite solid cast (Michael Gough is a butler, Donald Pleasence a solicitor) this is only a so-so comedy whodunit with scattered laughs. Aired as *No Place Like Homicide*. (DVD-Wham! USA)

What the Peeper Saw (1972) 2.0
New 22-year-old stepmom thinks 12-year-old stepson may have murdered his mother two years ago and is now targeting her. Icky thriller involving sexual tension between the two leads might have worked with more convincing performances and better-written characters. So-so film has good ending though. (BR-VCI)

What Ever Happened to Aunt Alice? (1969) 3.0
After her husband dies leaving her with no money, nasty Claire Marrable (Geraldine Page) resorts to hiring live-in housekeepers whom she eventually murders for their savings, and then buries the bodies in her garden. Her latest employee (Ruth Gordon) however is not all she appears to be. Page is great fun as a truly vile villain; Gordon is sympathetic as woman determined to find the truth about her friend. The final twist is terrific. (BR-Kino)

What Ever Happened to Baby Jane? (1962) 3.5
Former Hollywood star Blanche Hudson (Joan Crawford), an invalid due to accident in 1935, lives with her alcoholic, half-crazed sister Jane (Bette Davis), who never had the career she wanted. Having learned her sister plans to sell the house they share Jane terrorizes Blanche in series of vicious "pranks" that eventually turn deadly. Acting legends Crawford and Davis no doubt drew upon their well-known antagonism for this terrific, watershed thriller/dark comedy that led to series of films featuring stars of yesteryear. (BR-Warner Bros.)

What's the Matter with Helen? (1971) 2.5
Two women (Debbie Reynolds and Shelley Winters) whose teenage sons committed murder move to 1930s California to start over, opening a dance studio for young girls. Mysterious phone calls and an after-hours visit that leads to murder threaten the women's future. Good cast does well with a script that offers no real surprises. (BR-Shout! Factory)

When Every Day Was the Fourth of July (TV-1978) 3.0
Dan Curtis co-wrote, produced, and directed this courtroom mystery set in 1937 Bridgeport, Connecticut. When a mute (dubbed Snowman by the locals) is accused of murdering a candy storeowner, a nine-year-old begs her attorney father to defend him. Engrossing drama with strong cast and satisfying conclusion. (DVD-MPI with *The Long Days of Summer*)

When G-Men Step In (1938) 2.5
Racketeer who specializes in fake charities and phony lottery tickets is shocked to learn the brother he put through law school has joined the FBI! Columbia B-picture offers enjoyable fraternal cat-and-mouse game, even though it plays out as expected. (NA)

When Worlds Collide (1951) 3.0
Handsome George Pal production of planet Zyra and star Bellus heading towards Earth, and those who construct a rocket ship in hopes of averting doom. Well-done if unsubtle reworking of the Noah's Ark story for the space age with great effects work and fast pace. The scenes of destruction are utterly harrowing. (DVD-Paramount)

Where Time Began (1977) 2.0
Handsome but rather staid version of Jules Verne's *Journey to the Center of the Earth*. Quartet follows clues to secret entrance to Earth's center; face various perils including prehistoric monsters. The 1959 version is much livelier and more entertaining. (DVD-Code Red with *Encounter with the Unknown*)

The Whip and the Body (1963) 3.0
Christopher Lee stars as black sheep of noble family who returns when his ex-lover marries his brother. He also torments his father, the mother of a woman he drove to suicide, and his cousin, who is also in love with his brother. Part murder mystery, part ghost story, all luscious Italian gothic courtesy of director Mario Bava. (BR-Kino)

The Whip Hand (1951) 2.0
Magazine writer goes fishing in town where the trout don't bite, and the residents act strangely. The secret they're guarding involves former Nazi doctor and his various experiments. Nicely shot and frequently suspenseful. Elliott Reid isn't very good in the lead and that lessens the impact. (DVD-R-Warner Archive)

White Pongo (1945) 0.0
Before dying from jungle fever, delirious anthropologist claims to have seen a white gorilla, which could be the "missing link between man and monkey" according to Royal Society of Explorers member. Subsequent expedition battles nature and the natives while searching for the legendary beast. Poverty Row dreck from PRC blends talk, stock footage, a love triangle, and scenes of a stalking pale gorilla, resulting in extreme tedium for the viewer. (DVD-Alpha)

The White Spider (1963) 2.0
Gamblers with large insurance policies are dying in supposed accidents, and anyone who gets too nosey ends up dead too. The main villain is so badass that he wears an eyepatch *and* sunglasses and bears a scar on his left cheek. But that's just one of his *many* disguises. Overlong German *krimi* builds to a truly disappointing finale. Knowing they were after a master of disguise, you'd think the main Inspector would order any bearded, seemingly harmless character roaming about a murder scene to be detained! (DVD-R-Sinister Cinema)

Who Killed Gail Preston? (1938) 2.5
Rita Hayworth stars as band singer who is shot dead during her act. Virtually a scene-for-scene remake of *The Crime of Helen Stanley*, with the victim being a crooner instead of a dancer. Dwight Frye is one of the suspects. Fast-paced with clever method of murder. (NA)

Whoever Slew Auntie Roo? (1972) 2.5
Every Christmas, "Auntie Ruth" lets several children from the nearby orphanage stay over at her mansion Christmas Eve and Christmas night. However, she has a tragic past: her own daughter died in a freak accident…And the child's corpse is still in the house! Even worse, Ruth begins to believe one of the orphans is her daughter. Shelley Winters is great in the title role and the production design is gorgeous. Unfortunately, the story keeps showing how harmless Ruth really is, so the suspense isn't there. (BR-Kino)

The Wild Racers (1968) 1.0
Fabian plays obnoxious American racecar driver Joe Joe Quillico who travels the international circuit on his way to the Grand Prix while trying to avoid falling in love. Aggressive editing is probably supposed to convey Joe Joe's fast-paced, erratic life. (He's always in a hurry.) But it comes off pretentious and distracting. There's also no reason given to care about this guy. The result is an endurance test for the audience. (NA)

The Wild, Wild Planet (1966) 1.5
Sometime in the future, mysterious pairs that can shrink their targets to doll size kidnap thousands of Earthlings. The nefarious plot has something to do with tissue grafts, transplants, and perfection. Colorful Italian sci-fi is visually appealing but dramatically stagnant and at times silly. (Why the heck was that hall of mirrors at the space station?) Lead villain does earn his mad scientist club card though. (DVD-R-Warner Archive)

Willard (1971) 2.5
Nebbish Willard Stiles befriends rats Socrates and Ben (and 600 others), and in return they help him get even with cruel boss Ernest Borgnine. Good cast and interesting story helped launch a 1970s sub-genre of vengeful nerds and their pets. Hampered though by undistinguished direction and inappropriate score. Ben returned for a sequel. (BR-Shout! Factory)

Winter Kill (TV-1974) 2.0
Someone is slaying those he or she blames for fate of 18-year-old who was pregnant and troubled. Formulaic TV movie helped somewhat by lovely snow-covered locations and good cast, including Andy Griffith as the intrepid sheriff. The script is too familiar and predictable. (DVD-R-Warner Archive)

The Witch (1966) 2.0
Widow asks ladies' man Richard Johnson to catalogue the erotic writings of her late husband. When he meets her beautiful daughter Aura (Rosanna Schiaffino), he agrees for lustful reasons. He should have bolted when Aura freaks out over cats getting into the greenhouse. Instead, he sticks around and discovers other librarian is living there and becomes pawn in the women's bizarre games. Intriguing but also slow and off putting. Good ending, however. (DVD-Eclectic)

The Witches (1966) 3.0
Interesting Hammer effort about witchcraft at secluded school. New teacher Joan Fontaine tries to discover who is behind the

sinister goings on. Good cast and some memorable terror sequences. (BR-Shout! Factory)

The Witches Mountain (1972) 2.5
Photographer on assignment in the Pyrenees Mountains meets beautiful writer who agrees to accompany him. Unfortunately, mysterious events put a stop to their blooming romance. Beautiful, slow burn, atmospheric film has a decidedly nightmarish quality given the seeming incoherence. However, the story ultimately makes a certain sense when one considers the pre-credit murder of a cat-killing child in conjunction with the very last shot of the film, which reveals the hero's fate. (DVD-Mill Creek as part of *Chilling Classics: 50 Movie Pack*)

The Witchmaker (1969) 2.5
Psychic researcher brings his team to isolated cabin in Louisiana swamp where young women have been murdered and drained of blood. It turns out there is a coven nearby looking for a 13th member. Unique, beautiful, and atmospheric, hampered mainly by sluggish pacing. Great finale. (BR-Code Red)

The Witch's Curse (1962) 1.5
A hundred years after a condemned witch curses her accusers as she is burned at the stake, her descendant is threatened with a similar fate unless Maciste (Kirk Morris) can save her, which he attempts to do by traveling to hell. Morris is physically imposing as he tosses boulders, fights a lion, strangles a monstrous eagle, and performs other feats of strength. It's all for naught though because he lacks charisma, making him a bland hero and the film less than compelling. Italian sword and sandal flick no doubt "inspired" by the superior *Hercules in the Haunted World*. (DVD-Image with *Hercules against the Moon Men*)

The Witch's Mirror (1962) 2.5
Witch's goddaughter is murdered by her husband so she plan's revenge. Rather wild mix of mad scientist and ghost story genres makes this interesting, if not totally rewarding, viewing. As with most Mexican horror films of this period, the atmospherics are top notch. (DVD-Casa Negra)

The Witness Vanishes (1939) 2.5
Former newspaper owner escapes from sanatorium vowing to murder the four men who put him there. Soon obituaries are appearing *before* the victims' deaths. Meanwhile suspect's estranged daughter gets job at paper incognito. Final entry in Universal's "Crime Club" series is brisk and entertaining, if a tad obvious. (NA)

The Wizard of Mars (1965) 1.0
On New Year's Day 1975, Mars Probe One crashes on the red planet, leaving the four crewmembers to survive on four days' worth of oxygen. They explore caves, are nearly scorched by lava, and finally discover deserted village (after more than 45 sluggish minutes) and John Carradine's talking head. There are allusions to *The Wizard of Oz* including a golden road, a character named Dorothy, and completing an assigned task to return home. Visually interesting at times, with eerie music score, this is little more than talk, talk, and more talk delivered by mostly amateur cast. The dubbing makes some of them sound like cartoon characters. (VHS-Star Classics, Inc. as *Horrors of the Red Planet*)

The Wolf Man (1941) 4.0
Lon Chaney, Jr.'s signature role, Larry Talbot, a would-be hero who is bitten by Bela Lugosi's werewolf when trying to save a life. Hands down Universal's best horror film of the 1940s. Beautifully filmed and heartfelt, the Wolf Man may be the most tragic of the classic monsters because his human side is fully aware of what his beastly side is doing, and no one will believe him. The look on Claude Rains' face during the finale is shattering. (BR-Universal as part of *The Wolf Man: Complete Legacy Collection*)

The Woman in White (1948) 3.0
England 1851: painter arrives at Limmeridge House for his new job as drawing master for well-to-do family and encounters title character, allegedly an asylum escapee. He becomes engrossed in mystery regarding woman's identity while falling in love with his pupil. Intricately plotted Gothic melodrama is absorbing all the way, with a top-notch cast and satisfying denouement. (DVD-R-Warner Archive)

Woman Who Came Back (1945) 2.5
After being the only survivor of a bus accident, a woman believes a vengeful witch has possessed her. Above average psychological thriller in the Val Lewton tradition features good lead performance by Nancy Kelly. (DVD-Image)

The Woman Eater (1958) 2.0
A doctor returns from the Amazon jungle with a tree that eats only beautiful women, and its sap can bring the dead back to life! This British production is watchable thanks to George Coulouris' committed performance as the mad medico. However, since the tree is planted in the basement and does not budge, it hardly makes for a very exciting monster. (DVD-Image)

Women of the Prehistoric Planet (1966) 0.5
After ship crashes on unexplored planet thanks to a failed hijacking, a rescue team shows up 18 years later (thanks to the time paradox) and encounters a giant lizard, fatal acid bath, plush toy tarantula, and spear-throwing cavemen. There are, technically speaking, no women found on the planet, effectively negating the title, which is more interesting than anything found in this low-budget endurance test. (VHS-First Look Home Entertainment)

The World of the Vampires (1961) 2.0
Vampire sets his sights on pianist's girlfriend. Atmosphere galore and some unexpected plot turns help overcome poor special effects (check out those vampire masks). Probably only for fans of Mexican horror films though. (DVD-Beverly Wilshire)

World Without End (1956) 2.5
Returning from the first mission to Mars, astronauts are caught in time warp that propels them to a post-apocalyptic Earth, where they encounter giant spiders, mutants, and what's left

of civilized humankind living underground. Nicely mounted sci-fi manages to be surprisingly optimistic; major debit is the all-too-familiar jealously subplot. (BR-Warner Archive)

X (1963) 2.5
Scientist invents eye drops that help him see through solid objects, His dreams of learning the secrets of life are thwarted however when tragedy strikes, and he must hide out in carnival as sideshow act. Intriguing premise isn't satisfactorily developed, and Ray Milland isn't particularly sympathetic as the title character. Frequently listed as *X: The Man with the X-Ray Eyes*. (BR-Kino)

The X from Outer Space (1967) 1.0
Mars expedition returns with specimen that turns into gigantic chicken-type monster. Weak *kaiju eiga* features awful score that nearly undermines the whole production, too much time wasted on love triangle and other silliness that fills the void in between terrible effects sequences. Remember the moral of the story: all things must remain where they belong. (DVD-Criterion as part of *When Horror Came to Shochiku*)

X the Unknown (1956) 3.0
British soldiers in Scotland discover radioactive "mud monster" that grows as it consumes radioactive energy. American scientist Dean Jagger tries to stop it. Intense, straight-faced sci-fi from Hammer Film Productions is well directed and acted, with several terrifying moments, including a face melting! Balances explanatory and action scenes nicely. (BR-Shout! Factory)

Yog, Monster from Space (1970) 2.0
Gigantic squid, that can walk on its tentacles, plagues would-be resort island. The true villain is other worldly entity that can possess and mutate ordinary sea life, as well as control certain humans. Standard *kaiju eiga* with the novelty of watching seafood turn the tables. (DVD-Media Blasters as *Space Amoeba*)

Yongary, Monster from the Deep (1967) 2.0
South Korean take on Japanese *kaiju eiga* efforts. Nuclear blast from rocket launch frees ancient, oil-chugging monster. Clearly aimed at kids, with eight-year-old figuring significantly into the plot. Of course, lots of models and toys are blown up, stepped on, or burned. Highlight though is Yongary briefly dancing after realizing he's not dead after all. (BR-Kino)

Yor, the Hunter from the Future (1983) 1.5
Italian-lensed prehistoric adventure/fantasy about blonde-haired Yor who battles various beasts and men in search of his own origins. Lots of kicking, fighting, and screaming in this busy, noisy action flick; gives new meaning to the word cheesy. Takes a jarring turn in the last half hour or so that manages to throw *Superman* and *Star Wars* elements into the fondue. (BR-Mill Creek)

You'll Find Out (1940) 2.0
Although co-starring Boris Karloff, Bela Lugosi, and Peter Lorre, this is really a Kay Kyser & Band vehicle as Kay tries to thwart a plot against young lass about to inherit a lot of money. Our three boogiemen are in good form-and play it straight-but the mood is jovial. (DVD-Warner Bros. as part of *Karloff & Lugosi Horror Classics*)

You'll Like My Mother (1972) 3.0
Pregnant widow makes it a point to meet her mother-in-law, thinking she will be welcomed. Boy did she make a mistake. Tense, frequently nerve-wracking thriller with Patty Duke doing a marvelous job in the lead. Highly recommended to fans of 1970s suspense flicks. (BR-Shout! Factory)

Young Frankenstein (1974) 4.0
One of the all-time great horror comedies, which combines plot points and characters from the first three Universal *Frankenstein* films into a very funny, loving homage. Young Dr. Frankenstein (Gene Wilder) inherits the family castle and travels to Transylvania; discovers grandfather's notes about creating life. Terrific cast, especially Marty Feldman as Igor, and some marvelous set pieces, most notably a soft shoe with the Monster (Peter Boyle) and Frankenstein. (BR-Fox)

Zardoz (1974) 2.0
Sean Connery stars in this fu-

turistic tale as an Exterminator of mortals who has somehow invaded the Vortex, the world where the Immortals live in harmony and protection. There are those not thrilled about living forever and see Connery as their savior, able to bring about their deaths. Off putting sci-fi has some interesting ideas but is emotionally cold and thus largely uninvolving. (BR-Twilight Time)

Zombie (1979) 2.0
Tropic-set horror as scientist tries to find why locals are turning into zombies. Lucio Fulci is a god to some but most of his films are the very definition of the tail wagging the dog; in this case, the gruesome effects include the infamous splinter through the eye scene. However, the story is thin, and the camera lingers too long on some of the effects work. Then again, there is that zombie vs. shark sequence. (BR-Blue Underground)

Zombies of Mora Tau (1957) 2.0
Zombies in small African village zealously guard sunken diamonds. That does not stop the latest group of fortune seekers from trying to steal them. The zombies in this film are more frightening than in previous zombie films, which treated the undead as mindless slaves. Here they are impervious to bullets and are strong enough to break necks. However, the flat direction fails to build up any momentum. Still, Allison Hayes, as a flirtatious wife, is in the cast so... (BR-Arrow as part of *Cold War Creatures: Four Films from Sam Katzman*)

Zombies on Broadway (1945) 2.0
Horror-comedy with Bela Lugosi as scientist (what a surprise) on island of San Sebastian who can transform people into zombies. The comedy team of Wally Brown and Alan Carney show up looking for a real zombie to use in a nightclub's opening. Amusing but negligible film does have some nice links to *I Walked with A Zombie* (location, Sir Lancelot showing up). (DVD-Warner Bros. as part of *Karloff & Lugosi Horror Classics*)

Zontar, the Thing from Venus (TV-1966) 1.0
Venetian who has been plotting with scientist via "hyperspace hypnotism" hitches a ride on satellite and lands on Earth. It then cuts the power supply and sends out bat-like creatures to begin its takeover of humankind. This listless color remake of *It Conquered the World* is one of several remakes of 1950s AIP films made for TV syndication by director Larry Buchanan. The acting is poor and tension nonexistent. Sparks to life only in its final moments, when several people attack the bat creature in its cave. Good luck making it that far, though. (DVD-Retromedia with *The Eye Creatures*)

Appendix 2
Network Airings

While the focus of this book is on local airings unique to the Maryland/D.C. area, a handful of films aired only as part of network programming. Below is a list of those films that aired either as prime time network features, or as part of network late-night offerings, but never as part of local programming.

20,000 Leagues Under the Sea (1954) 3.5
The sea monster wreaking havoc on 1868 Pacific Ocean ships is the Nautilus, a creepily designed submarine helmed by Captain Nemo, who has declared war on warships. Classic version of Jules Verne novel; cast, production design, and effects work are all excellent. James Mason is a peerless Nemo. (He has an organ on board so he can play J. S. Bach's "Toccata & Fugue in D Minor"!) Giant squid attack remains a must-see. (BR-Disney)
02/23/74 8:00 PM Channels 11,4 Disney Night at the Movies
10/24/76 7:00 PM Channels 11,4 Walt Disney Night at the Movies

An American Werewolf in London (1981) 2.5
Werewolf attacks two American students hitchhiking their way through England. The one who didn't survive visits the one who did, warning him he will become a beast during the next full moon. A frustrating mix of highly effective terror sequences with ineffectual comedy and an uncertain lead performance by David Naughton. He doesn't seem sure whether he should be playing this straight or for laughs. And the ending is awful. (BR-Arrow)
01/09/87 12:00 AM Channel 11 CBS Late Movie

Beyond Evil (1980) 1.5
Architect and his wife take residence in haunted mansion where restless spirit quickly goes after the missus. Tacky horror with bad effects and mundane script. (BR-Vinegar Syndrome)
05/01/86 1:10 AM Channels 11,9 CBS Late Movie
03/11/87 1:10 AM Channels 11,9 CBS Late Movie

Beyond the Door (1974) 1.0
Woman carrying Satan's spawn starts behaving like Linda Blair from *The Exorcist*. Noisy, confusing, nonsensical, and protracted Italian rip-off of the classic possession film and *Rosemary's Baby* offers nothing new except maybe unusually foul-mouthed kids. Ridiculous garbage. (BR-Arrow)
11/09/79 12:40 AM Channel 45 CBS Late Movie
11/11/79 1:10 AM Channel 9 CBS Late Movie
01/30/81 11:30 PM Channel 45 CBS Late Movie
01/31/81 11:30 PM Channel 9 CBS Late Movie

Black Christmas (1974) 3.5
On Christmas Eve, a psychotic killer settles in the attic of a sorority house. Soon he starts taunting and murdering the inhabitants. This gem of a flick wasn't always as appreciated as it is today. Director Bob Clark creates and sustains tension from the first scene, when we see the killer climb into the attic. Obscene phone calls have never been as effective onscreen as they are here. Aired as *Stranger in the House*. (BR-Shout! Factory)
01/28/78 9:00 PM Channels 11,4 NBC Saturday Night at the Movies
02/04/79 11:30 PM Channel 4 NBC Late Night Movie

Blood and Roses (1960) 2.5
French take on J. Sheridan Le Fanu's novella *Carmilla*. When the cousin she loves becomes engaged to her best friend, Carmilla starts behaving strangely, perhaps because she's been possessed by her vampire ancestor. Handsome production tends to be self-consciously arty at times, disrupting the pacing. But the film still works as intriguing variation on the standard vampire tale. (VHS-Paramount)
07/15/75 11:30 PM Channel 2 CBS Late Movie

Christine (1983) 3.0
High school nerd (Keith Gordon) purchases and restores classic automobile which he names Christine. To thank him, she hunts down and murders his tormentors. Good film version of Stephen King's novel by director John Carpenter with some impressive effects. Gordon is excellent. (BR-Twilight Time)
04/18/87 9:00 PM Channels 11,9 CBS Saturday Night Movie

Claws (1977) 2.0
Logger who survived attack by "devil bear" five years ago plans to slay his nemesis after it reappears and attacks his son. Fairly intense thriller soured by too many flashbacks and lackluster performances by some of the supporting cast. (VHS-United American Video Corp)
03/17/81 1:10 AM Channels 2,9 CBS Late Movie
07/17/81 12:40 AM Channel 45 CBS Late Movie
07/18/81 12:40 AM Channel 9 CBS Late Movie

Crescendo (1970) 2.0
Student doing her thesis on late American composer comes to stay with his widow. There she also meets his son, who's confined to a wheelchair and seems to have mommy issues. Bland thriller from Hammer offers few surprises. (DVD-R-Warner Archive)
02/21/78 11:30 PM Channels 13, 7 Tuesday Movie of the Week
11/13/79 12:05 AM Channels 13, 7 Tuesday Movie of the Week

Dark Places (1974) 2.0
Flat, poorly edited ghost tale about a race to find hidden loot in a haunted estate, while spirit of the former owner slowly takes over that of the new one. Good cast includes Christo-

pher Lee and Joan Collins as scheming siblings. (DVD-R-Sinister Cinema)
12/18/85 12:40 AM Channel 9 CBS Late Movie
12/25/85 1:10 AM Channel 11 CBS Late Movie
07/17/86 1:10 AM Channels 11, CBS Late Movie

Echoes (1982) 2.0
The murderer from an artist's recurring dream starts invading his waking hours, creating problems in his current relationship. Not uninteresting blend of past life and possession motifs, with "hero" becoming more unpleasant as the story progresses. Loses its grip before the finale though. (VHS-Vid-America)
11/14/84 12:40 AM Channel 9 CBS Late Movie
11/21/84 1:10 AM Channel 11 CBS Late Movie

Embryo (1976) 2.0
Scientist tests experimental growth hormone on 12-week-old fetus, which accelerates development so that child is soon a beautiful adult female. Things start out pleasantly but take a very dark turn when the subject begins experiencing sudden pains. Interesting idea is unimaginatively developed, and the script's contrivances get to be a bit much. (DVD-Mill Creek as part of *B-Movie Blast: 50 Movie Pack*)
09/18/81 9:00 PM Channels 2,4 NBC Friday Night at the Movies
03/04/83 12:00 AM Channel 11 CBS Late Movie
12/03/83 11:30 PM Channel 9 CBS Late Movie
12/09/83 12:00 AM Channel 11 CBS Late Movie
03/24/86 1:10 AM Channels 11,9 CBS Late Movie
12/15/86 1:10 AM Channels 11,9 CBS Late Movie

Escape to Witch Mountain (1975) 3.0
Wealthy Ray Milland's minion Donald Pleasence pursues orphaned brother and sister with special powers, along with their cat Winky, since harnessing their gifts will add to Milland's fortunes. They stowaway aboard sympathetic Eddie Albert's Winnebago while trying to understand who they are and where they came from. Delightful Disney fantasy-adventure with thrills, laughs, and marvelous effects. Fine music score too. (BR-Disney)
02/17/80 7:00 PM Channels 11,4 Disney's Wonderful World
10/12/80 7:00 PM Channels 11,4 Disney's Wonderful World

The Fearless Vampire Killers (1967) 3.0
Eccentric professor and his amiable assistant hunt down vampires in Transylvania, searching for beauty kidnapped from the local inn. Attractively shot blending of horror and humor, with a memorable ending that provides a nice shiver down the spine. (I remember seeing this on June 15, 1976, after the Orioles game on Channel 13 had ended. The sting in the tale really freaked me out.) (BR-Warner Archive)
02/20/72 11:30 PM Channel 9 CBS Late Movie
05/31/74 11:30 PM Channel 20 CBS Late Movie
06/15/76 11:30 PM Channels 2,9 CBS Late Movie

The Final Conflict (1981) 1.0
Satan's son Damien is all grown up and eyeing the White House to carry out his father's will. Dreadful conclusion to *The Omen* trilogy is doomed right from the beginning, because the so-called religious folk trying to kill Damien don't seem to have even read the Book of Revelation! Otherwise, they would have been very aware of the "surprise" ending. Sam Neill fails to register as the supreme evilness he's supposed to be. (BR-Shout! Factory as part of *The Omen Collection*)
02/01/84 9:00 PM Channels 11,9 CBS Wednesday Night Movie

It Lives Again (1978) 1.5
As more mutant babies are born and police hunt them down, a group of parents and scientists try to protect the monstrous tykes. Disappointing sequel features few likeable characters and no new ideas. Ultimately dull and tedious. (BR-Shout! Factory as part of *It's Alive Trilogy*)
07/25/86 12:00 AM Channel 11 CBS Late Movie
07/26/86 11:30 PM Channel 9 CBS Late Movie
12/30/86 1:10 AM Channels 11,9 CBS Late Movie

It's Alive (1974) 3.0
Mutant newborn slays five people before disappearing from the hospital, now looking for its family. Deserving of its cult status, this schlock masterpiece from writer-director Larry Cohen blends suspense and horror with some social commentary along with fine Bernard Herrmann score. (BR-Shout! Factory as part of *It's Alive Trilogy*)
07/18/86 12:00 AM Channel 11 CBS Late Movie
07/19/86 11:30 PM Channel 9 CBS Late Movie
12/29/86 1:10 AM Channels 11,9 CBS Late Movie

Jaws II (1978) 2.5
Another summer season in Amity, another series of shark attacks. Again, the idiotic politicians ignore Chief Brody (Roy Scheider) until much death has occurred. Not particularly inspired, but there are some suspenseful sequences and a nice turn by Scheider reprising his role from the 1975 classic. (BR-Universal)
02/15/81 8:00 PM Channels 13, 7 ABC Sunday Night Movie

The Keeper (1976) 0.5
Christopher Lee runs an asylum for wealthy mental cases, conducting bizarre hypnosis experiments while arranging murders of his patients' relatives so he can inherit vast sums. But the police are on to him, and a private detective has been hired, so the Keeper's time appears to be running out. The entire budget must have been spent on hiring Lee because everything else about this thriller is the pits. (DVD-Substance)
12/19/85 12:40 AM Channel 9 CBS Late Movie
12/26/85 1:10 AM Channel 11 CBS Late Movie

Knife for the Ladies (1974) 2.0
Horror whodunit set in the 19th-century West about private detective hired to solve three knife murders (soon to be more). Interesting blend of genres ultimately falls flat, although there are some good moments along the way. Jack Elam is fun as the grouchy sheriff. Aired as *Silent Sentence*. (BR-Code Red)
02/24/86 12:40 AM Channel 9 CBS Late Movie

03/03/86 1:10 AM Channel 11 CBS Late Movie
08/05/86 1:10 AM Channels 11,9 CBS Late Movie

The Last Wave (1977) 3.0
Corporate tax lawyer who is defending five Aborigines accused of murder begins having visions and nightmares of what could be a coming apocalypse. Unique thriller is visually enthralling but decidedly enigmatic. (DVD-Criterion)
10/02/81 11:30 PM Channel 11 CBS Late Movie
10/03/81 11:30 PM Channel 9 CBS Late Movie
06/05/82 11:30 PM Channel 9 CBS Late Movie
06/11/82 12:00 AM Channel 11 CBS Late Movie

Looker (1981) 3.0
Someone is murdering plastic surgeon's patients, so he decides to investigate before the one he has feelings for becomes the next victim. Nifty blend of sci-fi and crime drama is more science prediction given how certain plot points have become reality. Albert Finney and James Coburn as hero and villain, respectively, make fine adversaries. (BR-Warner Archive)
12/02/83 9:00 PM Channel 4 NBC Friday Night at the Movies

Night of Dark Shadows (1971) 2.0
Married couple move into estate that is haunted by husband's ancestor and his lover, a witch hanged in 1810. The ghosts have evil plans for the new arrivals. Unconvincing possession tale at least has terrific sets and creepy atmosphere to offset mediocre script. Unfortunately, when the CBS Late Movie aired *House of Dark Shadows* on July 16, 1976, it was preempted locally. (BR-Warner Bros.)
06/13/77 12:30 AM Channel 9 CBS Late Movie

Night of the Lepus (1972) 2.0
Rabbit injected with experimental serum escapes from test lab and soon giant, man-eating bunnies threaten the world. It's hard to believe the people behind this film thought they could make fluffy pets scary. But they went for it and failed miserably. Still, the cast plays it straight and there is entertainment to be found. Who knew bunnies growled? (BR-Shout! Factory)
09/13/74 11:30 PM Channel 20 CBS Late Movie
10/17/75 11:40 PM Channel 2 CBS Late Movie
07/13/76 11:30 PM Channels 2,9 CBS Late Movie
08/24/76 11:30 PM Channels 2,9 CBS Late Movie

The Pack (1977) 3.0
A pack of stray dogs terrorizes and attacks island community. Solid entry in nature's revenge subgenre. The cast is great and there is genuine suspense during the film's cabin showdown. Aired as *The Long, Dark Night*. (DVD-R-Warner Archive)
03/19/86 1:10 AM Channel 11 CBS Late Movie
09/18/86 1:10 AM Channels 11,9 CBS Late Movie

Parts: The Clonus Horror (1979) 3.0
At a top-secret facility, clones are being raised in ignorant bliss since they will someday supply needed organs to their wealthy counterparts. When one clone gets too curious, his actions threaten the whole scheme! Well-made, tightly paced low-budget sci-fi with convincing premise. (DVD-Mondo Macabro as *Clonus*)

04/10/82 11:30 PM Channel 9 CBS Late Movie
08/18/82 12:00 AM Channels 11,9 CBS Late Movie

Patrick (1978) 2.5
New nurse becomes fascinated with patient who's been in a coma for three years. She doesn't realize he has developed psychokinetic abilities which he begins using to interfere with her life. Enjoyable shocker although some of the character's motivations and actions are a bit muddy. (BR-Severin)
09/03/83 11:30 PM Channel 9 CBS Late Movie
03/03/84 12:30 AM Channel 9 CBS Late Movie
03/09/84 12:00 AM Channel 11 CBS Late Movie
08/09/84 12:40 AM Channel 9 CBS Late Movie
08/16/84 1:10 AM Channel 11 CBS Late Movie

Phobia (1980) 2.5
Psychiatrist is distressed that his patients are being murdered, subjected to their phobias. Angry detective suspects the doc. But is he really the killer? Much-maligned horror whodunit directed by the great John Huston is a suitably intense thriller. (BR-Kino)
08/17/86 9:00 PM Channels 2,4 NBC Sunday Night at the Movies

Plague (1979) 2.0
Scientist's tests with bacteria on rats are the cause of outbreak of highly contagious, deadly plague, resulting in a manhunt for the carrier and a quarantine for the city. OK thriller has some good moments but tends to repeat itself too much. Available on Region 2 DVD. (NA)
03/06/82 11:30 PM Channel 9 CBS Late Movie
07/28/82 12:00 AM Channels 11,9 CBS Late Movie

The Possession of Joel Delaney (1972) 3.0
Shirley MacLaine plays spoiled woman whose brother is possessed by his best friend's murderous spirit. Engrossing thriller with fine performances and unsettling finale. (DVD-Legend Films)
03/08/82 12:00 AM Channel 7 ABC Movie of the Week
03/08/82 1:00 AM Channel 13 ABC Movie of the Week

The Premonition (1976) 2.5
Adoptive mother starts having visions of her daughter's birth mother, who is planning to kidnap the child with the help of her violent boyfriend. Eventually she can't distinguish between reality and hallucination. Atmospheric thriller with plenty of chilling moments. Script is a bit choppy and disjointed. Jeff Corey does well as an understanding detective. (BR-Arrow)
01/30/82 11:30 PM Channel 9 CBS Late Movie
02/05/82 12:00 AM Channel 11 CBS Late Movie
01/26/83 1:10 AM Channels 11,9 CBS Late Movie

Project X (1968) 2.0
William Castle produced and directed this futuristic thriller about elaborate attempt to retrieve crucial memory from cryogenically frozen spy. But somebody doesn't want that memory discovered. Interesting premise is let down by overly complicated plotting and lots of talk. (BR-Olive)

07/21/74 8:30 PM Channels 13, 7 ABC Sunday Night Movie
04/21/76 11:30 PM Channels 2,9 CBS Late Movie

Psycho II (1983) 3.0
Norman Bates is released from the asylum and allowed to return to his home and motel. Before long, however, Mother starts calling and the murders begin. Nicely done sequel is much different in tone, with Norman clearly the sympathetic character here. Good twists, creative scenes of violence, and moving performance by Anthony Perkins make this much better than anyone could have foreseen. (BR-Shout! Factory)
10/25/86 9:00 PM Channels 11,9 CBS Saturday Night Movie

The Psychopath (1966) 2.5
A killer is leaving dolls at the scenes of his crimes in this decent thriller by writer Robert Bloch. Margaret Johnson really hams it up as a wheelchair-bound suspect. Directed by Freddie Francis for Amicus. (BR-Kino)
07/23/73 11:30 PM Channel 2 CBS Late Movie
01/30/74 11:30 PM Channel 2 CBS Late Movie
12/17/74 11:30 PM Channels 2,20 CBS Late Movie

Rituals (1977) 3.0
Five doctor pals venture through Canadian mountains on their annual get-together, soon realizing someone with a grudge is hunting them. Riveting, intense thriller with utterly believable characters and plenty of harrowing moments. Great cast too. (BR-Scorpion Releasing)
02/26/80 1:10 AM Channels 2,9 CBS Late Movie
01/06/82 12:05 AM Channels 11,9 CBS Late Movie

Saturday the 14th (1981) 1.5
After family moves into creepy house they've inherited, the son finds and mistakenly opens the Book of Evil, unleashing all sorts of rubbery creatures. There are a few scattershot laughs in this mostly lame horror parody. (BR-Shout! Factory)
11/20/85 12:40 AM Channel 9 CBS Late Movie
11/27/85 1:10 AM Channel 11 CBS Late Movie

Scream, Blacula, Scream (1973) 2.0
Disappointing sequel finds Blacula revived and this time falling for woman who might be able to exorcise his demons. Blacula isn't as sympathetic this time out and the pacing is off. (BR-Shout! Factory with *Blacula*)
10/31/75 11:30 PM Channels 13, 7 ABC Wide World of Entertainment

The Sender (1982) 3.0
The new suicidal resident at the state mental facility has telepathic powers that cause others to live out his nightmares. A sympathetic psychiatrist tries to help. Solid spook tale with engaging performances, clever script, and well-timed shocks. (BR-Olive)
07/21/86 9:00 PM Channels 2,4 NBC Monday Night at the Movies

Shock Waves (1977) 2.0
When their cruise boat is damaged, passengers take shelter on island where Peter Cushing presides over abandoned hotel and Nazi zombies. Low budget but atmospheric chiller does only a so-so job with its basic idea, as it's draggy in the early going. A couple of annoying characters don't help matters either. John Carradine plays a crusty captain. (BR-Blue Underground)
11/29/78 11:30 PM Channels 2,9 CBS Late Movie
08/26/81 11:30 PM Channels 2,9 CBS Late Movie

Spasms (1983) 1.0
Oliver Reed has psychic link to demon snake that escapes from university research lab and goes slithering about the city. Lots of POV shots and dodgy performances, along with a "that's it?" ending. Reed makes funny faces. Look fast for a *The Texas Chain Saw Massacre* poster during attack on a co-ed. (BR-Code Red)
05/15/86 1:10 AM Channel 11 CBS Late Movie
02/10/87 1:10 AM Channels 11,9 CBS Late Movie

Spawn of the Slithis (1978) 1.0
In Venice, California, high school journalism teacher investigates brutal slayings committed by organic mud monster. Potentially fun throwback repeatedly sabotaged by overly talky script. Cool looking monster though. The police lieutenant comes across as a cross between Jon Lovitz and Jack Nicholson. (BR-Code Red as *Slithis*)
03/07/86 1:10 AM Channel 11 CBS Late Movie
08/08/86 12:30 AM Channel 11 CBS Late Movie
08/09/86 11:30 PM Channel 9 CBS Late Movie
12/02/86 1:10 AM Channels 11,9 CBS Late Movie

The Spiral Staircase (1975) 2.0
Five people with physical disabilities have been murdered in the last year. Enter mute woman, traumatized by witnessing her family die, who's trapped in house with the killer during violent thunderstorm. Tepid version of the classic story made bearable thanks to good cast. (DVD-R-Warner Archive)
07/08/81 11:30 PM Channels 2,9 CBS Late Movie
04/21/86 1:10 AM Channels 11,9 CBS Late Movie
09/16/86 1:10 AM Channels 11,9 CBS Late Movie

Teen Wolf (1985) 2.5
Teenager discovers werewolfery runs in the family, which he's able to use to his advantage, especially on the basketball court. Silly but enjoyable monster comedy gets by largely on the charms of star Michael J. Fox. (BR-Shout! Factory)
05/04/87 9:00 PM Channels 2,4 NBC Monday Night at the Movies

The Thing (1982) 4.0
Thawed alien that can change into human form attacks an Antarctic research team, making everyone suspicious of their co-workers while trying to survive the falling temperatures. Terrific updating of the 1951 classic from director John Carpenter, with jaw-dropping effects, tense atmosphere, and solid cast. Dismissed upon its original release, this is now considered

one of the best sci-fi horrors of the 1980s. (BR-Shout! Factory)
07/18/86 9:00 PM Channels 11,9 CBS Friday Night Movie
04/10/87 12:15 AM Channel 11 CBS Late Movie

The Thing with Two Heads (1972) 2.0
Ray Milland plays dying, brilliant, and racist doctor whose experiments of transplanting heads are turned against him when he finds his own noggin attached to Rosey Greer. Tongue-in-cheek sci-fi is fun thanks to game cast. Its credibility score is zero though. (BR-Olive)
08/30/74 12:15 AM Channel 20 CBS Late Movie

UFO: Target Earth (1974) 0.0
Low-budget ineptitude about boring investigation into possible alien signals coming from bottom of lake. Poorly acted, directed, and scripted; not even watchable on the so-bad-it's-good curve. Ending rips off *2001: A Spacey Odyssey*. (DVD-Mill Creek as part of *Nightmare Worlds: 50 Movie Pack*)
01/09/76 11:30 PM Channel 2 CBS Late Movie

When A Stranger Calls (1979) 3.0
Intense chiller about maniac who terrorizes a babysitter, serves his time, and then has trouble reentering society. Impressive juggling of horror and police procedural by director/co-writer Fred Walton. Opening 20 minutes is of course the best part. But there's still plenty reason to stick around after that. (BR-

Mill Creek with *Happy Birthday to Me*)
01/25/82 9:00 PM Channels 2, 4 NBC Monday Night at the Movies
06/22/84 9:00 PM Channels 2, 4 NBC Friday Night at the Movies

Without Warning (1980) 2.0
Alien hunts humans with teeth-bearing critters that look like mushrooms. Great B-movie cast lensed through Dean Cundey's camera can do only so much with mediocre material. Effective special effects. (BR-Kino)
04/04/84 12:40 AM Channel 9 CBS Late Movie
04/11/84 1:10 AM Channel 11 CBS Late Movie
07/09/84 12:40 AM Channel 9 CBS Late Movie
07/16/84 1:10 AM Channel 11 CBS Late Movie

The Woman Who Wouldn't Die (1964) 2.5
A wealthy woman's faithless husband and crooked attorney conspire to murder her. Things of course don't go as planned. Very similar in feel and plotting to the Hammer "twist thrillers" of the same period, this familiar tale is handled well enough by director Gordon Hessler, who happens to have helmed this viewer's favorite *Kolchak: The Night Stalker* episode, "The Spanish Moss Murders." Available on Region 2 DVD as *Catacombs*. (NA)
03/12/75 11:30 PM Channels 2,20 CBS Late Movie
06/16/75 11:30 PM Channels 2,20 CBS Late Movie

Bibliography

Interviews

Tracy Lewis Collins, Tammy Petrides, James Uhrin. Timonium, Maryland, June 23, 2018
Richard Dix, Richard Dyszel, George Lewis. Towson, Maryland, February 27, 1993 [Nostalgia Vision Horror Host Panel]
Richard Dyszel. Columbia, Maryland, April 22, 2019
George Lewis. Lutherville, Maryland, January 15, 1991 [Conducted by Gene Crowell]
Gregory William Mank. Towson, Maryland, May 1, 2019

Books

Heffernan, Kevin. *Ghouls, Gimmicks, and Gold: Horror Films and the American Movie Business, 1953–1968*; Durham and London, Duke University Press, 2004
Mank, Gregory William. *The Very Witching Time of Night: Dark Alleys of Classic Horror Cinema*; Jefferson, North Carolina, McFarland & Company, Inc., 2004
Monahan, Michael. *American Scary: Conversations with the Kings, Queens and Jesters of Late-Night Horror TV*; Baltimore, Maryland, Midnight Marquee Press, Inc., 2011
Watson, Elena M. *Television Horror Movie Hosts*; Jefferson, North Carolina, McFarland & Company, Inc., 1991

Film/DVD

Creature Feature: The Legacy Series (2003-2010; Cape Coral, Florida) DVD-R
Virginia Creepers. Directed by Sean Kotz and Christopher Valluzzo. (2009; New River Valley, Virginia: Horse Archer Productions, 2009) DVD-R

Websites

Chastain, George. *E-gor's Chamber of TV Horror Hosts*, 2019, www.egorschamber.com/tvhorrorhosts
Colton, David, *The Classic Horror Film Board*, Tapatalk, Inc., 2019, www.tapatalk.com/groups/monsterkidclassichorrorforum
Dyszel, Richard. *Countgore.com*, 2019, www.countgore.com
Milford, Keith. *SirGravesGhastly.com*, 2005, www.sirgravesghastly.com
None. *Newspapers+* by Ancestry, 2019, www.newspapers.com

Magazines and Trade Journals

The Baltimore Sun, The Capital, The Cumberland News, The Daily Mail, The Evening Star, Midnight Marquee, The Morning Herald, The News, The Robesonian, Scary Monsters, The Star-Democrat, TV Guide, The Washington Post

To see all
Midnight Marquee Press titles
visit our website at
http://www.midmar.com

Midnight Marquee Press, Inc.
9721 Britinay Lane
Baltimore, MD 21234
mmarquee@aol.com

www.ingramcontent.com/pod-product-compliance
Lightning Source LLC
Chambersburg PA
CBHW061109070526
44583CB00027B/3239